THE POP PIANO BOOK

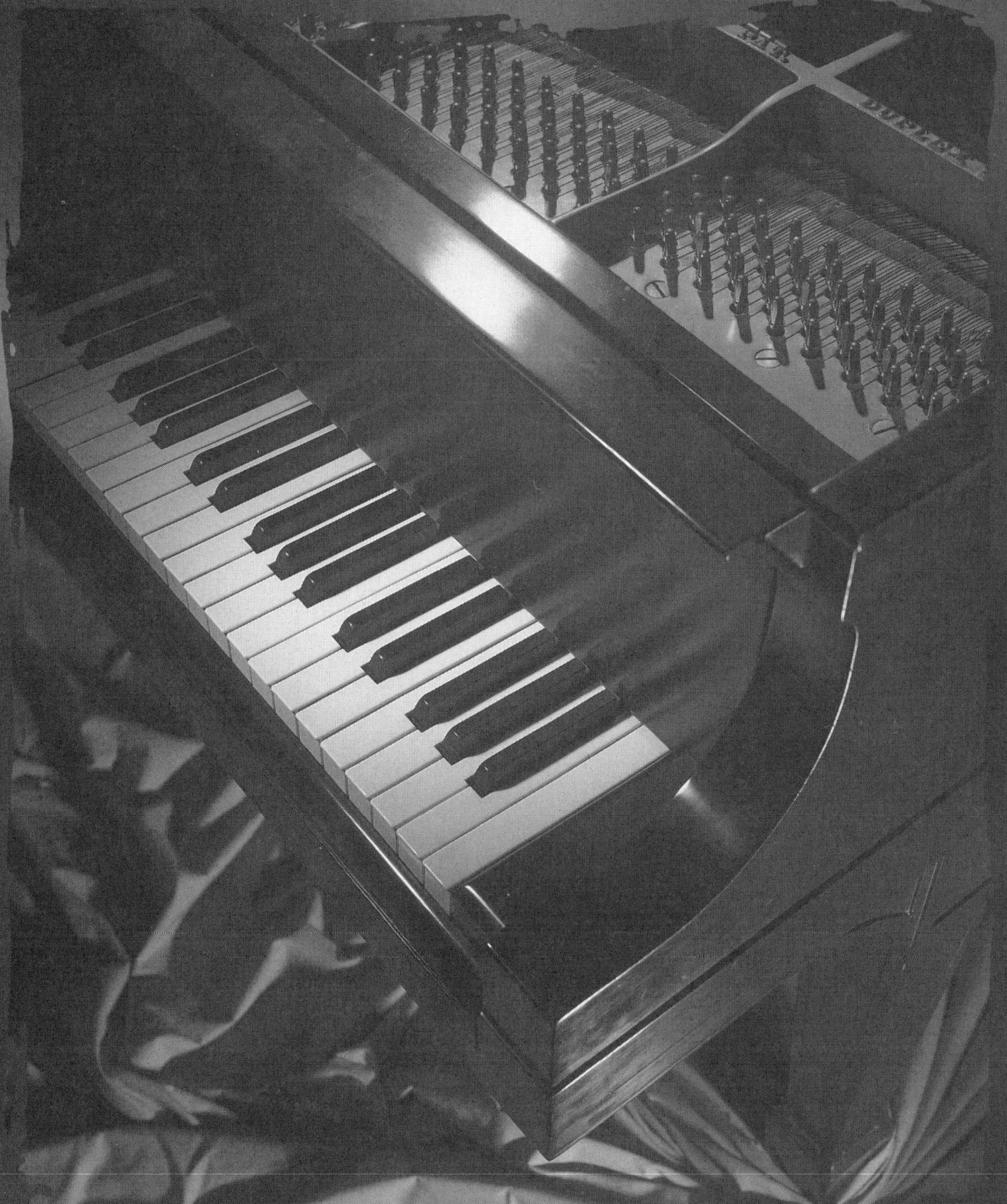

BY MARK HARRISON

ISBN 0-7935-9878-8

7777 W. Bluemound Rd. P.O. Box 13819 Milwaukee, WI 53213

Visit Hal Leonard Online at
www.halleonard.com

ENDORSEMENTS

"I'm very impressed with all the wonderful information this book. It's very well done and I like it a lot. I wish I could ve had this book while I was learning!"

Russell Ferrante

*- **Grammy**-winning **GRP** recording artist*
*- Keyboardist-composer with **Yellowjackets***

"Most how-to-play books in a particular style provide only ks or arrangements from which a student must extrapolate in der to figure out how the patterns fit into an actual performance. is isn't necessarily bad; you can assimilate a lot of spice into ur playing this way. But it does nothing to actually teach you w to play.

Mark Harrison's 498-page book is different. He breaks wn the licks and patterns that make up the various pop styles o their component elements. He explains these elements in ht of their harmonic and rhythmic functions. He provides a nple and enjoyable method for learning these basics in all keys. en he shows you how the basic elements combine to create e various styles. In the process of following his method, your nds can develop a tactile sense of the appropriate thing to do the appropriate time, and your ears can begin to recognize at's appropriate in order to guide your hands.

It makes a lot of sense, and it seems like something that uld come from having taught for years. No surprise: Harrison s done just that, and continues to do so, from his own music hool in Los Angeles.

His writing is warm, humorous, and clear. Practice ercises build gradually and in a very logical sequence. All of e exercises and musical examples are available as MIDI files on audio cassettes, for an additional fee. These materials are ell-prepared, and should be valuable for the notationally-allenged.

The styles covered are ballad, pop, rock, R&B, funk, w age, country, and gospel. Each style is thoroughly treated, t only to a level of detail that's musical. When you consider e amount of harmony and music theory that is included as an egral part of the approach, it's almost a course on composing pop styles.

This is the most accessible and valuable keyboard ethod available for those interested in popular styles. ginners will not be scared off by it. Weekend warriors who never ite got all 12 keys or all those chord extensions under their lts will benefit handsomely from it. Going through the method just plain fun. And at the end, almost anybody who puts a e effort into it should play better!"

Ernie Rideout

*- Assistant Editor, **KEYBOARD MAGAZINE***

"This is a really great method - and it's very up-to-date!"

David Goldblatt

- Top Los Angeles session keyboardist
*- Music director for **Diana Ross**, and **Dennis Miller** & **Chevy Chase** shows*
*- Movie soundtrack credits include "**Little Man Tate**"*

"This book is well laid out and very informative!"

Mark James

- Top Los Angeles- and Nashville-based songwriter
*- **Double-Grammy** winner for the country tune "Always On My Mind"*

"This is a very good and well-organized method!"

Dick Grove

*- **Grammy**-nominated former president of the internationally-acclaimed "**Grove School of Music**"*
*- Co-producer of the hit **Liz Story** album "**My Foolish Heart**"*
*- Los Angeles Jazz Society "**Jazz Educator of the Year**" in 1988.*

"*The Pop Piano Book* by Mark Harrison is a gem. There's nothing like it on the market!

The first section, which deals with contemporary harmonic and rhythmic concepts for piano, is worth the price alone. His explanation of modes is the clearest I've ever seen.

He's so experienced as a teacher, he's able to impart information in a highly organized and practical way. His warm personal style helps the student overcome 'information overload'. Learning one skill leads to the next with complete logic.

The second section contains crystal clear rhythmic and harmonic analysis of eight contemporary styles. Using the skills developed in the first section, these styles are accessible and the student can make music!

I highly recommend this book, and I congratulate Mark on the knowledge, experience and work he put into this valuable book."

Joyce Collins

- Internationally-renowned pianist, performer, recording artist and clinician
*- Many credits include **Grammy**-nominated albums and the movie "**Fabulous Baker Boys**"*
*- Los Angeles Jazz Society "**Jazz Educator of the Year**" in 1992.*

AUTHOR'S FOREWORD

Welcome to ***The Pop Piano Book.*** Let's start with a little trivia quiz:-

- **HAVE YOU EVER** bought the sheet music for a pop tune, only to be 'underwhelmed' by somebody else's arrangement, and unsure how to fix it or make it sound 'hipper'?
- **HAVE YOU EVER** tried to play a pop tune from a 'fake book' or leadsheet, only to be unsure how to interpret the chord symbols, or 'stuck in a rut' with your voicings?
- **HAVE YOU EVER** bought a so-called pop piano instruction book which contained some cool-sounding music examples, but no satisfactory explanation of how they were derived, or how to apply the concepts in different situations?
- **HAVE YOU EVER** wished you could spontaneously emulate the great keyboard players you hear on records, in modern styles such as pop-rock, funk, gospel etc.?
- **HAVE YOU EVER** become frustrated when performing your own tunes or songs, wishing you could interpret them in more stylistically appropriate and interesting ways?

If you answered **YES** to any of these questions, then the solution to your problems is in your hands! At last there is now a method available to help you **spontaneously create your own arrangements** in contemporary styles. In the years that I have been instructing keyboard students in both private and classroom situations, it has become clear to me that the essential foundation for these skills is a firm grasp of harmonic and rhythmic concepts. So the first part of the **Pop Piano Book** (**Chapters 1 – 10**) presents a step-by-step approach to these basic building blocks necessary to play contemporary styles. This is what I call the '**toolbox**' part of the book! At each stage the harmony and underlying concepts are explained, and reinforced with examples and practice routines in different stylistic settings.

The second part of the **Pop Piano Book** (**Chapters 11 – 18**) then presents and analyzes the components of each contemporary style, and gives you specific methods to construct your own accompaniment patterns and melody treatments in each style. These chapters contain hundreds of music examples, **all analyzed and explained**, with detailed cross-reference back to the first part of the book showing you the harmonic and rhythmic devices used in each case. Working through this text will enable you to sound convincing in these styles - **just reading from a chord chart** or from memory! Think of it - no longer will you be unsure about what to play - or be shackled to someone else's cheesy arrangement! Like all worthwhile goals, this learning process will take longer than five minutes (!) and involves some work - but the goal **is achievable** if you follow these methods!

The **Pop Piano Book** can be used by many levels of student, from serious beginner through to intermediate/advanced. You should ideally have some familiarity with treble and bass clef notation, major scales and key signatures, and basic chords. (**Chapter 1** contains a review of chords and scales used in contemporary styles). Here are some ways in which this book can be used:-

- Students can progress through each chapter in order, working through all the examples and practice assignments. This is the most thorough approach and is suitable for serious beginners through to intermediate level students. (Note to teachers - this approach is also suitable for classroom situations as well as private lessons - for example, I have divided this material into five ten-week segments when teaching group classes). If you are working sequentially through the book, the first main areas of 'playing work' are the rhythmic drills beginning on page 29 in **Chapter 2**, and the major scale 'contour' & diatonic triad exercises in **Chapter 3**. You can review review notation, harmony and rhythmic concepts as needed in **Chapter 1** and the first part of **Chapter 2** (i.e. pages 1 – 28), and of course you can also play through the music examples in this section if you wish!
- More advanced players can review any 'contemporary harmony' information in **Chapters 1 – 10** as necessary, before focusing on particular styles of interest in **Chapters 11 – 18**. Because **Pop Piano Book** is so extensively cross-referenced, it is actually possible to 'jump into' the book pretty much anywhere!
- All musicians (including composers, arrangers and other instrumentalists) can use this book as a harmonic and stylistic reference source. Use the Glossary as a look-up index!
- For those of you who don't care for all the analysis and explanation (and I know you're out there...) and who just want to play - well there's nearly **800 music examples** in this book (including all the different styles) for you to have fun with!

We have also created **compact discs**, **audio cassettes** and **standard MIDI files** of all the music examples in the book - you can speed up the learning process by 'hearing as well as seeing' the examples! Please see page ***viii*** for further information on how to order these products. Although the **Pop Piano Book** is primarily written from a piano-playing perspective, the ideas and concepts also substantially apply to synthesizers and electronic keyboards.

Good luck - and I look forward to helping you play the music you enjoy!

Mark Harrison

Harrison Music Education Systems

Los Angeles, California

ABOUT THE AUTHOR

MARK HARRISON is a keyboardist, composer and educator with over twenty years experience in the industry. Before moving to Los Angeles in 1987, Mark's musical career in his native London included appearances on British national (**BBC**) television as well as extensive club and studio experience. As an active composer for television in both England and the United States, his work is heard internationally in commercials for clients like **American Express** and **CNN**, as well as in numerous dramas and documentaries including **A & E**'s popular **American Justice** series.

Mark was commissioned by the music equipment manufacturers **Roland** and **Gibson** to compose and arrange music for their trade shows, and in 1996 Boston's renowned **Berklee College of Music** invited Mark to showcase his composition **First Light** with Berklee's faculty orchestra. Active in the Los Angeles music scene, Mark has performed with top professional musicians such as **Bruce Hornsby**'s drummer John Molo and **Yanni**'s bassist Rick Fierabracci. He leads and composes for the **Mark Harrison Quintet**, which performs regularly on the L.A. jazz circuit. After a recent show, **Music Connection** magazine noted that the Quintet "excelled at contemporary jazz" and that Mark "played with a high level of skill and passion that gave every song a soul".

After teaching at the internationally-acclaimed **Grove School of Music** for six years, Mark founded the **Harrison School of Music** (a successor institution to the Grove school) in Los Angeles. The Harrison School has since helped hundreds of students achieve their musical goals. Mark's groundbreaking keyboard method **The Pop Piano Book** is endorsed by Grammy-winners **Russell Ferrante** and **Mark James**, as well as other top professional musicians and educators. **Keyboard Magazine** calls his presentation style "warm, humorous and clear", and names The Pop Piano Book "the most accessible and valuable keyboard method available for those interested in popular styles".

Mark has also authored a complete series of instruction books for contemporary music theory and eartraining, which are "first class teaching texts" and "an excellent, plainspoken introduction to understanding music" according to **Jazz Times** magazine. The **Harrison Music Education Systems** product line is published internationally by **Hal Leonard Publications**. Mark's methods are also used and recommended at many educational institutions (including the internationally-famous **Berklee College of Music**) and his materials have been purchased by thousands of students in over twenty-five countries worldwide. Mark has written several 'master class' articles on contemporary rock, R&B and gospel piano styles for **Keyboard Magazine**, and he continues to be in demand as a uniquely effective contemporary music educator. He currently runs a busy private teaching studio in the Los Angeles area.

CDs, TAPES & MIDI FILES are available with this book!

The **Pop Piano Book** contains nearly **800** music examples! These examples are available in the following formats:

- recorded on ***compact discs*** (a set of five CDs)
- recorded on ***cassette tapes*** (a set of four tapes)
- as ***standard Midi files*** in PC or Mac format (a set of two floppy disks).

Speed up your learning process by **hearing** as well as **seeing** the music in this book! To order or inquire about these products, please contact us (see info at the bottom of the next page).

Here are some more products available from

HARRISON MUSIC EDUCATION SYSTEMS:

Contemporary Music Theory Level One Book

This introductory pop & jazz theory course covers music notation, major and minor scales, key signatures, intervals, triads, four-part chords, modes, diatonic chords, suspensions, and alterations of 3- and 4-part chords. Includes hundreds of written theory exercises, all with answers provided!

Contemporary Music Theory Level Two Book

This intermediate pop & jazz theory course covers 'II-V-I' progressions in major and minor keys, five-part chords, substitutions, harmonic analysis of pop & jazz tunes, voiceleading, use of 'upper structure' voicings, and pentatonic & blues scale applications. Includes hundreds of written theory exercises with answers!

Contemporary Music Theory Level Three Book *(available with CDs)*

This more advanced pop & jazz theory course presents the chord tones, extensions, alterations, and scale sources, for all major, minor, dominant and diminished chords. This information is then used to create voicings, polychords, and to harmonize melodies, using our 'contemporary shape concept'. This book is available with CDs of all music examples, and includes hundreds of written theory exercises with answers!

(more products available contd)

Contemporary Eartraining Level One Book *(available with CDs & cassettes)*

A modern eartraining approach to help you hear and transcribe melodies, rhythms, intervals, bass lines and basic chords (available with CDs and cassettes of vocal drills and exercises). Developed at the **Grove School of Music** in Los Angeles.

Contemporary Eartraining Level Two Book *(available with CDs & cassettes)*

A modern eartraining approach to help you hear and transcribe chord progressions, modes and key changes used in pop and jazz styles (available with CDs and cassettes of all exercises). Developed at the **Grove School of Music** in Los Angeles.

*If you would like to **order** or **inquire about our products**, or if you are interested in **private instruction with Mark Harrison** in the Los Angeles area, please call toll-free (in the U.S.):*

(4 6 3 7)

1-800-799-HMES

(Harrison Music Education Systems)

or visit our website at:

www.harrisonmusic.com

or write to us at:

HARRISON MUSIC EDUCATION SYSTEMS
P.O. BOX 56505, SHERMAN OAKS,
CA 91413, U.S.A.

SPECIAL ACKNOWLEDGEMENT

DICK GROVE

During the period from 1988 until 1992 I had the pleasure and privilege of teaching a wide range of courses at the **Grove School of Music**, in Los Angeles, California. From the time that **Dick Grove** founded this school in 1973 until the school's closure in 1992, his unique perspective on contemporary music influenced literally thousands of musicians and students from all around the world, as well as those of us on the faculty who were fortunate enough to work in this exceptional institution.

My experience on the Grove School faculty provided an ideal environment for me to develop and fine-tune my own concepts of how contemporary music should be taught, which in turn has helped me create my own series of instruction books and methods. Dick Grove's overall philosophy and concepts of contemporary music were very influential in this process, and I am proud to have been an integral part of the Grove School educational environment.

We were very saddened to hear of Dick's untimely death in December of 1998. I had the honor of speaking at a memorial service held for Dick in Los Angeles, which was attended by several hundred members of the 'Grove community'. Dick was a major influence and inspiration for my own educational career, and I know his legacy and spirit will continue to impact the many lives he has touched.

Mark Harrison

TABLE OF CONTENTS

The Pop Piano Book by Mark Harrison

SECTION 1 - Contemporary harmonic and rhythmic concepts for piano

SECTION 2 - Contemporary piano styles

--- NOTES ---

CHAPTER ONE

Scales and chords - review

Major scales

We will first of all review some concepts relating to major scales. This is the scale most easily understood by the ear, and is the basis for much of today's contemporary pop music. When teaching harmony and theory classes, I emphasise to students the importance of working with and memorizing the **interval relationships** (i.e. the whole-steps and half-steps) present in the major scale, as this approach most closely parallels how the ear relates to the scale. So don't just rely on your key signatures to figure out the notes in an **A** major scale (for example)!! If you know your intervals you can figure out any major scale - this is also the starting point to getting the 'contour' of the scale under your fingers, an essential step on the road to becoming a proficient player in all keys (see discussion of diatonic relationships in **Chapter 3**). Of course knowing your key signatures is important for notation reasons (reading and writing) but does not in my view represent the best way to memorize the contents of a major scale! The following example shows us the **C Major** scale, also indicating the intervals (whole-steps and half-steps) present:-

Figure 1.1. C Major scale interval construction

(**WS** = whole-step, **HS** = half-step).

Of course the above interval relationships work for all major scales, not just C Major!

The following examples are a summary of all the major scales, both with and without key signatures. It's very important that you learn the major scales and recognize their 'contour' on the keyboard - this is a vital 'cornerstone' of the approach that we will be developing!

Major scales with key signatures

Figure 1.2. - C major

Figure 1.3. - F major

Figure 1.4. - Bb major

FOR FURTHER INFORMATION ON THE THEORY CONCEPTS REVIEWED IN THIS CHAPTER, PLEASE REFER TO OUR CONTEMPORARY MUSIC THEORY LEVELS 1 & 2 BOOKS (SEE PAGE ix IN THIS BOOK).

CHAPTER ONE

Major scales with key signatures (contd)

Figure 1.5. - Eb major

Figure 1.6. - Ab major

Figure 1.7. - Db major

Figure 1.8. - Gb major

Figure 1.9. - Cb major

Figure 1.10. - G major

Figure 1.11. - D major

Figure 1.12. - A major

Figure 1.13. - E major

Figure 1.14. - B major

Figure 1.15. - F# major

Figure 1.16 - C# major

Major scales without key signatures

Figure 1.17. - C major

Figure 1.18. - F major

Figure 1.19. - Bb major

Figure 1.20. - Eb major

Figure 1.21. - Ab major

Figure 1.22. - Db major

Figure 1.23. - Gb major

Figure 1.24. - Cb major

Figure 1.25. - G major

Figure 1.26. - D major

Figure 1.27. - A major

Figure 1.28. - E major

Major scales without key signatures (contd)

Figure 1.29.
- B major

Figure 1.30.
- F# major

Figure 1.31.
- C# major

Modal scales

A modal scale can most conveniently be thought of as a **'displaced'** scale i.e. using a scale starting from a point other than the normal tonic or first note of that scale. This type of displacement is most typically applied to major scales in contemporary styles. Other scales however can also be 'displaced' in a similar manner (a good example being the 'modes' of a melodic minor scale, which are widely used in jazz styles). Each possible 'displacement' of a major scale has its own mode name, as illustrated in the following examples:-

- A C major scale starting on the note **D** (i.e. using D as the new tonic) would be referred to as a **D Dorian** mode (Dorian means major scale starting from its **2nd** degree):-

Figure 1.32.
- D Dorian

- A C major scale starting on the note **E** (i.e. using E as the new tonic) would be referred to as an **E Phrygian** mode (Phrygian means major scale starting from its **3rd** degree):-

Figure 1.33.
- E Phrygian

- A C major scale starting on the note **F** (i.e. using F as the new tonic) would be referred to as an **F Lydian** mode (Lydian means major scale starting from its **4th** degree):-

Figure 1.34.
- F Lydian

- A C major scale starting on the note G (i.e. using G as the new tonic) would be referred to as a **G Mixolydian** mode (Mixolydian means major scale starting from its **5th** degree):-

Figure 1.35.
- G Mixolydian

Modal scales (contd)

- A C major scale starting on the note **A** (i.e. using A as the new tonic) would be referred to as an **A Aeolian** mode (Aeolian means major scale starting from its **6th** degree):

Figure 1.36.
- A Aeolian

- A C major scale starting on the note **B** (i.e. using B as the new tonic) would be referred to as a **B Locrian** mode (Locrian means major scale starting from its **7th** degree):-

Figure 1.37.
- B Locrian

- A C major scale which is not displaced (i.e. still using the note C as the tonic) also has a mode name or description - this is referred to as a **C Ionian** mode (Ionian means major scale starting from its normal tonic):-

Figure 1.38.
- C Ionian
(= C Major)

Why do we use modes? Well, different interval relationships occur in the scale depending on which mode we use i.e. the expected major scale sequence of whole-steps and half-steps (see **Fig. 1.1.**) is modified in some way - thereby creating different responses on the part of the listener. Also the modes are used as scale sources for different chordal relationships (see following chord review in this Chapter). Subject to numerous variations/ exceptions the following stylistic observations could be made regarding the modes:-

- **Phrygian** and **Locrian** have a more 'altered' characteristic (these modes start with a half-step) and are generally reserved for more jazz-oriented and sophisticated styles.

- **Lydian**, **Mixolydian** and **Aeolian** are widely used in contemporary styles. (The bright 'major' sound of Lydian is a favourite for TV music and commercials - the 'natural minor' sound of Aeolian is widely used in rock styles).

- **Dorian** has a 'minor' sound and is found in jazz and some contemporary and fusion styles.

Each modal scale has a **'relative major'**, which is the original major scale which has been displaced to create the mode in question. For example, the relative major of all the previous examples (**1.32. - 1.38.**) is **C Major** - because all of these examples are displaced versions of C Major. I believe that using the 'relative major' concept is the key to working with modes for the keyboardist - if you know the 'relative major' of the mode that you're working with, then you're home free (assuming you know your major scales of course)! To illustrate this principle, here are some further examples of the different modes, but this time using the same starting note (C) and different relative major scales. Let's say we wanted to create a Dorian mode, but instead of starting a C major scale on D (as in Fig. **1.32.**) we still wanted to keep the starting note of C. We know that a Dorian mode means 'major scale starting from its 2nd degree', so we ask ourselves - "Which major scale has C as its 2nd degree?".

Modal scales (contd)

This would be a Bb major scale (if you're not sure about this, refer back to the intervals in **Fig. 1.1.** - Bb is a whole-step below C). So - to create a Dorian mode starting on C, we use a Bb major scale as follows:-

Figure 1.39. - C Dorian *(relative major is **Bb**)*

We can use the same principle to derive all of the previously described modal scales, but this time keeping **C** as the starting note in each case - therefore the relative major scale will change with each mode:-

Figure 1.40. - C Phrygian *(relative major is **Ab**)*

Figure 1.41. - C Lydian *(relative major is **G**)*

Figure 1.42. - C Mixolydian *(relative major is **F**)*

Figure 1.43. - C Aeolian *(relative major is **Eb**)*

Figure 1.44. - C Locrian *(relative major is **Db**)*

One good way to get this concept 'under your fingers' is to practise all of the modal scales which pass through a given note (effectively you'll be playing all the major scales which contain the note!) - i.e. the above examples in **Figs.1.39. - 1.44.** are all the modes which contain the note C. On the following page is an example of such an exercise:-

Modal scales (contd)

Figure 1.45.
- Modal Exercise

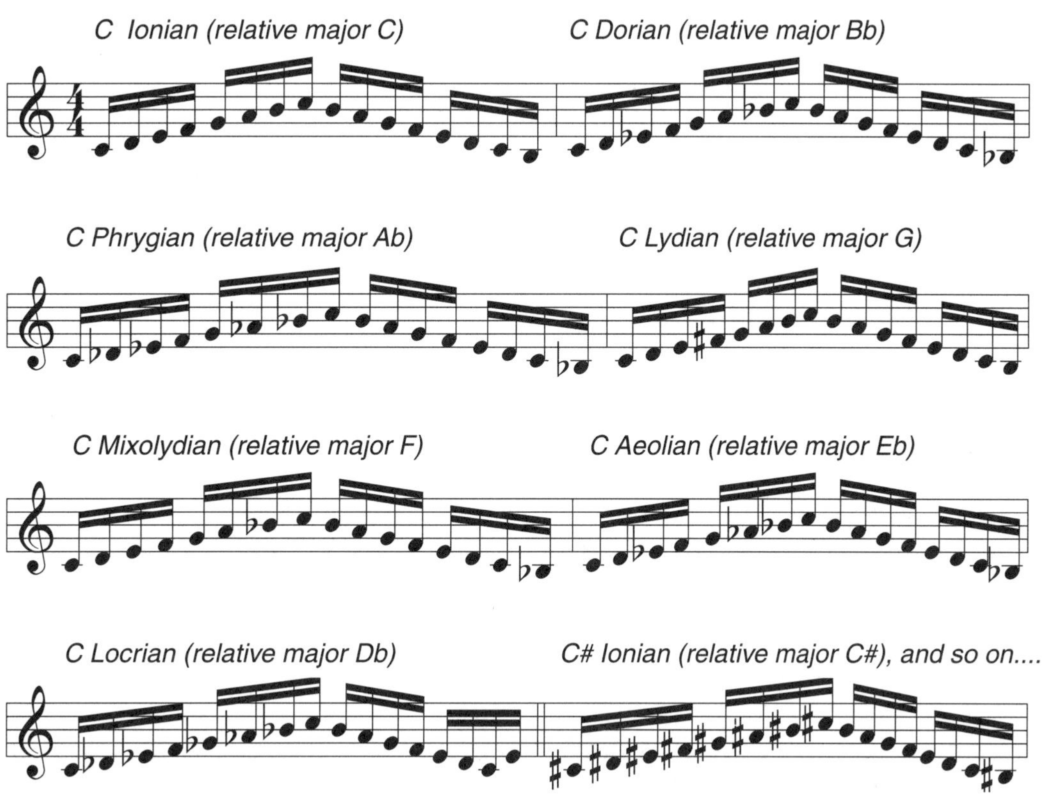

Once you get to **C# Ionian** (the last measure above), you should then play all the modes passing through **C#** in the same manner as you did all the modes passing through **C** (as above). You should then continue to ascend chromatically through all the possible starting notes (i.e. continue thru D, Eb, E etc.) in the same way! Another good variation is to cover a greater range on each mode (2, 3 or 4 octaves) ascending and descending.

(Don't forget that any sharps or flats are 'in force' for the remainder of the measure in which they occur).

Have fun!

CHAPTER ONE

Minor scales

There are three types of minor scales the contemporary keyboardist needs to be familiar with - **melodic, harmonic and natural**. In classical theory minor scales can have different ascending and descending forms - however this does not apply to contemporary applications! One convenient way to derive the minor scales is to modify a major scale as required. If we take a C major scale and lower the 3rd degree by half-step, we create a **C melodic minor** scale:-

Figure 1.46.
- C melodic minor
(C major scale with b3)

If we keep the flatted 3rd and additionally lower the 6th degree by half-step, we create a **C harmonic minor** scale:-

Figure 1.47.
- C harmonic minor
(C major scale with b3,b6)

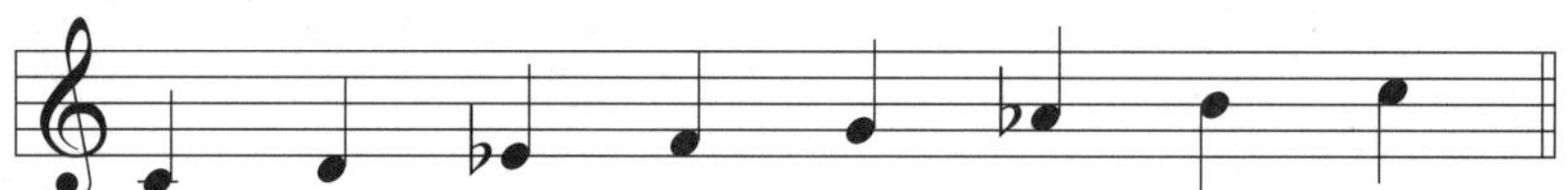

If we keep the flatted 3rd and 6th, and additionally lower the 7th degree by half-step, we create a **C natural minor** scale:-

Figure 1.48.
- C natural minor
(C major scale with b3,b6,b7)

As with the modal scales, the minor scales have different impressions and stylistic usages. Again subject to numerous variations and exceptions, the following observations could be made regarding the minor scales:-

- **Melodic** minor scales are used extensively in jazz, fusion and latin styles.
- **Harmonic** minor scales are generally found in ethnic styles (and some jazz styles).
- **Natural** minor scales are used extensively in contemporary pop and rock styles.

We briefly need to review the concept of **relative minor**. Each major key (see major scales with key signatures in **Figs. 1.2. - 1.16.**) has a corresponding relative minor key which shares the same key signature. The relative minor for a major key can be found by taking the **6th degree** of the relevant major scale. For example, let's say we wanted to know the relative minor of Ab major - well the 6th degree of Ab major is F (see **Fig. 1.6.**), and so F minor is the relative minor of Ab major and would share the same key signature (four flats). Don't forget that if you use a minor key signature with no accidentals (extra sharps or flats), then a **natural minor scale is what you get**. For example, in **Fig. 1.48.** above we derived the C natural minor scale. C is the relative minor (6th degree of) Eb major, and so the keys of Eb major and C minor would share the same key signature (three flats). So starting a scale on C within the discipline of the Eb major/C minor key signature will yield a C natural minor scale, as follows:-

Minor scales (contd)

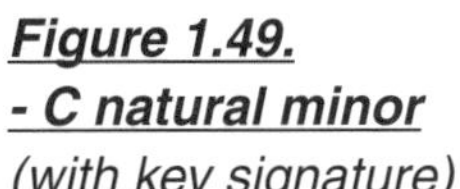

Figure 1.49.
- C natural minor
(with key signature)

(Note that the natural minor scale is identical to the Aeolian mode - see **Fig. 1.43.**). If we wanted to make use of either C harmonic or C melodic minor scales, and the minor key key signature (in this case three flats) was in force, then we would need to **contradict the key signature** with either one or two accidentals, as follows:-

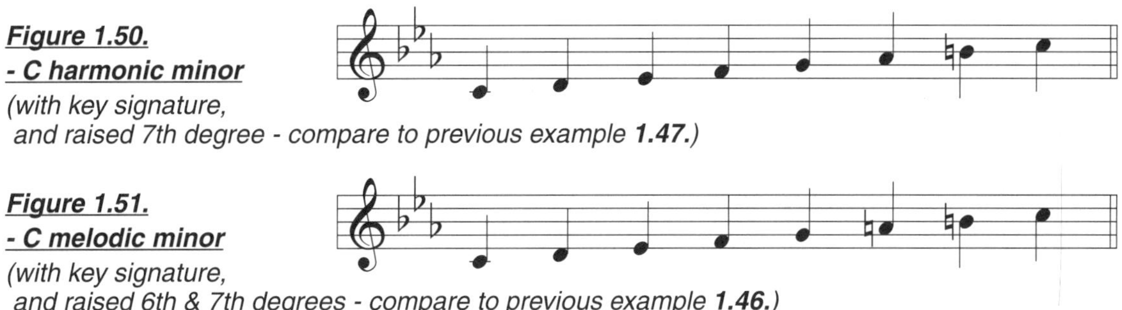

Figure 1.50.
- C harmonic minor
*(with key signature, and raised 7th degree - compare to previous example **1.47.**)*

Figure 1.51.
- C melodic minor
*(with key signature, and raised 6th & 7th degrees - compare to previous example **1.46.**)*

Pentatonic scales

Pentatonic scales are widely used in all forms of contemporary rock and pop music as well as jazz styles, as we will see in later chapters. One convenient way to derive a pentatonic scale is to take a major scale and **remove the 4th and 7th** degrees. When teaching harmony classes I refer to this as a 'major scale with the teeth pulled' (!) as the 4th and 7th degrees are the active and 'leading' half-steps in the scale - by removing these scale degrees the resulting scale has a less 'leading' quality and is more easily able to 'float' over different harmonies. Here is an example of a **C pentatonic** scale:-

Figure 1.52.
C pentatonic
(C major with 4th and 7th degrees removed)

Here for your reference are all of the pentatonic scales (getting these 'under your fingers' is very desirable as they are a tremendously useful source for patterns, embellishments, solo ideas etc. - as we shall see!):-

Figure 1.53.
F pentatonic

Figure 1.54.
Bb pentatonic

Pentatonic scales (contd)

Pentatonic scales (contd)

One other pentatonic variation we need to consider is the **minor pentatonic** scale. This can be considered as a 'mode' of a pentatonic scale, but starting on the relative minor instead of the normal tonic. For example, we have already derived an **Eb pentatonic** scale (see **Fig. 1.55.**) - and the relative minor of Eb is C minor (see previous section reviewing relative minor). So an Eb pentatonic scale built from C we will call a '**C minor pentatonic scale**' as follows:-

Figure 1.67.
- C minor pentatonic
(Eb pentatonic scale built from C)

The minor pentatonic scale is widely encountered in contemporary pop and rock styles.

Blues scales

If we add a half-step 'connector' or passing tone between the 3rd and 4th degrees of a minor pentatonic scale, we derive what is commonly known as the **'blues scale'**, which is also widely encountered in many contemporary and jazz idioms. Here is an example of the C blues scale:-

Figure 1.68.
- C Blues
(C minor pentatonic with added half-step passing tone between 3rd and 4th scale degrees)

As with the previous pentatonic scales, it is very useful to have these minor pentatonics and blues scales 'under your fingers'. Practise them in all keys (of course)!!

CHAPTER ONE

Three-note chords (triads)

There are four different 'triads' (three-note chords) in common usage - **major**, **minor**, **augmented** and **diminished**. It is useful to be aware of the interval relationships present in these triads, as illustrated below. Another approach is to consider the major triad as consisting of the 1st, 3rd and 5th degrees of a major scale, and then to modify the major triad to obtain the other types of triad:-

Figure 1.69.
- C major triad
(Intervals are Ma3rd and Per5th with respect to root of chord - can be derived by taking 1st, 3rd & 5th degrees of major scale).

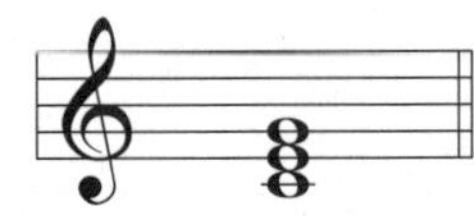

Figure 1.70.
- C minor triad
(Intervals are Mi3rd and Per5th with respect to root of chord - can be derived by taking major triad and flatting the 3rd by half-step)

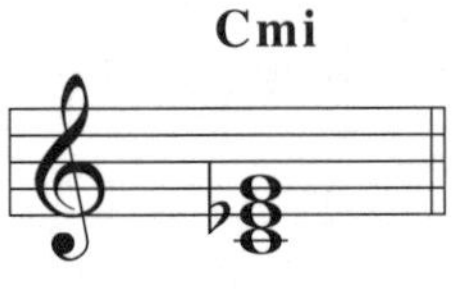

Cmi

Figure 1.71.
- C augmented triad
(Intervals are Ma3rd and Aug5th with respect to root of chord - can be derived by taking major triad and sharping the 5th degree by half-step)

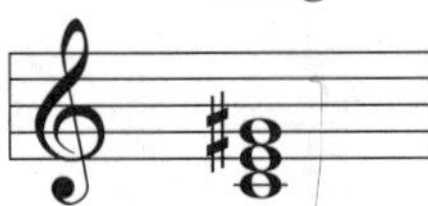

Figure 1.72.
- C diminished triad
(Intervals are Mi3rd and Dim5th with respect to root of chord - can be derived by taking major triad and flatting the 3rd & 5th degress by half-step)

A major (or minor) triad can also be suspended - this means that the 3rd of the chord has been replaced by the note which is a perfect 4th interval above the root of the chord. For example, to change a **C major** triad to **C sus**, the note E would be replaced by the note F as in the following example:-

Figure 1.73.
- C sus
(Intervals are Per4th and Per5th with respect to root of chord)

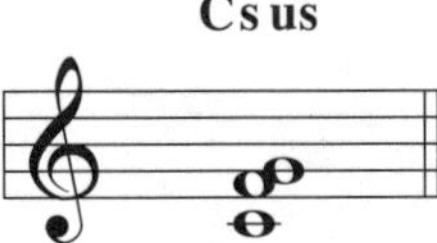

Depending upon the harmonic style, the 'suspension' might well resolve to a major or minor triad - see **Chapter 9** for further information.

Triads (contd)

Another important point I stress when teaching harmony classes is that chords are not simply 'disconnected' stacks of pitches - they all have a function or purpose within a **key center relationship**. For example, we could build triads (3-note chords) from each note in a major scale, all the time making sure that we did not move outside the restriction of that scale. Such chords are known as **diatonic triads** (diatonic means belonging to a major scale or key area). When we do this, different triad qualities (major, minor etc.) result from the different scale degrees as follows:-

Figure 1.74. Diatonic triads from C major

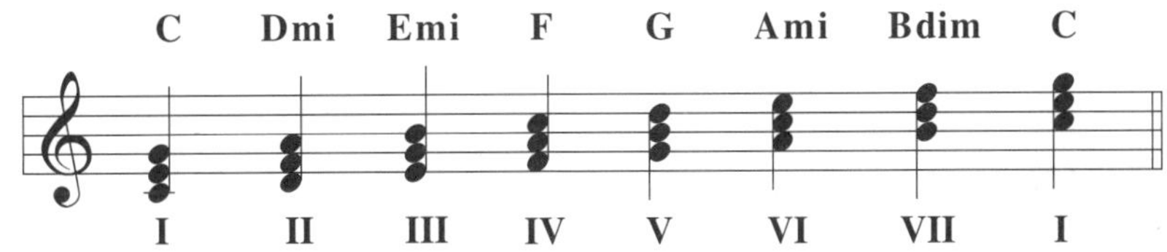

This gives us another important angle on minor triads for example - a minor triad will occur 'naturally' from the 2nd, 3rd and 6th degrees of a major scale as above, as well as by taking a major triad and flatting the 3rd as previously discussed.

Four-note chords

Four-note (or four-part) chords can be considered from the point of view of adding some kind of 6th or 7th interval to one of the triads previously discussed. (See following examples):-

If we add a major 7th interval to a major triad, we get a **major 7th** chord.

Figure 1.75. C major 7th
(intervals are Ma3rd, Per5th and Ma7th with respect to the root)

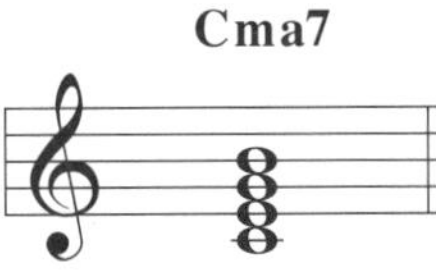

If we add a major 6th interval to a major triad, we get a **major 6th** chord.

Figure 1.76. C major 6th
(intervals are Ma3rd, Per5th and Ma6th with respect to the root)

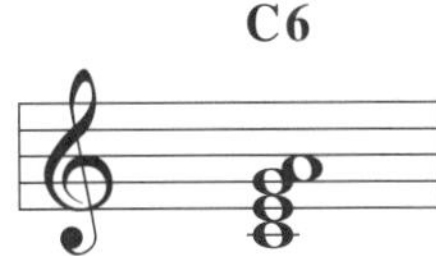

If we add a minor 7th interval to a major triad, we get a **dominant 7th** chord.

Figure 1.77. C (dominant) 7th
(Intervals are Ma3rd, Per5th and Mi7th with respect to the root)

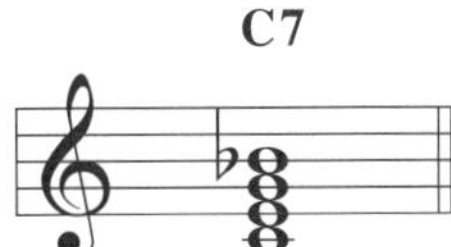

Four-note chords (contd)

If we add a minor 7th interval to a suspended triad, we get a **suspended dominant 7th** chord.

Figure 1.78.
C suspended (dominant) 7th
(Intervals are Per4th, Per5th and Mi7th with respect to the root)

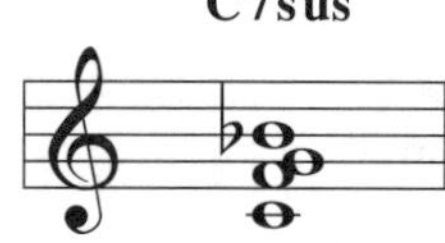

If we add a minor 7th interval to a minor triad, we get a **minor 7th chord**.

Figure 1.79.
C minor 7th
(Intervals are Mi3rd, Per5th and Mi7th with respect to the root)

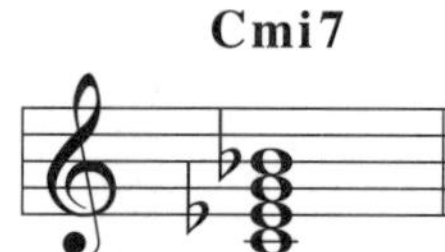

If we add a major 7th or 6th interval to a minor triad, we get a **minor major 7th** or **minor 6th chord**.

Figure 1.80.
C minor major 7th & C minor 6th
(Intervals are Mi3rd, Per5th, and Ma7th or Ma6th with respect to the root)

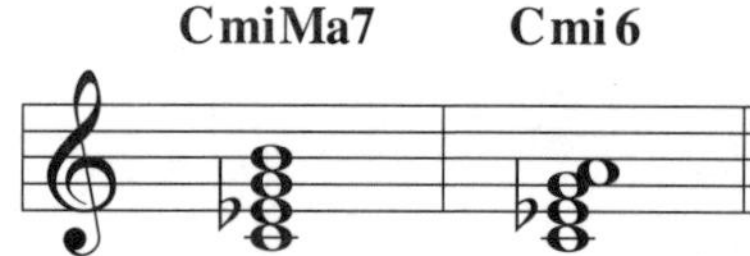

If we add a diminished 7th (equivalent to a major 6th) interval to a diminished triad, we get a **diminished 7th** chord.

Figure 1.81.
C diminished 7th
(Intervals are Mi3rd, Dim5th and Dim7th with respect to the root)

One important common factor to the above four-note chords (except the diminished 7th) is the presence of the perfect 5th. It is therefore the different permutations of the **3rd** and **6th/7th** which define the chord quality. However, on major 7th, minor 7th and dominant 7th chords the **5th** may additionally be **'altered'** as follows:-

Figure 1.82. Altered 5ths on a C major 7th chord

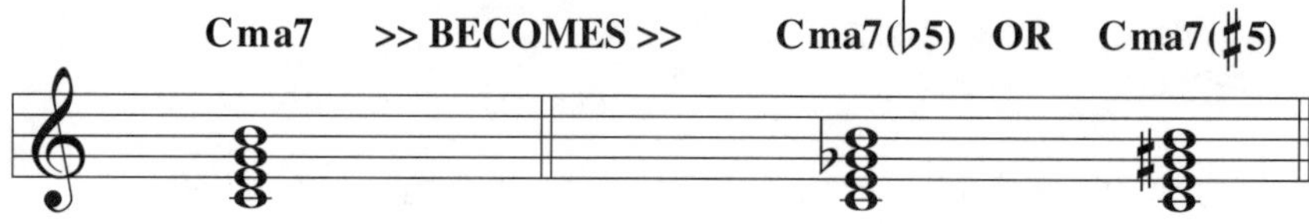

Figure 1.83. Altered 5ths on a C minor 7th chord

Four-note chords (contd)

Figure 1.84. Altered 5ths on a C dominant 7th chord

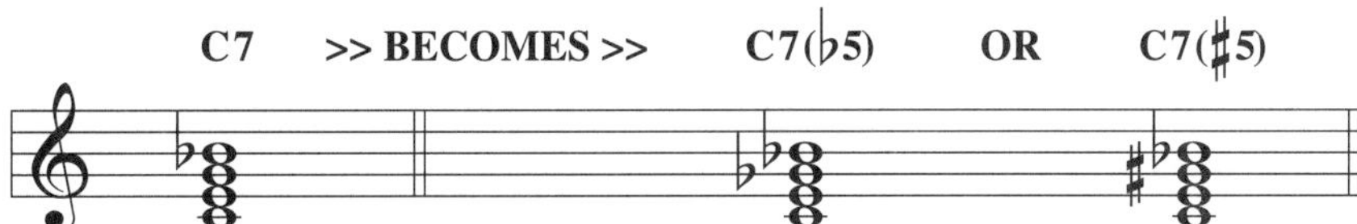

As with the diatonic triads, it is important to know the **diatonic four-part** relationships within a major scale. Again these chords are being built within the restriction of the scale as follows:-

Figure 1.85. Diatonic four-note chords in C major

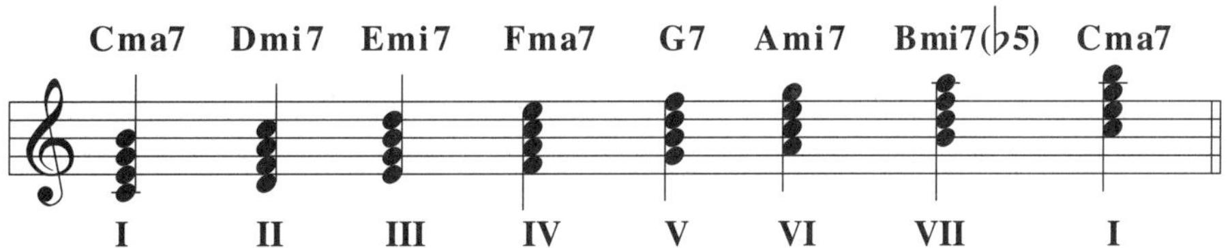

The modal scales created when 'displacing' a C major scale (see **Figs. 1.32. - 1.37.**) can be considered as scale sources for the above diatonic four-part chords. For example, **D Dorian** can be the scale source for the **Dmi7** chord, **E Phrygian** can be the scale source for the **Emi7** chord, and so on. This enables us to build a (modal) scale source from the root of each diatonic chord, which can be helpful in playing situations.

A complete presentation of every diatonic and substitute relationship in major and minor keys is somewhat beyond the scope of this brief review chapter! However we can add the following observations:-

- The 'dominant' 7th chord is so-called because of its very active and leading quality. It is normally built from the **5th degree** of the key area (see above) and typically would resolve to the tonic, or chord built from the 1st degree. The 'suspended' form (see **Fig. 1.78.**) is less active/leading and is frequently used in modern pop styles.
- In styles using four-part chords and above, the **II**(mi7)/**V**(7)/**I**(ma7) are often viewed as the primary or definitive chords (in major keys). Other diatonic chords could be seen as substitutes (typically **IV** for **II**, **VII** for **V**, and **III** or **VI** for **I**).
- The mi6 and miMa7 chords described earlier are typically found in minor key applications (often built from the tonic or 1st degree of a minor key) and are usually derived from melodic minor scales.
- The 'altered' chords above are the result of modifying the 5th of a four-part chord while leaving the 3rd & 7th intact. This will typically occur in minor key applications. The 'altered' minor 7th chord is frequently built on the 2nd degree of a minor key, and the 'altered' dominant 7th chord is frequently built on the 5th degree of a minor key.

Five-note chords

We can also add 9ths to all of the previous chord possibilities. This gives a 'fuller' and more sophisticated sound and is appropriate for many modern styles. Generally the rule is that we add a **major 9th** with respect to the root of the chord. The only exception to this (at least in conventional tonal idioms!) is on the dominant 7th chord, where an 'altered' 9th is possible. This is generally reserved for jazz, latin and more sophisticated R'n'B styles. Here are the commonly used '9th' chords:-

Figure 1.86. Creating Cma9 by adding a 9th to Cma7

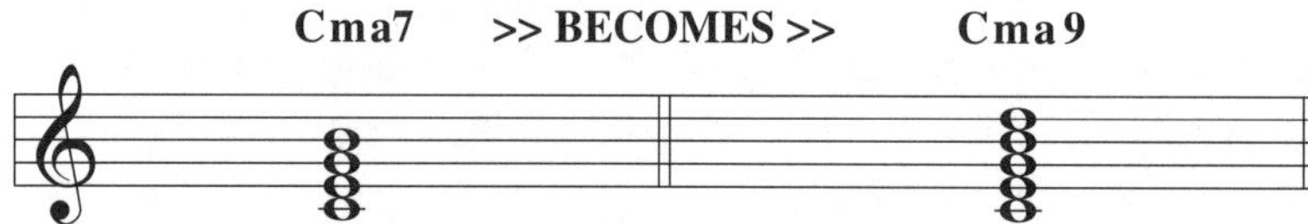

Figure 1.87. Creating Cmi9 by adding a 9th to Cmi7

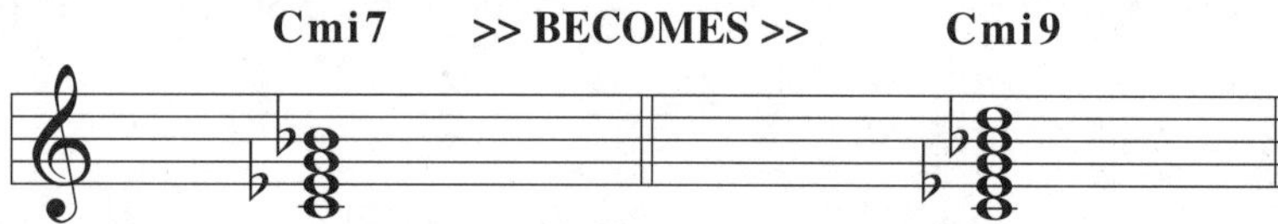

Figure 1.88. Creating C9 (C dominant 9th) by adding a 9th to C7

Figure 1.89. Creating C9sus by adding a 9th to C7sus

Figure 1.90. Creating C69 by adding a 9th to C6

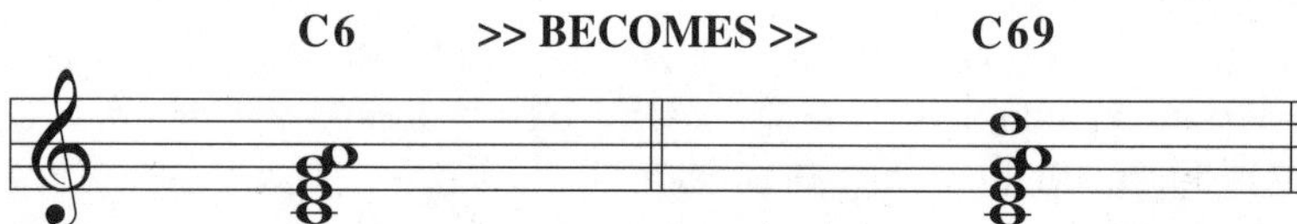

Figure 1.91. Creating CmiMa9 by adding a 9th to CmiMa7

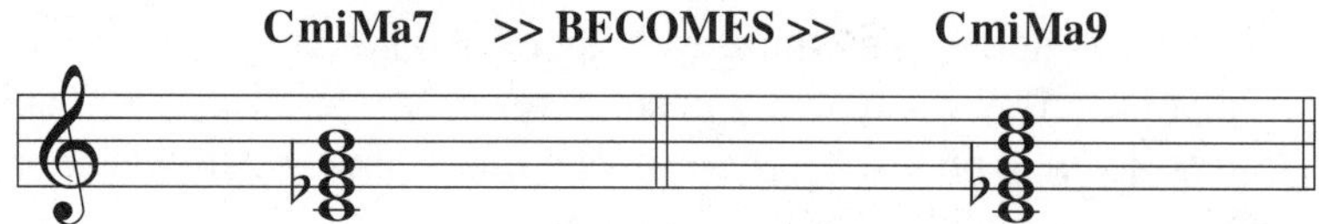

Five-note chords (contd)

Figure 1.92. Creating Cmi69 by adding a 9th to Cmi6

It is also possible to add a (major) 9th to a major or minor triad, **without** including the 6th or 7th of the chord. This is called an **'add9'** chord, and is widely used in contemporary styles - see following examples:-

Figure 1.93. Creating C(add9) by adding a 9th to C (major triad)

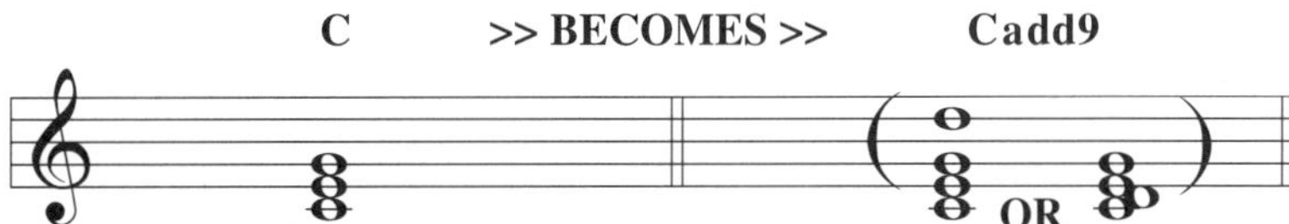

Figure 1.94. Creating Cmi(add9) by adding a 9th to Cmi

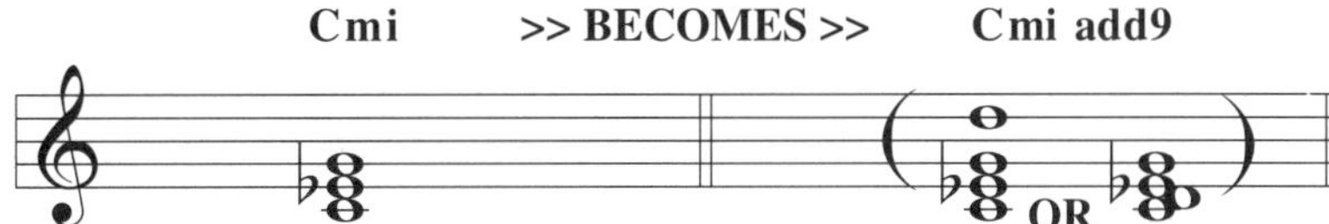

Finally, as mentioned above we can add an **'altered' 9th** (instead of a major 9th) to a dominant 7th chord, in more sophisticated music styles. See following examples:-

Figure 1.95. Altering the 9th on a C (dominant) 9th chord

As we said before, the dominant chord is generally functioning as a V chord in a key - the above 'altered' dominants are normally used in minor key applications.

CHAPTER ONE

Circle-of-fifths and circle-of-fourths

In this book the term 'circle-of-fifths' refers to a sequence of keys, scales or chords as follows:-

C - F - Bb - Eb - Ab - Db (C#) - Gb (F#) - Cb (B) - E - A - D - G - C

Also the term 'circle-of-fourths' refers to a sequence of keys, scales or chords as follows:-

C - G - D - A - E - B (Cb) - F# (Gb) - C# (Db) - Ab - Eb - Bb - F - C

Alternative enharmonic names are shown in parentheses. The above sequences could of course start and end at any point - here they are just shown starting and ending on C for reference.

There are certainly a number of different ways of looking at the 'circle' and it may well be that you have not encountered the above interpretation! I often find that people are tempted to refer to the first line above (i. e. **C - F - Bb** etc) as 'circle of fourths', as it would seem that C to F is a 4th interval, and so on. Well it is if you are considering the intervals as **ascending**, but if you think of the intervals as **descending** then C down to F is a 5th interval! So in classroom teaching situations, I consider an 'interval based' method for labelling the 'circles' rather unsatisfactory given these different interpretations.

I prefer instead to consider the 'harmonic' aspects of the circle. If we consider each stage on the circle as a new 'key area', then the relationship of the immediately preceding stage to the current stage is either a **5 to 1** relationship or a **4 to 1** relationship. For example in the top line above, C to F is a **5 to 1** relationship (in the key of **F** where we have landed; C is the **5th degree** of the F major scale) - so we call this **'circle-of-fifths'**. In the second line above, C to G is a **4 to 1** relationship (in the key of **G** where we have landed; C is the **4th degree** of the G major scale) - so we call this **'circle-of-fourths'**. This method neatly sidesteps any interval problems - for example C to F can always be considered a **5 to 1** relationship, regardless of the interval direction (i.e. ascending or descending) between C and F.

Some of the underlying harmony and eartraining principles behind this approach are beyond the scope of this brief review chapter! (Check out our **Contemporary Music Theory** books for a fuller explanation). It's my belief that the above method not only makes labelling the directions on the circle more 'foolproof' but also more closely parallels how the ear relates to the resolutions which occur as we traverse around the circle. However, it's really only terminology - don't worry if you initially learned it a different way! In this book the 'circles' are used as sequences of scales or chords to practise certain routines in, and as frameworks for various chord voiceleading ideas and exercises. So if you're not sure what I mean by 'circle-of-fifths' of 'circle-of-fourths' when I refer to them in later chapters, then refer to the top of this page as necessary!

Rhythmic concepts and notation - review

Notation of rhythmic values

First of all we will review rhythmic notation concepts for notes and rests. Here we are focusing on the duration i.e. how many beats the note or rest will last. The different note durations we will be working with are illustrated as follows:-

Figure 2.1.
- Whole note
(lasts for four beats)

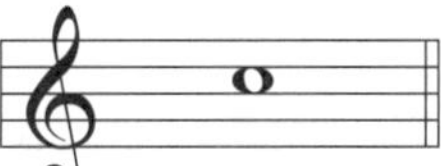

Figure 2.2.
- Half note
(lasts for two beats)

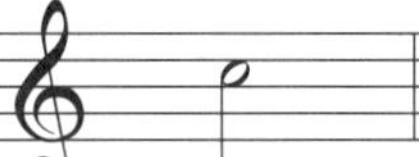

Figure 2.3.
- Dotted half note
(lasts for three beats)

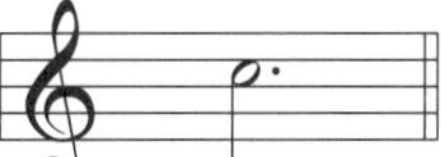

Figure 2.4.
- Quarter note
(lasts for one beat)

Figure 2.5.
- Dotted quarter note
(lasts for one & a half beats)

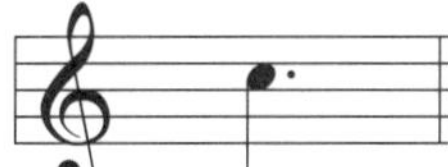

Figure 2.6.
- Eighth note
(lasts for half a beat)

Figure 2.7.
- Dotted eighth note
(lasts for three-quarters of a beat)

Figure 2.8.
- Sixteenth note
(lasts for a quarter of a beat)

Notice that the 'dotted' rhythms **add half as much again** to the original duration of the note. Now we will review all of the corresponding rests for the above durations. (The rest of course indicates silence or no sound from the instrument/part in question).

Notation of rhythmic values (contd)

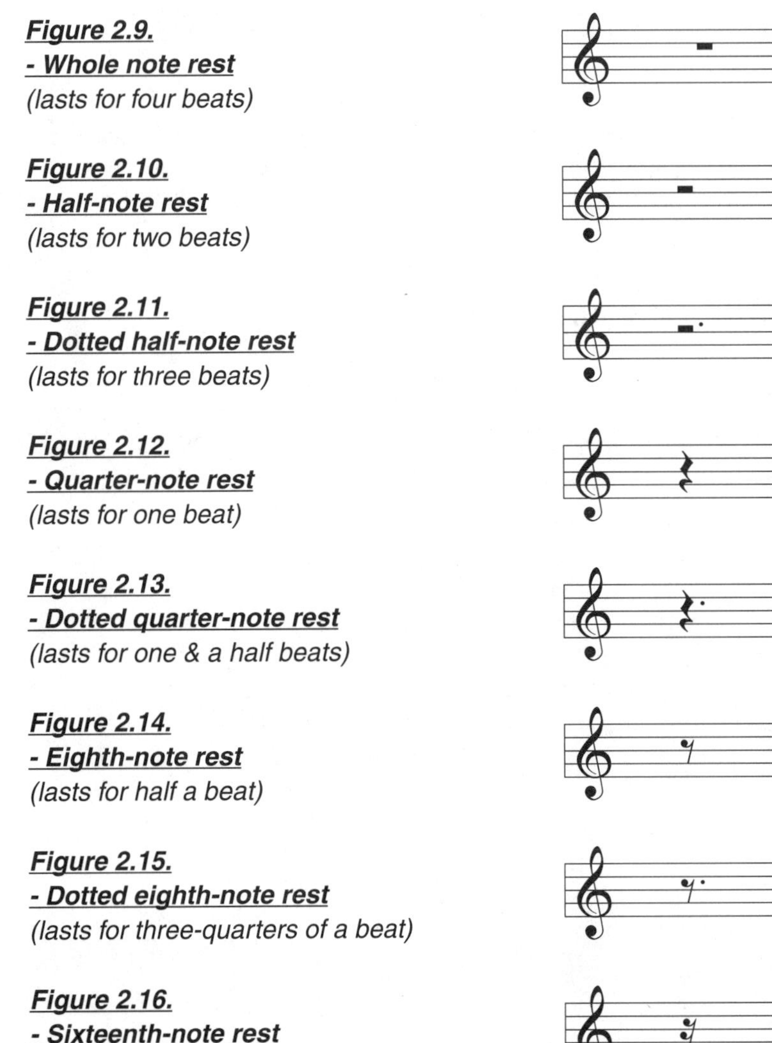

Figure 2.9.
- Whole note rest
(lasts for four beats)

Figure 2.10.
- Half-note rest
(lasts for two beats)

Figure 2.11.
- Dotted half-note rest
(lasts for three beats)

Figure 2.12.
- Quarter-note rest
(lasts for one beat)

Figure 2.13.
- Dotted quarter-note rest
(lasts for one & a half beats)

Figure 2.14.
- Eighth-note rest
(lasts for half a beat)

Figure 2.15.
- Dotted eighth-note rest
(lasts for three-quarters of a beat)

Figure 2.16.
- Sixteenth-note rest
(lasts for a quarter of a beat)

Time signatures

The time signature in a piece of music indicates how many beats in the measure, and what type of note 'gets the beat' i.e. which rhythmic unit are we counting in - typically either half, quarter or 8th notes. The different numbers within the time signature have the following functions:-

- the **top** number indicates how many beats in the measure
- the **bottom** number indicates which rhythmic unit 'gets the beat'.

The majority of contemporary music is notated in **4/4** time - also known as **common** time. This time signature is telling us that there are four beats in the measure, and that we are 'counting' in quarter notes i.e. the beat is felt in units of a quarter note. Here is a list of important time signatures that we should review:-

Time signatures - (contd)

Figure 2.17. - 4/4 time
(four beats to the measure - quarter note gets the beat)

Figure 2.18. - Common time
(same as 4/4)

Figure 2.19. - 2/2 time
(two beats to the measure - half note gets the beat)

Figure 2.20.- 'Cut' time
(same as 2/2)

Figure 2.21. - 3/4 time
(three beats to the measure - quarter note gets the beat)

Figure 2.22. - 6/8 time
(six beats to the measure - eighth note gets the beat)

Figure 2.23. - 9/8 time
(nine beats to the measure - eighth note gets the beat)

Figure 2.24. - 12/8 time
(twelve beats to the measure - eighth note gets the beat)

There are of course many other possibilities for time signatures - however the preceding examples are those most frequently encountered in contemporary styles. Notice that in the last 3 examples (**6/8**, **9/8** & **12/8**), the number of beats was divisible by 3 - this will frequently imply a **triplet subdivision** (see discussion later in this chapter). In this case although the beat technically is an eighth note, an emphasis or 'pulse' is felt every **3** eighth notes i.e. on the **dotted quarter note**. (**3/4** time signatures used in slow gospel are often referred to as having a **9/8** "feel" - see **Chapter 17**).

The sum of all the rhythmic values (notes and rests) must equal the total rhythmic value indicated in the time signature. Here are some examples of this principle, which also demonstrate a type of rhythmic notation using 'slashes' instead of conventional noteheads. This is frequently encountered in fake books and contemporary charts as a way of indicating the rhythm required (typically according to specified chord changes), but without actually writing the notes out, as folllows:-

Time signatures (contd)

Figure 2.25.
Incorrect rhythmic sum example 1
(time signature says four beats - sum of rhythmic values is four & a half beats)

Figure 2.26.
Incorrect rhythmic sum example 2
(time signature says four beats - sum of rhythmic values is three & a half beats)

Figure 2.27.
Correct rhythmic sum example 1

Figure 2.28.
Correct rhythmic sum example 2

Rhythmic subdivisions

In contemporary applications it is very important to be in control of the **rhythmic subdivision** - this is the smallest regularly-occurring rhythmic unit in the arrangement. This will almost always either be an eighth note, eighth note triplet, sixteenth note, or sixteenth note triplet. From the keyboardist's point of view, managing the rhythmic subdivision and being able to play (and alter) the subdivision at will, are vital goals to work towards - the exercises in this chapter (and throughout the book) will help you achieve this! Subject to numerous variations and exceptions, the different subdivisions are used in the following styles:-

- Eighth note ('straight 8ths')	- pop, rock, country, new age
- Eighth note triplet ('swing 8ths')	- pop & rock shuffles, blues, gospel, country
- Sixteenth note ('straight 16ths')	- R'n'B, funk, fusion, some rock & new age
- Sixteenth note triplet ('swing 16ths')	- hip-hop, funk, reggae

In a '**swing 8ths**' subdivision, the first pair of eighth notes are subdividing the beat in a two-thirds/one-third fashion, as opposed to '**straight 8ths**' which divides the beat exactly in half. This may be indicated on the music by using this symbol as illustrated, on the top of a chart. In this way the eighth notes in the chart are simply **re-interpreted** in a 'swing 8ths' style, and it is not necessary to make further changes to the music itself. This is further demonstrated by the following examples:-

Figure 2.29.
'Straight 8ths' rhythm example
(Cassette Tape Example 1)

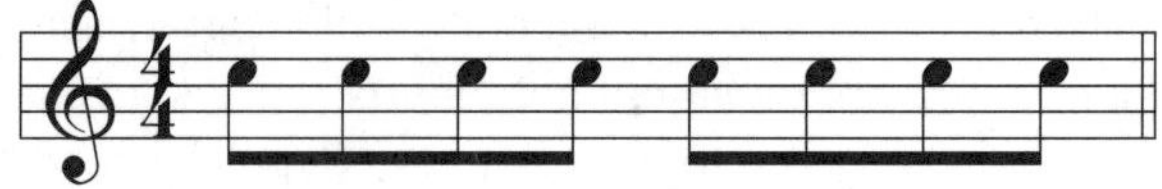

Rhythmic subdivisions (contd)

This can of course be re-interpreted in a 'swing 8ths' fashion. This interpretation could then be notated in one of the following ways:-

Figure 2.30.
'Swing 8ths' rhythm example
(with 'swing 8ths' symbol above music)
(CASSETTE TAPE EXAMPLE 2)

Figure 2.31.
'Swing 8ths' rhythm example
(triplet signs used within the music)
(CASSETTE TAPE EXAMPLE 2)

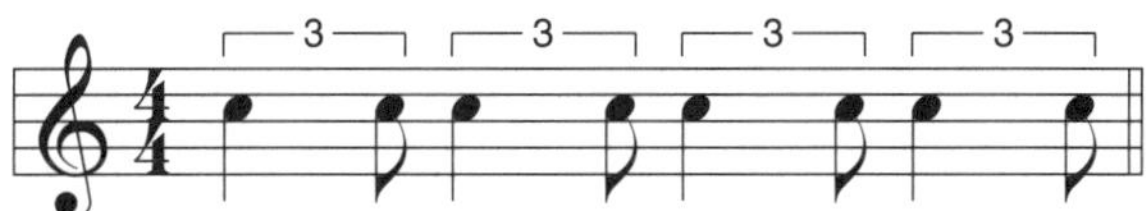

Which of the 'swing 8ths' notation examples would you rather read? I think the example in **Fig. 2.30.** is a little friendlier! As we said earlier, the 'swing 8ths' interpretation means that each beat is subdivided in a two-thirds/one-third fashion. Another way of looking at this is that we are accessing the **first and third triplet subdivisions of the beat**. However, there will be times when we need to access the **second** triplet subdivision. In this case, using the 'swing 8ths' symbol above the music as in **Fig. 2.30.** will not achieve the desired result - we have no choice but to put triplets in the music itself (assuming we stay in **4/4** time). Look at the following example in which all of the triplet subdivisions are required:-

Figure 2.32.
Eighth note rhythm example
(using all triplet subdivisions)
(CASSETTE TAPE EXAMPLE 3)

Clearly this is rather 'inelegant' and fatiguing to read. So - using the 'swing 8ths' symbol (as in **Fig. 2.30.**) is very convenient in typical pop, rock and blues shuffle situations where generally the two-thirds/one-third beat subdivision is required - but if all three triplet subdivisions are required (particularly if the **second** subdivision is needed) then we need to use triplet signs in order to stay in **4/4** time. A better alternative in this case however might well be to change the time signature. If we change the bottom number to **8** (implying eighth notes) and the top number to a multiple of **3** (typically **6**, **9** or **12**), then this will expose all of the triplet subdivisions and it will not be necessary to place triplets within the music itself. (See the **6/8**, **9/8** and **12/8** key signature examples in **Figs. 2.22. - 2.24.**) We will now re-notate the above example in **12/8** time as follows:-

Figure 2.33.
Eighth note rhythm example
*(using all subdivisions in **12/8** time)*
(CASSETTE TAPE EXAMPLE 3)

This is easier to deal with than the previous example! So - when all the triplet subdivisions are required within the beat (or particularly the **2nd** triplet as discussed), consider using **12/8** time as an alternative to **4/4** with triplet signs. In the above example we will most probably still feel four 'pulses' per measure (see previous comments regarding **12/8** time).

Rhythmic subdivisions (contd)

One style in which all the eighth-note triplet subdivisions are required, would be a 'traditional' or 50s-style rock'n'roll setting. Here's a comping pattern example in this style, first in **12/8** time, then in **4/4** time with triplet signs:-

Figure 2.34. 50s-style rock'n'roll example using 12/8 time
(Cassette Tape Example 4)

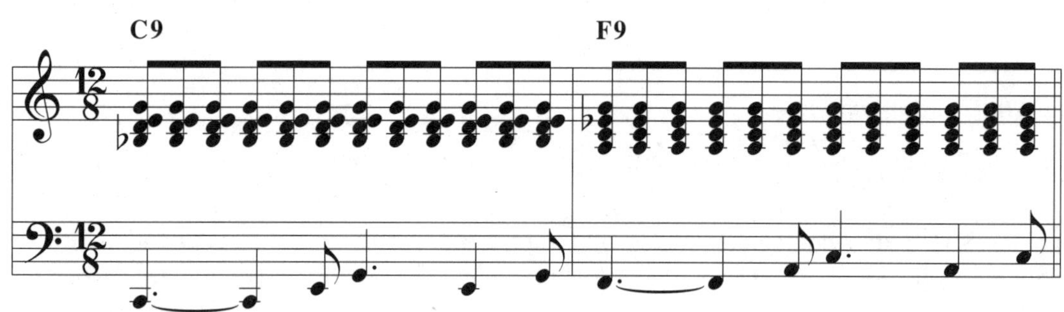

Notice that in the above example the 'pulse' is actually felt on the **dotted quarter note**. This is very typical in **12/8** musical styles. Now the same idea but notated in **4/4** with triplets:-

Figure 2.35. 50s-style rock'n'roll example using 4/4 time
(Cassette Tape Example 4)

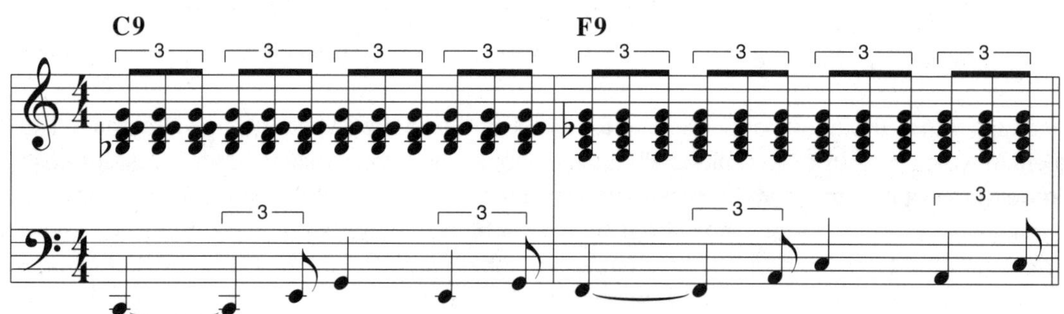

Again, it's important to emphasize that the above two examples **sound the same** - they are just notated differently!

On the following page is another example of a 'comping' figure using an eighth note subdivision. This is in a **pop-rock** style using an alternating triad concept in the right hand against a repetitive root in the left hand. (We will examine pop-rock styles in detail in **Chapter 12**). Notice that again we could again play this example in a 'straight 8ths' or 'swing 8ths' fashion - that's just a matter of how we choose to interpret the eighth notes!

Rhythmic subdivisions (contd)

Figure 2.36. 'Pop-rock' example using eighth note subdivision
(CASSETTE TAPE EXAMPLE 5 - 'STRAIGHT 8THS')
(CASSETTE TAPE EXAMPLE 6 - 'SWING 8THS')

Turning now to sixteenth-note rhythms, we said that there were basically two types of treatment, namely 'straight 16ths' and 'swing 16ths'. The concept here is very similar to the above discussions concerning eighth notes, but now applied at the sixteenth note level. In a '**straight 16ths**' situation, each 16th note gets exactly one-quarter of the beat (or one-half of an eighth note). In a '**swing 16ths**' subdivision, each pair of 16th notes are dividing the **eighth note** in a two-thirds/one-third fashion. This may be indicated on the music by using this symbol as illustrated, on the top of a chart. In this way the sixteenth notes in the chart are simply re-interpreted in a 'swing 16ths' style, and it is not necessary to make further changes to the music itself. This is further demonstrated by the following examples:-

Figure 2.37.
'Straight 16ths' rhythm example
(CASSETTE TAPE EXAMPLE 7)

This can then be re-interpreted in a 'swing 16ths' fashion and notated in one of the following ways:-

Figure 2.38.
'Swing 16ths' rhythm example
(with 'swing 16ths' symbol above music)
(CASSETTE TAPE EXAMPLE 8)

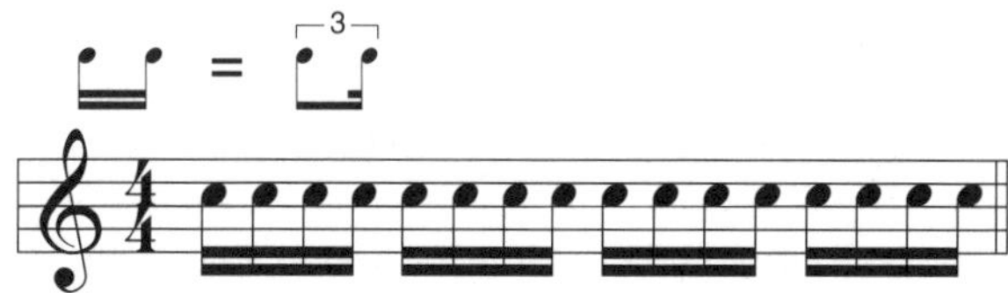

Rhythmic subdivisions (contd)

Figure 2.39.
'Swing 16ths' rhythm example
(triplet signs used within the music)
(CASSETTE TAPE EXAMPLE 8)

Again I think the first 'swing 16ths' example (**Fig. 2.38.**) looks a little friendlier! Now we will look at a 'comping' pattern using a sixteenth note subdivision. This is in a **funk** style, using a rhythmic alternation between left and right hands. (This type of 'funk' keyboard part is covered in detail in **Chapter 15**). We can interpret this example in either 'straight 16ths' or 'swing 16ths':-

Figure 2.40. 'Funk' example using sixteenth note subdivision
(CASSETTE TAPE EXAMPLE 9 - 'STRAIGHT 16THS')
(CASSETTE TAPE EXAMPLE 10 - 'SWING 16THS')

'Counting' rhythms

It is important for the beginning/intermediate player to be able to '**count**' their way through a rhythm if necessary. This is the key to working out a rhythm that the player may not have seen before. More experienced players will not need to 'count' because they will recognize rhythmic phrases (especially in contemporary applications, the same rhythms show up again and again!) and because they will recognize the **anticipations** which are occurring (see following section).

One good way to approach counting eighth note rhythms is to think of **downbeats** and **upbeats**. The downbeats are where the quarter notes fall, and are typically referred to (in **4/4** time) as **1**, **2**, **3** and **4**. The upbeats are where the eighth notes are occurring in between, and are typically counted using an '**&**' after each downbeat, as in the following example:-

Figure 2.41.
Eighth note rhythm example
(with counting)

A similar concept applies to the counting of sixteenth note rhythms, only now we have more subdivisions to consider. Effectively we need to fit an extra subdivision **in between** all of the rhythmic events in the above example. When counting, it is customary to refer to the **2nd** sixteenth note within the beat as '**e**', and the **4th** sixteenth note as '**a**', as follows:-

'Counting' rhythms (contd)

Figure 2.42.
Sixteenth note rhythm example
(with counting)

The same counting ideas can be applied to either 'straight' or 'swing' subdivisions for eighth notes or sixteenth notes. In an eighth note subdivision, beats **1 and 3** are often considered to be the most important or **primary** beats. In a sixteenth note 'feel' however, each beat (1, 2, 3 and 4) can have equal importance, due to the increased number of subdivisions available.

Rhythmic anticipations

An important technique for the writing, reading and performance of contemporary styles is to understand and apply **rhythmic anticipations**. In an eighth note subdivision, an anticipation occurs when a rhythmic event falls on an **upbeat** (i.e. one of the '&s' or eighth notes between the downbeats - see **Fig. 2.41.**) and is then followed by a rest on the following downbeat or is sustained through the following downbeat. This subjectively has the effect of 'shifting' the downbeat an eighth note to the left, and is widely used in contemporary styles. This is demonstrated in the following example, which also includes the rhythmic 'counting' for reference:-

Figure 2.43. Eighth note anticipation example (pop-rock style)
(Cassette Tape Example 11)

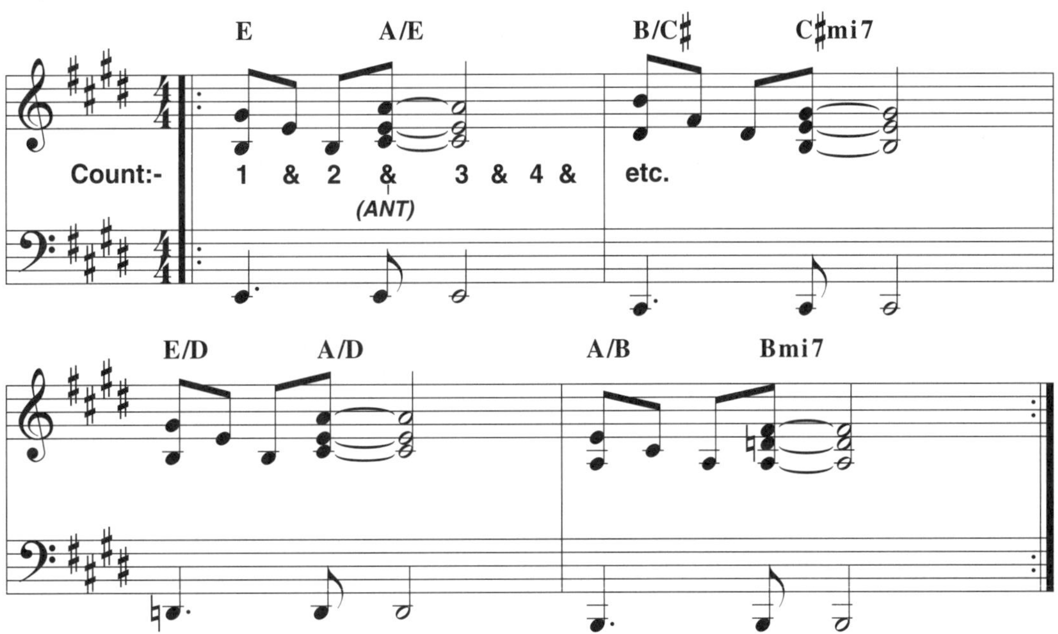

Note the description '**ANT**' in the first measure which signifies an anticipation. In this case the right-hand triad is **anticipating** beat **3** (i.e. landing an eighth note earlier on the '**& of 2**' and sustaining through beat **3**). However the left hand is still landing on the downbeat. This is a very typical feature of contemporary pop and R'n'B styles (the right hand anticipating the left hand).

Rhythmic anticipations (contd)

Similar concepts apply when dealing with anticipations in a sixteenth note subdivision or 'feel' - however there are now more anticipations available within the measure. Refer back to the sixteenth note 'counting' example (**Fig. 2.42.**) - as you saw we can count the sixteenth note subdivision using "1 e & a 2 e & a" etc. An anticipation occurs in a sixteenth note subdivision in the following situations:-

a) A rhythmic event falls on an '<u>e</u>' (2nd sixteenth note within the beat) and is then followed by a rest on, or is sustained through, the following '<u>&</u>' (3rd sixteenth note within the beat).

b) A rhythmic event falls on an '<u>a</u>' (4th sixteenth note within the beat) and is then followed by a rest on, or is sustained through, the following <u>**downbeat**</u> (i.e. 1, 2, 3 or 4).

Again this has the subjective effect of 'shifting' the rhythmic event one sixteenth note to the left. This is a staple ingredient in contemporary R'n'B and funk styles. The following is an example of an R'n'B ballad figure using anticipations (and showing the 'counting' for reference):-

<u>Figure 2.44. Sixteenth note anticipation example (R'n'B ballad style)</u>
(Cassette Tape Example 12)

Note again the description '<u>**ANT**</u>' in the first measure which signifies an anticipation. In this case the right-hand voicing is <u>**anticipating**</u> beat **3**, by landing on the last 16th note of beat **2**. Again notice that the left hand is still landing on the downbeat - as we said this is typical in R'n'B keyboard styles (see **Chapters 14** & **15** for further details).

Rhythmic drills

In this section we will construct a series of exercises to help you get these rhythms 'under your fingers'. We will first of all look at individual routines for left hand and right hand, and then we will combine the hands together in different rhythmic combinations. <u>**Rhythmic consistency and independence between the hands are essential attributes for the contemporary keyboardist!**</u> Each 'eighth note subdivision' exercise can be performed in 'straight 8ths' or 'swing 8ths', and each 'sixteenth note subdivision' exercise can be performed in 'straight 16ths' or 'swing 16ths'. You should practise these examples with a metronome or drum machine, starting at a slow tempo at first, and then gradually increasing the tempo. Firstly we will look at some rhythmic drills for the right hand:-

Rhythmic drills (contd)

Figure 2.45. Right hand drill #1 - Whole notes

(CASSETTE TAPE EXAMPLE 13)

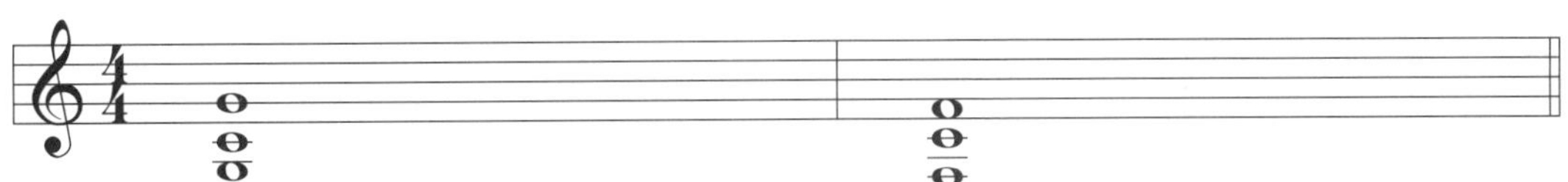

Figure 2.46. Right hand drill #2 - Half notes

(CASSETTE TAPE EXAMPLE 14)

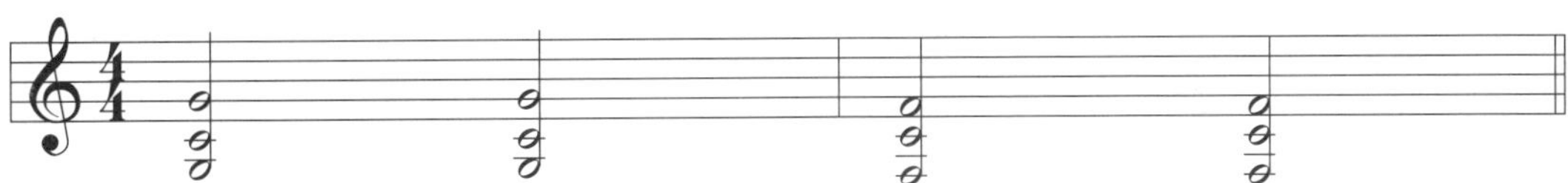

Figure 2.47. Right hand drill #3 - Quarter notes

(CASSETTE TAPE EXAMPLE 15)

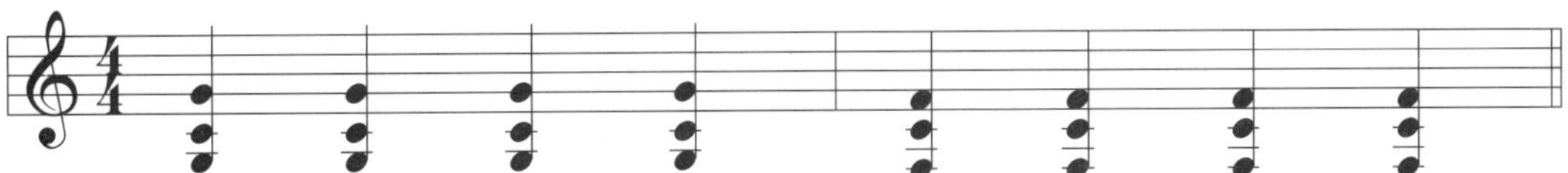

Figure 2.48. Right hand drill #4 - Eighth notes

(CASSETTE TAPE EXAMPLE 16 - 'STRAIGHT 8THS')
(CASSETTE TAPE EXAMPLE 17 - 'SWING 8THS')

Figure 2.49. Right hand drill #5 - Eighth notes with anticipations

(CASSETTE TAPE EXAMPLE 18 - 'STRAIGHT 8THS')
(CASSETTE TAPE EXAMPLE 19 - 'SWING 8THS')

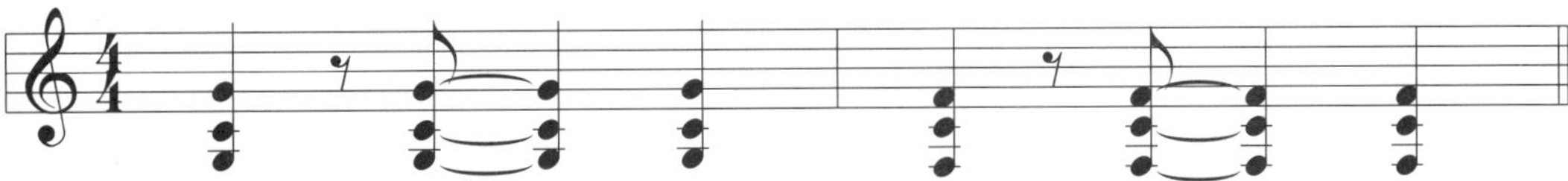

Figure 2.50. Right hand drill #6 - Sixteenth notes with anticipations

(CASSETTE TAPE EXAMPLE 20 - 'STRAIGHT 16THS')
(CASSETTE TAPE EXAMPLE 21 - 'SWING 16THS')

Rhythmic drills (contd)

Now we will look at some rhythmic drills for the left hand as follows:-

Figure 2.51. Left hand drill #1 - Whole notes
(Cassette Tape Example 22)

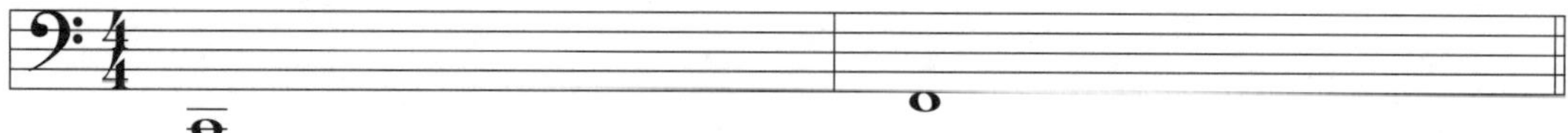

Figure 2.52. Left hand drill #2 - Half notes
(Cassette Tape Example 23)

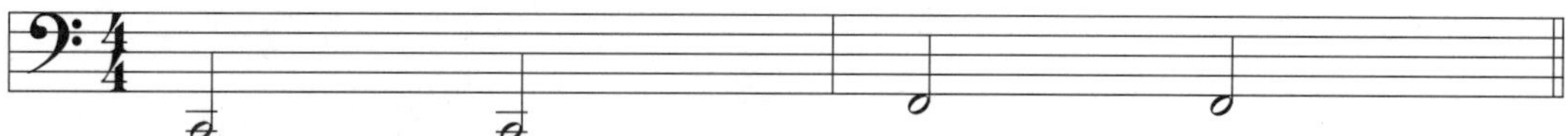

Figure 2.53. Left hand drill #3 - Quarter notes
(Cassette Tape Example 24)

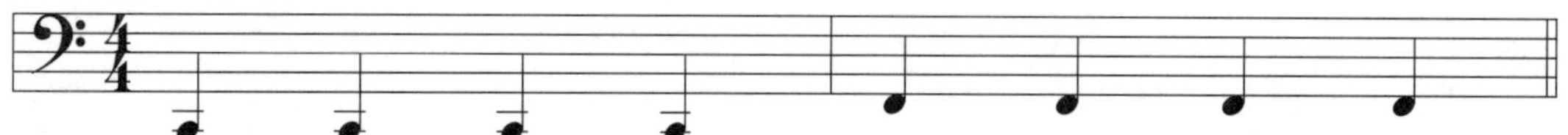

Figure 2.54. Left hand drill #4 - Eighth notes
(Cassette Tape Example 25 - 'Straight 8ths')
(Cassette Tape Example 26 - 'Swing 8ths')

Figure 2.55. Left hand drill #5 - Eighth notes with anticipations
(Cassette Tape Example 27 - 'Straight 8ths')
(Cassette Tape Example 28 -'Swing 8ths')

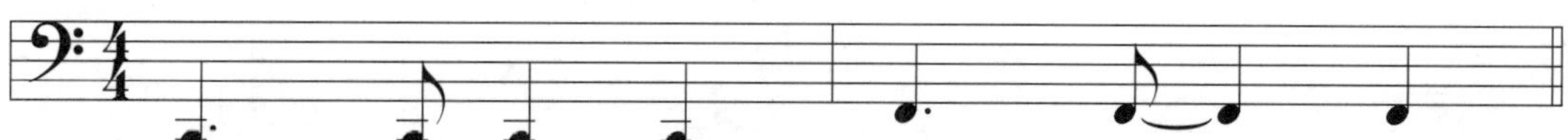

Figure 2.56. Left hand drill #6 - Sixteenth notes (with anticipations)
(Cassette Tape Example 29 - 'Straight 16ths')
(Cassette Tape Example 30 - 'Swing 16ths')

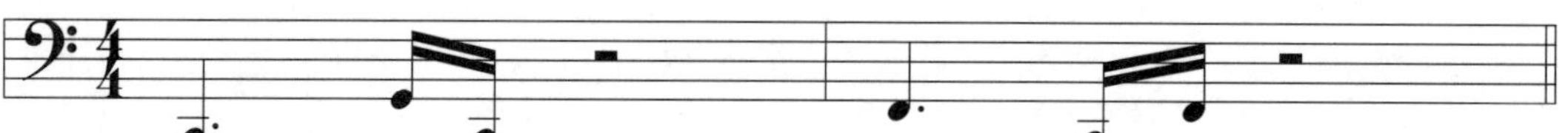

Rhythmic drills (contd)

When you are comfortable with the preceding exercises, the next stage is to combine the various rhythms together using both hands. This provides an essential foundation for the rhythmic independence and co-ordination needed by the contemporary keyboardist! Again, in the drills involving eighth- or sixteenth-note subdivisions, you should practice these in both a 'straight' and 'swing' fashion, and both treatments are contained on the tapes for your reference. As with the previous drills, start at a slow tempo as necessary and gradually increase the tempo as your progress allows. We will start by combining whole notes in the left hand with various rhythms in the right hand, as follows:-

Figure 2.57. Left/right hand drill #1 - Whole notes in left hand, quarter notes in right hand
(Cassette Tape Example 31)

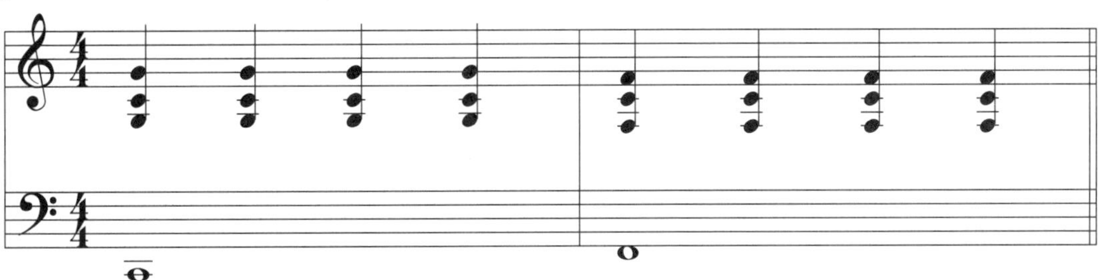

Figure 2.58. Left/right hand drill #2 - Whole notes in left hand, eighth notes in right hand
(Cassette Tape Example 32 - 'Straight 8ths')
(Cassette Tape Example 33 - 'Swing 8ths')

Now we will look at some drills using half notes in the left hand as follows:-

Figure 2.59. Left/right hand drill #3 - Half notes in left hand, quarter notes in right hand
(Cassette Tape Example 34)

Rhythmic drills (contd)

Figure 2.60. Left/right hand drill #4 - Half notes in left hand, eighth notes in right hand
(CASSETTE TAPE EXAMPLE 35 - 'STRAIGHT 8THS')
(CASSETTE TAPE EXAMPLE 36 - 'SWING 8THS')

Figure 2.61. Left/right hand drill #5 - Half notes in left hand, eighth note anticipations in right hand
(CASSETTE TAPE EXAMPLE 37 - 'STRAIGHT 8THS'
(CASSETTE TAPE EXAMPLE 38 - 'SWING 8THS')

Figure 2.62. Left/right hand drill #6 - Half notes in left hand, 16th note anticipations in right hand
(CASSETTE TAPE EXAMPLE 39 - 'STRAIGHT 16THS')
(CASSETTE TAPE EXAMPLE 40 - 'SWING 16THS')

Now we will look at some drills using quarter notes in the left hand as follows:-

Rhythmic drills (contd)

Figure 2.63. Left/right hand drill #7 - Quarter notes in left hand, whole notes in right hand
(CASSETTE TAPE EXAMPLE 41)

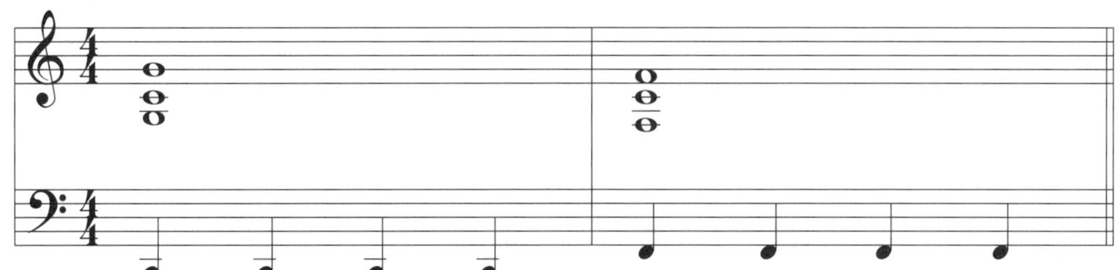

Figure 2.64. Left/right hand drill #8 - Quarter notes in left hand, half notes in right hand
(CASSETTE TAPE EXAMPLE 42)

Figure 2.65. Left/right hand drill #9 - Quarter notes in left hand, eighth notes in right hand
(CASSETTE TAPE EXAMPLE 43 - 'STRAIGHT 8THS')
(CASSETTE TAPE EXAMPLE 44 - 'SWING 8THS')

Figure 2.66. Left/right hand drill #10 - Quarter notes in left hand, 8th note anticipation in right hand
(CASSETTE TAPE EXAMPLE 45 - 'STRAIGHT 8THS')
(CASSETTE TAPE EXAMPLE 46 - SWING 8THS')

Rhythmic drills (contd)

Figure 2.67. Left/right hand drill #11 - Quarter notes in left hand, 16th note anticipation in right hand
(CASSETTE TAPE EXAMPLE 47 - 'STRAIGHT 16THS')
(CASSETTE TAPE EXAMPLE 48 - 'SWING 16THS')

Now we will look at some drills using eighth notes in the left hand as follows:-

Figure 2.68. Left/right hand drill #12 - Eighth notes in left hand, whole notes in right hand
(CASSETTE TAPE EXAMPLE 49 - 'STRAIGHT 8THS')
(CASSETTE TAPE EXAMPLE 50 - 'SWING 8THS')

Figure 2.69. Left/right hand drill #13 - Eighth notes in left hand, half notes in right hand
(CASSETTE TAPE EXAMPLE 51 - 'STRAIGHT 8THS')
(CASSETTE TAPE EXAMPLE 52 - 'SWING 8THS')

Rhythmic drills (contd)

Figure 2.70. Left/right hand drill #14 - Eighth notes in left hand, quarter notes in right hand

(Cassette Tape Example 53 - 'Straight 8ths')
(Cassette Tape Example 54 - 'Swing 8ths')

The following two examples now use eighth note anticipations in the left hand:-

Figure 2.71. Left/right hand drill #15 - 8th note anticipations in left hand, whole notes in right hand

(Cassette Tape Example 55 - 'Straight 8ths')
(Cassette Tape Example 56 - 'Swing 8ths')

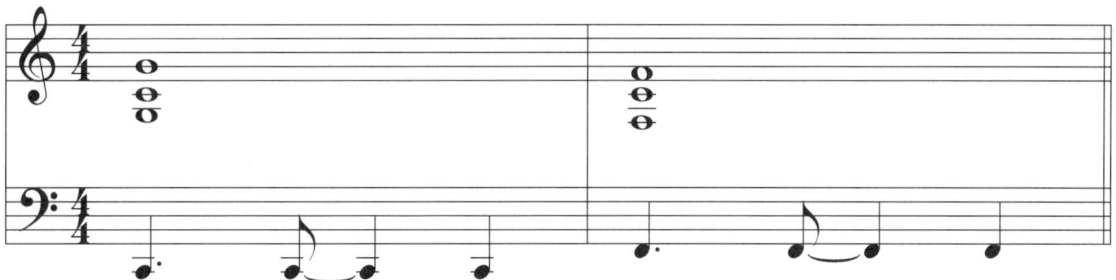

Figure 2.72. Left/right hand drill #16 - 8th note anticipations in left hand, eighth notes in right hand

(Cassette Tape Example 57 - 'Straight 8ths')
(Cassette Tape Example 58 - 'Swing 8ths')

Rhythmic drills (contd)

Finally we have an example using a sixteenth note anticipation in the left hand as follows:-

Figure 2.73. Left/right hand drill #17 - 16th note anticipations in left hand, whole notes in right hand
(Cassette Tape Example 59 - 'Straight 16ths')
(Cassette Tape Example 60 - 'Swing 16ths')

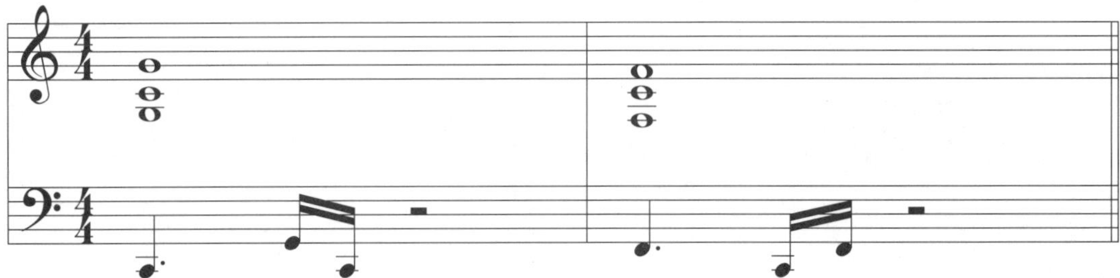

If you can master the exercises in this section, you will be developing the rhythmic co-ordination and hand independence necessary to perform in contemporary styles. Good luck - and have fun!

Practice directions:-

- **Practice and count the following rhythmic examples:-**
  - **'straight eighths' as in Figs. 2.29.**
  - **'swing eighths' as in Figs. 2.30 & 2.31.**
  - **'straight sixteenths' as in Fig. 2.37.**
  - **'swing sixteenths' as in Figs. 2.38. & 2.39.**

  *You can play a single repeated note in either hand to practice these rhythms. Count while you are playing! (see **Figs. 2.41. & 2.42.**)*
- **You may optionally play through the different style examples in Figs. 2.34. - 2.36., 2.40. & 2.43. - 2.44.**

  These are a taste of things to come, in the second part of the book!
- **Practice the rhythmic drills as follows:-**
  - **right hand drills as in Figs. 2.45. - 2.50.**
  - **left hand drills as in Figs. 2.51. - 2.56.**
  - **right & left hand drills as in Figs. 2.57. - 2.73.**

  Examples with 8th note subdivisions should be practiced in 'straight' and 'swing' 8ths, and examples with 16th note subdivisions should be practiced in 'straight' and 'swing' 16ths. Use a metronome for these drills - as slow as necessary at first - then gradually increase the tempo as your facility improves!

Diatonic triads and four-part chords

Introduction

Familiarity with diatonic chord forms in all keys is vital to the contemporary keyboardist. (As discussed in **Chapter 1**, the term 'diatonic' means belonging to a major scale or key area). Exercises using diatonic chords are an excellent way to get the 'contour' or shape of a major scale under your fingers. The term 'contour' here refers to the shape created by the sequence of black and white keys in a scale - this shape is unique for each major scale. Let's say you were playing through a leadsheet in the key of A major - well, if you had to look at the key signature to figure out which sharps you needed to play, this would clearly be a very inefficient and undesirable method! (As I said in **Chapter 1**, we need to know our key signatures for notation purposes, but this is not the best concept when applied to our instrument). Instead we need to develop a tactile and instinctive understanding of the 'keyboard geography' of each major scale/key area - that way our understanding of the scale 'contour' becomes a filter through which we play in each key as required. Of course playing the scales in all keys will help to develop this concept, and as such this is always a useful addition to your personal practice schedule. In this chapter I have approached this topic from another angle - harmonic exercises using diatonic triads and four-part chords from all major scales. This is a very practical vehicle for this purpose, as a great percentage of today's pop styles use this kind of diatonic harmony. As well as aiding your 12-key familiarity, these exercises will also develop your ability to transpose from one key to another - a great asset for a contemporary keyboardist!

When playing these diatonic chord exercises there are generally two approaches to use. The first approach says, "I know what my **major scale contour** is, and I am working within that restriction when building my chords". I think this approach is not only the most productive for the keyboardist, but also reflects a better understanding of diatonic harmony - it is the major scale which is 'giving us' the diatonic chords, and these chords are simply incomplete representations of the scale at any given point. Another approach says, "I know what the root of my diatonic chord should be (from the major scale) and I know the chord quality I need to build from that scale". For example, for diatonic triads (see **Fig. 1.74.**) this would be a **major triad** from the 1st degree, a **minor triad** from the 2nd degree etc., and for diatonic four-part chords (see **Fig. 1.85.**) this would be a **major 7th** from the 1st degree, a **minor 7th** from the 2nd degree and so on. This angle will reinforce your knowledge of diatonic chord relationships and may initially prove useful in some of the keys with which you are less familiar!

Major scale 'contour'

The following exercise is designed to help you develop the major scale 'contour' in all keys. This is a great preparation for all of the subsequent diatonic 3-part and 4-part exercises. The idea is to play all pitches in the major scale at once - three notes in the left hand and five in the right hand. I think you'll agree that this is a rather ugly sound! As I said though, the whole point is to develop a tactile sense of the contour or 'shape' of each scale. **DO NOT** think about the key signature when playing this exercise (or for that matter when playing any of these diatonic chord exercises). Instead, always be aware of the intervals (whole-steps and half-steps) present in each major scale (review **Fig. 1.1.** as necessary). See exercise on following page:-

For further information on diatonic triads and four-part chords, please refer to Chapters 4 & 7 of our Contemporary Music Theory Level 1 book (see page ix in this book).

Major scale 'contour' (contd)

Figure 3.1. Major scale 'contour' exercise
(Cassette Tape Example 61)

Diatonic triads

A tremendous amount of contemporary music is based on diatonic triad (or 4-part chord) structures. As we saw in **Chapter 1** (see **Fig. 1.74.**), 'diatonic' means belonging to a major scale or key area - so these diatonic triads occur naturally within a major scale. As well as being an important asset when playing pop music structures and transposing keys, playing these diatonic chords will also develop our scale 'contour' awareness as discussed above. Here for your reference are the diatonic triads in all major keys:-

Figure 3.2. - C Major

Figure 3.3. - F Major

Diatonic triads (contd)

Diatonic triads (contd)

Figure 3.13. - E Major

Figure 3.14. - B Major

Figure 3.15. - F# Major

Figure 3.16. - C# Major

Diatonic triad exercises

We will now begin to use these diatonic triads in exercise drills. These will be in different 'settings', with left and right hands playing the chords in either a 'concerted' (all the notes played together) or 'arpeggiated' (broken chord style) manner. For the time being we are using the triads in root position - more on inversions in **Chapter 4**! Each of the following practise settings is illustrated in the key of C - however of course we will be applying these in all keys!

Figure 3.17. Diatonic triad setting #1 - 'Concerted' right hand

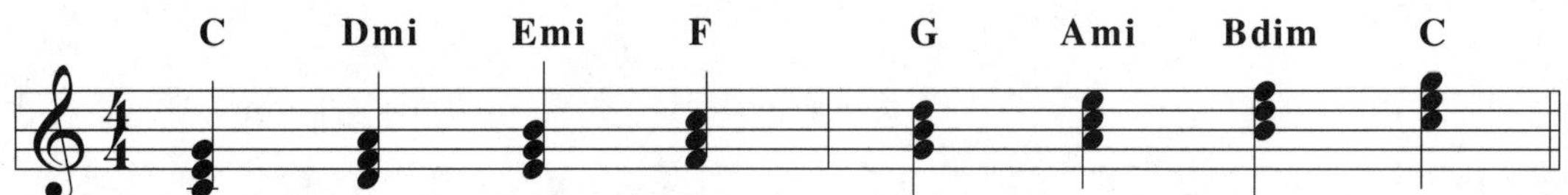

Figure 3.18. Diatonic triad setting #2 - 'Concerted' left hand

Diatonic triad exercises (contd)

Figure 3.19. Diatonic triad setting #3 - 'Arpeggiated' right hand

Figure 3.20. Diatonic triad setting #4 - 'Arpeggiated' left hand

Figure 3.21. Diatonic triad setting #5 - 'Concerted' left and right hands

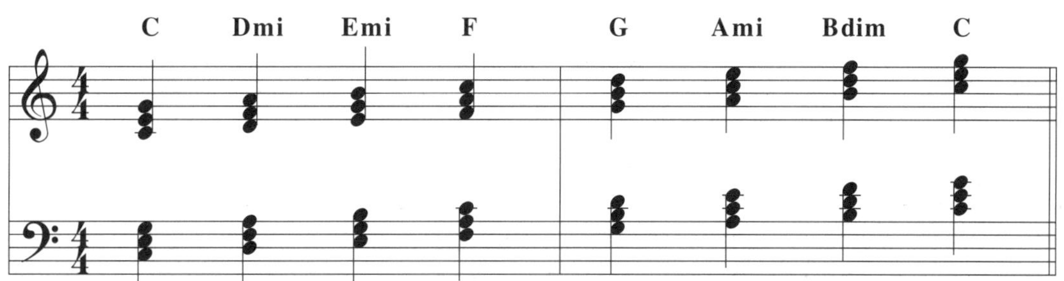

Figure 3.22. Diatonic triad setting #6 - 'Concerted' left hand, 'arpeggiated' right hand

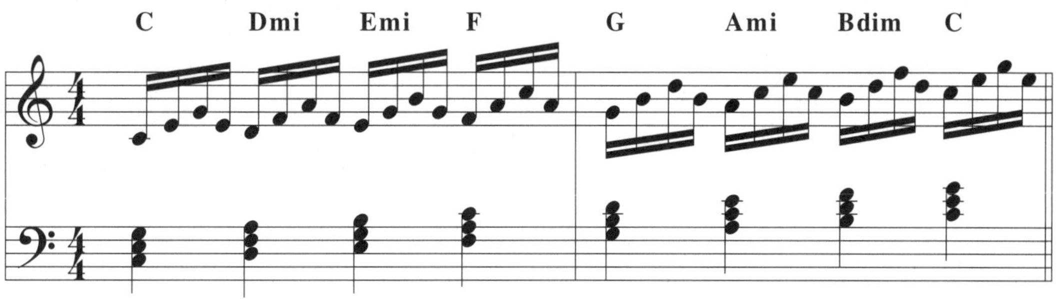

Diatonic triad exercises (contd)

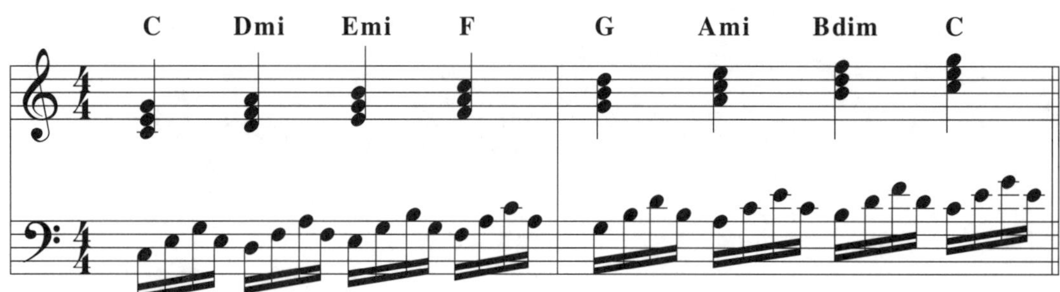

Figure 3.23. Diatonic triad setting #7 - 'Arpeggiated' left hand, 'concerted' right hand

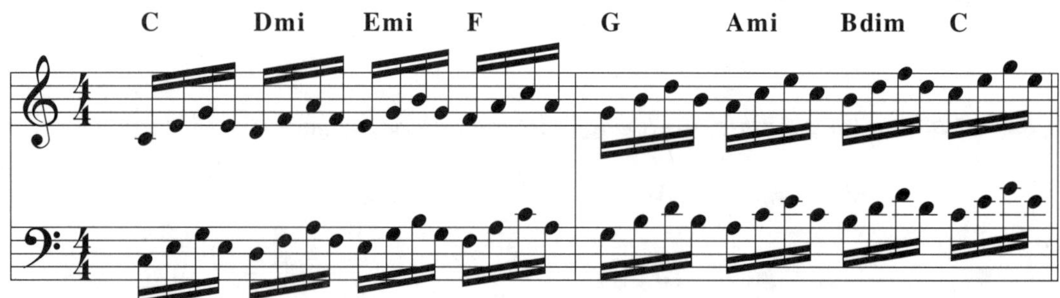

Figure 3.24. Diatonic triad setting #8 - 'Arpeggiated' left and right hands

Practice directions:-

- ***Practice the 'major scale contour' exercise in Fig. 3.1.***
  *(This is a useful warm-up before any of the '**diatonic chord**' exercises).*
- ***Practice the diatonic triad settings #1 - #8 (as shown in Figs. 3.17. - 3.24.) in all keys.***
  *(Circle-of-5ths or Circle-of-4ths can be used as a sequence of keys for practice - see **p18**).*

For space reasons I have not illustrated all of the above settings in every key! Besides, I don't think that these should be reading exercises - they should be approached from a key-center or '**contour**' point of view. However, I have provided one example of each setting, in a selection of different keys as follows:-

Diatonic triad exercises (contd)

Figure 3.25. Diatonic triad setting #1 - 'Concerted' right hand (Key of D)
(CASSETTE TAPE EXAMPLE 62)

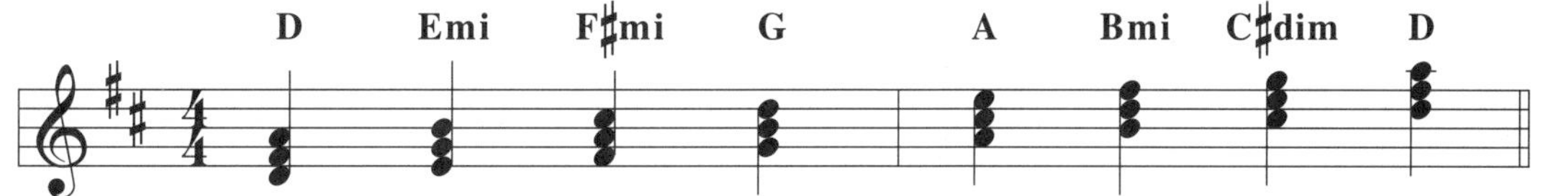

Figure 3.26. Diatonic triad setting #2 - 'Concerted' left hand (Key of E)
(CASSETTE TAPE EXAMPLE 63)

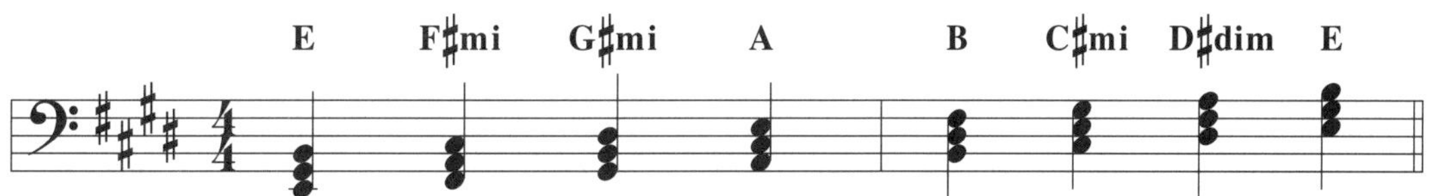

Figure 3.27. Diatonic triad setting #3 - 'Arpeggiated' right hand (Key of Bb)
(CASSETTE TAPE EXAMPLE 64)

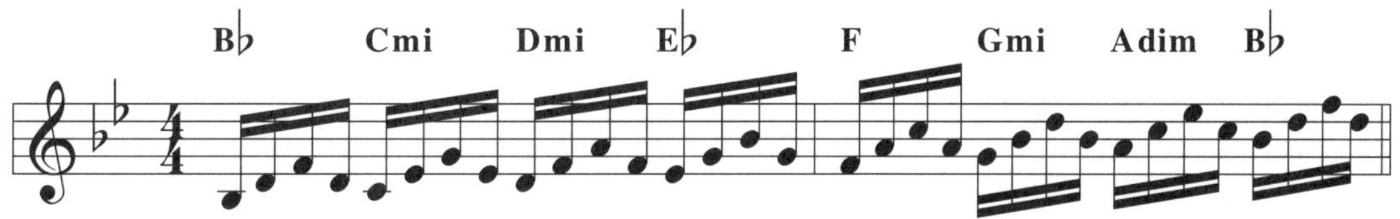

Figure 3.28. Diatonic triad setting #4 - 'Arpeggiated' left hand (Key of Db)
(CASSETTE TAPE EXAMPLE 65)

Diatonic triad exercises (contd)

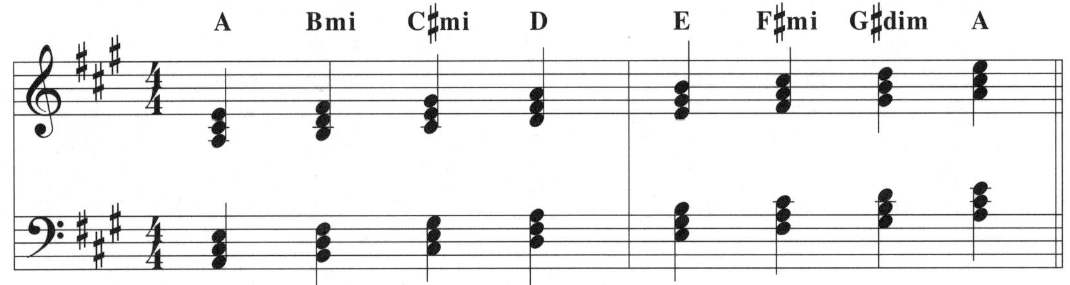

Figure 3.29. Diatonic triad setting #5 - 'Concerted' left and right hands (Key of A)
(Cassette Tape Example 66)

Figure 3.30 Diatonic triad setting #6 - 'Concerted' left hand, 'arpeggiated' right hand (Key of B)
(Cassette Tape Example 67)

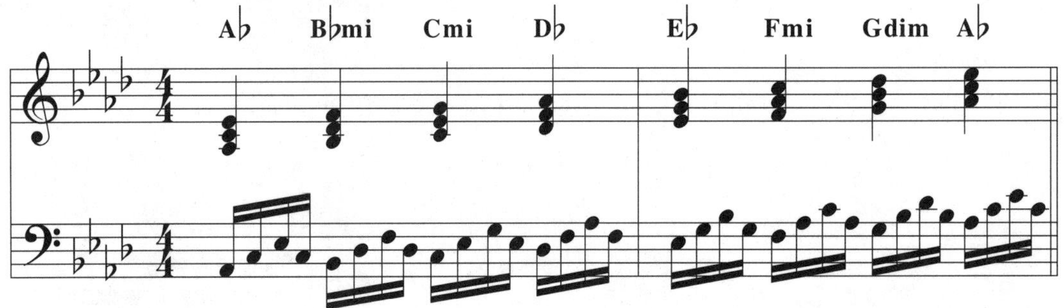

Figure 3.31. Diatonic triad setting #7 - 'Arpeggiated' left hand, 'concerted' right hand (Key of Ab)
(Cassette Tape Example 68)

Diatonic triad exercises (contd)

Figure 3.32. Diatonic triad setting #8 - 'Arpeggiated' left and right hands (Key of Eb)
(Cassette Tape Example 69)

Diatonic four-part chords

We will now expand the above concepts to include four-part diatonic relationships. We saw how these chords were constructed within a major key in **Chapter 1** (see **Fig. 1.85.**). We will now learn and apply these diatonic 4-part chords in all keys in a similar fashion as for the diatonic triads. Here for your reference are the diatonic four-part chords in all the major keys:-

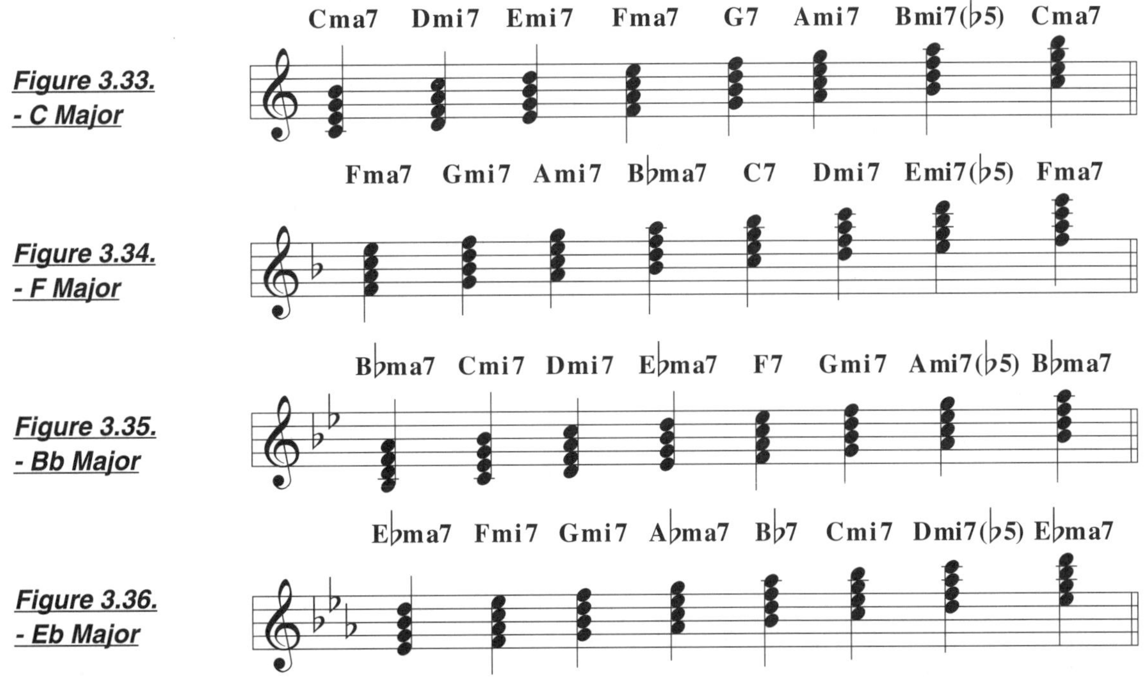

Diatonic four-part chords (contd)

Diatonic four-part chords (contd)

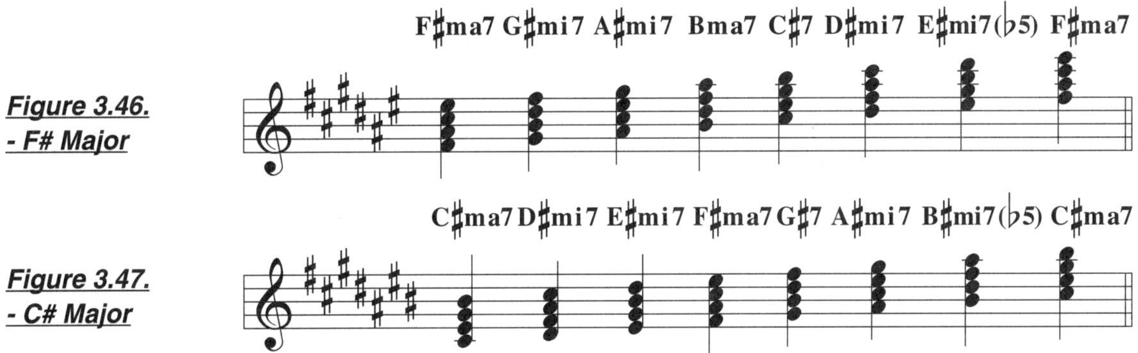

Figure 3.46. - *F# Major*

Figure 3.47. - *C# Major*

Diatonic 4-part chord exercises

Now we will use the diatonic 4-part chords in exercise drills. As with the diatonic triads, we will be practising these 4-part chords in different 'settings'. Again we will for the time being be focusing on root-position structures. As before, each of the following settings is illustrated in the key of C and will then be applied in all other keys:-

Figure 3.48. Diatonic 4-part setting #1 - 'Concerted' right hand

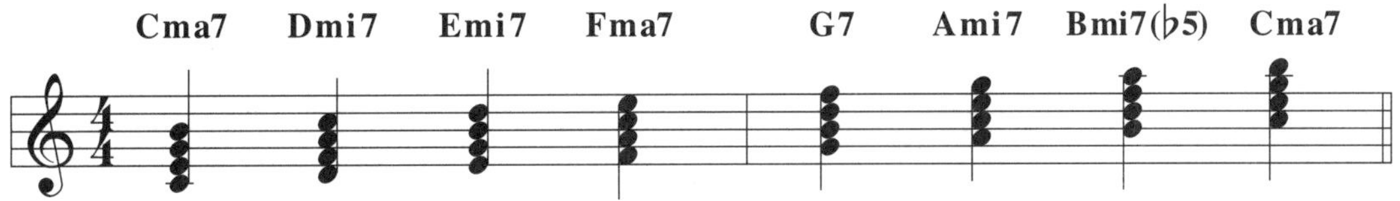

Figure 3.49. Diatonic 4-part setting #2 - 'Concerted' left hand

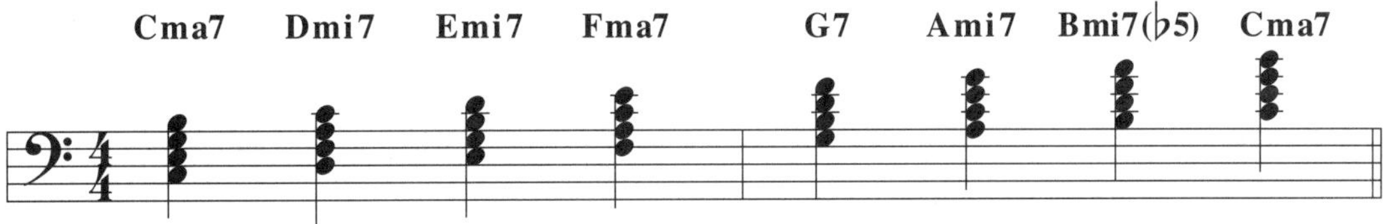

Figure 3.50. Diatonic 4-part setting #3 - 'Arpeggiated' right hand

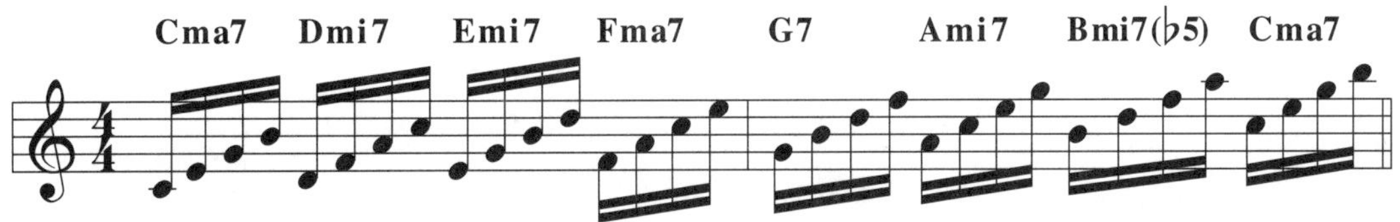

Diatonic 4-part chord exercises (contd)

Figure 3.51. Diatonic 4-part setting #4 - 'Arpeggiated' left hand

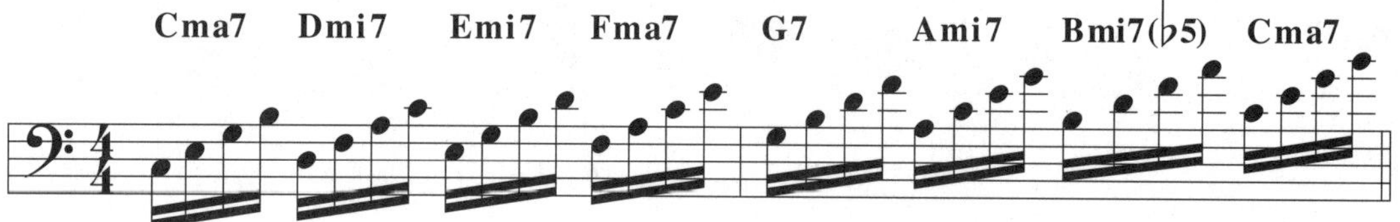

Figure 3.52. Diatonic 4-part setting #5 - 'Concerted' left and right hands

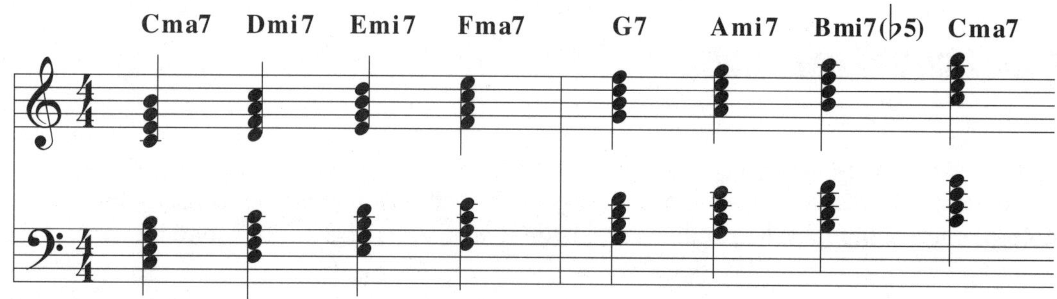

Figure 3.53. Diatonic 4-part setting #6 - 'Concerted' left hand, 'arpeggiated' right hand

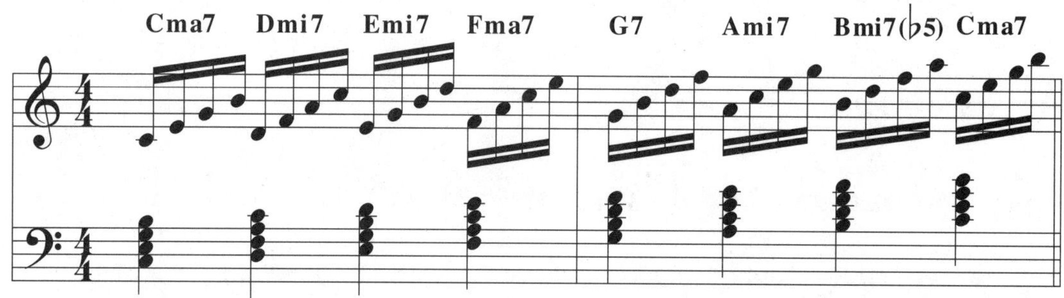

Figure 3.54. Diatonic 4-part setting #7 - 'Arpeggiated' left hand, 'concerted' right hand

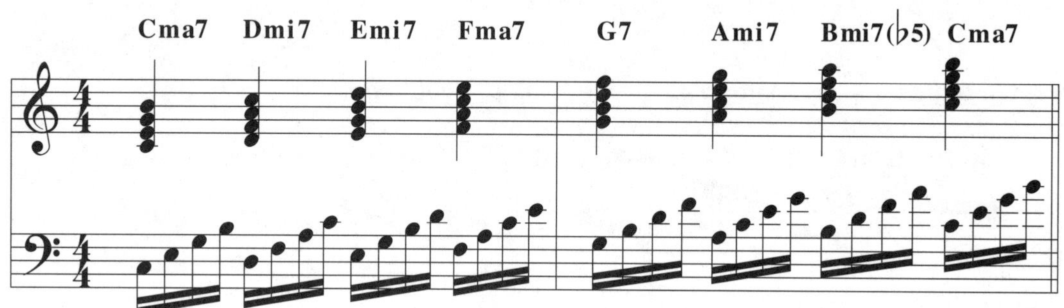

Diatonic 4-part chord exercises (contd)

Figure 3.55. Diatonic 4-part setting #8 - 'Arpeggiated' left and right hands

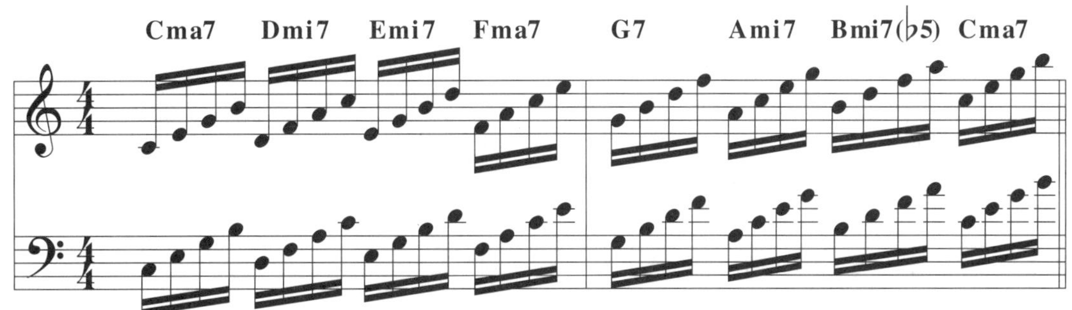

Practice directions:-

- ***Practice the diatonic 4-part settings #1 - #8 (as shown in Figs. 3.48. - 3.55.) in all keys.***
  *(Circle-of-5ths or Circle-of-4ths can be used as a sequence of keys for practice - see p**18**).*

Again for space reasons I have not illustrated all of the settings in every key - here is one example of each setting, in a selection of different keys as follows:-

Figure 3.56. Diatonic 4-part setting #1 - 'Concerted' right hand (Key of F)
(Cassette Tape Example 70)

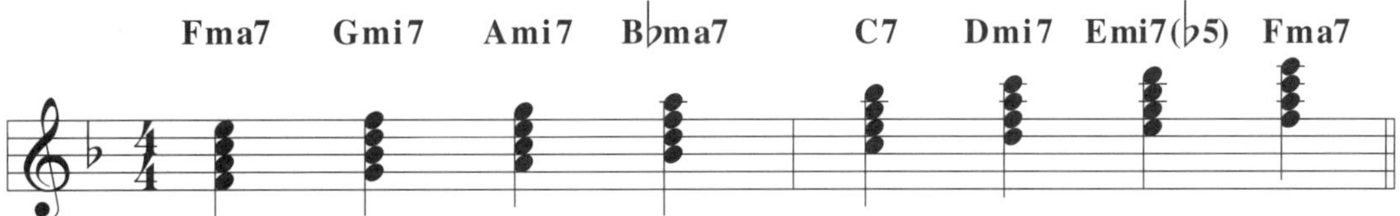

Figure 3.57. Diatonic 4-part setting #2 - 'Concerted' left hand (Key of A)
(Cassette Tape Example 71)

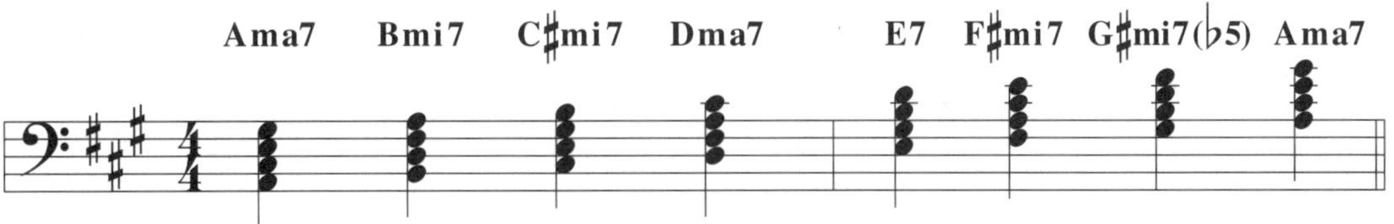

Diatonic 4-part chord exercises (contd)

Figure 3.58. Diatonic 4-part setting #3 - 'Arpeggiated' right hand (Key of G)
(Cassette Tape Example 72)

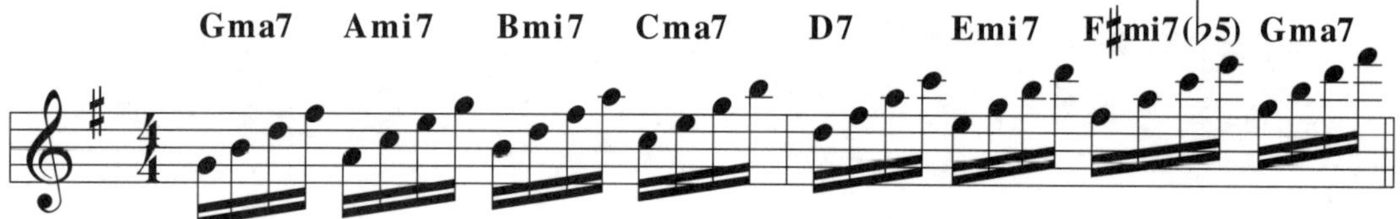

Figure 3.59. Diatonic 4-part setting #4 - 'Arpeggiated' left hand (Key of Eb)
(Cassette Tape Example 73)

Figure 3.60. Diatonic 4-part setting #5 - 'Concerted' left and right hands (Key of E)
(Cassette Tape Example 74)

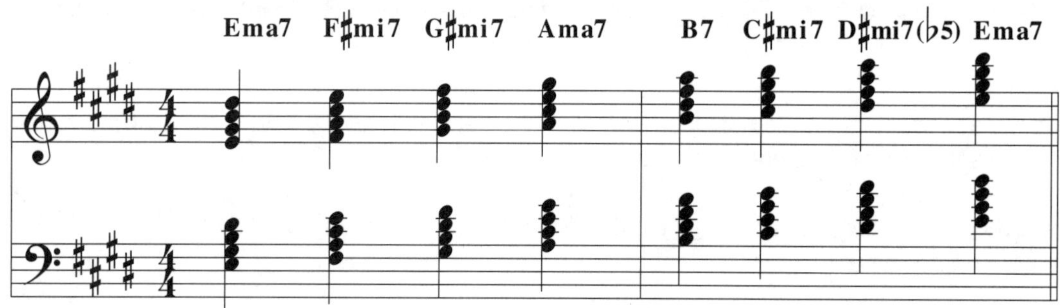

Figure 3.61. Diatonic 4-part setting #6 - 'Concerted' left hand, 'arpeggiated' right hand (Key of D)
(Cassette Tape Example 75)

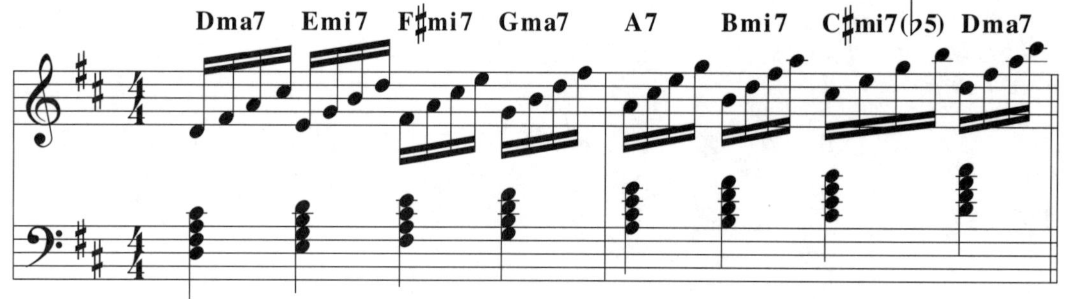

Diatonic 4-part chord exercises

Figure 3.62. Diatonic 4-part setting #7 - 'Arpeggiated' left hand, 'concerted' right hand (Key of Gb)
(*Cassette Tape Example 76*)

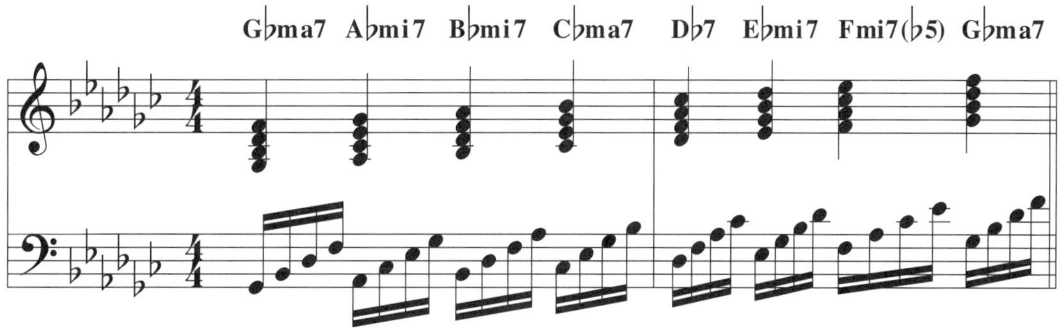

Figure 3.63. Diatonic 4-part setting #8 - 'Arpeggiated' left and right hands (Key of Db)
(*Cassette Tape Example 77*)

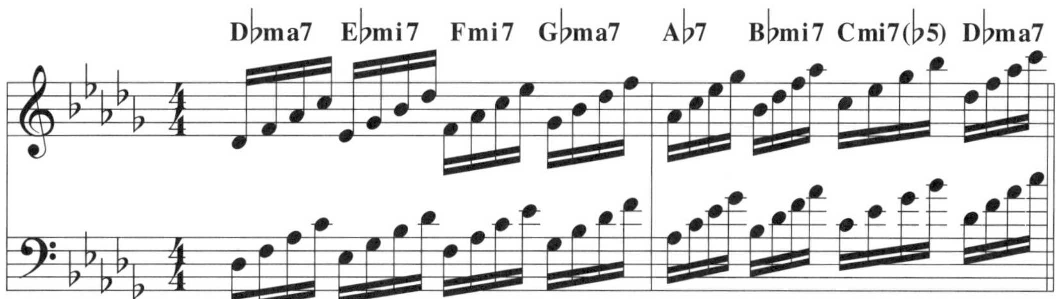

--- NOTES ---

Triads - inversions and voiceleading

Introduction

One of the very fundamental techniques a contemporary keyboardist must acquire is the ability to play triads and their inversions in a spontaneous fashion. This is primarily a right-hand consideration, and requires an understanding of '**voiceleading**' principles. Voiceleading means moving from one chord voicing to the next in a smooth manner horizontally i.e. without unnecessary interval leaps. This is achieved by the use of chord inversions as required. For example, here is a simple progression using root-position triads:-

Figure 4.1. Root position triad example (no voiceleading used)
(CASSETTE TAPE EXAMPLE 78)

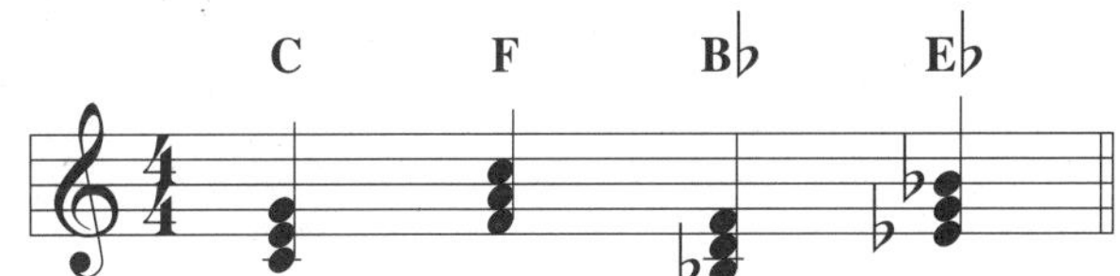

As you play this example (or listen to the tape) you can hear that it has a rather 'choppy' or disconnected feel from left to right - this is because the use of root-position triads forces us to make large interval skips. Now here is an example of the same progression using 'voiceleading' - going to the closest inversion of each successive chord as follows:-

Figure 4.2. Inverted triad example (voiceleading used)
(CASSETTE TAPE EXAMPLE 79)

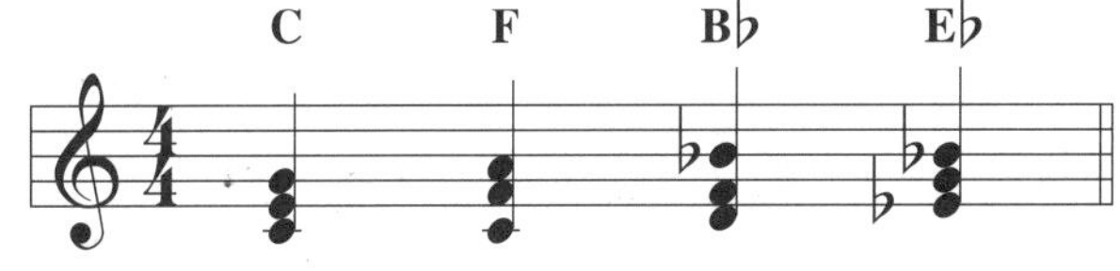

You'll notice that this example sounds much 'smoother' and more musical. To be able to voicelead spontaneously in contemporary styles, it is necessary to become familiar with all inverted triads **as shapes in their own right** and not just as variations on a root-position triad. For example, in **Fig. 4.2.** above we used a 2nd inversion F major triad following the C triad, as this resulted in good voiceleading. If we had to pause to figure out what a 2nd inversion F triad was by first considering a root-position F triad and then inverting it - well, by the time we've figured it out, it's probably too late to execute it in tempo! The secret is to **bypass this process** by getting an intuitive understanding of all triad inversions into our 'muscle memory' i.e. into our hands so we don't have to think about it all the time! This is the key to successful voiceleading and is one of the main goals of the exercises in this chapter. Later we shall see that these voiceled triads will become the '**upper structures**' of various different chords overall (see **Chapter 5**) - this is essentially how a lot of 'pop' harmony is created - however the voiceleading of the upper triads frequently works in the same way, as detailed in this chapter.

Major triad inversions

We will first become familiar with inverted major triads in all keys. We will use the terms '**root position**', '**first inversion**' and '**second inversion**' as follows:-

Figure 4.3. C major triad (root position and inversions)
(CASSETTE TAPE EXAMPLE 80)

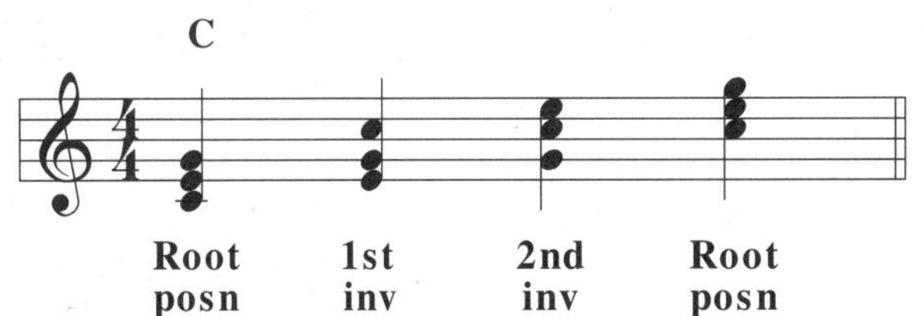

FOR FURTHER INFORMATION ON VOICELEADING OF TRIADS, PLEASE REFER TO CHAPTER 6 OF OUR CONTEMPORARY MUSIC THEORY LEVEL 2 BOOK (SEE PAGE ix IN THIS BOOK).

Major triad inversions (contd)

One convenient way to relate to these inversion terms is to consider where the root of the triad is in each inversion, as follows:-

In **root position**:- The **root** of the triad is on the **bottom** (with 3rd and 5th above).
In **1st inversion**:- The **root** of the triad is on the **top** (with 3rd and 5th below).
In **2nd inversion**:- The **root** of the triad is in the **middle** (with 5th below and 3rd above).

As a warm-up exercise we will play major triad inversions (as in **Fig. 4.3.**) in all keys around the circle-of-fifths, as follows (accidentals are repeated for each chord for your convenience):-

Figure 4.4. Major triads (root position and inversions) around the circle-of-fifths
(Cassette Tape Example 81)

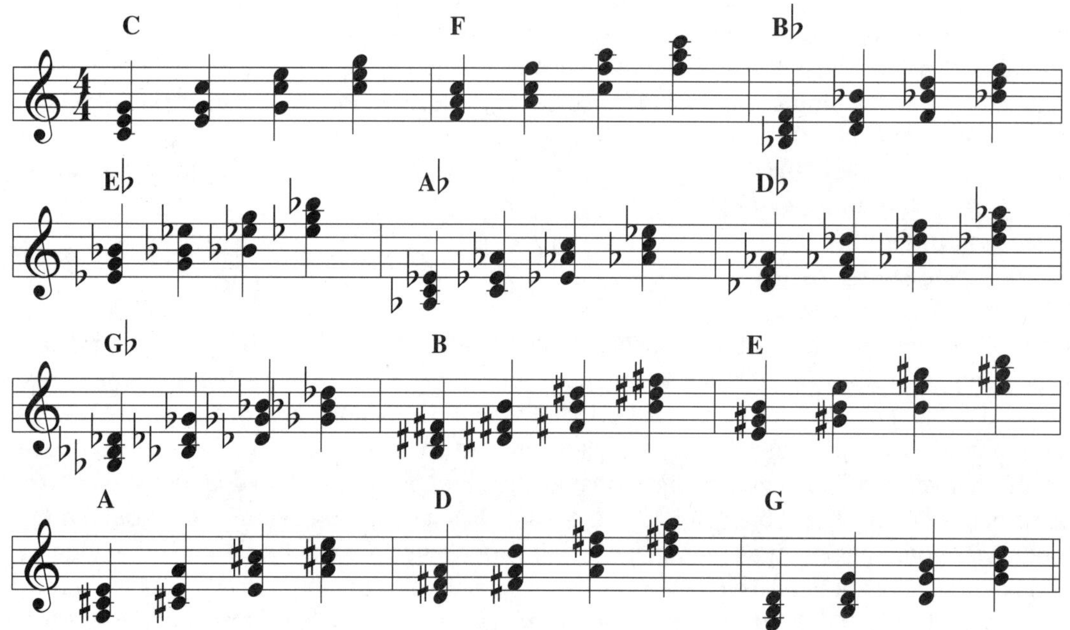

The next stage is to target the **1st** and **2nd** inversion triads without playing the root position triad first. If we do this for example in a circle-of-fifths sequence around the keys, we notice that the different inverted triads exhibit '**keyboard contour**' characteristics i.e. specific groupings of black and white notes on the keyboard. Let's look first of all at **first inversion** major triads around the circle-of-fifths, and then analyse the black/white key groups involved:-

Major triad inversions (contd)

Figure 4.5. First inversion major triads around the circle-of-fifths
(CASSETTE TAPE EXAMPLE 82)

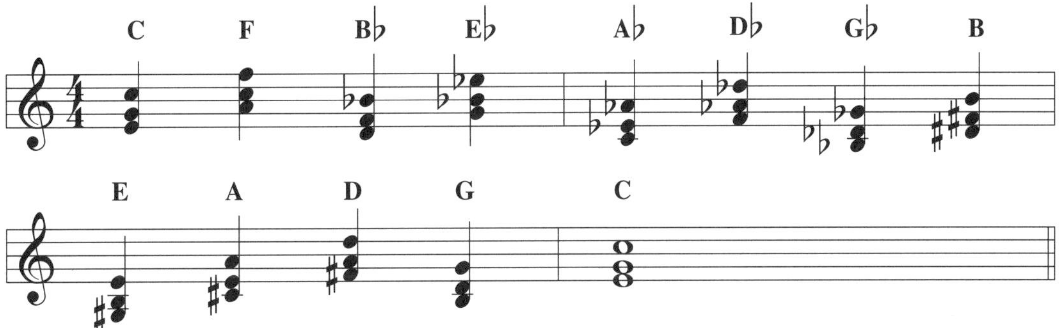

There are twelve different triads in this example - however there are only six different 'keyboard contours' i.e. configurations of black and white notes. For example, the 1st inversion Eb triad above has a white-black-black key configuration from bottom to top - exactly the same as for the following Ab and Db triads - so your hand will see these shapes **exactly the same** from a finger position standpoint. Here's the full analysis of the white/black key configurations in the above example:-

Major triads (1st inversion)	White-Black key configuration (bottom to top)
C, F	White - White - White
Bb	White - White - Black
Eb, Ab, Db	White - Black - Black
Gb	Black - Black - Black
B	Black - Black - White
E, A, D	Black - White - White
G, C	White - White - White

Seeing each inversion as part of a 'contour group' like this will help you get these shapes 'under your fingers'. Now let's look at **second inversion** major triads from the same perspective:-

Figure 4.6. Second inversion major triads aound the circle-of-fifths
(CASSETTE TAPE EXAMPLE 83)

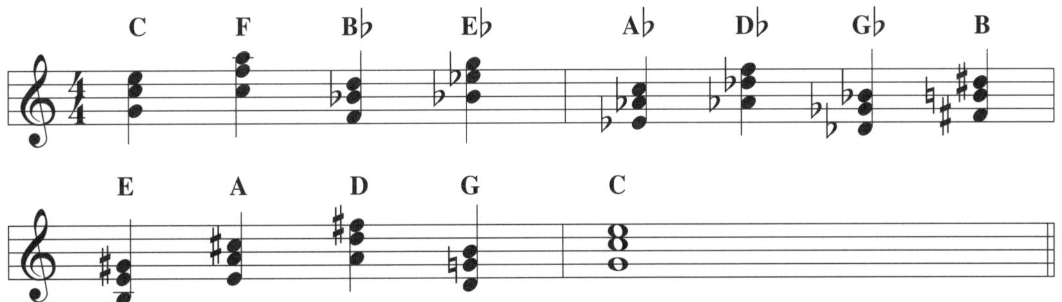

Major triad inversions (contd)

Major triads (2nd inversion)	White-Black key configuratrion (bottom to top)
C, F	White - White - White
Bb	White - Black - White
Eb, Ab, Db	Black - Black - White
Gb	Black - Black - Black
B	Black - White - Black
E, A, D	White - White - Black
G, C	White - White - White

PRACTICE DIRECTIONS:-

- ***Practice major triads in all inversions as in Fig. 4.4.***
- ***Practice first inversion major triads as in Fig. 4.5.***
  (for variation in sequence of keys, use circle-of-4ths)
- ***Practice second inversion major triads as in Fig. 4.6.***
  (for variation in sequence of keys, use circle-of-4ths)

Minor triad inversions

We will now turn our attention to minor triads. Similar inversion terminology and concepts will apply. Again we will start out by playing minor triad inversions in all keys around the circle-of-fifths as follows:-

Figure 4.7. Minor triads (root position and inversions) around the circle-of-fifths
(CASSETTE TAPE EXAMPLE 84)

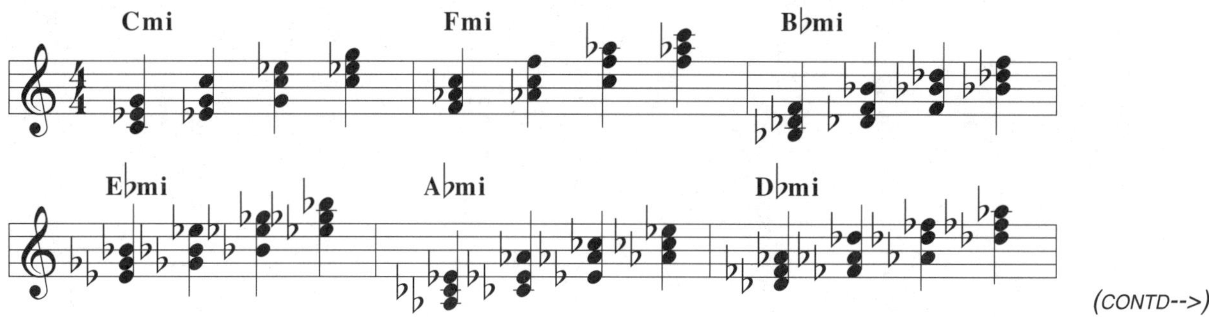

(CONTD-->)

Minor triad inversions (contd)

Figure 4.7. Minor triads (root position and inversions) around the circle-of-fifths (contd)

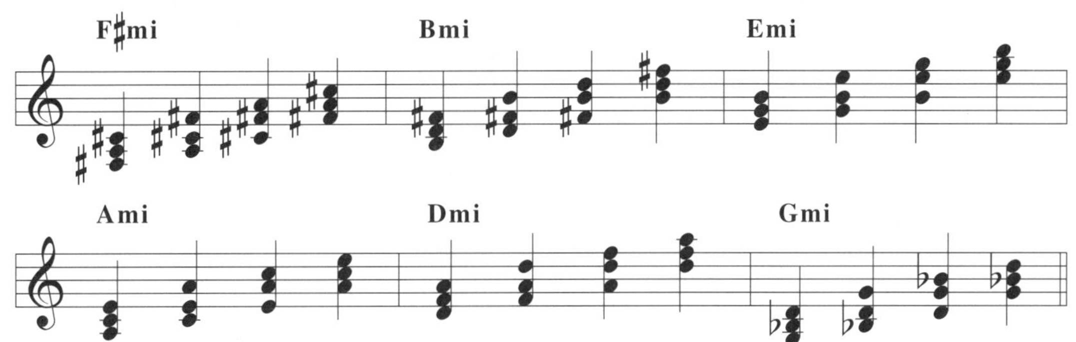

As with the major triads, we will now focus on the first inversion and then second inversion minor triads and their respective '**keyboard contours**' or configurations of black and white keys, as follows:-

Figure 4.8. First inversion minor triads around the circle-of-fifths
(Cassette Tape Example 85)

Minor triads (1st inversion)	White-Black key configuration (bottom to top)
Cmi, Fmi	Black - White - White
Bbmi	Black - White - Black
Ebmi	Black - Black - Black
Abmi, Dbmi, F#mi	White - Black - Black
Bmi	White - Black - White
Emi, Ami, Dmi	White - White - White
Gmi, Cmi	Black - White - White

Minor triad inversions (contd)

Figure 4.9. Second inversion minor triads around the circle-of-fifths
(Cassette Tape Example 86)

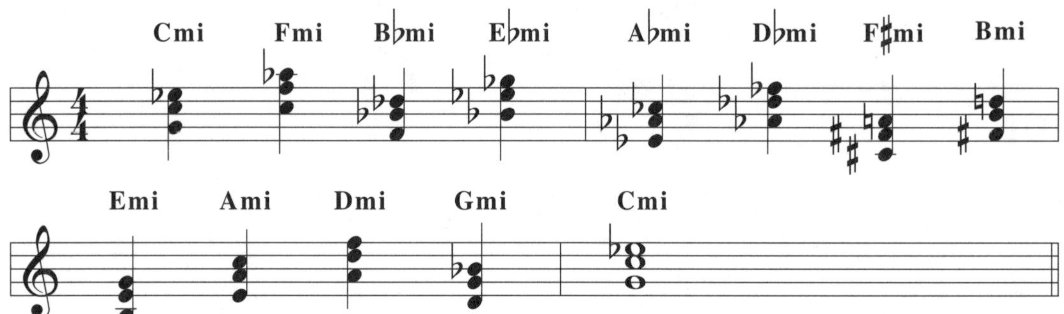

Minor triads (2nd inversion)	White-Black key configuration (bottom to top)
Cmi, Fmi	White - White - Black
Bbmi	White - Black - Black
Ebmi	Black - Black - Black
Abmi, Dbmi, F#mi	Black - Black - White
Bmi	Black - White - White
Emi, Ami, Dmi	White - White - White
Gmi, Cmi	White - White - Black

Practice directions:-

- ***Practice minor triads in all inversions as in Fig. 4.7.***
- ***Practice first inversion minor triads as in Fig. 4.8.***
  (for variation in sequence of keys, use circle-of-fourths)
- ***Practice second inversion minor triads as in Fig. 4.9.***
  (for variation in sequence of keys, use circle-of-fourths)

Inverting triads below melody

Very frequently in contemporary applications we are required to invert a major or minor triad below a given melody or 'top note'. This triad may then in turn be part of a larger chord form or structure (see following chapter). The goal of the exercises in this section is for you to be able to 'see' all of the triads which contain a given note, and then to be able to invert the triads below that note. For example, if we were to take the note C, we find that it is contained in 3 major and 3 minor triads as follows:-

Figure 4.10. Major and minor triads containing the note C
(Cassette Tape Example 87)

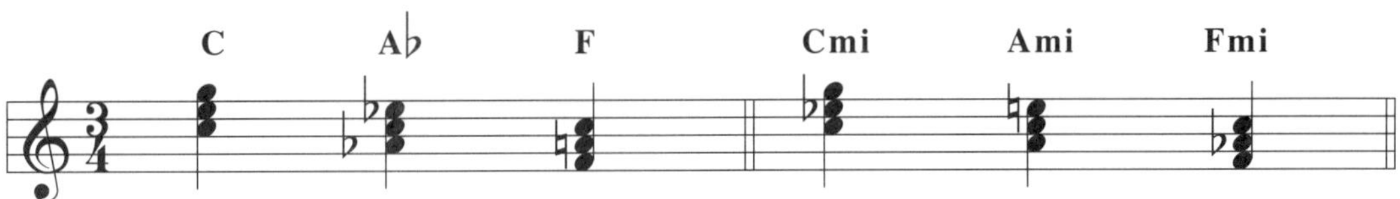

If however we wanted to keep the note C on top throughout, we would need to invert the triads as follows:-

Figure 4.11. Major and minor triads containing the note C (inverted to keep C on top)
(Cassette Tape Example 88)

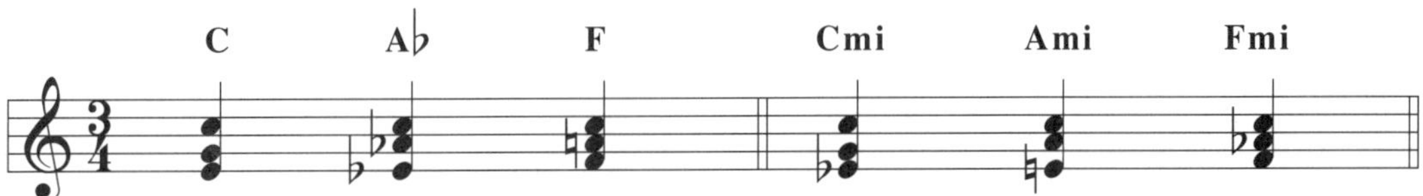

Notice that different inversions are required of the respective triads in order to accommodate the note C on top. (Refer to inversion explanation in **Fig. 4.3.** if necessary). These situations can be summarized as follows:-

- C is the **root** of C major - this triad is in **1st inversion.**
- C is the **3rd** of Ab major - this triad is in **2nd inversion.**
- C is the **5th** of F major - this triad is in **root position.**
- C is the **root** of C minor - this triad is in **1st inversion.**
- C is the **3rd** of A minor - this triad is in **2nd inversion.**
- C is the **5th** of F minor - this triad is in **root position.**

The next exercise will assist you in inverting major or minor triads below any top note. Again the purpose of this is to assimilate the 'shape' or keyboard contour of these triads, in order to use them when voiceleading spontaneously. The following top notes are presented in a circle-of-fifths sequence - although all of the triad voicings are provided for your reference, you should approach this exercise (like most of the exercises in **Section 1** of this book) from a shape-recognition standpoint i.e. try to get away from reading the notes all the time!

Inverting triads below melody (contd)

Figure 4.12. Major and minor triads inverted below top notes in circle-of-fifths sequence
(Cassette Tape Example 89)

Practice directions:-

- ***Practice major and minor triad inversions below all possible 'top notes' as in Fig. 4.12.***
  (Can also use random top-note sequences as well as circle-of-5ths)

Major triad voiceleading

Now we will consider the voiceleading of major triads around the circle-of-fifths and circle-of-fourths. The ability to do this spontaneously (from any starting inversion) is a crucial component of the method we are establishing. As we will see later, each triad can be used in a variety of different vertical structures - however this type of 'upper structure' voiceleading is typically a common factor. When looking at voiceled triads around the circle, we will become familiar with all starting inversions in order to cover all voiceleading options. When voiceleading these triads around the circle-of-5ths or 4ths there are generally two approaches to use, as follows:-

- consider the **sequence of inversions being used** i.e. do we need a root-position triad followed by a 2nd inversion, followed by a 1st inversion, and so on in a repeating cycle (see **Fig. 4.13.** below).

- consider the **commontone between successive triads** i.e. in **Fig. 4.13.** below, the bottom note is common between the first 2 triads, the middle note is common between the next 2 triads, and the top note is common between the next 2 triads - this sequence of commontones (bottom, middle, top) then repeats afterwards.

Figure 4.13. Major triads voiceled around circle-of-fifths - starting with C triad in root position
(Cassette Tape Example 90)

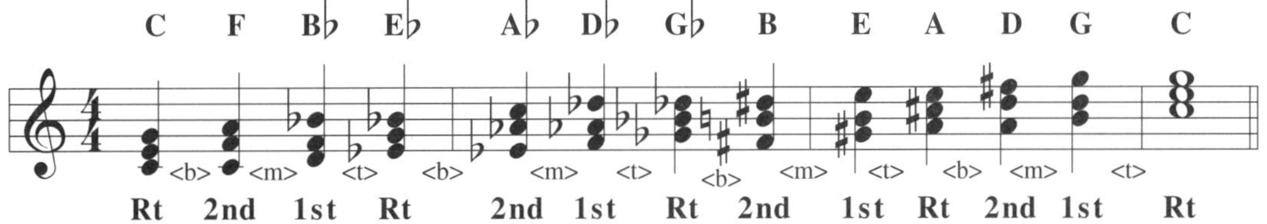

The circle-of-fifths voiceleading generally works best when the top note is either static or moving in an ascending direction. Notice that underneath the example I have indicated which inversion (**Rt**, **1st**, or **2nd**) is required for each triad. You will already have become familiar with these inversions through the exercises earlier in this chapter - so you should now be able to fit them into the above pattern! I have also indicated in parentheses which note is common between successive triads (either bottom, middle or top - represented as <b>, <m> or <t> respectively). This approach is useful when finding your way from one inversion to another. Notice also that the previous example started with a C major triad in root position. This meant that we used the next F triad in second inversion, and so on. However, had we started from a C triad in first inversion, in order to maintain the voiceleading direction we would need a root position F triad afterwards. In other words all subsequent inversions would be displaced, as follows:-

Figure 4.14. Major triads voiceled around circle of fifths - starting with C triad in 1st inversion
(Cassette Tape Example 91)

Major triad voiceleading (contd)

Compare **Fig. 4.14.** to **Fig. 4.13.** and you'll see that the inversions and commontones indicated have all been displaced. This is also the case when starting with a second inversion C major triad, as follows:-

Figure 4.15. Major triads voiceled around circle-of-fifths - starting with C triad in 2nd inversion
(Cassette Tape Example 92)

Again the inversions and commontones are indicated. The previous three examples (**Figs. 4.13. - 4.15.**) together contain **all** inversions of **all** major triads, in voiceled contexts. Now we will look at the corresponding patterns moving in circle-of-fourths, again from each starting inversion. The circle-of-fourths voiceleading generally works best when the top note is either static or moving in a descending direction. Again all inversions and commontone relationships are indicated, as follows:-

Figure 4.16. Major triads voiceled around circle-of-fourths - starting with C triad in root position
(Cassette Tape Example 93)

Figure 4.17. Major triads voiceled around circle-of-fourths - starting with C triad in 1st inversion
(Cassette Tape Example 94)

Figure 4.18. Major triads voiceled around circle-of-fourths - starting with C triad in 2nd inversion
(Cassette Tape Example 95)

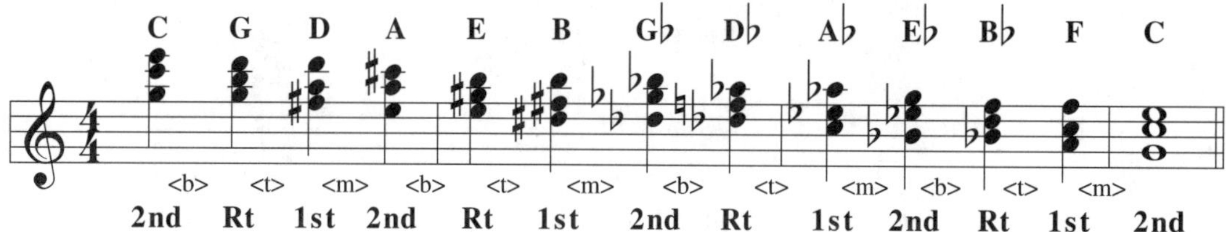

Major triad voiceleading (contd)

PRACTICE DIRECTIONS:-

- ***Practice major triad voiceleading around the circle-of-fifths as in Figs. 4.13. - 4.15.***
- ***Practice major triad voiceleading around the circle-of-fourths as in Figs. 4.16. - 4.18.***

(Left hand may optionally double right hand, 1 octave lower)

Minor triad voiceleading

Now we have equivalent exercises for minor triads voiceled around the circle-of-fifths and circle-of-fourths in all starting inversions. The inversions and commontones are indicated in a similar fashion to the major triads, as follows:-

Figure 4.19. Minor triads voiceled around circle-of-fifths - starting with Cmi triad in root position
(CASSETTE TAPE EXAMPLE 96)

Figure 4.20. Minor triads voiceled around circle-of-fifths - starting with Cmi triad in 1st inversion
(CASSETTE TAPE EXAMPLE 97)

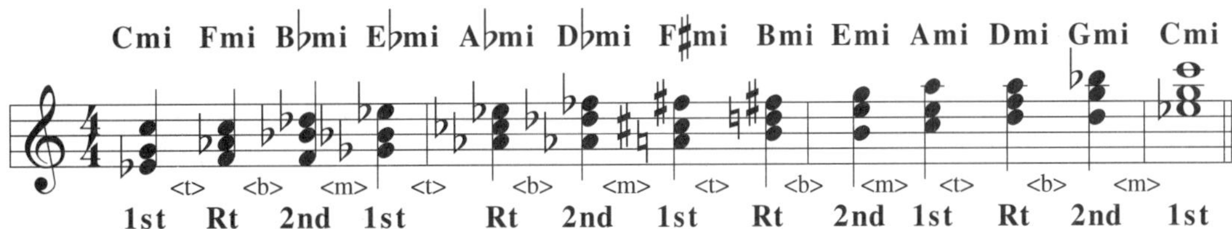

Figure 4.21. Minor triads voiceled around circle-of-fifths - starting with Cmi triad in 2nd inversion
(CASSETTE TAPE EXAMPLE 98)

Minor triad voiceleading (contd)

Figure 4.22. Minor triads voiceled around circle-of-fourths - starting with Cmi triad in root position
(Cassette Tape Example 99)

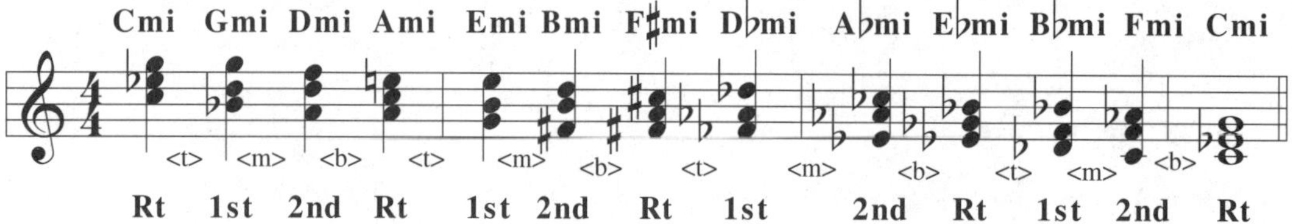

Figure 4.23. Minor triads voiceled around circle-of-fourths - starting with Cmi triad in 1st inversion
(Cassette Tape Example 100)

Figure 4.24. Minor triads voiceled around circle-of-fourths - starting with Cmi triad in 2nd inversion
(Cassette Tape Example 101)

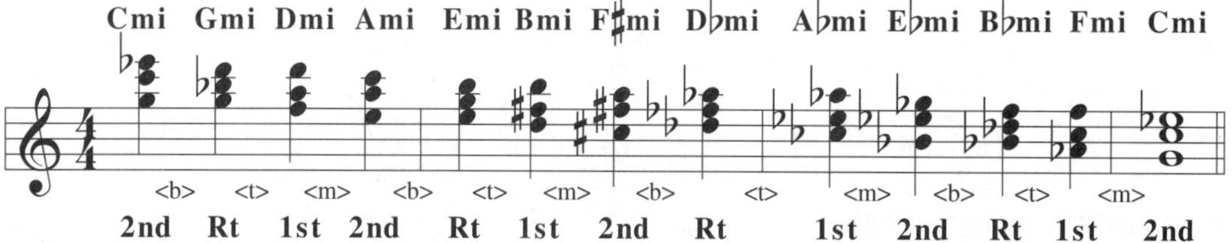

Practice directions:-

- ***Practice minor triad voiceleading around the circle-of-fifths as in Figs. 4.19. - 4.21.***
- ***Practice minor triad voiceleading around the circle-of-fourths as in Figs. 4.22. - 4.24.***

(Left hand may optionally double right hand, 1 octave lower)

Creating & using triad-over-root chords

Introduction

We can now apply the triad voiceleading learnt in the last chapter to '**triad-over-root**' chords, i.e. creating an overall structure by placing the triad over a root in the bass voice. This vertical concept is the basis for a great deal of today's pop music harmony. Each major or minor triad could be placed over any one of twelve different pitches - however some of the resulting sounds are too dissonant for modern contemporary styles. From these overall choices, there are seven different roots which when placed below the major triad, result in useful and often-used combinations for mainstream pop music. Similarly, there are seven different minor-triad-over-root structures to consider. These sounds are illustrated below, using **C major** or **C minor** as the upper triad in each case - however of course these principles will apply to all major and minor triads:-

Figure 5.1. C major triad with C in bass voice
(CASSETTE TAPE EXAMPLE 102)

This combination creates a simple unaltered **major triad**. In later chapters we will refer to this as a **1-3-5** upper structure, as (with respect to the C in the bass) the triad represents the root, 3rd and 5th of the overall major chord.

Figure 5.2. C major triad with D in bass voice
(CASSETTE TAPE EXAMPLE 103)

This combination creates a **dominant 11th** suspension, often functioning as a 'softer' and less leading form of dominant (**V**) chord in contemporary styles. Other symbols for this chord are **D11** or **D9sus**. Another interpretation of this chord is as an incomplete (no 3rd or 5th) **minor 11th** chord. In later chapters we will refer to this combination as a **b7-9-11** upper structure, as (with respect to the D in the bass) the triad represents the b7th, 9th and 11th of the overall suspended (or minor) chord.

Figure 5.3. C major triad with E in bass voice
(CASSETTE TAPE EXAMPLE 104)

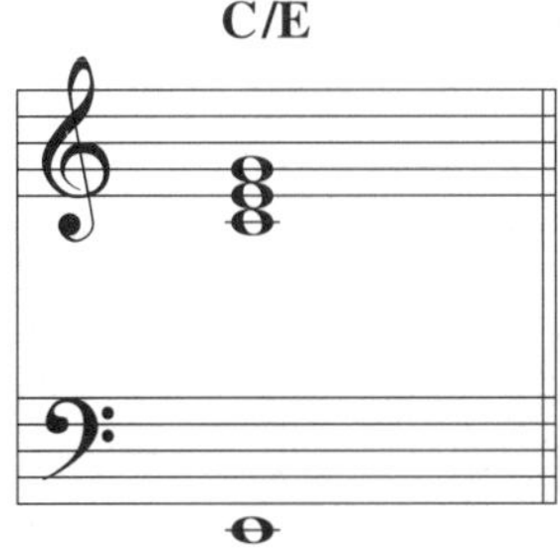

This combination creates an **inverted major chord** over the third - this chord will function and will be heard as an inverted C chord, and so in later chapters we will still refer to it as a **1-3-5** upper structure, but over the 3rd in the bass. In this configuration the inverted C chord sounds 'unstable', and the root generally wants to move scalewise (or by circle-of-fifths) to the root of the next chord. Sometimes the alternate chord symbol **Emi(#5)** is encountered - although this is technically correct, the symbol **C/E** is more likely to reflect how the chord is 'heard' and used.

FOR FURTHER INFORMATION ON CREATING & USING TRIAD-OVER-ROOT CHORDS, PLEASE REFER TO CHAPTER 7 OF OUR CONTEMPORARY MUSIC THEORY LEVEL 2 BOOK (SEE PAGE ix IN THIS BOOK).

Introduction - triad-over-root chords (contd)

Figure 5.4. C major triad with F in bass voice
(Cassette Tape Example 105)

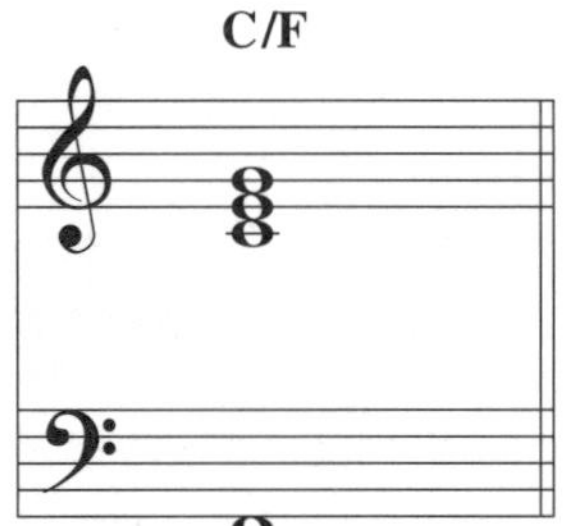

This combination creates a **major 9th** chord but with the 3rd omitted. Alternate chord symbols in this case would be **Fma9(no3)** or **Fma9(omit3)**. Without the 3rd this major chord has a more transparent and 'modern' sound. In later chapters we will refer to this combination as a **5-7-9** upper structure, as (with respect to the F in the bass) the triad represents the 5th, 7th and 9th of the overall major chord.

Figure 5.5. C major triad with G in bass voice
(Cassette Tape Example 106)

This combination creates an **inverted major chord** over the 5th - this chord will function and be heard as an inverted **C** chord rather than a G chord, and so in later chapters we will still refer to it as a **1-3-5** upper structure, but over the 5th in the bass. In this configuration the inverted C chord sounds fairly 'stable' and is widely used especially in gospel styles.

Figure 5.6. C major triad with A in bass voice
(Cassette Tape Example 107)

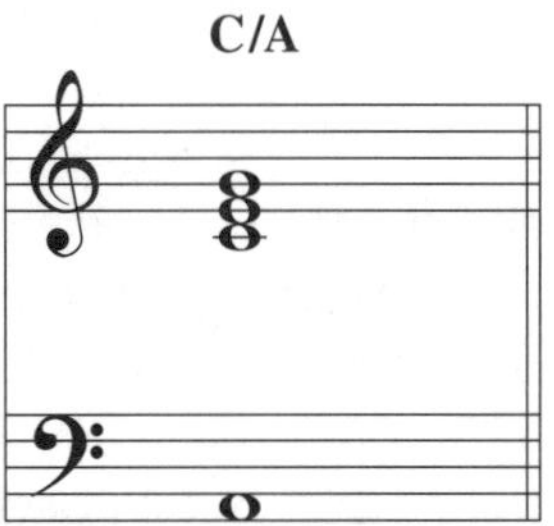

This combination creates a fully-defined **minor 7th** chord - alternate chord symbol in this case would be **Ami7**. This chord is typically functioning as a **II**, **III** or **VI** in major keys or a **I** or **IV** in minor keys. In later chapters we will refer to this combination as a **b3-5-b7** upper structure, as (with respect to the A in the bass) the triad represents the b3rd, 5th and b7th of the overall minor chord.

Figure 5.7. C major triad with Bb in bass voice
(Cassette Tape Example 108)

This combination is heard and used in two ways:-

- as an **inverted dominant chord** (in this case **C7**) over the seventh. This usage will be referred to in later chapters as a **1-3-5** upper structure, but over the 7th of the chord in the bass.
- as an incomplete **major 13th chord** (in this case a **Bbma13** without the 3rd, 5th or 7th). This usage will be referred to in later chapters as a **9-#11-13** upper structure, as (with respect to Bb in the bass) the triad represents the 9th, raised 11th and 13th of the overall major chord.

Introduction - triad-over-root chords (contd)

Figure 5.8. C minor triad with C in bass voice
(CASSETTE TAPE EXAMPLE 109)

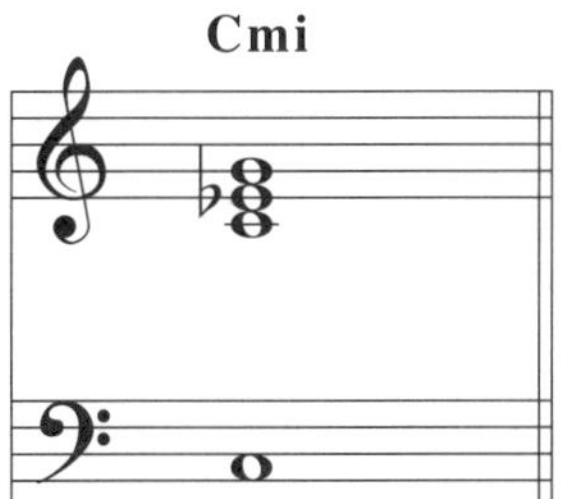

This combination creates a simple unaltered **minor triad** (a **1-b3-5** upper structure).

Figure 5.9. C minor triad with Eb in bass voice
(CASSETTE TAPE EXAMPLE 110)

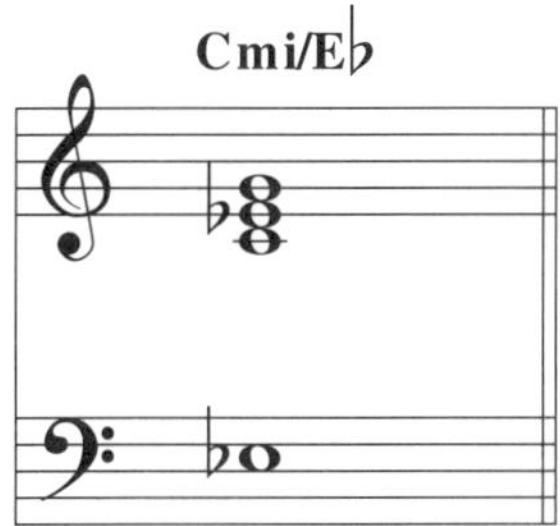

This combination creates an **inverted minor chord** over the third - this chord will generally function and be heard as an inverted **Cmi** chord, and so in later chapters we will still refer to it as a **1-b3-5** upper structure, but over the 3rd in the bass. There is also a possible alternative **major 6th** chord implication (in this case **Eb6**).

Figure 5.10. C minor triad with F in bass voice
(CASSETTE TAPE EXAMPLE 111)

This combination creates an incomplete or non-definitive **9th chord** (a **5-b7-9** upper structure) which could imply a minor or dominant 9th structure depending on the context.

Figure 5.11. C minor triad with G in bass voice
(CASSETTE TAPE EXAMPLE 112)

This combination creates an **inverted minor chord** over the 5th - this chord will function and be heard as an inverted **Cmi** chord rather than a G chord, and so in later chapters we will still refer to it as a **1-b3-5** upper structure, but over the 5th in the bass.

Introduction - triad-over-root chords (contd)

Figure 5.12. C minor triad with Ab in bass voice
(Cassette Tape Example 113)

This combination creates a fully-defined **major 7th** chord (a 3-5-7 upper structure) - alternate chord symbol in this case would be **Abma7**. This chord is typically functioning as a **I** or **IV** in major keys or a **bIII** or **bVI** in minor keys.

Figure 5.13. C minor triad with A in bass voice
(Cassette Tape Example 114)

This combination creates a fully-defined '**minor 7th with flatted 5th**' chord (a **b3-b5-b7** upper structure) - alternate chord symbol in this case would be **Ami7(b5)**. Generally reserved for more sophisticated styles, this chord typically functions as a **VII** in major keys or a **II** or **VI** in minor keys.

Figure 5.14. C minor triad with Bb in bass voice
(Cassette Tape Example 115)

This combination is heard and used as a **minor 7th** chord inverted over the 7th. Typically this is used to accommodate a specific root melody or voiceleading.

In mainstream contemporary styles the major-triad-over-root combinations are generally used more frequently than the minor-triad-over-root combinations - however all of these structures are useful and should be learnt and practiced. The remainder of this chapter now deals with the application of these chords in various voiceleading and rhythmic settings.

Progressions using major-triad-over-root chords

We will now apply the circle-of-fifths and circle-of-fourths voiceleading concepts presented in the last chapter, to major-triad-over-root chords in progressions. Each vertical usage of the major triad (presented in **Figs. 5.1.** through **5.7.**) is shown below in both a circle-of-fifths and circle-of-fourths progression context. Notice that in each of these examples, the vertical sound (overall chord quality) **remains the same** throughout each progression:-

Figure 5.15. Basic major triad (1-3-5 upper structure - see Fig. 5.1.) moving around circle-of-5ths (*Cassette Tape Example 116*)

Figure 5.16. Dominant 11th suspension (b7-9-11 upper structure - see Fig. 5.2.) moving around circle-of-5ths (*Cassette Tape Example 117*)

Figure 5.17. Major triad inverted over 3rd (see Fig. 5.3.) moving around circle-of-5ths (*Cassette Tape Example 118*)

Progressions using major-triad-over-root chords (contd)

Figure 5.18. Major 9th chord without the 3rd (5-7-9 upper structure - see Fig. 5.4.) moving around circle-of-5ths (CASSETTE TAPE EXAMPLE 119)

Figure 5.19. Major triad inverted over 5th (see Fig. 5.5.) moving around circle-of-5ths (CASSETTE TAPE EXAMPLE 120)

Figure 5.20. Minor 7th chord (b3-5-b7 upper structure - see Fig. 5.6.) moving around circle-of-5ths (CASSETTE TAPE EXAMPLE 121)

Progressions using major-triad-over-root chords (contd)

Figure 5.21. Inverted Dominant 7th or Lydian chord (9-#11-13 upper structure - see Fig. 5.7.) moving around circle-of-5ths (CASSETTE TAPE EXAMPLE 122)

Figure 5.22. Basic major triad (1-3-5 upper structure - see Fig. 5.1.) moving around circle-of-4ths (CASSETTE TAPE EXAMPLE 123)

Figure 5.23. Dominant 11th suspension (b7-9-11 upper structure - see Fig. 5.2.) moving around circle-of-4ths (CASSETTE TAPE EXAMPLE 124)

Progressions using major-triad-over-root chords (contd)

Figure 5.24. Major triad inverted over 3rd (see Fig. 5.3.) moving around circle-of-4ths *(Cassette Tape Example 125)*

Figure 5.25. Major 9th chord without the 3rd (5-7-9 upper structure - see Fig. 5.4.) moving around circle-of-4ths *(Cassette Tape Example 126)*

Figure 5.26. Major triad inverted over 5th (see Fig. 5.5.) moving around circle-of-4ths *(Cassette Tape Example 127)*

Progressions using major-triad-over-root chords (contd)

Figure 5.27. Minor 7th chord (b3-5-b7 upper structure - see Fig. 5.6.) moving around circle-of-4ths *(Cassette Tape Example 128)*

Figure 5.28. Inverted Dominant 7th or Lydian chord (9-#11-13 upper structure - see Fig. 5.7.) moving around circle-of-4ths *(Cassette Tape Example 129)*

Practice directions:-

- ***Practice all major-triad-over-root combinations around the circle-of-fifths as shown in Figs. 5.15. - 5.21.***
- ***Practice all major-triad-over-root combinations around the circle-of-fourths as shown in Figs. 5.22. - 5.28.***

*For extra practice - try these exercises using different starting inversions of the first upper C triad (see **Figs. 4.13. - 4.18.**), and in general starting/finishing at different points around the circle!*

Progressions using major-triad-over-root chords (contd)

We can now begin to apply rhythmic or 'comping' settings in different contemporary styles to these major-triad-over-root progressions. In the second part of this book we will address these styles in more detail - however for now these patterns will represent a useful and realistic way to apply these chord structures. For example, if we took the **Minor 7th** chord progression around the circle-of-fifths (as illustrated in **Fig. 5.20.**), we could apply some different contemporary styles to this sequence as follows:-

Figure 5.29. 'Pop-rock' pattern using minor 7th chords around circle-of-fifths
(Cassette Tape Example 130)

Progressions using major-triad-over-root chords (contd)

Figure 5.30. 'Funk' pattern using minor 7th chords around the circle-of-fifths
(Cassette Tape Example 131)

Progressions using major-triad-over-root chords (contd)

Figure 5.31. 'Pop ballad' pattern using minor 7th chords around the circle-of-fifths
(Cassette Tape Example 132)

The contemporary styles referred to in these examples (**Pop Ballad**, **Pop-Rock** & **Funk**) will be covered in detail in **Chapters 11**, **12** & **15** respectively.

Any of these patterns (plus others to be developed later) can be applied to any of the major-triad-over-root progressions around the circle-of-fifths and circle-of-fourths as presented in **Figs. 5.15. - 5.28**. Here are some examples of how this works, just showing the first three measures of each:-

Figure 5.32. 'Pop-rock' pattern using major 9th (no 3rd) chords, around circle-of-4ths (using Fig. 5.25. voiceleading) *(Cassette Tape Example 133)*

Progressions using major-triad-over-root chords (contd)

Figure 5.33. 'Funk' pattern using dominant 11th suspensions, around circle-of-4ths (using Fig. 5.23. voiceleading) *(Cassette Tape Example 134)*

Figure 5.34. 'Pop ballad' pattern using major triads inverted over 3rd, around circle-of-5ths (using Fig. 5.17. voiceleading) *(Cassette Tape Example 135)*

Practice directions:-

- ***Practice minor 7th chords around the circle-of-fifths in the pop-rock, funk and pop ballad settings as in Figs. 5.29. - 5.31.***
- ***Work on spontaneously combining stylistic settings with the different chord structures by choosing one option from each of the following categories:***
    - ***a major-triad-over-root chord (from the seven types available)***
    - ***a stylistic setting (pop-rock, funk, or pop ballad)***
    - ***a direction around the circle (i.e. 4ths or 5ths)***

Figs. 5.32. - 5.34. *are three partial examples of the various combinations available. Have fun!!*

Progressions using major-triad-over-root chords (contd)

Of course there are many different ways to combine these chord structures into progressions. One way to begin experimenting with your own progressions is to vary the overall chord quality (from the seven major-triad-over-root choices available) within the chord sequence, while still maintaining **circle-of-fifths** or **circle-of-fourths** voiceleading in the upper triads. This type of harmony occurs all the time in contemporary pop music and is largely the result of making 'ear' decisions. The following diagram represents the major-triad-over-root choices, together with an example of a progression using the above idea:-

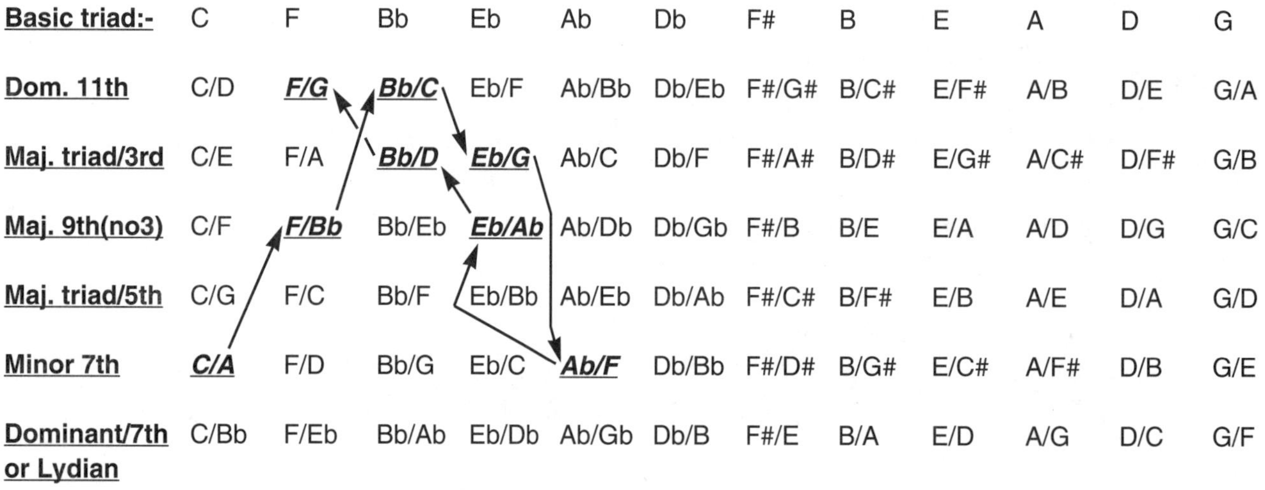

Basic triad:-	C	F	Bb	Eb	Ab	Db	F#	B	E	A	D	G
Dom. 11th	C/D	***F/G***	***Bb/C***	Eb/F	Ab/Bb	Db/Eb	F#/G#	B/C#	E/F#	A/B	D/E	G/A
Maj. triad/3rd	C/E	F/A	***Bb/D***	***Eb/G***	Ab/C	Db/F	F#/A#	B/D#	E/G#	A/C#	D/F#	G/B
Maj. 9th(no3)	C/F	***F/Bb***	Bb/Eb	***Eb/Ab***	Ab/Db	Db/Gb	F#/B	B/E	E/A	A/D	D/G	G/C
Maj. triad/5th	C/G	F/C	Bb/F	Eb/Bb	Ab/Eb	Db/Ab	F#/C#	B/F#	E/B	A/E	D/A	G/D
Minor 7th	***C/A***	F/D	Bb/G	Eb/C	***Ab/F***	Db/Bb	F#/D#	B/G#	E/C#	A/F#	D/B	G/E
Dominant/7th or Lydian	C/Bb	F/Eb	Bb/Ab	Eb/Db	Ab/Gb	Db/B	F#/E	B/A	E/D	A/G	D/C	G/F

The descriptions on the left summarize the seven major-triad-over-root qualities discussed so far. Across the top line are the major triads moving around the circle-of-fifths (moving left-to-right) or circle-of-fourths (moving right-to-left). Underneath each triad in the columns are the different vertical structures using that triad respectively (refer to **Figs. 5.1. - 5.7.** as necessary). I have indicated a short eight-chord progression on the table with underlined chord symbols and arrows connecting between chords. From one chord to the next, the upper triads are moving in a circle-of-fifths or circle-of-fourths fashion - however unlike the practice progressions (see **Figs. 5.15. - 5.28.**) the chord quality is now being varied between one chord and the next, resulting in different root intervals. As you can see there are a huge number of ways this can be done within the above possibilities - **feel free to experiment and create your own ideas!** Here now is a rhythmic setting of the above example:-

Figure 5.35. 'Pop-rock' pattern using triad-over-root progression example
(CASSETTE TAPE EXAMPLE 136)

(CONTD-->)

Progressions using major-triad-over-root chords (contd)

Figure 5.35. (contd)

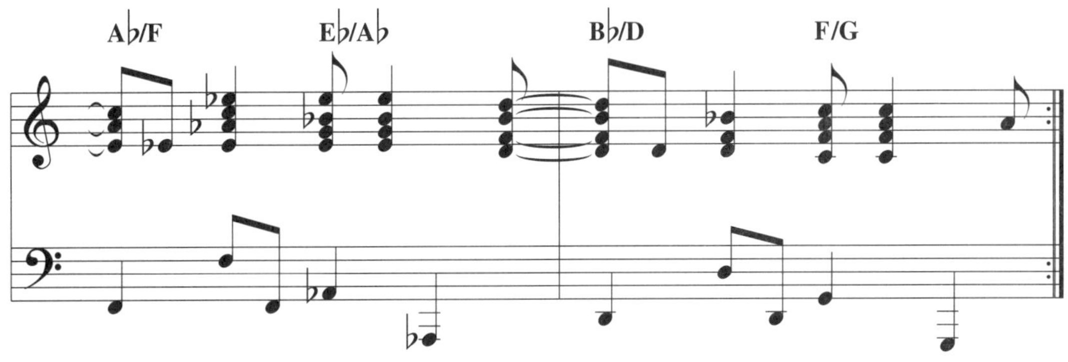

Progressions using minor-triad-over-root chords

Although the minor-triad-over-root combinations (see **Figs. 5.8. - 5.14.**) are not as widely used as the major triad combinations, they are still useful and it is desirable to get these 'under your fingers'. In a similar fashion as for the major triads, here are some of the minor-triad-over-root combinations around the circle-of-fifths and circle-of-fourths:-

Figure 5.36. Basic minor triad (1-b3-5 upper structure - see Fig. 5.8.) moving around circle-of-5ths *(Cassette Tape Example 137)*

Figure 5.37. Major 7th chord (3-5-7 upper structure - see Fig. 5.12.) moving around circle-of-5ths *(Cassette Tape Example 138)*

Progressions using minor-triad-over-root chords (contd)

Figure 5.38. Incomplete 9th chord (5-b7-9 upper structure - see Fig. 5.10.) moving around circle-of-5ths (CASSETTE TAPE EXAMPLE 139)

Figure 5.39. Basic minor triad (1-b3-5 upper structure - see Fig. 5.8.) moving around circle-of-4ths (CASSETTE TAPE EXAMPLE 140)

Figure 5.40. Major 7th chord (3-5-7 upper structure - see Fig. 5.12.) moving around circle-of-4ths (CASSETTE TAPE EXAMPLE 141)

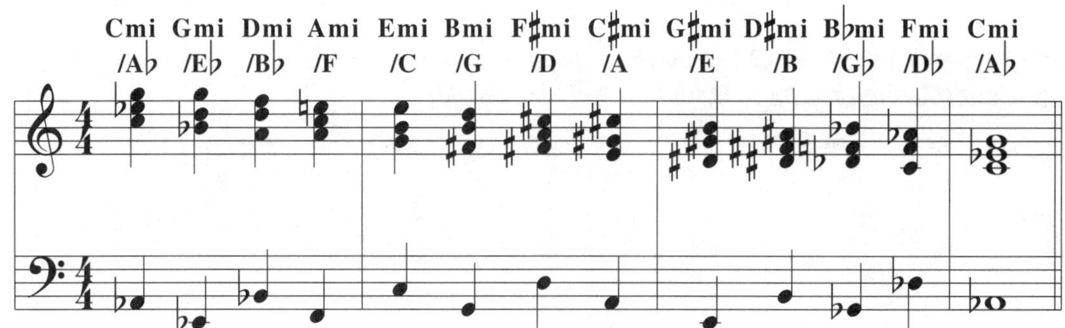

Progressions using minor-triad-over-root chords (contd)

Figure 5.41. Incomplete 9th chord (5-b7-9 upper structure - see Fig. 5.10.) moving around circle-of-4ths *(Cassette Tape Example 142)*

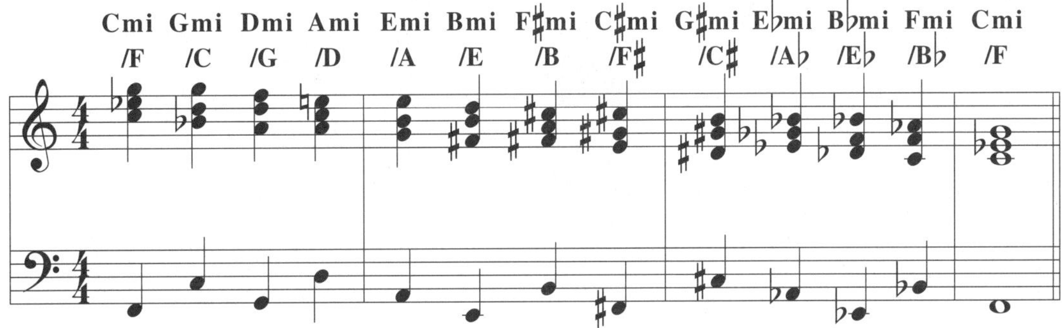

As you saw in the introduction to this chapter (**Figs. 5.8. - 5.14.**), the minor triad can also be inverted over the **3rd**, **5th** or **7th**, or it can be built from the **3rd** of a **minor 7th(b5)** chord. Feel free to experiment with these combinations around the circle-of-fifths and circle-of-fourths if you like! We can also apply rhythmic settings to these minor-triad-over-root progressions, in a similar fashion as was done for major triads. Here are two examples, again showing the first three measures of each:-

Figure 5.42. 'Pop ballad' pattern using major 7th chords, around circle-of-4ths (using Fig. 5.40. voiceleading) *(Cassette Tape Example 143)*

Figure 5.43. 'Pop-rock' pattern using incomplete 9th chords, around circle-of-5hs (using Fig. 5.38. voiceleading) *(Cassette Tape Example 144)*

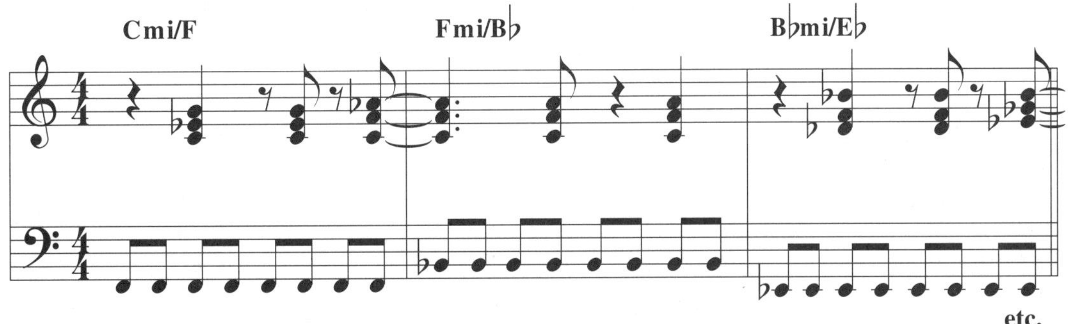

Progressions using minor-triad-over-root chords (contd)

PRACTICE DIRECTIONS:-

- ***Practice the minor-triad-over-root combinations around the circle-of-fifths and circle-of-fourths as shown in Figs. 5.36. - 5.41.***
  *(You may optionally work on the remaining minor-triad-over-root chords as detailed in **Figs. 5.8. - 5.14.** around the circle-of-fifths and circle-of-fourths)*
- ***Practice the minor-triad-over-root stylistic settings as shown in Figs. 5.42. - 5.43.*** *(continuing around the circle-of-fourths and circle-of-fifths)*
- ***Work on spontaneously combining stylistic settings with different minor-triad-over-root chords, in a similar fashion as for the major triads*** *(refer to practice directions on p.77).*

As you can see, a great many options for chord progressions become available when we start combining major-triad-over-root and minor-triad-over-root structures together. Have fun experimenting with these, which are the foundation of a significant percentage of today's contemporary music!

Four-part chords - inversions and voiceleading

Introduction

In a similar fashion as for the triads detailed in **Chapter 4**, we also need to work on four-part chords and their inversions. We will also be considering how to 'voicelead' these chords in this chapter, which then prepares us for using four-part-chord-over-root structures in progressions as detailed in the following chapter. Here we will focus for now on **Major 7th** and **Minor 7th** four-part 'shapes' - these are the most useful in contemporary situations as they can be placed over various roots in the bass register (i.e. they are 'plural' to a number of larger chord structures).

As previously described, voiceleading means moving from one chord voicing to the next in a smooth manner horizontally i.e. without any unnecessary interval skips. Again this is achieved by using chord inversions as required. Here is a simple progression using root-position four-part chords:-

Figure 6.1. Root position Ma7th example (no voiceleading used)
(Cassette Tape Example 145)

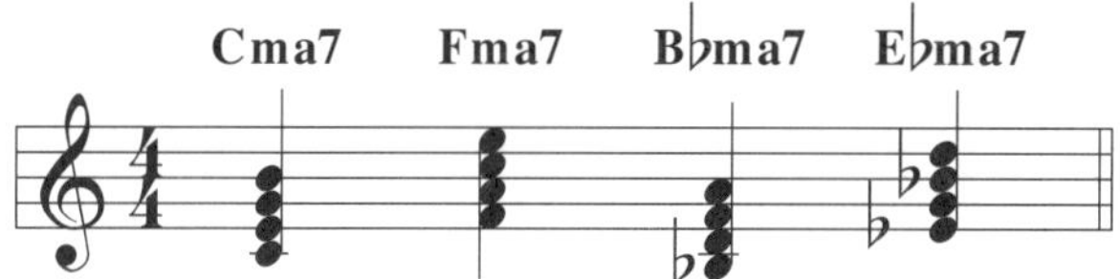

As with the previous root-position triad example (see **Fig. 4.1.**), this has a rather disconnected sound from left to right - the use of root-position major 7th chords forces us to make large interval skips. Now here is the same progression using 'voiceleading' - going to the closest inversion of each successive chord as follows:-

Figure 6.2. Inverted Ma7th example (voiceleading used)
(Cassette Tape Example 146)

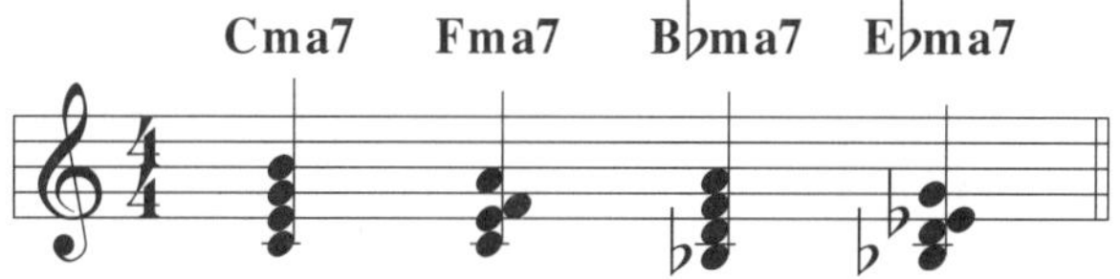

As with the major triad inversions, we need to work on becoming familiar with inversions of these four-part chords **as shapes in their own right** and not just as variations on a root-position four-part chord. This is the key to spontaneously using these shapes - particularly in the context of four-part-chord-over-root structures as detailed in the next chapter.

Major 7th chord inversions

We will first become familiar with inverted **major 7th** chords in all keys. Similar inversion terminology as for triads will apply, except that we now have an additional '**third inversion**' to consider. We will use the terms '**root position**', '**first inversion**', '**second inversion**' and '**third inversion**' as shown on the following page:-

For further information on voiceleading of four-part chords, please refer to Chapter 6 of our Contemporary Music Theory Level 2 book (see page ix in this book).

Major 7th chord inversions (contd)

Figure 6.3. C major 7th chord (root position and inversions)
(Cassette Tape Example 147)

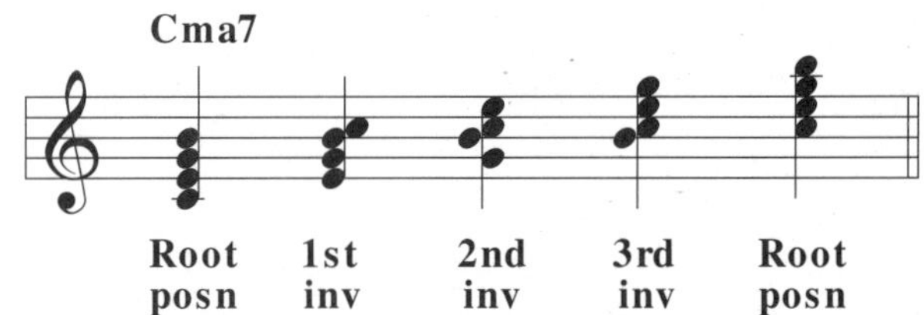

Notice that the 1st inversion chord has a half-step (minor 2nd) at the top - this 'exposed' dissonance makes this inversion less useful than the others. Again a convenient way to relate to each of these inversion terms is to consider where the root of the major 7th chord is, in each inversion as follows:-

In **root position**:- The **root** is on the **bottom** (with 3rd, 5th and 7th above)
In **1st inversion**:- The **root** is on the **top** (with 3rd, 5th and 7th below)
In **2nd inversion**:- The **root** is the **2nd note from the top** (with 3rd above, & 5th & 7th below)
In **3rd inversion**:- The **root** is the **2nd note from the bottom** (with 3rd & 5th above, & 7th below)

As a warm-up exercise we will play major 7th chord inversions (as in **Fig. 6.3.**) in all keys around the circle-of-fifths, as follows (accidentals are repeated for each chord for your convenience):-

Figure 6.4. Major 7th chords (root position and inversions) around circle-of-fifths
(Cassette Tape Example 148)

Major 7th chord inversions (contd)

The next stage is to target specific inversions without playing the root position chord first. (We will omit the less musically useful **1st inversion**, and focus on the **2nd** and **3rd inversions**). Again, as with the inverted triads (see **Figs. 4.5. - 4.6.**), we notice that the different inverted four-part chords exhibit different 'keyboard contour' characteristics i.e. specific groupings of black and white keys on the keyboard. Here then are the 2nd and 3rd inversion major 7th chords in all keys:-

Figure 6.5. Second inversion major 7th chords around circle-of-fifths
(Cassette Tape Example 149)

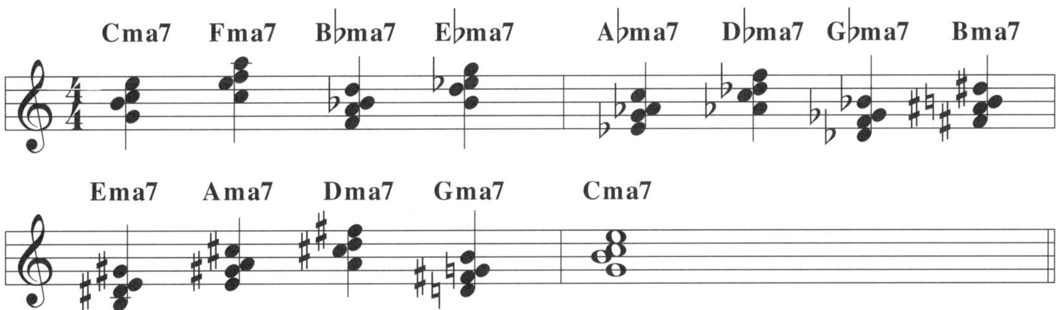

Figure 6.6. Third inversion major 7th chords moving around circle-of-fifths
(Cassette Tape Example 150)

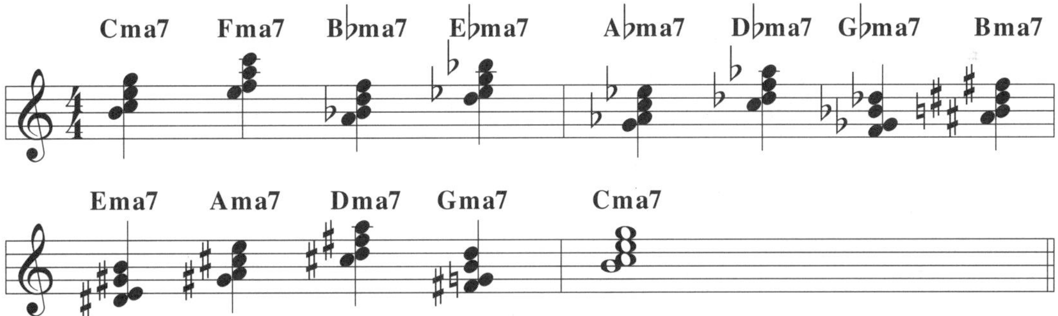

Practice directions:-

- ***Practice major 7th chords in all inversions as in Fig. 6.4.***
- ***Practice 2nd inversion major 7th chords as in Fig. 6.5.***
  (for variation in sequence of keys, use circle-of-fourths)
- ***Practice 3rd inversion major 7th chords as in Fig. 6.6.***
  (for variation in sequence of keys, use circle-of-fourths)

CHAPTER SIX

Minor 7th chord inversions

We will now turn our attention to **minor 7th chord** shapes. Similar inversion terminology and concepts will apply. Again we will start out by playing minor 7th chord inversions in all keys around the circle-of-fifths:-

Figure 6.7. Minor 7th chords (root position and inversions) around circle-of-fifths
(Cassette Tape Example 151)

As with the major 7th chords, we will now target the **2nd** and **3rd** inversion minor 7th chords as follows:-

Figure 6.8. Second inversion minor 7th chords around circle-of-fifths
(Cassette Tape Example 152)

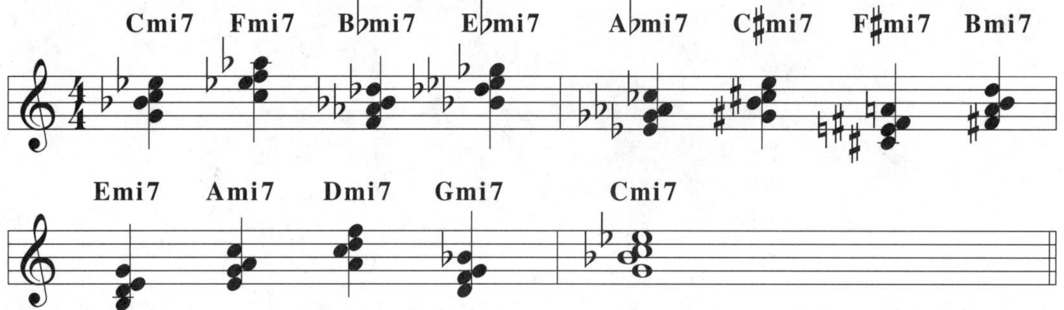

Minor 7th chord inversions (contd)

Figure 6.9. Third inversion minor 7th chords around circle-of-fifths
(Cassette Tape Example 153)

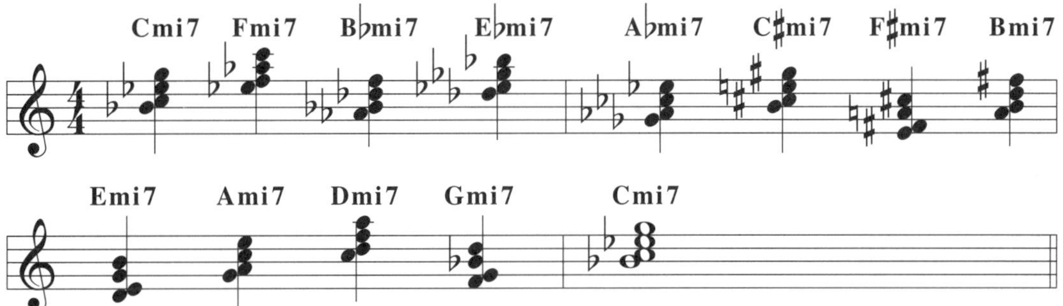

Practice directions:-

- ***Practice minor 7th chords in all inversions as in Fig. 6.7.***
- ***Practice 2nd inversion minor 7th chords as in Fig. 6.8.***
  (for variation in sequence of keys, use circle-of-fourths)
- ***Practice 3rd inversion minor 7th chords as in Fig. 6.9.***
  (for variation in sequence of keys, use circle-of-fourths)

Major 7th chord voiceleading

Now we will consider the voiceleading of **major 7th** chords around the circle-of-fifths and circle-of-fourths. As with the triad voiceleading, it is important to develop the ability to spontaneously voicelead these shapes from different starting inversions, and to do this we can again consider two different approaches:-

- consider the **sequence of inversions being used**. With these four-part chord shapes, we are generally alternating between **root position** and **2nd inversion** successively around the circle-of-fifths and circle-of-fourths.

- consider the **commontones between successive chords.** With these four-part chord shapes, normally two notes out of the four remain common between successive chords around the circle-of-fifths or circle-of-fourths. The other two tones will move by parallel whole-step (major 2nd).

We see these principles at work in the following example:-

Major 7th chord voiceleading (contd)

Figure 6.10. Major 7ths voiceled around circle-of-fifths - starting with Cma7 in root position
(Cassette Tape Example 154)

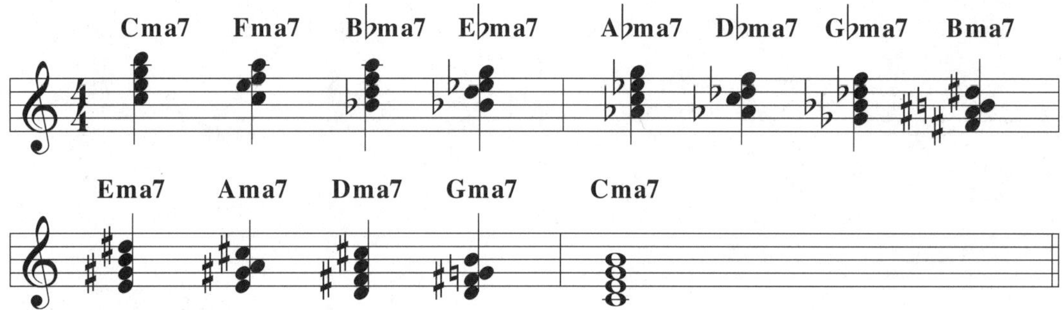

Notice that in this case the sequence of inversions is root position-2nd inversion-root position-2nd inversion etc. repeated throughout the sequence. Also observe that between the first two chords (**Cma7** and **Fma7**) the bottom two notes remained common (**C** and **E**) while the top two notes moved by parallel whole step (**B to A** and **G to F**). Similarly between the next two chords, the pattern is reversed - now the top two notes remain common while the bottom two move by whole-step etc. This pattern again repeats throughout the sequence. As you can see this type of circle-of-fifths voiceleading generally results in a descending voiceleading direction for these four-part chords. Now we will start the same sequence from a second inversion **Cma7** chord, and all the subsequent inversions and commontone relationships are correspondingly displaced as follows:-

Figure 6.11. Major 7ths voiceled around circle-of-fifths - starting with Cma7 in 2nd inversion
(Cassette Tape Example 155)

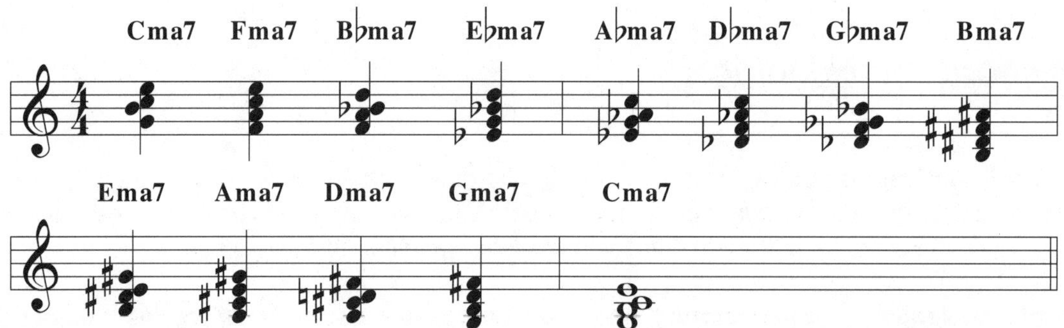

As you can see the inversion sequence and commontone patterns have been reversed. Now we will look at major 7th chords voiceled around the circle-of-fourths. In this situation, these four-part shapes generally voicelead in an ascending direction, as follows:-

Major 7th chord voiceleading (contd)

Figure 6.12. Major 7ths voiceled around circle-of-fourths - starting with Cma7 in root position
(Cassette Tape Example 156)

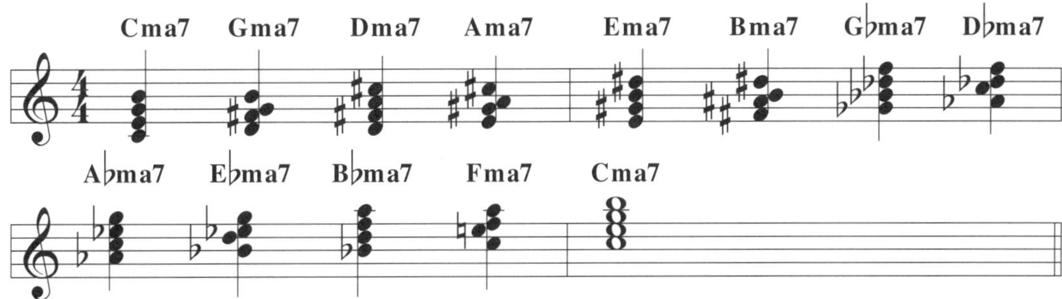

Figure 6.13. Major 7ths voiceled around circle-of-fourths - starting with Cma7 in 2nd inversion
(Cassette Tape Example 157)

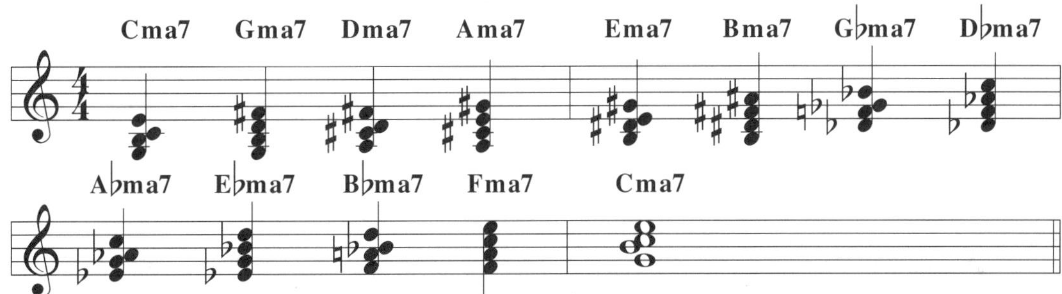

Practice directions:-

- ***Practice major 7th chords voiceleading around the circle-of-fifths as in Figs. 6.10. and 6.11.***
- ***Practice major 7th chords voiceleading around the circle-of-fourths as in Figs. 6.12. and 6.13.***
  (Left hand may optionally double right hand, 1 octave lower)

CHAPTER SIX

Minor 7th chord voiceleading

Now we have equivalent routines for **minor 7th** chords voiceleading around the circle-of-fifths and circle-of-fourths. The sequence of inversions (alternating root position and 2nd inversion) and commontone aspects (two commontones per chord change, with remaining two notes moving by parallel whole-step) is similar to the major 7th chord exercises, as follows:-

Figure 6.14. Minor 7ths voiceled around circle-of-fifths - starting with Cmi7 in root position
(Cassette Tape Example 158)

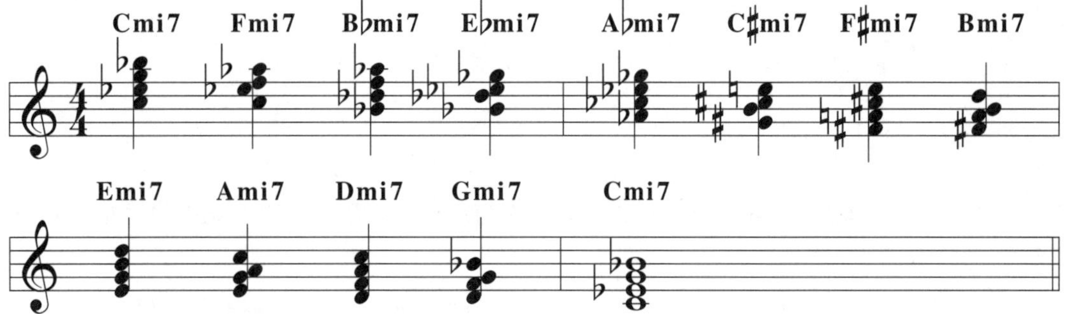

Figure 6.15. Minor 7ths voiceled around circle-of-fifths - starting with Cmi7 in 2nd inversion
(Cassette Tape Example 159)

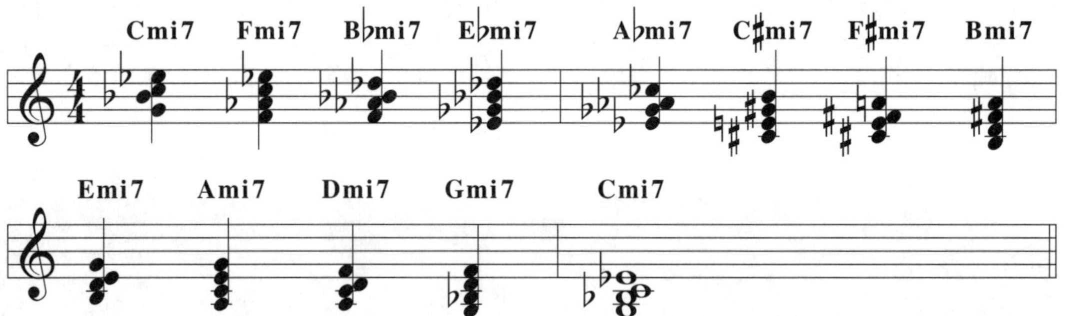

Figure 6.16. Minor 7ths voiceled around circle-of-fourths - starting with Cmi7 in root position
(Cassette Tape Example 160)

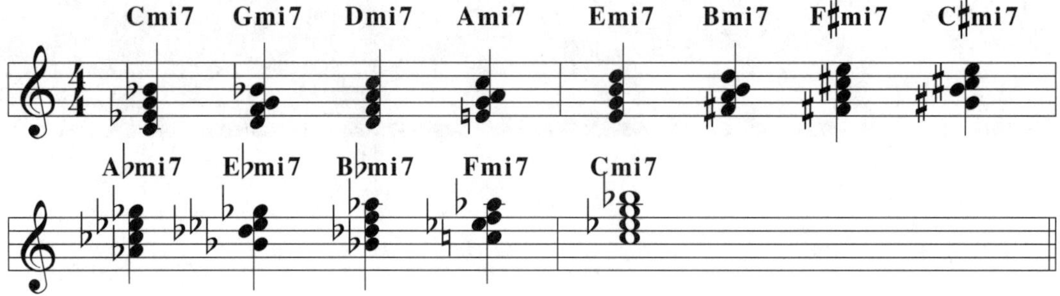

Minor 7th chord voiceleading (contd)

Figure 6.17. Minor 7ths voiceled around circle-of-fourths - starting with Cmi7 in 2nd inversion
(Cassette Tape Example 161)

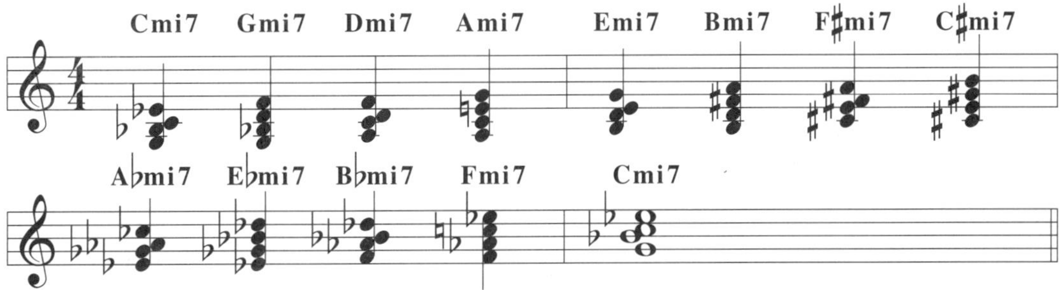

Practice directions:-

- ***Practice minor 7th chords voiceleading around the circle-of-fifths as in Figs. 6.14. and 6.15.***
- ***Practice minor 7th chords voiceleading around the circle-of-fourths as in Figs. 6.16. and 6.17.***
  (Left hand may optionally double right hand, 1 octave lower)

--- NOTES ---

Creating & using 4-part-over-root chords

Introduction

We can now apply the four-part voiceleading learnt in the previous chapter, to creating '**four-part-over-root** chords - this involves using a four-part structure over another root in the bass, creating a **five-part chord** overall. Again as with the previously studied triad-over-root forms (which created **four-part chords** overall) in **Chapter 5**, these voicings are widely used in contemporary styles. The **major 7th** and **minor 7th** four-part structures already presented will now be used as 'upper structures' of larger chord forms. There are various choices of root notes below these four-part chords - however for now we will focus on two usages each for major 7th and minor 7th 'upper structures' which are the most useful and frequently used. These sounds are illustrated below, using **Cma7** or **Cmi7** as the upper chord in each case:-

Figure 7.1. Cma7 chord with A in bass voice
(CASSETTE TAPE EXAMPLE 162)

This combination creates a fully-defined **minor 9th** chord - alternate chord symbol in this case is **Ami9**. In later chapters we will refer to this as a **b3-5-b7-9** upper structure, as (with respect to the A in the bass) the 4-part shape represents the b3rd, 5th, b7th & 9th of the overall minor chord.

Figure 7.2. Cma7 chord with D in bass voice
(CASSETTE TAPE EXAMPLE 163)

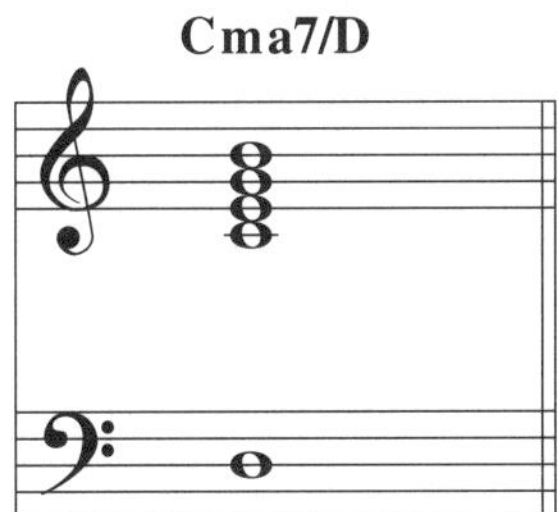

This combination creates a **dominant 13th suspension**, similar to the (triad-over-root) dominant 11th suspension in **Fig. 5.2.**, but with the extra sophistication of the 13th. Alternate chord symbol in this case is **D13sus**. In later chapters we will refer to this combination as a **b7-9-11-13** upper structure, as (with respect to the D in the bass) the 4-part shape represents the b7th, 9th, 11th & 13th of the overall suspended chord.

Figure 7.3. Cmi7 chord with Ab in bass voice
(CASSETTE TAPE EXAMPLE 164)

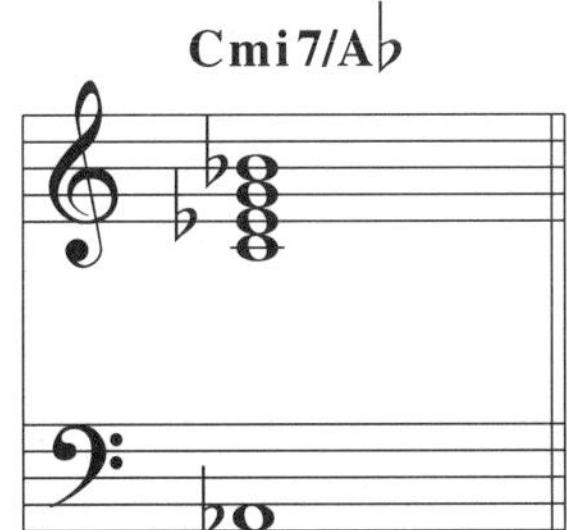

This combination creates a fully-defined **major 9th** chord - alternate chord symbol in this case is **Abma9**. In later chapters we will refer to this as a **3-5-7-9** upper structure, as (with respect to Ab in the bass) the 4-part shape represents the 3rd, 5th, 7th & 9th of the overall major chord.

FOR FURTHER INFORMATION ON CREATING & USING 4-PART-OVER-ROOT CHORDS, PLEASE REFER TO CHAPTER 8 OF OUR CONTEMPORARY MUSIC THEORY LEVEL 2 BOOK (SEE PAGE ix IN THIS BOOK).

Introduction - 4-part-over-root chords (contd)

Figure 7.4. Cmi7 chord with F in bass voice
(Cassette Tape Example 165)

This combination creates a **dominant 11th suspension**, very similar to the (triad-over-root) 11th chord in **Fig. 5.2.**, but with the addition of the 5th of the chord. Alternate chord symbols in this case are **F11** or **F9sus**. Another interpretation of this chord is as an incomplete (no 3rd) **minor 11th** chord. In later chapters we will refer to this combination as a **5-b7-9-11** upper structure, as (with respect to the F in the bass) the 4-part shape represents the 5th, b7th, 9th & 11th of the suspended (or minor) chord.

Progressions using major-7th-over-root chords

In a similar fashion as for the triad-over-root structures (see **Chapter 5**), we will now apply the circle-of-fifths and circle-of-fourths voiceleading concepts presented in the last chapter, to major-7th-over-root chords in progressions. Both vertical usages of the major 7th chord (presented in earlier examples **7.1.** and **7.2.**) are shown below in a circle-of-fifths and circle-of-fourths progression context. Again notice that in each of these examples, the vertical sound (overall chord quality) **remains the same** throughout each progression:-

Figure 7.5. Minor 9th chord (see Fig. 7.1.) moving around circle-of-fifths
(Cassette Tape Example 166)

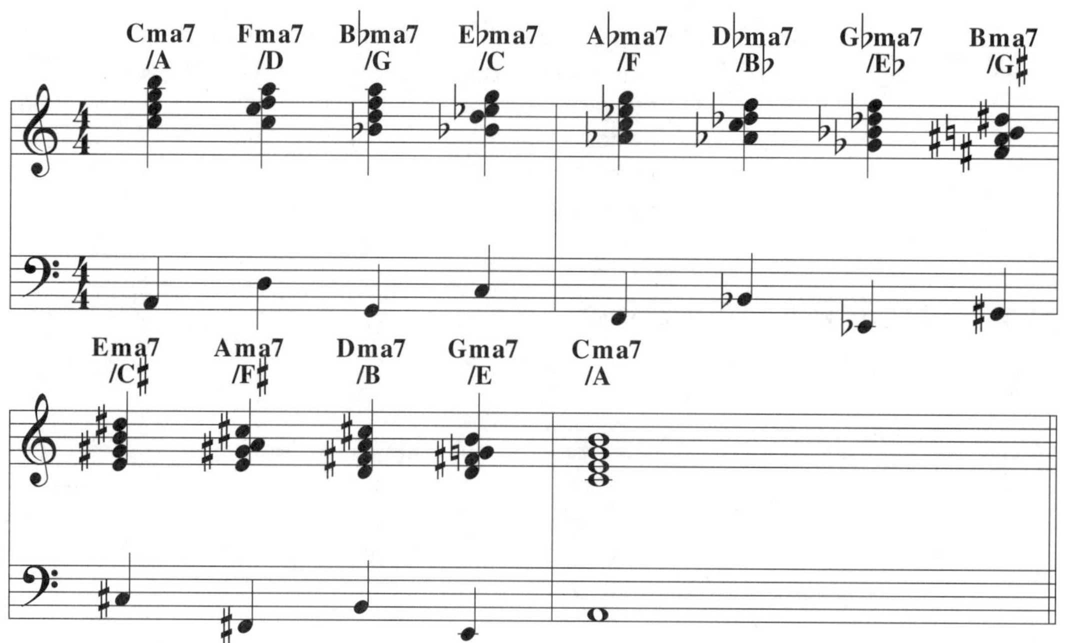

Progressions using major-7th-over-root chords (contd)

Figure 7.6. Dominant 13th suspension (see Fig. 7.2.) moving around circle-of-fifths
(CASSETTE TAPE EXAMPLE 167)

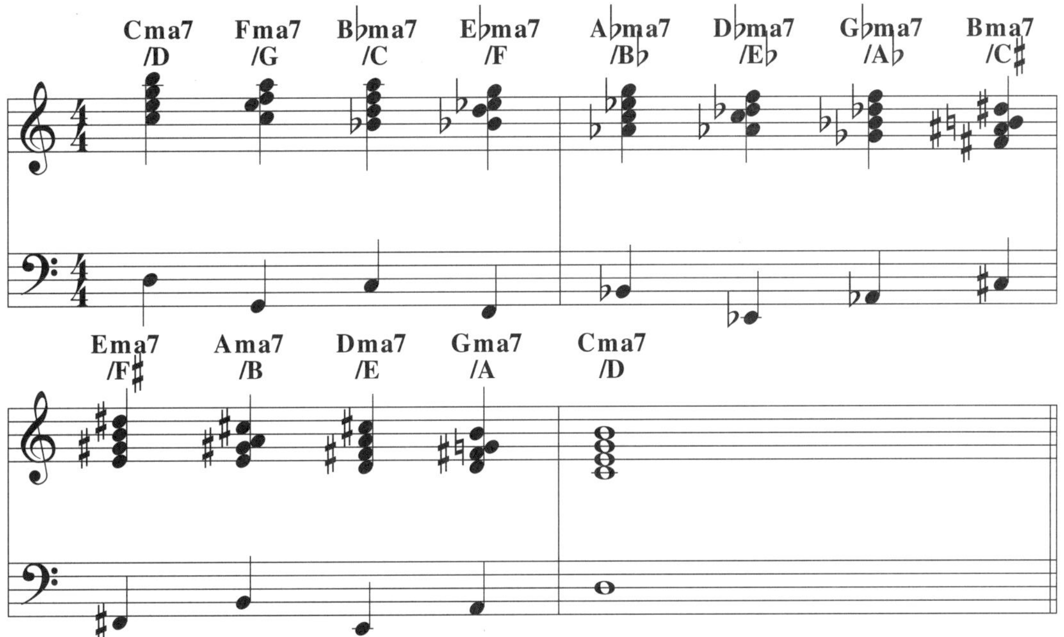

Figure 7.7. Minor 9th chord (see Fig. 7.1.) moving around circle-of-fourths
(CASSETTE TAPE EXAMPLE 168)

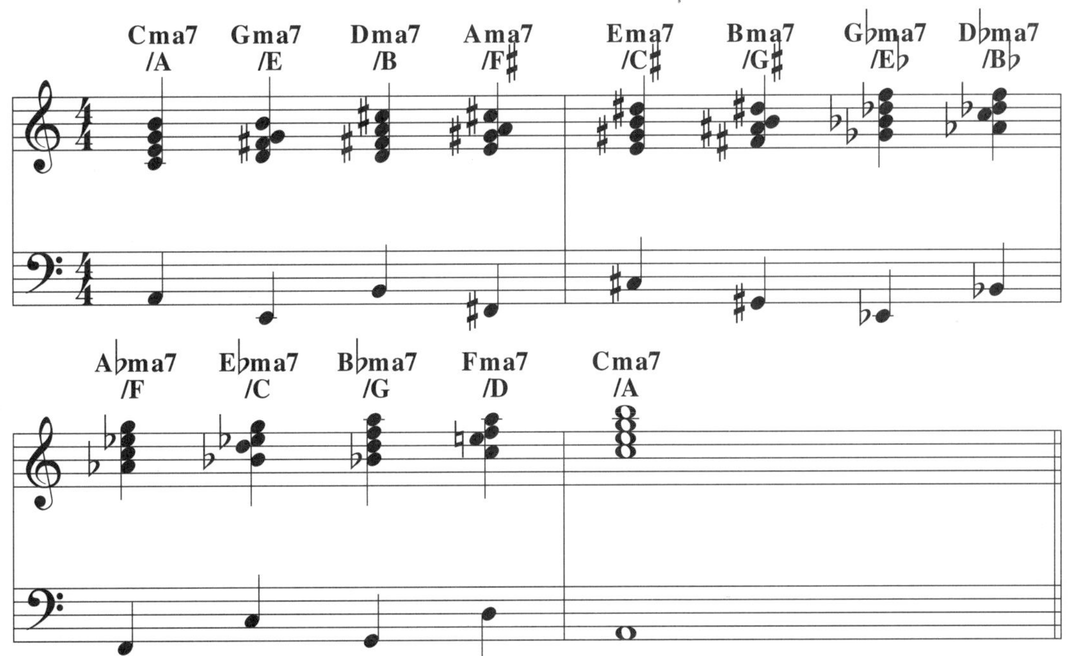

Progressions using major-7th-over-root chords (contd)

Figure 7.8. Dominant 13th suspension (see Fig. 7.2.) moving around circle-of-fourths
(Cassette Tape Example 169)

Practice directions:-

- **Practice major-7th-over-root combinations around the circle-of-fifths as shown in Figs. 7.5. and 7.6.**
- **Practice major-7th-over-root combinations around the circle-of-fourths as shown in Figs. 7.7. and 7.8.**

*As a practice variation - voicelead the upper structures beginning with the Cma7 shape in 2nd inversion, as shown in **Figs. 6.11. and 6.13.***

Progressions using major-7th-over-root chords (contd)

As with the previous triad-over-root chords, we can now begin to apply different rhythmic or 'comping' settings to these four-part-over-root structures. The patterns detailed in **Chapter 5** (pop-rock, funk, pop ballad) can all be applied to these chords, and you are encouraged to experiment with these. Here are a couple of new patterns using the minor 9th chord derived in **Fig. 7.1.** and then taken around the circle-of-fifths in **Fig. 7.5.**:-

Figure 7.9. 'Reggae' pattern using minor 9th chords around circle-of-fifths

(Cassette Tape Example 170)

(Note the '**swing 8ths**' symbol at the top of the chart - review **Fig. 2.30.** and accompanying text as necessary).

Cma7/A Fma7/D B♭ma7/G

E♭ma7/C A♭ma7/F D♭ma7/B♭

G♭ma7/E♭ Bma7/G♯ Ema7/C♯

Ama7/F♯ Dma7/B Gma7/E Cma7/A

Progressions using major-7th-over-root chords (contd)

Figure 7.10. 'Arpeggiated pop-rock' pattern using minor 9th chords around circle-of-fifths

(Cassette Tape Example 171)

Any of these patterns (plus others developed in **Chapter 5**) can now be applied to the major-7th-over-root progressions around the circle-of-fifths and circle-of-fourths as presented in **Figs. 7.5. - 7.8**. Here are some examples of these combinations, just showing the first three measures of each:-

Progressions using major-7th-over-root chords (contd)

Figure 7.11. 'Reggae' pattern using dominant 13th suspensions, around circle-of-fourths (using Fig. 7.8. voiceleading) *(Cassette Tape Example 172)*

Figure 7.12. 'Arpeggiated pop-rock' pattern using dominant 13th suspensions, around circle-of-fifths (using Fig. 7.6. voiceleading) *(Cassette Tape Example 173)*

Practice directions:-

- ***Practice minor 9th chords around the circle-of-fifths in the reggae and arpeggiated pop-rock settings as in Figs. 7.9. and 7.10.***
- ***Work on spontaneously combining stylistic settings with the 4-part-over-root chord structures by choosing one option from each of the following categories:-***
    - ***a major-7th-over-root chord (either a minor 9th chord or dominant 13th suspension overall)***
    - ***a stylistic setting*** *(reggae and arpeggiated pop-rock presented in this chapter - you can also use the funk, pop-rock and pop ballad settings from* ***Chapter 5****)*
    - ***a direction around the circle (4ths or 5ths)***

Figs. 7.11. *and* ***7.12.*** *are partial examples of the various combinations available. Have fun!!*

Progressions using minor-7th-over-root chords

The minor-7th-over-root chords (see **Figs. 7.3.** and **7.4.**) are now voiceled around the 'circles' as follows:-

Figure 7.13. Major 9th chord (see Fig. 7.3.) moving around circle-of-fifths
(CASSETTE TAPE EXAMPLE 174)

Figure 7.14. Dominant 11th suspension (see Fig. 7.4.) moving around circle-of-fifths
(CASSETTE TAPE EXAMPLE 175)

Progressions using minor-7th-over-root chords (contd)

Figure 7.15. Major 9th chord (see Fig. 7.3.) moving around circle-of-fourths

(CASSETTE TAPE EXAMPLE 176)

Figure 7.16. Dominant 11th suspension (see Fig. 7.4.) moving around circle-of-fourths

(CASSETTE TAPE EXAMPLE 177)

Progressions using minor-7th-over-root chords (contd)

Again as with the previous major-7th-over-root chords, we can now begin to experiment with different rhythmic or 'comping' settings. The rhythmic patterns in this chapter (reggae and arpeggiated pop-rock) plus those presented in **Chapter 5** can all be applied to the minor-7th-over-root chords. Here are some examples of these combinations, just showing the first three measures of each:-

Figure 7.17. 'Reggae' pattern using major 9th chords, around circle-of-fifths (using Fig. 7.13. voiceleading) *(Cassette Tape Example 178)*

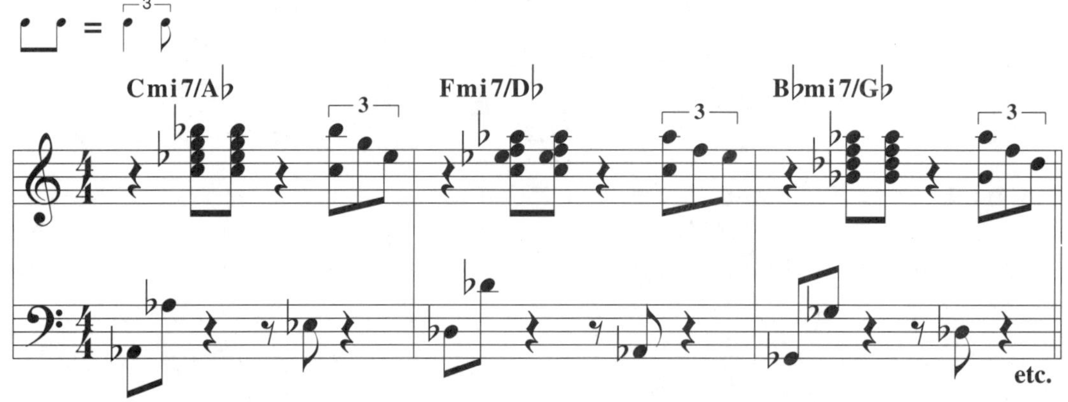

Figure 7.18. 'Arpeggiated pop-rock' pattern using dominant 11th suspensions, around circle-of-fourths (using Fig. 7.16. voiceleading) *(Cassette Tape Example 179)*

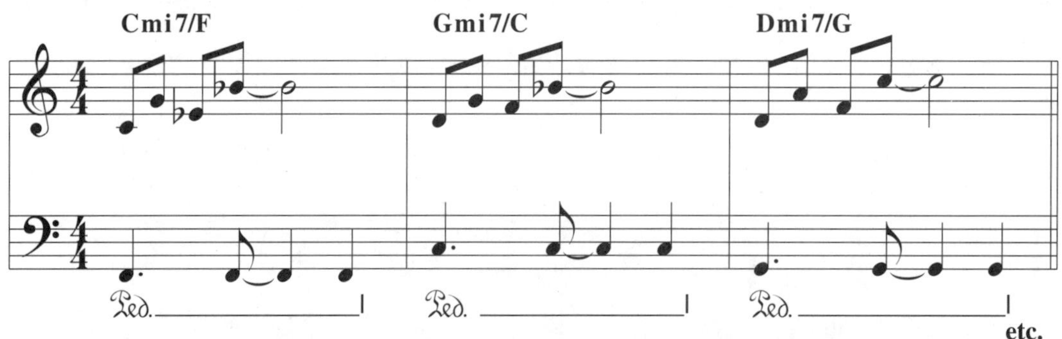

PRACTICE DIRECTIONS:-

- ***Practice the minor-7th-over-root combinations around the circle-of-fifths and circle-of-fourths as in Figs. 7.13. - 7.16.*** *(Use upper voiceleading in **Figs. 6.15.** and **6.17.** as a practice variation).*
- ***Work on spontaneously combining stylistic settings with different minor-7th-over-root chords, in a similar fashion as for the major-7th-over-root chords*** *(see practice directions **p.99**)* ***Figs. 7.17.*** *and* ***7.18.*** *are partial examples of the various combinations.*

Triad resolutions using added 9ths

Introduction

We have already seen that using triads as 'upper structures' of different chords is an integral part of contemporary music styles. Now we begin to look at the interior resolutions which can occur within a triad. These resolutions can add interior motion and interest when voiceleading through chord progressions. In this chapter we will focus on resolving the 9th to the root (referred to as a '**9 to 1**' resolution) within major and minor triads, and we will then in turn use this new structure in conjunction with different roots in the bass register in a similar fashion as the various triad-over-root chords presented in **Chapter 5**.

'9 to1' resolutions within major triads

We can resolve the 9th to the root within a major triad as follows:-

Figure 8.1. '9 to 1' resolution within C major triad
(Cassette Tape Example 180)

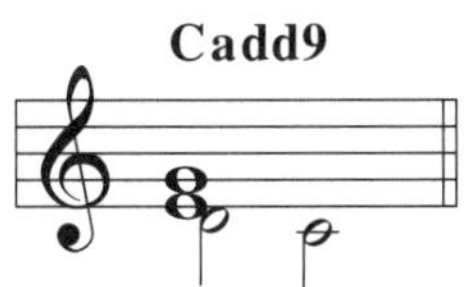

Note that in this case we have resolved to a root-position C major triad. In **Chapter 4** we worked on inverting triads, and we recall that there are 3 inversion options for this major triad i.e. root position, first inversion and second inversion as in **Fig 4.3**. We can therefore use this this '**9 to 1**' resolution within any inversion of this triad, as follows:-

Figure 8.2. '9 to 1' resolution within all inversions of C major triad
(Cassette Tape Example 181)

You'll see that the notation style here effectively combines two 'parallel systems' onto one staff - for each inversion, the 3rd and 5th of the chord last for one beat, **during which** the 9th and the root occupy half a beat each. As with our work on inverted triads earlier, it is important to conceptualize each of the above resolutions as separate entities and not just as variations on a root-position resolution. Each inversion using this resolution can be considered from the standpoint of where the '**9 to 1**' movement is occurring in each case, as follows:-

'9 to1' resolutions within major triads (contd)

In **root position**:-	The **9 to 1** is on the **bottom** (with 3rd and 5th above)
In **1st inversion**:-	The **9 to 1** is on the **top** (with 3rd and 5th below)
In **2nd inversion**:-	The **9 to 1** is in the **middle** (with 5th below and 3rd above)

Here now are some routines to help you conceptualize these different resolution settings, again using the circle-of-fifths as a practice sequence:-

Figure 8.3. Root position major triad '9 to1' resolutions around circle-of-fifths
(Cassette Tape Example 182)

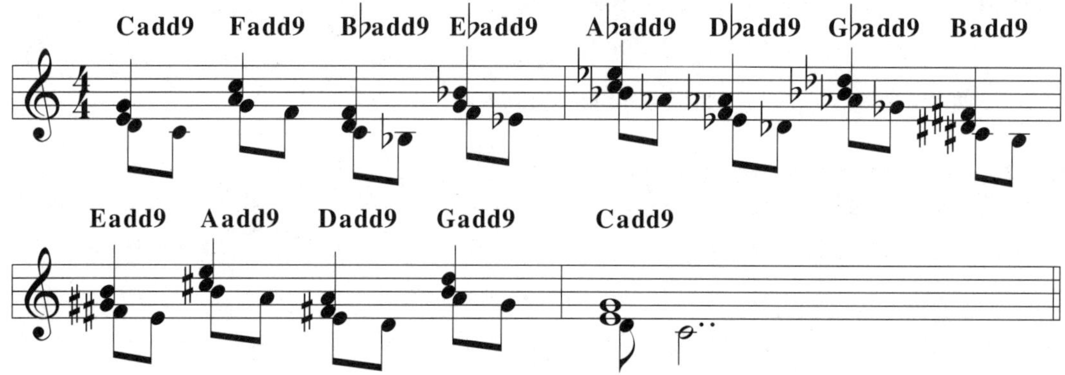

Figure 8.4. 1st inversion major triad '9 to1' resolutions around circle-of-fifths
(Cassette Tape Example 183)

'9 to 1' resolutions within major triads (contd)

Figure 8.5. 2nd inversion major triad '9 to 1' resolutions around circle-of-fifths
(Cassette Tape Example 184)

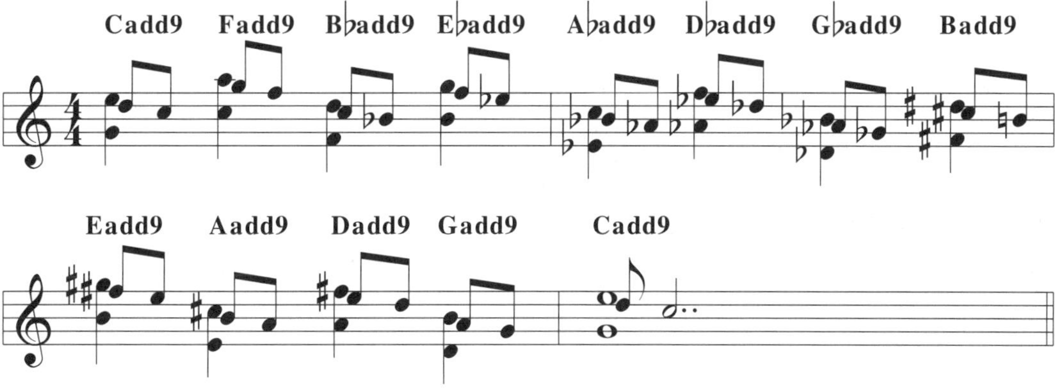

Now we will work on incorporating these resolutions into a voiceleading context. In **Chapter 4** we used 'voiceleading' (i.e. moving to the closest inversion) to connect smoothly between one chord and the next. We used voiceleading to move between triads around the circle-of-fifths as follows:-

Figure 8.6. Major triads voiceled around the circle-of-fifths
(Cassette Tape Example 79 - see Chapter 4)

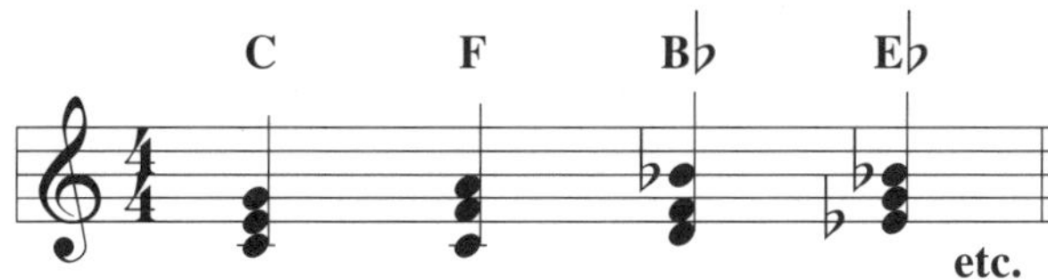

If we now apply '**9 to 1**' resolutions within these triads **using the same inversions as above for voiceleading purposes**, we derive the following:-

Figure 8.7. Major triads voiceled around the circle-of-fifths, using '9 to 1' resolutions
(Cassette Tape Example 185)

The ability to add these resolutions spontaneously within voiceled triads is I find a tremendous asset when improvising accompaniments in contemporary styles, especially when these structures are then combined with different roots in the bass register. Here now is the previous example in **Fig. 8.7.**, (starting with C major in root position), continuing around the circle-of-fifths:-

'9 to 1' resolutions within major triads (contd)

Figure 8.8. Major triad '9 to 1' resolutions voiceled around circle-of-fifths, starting with C major triad in root position *(Cassette Tape Example 186)*

We know from our work on voiceleading triads (see **Chapter 4, Figures 4.13. to 4.15.**) that if we change the starting inversion during these routines, we then displace all subsequent inversions. Here now is the above voiceled sequence but starting on the different inversions of the first (C major) triad:-

Figure 8.9. Major triad '9 to 1' resolutions voiceled around circle-of-fifths, starting with C major triad in 1st inversion *(Cassette Tape Example 187)*

Figure 8.10. Major triad '9 to 1' resolutions voiceled around circle-of-fifths, starting with C major triad in 2nd inversion *(Cassette Tape Example 188)*

'9 to 1' resolutions within major triads (contd)

PRACTICE DIRECTIONS:-

- ***Practice root position, 1st inversion and then 2nd inversion major triad '9 to 1' resolutions around the circle-of-fifths as in Figs. 8.3. - 8.5.***
  (for variation in sequence of keys, use circle-of-fourths)
- ***Practice voiceleading the major triad '9 to 1' resolutions around the circle-of-fifths from each starting position as in Figs. 8.8. - 8.10.***
  (as a variation, you can play each routine 'backwards' in a circle-of-fourths sequence using descending voiceleading)

Using '9 to 1' resolutions within major-triad-over-root chords

These resolution ideas now really come to life when applied to major-triad-over-root chords within a progression. We know from our work in **Chapter 5** that there are various major-triad-over-root combinations available. We will now see what happens when we apply '**9 to 1**' resolutions to some of these, as follows:-

Figure 8.11. C major triad with C in bass voice (see Fig. 5.1.)
(CASSETTE TAPE EXAMPLE 102)

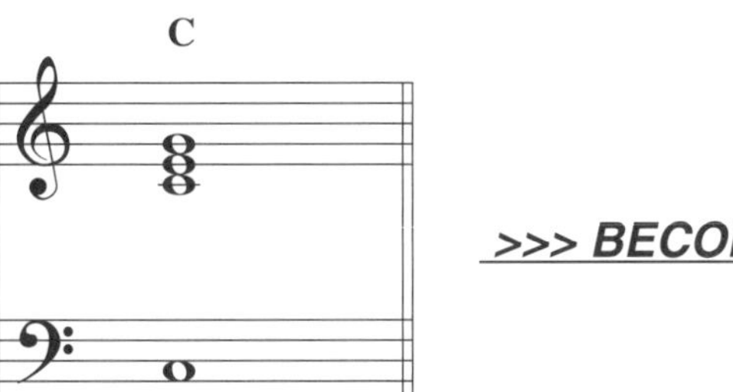

>>> BECOMES >>>

Figure 8.12. C major '9 to 1' resolution with C in bass voice
(CASSETTE TAPE EXAMPLE 189)

Using '9 to 1' resolutions within major-triad-over-root chords (contd)

Figure 8.13. C major triad with A in bass voice (see Fig. 5.6.)
(Cassette Tape Example 107)

Figure 8.14. C major '9 to 1' resolution with A in bass voice
(Cassette Tape Example 190)

In **Chapter 5** (**Fig. 5.6.**) we saw that a C major triad with A in the bass created an **Ami7** chord overall. The '**9 to 1**' resolution within the upper triad here effectively becomes an '**11 to 3**' or '**4 to 3**' movement within the overall minor chord. The added 11th to this minor chord can be represented by symbols such as **Ami11**, **Ami7(11)**, **Ami7(add11)**, **Ami7(sus4)**, **Ami7sus** etc. Now another resolution example:-

Figure 8.15. C major triad with F in bass voice (see Fig. 5.4.)
(Cassette Tape Example 105)

Figure 8.16. C major '9 to 1' resolution with F in bass voice
(Cassette Tape Example 191)

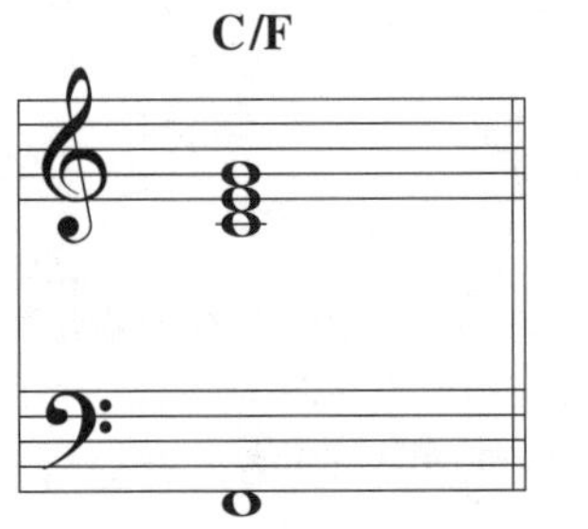

>>> BECOMES >>>

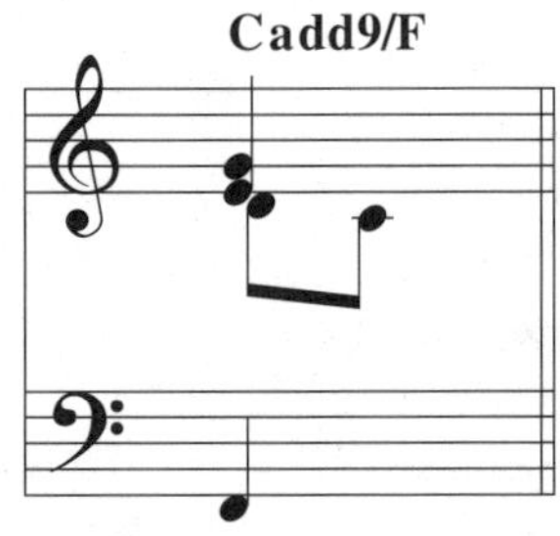

Again in **Chapter 5** (**Fig. 5.4.**) we saw that a C major triad with F in the bass created an **Fma9(no3)** chord overall. The '**9 to 1**' resolution within the upper triad here effectively becomes a '**13 to 5**' or '**6 to 5**' movement within the overall major chord. The added 13th (6th) to this major chord can be represented by symbols such as **Fma7(add6)**, **Fma9(add6)**, **Fma13** etc. Back in **Chapter 5** we also worked on various other major-triad-over-root combinations - feel free to experiment with '**9 to 1**' resolutions within the upper triads on these!

Now we will combine the vertical structures just presented (**Figs. 8.12., 8.14. & 8.16.**) with the voiceleading concepts as shown in **Figs. 8.8. - 8.10.** In other words, we will now voicelead these vertical structures around the circle-of-fifths, as follows:-

Using '9 to 1' resolutions within major-triad-over-root chords (contd)

Figure 8.17. Major chord '9 to 1' resolutions (see Fig. 8.12.) voiceled around circle-of-fifths
(CASSETTE TAPE EXAMPLE 192)

Figure 8.18. Minor chord '11 to 3' resolutions (see Fig. 8.14.) voiceled around circle-of-fifths
(CASSETTE TAPE EXAMPLE 193)

Using '9 to 1' resolutions within major-triad-over-root chords (contd)

Figure 8.19. Major chord '13 to 5' resolutions (see Fig. 8.16.) voiceled around circle-of-fifths
(Cassette Tape Example 194)

Now we'll see an application of the previous '**11 to 3**' movement on minor chords (see **Figs. 8.14. & 8.18.**) within a pop-rock rhythmic setting first seen in **Chapter 5** - the following example is based on **Fig. 5.29:-**

Figure 8.20. Pop-rock pattern using minor chord '11 to 3' resolutions, around circle-of-fifths
(Cassette Tape Example 195)

(CONTD-->)

Using '9 to 1' resolutions within major-triad-over-root chords (contd)

Figure 8.20. (contd)

PRACTICE DIRECTIONS:-

- ***Practice voiceleading the '9 to 1' resolutions within major-triad-over-root chords around the circle-of-fifths, as in Figs. 8.17. - 8.19.***
- *Practice variations:-*
    - *change the root by using other major-triad-over-root combinations as in **Chapter 5 Figs. 5.1. - 5.7.***
    - *change the first triad inversion in the routine (see **Figs. 8.9.** & **8.10.**)*
    - *change sequence of keys i.e. use circle-of-fourths*
- ***Practice the pop-rock rhythmic setting for minor chord '11 to 3' resolutions around the circle-of-fifths as in Fig. 8.20.***
- ***Experiment with combining different stylistic settings i.e. from Chapter 5, with different major-triad-over-root chords using resolutions.***

CHAPTER EIGHT

'9 to 1' resolutions within minor triads

Now we will turn our attention to minor triads. We can resolve the 9th to the root within the minor triad as follows:-

Figure 8.21. '9 to 1' resolution within C minor triad
(Cassette Tape Example 196)

In this case we have resolved to a root-position minor triad - but as for the major triad we know there are three possible inversions to consider (see **Fig. 4.7.**) - we can therefore use the '**9 to 1**' resolution within any inversion of the minor triad, as follows:-

Figure 8.22. '9 to 1' resolution within all inversions of C minor triad
(Cassette Tape Example 197)

Similar inversion and notation concepts apply as for the major triad resolutions (see text following **Fig. 8.2**). Here now are some routines to familiarize you with these minor triad resolution settings:-

Figure 8.23. Root position minor triad '9 to 1' resolutions around circle-of-fifths
(Cassette Tape Example 198)

'9 to 1' resolutions within minor triads (contd)

Figure 8.24. 1st inversion minor triad '9 to 1' resolutions around circle-of-fifths
(CASSETTE TAPE EXAMPLE 199)

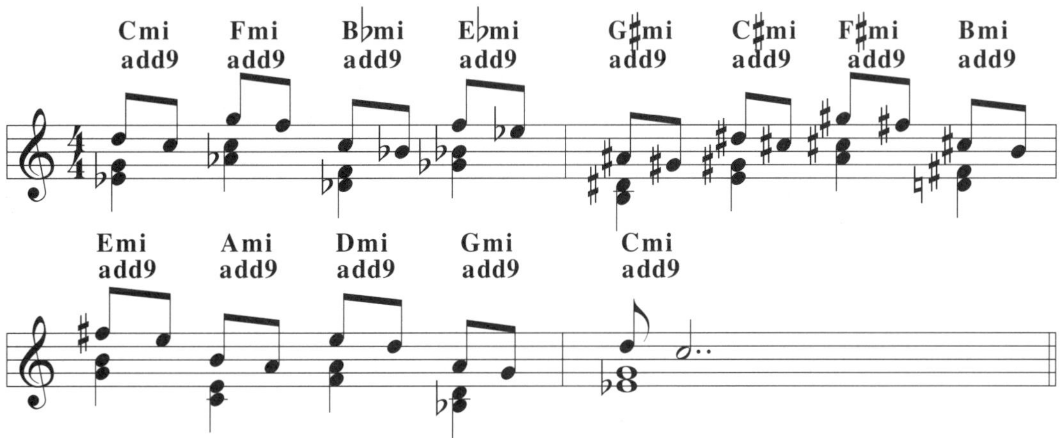

Figure 8.25. 2nd inversion minor triad '9 to 1' resolutions around circle-of-fifths
(CASSETTE TAPE EXAMPLE 200)

In a similar fashion as for the major triad resolutions, we will now work on voiceleading these minor triad '**9 to 1**' resolutions around the circle-of-fifths. (Refer to the text accompanying **Figs. 8.6.** and **8.7.** as necessary). Again this will be very useful particularly when we begin to apply roots in the bass register below these structures. Here now are the voiceled minor triad resolutions, the first example starting with C minor in root position, and subsequent examples starting with 1st and then 2nd inversion (again notice that all subsequent inversions are correspondingly displaced):-

'9 to 1' resolutions within minor triads (contd)

Figure 8.26. Minor triad '9 to 1' resolutions voiceled around circle-of-fifths, starting with C minor triad in root position (CASSETTE TAPE EXAMPLE 201)

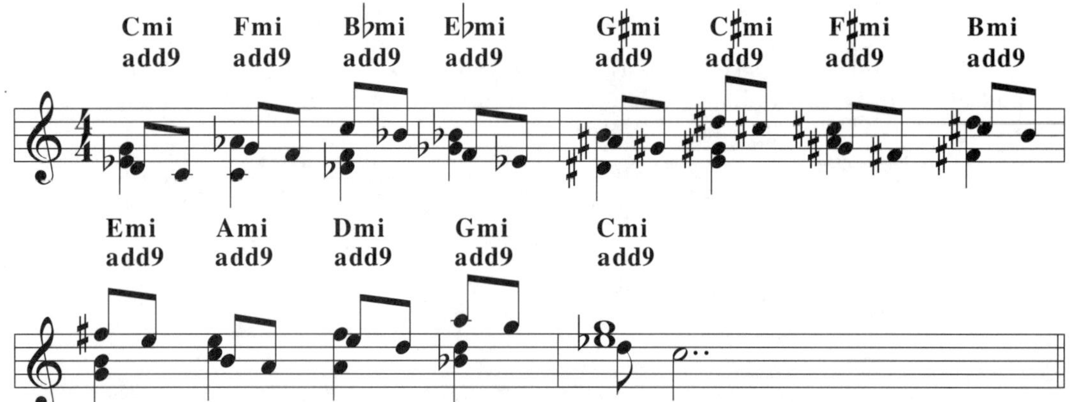

Figure 8.27. Minor triad '9 to 1' resolutions voiceled around circle-of-fifths, starting with C minor triad in 1st inversion (CASSETTE TAPE EXAMPLE 202)

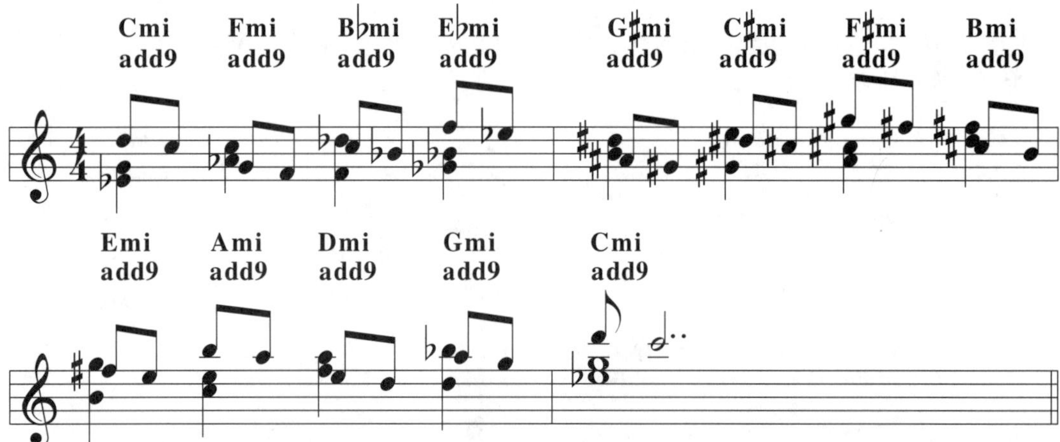

Figure 8.28. Minor triad '9 to 1' resolutions voiceled around circle-of-fifths, starting with C minor triad in 2nd inversion (CASSETTE TAPE EXAMPLE 203)

'9 to 1' resolutions within minor triads (contd)

PRACTICE DIRECTIONS:-

- ***Practice root position, 1st inversion and then 2nd inversion minor triad '9 to 1' resolutions around the circle-of-fifths as in Figs. 8.23. - 8.25.***
  (for variation in sequence of keys, use circle-of-fourths)
- ***Practice voiceleading the minor triad '9 to 1' resolutions around the circle-of-fifths from each starting position as in Figs. 8.26. - 8.28.***
  (as a variation, you can play each routine 'backwards' in a circle-of-fourths sequence using descending voiceleading)

Using '9 to 1' resolutions within minor-triad-over-root chords

As with the major triad structures, we will now apply resolutions within minor-triad-over-root chords within progressions. Again we know from **Chapter 5** that there are various minor-triad-over-root combinations available. Here are '**9 to 1**' resolutions applied to some of these:-

Figure 8.29. C minor triad with C in bass voice (see Fig. 5.8.)
(CASSETTE TAPE EXAMPLE 109)

Figure 8.30. C minor '9 to 1' resolution with C in bass voice
(CASSETTE TAPE EXAMPLE 204)

Using '9 to 1' resolutions within minor-triad-over-root chords (contd)

Figure 8.31. C minor triad
with Ab in bass voice (see Fig. 5.12.)
(CASSETTE TAPE EXAMPLE 113)

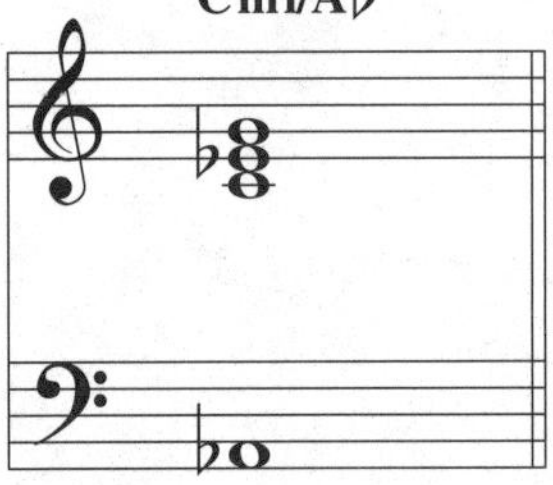

Cmi/A♭

>>> BECOMES >>>

Figure 8.32. C minor '9 to 1' resolution
with Ab in bass voice
(CASSETTE TAPE EXAMPLE 205)

In **Chapter 5** (**Fig. 5.12.**) we saw that a C minor triad with Ab in the bass created an **Abma7** chord overall. The '**9 to 1**' resolution within the upper triad here effectively becomes a '**#11 to 3**' or '**#4 to 3**' movement within the overall major chord (the note D is a sharped 4th or 11th with respect to the root of Ab). The added **#11th** to this major chord can be represented by symbols such as **Abma7(#11)**, **Ab Lydian** etc. Now another resolution example:-

Figure 8.33. C minor triad
with F in bass voice (see Fig. 5.10.)
(CASSETTE TAPE EXAMPLE 111)

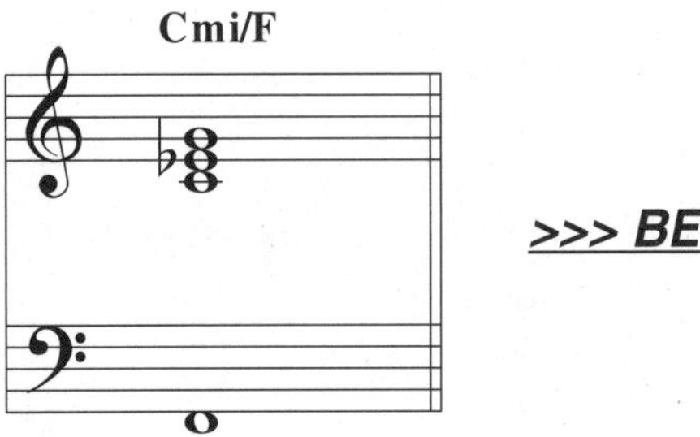

>>> BECOMES >>>

Figure 8.34. C minor '9 to 1' resolution
with F in bass voice
(CASSETTE TAPE EXAMPLE 206)

Again in **Chapter 5** (**Fig. 5.10.**) we saw that a C minor triad with F in the bass created an incomplete 9th chord form that could imply **Fmi9**, **F9** or **F9sus** depending on the context. The '**9 to 1**' resolution within the upper triad effectively becomes a '**13 to 5**' or '**6 to 5**' movement within the overall chord, creating possible **Fmi13**, **F13** or **F13sus** implications again depending on context. Back in **Chapter 5** we also worked on various other minor-triad-over-root combinations - feel free to experiment with '**9 to 1**' resolutions within the upper triads on these!

In a similar fashion to the major triad structures, we will now combine the vertical structures just presented (**Figs. 8.30., 8.32.** and **8.34.**) with the voiceleading around the circle-of-fifths as shown in **Figs. 8.26. - 8.28.**, as follows:-

Using '9 to 1' resolutions within minor-triad-over-root chords (contd)

Figure 8.35. Minor chord '9 to 1' resolutions (see Fig. 8.30.) voiceled around circle-of-fifths

(CASSETTE TAPE EXAMPLE 207)

Figure 8.36. Major chord '#11 to 3' resolutions (see Fig. 8.32.) voiceled around circle-of-fifths

(CASSETTE TAPE EXAMPLE 208)

Using '9 to 1' resolutions within minor-triad-over-root chords (contd)

Figure 8.37. Incomplete 9th chord '13 to 5' resolutions (see 8.34.) voiceled around circle-of-fifths
(CASSETTE TAPE EXAMPLE 209)

PRACTICE DIRECTIONS:-

- **Practice voiceleading the '9 to 1' resolutions within minor-triad-over-root chords around the circle-of-fifths, as in Figs. 8.35. - 8.37.**
- *Practice variations:-*
  - *change the root by using other minor-triad-over-root combinations as in* **Chapter 5 Figs. 5.8. - 5.14.**
  - *change the first triad inversion in the routine (see* **Figs. 8.24. & 8.25.***)*
  - *change sequence of keys i.e. use circle-of-fourths*
- **Experiment with combining different stylistic settings i.e. from Chapter 5, with different minor-triad-over-root chords using resolutions.**

CHAPTER NINE

Triad resolutions using suspended 4ths

Introduction

Now in this chapter we will focus on moving from the 4th to the 3rd (referred to as a '**4 to 3**' resolution) within major and minor triads. The concepts detailed in the last chapter concerning '**9 to 1**' resolutions also substantially apply to these '**4 to 3**' resolutions, as follows:-

- each '**4 to 3**' resolution within a major or minor triad can be played in root position, 1st or 2nd inversion.
- using inversions it is possible to voicelead these resolutions, for example around the circle-of-fifths.
- these resolutions can be used (and voiceled) as the upper part of triad-over-root structures.

'4 to 3' resolutions within major and minor triads

First of all we'll look at all inversions of the '**4 to 3**' resolution within major and minor triads:-

Figure 9.1. '4 to 3' resolutions within all inversions of C major triad
(Cassette Tape Example 210)

Figure 9.2. '4 to 3' resolutions within all inversions of C minor triad
(Cassette Tape Example 211)

Cmi
sus(4-3)

Here now for your reference are all the '**4 to 3**' resolutions within major and minor triads, presented in root position moving around the circle-of-fifths. For space reasons I have not shown all the inversions this time! As you can see above, each resolution can be played also in 1st and 2nd inversion and you are encouraged to also practice these around the circle-of-fifths (refer to the inverted '**9 to 1**' resolutions in **Figs. 8.4., 8.5., 8.24.** and **8.25.** as necessary).

'4 to 3' resolutions within major and minor triads (contd)

Figure 9.3. Root position major triad '4 to 3' resolutions around circle-of-fifths
(Cassette Tape Example 212)

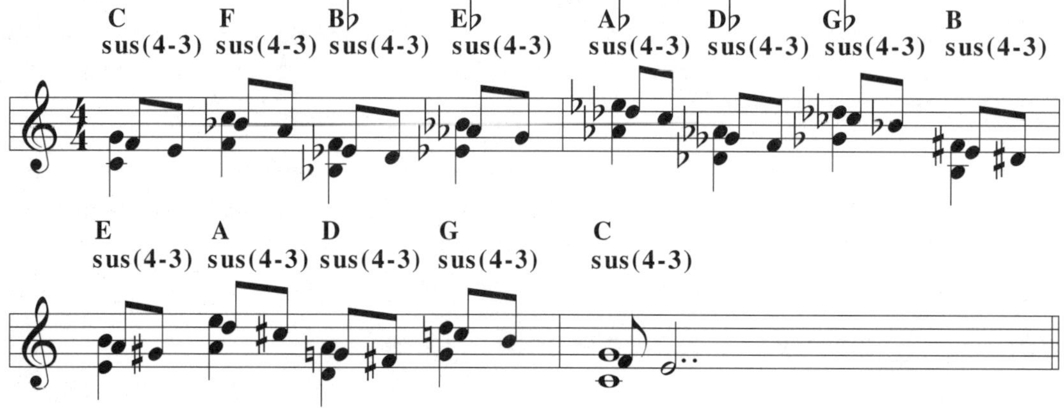

Figue 9.4. Root position minor triad '4 to 3' resolutions around circle-of-fifths
(Cassette Tape Example 213)

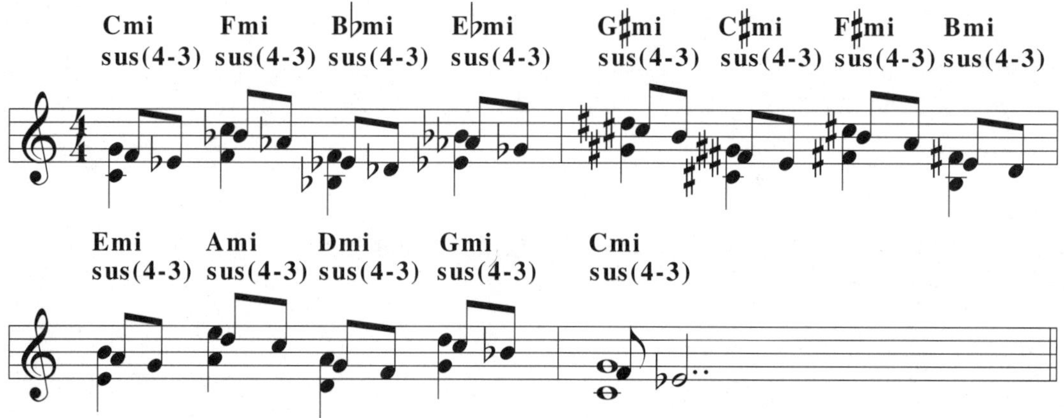

Again as with the '**9 to 1**' resolutions, it is now possible to voicelead these '**4 to 3**' resolutions within triads, for example around the circle-of-fifths. (Refer to **Chapter 8, Figs. 8.8. - 8.10.** and **8.26. - 8.28.** as required). As with the '**9 to 1**' voiceleading examples it is possible to start on any inversion - again for space reasons I have just presented the '**4 to 3**' voiceleading examples starting in root position - you should however experiment with different starting inversions as in the above-mentioned **Chapter 8** examples. Here now are voiceled examples of '**4 to 3**' resolutions within major and minor triads, around the circle-of-fifths:-

'4 to 3' resolutions within major and minor triads (contd)

Figure 9.5. Major triad '4 to 3' resolutions voiceled around circle-of-fifths
(CASSETTE TAPE EXAMPLE 214)

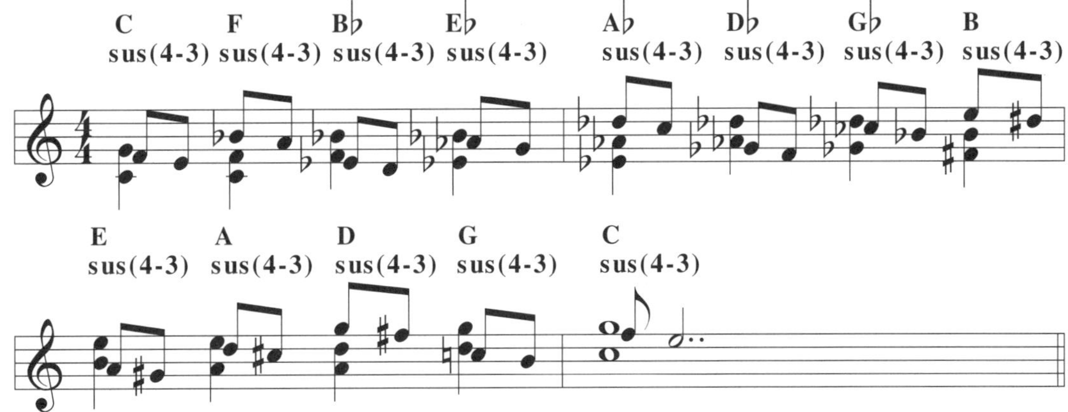

Figure 9.6. Minor triad '4 to 3' resolutions voiceled around circle-of-fifths
(CASSETTE TAPE EXAMPLE 215)

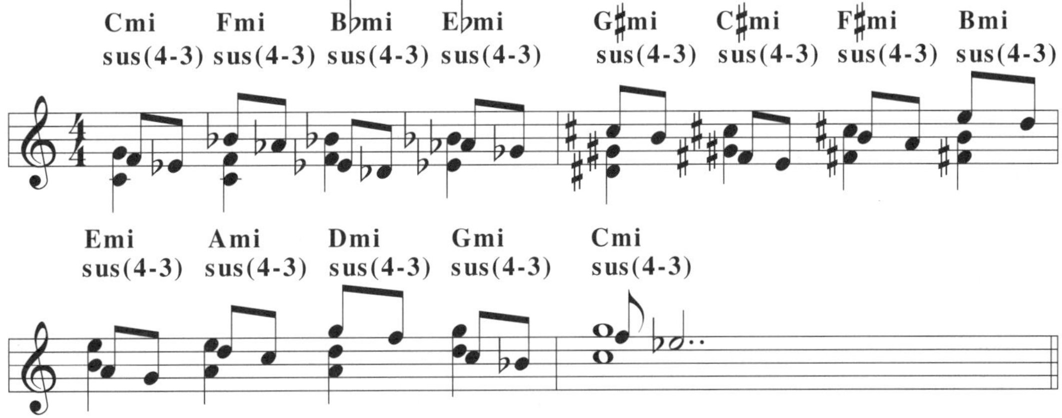

Using '4 to 3' resolutions within triad-over-root chords

As with the '**9 to 1**' resolutions (see **Chapter 8 Figs. 8.11. - 8.16.**), we can now apply these '**4 to 3**' movements within major-triad-over-root and minor-triad-over-root structures. Again there were a number of triad-over-root chords presented in **Chapter 5** and you are encouraged to apply resolutions within the upper triads on these! Here are some examples to get you started:-

Using '4 to 3' resolutions within triad-over-root chords

Figure 9.7. C major '4 to 3' resolution with A in bass voice
(CASSETTE TAPE EXAMPLE 216)

This resolution within a **C/A** or **Ami7** chord (see **Fig. 5.6.**) creates an **Ami7(#5)** resolving back to **Ami7**. Again the upper triad resolution could be in any inversion (see **Fig. 9.1.**) - try using different resolution inversions over the root! (2nd inversion is widely used, giving the moving '**4 to 3**' line on top).

Figure 9.8. C major '4 to 3' resolution with D in bass voice
(CASSETTE TAPE EXAMPLE 217)

This resolution within a **C/D** chord (see **Fig. 5.2.**) creates a **Dmi7(11)** or **Dmi7(add11)** resolving back to a **C/D** or incomplete **Dmi11**. Although the chord **C/D** typically functions as a dominant suspension, this resolution is generally heard in a minor context (with the moving line as the 3rd to the 9th of the overall mnior chord) rather than as a dominant chord.

Figure 9.9. C minor '4 to 3' resolution with Ab in bass voice
(CASSETTE TAPE EXAMPLE 218)

This resolution within a **Cmi/Ab** or **Abma7** chord (see **Fig. 5.12.**) creates an **Abma7(add6)** or **Abma13** resolving back to **Abma7**. The 6th (13th) and the 7th can generally be combined as desired on the major chord.

We will now work on voiceleading some of these '**4 to 3**' resolutions within triad-over-root chords, around the circle-of-fifths, as follows:-

Using '4 to 3' resolutions within triad-over-root chords (contd)

Figure 9.10. Minor chord '#5 to 5' resolution (see Fig. 9.7.) voiceled around circle-of-fifths
(Cassette Tape Example 219)

Figure 9.11. Major chord '6 to 5' resolution (see Fig. 9.9.) voiceled around circle-of-fifths
(Cassette Tape Example 220)

(CONTD-->)

Using '4 to 3' resolutions within triad-over-root chords (contd)

Figure 9.11. (contd)

PRACTICE DIRECTIONS:-

- ***Practice root position, 1st inversion and 2nd inversion major triad '4 to 3' resolutions around the circle-of-fifths.***
  *Root position major '4 to 3' resolutions around the circle-of-fifths are shown in **Fig. 9.3.** - 1st and 2nd inversion major '4 to 3' resolutions within a C major triad are shown in **Fig. 9.1.***
- ***Practice root position, 1st inversion and 2nd inversion minor triad '4 to 3' resolutions around the circle-of-fifths.***
  *Root position minor '4 to 3' resolutions around the circle-of-fifths are shown in **Fig. 9.4.** - 1st and 2nd inversion minor '4 to 3' resolutions within a C minor triad are shown in **Fig. 9.2.***
- ***Practice voiceleading the major and minor '4 to 3' resolutions around the circle-of-fifths as in Figs. 9.5. & 9.6.***
  These examples start with a root position C major and C minor triad respectively. Experiment with different starting inversions for the first triad.
- ***Practice voiceleading the major and minor '4 to 3' resolutions within the triad-over-root examples, around the circle-of-fifths as in Figs. 9.10. & 9.11.***
  *Experiment with '4 to 3' resolutions within different triad-over-root contexts as in **Chapter 5**, around the circle-of-fifths and circle-of-fourths.*
- ***Experiment with different stylistic settings as in Chapter 5, using '4 to 3' resolutions in triad-over-root chords.***
  *For example - **Fig. 8.20.** is a variation of the 'pop-rock' setting using '9 to 1' resolutions within an overall minor chord structure. Have fun!!*

Chord 'shapes' using fourth intervals

Introduction

Finally in the 'harmonic concepts' part of this book we will look at the application of chord 'shapes' using fourth intervals. The perfect 4th interval used harmonically creates an open, hollow and transparent sound which is widely used in contemporary styles. If we 'stack' one perfect 4th on top of another, we get a uniquely useful chord 'shape' which I refer to in this chapter as a '**double 4th**':-

Figure 10.1. 'Double 4th' example built from G
(Cassette Tape Example 221)

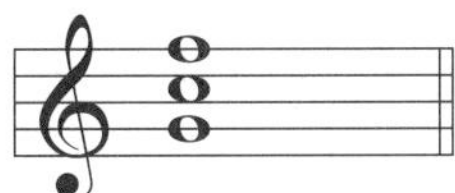

Notice that I have not placed a chord symbol over this example. You may initially hear this as having a suspended quality, and indeed if you refer back to **Fig. 9.1.** you'll notice that the above notes equate to a 2nd inversion '**4 to 3**' in major, prior to the resolution occurring. As we will see in this chapter however, this is only one of the many functions of this 'double 4th' shape. We will also be considering inversion and voiceleading aspects of 'double 4th' structures.

Double-4th-over-root chords

The double 4th interval configuration can be found over many different roots, as follows:-

Figure 10.2. 'Double 4th' example showing different roots available
(Cassette Tape Example 222)

All of the above 'double-4th-over-root' combinations create legitimate and useful chord forms. We will now analyze each of the combinations, starting with the double 4th over C in the root, and then proceeding from left to right within the above example. In each case we will derive a chord symbol for the overall combination, and comment on the quality and function of the chord.

Double-4th-over-root chords (contd)

Figure 10.3. Double 4th 'G-C-F' with C in bass voice
(Cassette Tape Example 223)

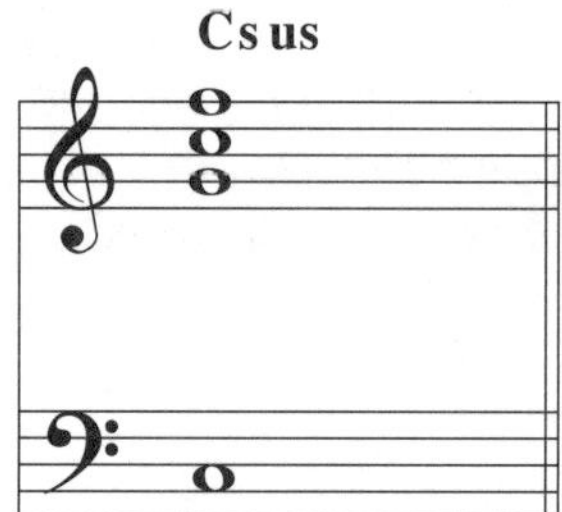

This combination creates a simple **suspended** chord, which typically may resolve back to a major or minor chord (see discussion of '**4 to 3**' resolutions in **Chapter 9**). This can be referred to as a **5-1-11** combination, as from bottom to top the double 4th represents the 5th, tonic and 11th with respect to the root.

Figure 10.4. Double 4th 'G-C-F' with Db in bass voice
(Cassette Tape Example 224)

This combination creates a **major 7th** chord with a **raised 11th** (or flatted 5th). This altered tone on the major chord creates a sophisticated sound. This can be referred to as a **#11-7-3** combination, as from bottom to top the double 4th represents the #11th, 7th and 3rd with respect to the root.

Figure 10.5. Double 4th 'G-C-F' with D in bass voice
(Cassette Tape Example 225)

This combination creates a **minor 7th** chord with an **added 11th**. (Sometimes the symbol **Dmi11** may be used). This is a great way to make a minor 7th chord sound more 'hip' and will not normally cause any harmonic conflicts. This can be referred to as an **11-b7-b3** combination, as from bottom to top the double 4th represents the 11th, b7th and b3rd with respect to the root.

Figure 10.6. Double 4th 'G-C-F' with Eb in bass voice
(Cassette Tape Example 226)

This combination creates a **major 69** chord. It is a rounded, open sound found in new age as well as jazz styles. This can be referred to as a **3-6-9** combination, as from bottom to top the double 4th represents the 3rd, 6th and 9th with respect to the root.

Double-4th-over-root chords (contd)

Figure 10.7. Double 4th 'G-C-F' with F in bass voice

(Cassette Tape Example 227)

This combination creates an **added 9th** chord without the 3rd, and will often have a major implication (although the 'neutral' quality allows it to be used on minor, dominant or suspended chords in the right context). This one is great for keyboardists in rock bands (see **Chapter 12**) as well as being useful in other styles i.e. new age (see **Chapter 13**). This can be referred to as a **9-5-1** combination, as from bottom to top the double 4th represents the 9th, 5th and tonic with respect to the root.

Figure 10.8. Double 4th 'G-C-F' with G in bass voice

(Cassette Tape Example 228)

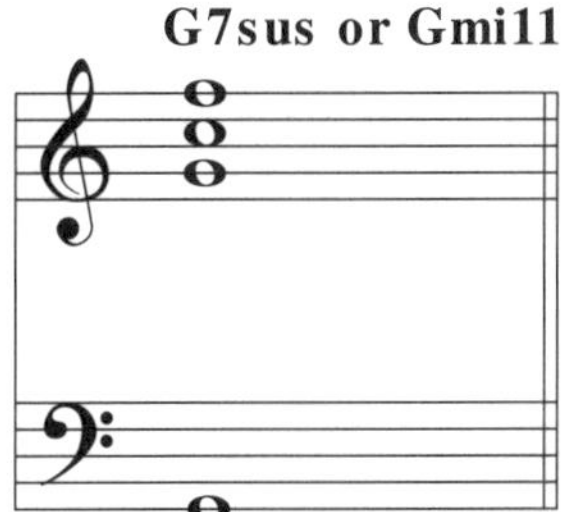

This combination creates a **suspended dominant 7th** (or in some cases an incomplete **minor 11th**) chord. Suspended dominants are widely used in today's pop styles. This can be referred to as a **1-11-b7** combination, as from bottom to top the double 4th represents the tonic, 11th and b7th with respect to the root.

Figure 10.9. Double 4th 'G-C-F' with Ab in bass voice

(Cassette Tape Example 229)

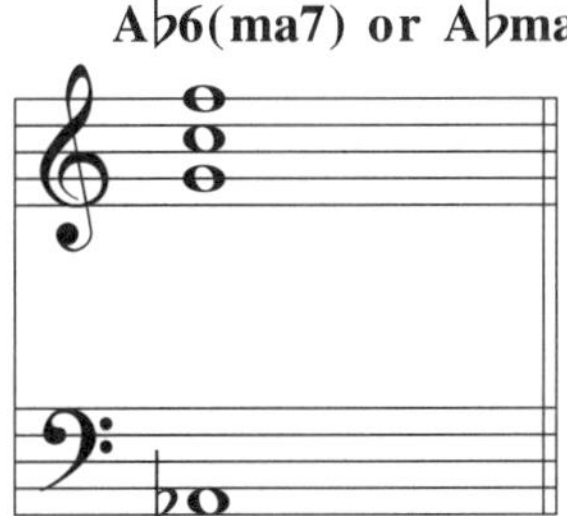

This combination creates a **major chord** with both the 6th (13th) and 7th present, and has a sophisticated sound. This can be referred to as a **7-3-6** combination, as from bottom to top the double 4th represents the 7th, 3rd and 6th(13th) with respect to the root.

Figure 10.10. Double 4th 'G-C-F' with A in bass voice

(Cassette Tape Example 230)

This combination will be heard and used in two ways:-

- as a **minor 7th** chord with a **raised 5th**. In this context it can be referred to as a **b7-b3-#5** combination, as from bottom to top the double 4th represents the b7th, b3rd and #5th of the chord.
- as a **major (add9)** chord inverted over the **3rd** (i.e. in this case an **Fadd9/A**). In this context it can be referred to as a **9-5-1** combination (see **Fig. 10.7.**), but inverted over the 3rd.

Double-4th-over-root chords (contd)

Figure 10.11. Double 4th 'G-C-F' with Bb in bass voice

(CASSETTE TAPE EXAMPLE 231)

This combination creates a **69 chord** without the 3rd, and will usually have a major implication even though the 3rd is not used. (To be strictly accurate the symbol **Bb69(no3)** might be used). The rather 'neutral' sound produced is particularly useful in new age styles. This can be referred to as a **6-9-5** combination, as from bottom to top the double 4th represents the 6th, 9th and 5th with respect to the root. Sometimes this combination is also used over a dominant or suspended dominant chord, in which case the 6th becomes a 13th. (However, the dominant chord normally needs the b7th in addition, to be 'fully definitive').

You are encouraged to play through all of the above combinations to get the sounds 'into your ear'. As with previous triad- and 4-part-over-root chords, we can now practice these structures in different keys, for example around the circle-of-5ths/4ths. To save space I have just presented two of the above combinations in this manner - however of course you should experiment with the remaining chords moving around the 'circles':-

Figure 10.12. Double 4th '9-5-1' combination (see 10.7.) moving around circle-of-fifths

(CASSETTE TAPE EXAMPLE 232)

Double-4th-over-root chords (contd)

Figure 10.13. Double 4th '11-b7-b3' combination (see 10.5.) moving around circle-of-fourths
(CASSETTE TAPE EXAMPLE 233)

Double 4th inversions

These double 4th 'shapes', like triads and four-part chords, can also be inverted. Any of the preceeding double-4th-over-root chords could be constructed with an inverted double 4th as the upper structure. Here is an example of double 4th inversions:-

Figure 10.14. Double 4th 'C-F-Bb' in all inversions
(CASSETTE TAPE EXAMPLE 234)

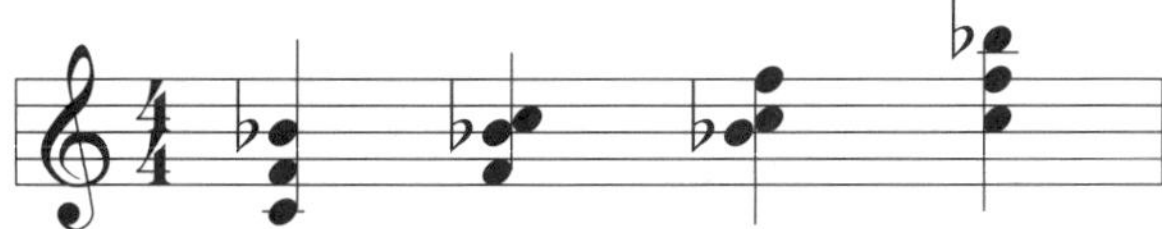

Note that in inverted positions this 'shape' consists of a whole-step and a fourth interval, rather than two fourth intervals - however the basic hollow quality and projection of the 'shape' remain intact. Here now for your reference are all inversions of all double 4th structures, starting with the above example and then moving the bottom note around the circle-of-fifths:-

Double 4th inversions (contd)

Figure 10.15. All double 4th inversions (bottom note moving around circle-of-fifths)
(Cassette Tape Example 235)

Double-4th-over-root chord progressions

Now we'll see how these inverted double 4ths might be used within double-4th-over-root chords in a progression context. Hear how a fairly ordinary chord progression is made more stylish and modern using these structures, which are now voiceled from left to right:-

Figure 10.16. Progression example (in C) using double-4th-over-root chords
(Cassette Tape Example 236)

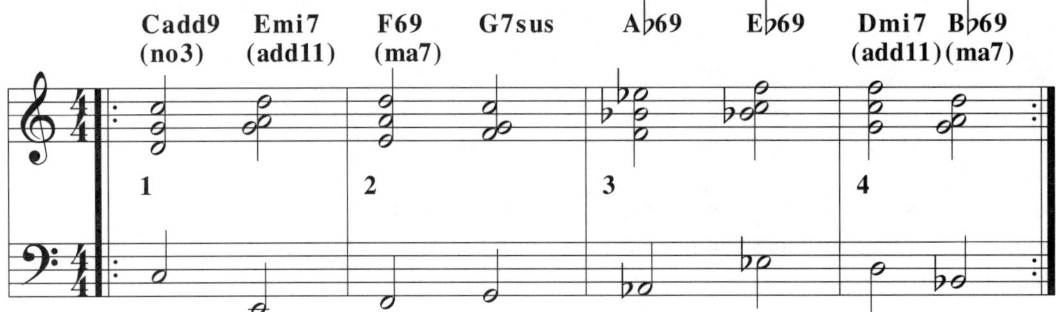

Double-4th-over-root chord progressions (contd)

I mentioned 'key of C' in the heading as the progression does repeat back to C which is heard as 'home-base' - however there are some chromatic notes (to the key of C) within the sequence of course. We can analyze each voicing in the previous example as follows:-

- Measure 1
- The first chord **Cadd9(no3)** is using a <u>**9-5-1**</u> combination (see **Fig. 10.7.**) with the double 4th in root position, giving the root of the overall chord (C) as a top-note.
- The second chord **Emi7(add11)** is using an <u>**11-b7-b3**</u> combination (see **Fig. 10.5.**) with the double 4th in 2nd inversion, giving the 7th of the overall chord (D) as a top-note.

- Measure 2
- The first chord **F69(ma7)** is using a <u>**7-3-6**</u> combination (see **Fig. 10.9.**) with the double 4th in root position, giving the 6th of the overall chord (D) as the top-note.
- The second chord **G7sus** is using a <u>**1-11-b7**</u> combination (see **Fig. 10.8.**) with the double 4th in 2nd inversion, giving the 11th(4th) of the overall chord (C) as the top-note.

- Measure 3
- The first chord **Ab69** is using a <u>**6-9-5**</u> combination (see **Fig. 10.11.**) with the double 4th in root position, giving the 5th of the overall chord (Eb) as the top-note.
- The second chord **Eb69** is also using a <u>**6-9-5**</u> combination (see **Fig. 10.11.**) with the double 4th in 2nd inversion, giving the 9th of the overall chord (F) as the top-note.

- Measure 4
- The first chord **Dmi7(add11)** is using an <u>**11-b7-b3**</u> combination (see **Fig. 10.5.**) with the double 4th in root position, giving the 3rd of the overall chord (F) as the top-note.
- The second chord **Bb69(ma7)** is using a <u>**7-3-6**</u> combination (see **Fig. 10.9.**) with the double 4th in 2nd inversion, giving the 3rd of the overall chord (D) as the top-note.

As an exercise it would be a good idea to transpose this progression into other keys. To do this, you first of all need to be aware of what the roots are in the new key (i.e. in this case figure out the <u>**I**</u>, <u>**III**</u>, <u>**IV**</u>, <u>**V**</u>, <u>**bVI**</u>, <u>**bIII**</u>, <u>**II**</u>, and <u>**bVII**</u> in the new key), and then be sufficiently familiar with the vertical forms and voiceleading to construct the required chords on these roots. For example, here is the same progression in the key of <u>**A**</u>:-

<u>Figure 10.17 Progression example (in A) using double-4th-over-root chords</u>
(Cassette Tape Example 237)

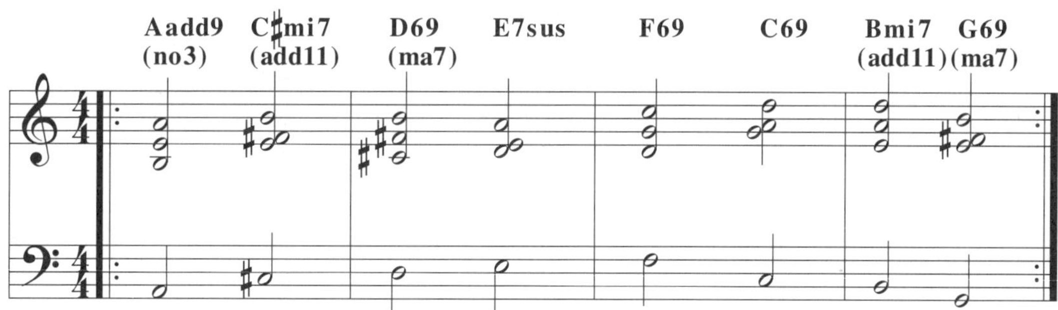

It is also possible to superimpose a stylistic setting on this progression. In the next example (back in the key of <u>**C**</u>) in a pop/new age setting, the upper double 4ths are arpeggiated with an eighth-note subdivision. Use the sustain pedal during each chord change as necessary:-

Double-4th-over-root chord progressions (contd)

Figure 10.18. Pop/new age pattern using double-4th-over-root chords
(Cassette Tape Example 238)

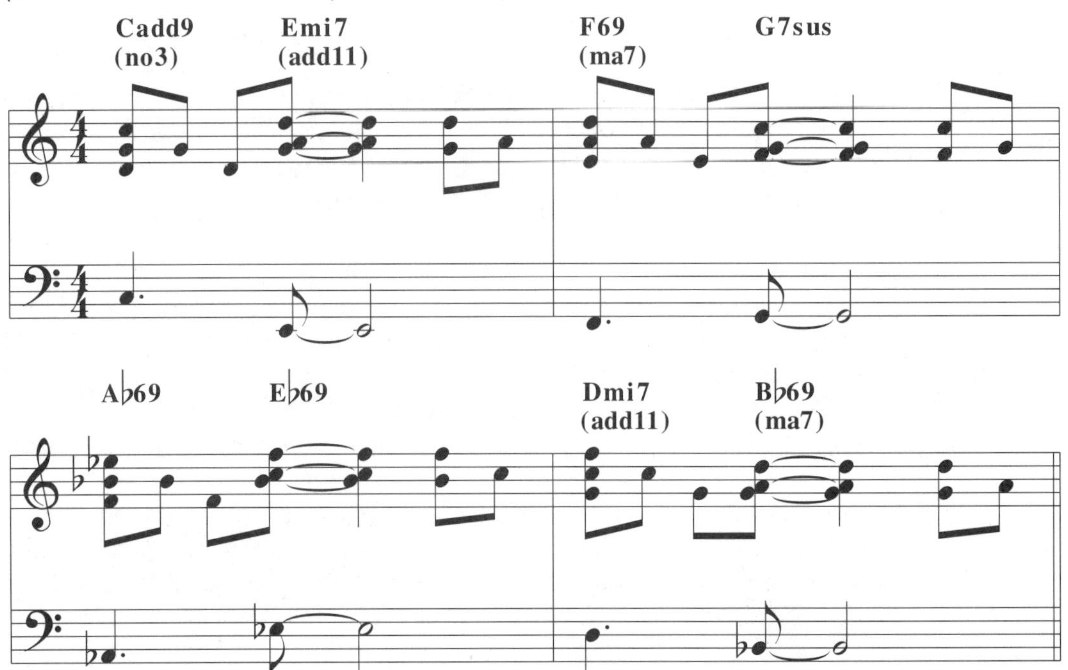

(See **Chapter 13** for more detail regarding new age styles!).

Practice directions:-

- ***Practice double-4th-over-root combinations as in Figs. 10.3. - 10.11. around the circle-of-fifths and circle-of-fourths.***
  Fig. 10.12. *shows the* ***9-5-1*** *combination moving around the circle-of-fifths.*
  Fig. 10.13. *shows the* ***11-b7-b3*** *combination moving around the circle-of-fourths.*
- ***Practice double 4ths in all inversions around the circle-of- fifths as in Fig. 10.15.***
- ***Practice the double-4th-over-root chord progression shown in Fig. 10.16. in all keys.***
  Fig. 10.16. *shows this progression in the key of* ***C****.*
  Fig. 10.17. *shows this progression in the key of* ***A****.*
- ***Practice the pop/new age stylistic setting using double-4th-over-root chords as in Fig. 10.18.***
  Experiment with this setting in different keys!

CHAPTER ELEVEN

Pop Ballad

Introduction

Now in the second half of this book we will deal with the various contemporary styles, using the building blocks and devices studied in the earlier chapters. We begin with a study of **Pop Ballad** styles, which generally use a 'straight-eighths' rhythmic subdivision (see text accompanying **Fig. 2.29.**) at a slow-to-medium tempo. Contemporary ballad styles can typically use 8th-note or 16th-note subdivisions - however from a playing standpoint we need to make a distinction between ballads primarily using 8th-note subdivisions, with perhaps some 16ths as rhythmic embellishments (dealt with in this **Pop Ballad** chapter) and ballads built around 16th-note subdivisions and making use of 16th-note anticipations (dealt with in **Chapter 14 - R'n'B Ballad**). This is mainly a technical distinction at this point, as different playing devices and 16th-note anticipation concepts will be required in the more rhythmically challenging R'n'B ballad style than in the more straightforward Pop Ballad style. Many of today's ballads feature a 16th-note anticipation concept, which technically for our purposes puts them in the R'n'B ballad category - however a good percentage of modern ballads (as well as a lot of 'older' pop ballads by artists such as the Beatles) are still organized around an eighth-note subdivision. Review **Chapter 2** as necessary for information on rhythmic subdivisions and anticipations.

In all the contemporary styles addressed (beginning with Pop Ballad) we need to discuss the roles of the left and right hands. In most cases the left hand is providing harmonic and rhythmic support to the right hand, playing the roots of the chords (or a basic chord tone) on the primary beats of the measure and/or at the points of chord change. The left hand may additionally be providing rhythmic subdivision and forward motion, for example by arpeggiating the chord. The right hand part is generally built around the tones of the chord (or the upper part of chord forms which are larger than triads i.e. seventh chords and above) and will normally be providing an eighth-note subdivision in various ways as detailed in this chapter. If we are additionally responsible for playing the melody (as opposed to accompanying ourselves or another singer/instrumentalist) then the issue becomes one of supporting the melody with one of various techniques in the right hand, within the harmonic discipline of the chord sequence - again detailed in this chapter.

Pop ballad accompaniment

We will first of all address various ways of constructing accompaniments (often referred to as 'comping' through the changes) in a pop ballad style. Notice that we are **not** talking here about reading someone else's arrangement, but instead manufacturing your own arrangement spontaneously from the chords provided and using your understanding of the style. (Apart from not wanting to limit ourselves to another person's arrangement, often the written sheet music when available is misleading or just plain wrong, as I'm sure you may have found!) So typically we are trying to create a finished product from a chord chart or 'leadsheet', as in the example on the following page:-

Pop ballad accompaniment (contd)

Figure 11.1. Eight measure leadsheet example

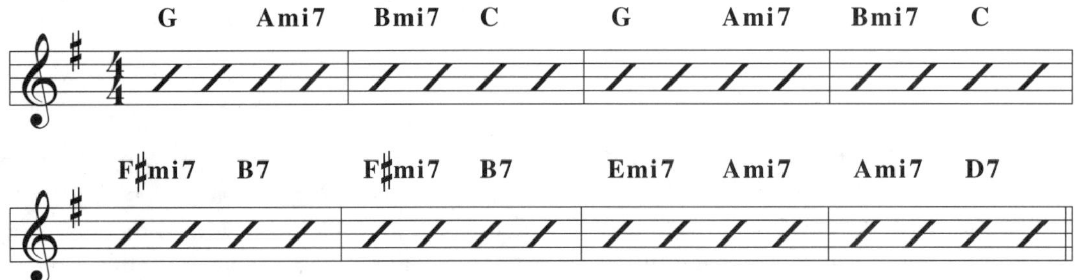

Our first order of business will be to determine the harmonic structure of the right-hand part. By this I mean we need to figure out which part of the overall chord to play in the right hand, and then to invert the results as necessary to ensure smooth voiceleading from left to right. For the moment we will mainly work with three-part (triad) upper voicing structures. Here's how we choose which part of the overall chord to play in the **right hand**:-

- On the **triad chord symbols** (i.e. the **G** and **C** major chords above) the right hand can play a triad containing the root, 3rd & 5th of the chord. On these major chords, we refer to this voicing as a **1-3-5** upper structure (see **Fig. 5.1.**).
- On the **seventh chord symbols** the right hand can play one of the following:-
  - a triad containing the 3rd, 5th and 7th of the chord. On a minor 7th chord, we refer to this voicing as a **b3-5-b7** upper structure (see **Fig. 5.6.**) which can be 'built from' the 3rd of the overall chord.
  - a 4-part shape containing the root, 3rd, 5th and 7th of the chord. On the dominant 7th chord, we will refer to this as a **1-3-5-b7** upper structure.

Generally using the triad 'built from' the 3rd is a preferred solution on **seventh** chord symbols - however, on the dominant chords the 4-part **1-3-5-b7** structure is a useful alternative to the diminished triad 'built from' the 3rd of this chord (see measure 5 comments on following page). None of these upper structure choices 'upgrades' the chord symbols shown (i.e. no other chord extensions have been added). This type of basic 3- & 4-part chord solution is suitable for simple pop ballad styles. However, as we work through **Section 2** of this book we will see many situations where a choice of voicing has 'upgraded' the chord symbol with added extensions. Having now decided which 'upper structure' to use on each chord in the above example, we still need to voicelead between one structure and the next. One of many right-hand voicing solutions for this is as follows:-

Figure 11.2. Upper structure voiceleading for leadsheet in Fig. 11.1. - first example
(CASSETTE TAPE EXAMPLE 239)

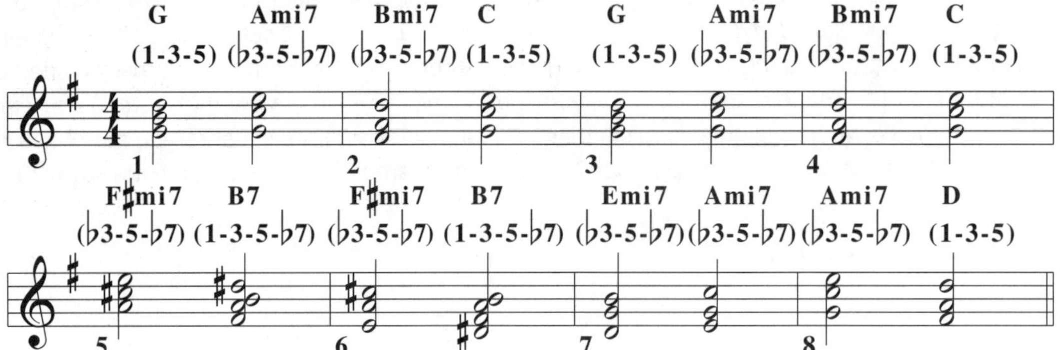

Pop ballad accompaniment (contd)

Notice in the previous example that the upper structures used on the minor 7th chords (referred to here as **b3-5-b7** voicings) do not by themselves define the chord - they need to be placed **over the roots of the original chords in the bass register** to create the overall chord indicated on the leadsheet. (Listen to the cassette tape example, playing the above 'upper structure' triads both with and without the roots in the bass register). Now we will look at each measure in **Fig. 11.2.** and analyze the upper structures and voiceleading used:-

- Measure 1

- On the **G** chord we are using a **1-3-5** upper structure (a root position **G** triad - see **Fig. 5.1.**). The starting inversion of the triad is arbitrary - typical registers are in, or a little below, the treble staff. Once we have chosen our starting inversion though, we generally need to voicelead i.e. move to the closest inversion of the next 'upper structure'.
- On the **Ami7** chord we are using a **b3-5-b7** upper structure (a 2nd inversion **C** triad - see **Fig. 5.6.** which showed that a C triad with A in the bass created an Ami7 overall). We also need to voicelead correctly from the previous G triad - the closest inversions of the required C triad are 1st or 2nd inversion (see **Fig. 4.3.** as necessary). Notice the upper structure movement here (G to C) is of a circle-of-fifths nature (see end of **Fig. 4.15.**) even though the overall chord change is from **G** to **Ami7**.

- Measure 2

- On the **Bmi7** chord we are again using a **b3-5-b7** upper voicing - now the upper shape is a **D** major triad, this time in 1st inversion to voicelead closely from the previous chord.
- On the **C** chord we are again using a **1-3-5** upper structure, now with the upper **C** triad in 2nd inversion to voicelead from the previous D triad.

- Measures 3-4

- As for measures 1-2.

- Measure 5

- On the **F#mi7** chord we are again using a **b3-5-b7** upper structure - now the upper shape is an **A** major triad, in root position to voicelead closely from the previous C triad.
- On the **B7** chord we are using a four part **1-3-5-b7** voicing as a variation. (Refer to **Fig. 1.77.** for how to construct the dominant 7th chord as necessary). Although generally we might prefer not to voice the root in the right hand on four-part chords (i.e. to just use the 3rd, 5th & 7th), the basic dominant chord is sometimes an exception, as the 3rd, 5th & 7th of this chord together create a diminished triad which is a rather 'angular' sound - using the root also in the upper structure gives a more rounded effect. Note that this will not be a consideration on the **suspended** dominant chord forms (see **Figs. 5.2.**, **7.2.** & **7.4.**) used on various subsequent examples. The basic **B7** dominant shape is used here in 2nd inversion to voicelead closely from the previous A triad.

- Measure 6

- On the **F#mi7** chord we are again using a **b3-5-b7** upper structure - the upper **A** triad is now in 2nd inversion to continue a downward voiceleading direction from the previous B7 chord.
- On the **B7** chord we are again using a four-part **1-3-5-b7** voicing - now in 1st inversion to continue a downward voiceleading direction from the previous A triad.

- Measure 7

- On the **Emi7** chord we are again using a **b3-5-b7** upper structure - now the upper shape is a **G** major triad, in 2nd inversion to voicelead closely from the previous B7.
- On the **Ami7** chord we are again using a **b3-5-b7** upper structure - now the upper shape is a **C** major triad, in 1st inversion to voicelead closely from the previous G triad. Notice the upper structure movement here (between the G & C upper triads) is again of a circle-of-fifths nature (see end of **Fig. 4.14.**).even though the overall chord movement is from **Emi7** to **Ami7**.

Pop ballad accompaniment (contd)

- Measure 8 - On the **Ami7** chord we are again using a **b3-5-b7** upper voicing - the upper C triad is now in 2nd inversion to give some variation and movement from the previous chord.
- On the **D** chord we are returning to a **1-3-5** upper structure, now with the D triad in 1st inversion to voicelead closely from the previous C triad.

This upper structure voiceleading example could then form the basis of an accompaniment pattern. Let us again review how we got to this point - we looked at the chord changes and did two things:-

FIRST:- We looked at each chord symbol and decided which part of the chord to play in the right hand. On the **triad chord symbols** we 'built' a triad from the root of the chord (these were **1-3-5** upper structures on the major chords). On the **seventh chord symbols** we generally 'built' a triad from the 3rd of the chord (i.e. the **b3-5-b7** upper structures on the minor 7th chords), except on the dominant 7th chords where we used the **1-3-5-b7** 4-part upper structure alternative. All of these choices enable us to stay 'within' the chord symbols, avoiding upper chord extensions which are inappropriate in a simple pop style.

SECOND:- We then inverted each successive upper structure to voicelead according to our intended direction from left to right. Generally we might aim for fairly static voiceleading (as in measures **1-4** from the previous example) - however we can also try ascending or descending directional ideas (as in measures **5-8**). **WE WILL NOT BE ABLE TO DO THIS UNLESS WE KNOW ALL OF OUR TRIAD INVERSIONS!!!** The main focus of the exercises in **Chapter 4** is to accomplish this. **Chapter 5** then works with numerous triad-over-root combinations - these give you the necessary 'upper structure' voicings that we have now started to work with.

Now let's look at a comping pattern using the above upper structures and voiceleading. This first ballad style features a type of 'rocking' right-hand motion back and forth. The upper fingers of the right hand are playing all of the notes in the upper structure except for the bottom note, on the downbeats (i.e. **1** & **2** & **3** & **4** &) of each measure, while the thumb of the right hand is playing the bottom note of the upper structure on each upbeat (i.e. 1 **&** 2 **&** 3 **&** 4 **&**). The left hand meanwhile is playing a simple dotted quarter-eighth-half note pattern based on the roots of the chords. As with all the patterns in this chapter, you generally need to depress the sustain pedal for the duration of each chord (but don't forget to release between chords!). As you look at this example, compare the right hand part to **Fig. 11.2.** - notice that the right hand upper structures and voiceleading are the same:-

Figure 11.3. Pop ballad comping pattern #1 (based on Fig. 11.2. voiceleading)
(CASSETTE TAPE EXAMPLE 240)

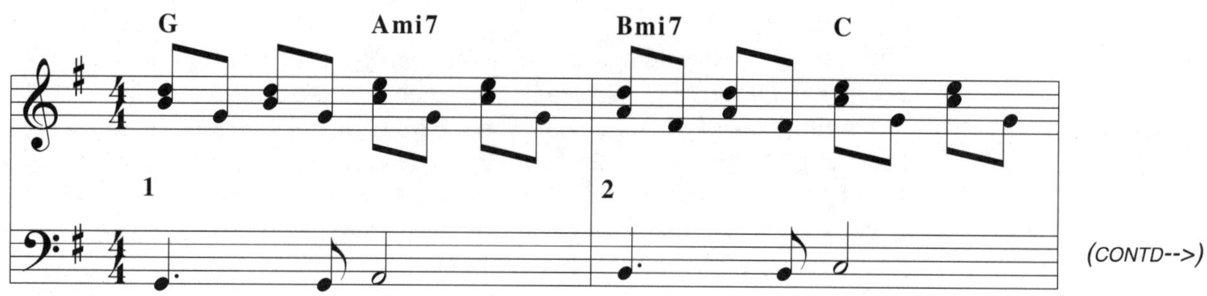

(CONTD-->)

Pop ballad accompaniment (contd)

Figure 11.3. (contd)

Again it's worth repeating that that the notes played in the right hand in the above example are derived from the original voiceleading choices as in **Fig. 11.2.** Now let's see what would happen if this voiceleading were varied, and how that would affect the execution of the above comping pattern. Let's say the voiceleading for the first 2 measures of the progression was changed as follows:-

Figure 11.4. Upper structure voiceleading variation #1 (first 2 measures)

(Cassette Tape Example 241)

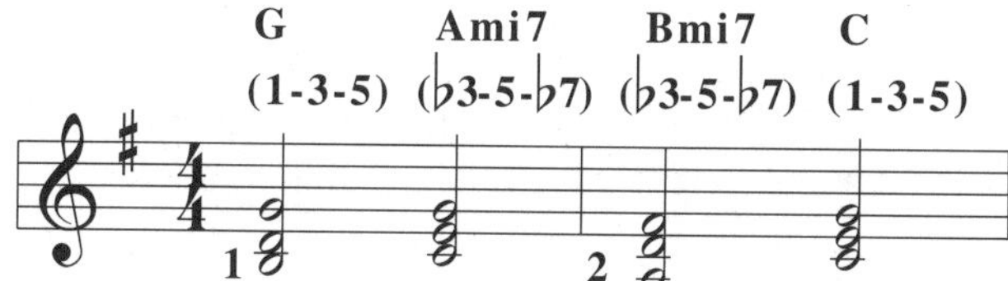

Pop ballad accompaniment (contd)

Notice that the upper structures in measures 1-2 as detailed in the text accompanying **Fig.11.2**. have now been inverted differently. The starting **G** triad is now in 1st inversion, which means that the following **C** triad (a **b3-5-b7** upper structure on the **Ami7** chord) is best used in root position to voicelead closely from the previous triad - again this is a circle-of-fifths type of voiceleading. Now the subsequent **D** triad (a **b3-5-b7** upper structure on the **Bmi7** chord) is used in 2nd inversion again to voicelead from the previous triad. Finally we return to the same root position **C** triad, this time being used as a **1-3-5** upper structure of the overall C major chord. Here's how the first two measures of the last comping pattern would look using the above voiceleading variations:-

Figure 11.5. Pop ballad comping pattern #1 variation #1 (based on Fig. 11.4. voiceleading)
(Cassette Tape Example 242)

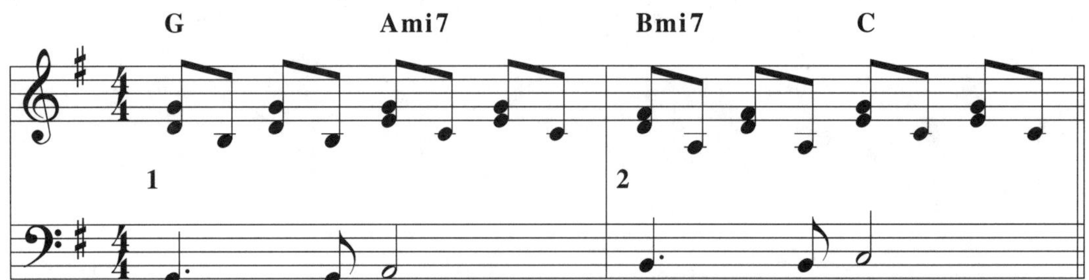

Now we'll look at some other variation techniques which can be applied to this basic comping style. One way to make the right hand voicing 'fuller' is to play three notes on each down beat instead of two. In terms of using triad upper structures, this involves playing all three triad tones with the upper fingers of the right hand on each downbeat, and doubling the top note of the triad an octave lower, with the thumb of the right hand on each upbeat. This is a subtle but effective variation which increases the energy level or momentum of the arrangement. Again here are the first 2 measures of the pattern with this variation (based on the original voiceleading):-

Figure 11.6. Pop ballad comping pattern #1 variation #2 (triads on downbeats & doubling top note)
(Cassette Tape Example 243)

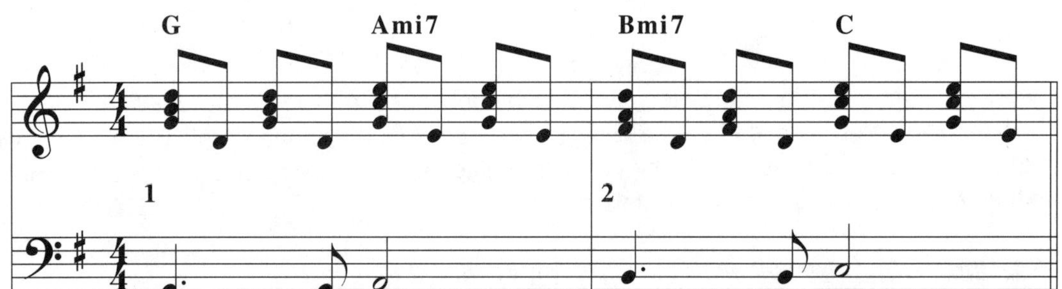

The upper structure harmony used here (**1-3-5** on the **G** & **C** chords, **b3-5-b7** on the **Ami7** & **Bmi7** chords) is again the same as for measures 1-2 of **Fig. 11.2**. Now we'll look at ways to make this pattern a little more sophisticated. One of the main techniques which is available is the use of interior resolutions within upper structure triads (refer to **Chapter 8** as necessary). One example of using some '**9 to 1**' resolutions within these upper triads on this progression is as follows:-

Pop ballad accompaniment (contd)

Figure 11.7. Pop ballad comping pattern #1 variation #3 ('9 to 1' resolution first example)
(Cassette Tape Example 244)

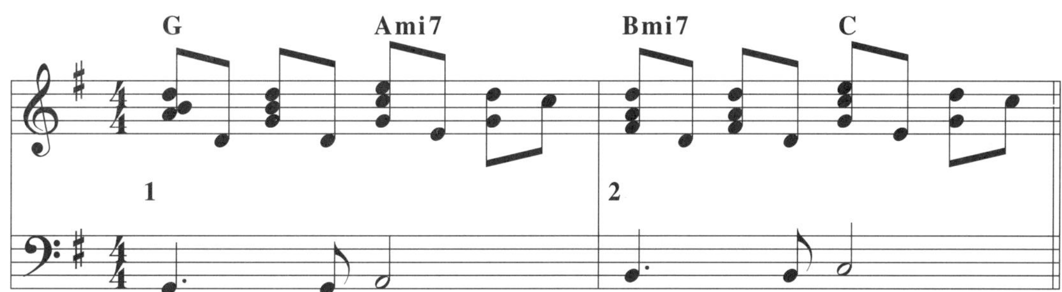

Let's look at each measure in the above example and analyze the interior resolutions and voiceleading which were used:-

- Measure 1 - On the **G** chord we are using a '**9 to 1**' resolution (see **Fig. 8.12.**) within the **1-3-5** upper structure i.e. just the basic triad, in root position. Notice that in this setting the 9th of the chord is played on beat **1**, resolving to the root of the chord on beat **2**. Again as with the previous example in **Fig. 11.6.** the top note of the upper triad is 'doubled' with the thumb on the upbeats.

- On the **Ami7** chord (during beat **4**) we are using a '**9 to 1**' resolution within the **b3-5-b7** upper structure (i.e. a C triad) of the overall Ami7 chord - refer to text accompanying **Fig. 8.14.** as necessary. As we saw in **Chapter 8**, this gives us the sophisticated sound of the 11th moving to the 3rd, with respect to the overall minor chord. The resolution in this case is occurring within a 1st inversion upper C triad, for voiceleading purposes - review **Fig. 8.18.** to see that this '11th to 3rd' movement on the overall minor 7th chord can occur within any inversion of the upper triad. Notice also that the resolution rhythm on the Ami7 chord is different to the preceeding G chord - here the 9th of the upper triad (11th of the overall Ami7) falls on beat **4**, resolving to the root of the upper triad (3rd of the overall Ami7) on the '**& of 4**'. Effectively we have an inversion change of the upper C triad, from 2nd inversion on beat **3** to 1st inversion on beat **4** with the '**9 to 1**' happening on top - also notice that we did not restrike the note E (below G & D) on beat **4**, as might have been expected on a '**9 to 1**' resolution within a C triad - this is because the thumb has just played E on the '**& of 3**', and therefore we get a better pianistic 'flow' with just the two notes in the right hand on beat **4**.

- Measure 2 - On the **Bmi7** chord we are just using the normal **b3-5-b7** upper structure, without any interior resolutions. The top note is doubled in the same manner as in measure 2 of **Fig. 11.6.**

- On the **C** chord we are using a '**9 to 1**' resolution within the **1-3-5** basic triad structure. Similar inversion, resolution and rhythmic concepts apply as for the C triad used as the **b3-5-b7** upper structure of the Ami7 chord in measure 1.

Now we'll look at more variations using '**9 to 1**' resolutions within the upper structure triads:-

Pop ballad accompaniment (contd)

Figure 11.8. Pop ballad comping pattern #1 variation #4 ('9 to 1' resolution second example)
(Cassette Tape Example 245)

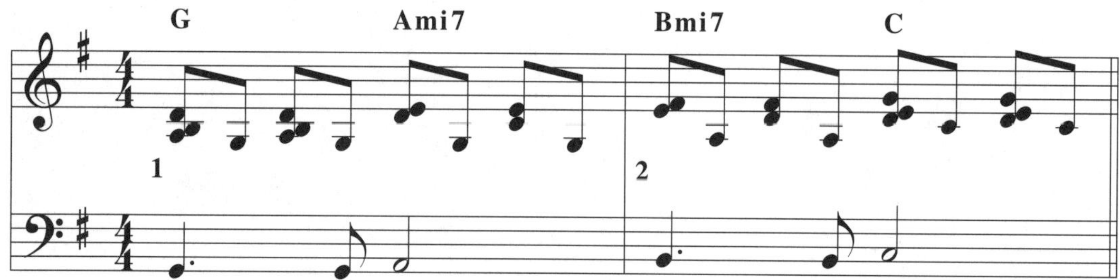

Again we'll look at each measure and analyze the interior resolutions and voiceleading:

- Measure 1

- On the **G** chord we are using a '**9 to 1**' resolution (see **Fig. 8.12.**) within the **1-3-5** upper structure i.e. just the basic triad, in root position. Notice that in this setting the 9th of the chord is played on the downbeat, resolving to the root of the chord on the upbeat. This is an extremely typical pop ballad device popularized by artists such as Barry Manilow for example.
- On the **Ami7** chord we are using a '**9 to 1**' resolution within the **b3-5-b7** upper structure (i.e. a C triad) of the overall Ami7 chord (see **Fig. 8.14.**). The resolution in this case is occurring within a 2nd inversion upper C triad, for voiceleading purposes. Notice also that the resolution rhythm on the Ami7 chord is different to the preceding G chord - here the 9th of the upper triad (11th of the overall Ami7) falls on beat **3**, resolving to the root of the upper triad (3rd of the overall Ami7) on beat **4**.

- Measure 2

- On the **Bmi7** chord we are again using a '**9 to 1**' resolution within the **b3-5-b7** upper structure (i.e. a D triad) of the overall Bmi7 chord. Similar inversion, resolution and rhythmic concepts apply as for the preceeding Ami7.
- On the **C** chord we are using a '**9 to 1**' resolution within the **1-3-5** basic triad structure. Similar inversion, resolution and rhythmic concepts apply as for the G major chord in measure 1.

And another variation with resolutions, this time using more upper structure inversion changes:-

Figure 11.9. Pop ballad comping pattern #1 variation #5 ('9 to1' resolution third example)
(Cassette Tape Example 246)

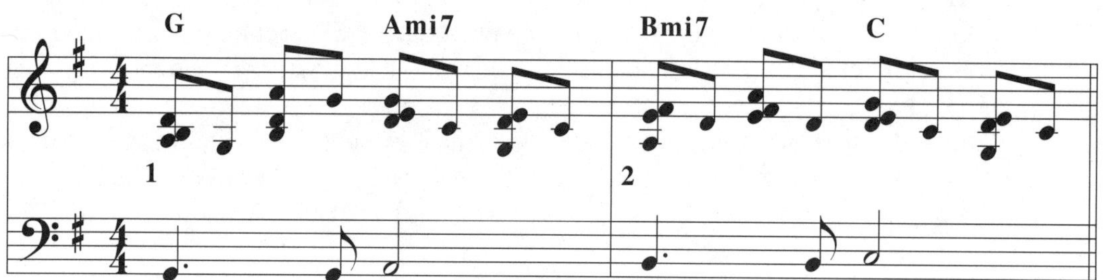

Pop ballad accompaniment (contd)

Again we'll look at each measure and analyze the interior resolutions and voiceleading:-

- Measure 1

- On the **G** chord we are using two successive '**9 to 1**' resolutions within the **1-3-5** upper structure (i.e. the basic G triad). The two resolutions occur within a root position, and then a 1st inversion, G triad on beats **1** & **2** respectively. (Review **Chapter 8** as necessary regarding resolutions within different inversions of upper structure triads).
- On the **Ami7** chord we are again using two successive '**9 to 1**' resolutions, this time within the **b3-5-b7** upper structure (i.e. a C triad) of the Ami7 chord. The two resolutions occur within root position and 2nd inversion C triads, on beats **3** & **4** respectively.

- Measure 2

- On the **Bmi7** chord we are again using two successive '**9 to 1**' resolutions within the **b3-5-b7** upper structure (a D triad). The two resolutions occur within 2nd inversion and root position D triads, on beats **1** & **2** respectively.
- On the **C** chord we are again using two successive '**9 to 1**' resolutions within the **1-3-5** upper structure (i.e. the basic C triad). Similar inversion and resolution concepts apply as for the previous C triad used on the Ami7 chord in measure 1.

You can hear that this example has a lot of interior motion and interest - however the 'busy' nature and the uneven voiceleading may make it unsuitable for a number of applications! Let's summarize the decisions to be made when applying these interior resolutions:-

- We need to establish which inversion of the upper structure triad the interior resolution is going to occur in. As you can see we will generally voicelead these inversions from left to right, however sometimes more movement may be desirable, as in **Fig. 11.9.**
- We need to establish where the resolutions are to occur rhythmically. Mostly this will be between the downbeat and the following upbeat (as in **Fig. 11.8.**, 1st & 4th chords) or between successive downbeats (as in **Fig. 11.7.**, 1st chord).
- We need to decide where and how frequently to use this device. Unfortunately there are no 'set rules' for this - it's largely a stylistic judgement call which you'll develop the ability to make as you experiment and work with the techniques. As with all stylistic devices - don't overdo it!

Now we'll look at a further variation based on **Fig. 11.6.** using 16th-note arpeggiated embellishments:-

Figure 11.10. Pop ballad comping pattern #1 variation #6 (16th-note arpeggios)
(Cassette Tape Example 247)

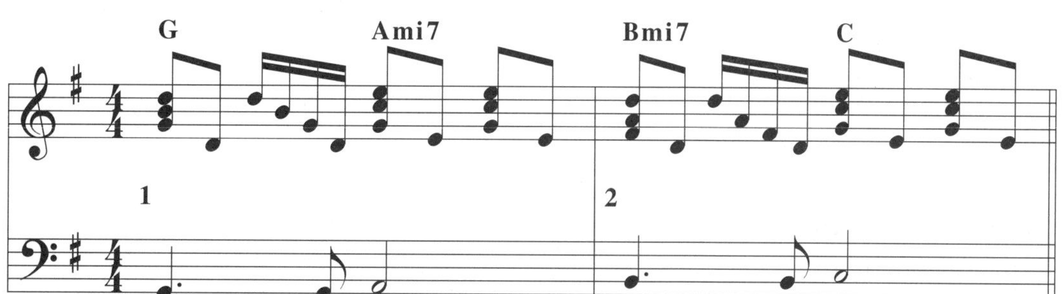

Pop ballad accompaniment (contd)

Notice that the preceding example is structurally the same as **Fig. 11.6.**, except that a descending 16th-note arpeggio is now used on beat **2** of the first measure (arpeggiating the **1-3-5** upper structure on the **G** chord) and beat **2** of the second measure (arpeggiating the **b3-5-b7** upper structure on the **Bmi7** chord). This again is another good way to build intensity in a pop ballad arrangement. However, 16th-note subdivisions should not be overdone on a pop ballad which is basically constructed around an eighth-note subdivision - see rhythmic discussion at the beginning of this chapter. Again once you have decided which inversion of which upper structure to apply to each chord, these embellishments can be freely applied according to your taste - again don't overdo it!

PRACTICE DIRECTIONS:-

- ***Practice the upper structure voiceleading example Fig. 11.2.***
- ***Practice the comping pattern #1 based on above voiceleading, as shown in Fig. 11.3.***
- ***Play the first 2 measures of the voiceleading variation #1 in Fig. 11.4., and work on spontaneously voiceleading the upper structures for the remainder of the progression, from this starting point.***
- ***Play comping pattern #1 variation #1 (based on above voice-leading variation) in Fig. 11.5., and continue this pattern and voiceleading idea through the remainder of the progression.***
- ***Play comping pattern #1 variations #2 - #6 (as in Figs. 11.6. - 11.10.) and again work on continuing these patterns respectively through the remainder of the progression.***
  *(The original chord sequence for the above progression is shown in **Fig. 11.1.**)*
- ***Work on applying these patterns and upper structure voice-leading concepts to other tunes of your choice, and to the practice progressions at the end of this chapter.***

Now we will turn our attention to another widely-used pop ballad accompaniment device, using what is known as an **arpeggiated left hand** concept. It is extremely useful to be able to play an arpeggiated left hand pattern 'on demand' through any set of chord changes. These left hand arpeggios provide rhythmic subdivision (generally eighth-notes) and forward motion for an arrangement. They are generally most effective when built around open triads, as follows:-

Pop ballad accompaniment (contd)

Figure 11.11. Left hand arpeggio example (using C major)
(Cassette Tape Example 248)

Figure 11.12. Left hand arpeggio example (using D minor)
(Cassette Tape Example 249)

By 'open triad' we mean a triad with the middle note raised one octave. This gives the chord more 'span' and projection and is especially effective in the lower registers where the left hand is generally operating. Notice that raising the middle note one octave can occur on a triad in any inversion. **Fig. 11.11.** above is based on a **C major** chord. In the first measure of this example, we start out with a C triad in root position, and then raise the middle note (the 3rd) by an octave to get the **1-5-3-5** pattern (the **3rd** of the chord is now technically a major 10th interval above the root). However, in the next measure we start out with a C triad in 1st inversion (i.e. E-G-C from bottom to top) - so when we raise the middle note by an octave, it is now the 5th of the triad (G), resulting in the **3-1-5-1** pattern. Similarly, starting with a 2nd inversion triad yields the subsequent **5-3-1-3** pattern (a little harder to play, due to the larger interval stretch). As with the previous pop ballad examples, these arpeggios generally require the sustain pedal to be depressed for the duration of each chord. The other example (**Fig. 11.12.** above) uses the same harmonic concepts on a **D minor** chord (again note that in the first **1-5-b3-5** pattern, the **b3rd** of the chord is now a minor 10th interval above the root).

Most often then either the root, 3rd or 5th will be on the bottom of these arpeggiated patterns, although occasionally the 7th may be used to facilitate a descending bass line movement for example. The examples above also represent the most useful range of these left hand arpeggios - generally you don't want to go much below the C which is 2 octaves below Middle C, for the lowest note of the pattern - similarly you don't want to use a starting note much higher than the C below Middle C, as then the left hand is starting to occupy the melodic register, and perhaps then getting in the way of the right hand.

We'll now apply this kind of left hand arpeggiated idea to the previous chord progression (first shown in **Fig 11.1.**). This is a simple setting with the right hand playing half-note chords, again using upper structures and voiceleading from left to right. Notice the static nature of the right hand part gives us a good chance to check out the inversions and voiceleading used on these upper structures, which is different to the previous settings - so the following example is also a (right hand) voiceleading variation on the original progression:-

Pop ballad accompaniment (contd)

Figure 11.13. Pop ballad comping pattern #2 (left hand arpeggios, right hand half-notes) - incorporating Upper structure voiceleading variation #2 *(Cassette Tape Example 250)*

Again we'll analyze the right and left hand devices in each measure as follows:-

Pop ballad accompaniment (contd)

- Measure 1

- On the **G** chord, the right hand is using a basic **1-3-5** upper structure in 2nd inversion. The left hand is using a **1-5-3-5** arpeggio pattern.
- On the **Ami7** chord, the right hand is using a **b3-5-b7** upper structure (a C triad) in 1st inversion. The left hand is using a **1-5-b3-5** arpeggio pattern.

- Measure 2

- On the **Bmi7** chord, the right hand is again using a **b3-5-b7** upper structure (a D triad) in 1st inversion. The left hand is again using a **1-5-b3-5** arpeggio pattern.
- On the **C** chord, the right hand is using a basic **1-3-5** upper structure in 2nd inversion. The left hand is again using a **1-5-3-5** arpeggio pattern.

- Measure 3

- On the **G** chord, the right hand is using a basic **1-3-5** voicing in root position. The left hand is again using a **1-5-3-5** arpeggio pattern.
- On the **Ami7** chord, the right hand is using a **b3-5-b7** upper structure (a C triad) in 2nd inversion. The left hand is again using a **1-5-b3-5** arpeggio pattern.

- Measure 4

- On the **Bmi7** chord, the right hand is again using a **b3-5-b7** upper structure (a D triad) in 2nd inversion. The left hand is again using a **1-5-b3-5** arpeggio pattern.
- On the **C** chord, the right hand is using a basic **1-3-5** voicing in 2nd inversion. The left hand is again using a **1-5-3-5** arpeggio pattern.

- Measure 5

- On the **F#mi7** chord, the right hand is again using a **b3-5-b7** upper structure (an A triad), in root position. The left hand is now using a variation of the previous idea - a **1-b7-b3-b7** arpeggio pattern. This is an effective variation giving a more 'definitive' sound on **minor 7th** chords.
- On the **B7** chord, the right hand is now using a four-part **1-3-5-b7** structure (see **Fig. 11.2.** measure 5 comments) in 2nd inversion. The left hand is using another variation - this time a **1-5-b7-5** pattern again sometimes used on minor and dominant chords - chosen here mainly for voiceleading reasons, to lead better into the next chord.

- Measure 6

- On the **F#mi7** chord, the right hand is again using a **b3-5-b7** upper structure (an A triad), this time in 2nd inversion. The left hand is again using a **1-b7-b3-b7** pattern.
- On the **B7** chord, the right hand is again using a **1-3-5-b7** structure, this time in 1st inversion. The left hand is again playing a **1-5-b7-5** arpeggio pattern.

- Measure 7

- On the **Emi7** chord, the right hand is again using a **b3-5-b7** upper structure (a G triad), in 2nd inversion. The left hand has reverted back to the **1-5-b3-5** arpeggio pattern.
- On the **Ami7** chord, the right hand is again using a **b3-5-b7** upper structure (a C triad), in 1st inversion. The left hand is again playing a **1-5-b3-5** arpeggio pattern.

- Measure 8

- On the **Ami7** chord, the right hand is again using a **b3-5-b7** upper structure (a C triad), in 2nd inversion to give some variation and movement from the previous chord. The left hand is again playing a **1-5-b3-5** arpeggio pattern.
- On the **D** chord - this for variation has been changed to a **D/F#** chord, i.e. inverted over the 3rd. This is a common harmonic embellishment in pop styles, and would work well here if we were repeating back to the beginning of the progression, as it would allow the root to resolve up by half-step into the G major chord. This is especially suitable for the left hand arpeggio, as we can now use the **3-1-5-1** pattern. The right hand is using a basic **1-3-5** upper structure (in 1st inversion), which is a good choice when inversions are being used in the bass voice.

Now we'll vary the previous example by doubling the top note in the upper triad to get a fuller sound, in a similar fashion to variation #2 on the first pattern (**Fig. 11.6.**):-

Pop ballad accompaniment (contd)

Figure 11.14. Pop ballad comping pattern #2 variation #1 (doubling top note)
(CASSETTE TAPE EXAMPLE 251)

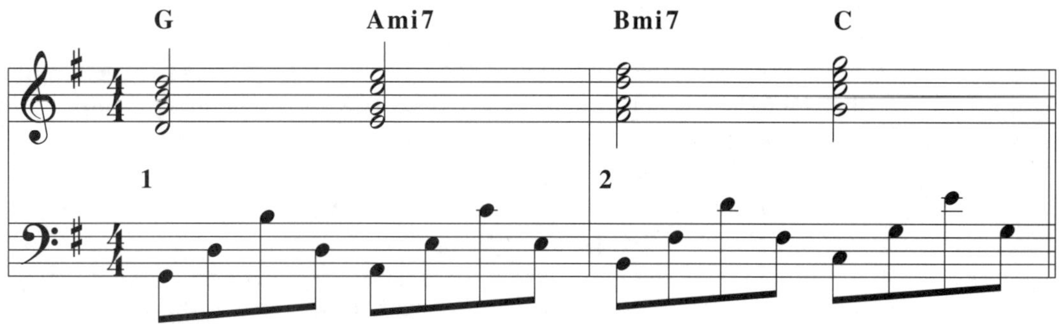

This is again a useful way to increase the energy level of the arrangement. Another right hand variation would be to play upper structure triads on each downbeat, as follows:-

Figure 11.15. Pop ballad comping pattern #2 variation #2 (quarter-note upper triads)
(CASSETTE TAPE EXAMPLE 252)

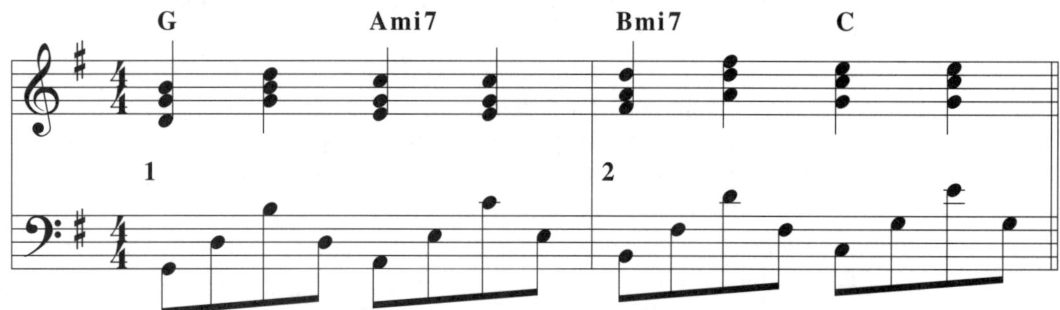

Notice in the above example we changed inversions of the upper triads within the same chord, i.e. in the first measure we are using a **1-3-5** upper structure on the **G** major chord, starting in 2nd inversion on beat **1** and then moving to root position on beat **2**. Also in the second measure we are using a **b3-5-b7** voicing on the **Bmi7** chord, starting in 1st inversion on beat **1** and moving to 2nd inversion on beat **2**. This type of upper structure inversion change (while not always appropriate) can add motion and interest to an accompaniment.

Our next right hand variation (still using an arpeggiated left hand) uses what I call a '**parallel interval**' approach. This involves playing tones of a triad separated by 6th (or 5th) intervals together. For example, the root up to the 5th of the triad constitutes a 5th interval (referred to in the following example as **1-5**). The 3rd up to the root of the triad constitutes a 6th interval (referred to in the following example as **3-1**). The 5th up to the 3rd of the triad also constitutes a 6th interval (referred to in the following example as **5-3**). These intervals can then be manipulated in a pattern, either sequentially i.e. **1-5** followed by **5-3**, **5-3** followed by **3-1** etc. or in conjunction with the remaining single tone in the triad i.e. **1-5** followed by **3**, **3-1** followed by **5**, or **5-3** followed by **1**. These movements are shown within C major and D minor triads in the following example:-

Pop ballad accompaniment (contd)

Figure 11.16. 'Parallel interval' pattern example on C major and D minor triads
(CASSETTE TAPE EXAMPLE 253)

We can now see some of these interval ideas at work on the following 'comping' variation:-

Figure 11.17. Pop ballad comping pattern #2 variation #3 ('parallel' intervals)
(CASSETTE TAPE EXAMPLE 254)

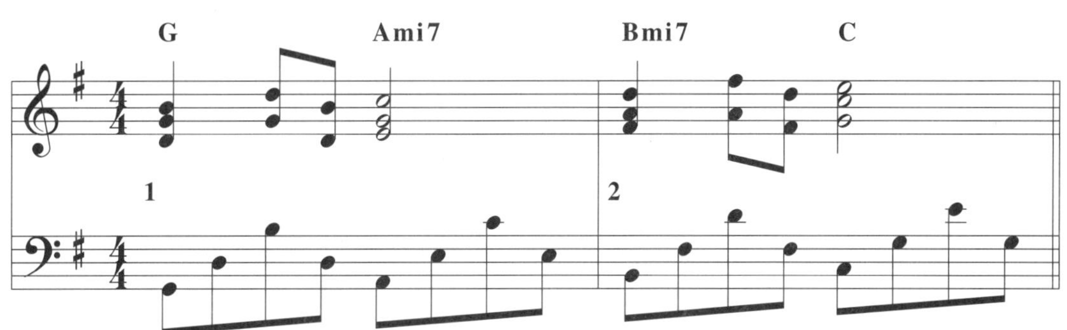

In measure **1** on the **G** chord we have a **1-5** followed by a **5-3** interval coupling movement, which leads into the next chord (C triad upper structure on Ami7). In measure **2** on the **Bmi7** chord we have a **5-3** followed by a **3-1** interval (within the D triad upper structure) leading into the next C major chord. These interval movements are very effective within triad-over-root contexts as you can see on the above Bmi7 chord. Now we will look at another comping variation using '**9 to 1**' resolutions within the upper triads, against an arpeggiated left hand as follows:-

Figure 11.18. Pop ballad comping pattern #2 variation #4 ('9 to 1' resolutions)
(CASSETTE TAPE EXAMPLE 255)

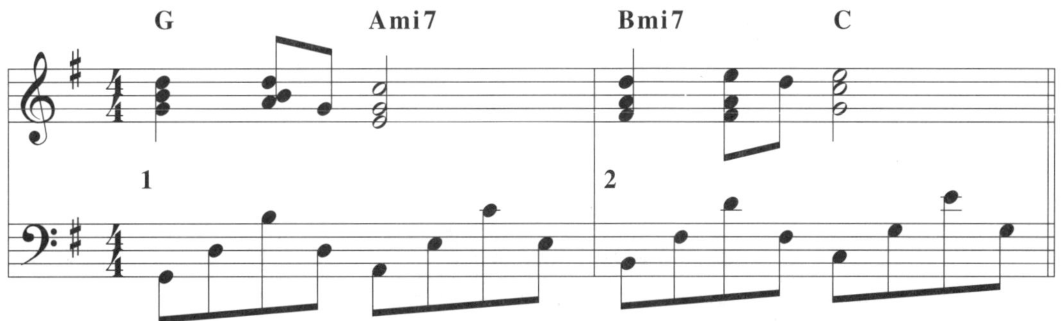

Pop ballad accompaniment (contd)

In the previous **Fig. 11.18.**, in measure **1** on the **G** chord we have a root position '**9 to 1**' resolution within the basic **1-3-5** upper structure, beginning on beat **2** and resolving on the '**& of 2**'. (Refer to **Fig. 8.2.** as necessary). In measure **2** on the **Bmi7** chord we have a 2nd inversion '**9 to 1**' resolution within the **b3-5-b7** (D major triad) upper structure (see **Fig. 8.14.**), used in a rhythmically similar manner to measure 1.

The next variations have some arpeggiation of the upper structures in the right hand, against the same arpeggiated left hand. Some care is necessary in this approach, as both hands arpeggiating continuously can be monotonous and distracting. Arpeggiated non-continuous embellishments in the right hand however, can be effective (with an arpeggiated left hand) if used sparingly. Here's an example with eighth notes in the right hand:-

Figure 11.19. Pop ballad comping pattern #2 variation #5 (right hand eighth-note arpeggios)
(Cassette Tape Example 256)

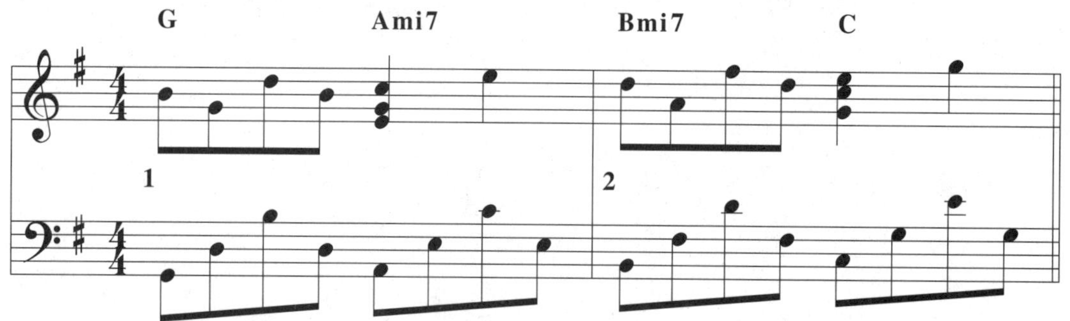

In measure 1 on the **G** chord we have a **3-1-5-3** pattern (i.e. the 3rd, root, 5th & 3rd in sequence) of the basic **1-3-5** triad upper structure in the right hand, across beats **1** and **2**. In measure 2 on the **Bmi7** chord we have a **1-5-3-1** pattern (i.e. the root, 5th, 3rd and root in sequence) of a D major triad in the right hand, which is in turn the **b3-5-b7** upper structure of the overall Bmi7 chord. The roots, 3rds and 5ths of these upper structure triads can be freely mixed and combined together for these arpeggiated right hand embellishments. (The later Pop Ballad comping pattern **#3** and variations, feature more right hand arpeggiation). Now we have an example with some 16th-note arpeggiation in the right hand:-

Figure 11.20. Pop ballad comping pattern #2 variation #6 (right hand 16th-note arpeggios)
(Cassette Tape Example 257)

Pop ballad accompaniment (contd)

In the previous **Fig. 11.20.**, in measure 1 on the **G** chord we have a **5-1-3-5** pattern (within the basic **1-3-5** triad upper structure) in the right hand, using 16th-note subdivisions of beat **2**. In measure **2** on the **Bmi7** chord we have a **3-5-1-3** pattern within a D major triad in the right hand, which again is in turn the **b3-5-b7** upper structure of the overall Bmi7 chord. Again we are using 16th-note subdivisions throughout beat **2** of the measure. Previous comments regarding the use of 16th-note subdivisions on pop ballads also apply here - refer as necessary to the introduction and text accompanying **Fig. 11.10.** in this chapter.

Finally in this section introducing left-hand arpeggiation, we will look at another 8-measure progression example. This progression features a number of inversions in the bass voice i.e. the left hand arpeggio will sometimes be landing on the 3rd, 5th or 7th of the chord at the points of chord change. This device is widely used in pop ballad styles to achieve a more melodic or 'scalewise' bass line movement - refer to inverted left hand inverted arpeggio examples in **Figs. 11.11.** and **11.12.** as necessary. Notice we have also used some right hand single-note embellishments or 'fills' between the various upper structures, as follows:-

Figure 11.21. 8-measure progression example using left hand arpeggiation with inversions
(CASSETTE TAPE EXAMPLE 258)

C G/B Ami Emi/G
1 2

F C/E Dmi F/C
3 4

G/B F/A G G/F
5 6

(CONTD-->)

Pop ballad accompaniment (contd)

Figure 11.21. (contd)

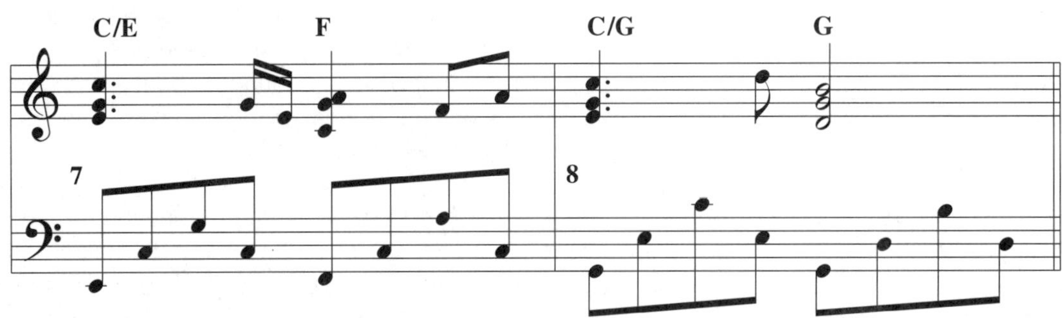

In the preceding example, the right hand part is based around a simple **1-3-5** (or **1-b3-5**) triad upper structure on each chord (including some inversions over the 3rd or 5th of the chord in the left hand - review **Figs. 5.3., 5.5. & 5.9.** as necessary). We can further analyze the right and left hand devices used, as follows:-

- Measure 1

- On the **C** chord, the right hand upper triad is in 2nd inversion, followed by a partial arpeggiated embellishment using two 16th-notes (root and 3rd of the chord). These begin on the '**& of 2**' and lead into beat **3**. The left hand is using a **1-5-3-5** pattern.
- On the **G/B** chord, the right hand upper triad is in root position to voicelead from the previous upper structure (in a circle-of-fourths fashion - see **Fig. 4.18.**). The left hand is playing a **3-1-5-1** pattern, enabling the bass notes at the points of chord change (i.e. beats **1** & **3** here) to move in a descending 'scalewise' manner.

- Measure 2

- On the **Ami** chord, the right hand upper triad upper triad is in 2nd inversion, to voice-lead from the previous chord. Again a partial arpeggiated embellishment using two 16th-notes (root and 3rd of chord) occurs on the '**& of 2**' leading into beat **3**. The left hand is using a **1-5-b3-5** pattern.
- On the **Emi/G** chord, the right hand upper triad is in root position to voicelead from the previous chord (in a circle-of-fourths fashion - see **Fig. 4.24**). The left hand is playing a **b3-1-5-1** pattern, again enabling the bass line to move in a descending manner.

- Measure 3

- On the **F** chord, the right hand upper triad is in 2nd inversion to voicelead from the previous chord. Again a 16th-note embellishment (using the root and 3rd of the chord) is leading into beat **3**. The left hand is playing a **1-5-3-5** pattern.
- On the **C/E** chord, the right hand is now using a 'parallel interval' approach within the upper C triad (see **Figs. 11.16. & 11.17**). The **1-5** coupling is played on beat **3** and the **3-1** coupling is played on beat **4**. The left hand is using a **3-1-5-1** pattern, again maint-aining the descending bass movement.

- Measure 4

- On the **Dmi** chord, the right hand upper triad is in 1st inversion to voicelead from the previous chord. The left hand is playing a **1-5-b3-1** pattern, ending on the root of the chord an octave higher than the start of the pattern. This is in order to voicelead into the bass voice of the next chord - a C below Dmi7.
- On the **F/C** chord, the right hand upper triad is now in first inversion, continuing the previous ascending voiceleading direction. The 16th-note embellishment beginning on the '**& of 4**' functions as a melodic connection between the note F (on top of the F triad on beat **3**) and the note D (on top of the G triad on beat **1** in measure 5). The left hand

Pop ballad accompaniment (contd)

- Measure 4 (contd) is using a **5-3-1-3** pattern, again to enable the bass voice to descend melodically into the next chord.

- Measure 5
- On the **G/B** chord, the right hand upper triad is now in root position, again followed by a 16th-note melodic embellishment (moving from the 9th to the 3rd of the G chord) leading into the next chord. The left hand is using a **3-1-5-1** pattern.
- On the **F/A** chord, the right hand upper triad is again in root position to voicelead from the previous chord. The 6th of the F chord (D) is used as a single 8th-note embellishment on the '**& of 4**', leading into the next chord. The left hand is again using a **3-1-5-1** pattern.

- Measure 6
- On the **G** chord, the right hand upper triad is now in 2nd inversion to voicelead from the previous chord. The left hand is using a **1-5-3-5** pattern.
- On the **G/F** chord, the right hand is again using a 'parallel interval' approach. The **5-3** coupling is played on beat **3**, and the **1-5** coupling is played on beat **4**. The left hand is using a **b7-5-3-5** pattern, again enabling the chord to be placed 'over' the 7th. Note that this G/F is actually functioning as an inverted **G7** dominant chord, leading to the following (inverted) C major chord - also see **Fig. 5.7.** comments.

- Measure 7
- On the **C/E** chord, the right hand upper triad is in 1st inversion to voicelead from the previous chord. A partial 16th-note arpeggio (using the 5th and 3rd of the chord) is again placed on the '**& of 2**' leading into beat **3**. The left hand is using a **3-1-5-1** pattern.
- On the **F** chord, the right hand is using a 2nd inversion '**9 to 1**' resolution (within the basic **1-3-5** upper triad) - see **Fig. 8.17**. The resolution continues into a partial arpeggio (using the root and 3rd of the chord) this time using 8th-notes, starting on beat **4**. The left hand is using a **1-5-3-5** pattern.

- Measure 8
- On the **C/G** chord, the right hand upper triad is now in 1st inversion. The 9th of the C chord (D) is used as a single 8th-note embellishment on the '**& of 4**', in a similar manner as for measure 5. The left hand is using a **5-3-1-3** pattern.
- On the **G** chord, the right hand upper triad is now in 2nd inversion, again using a circle-of-fourths type voiceleading from the previous upper triad (see **Fig. 4.17**). The left hand is using a **1-5-3-5** pattern.

Again it's a useful exercise to isolate the bass line used at the points of chord change, i.e. on beats **1** and **3** in this example. We get a descending pattern (C to B to A to G to F, etc) creating inversions beneath simple diatonic chord forms - an extremely typical pop ballad harmonic setting.

(See over for practice directions on this section, focusing on left hand arpeggiated comping).

Pop ballad accompaniment (contd)

PRACTICE DIRECTIONS:-

- ***Practice the left hand arpeggios in Figs. 11.11 and 11.12., and the right hand 'parallel intervals' in Fig. 11.16., in all keys.***
  (For sequence of keys, use circle-of-fifths or circle-of-fourths)
- ***Practice the comping pattern #2 using left hand arpeggios and voiceleading variation #2, as shown in Fig. 11.13.***
- ***Play comping pattern #2 variations #1 - #6 (as in Figs. 11.14., 11.15. and 11.17. - 11.20.) and work on continuing these patterns respectively throughout the progression.***
  *(The original chord sequence is shown in **Fig. 11.1.**)*
- ***Practice the 8-measure inverted left hand arpeggio example in Fig. 11.21.***
- ***Work on applying these patterns and concepts to other tunes of your choice, and to the practice progressions at the end of this chapter.***

Now we will look at another way to 'comp' over the progression first seen in **Fig. 11.1.**, this time using arpeggios in the right hand. Again these arpeggios will bring rhythmic subdivision and forward motion to an arrangement. We will base these next patterns on a new upper structure voiceleading variation in the right hand, as follows:-

Figure 11.22. Upper structure voiceleading variation #3 (based on progression in Fig. 11.1.)
(CASSETTE TAPE EXAMPLE 259)

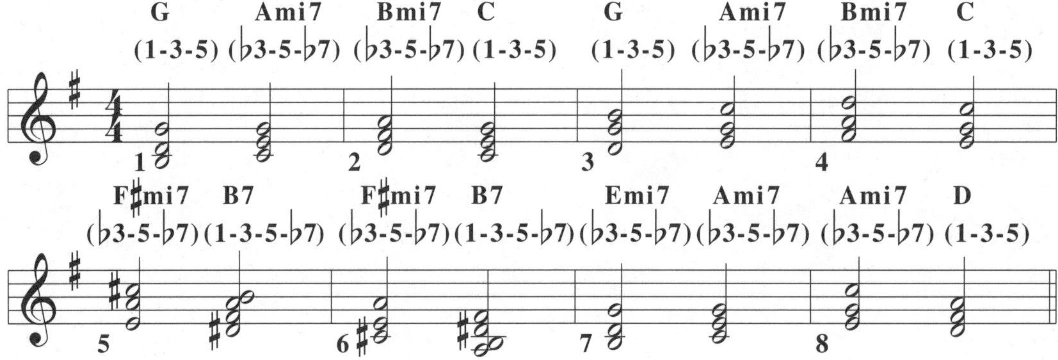

We can compare and contrast this voiceleading example with the previous upper structure voiceleading shown on the same progression in **Figs. 11.2.** and **11.13.** The upper structures used are the same, however the

Pop ballad accompaniment (contd)

inversions and voiceleading used are different in each case. Even while using the same set of upper structures, there are numerous possibilities for which inversions to use, depending upon the voiceleading intention (static, ascending, descending etc.) - you are encouraged to experiment! Generally speaking in mainstream contemporary styles, you should first choose your upper structures for each chord and then voicelead within the resulting restrictions. In the previous example (**Fig. 11.22.**) the upper structures have all been indicated (i.e. **1-3-5**, **b3-5-b7** etc). in a similar manner as for **Fig. 11.2**. Now we will look at this voiceleading used in a right-hand arpeggio context, as follows:-

Figure 11.23. Pop ballad comping pattern #3 (right hand arpeggios, based on Fig. 11.22. voiceleading *(Cassette Tape Example 260)*

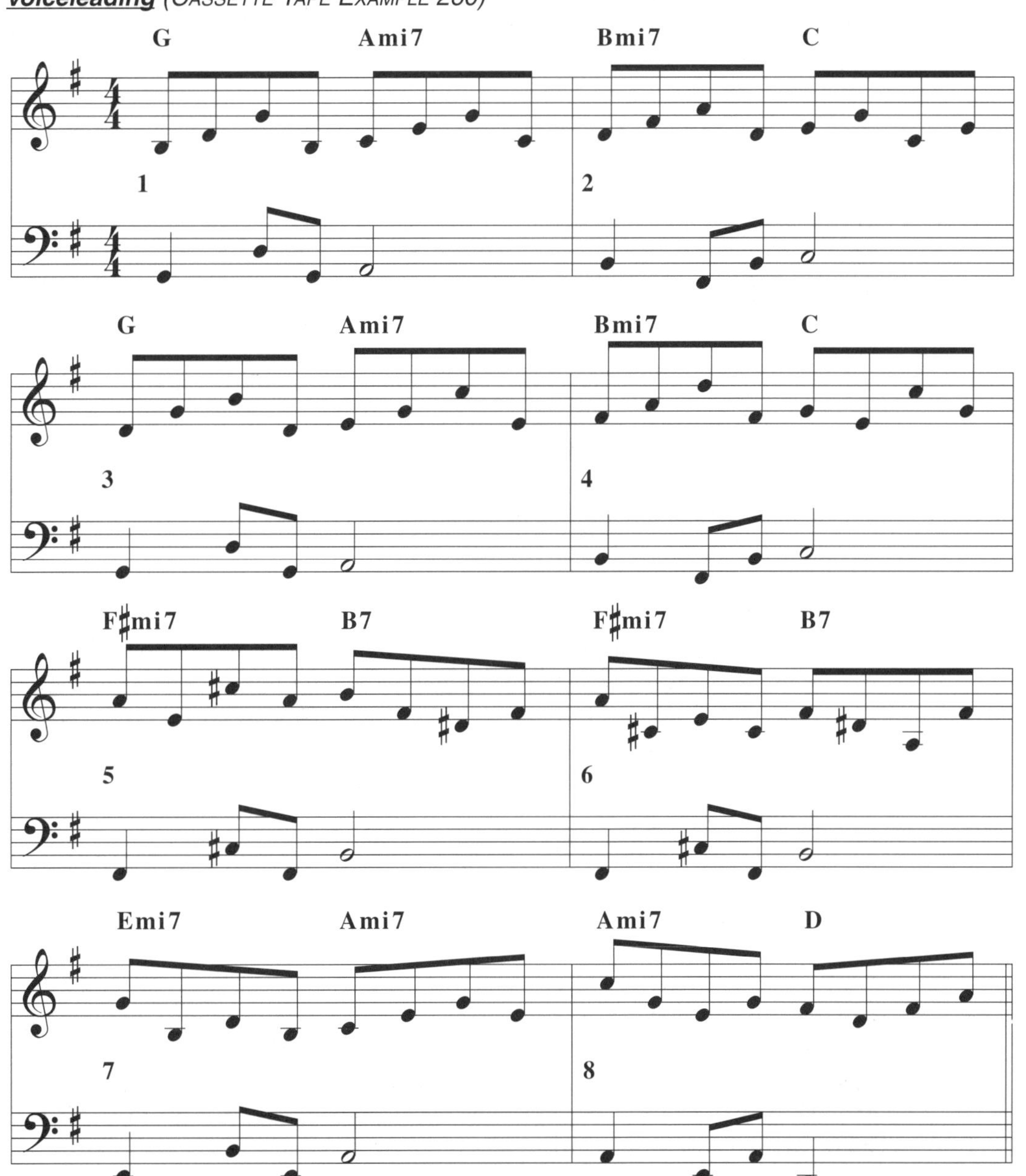

Pop ballad accompaniment (contd)

Notice that in the previous **Fig. 11.23.**, the left hand in addition to playing the roots of the chords at the points of chord change (beats **1** & **3**), is also playing some 8th-note 'pickups' into beat **3**. In this example these consist of the 5th of the chord on beat **2** and the root of the chord on the '**& of 2**'. This optional embellishment leads effectively into beat **3** of each measure. Notice the relationship between the voiceleading in **Figs. 11.22.** and **11.23**. - the same upper structure inversions are used. The pattern in which the right hand arpeggiates these upper structures can be varied arbitrarily, but may be influenced by such factors as the need to connect the arpeggiated line through the chord changes. For instance, in the previous example the last note of an arpeggiated chord generally connected into the first note of the next arpeggiated chord by a half-step or whole-step interval. While not always essential, this can certainly add fluency to an accompaniment. Let's now analyze the specific right hand pattern used on each upper structure in the previous example (again using numbers to indicate which 'parts' of the right hand upper structure are being arpeggiated, as first seen in **Fig. 11.19.**):-

- Measure 1

- On the **G** chord, the right hand is playing a **3-5-1-3** pattern within the basic **1-3-5** upper structure. The pattern ended on the 3rd of the G chord in order to voicelead into the root of the C triad (the **b3-5-b7** upper structure on the next Ami7 chord) by half-step.
- On the **Ami7** chord, the right hand is playing a **1-3-5-1** pattern within a C major triad, which is in turn the **b3-5-b7** upper structure of the overall Ami7 chord. The pattern ended on the root of the upper C triad (3rd of the Ami7 chord) in order to voicelead into the root of the D triad (the **b3-5-b7** upper structure on the next Bmi7 chord) by whole-step.

- Measure 2

- On the **Bmi7** chord, the right hand is again playing a **1-3-5-1** pattern within a D major triad, which is in turn the **b3-5-b7** upper structure of the overall Bmi7 chord. The pattern ended on the root of the upper D triad (3rd of the overall Bmi7 chord) in order to voicelead into the 3rd of the next C major chord, by whole-step.
- On the **C** chord, the right hand is playing a **3-5-1-3** pattern within the basic **1-3-5** upper structure. The pattern ended on the 3rd of the C chord in order to voicelead into the 5th of the next G major chord, by whole-step.

- Measure 3

- On the **G** chord, the right hand is playing a **5-1-3-5** pattern within the basic **1-3-5** upper structure. The pattern ended on the 5th of the G chord in order to voicelead into the 3rd of the C triad (the **b3-5-b7** upper structure on the next Ami7 chord) by whole-step.
- On the **Ami7** chord, the right hand is playing a **3-5-1-3** pattern within a C major triad, which is in turn the **b3-5-b7** upper structure of the overall Ami7 chord. The pattern ended on the 3rd of the upper C triad (5th of the Ami7 chord) in order to voicelead into the 3rd of the D triad (the **b3-5-b7** upper structure on the next Bmi7 chord) by whole-step.

- Measure 4

- On the **Bmi7** chord, the right hand is again playing a **3-5-1-3** pattern within a D major triad, which is in turn the **b3-5-b7** upper structure of the overall Bmi7 chord. The pattern ended on the 3rd of the upper D triad (5th of the overall Bmi7 chord) in order to voicelead into the 5th of the next C major chord, by half-step.
- On the **C** chord, the right hand is playing a **5-3-1-5** pattern within the basic **1-3-5** upper structure. The pattern ended on the 5th of the C chord in order to voicelead into the root of the A triad (the **b3-5-b7** upper structure on the next F#mi7 chord) by whole-step.

- Measure 5

- On the **F#mi7** chord, the right hand is playing a **1-5-3-1** pattern within an A major triad, which is in turn the **b3-5-b7** upper structure of the overall F#mi7 chord. The pattern ended on the root of the upper A triad (3rd of the overall F#mi7 chord) in order to voicelead into the root of the next B7 chord, by whole-step.

Pop ballad accompaniment (contd)

- Measure 5 (contd) - On the **B7** chord, the right hand is playing a **1-5-3-5** pattern, just using 3 notes from the **1-3-5-b7** upper structure. On this occasion there is a minor 3rd interval between the ending note of the pattern (F#, the 5th of the chord) and the first note on the next chord.

- Measure 6 - On the **F#mi7** chord, the right hand is playing a **1-3-5-3** pattern within an A major triad, which is in turn the **b3-5-b7** upper structure of the overall F#mi7 chord. On this occasion there is a perfect 4th interval between the ending note of the pattern (C#, the 5th of the overall F#mi7 chord) and the first note on the next chord.

- On the **B7** chord, the right hand is playing a **5-3-7-5** pattern, again just using 3 notes from the **1-3-5-b7** (4-part) upper structure. The pattern ended on the 5th of the B7 chord in order to voicelead into the root of the G triad (the **b3-5-b7** upper structure on the next Emi7 chord) by half-step.

Measure 7 - On the **Emi7** chord, the right hand is playing a **1-3-5-3** pattern within a G major triad, which is in turn the **b3-5-b7** upper structure of the overall Emi7 chord. The pattern ended on the 3rd of the upper G triad (5th of the overall Emi7 chord) in order to voice-lead into the root of the C triad (the **b3-5-b7** upper structure on the next Ami7 chord) by half-step.

- On the **Ami7** chord, the right hand is playing a **1-3-5-3** pattern within a C major triad, which is in turn the **b3-5-b7** upper structure of the overall Ami7 chord. The arpeggiation of the C triad continues into the next measure.

- Measure 8 - On the **Ami7** chord, the right hand is playing a **1-5-3-5** pattern within a C major triad, which is in turn the **b3-5-b7** upper structure of the overall Ami7 chord. The pattern ended on the 5th of the upper C triad (7th of the overall Ami7 chord) in order to voice-lead into the 3rd of the next D major chord, by half-step.

- On the **D** chord, the right hand is playing a **3-1-3-5** pattern within the basic **1-3-5** upper structure.

Now we will vary the previous comping pattern **#3** in various ways. The first variation consists of applying an interval coupling on the 2nd beat of each chord change i.e. in this case on beats **2** and **4** of each measure:-

Figure 11.24. Pop ballad comping pattern #3 variation #1 (adding 6th interval couplings)
(Cassette Tape Example 261)

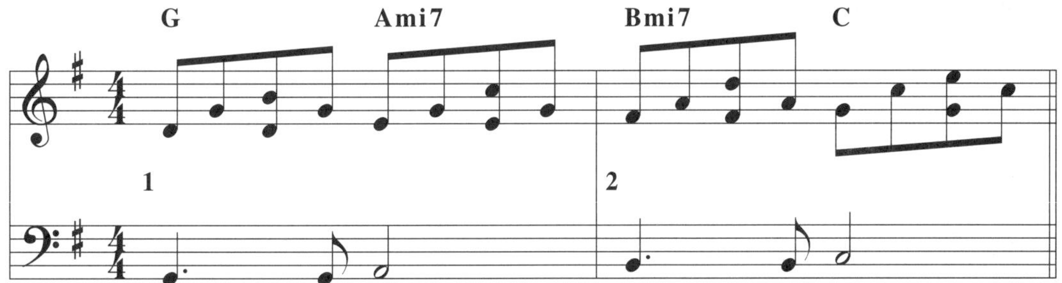

Refer to Fig. **11.16.** and accompanying text for discussion of 'parallel intervals' - here we have **5-3** and **3-1** interval couplings within the upper structure triads, on beats **2** & **4**. This gives a broader and fuller effect to the accompaniment. (The left hand has reverted to a basic dotted quarter-eighth-half note pattern using the roots of the chords). Now we'll look at a variation using 'added 9ths' within the right hand arpeggios. Typically the 9th

Pop ballad accompaniment (contd)

can be added as an embellishment tone within upper structure major triads. Note that we are talking about the 9th **with respect to the upper triad** - this of course may represent some other extension of the overall chord (as we saw in **Chapter 8, Figs 8.14.** & **8.16**). Often within the upper triad, the 9th will move down to the root or up to the 3rd, as in the following example:-

Figure 11.25. Pop ballad comping pattern #3 variation #2 (added 9ths in right hand arpeggios)
(CASSETTE TAPE EXAMPLE 262)

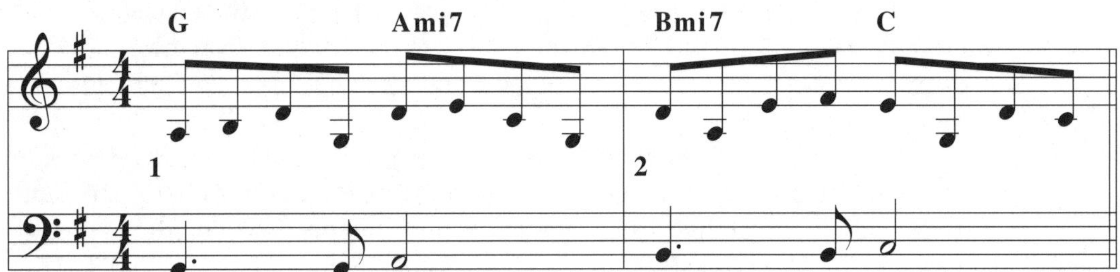

Here the added 9ths were used within the upper triads as follows:-

- Measure 1

- On the **G** chord the 9th of the **1-3-5** upper G triad (A) is placed on beat **1**, resolving to the 3rd of the triad (B) on the '**& of 1**'.
- On the **Ami7** chord the 9th of the **b3-5-b7** upper C triad (D) is placed on beat **3**, resolving to the 3rd of the triad (E) on the '**& of 3**'. Note that this represents an '**11 to 5**' movement within the overall Ami7 chord.

- Measure 2

- On the **Bmi7** chord the 9th of the **b3-5-b7** upper D triad (E) is placed on beat **2**, resolving to the 3rd of the triad (F#) on the '**& of 2**'. Note that this again represents an '**11 to 5**' movement within the overall Bmi7 chord.
- On the **C** chord the 9th of the **1-3-5** upper C triad (D) is placed on beat **4**, resolving to the root of the triad (C) on the '**& of 4**'.

Again there are numerous ways that the 9th of an upper triad can be combined together with the other triad tones, and you are encouraged to experiment. Now we will see an example combining some 'added 9th' ideas with 16th-note embellishments, as follows:-

Figure 11.26. Pop ballad comping pattern #3 variation #3 (added 9ths with 16th-notes)
(CASSETTE TAPE EXAMPLE 263)

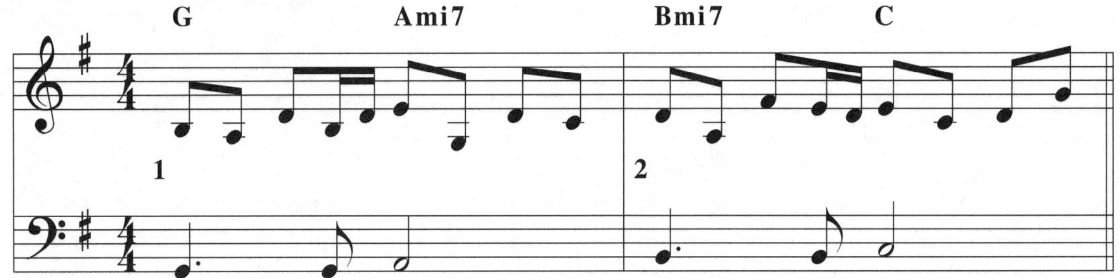

Pop ballad accompaniment (contd)

In the previous **Fig.11.26.**, the added 9ths and 16th-notes were used within the upper triads as follows:-

- Measure 1
- On the **G** chord the 9th of the **1-3-5** upper G triad (A) is now placed between the 3rd and 5th of the chord, which in turn fall on beats **1** & **2** respectively. Two 16th-notes (using the 3rd & 5th of the chord) begin on the '**& of 2**' and lead into beat **3**.
- On the **Ami7** chord the 9th of the **b3-5-b7** upper C triad (D) is now placed on beat **4**, resolving to the root of the triad (C) on the '**& of 4**'. Note that this represents an '**11 to 3**' movement within the overall Ami7 chord (see **Fig. 8.14.**).

- Measure 2
- On the **Bmi7** chord the 9th of the **b3-5-b7** upper D triad (E) is part of the 16th-note embellishment, landing on the '**& of 3**' and resolving to the root of the triad (D) on the last 16th note of beat **4**. Note that this again represents an '**11 to 3**' movement within the overall Bmi7 chord.
- On the **C** chord the 9th of the **1-3-5** upper C triad (D) is now placed between the root and 5th of the chord, this time landing on beat **4**.

Now the next variation is using 8th-note anticipations within the arpeggiated pattern, in the right hand. Again we are using different inversions of the same upper structures (**1-3-5** on the **G** and **C** chords, **b3-5-b7** on the **Ami7** and **Bmi7** chords) as follows:-

Figure 11.27. Pop ballad comping pattern #3 variation #4 (8th-note anticipations)
(Cassette Tape Example 264)

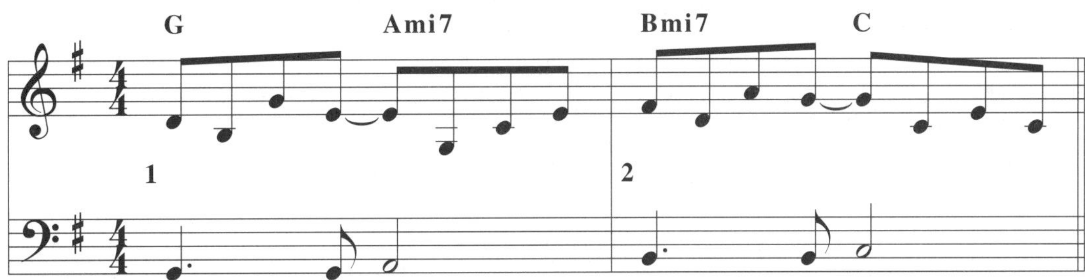

Notice in measure 1 that the note E (3rd of the **b3-5-b7** upper C triad on the Ami7 chord) falls on the '**& of 2**' and is tied over to beat **3**. **This note effectively 'belongs' to the next chord** even though it came before beat 3. Similarly in measure 2 the note G (5th of the **1-3-5** upper C triad on the C major chord) falls on the '**& of 2**' again anticipating beat **3**. Notice that the root however still landed on the downbeat in each case (i.e. on beat **3**). Anticipations in the right hand while landing on downbeats in the left hand, is typical of many contemporary applications. Review **Fig. 2.43**. and accompanying text as necessary for discussion of eighth-note anticipation concepts.

Now we will put many of these patterns and variations into practice as we construct a comping pattern for the following 32-measure progression (taken from a well-known pop ballad!). First of all we'll look at the leadsheet, showing the basic form and the chord symbols, which is the typical starting point in contemporary situations - see following page:-

Pop ballad accompaniment (contd)

Figure 11.28. Pop ballad leadsheet example (32 measures)

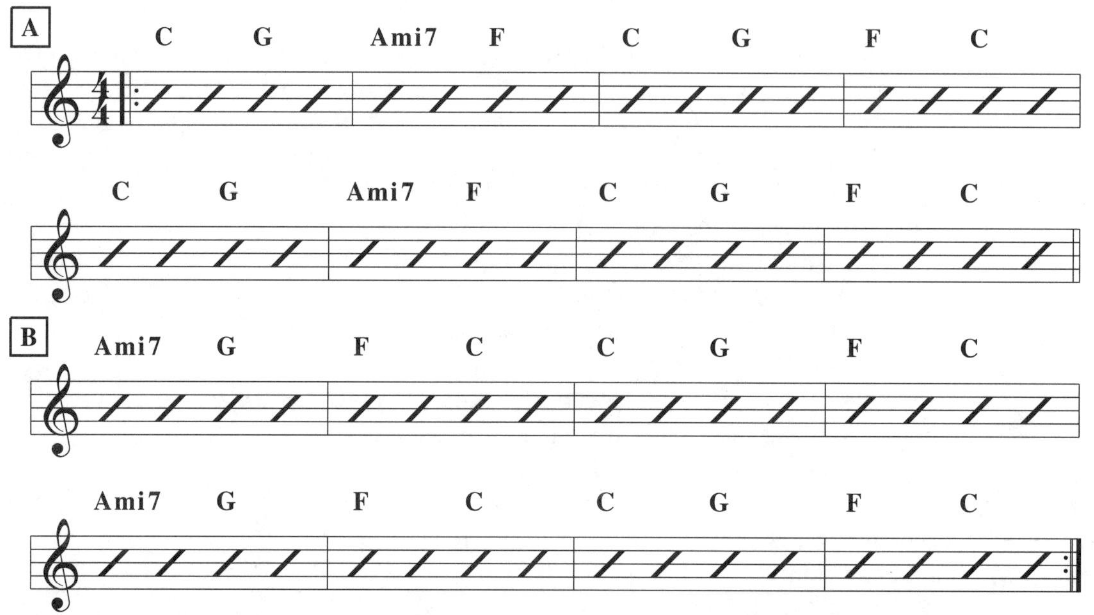

Notice the overall form consists of an 8-measure **A** section followed by an 8-measure **B** section, and then we repeat back to the top and go through the **A** and **B** sections one more time, giving 32 measures in total. One way to keep track of this form is to label the sections **A1**, **B1**, **A2** and **B2** respectively, which is what I have done on the subsequent comping solution. Notice how each section of the following example uses the various patterns and devices discussed to build the energy level of the arrangement from beginning to end, as follows:-

Figure 11.29. Pop ballad accompaniment solution for Fig. 11.28. leadsheet
(Cassette Tape Example 265)

Pop ballad accompaniment (contd)

Figure 11.29. (contd).

Pop ballad accompaniment (contd)

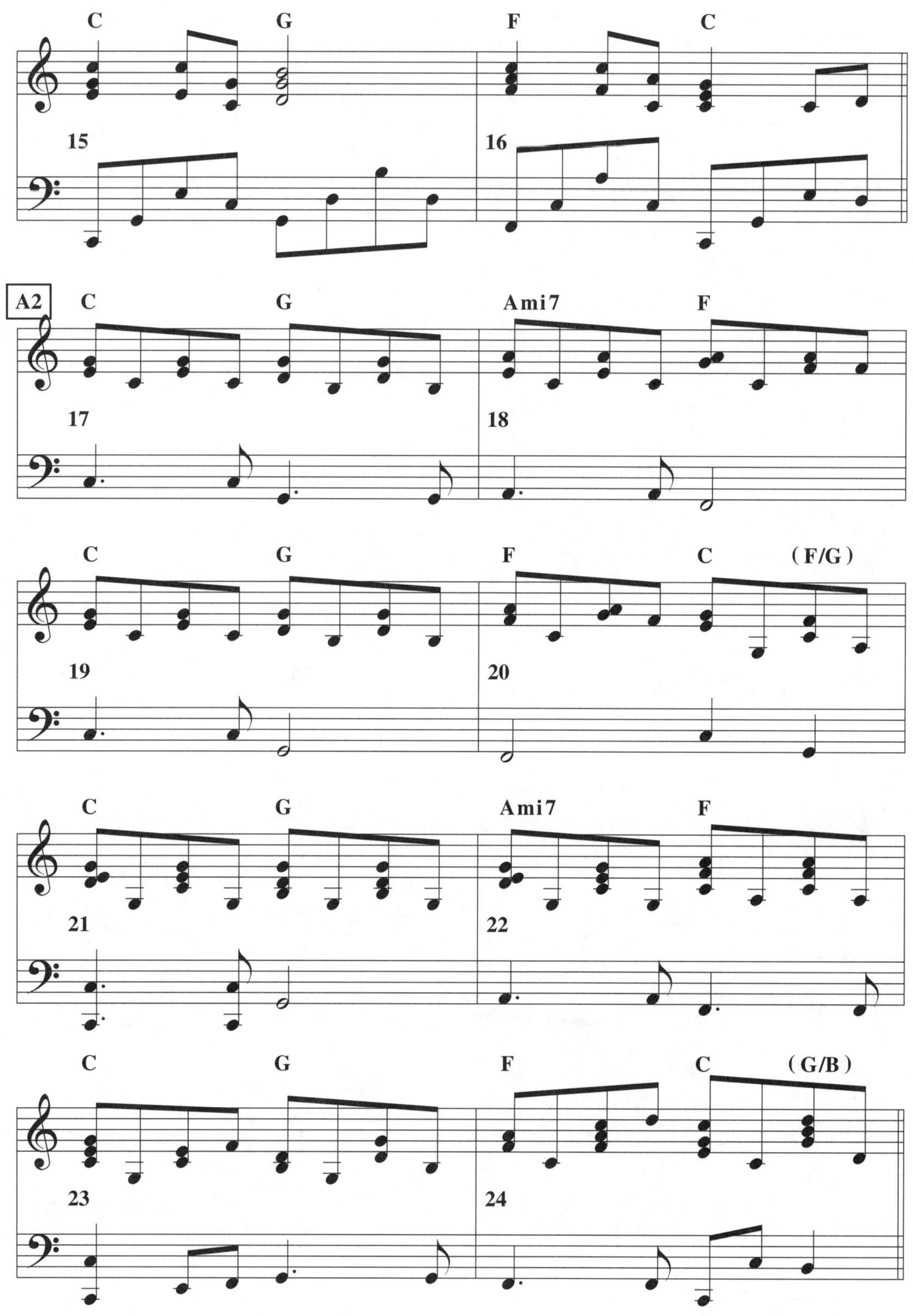

Figure 11.29. (contd).

Pop ballad accompaniment (contd)

Figure 11.29. (contd)

We will now analyse the devices used in the above accompaniment example as follows:-

- A1 section (measures 1 - 8) Here we start off with an arpeggiated right hand against a simple left hand (playing the roots of the chords using half-notes on each chord change) - see **Fig. 11.23**. The right hand is using simple **1-3-5** upper triad structures, except for the **Ami7** chord where a **b3-5-b7** (C triad) upper structure has been used. Again notice that the arpeggiated tones at the point of chord change,

Pop ballad accompaniment (contd)

Analysis of Fig. 11.29. contd.

- A1 section (contd) are generally connecting by half-step or whole-step. Note that the 9th of the upper C triad on the **Ami7** chord is used on the '**& of 2**' in measure 2, to connect into the 5th (C) of the next chord. As a variation, for the **C** chord in measure 4 the **1-3-5** triad is played on beat **3**, followed by a '**9 to 1**' embellishment using 8th-notes. In measures **5** - **8** we are using a coupling-based variation of the right hand arpeggios, as in **Fig. 11.24**. We are using **1-5**, **3-1** or **5-3** couplings (within each upper triad) on beats **2** & **4**. As a variation there is a **9-5** coupling on the **F** chord in measure **8** (beat **2**), with the 9th resolving to the root on the '**& of 2**'. In this section the left hand is now using a dotted half-eighth-half note pattern using the roots of the chords. As a variation we have two quarter-note chords on beats **3** & **4** of measure **8**. The additional **G/B** chord is a harmonic embellishment, providing a descending bass line to lead into the next Ami7 chord.

- B1 section (measures 9 - 16) Now we are using a **1-5-b3-5** and **1-5-3-5** arpeggiated patterns in the left hand, below half-note upper structure triads in the right hand, as in **Fig. 11.13**. Additionally we have a '**9 to 1**' embellishment on the **F** chord in measure 12. In measures 13 -16 we are using some 'parallel interval' couplings within the right hand upper structures, as in **Fig. 11.17.** Again different combinations of **3-1**, **1-5** and **5-3** couplings are being used, within these upper structure triads.

- A2 section (measures 17 - 24) Now we have a right-hand comping pattern using a 'rocking' motion back and forth (see **Fig. 11.3**. and accompanying text). Within the upper structure inversion chosen, the right hand is playing all of the notes except for the bottom one, on the downbeats - and then playing the bottom note of the upper structure with the thumb on the upbeats. Initially in measures 17 - 20 the right hand is playing 2 notes on each downbeat, increasing to 3 notes during measures 21 - 24 as the top note of each upper triad inversion is now doubled with the thumb. The left hand meanwhile initially reverts back to a dotted quarter-eighth-half note pattern playing the roots of the chords. In measures 21 - 24 the left hand is building more intensity by using some octaves (measures 21 & 23), using eighth-notes on the '**& of 2**' and the '**& of 4**' (as in measure 22), and using connecting tones into the root of the next chord (as in measures 23 & 24). The right hand is also doing some '**9 to 1**' resolutions within the upper triads, on the **F** chord (measures 18 & 20), and within the upper C triad used on the **C** chord (measure 21) and the **Ami7** chord (measure 22). Again some embellishment chords have been added to the original leadsheet. The **F/G** chord on beat **4** of measure 20 is a suspended dominant (see **Fig. 5.2**.) leading back to the following C major chord. The **G/B** chord on beat **4** of measure 24 is again connecting between the C chord and the following Ami7 - see previous comments on measure **8**.

- B2 section (measures 25 - 32) Now starting in measure 25 the right hand is using a combination of quarter-note triads with top-note doubled (see **Fig. 11.14**.), 16th-note arpeggiated embellishments (see **Fig. 11.20**.), '**9 to 1**' upper triad resolutions (see **Fig. 11.18**.) and 'parallel interval' couplings (see **Fig. 11.17**). Together with the arpeggiated pattern resuming in the left hand, this again serves to build the energy level. From measure 29 the right hand resumes the 'rocking back and forth' eigth-note pattern with 3 notes on each downbeat (see **Fig. 11.6**.) together with some 16th-note embellishments. Here the left hand is using a variation of the arpeggiated pattern - playing the root-5th of each chord at the points of chord change, and arpeggiating chord tones during beats **2** & **4**. In measure 31 we have some harmonic embellishments - the additional **C/E** and **F** chords giving a strong bass line movement into the following G chord. Notice at this point that the arrangement is at maximum intensity due to the use of these various devices!

Pop ballad accompaniment (contd)

PRACTICE DIRECTIONS:-

- ***Practice the comping pattern #3 using right hand arpeggios within voiceleading variation #3, as shown in Fig. 11.23.***
- ***Practice comping pattern #3 variations #1 - #4 (as in Figs. 11.24. - 11.27.) and work on continuing these patterns respectively throughout the progression.***
  (The original chord sequence is shown in ***Fig. 11.1.****)*
- ***Practice the 32-measure accompaniment solution example as shown in Fig. 11.29.***
- ***Work on applying accompaniment patterns and concepts to other tunes of your choice, and to the practice progressions at the end of this chapter.***

Pop ballad melody

Now we will turn our attention to pop ballad situations where we are required to play the melody, as opposed to providing an accompaniment while singing, or for another vocalist/instrumentalist. Not all contemporary styles lend themselves to solo piano renditions of the melody, not least because some styles are less 'melodic' than others! Pop ballads however, frequently have strong and commercial melodies, which make them suitable for solo piano treatment. What we will do in this section is to take a typical pop ballad leadsheet with melody and chord symbols, and then present different playing devices to support the melody. In all cases we must ensure that the melody 'projects' and that what we do does not detract from, but rather complements and supports the melody. To this end we are initially concerned with right-hand devices to use below the melody. Here is the leadsheet example we are working with:-

Figure 11.30. Eight measure (melody) leadsheet example

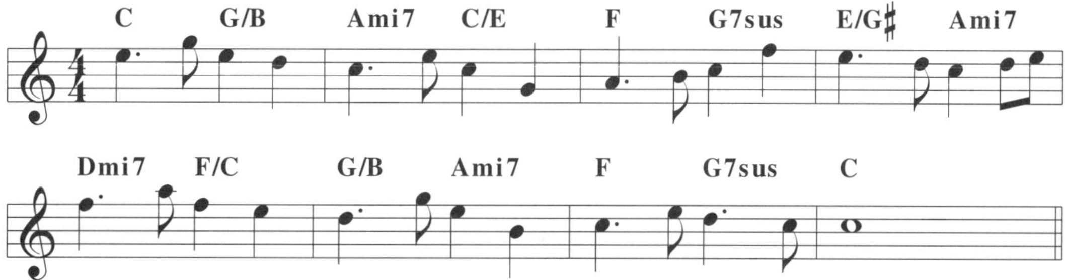

Pop ballad melody (contd)

Notice in the preceeding leadsheet that the melody and the chords (except for the **E/G#**) are all diatonic to the key signature (C major). The 'slash' chords are all basic triads inverted over the 3rd or 5th of the chord, to facilitate melodic bass line movement. The **G7sus** chord is a 'soft' or suspended dominant, typically voiced by building a **b7-9-11** upper structure triad i.e. in this case an F triad over G in the bass (see **Fig. 5.2.**).

The simplest melodic treatment of this leadsheet would be to play a single-note melody in the right hand, supported by 3-part triad voicings in the left hand. Even within this simple setting we should ensure that the left hand triads voicelead from left to right, as follows:-

Figure 11.31. Pop ballad melody version #1 (right hand single notes, left hand closed triads)
(Cassette Tape Example 266)

In the heading I have referred to these as 'closed triads' as their total span is less than one octave - as opposed to the 'open triads' with a span of greater than one octave, which we first encountered in **Fig. 11.11.** Notice the starting (2nd) inversion of the first C triad is around the middle C area - this is a good position for a closed triad - the melody is generally high enough in the staff that we have room to use this register in the left hand. Had the melody been shown an octave lower, to use this setting we would need to transpose the melody into the register shown, as the left hand closed triads become too 'muddy' when used in the fundamental or bass register. The use of slash chords on the leadsheet is primarily to control the root melody - however this closed triad setting does not really provide a root voice, therefore it is not particularly necessary to invert the closed triads to get the note 'on the right of the slash' on the bottom - however as soon as we have some root motion i.e. by using open triads or arpeggios in the left hand, this will become a requirement. Notice the harmonic concept in the left hand is generally to voicelead basic **1-3-5** (or **1-b3-5**) triad structures on each chord, with the exception of the **G7sus** chord - here the simple closed voicing is to play a **1-4-5** structure, the note C functioning as the 11th (or suspension) on the chord - review **Figs. 1.73. & 1.78.** as necessary. Now we will look at a second version, still using a single-note right hand melody, but with **open triads** in the left hand. Don't worry if you can't stretch the 10th intervals in the left hand - these voicings can be quickly 'rolled' from bottom to top, and sustained with the pedal:-

Pop ballad melody (contd)

Figure 11.32. Pop ballad melody version #2 (right hand single notes, left hand open triads)
(Cassette Tape Example 267)

Notice in this example that the left hand is playing a **1-5-3** or **3-1-5** open triad on the major chords, and a **1-5-b3** open triad on the minor chords, except for the following stuations:-

- On the **G7sus** chords in measures **3 & 7**, the left hand is playing a **root-b7th** interval coupling. This is a popular and effective left hand solution on minor and dominant chords. This device should not be used too low as it will get 'muddy' - your ears will be the final judge.
- On the **F/C** chord in measure 5, the left hand is playing a **5-3** interval coupling, placing the 5th on the bottom as required by the chord symbol. In this case the open triad would be a **5-3-1** from bottom to top, requiring an 11th interval stretch which I think you'll agree is rather uncomfortable! (although this could be arpeggiated of course). In this case the **5-3** voicing is sufficient to define the chord.

In the next example, the left hand is now **arpeggiating open triads** (a technique we first saw in **Figs. 11.11.** and **11.12.**) again below a single note melody:-

Figure 11.33. Pop ballad melody version #3 (right hand single notes, left hand arpeggios)
(Cassette Tape Example 268)

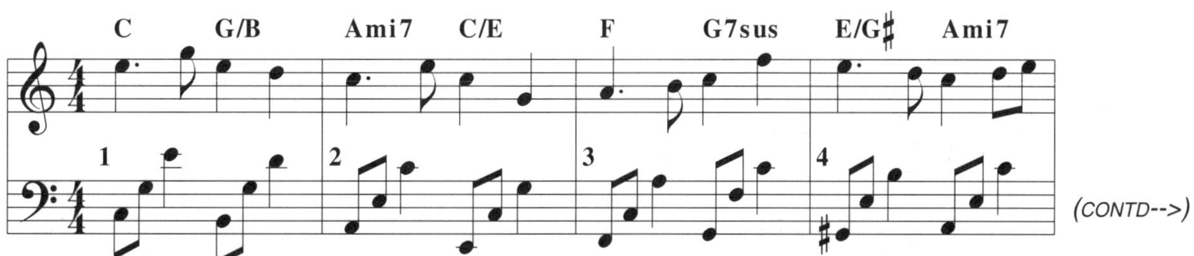

(CONTD-->)

Pop ballad melody (contd)

Figure 11.33. (contd)

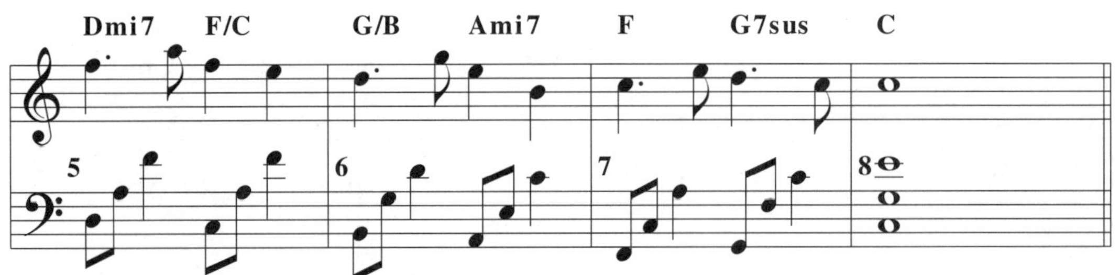

Again in this example the left hand arpeggio is using either **1-5-3**, **3-1-5** or **1-5-b3** patterns, except for the following situations:-

- On the **G7sus** chords in measures **3** & **7**, the left hand is playing a **1-b7-11** pattern. This is an effective choice on suspended dominant chords.
- On the **F/C** chord in measure **5**, the left hand is playing a **5-3-1** pattern (see **Fig. 11.11.**) to facilitate the bass line movement required by the leadsheet.
  (Note that the **1-b7-b3** left hand pattern first used on minor 7th chords in **Fig. 11.13.**, would be an effective alternative to the **1-5-b3** pattern used on the minor chords in this example).

The next setting involves placing a **triad under the melody note** in the right hand, at the points of chord change. This again will require us to know our triad inversions - see **Chapter 4** and the discussion accompanying **Fig. 11.2.** in this chapter. The basic method we use is as follows:-

- Look at the melody notes at the points of chord change. Decide whether the melody note is within the chord (or within the upper structure triad you wish to use on the chord).
  - If the melody note is within the chord or desired upper triad, then **invert that triad below the melody at the point of chord change**. The notes (of the triad) added below melody will then be sustained for the remaining time the chord is 'in force', i.e. by using the sustain pedal. Any remaining melody notes occurring within the same chord duration, can be played generally as single notes and will be heard in the context of the harmonic 'pad' already established. Again this will normally require the sustain pedal to be used for the duration of each chord change.
  - If the melody note is not within the chord or desired upper triad, then find the closest inversion of the upper structure below the melody, and then **substitute the melody note for the top note of that triad, placing the remaining tones of the triad below the melody**. Very often the melody will then resolve into a chord tone in any case - the out-of-chord tone thereby functioning as a neighbour tone (or upper extension).
- We may optionally repeat other tones from the upper structure used, below the melody other than at the points of chord change - this will depend on the register and rhythmic intensity of the melody i.e. generally the busier the melody is, the less we need to use supporting devices in the right hand.

We'll now see these concepts at work on the next melody version, which places triads below melody. Again we are mainly using basic **1-3-5** triad upper structures (including inversions over the 3rd or 5th in the left hand - see **Figs. 5.3. & 5.5.**), except for the **b3-5-b7** (C triad) used on the **Ami7**, the **b3-5-b7** (F triad) used on the **Dmi7**, and the **b7-9-11** (F triad) used on the **G7sus**. The left hand arpeggios are the same as for **Fig. 11.33.**:-

Pop ballad melody (contd)

Figure 11.34. Pop ballad melody version #4 (triad below melody)
(Cassette Tape Example 269)

Generally in the above example we are inverting the previously described upper structure triads below melody at the points of chord change, with the following variations:-

- On the inverted **G** chord in measure 1, the melody note E at the point of chord change is an out-of-chord tone (here the basic **1-3-5** G triad upper structure is a preferred choice over the 3rd in the root voice - see **Fig. 11.13.** measure 8 comments). This is therefore the second situation described in the inset paragraph on the previous page - we find the nearest inversion of the G triad below melody (root position in this case) and then **substitute** the note E for the note D which would otherwise have been played. Notice that the note E resolves to the note D in any case on beat **4** of the measure. The note E is a 6th with respect to the G chord 'in force'.

Pop ballad melody (contd)

- We can interpret the melody treatment on the **G7sus** chord in measure **7** in the same way. The melody note D is not wthin the **b7-9-11** upper F triad to be used (a preferred upper structure solution on the suspended dominant chord) - so we invert the F triad below D in the melody (i.e. in root position) and then **substitute** the note D for the note C at the point of chord change. Again later in the measure the melody resolves to the triad tone (C). The note D is a 5th with respect to the G7sus chord 'in force'.
- Additional triad tones have been added below melody during the inverted **C** chord in measure 2 and during the **Ami7** chord in measure 6. On beat **4** in measure 2, the 3rd (E) has been added below the 5th(G) in the melody. On beat **4** in measure 6, the note G (5th of the upper C triad - 7th of the overall **Ami7** chord) has been added below the note B in the melody. At this point the note B is an out-of-upper-triad melody note, functioning as the 9th of the overall **Ami7** chord.

Now we will consider another right-hand melody support device - placing a **diatonic interval** below the melody. Favourite intervals for this are 3rds and 6ths, due to their warm consonant quality. When we place 3rds or 6ths below a melody, one of three situations will occur:-

1) The interval placed below the melody is a basic chord tone with respect to the chord symbol 'in force' (or is within an upper structure being used). This is the safest result as everything is consistent with the chord symbol.
2) The interval placed below melody is not a basic chord tone, but is an available upper extension or passing tone on the chord. In these cases, it becomes a stylistic judgement call as to whether the upper extension is acceptable - it could for example result in a sophisticated sound which is inappropriate in simpler pop styles.
3) The interval placed below melody is not available on this chord, for example one of the following:-
    - A tone which is a half-step above the bass voice on the chord (creating a 'minor 9th' interval between the bass voice and the interval below melody).
    - The (major) 3rd on a suspended chord. The suspension creates a 4th (or 11th). The 3rd and 4th (11th) are mutually exclusive.
    - The perfect 4th (11th) on a major (or unsuspended dominant) chord. As above, the 3rd and 4th (11th) are mutually exclusive.

   In these cases it is best to modify the interval placed below the melody so that the note conforms to the chord symbol. Typical solutions are to expand a 3rd interval below melody to a 4th, and to reduce a 6th interval below melody to a 5th. This may also be done when the **2nd condition** above occurs (upper tension tone created) and it is decided that the upper tension/passing tone is inappropriate.

The first '**diatonic interval below melody**' example we will look at, features 'consistent' 6ths below the melody throughout. Although this does not create any problems in the **3rd category** above (i.e. notes not available on this chord), there are a number of intervals which fall into the **2nd category** i.e. some upper chord extensions are created. Each of these situations is analyzed, and then in the subsequent example all of the 'questionable' 6th intervals are changed to 5th intervals in order to conform better to the chord symbols. Listen closely to the difference between these two settings, beginning with the example on the following page:-

(Note that in the following melody examples in **Figs. 11.35. - 11.39.**, we are continuing to use the open triad pattern in the left hand which was first derived in **Fig. 11.33.**).

Pop ballad melody (contd)

Figure 11.35. Pop ballad melody version #5 ('consistent' 6ths below melody)
(Cassette Tape Example 270)

In this case, for about two-thirds of the above melody notes, placing a diatonic 6th below the melody causes no problems with respect to the chord symbol. However, in the following cases upper tension tones were added as follows:-

- On the **G** melody note in measure 1, the 6th below creates B which is a major 7th on the **C** chord in force. The 7th is of course available on the major chord, but will be inappropriate if a more basic 'triadic' sound is desired.
- On the **D** melody note in measure 1, the 6th below creates F which is a minor 7th on the inverted **G** chord, effectively creating a dominant 7th implication overall - this may be too 'leading' in simpler styles.

Pop ballad melody (contd)

- On the **G** melody note in measure 2, the 6th below G creates B, a major 7th on the inverted **C** chord - see measure 1 comments.
- On the **C** melody note in measure 3, the 6th below C creates E, the 13th on the **G7sus** chord.This is a sophisticated sound (don't forget this is always a 13th on a dominant chord - never a 6th!).
- On the **D** melody note on beat **4** of measure 4, the 6th below creates F, technically the #5th on the **Ami7** chord. The melody itself here is an upper extension (11th) of the chord. The note F here can be thought of as a passing tone, connecting the 5th (E) and 7th(G) of the overall Ami7 chord respectively.
- On the **E** melody note in measure **5**, the 6th below creates G, the 9th of the inverted **F** chord. Although the 9th is normally a safe extension, sometimes this can dilute the strength of inverted triads (i.e. over the 3rd or 5th in the bass) in simpler styles.
- On the **D** melody note in measure **6**, the 6th below creates F, effectively creating an inverted **G7** chord - see measure 1 comments.
- On the **B** melody note in measure **6**, the 6th below creates D, the 11th of the **Ami7** chord. The melody itself here is an upper extension (9th) of the chord. The 11th is normally a safe extension on minor 7th chords, however a more sophisticated effect is created.
- On the **C** melody note on beat **1** of measure 7, the 6th below creates E, the 7th of the **F** major chord - see measure 1 comments on C major.
- On the **C** melody note on the '**& of 4**' in measure **7**, the 6th below again creates E, which this time is the 13th on the **G7sus** chord - see measure 3 comments.

Now in the following setting, each of the above 'questionable' 6ths has been made into a (perfect) 5th interval. In each case the note created is more 'inside' the chord and therefore gives a simpler, more definitive result (amended intervals are indicated with '**' on the example):-

Figure 11.36. Pop ballad melody version #6 (6ths and 5ths below melody)
(Cassette Tape Example 271)

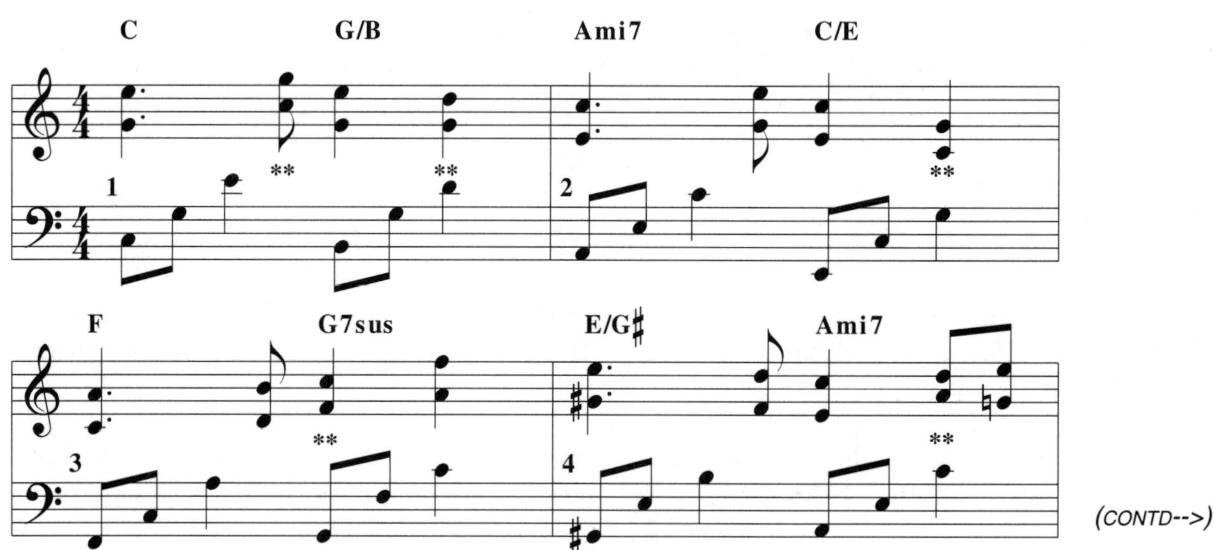

(CONTD-->)

Pop ballad melody (contd)

Figure 11.36. (contd)

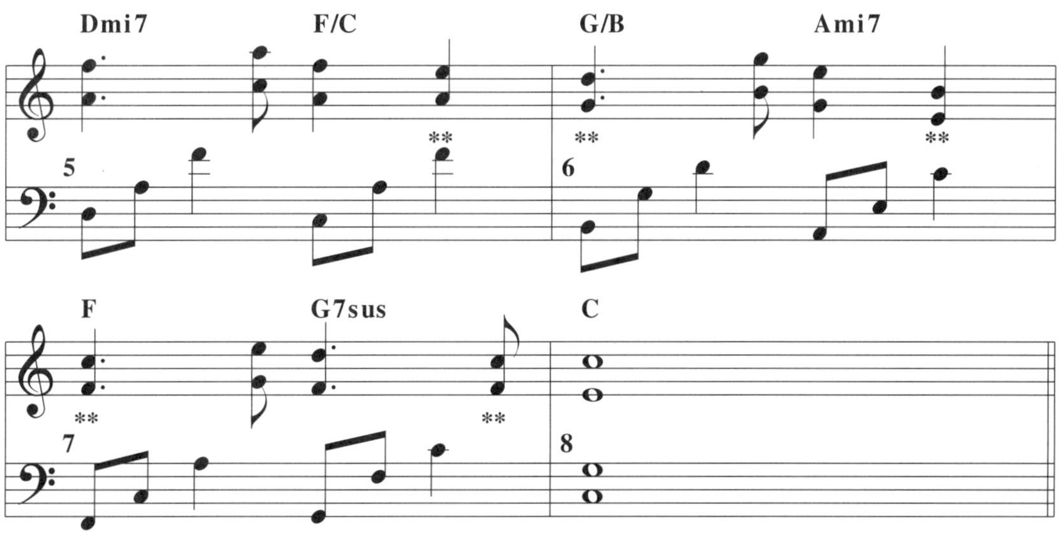

Play and listen to the two preceding examples to hear and understand the differences! Now we will look at diatonic 3rd intervals below melody. If diatonic 3rd intervals were used throughout the above melody, we would have a number of notes created which were incompatible with the chords (i.e. in the **3rd category** discussed in the text preceding **Fig. 11.35.**) - so instead of creating 3rds in these cases we have created perfect 4th intervals instead. In addition some 'questionable' 3rds (the **2nd category**) have also been replaced with 4ths for stylistic and definition reasons, as in the following example:-

Figure 11.37. Pop ballad melody version #7 (3rds and 4ths below melody)

(Cassette Tape Example 272)

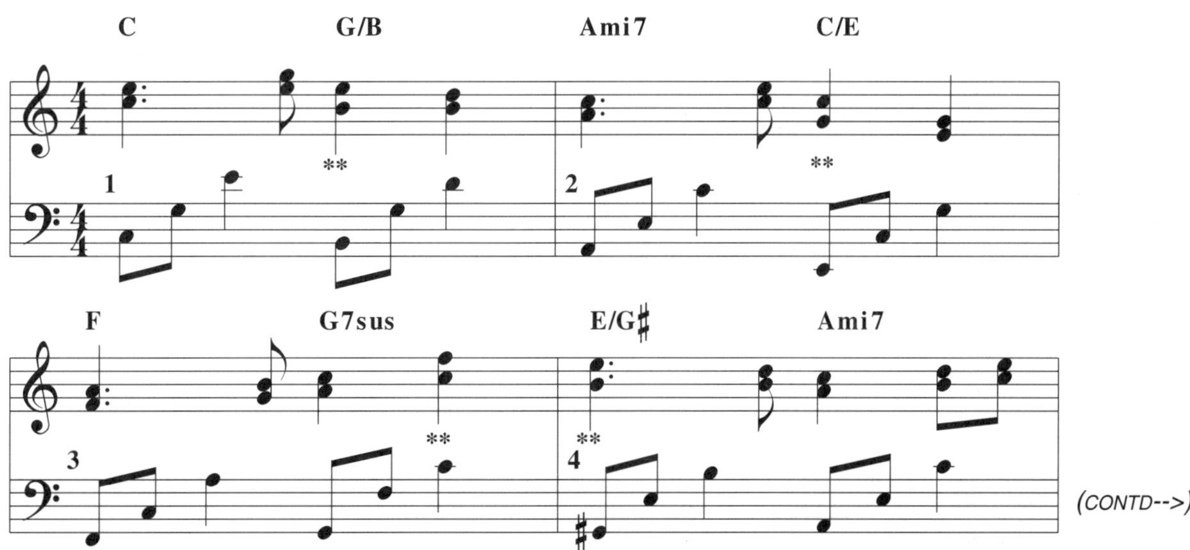

Pop ballad melody (contd)

Figure 11.37. (contd)

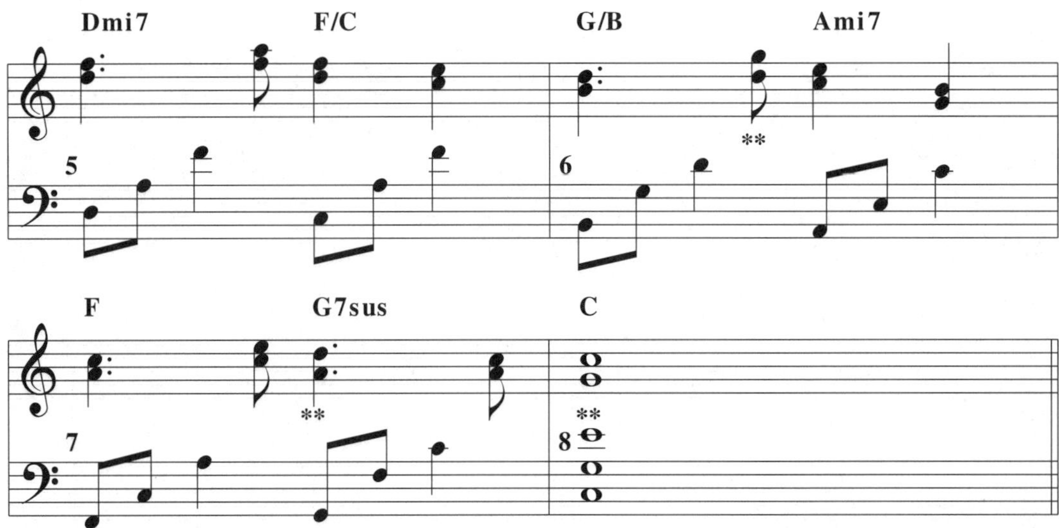

Again in most instances the diatonic 3rds worked within the confines of the chords - however in the places marked with '**', the 3rds were replaced with 4ths as follows:-

- On the **E** melody note on beat **3** of measure 1, the 3rd below would have created C which is a 4th (11th) on the inverted **G** major chord. This is incompatible with the major chord, so the interval is changed to a perfect 4th below melody which creates the note B (the 3rd of the G major chord).
- On the **C** melody note on beat **3** of measure 2, the 3rd below would have created A which is a 6th on the inverted **C** major chord. Although technically available, the 6th on the major chord can sound dated when used without the 9th, and especially does not sound strong on a triad inverted over the 3rd or 5th in the bass voice. The interval is changed to a 4th below melody, creating G (the 5th of the C major chord).
- On the **F** melody note in measure 3, the 3rd below would have created D which is a 5th on the **G7sus** chord. Although this is not a problem, it is much stronger to place the 4th (11th) below the melody on this suspension. The interval is changed to a 4th below melody, creating C (the 11th of the suspension).
- On the **E** melody note on beat **1** of measure 4, the 3rd below would have created C which is the raised 5th of the inverted **E** chord. This is a sophisticated sound actually implying an altered dominant quality - and potentially in conflict with the B in the left hand arpeggio landing on beat **2**. It's safer in simpler styles to make this a 4th below melody, creating B (the 5th of the E major chord).
- On the **G** melody note in measure 6, the 3rd below would have created E which is a 6th on the inverted **G** major chord - refer to measure 2 comments - the 6th of the chord is changed to the 5th.
- On the **D** melody note in measure 7, the 3rd below would have created B which is the 3rd of a G chord - this is incompatible with the **G7sus** which specifically excludes the 3rd in favour of the 4th (11th). The interval is changed to a 4th below melody, creating A (the 9th of the dominant suspension).
- On the **C** melody note in measure 8, the 3rd below would have created A which is the 6th of the **C** major chord - refer to measure 2 comments - the 6th of the chord is changed to the 5th.

Now we'll look at a setting using **octaves** to support the melody in the right hand. This is a useful way to build the energy of an arrangement without increasing the harmonic density (number of pitches played at once):-

Pop ballad melody (contd)

Figure 11.38. Pop ballad melody version #8 (octaves below melody)

(CASSETTE TAPE EXAMPLE 273)

Pianistically the right hand 'locks' into the same interval pattern throughout - as with all of these legato ballad styles, versions using octaves like this will especially rely on the use of the sustain pedal for the duration of each chord, to create a smooth effect. Here there are no additional harmony considerations as we are only doubling the existing melody. However, one other useful variation of this is the **'filled-in' octave** approach, where a chord tone is added in between the original melody and the doubled melody i.e. within the octave. It is quite normal in this approach to vary the intervals between the melody and the 'harmony note', in order to get good definition within the chord - generally basic chord tones are used (roots, 3rds, 5ths & 7ths) as follows:-

Pop ballad melody (contd)

Notice that the right hand is in a higher register - another reason to pick a harmony note (between each octave) which is a basic chord tone, as this will project and define better in simpler styles. Again we will definitely need to use the sustain pedal to get a smooth result! Here is an analysis of the notes chosen to 'fill-in' the octaves under each melody note:-

Pop ballad melody (contd)

- Measure 1

- On beat **1**, on the **C** chord below **E** in the melody we have added G - the 5th of the chord and a 6th interval below melody.
- On the '**& of 2**', on the **C** chord below **G** in the melody we have added C - the root of the chord and a 5th interval below melody.
- On beat **3**, on the inverted **G** chord below **E** in the melody we have added G - the root of the chord and a 6th interval below melody.
- On beat **4**, on the inverted **G** chord below **D** in the melody we have again added G - the root of the chord, now a 5th interval below melody.

- Measure 2

- On beat **1**, on the **Ami7** chord below **C** in the melody we have added G - the 7th of the chord and a 4th interval below melody. Viewed in the context of the **b3-5-b7** upper C major triad, the 5th of this triad (G) has been added below the root (C).
- On the '**& of 2**', on the **Ami7** chord below **E** in the melody we have again added G - the 7th of the chord and a 6th interval below melody. Viewed in the context of the **b3-5-b7** upper C major triad, the 5th of this triad (G) has been added below the 3rd (E).
- On beat **3**, on the inverted **C** chord below **C** in the melody we have added G - the 5th of the chord and a 4th interval below melody.
- On beat **4**, on the inverted **C** chord below **G** in the melody we have added C - the root of the chord and a 5th interval below melody. (Notice during the C/E chord we are just using roots and 5ths in the right hand - this is very effective when the major chord is inverted over the 3rd in the bass voice).

- Measure 3

- On beat **1**, on the **F** chord below **A** in the melody we have added C - the 5th of the chord and a 6th interval below melody.
- On the '**& of 2**', on the **F** chord below **B** in the melody we have added the note G. The melody note here is an upper tension tone, technically the 'raised 11th' with respect to the F chord. The note G (9th of the chord) placed below melody gives good support to this upper extension, and enables a 'contrary motion' voiceleading to occur into the following G7sus voicing.
- On beat **3**, on the **G7sus** chord below **C** in the melody we have added F - the 7th of the chord and a 5th interval below melody. Viewed in the context of the **b7-9-11** upper F major triad, the root of this triad (F) has been added below the 5th (C).
- On beat **4**, on the **G7sus** chord below **F** in the melody we have added C - the 11th of the chord and a 4th interval below melody. Viewed in the context of the **b7-9-11** upper F major triad, the 5th of this triad (C) has been placed below the root (F).

- Measure 4

- On beat **1**, on the inverted **E** chord below **E** in the melody we have added B - the 5th of the chord and a 4th interval below melody. (Again here the root and 5th of the triad is effective over the 3rd in the bass voice).
- On the '**& of 2**', on the inverted **E** chord below **D** in the melody we have added G# - the 3rd of the chord and an augmented 4th interval below melody. This voicing is momentarily combining together the major 3rd and minor 7th of an E chord, thereby creating a dominant quality. Combining the 3rd and 7th of the dominant together in the right hand, creates an active and leading sound.
- On beat **3**, on the **Ami7** chord below **C** in the melody we have added G - the 7th of the chord and a 4th interval below melody. Viewed in the context of the **b3-5-b7** upper C major triad, the 5th of this triad (G) has been placed below the root (C).

Pop ballad melody (contd)

Analysis of Fig. 11.39. contd.

- Measure 4 (contd)
- On beat **4**, on the **Ami7** chord below **D** in the melody we have added G - the 7th of the chord and a 4th interval below melody.
- On the '**& of 4**', on the **Ami7** chord below **E** in the melody we have added C - the 3rd of the chord and a 3rd interval below melody. Viewed in the context of the **b3-5-b7** upper C major triad, the root of this triad (C) has been placed below the 3rd (E).

- Measure 5
- On beat **1**, on the **Dmi7** chord below **F** in the melody we have added A - the 5th of the chord and a 6th interval below melody. Viewed in the context of the **b3-5-b7** upper F major triad, the 3rd of this triad (A) has been placed below the root (F).
- On the '**& of 2**', on the **Dmi7** chord below **A** in the melody we have added C - the 7th of the chord and a 6th interval below melody. Viewed in the context of the **b3-5-b7** upper F major triad, the 5th of this triad (C) has been placed below the 3rd (A).
- On beat **3**, on the inverted **F** chord below **F** in the melody we have added A - the 3rd of the chord and a 6th interval below melody.
- On beat **4**, on the inverted **F** chord below **E** in the melody we have again added A - the 3rd of the chord, now a 5th interval below melody.

- Measure 6
- On beat **1**, on the inverted **G** chord below **D** in the melody we have added G - the root of the chord and a 5th interval below melody.
- On the '**& of 2**', on the inverted **G** chord below **G** in the melody we have added B - the 3rd of the chord and a 6th interval below melody.
- On beat **3**, on the **Ami7** chord below **E** in the melody we have added G - the 7th of the chord and a 6th interval below melody - again this interval is within the **b3-5-b7** triad.
- On beat **4**, on the **Ami7** chord below **B** in the melody we have again added G - the 7th of the chord, now a 3rd interval below melody.

- Measure 7
- On beat **1**, on the **F** chord below **C** in the melody we have added A - the 3rd of the chord and a 3rd interval below melody.
- On the '**& of 2**', on the **F** chord below **E** in the melody we have added G - the 9th of the chord and a 6th interval below melody.
- On beat **3**, on the **G7sus** chord below **D** in the melody we have added F - the 7th of the chord and a 6th interval below melody.
- On the '**& of 4**', on the **G7sus** chord below **C** in the melody we have added F - the 7th of the chord and a 5th interval below melody - again this interval is within the **b7-9-11** triad.

- Measure 8
- On beat **1**, on the **C** chord below **C** in the melody we have added E - the 3rd of the chord and a 6th interval below melody.

Again notice that in most cases during the previous example, the extra note added 'within the octave' in the right hand was a basic chord tone i.e. **root**, **3rd**. **5th** or **7th** of the overall chord. This 'filled-in octave' approach is a very effective way to add breadth and color to an arrangement.

Now we will look at the next melody support device - **arpeggiating** the chord tones in the right hand. From a pianistic point of view, it is important that the melody 'projects' and is not submerged within the arpeggios being played. The concept here is harmonically similar to 'triads below melody' (see **Fig. 11.34**.) except that the triad tones are now arpeggiated below the melody, on the eighth-note subdivisions where the melody does not 'attack' i.e. where a melody note does not occur. We will first see this combined with a simple bass line in the left hand:-

Pop ballad melody (contd)

Figure 11.40. Pop ballad melody version #10 (arpeggios below melody, root in left hand)
(CASSETTE TAPE EXAMPLE 275)

Notice the relationship between this example and **Fig. 11.34**. (triads below melody) - we have taken the same right hand triads and now arpeggiated them below melody. As in previous versions of this melody, the right hand is mainly using **1-3-5** triad upper structures (including inversions over the 3rd or 5th in the bass voice), except for the minor 7th chords where a **b3-5-b7** is used, and the dominant 7th suspension where a **b7-9-11** is used - see text accompanying **Fig. 11.34**. The melody is shown with upward stems, and the supporting arpeggiated tones are shown with downward stems. The extra notes have been added **on all eighth-note subdivisions between the rhythmic attacks in the melody.** For example, in the measure 1 the first melody note E lands on beat **1**, and the second melody note G lands on the '**& of 2**'. Therefore there are 2 8th-note subdivisions between

Pop ballad melody (contd)

these two attacks, namely on the '**& of 1**' and on beat **2**. In both of these places an arpeggiated tone was added, derived from the basic <u>**1-3-5**</u> triad inverted below melody. Similarly on beats **3** & **4** of the measure, there are melodic attacks, so the 'open' eighth-note subdivisions are on the '**& of 3**' and the '**& of 4**'. Again a supporting tone (this time G from the upper G triad) has been added in these rhythmic spaces. These extra notes can be chosen arbitrarily from the upper triad placed below melody - in **Fig. 11.40.**, where there was room for two consecutive supporting tones (downward stems in right hand), they ascended within the triad i.e. G up to C within a C triad in measure **1** - however this could also have been done in a descending manner. Again for this to work properly, the supporting tones must be at a lower dynamic level than the melody, and as with most pop ballad styles you will need to depress the sustain pedal for the duration of each chord. The left hand in the previous example was playing a simple dotted quarter-eighth-half note pattern using the roots of the chords - when first using this 'arpeggio under melody' concept in the right hand, it's easier to combine it with a more basic left hand pattern to get started. However, this right hand idea can also be used with an arpeggiated left hand, as follows:-

Figure 11.41. Pop ballad melody version #11 (arpeggios below melody, and in left hand)
(Cassette Tape Example 276)

(CONTD-->)

Pop ballad melody (contd)

Figure 11.41. (contd)

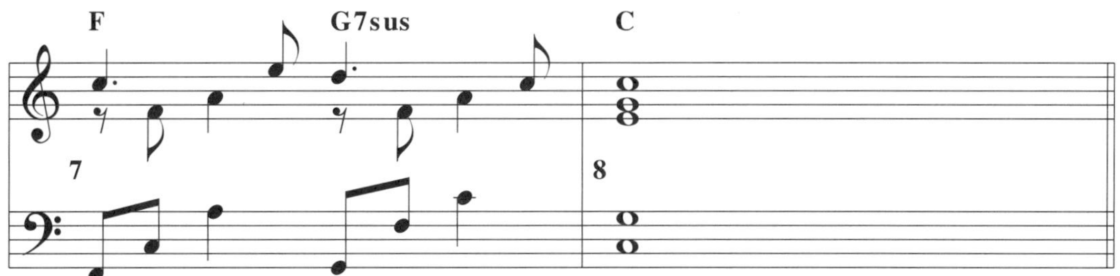

In this example the right hand 'arpeggio under melody' technique is the same as the previous pattern (**Fig. 11.40.**), however the left hand is now arpeggiating open triads as first shown in **Fig. 11.33**. This creates a very saturated, rhythmically subdivided sound - again you have to ensure pianistically that all the arpeggiation doesn't 'bury' the melody!

Now in the next section we are adapting the accompaniment device first shown in **Fig. 11.3**. (a 'rocking' back-and-forth motion in the right hand, using the top notes of a triad on downbeats and the bottom note of the triad on the upbeats) to support the melody. This motion will occur **within the upper structure triad inverted below melody.** In the first setting, only one other tone is being added below the melody on the downbeats. In the second (more challenging) setting, both remaining tones of the upper triad are placed below the melody on the downbeats, leaving the thumb to double the melody note (or play the nearest available triad tone) an octave below, on the upbeats. This requires some rapid hand position changes, and again will normally involve the use of the sustain pedal to achieve a smooth effect. Let's look at the first of these settings:-

Figure 11.42. Pop ballad melody version #12 (alternating right hand motion below melody, #1)

(Cassette Tape Example 277)

Pop ballad melody (contd)

Figure 11.42. (contd)

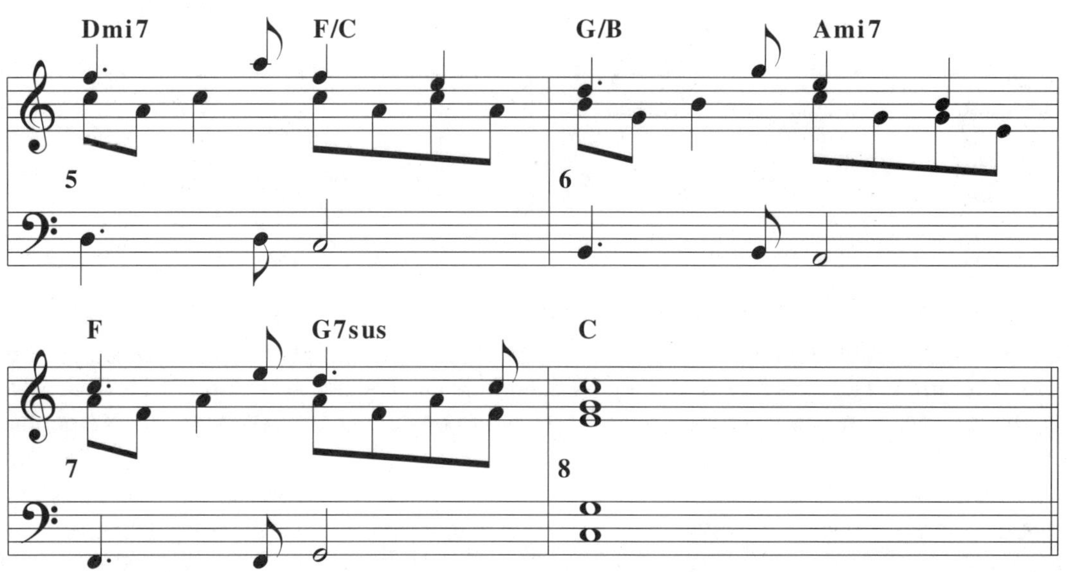

Again it is useful to compare this example to **Fig. 11.34**. (triads below melody) - notice that the upper triads used are exactly the same. In this setting, the nearest triad tone underneath the melody is played on every downbeat for the duration of that melody note. For example, in measure **1** the first melody E is supported by a C triad and lasts for one and a half beats (i.e. until the **'& of 2'**). The nearest triad tone below melody is the note C, which is therefore played on the downbeats (i.e. beats **1** & **2**) until the next melody note. The thumb of the right hand then plays the remaining (i.e. lowest) triad tone on the upbeats - again looking at measure **1**, the thumb is playing the note G (the lowest tone of this inverted C triad) on the **'& of 1'** following the melody note. In this example, if a melody note occurs on an upbeat, then no supporting tones are placed below (although you are of course encouraged to experiment as desired!). Looking at the second half of measure **1**, as we have already seen the melody note G on beat **3** is an out-of-chord tone (see text accompanying **Fig. 11.34**.) - we are still using an upper G triad, but substituting the melody note (E) for the top note of the triad (D). So the nearest triad tone below melody is B, which is placed on the downbeats (**3** & **4**), and the bottom note of the triad (G) is played on the upbeats (**'& of 3'** and **'& of 4'**). Here now is the second setting, using a development of this concept:-

Figure 11.43. Pop ballad melody version #13 (alternating right hand motion below melody ,#2)
(Cassette Tape Example 278)

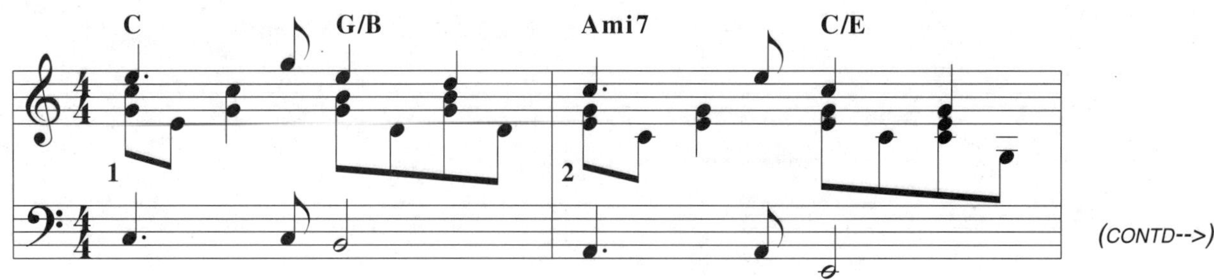

(CONTD-->)

Pop ballad melody (contd)

Figure 11.43. (contd)

Looking again at measure 1 in this example, now both remaining triad tones of the upper C triad (C and G) are placed below the melody, on beats **1** & **2**. Now the thumb is doubling the melody an octave lower on the upbeat i.e. playing the note E an octave below the melody on the '**& of 1**' in this measure. Again no supporting tones are placed under melody notes which land on upbeats, for example the G in the melody on the '**& of 2**' in measure 1. As we said, this is a challenging style in which to support the melody - you will need to change the right hand position fairly quickly - so again don't forget to use the sustain pedal as necessary during each chord, for a smooth result. Even in conjunction with this simple left hand pattern, this right hand device conveys a good sense of rhythmic motion and is useful for building the energy level of an arrangement. As before, you need to ensure that the melody 'projects' pianistically and is not lost within the other supportive tones being played by the right hand.

That's all of the melody examples! There now follows the practice directions summary for this section, and some practice 'charts' for you to use when working on the pop ballad accompaniment and melody devices. Remember - this is how you take control of a leadsheet or chart - rather than be the 'prisoner' of someone else's arrangement - you should strive to become as spontaneous as possible with these methods!

Pop ballad melody (contd)

PRACTICE DIRECTIONS:-

- ***Practice pop ballad melody versions #1 and #2 (Figs. 11.31. & 11.32.), using left hand closed and open triads with a right hand single note melody.***
- ***Practice pop ballad melody version #3 (Fig. 11.33.), using left hand open triad arpeggios with a right hand single note melody.***
  In particular, note the chord tones i.e. 1-5-10, 3-1-5 etc. used by the left hand.
- ***Practice pop ballad melody version #4 (Fig. 11.34.), using left hand as above with triads below melody in right hand.***
  In particular, note the upper structure triad used in the right hand below melody i.e. 1-3-5, b3-5-b7, b7-9-11 etc.
- ***Practice pop ballad melody versions #5, #6 & #7 (Figs. 11.35. - 11.37.), using left hand as above with interval couplings below melody in right hand.***
- ***Practice pop ballad melody versions #8 & #9 (Figs. 11.38. and 11.39.), using left hand as above, first with octaves and then 'filled-in' octaves below melody in right hand.***
- ***Practice pop ballad melody versions #10 & #11 (Figs. 11.40. and 11.41.), with different left hand patterns combined with arpeggios below melody in right hand.***
- ***Practice pop ballad melody versions #12 & #13 (Figs. 11.42. and 11.43.), using a basic left hand root pattern with 'alternating eighth-note' triad tones below melody in right hand.***
- ***Work on applying these 'melody support' devices to other tunes of your choice, and to the practice leadsheets at the end of this chapter.***

Figure 11.44. Practice leadsheet #1 (chords only - for 'comping' practice)

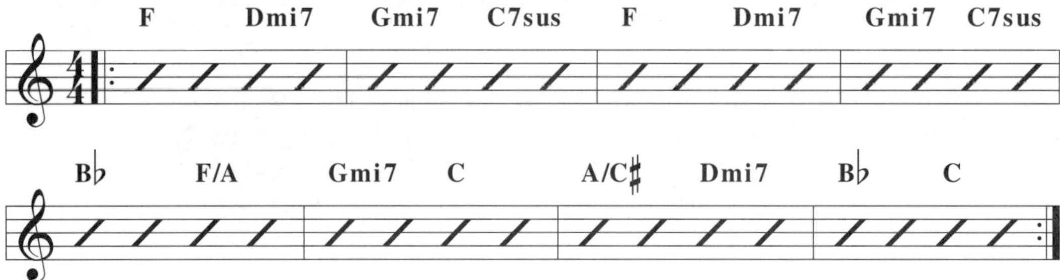

Pop ballad practice examples

Figure 11.45. Practice leadsheet #2 (chords only - 'for 'comping' practice)

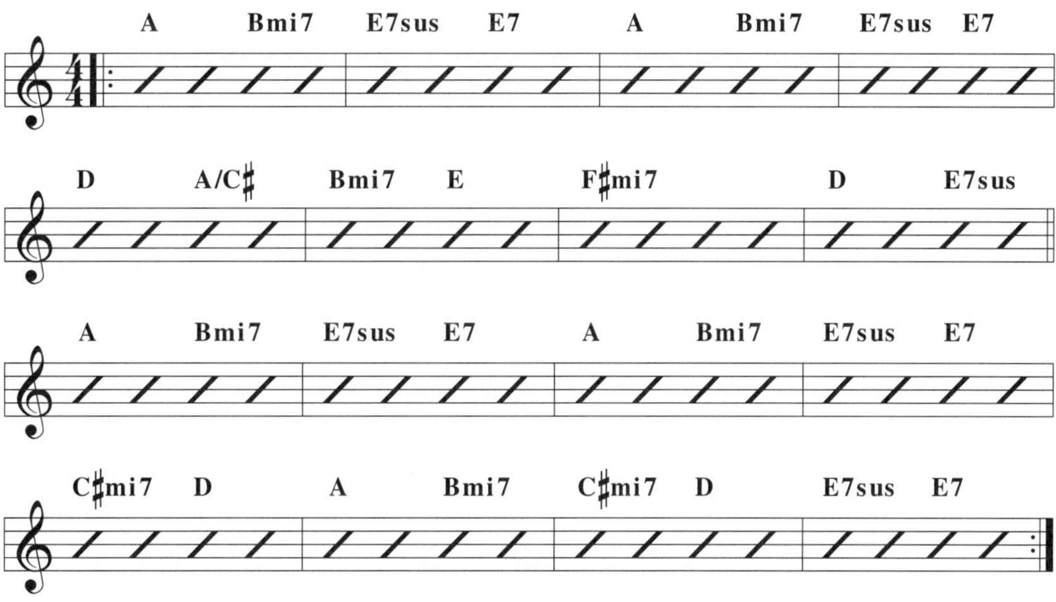

Figure 11.46. Practice leadsheet #3 (chords only - for 'comping' practice)

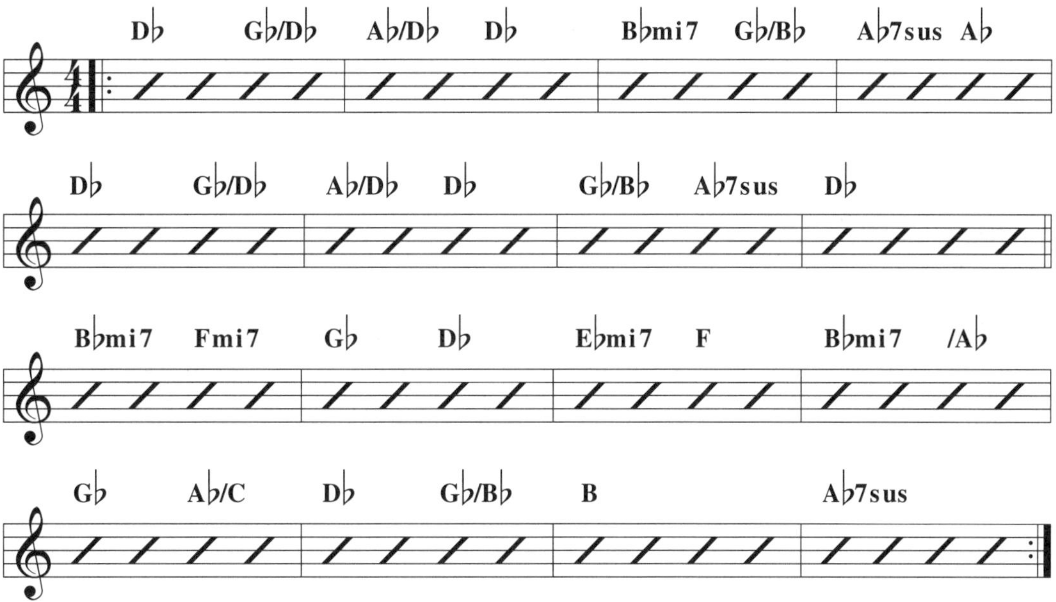

Pop ballad practice examples (contd)

Figure 11.47. Practice leadsheet #4 (melody & chords, for 'melody treatment' or 'comping' practice)

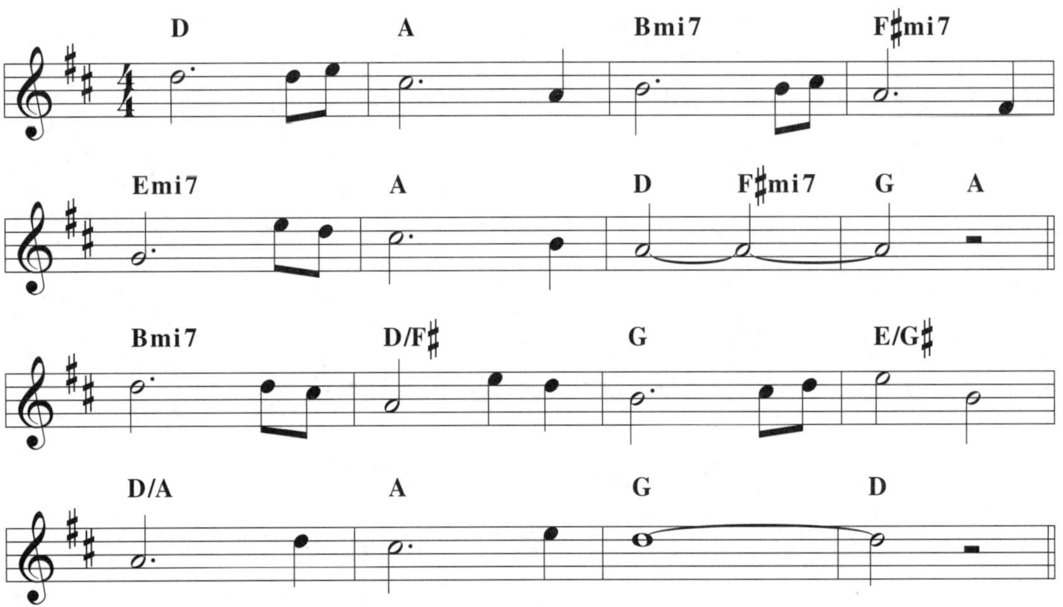

Figure 11.48. Practice leadsheet #5 (melody & chords, for 'melody treatment' or 'comping' practice)

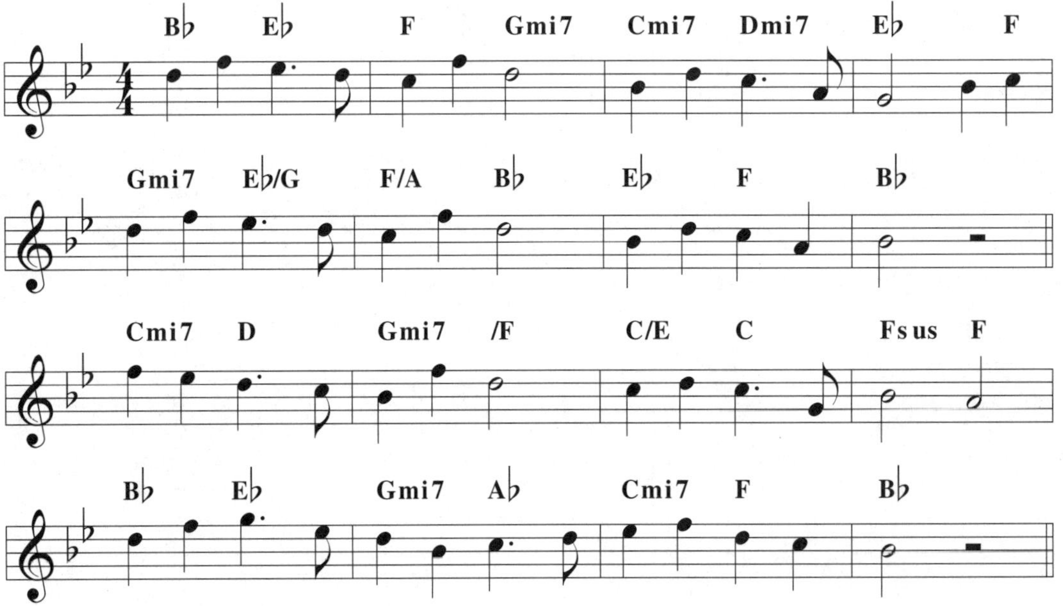

Pop-Rock and Hard Rock

Introduction

The next contemporary style to be examined is pop-rock. This style typically features eighth-note rhythmic subdivisions at medium-to-fast tempos. Most pop-rock applications will be using straight-eighth notes (see text accompanying **Fig. 2.29**.) although a smaller percentage will be using swing-eighth notes (see text accompanying **Figs. 2.30. & 2.31**.), also referred to as a 'shuffle' in this style. A large percentage of today's music falls into the pop-rock category, ranging from the 'softer' style of Christopher Cross, Mike Post etc. through to artists such as Richard Marx, Heart, and Foreigner, as well as the 'harder' rock sounds from bands such as Van Halen, Toto etc. In band settings these styles are characterized by driving repetitive rhythm section grooves. The harder rock examples are often built around the 'heavy' guitar sounds associated with the style, implying simpler harmonic forms i.e. root-5ths of chords. More mainstream pop-rock styles will however use various triad, pentatonic and shape-based concepts in the harmony.

In adapting the pop-rock style to solo piano, we find that the left hand is providing the rhythmic drive and definition required, typically by playing patterns based around the root of the chord (or an inversion) using eighth-note subdivisions. The right hand parts are usually based around triads, chord 'shapes' using fourth intervals (see **Chapter 10**) or fourth intervals built from the minor pentatonic scale (see **Fig. 1.67.** and later explanation in this chapter). These right hand devices generally use a lot of eighth-note anticipations (see text accompanying **Fig. 2.43**.) in conjunction with the left hand parts which land more on the downbeats (especially the 'primary' beats **1** & **3**). The right hand can also invert the various right-hand triads and 'shapes' to accommodate a melody if required - see text at the end of this chapter. Unlike the pop ballad styles studied in the last chapter, when playing pop-rock we generally do **not** use the sustain pedal, as it can detract from the rhythmic 'drive' required.

Pop-rock left hand patterns

We will first look at some left hand patterns. Again these typically feature driving eighth-note rhythms and use of octaves, as follows:-

Figure 12.1. Pop-rock left hand pattern #1 - all eighth-note subdivisions using single root
(Cassette Tape Example 279)

This is the basic pop-rock left hand pattern, providing rhythmic and harmonic definition.

Figure 12.2. Pop-rock left hand pattern #2 - all eighth-notes using doubled octaves
(Cassette Tape Example 280)

As above, but using octaves for a fuller and heavier effect.

Pop-rock left hand patterns (contd)

Figure 12.3. Pop-rock left hand pattern #3 - all quarter note subdivisions using single root
(Cassette Tape Example 281)

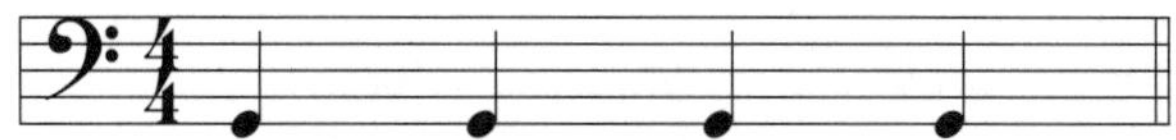

This provides a strong rhythmic foundation on the downbeats. The right hand will generally need to play 8th-note subdivisions/anticipations.

Figure 12.4. Pop-rock left hand pattern #4 - all quarter notes using doubled octaves
(Cassette Tape Example 282)

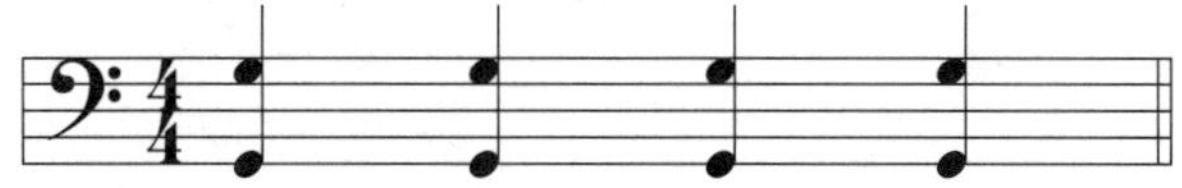

As above, but using octaves for a fuller and 'heavier' effect.

Figure 12.5. Pop-rock left hand pattern #5 - eighth note alternating octaves
(Cassette Tape Example 283)

This eighth-note pattern has a busy and rhythmically driving effect.

Figure 12.6. Pop-rock left hand pattern #6 - dotted quarter-eighth note pairs
(Cassette Tape Example 284)

This pattern is covering the primary beats (**1** & **3**) and providing an 8th-note 'pickup' into each one.

Figure 12.7. Pop-rock left hand pattern #7 - quarter note followed by eighth-note octaves
(Cassette Tape Example 285)

As above but now adding the higher octave on the 'backbeats' i.e. beats **2** & **4**.

Figure 12.8. Pop-rock left hand pattern #8 - eighth notes with upper octave on backbeats
(Cassette Tape Example 286)

A busier version of the previous pattern, now using the remaining 8th-note subdivisions.

All of these patterns will work in a 'straight 8ths' rhythmic subdivision, and the first five patterns (in **Figs. 12.1. - 12.5.**) will also sound good using a 'swing 8ths' rhythmic subdivision. In the remainder of this chapter we will use and combine these various left hand patterns as required. Again don't forget that in this style, the left hand is responsible for providing a solid, driving rhythmic foundation as well as basic harmonic definition.

Pop-rock alternating triad concepts

A great deal of the harmony used in pop-rock styles is based around the use of alternating triads. This involves 'alternating' two or more triads over a single root voice, for the duration of a chord. In this section we will focus on major, minor and dominant/suspended chords to see what alternating triads are available on each. From a keyboardist's point of view, these triads are then played in the right hand using eighth-note anticipations, playing off the downbeats established by the left hand part. An important point to keep in mind is that, while the use of these triads adds a stylistic element to the music, the exact chord symbols or voicings will rarely be shown on a leadsheet - so often it will be up to you to bring this element to the music by looking at the basic chord type and figuring out which alternating triad devices will work! The voiceleading between the alternating triads on each chord, will typically occur in a circle-of-fifths or circle-of-fourths fashion - see **Chapter 4**.

The following examples are labelled using a numerical 'formula' describing the relationship of the upper triads to the root of the overall chord. However, another important angle to keep in mind is how the alternating triads fit into the key of the song. In most cases the choice of triads needs to be diatonic to (i.e. fit within) the major or minor key that the song is using. Viewed from this perspective, the alternating triads are often the **1**, **4** and **5** of the major key area, used over various diatonic roots from the same scale source. In the following examples, note that everything is diatonic to a C major scale and that the upper triads used are the **1**, **4** and **5** (i.e. C, F and G) of the scale - however with respect to each type of chord, different vertical relationships are created:-

Figure 12.9. '5 to 1' alternating triads on major chord
(Cassette Tape Example 287)

With respect to the overall **C** chord, the upper **G** triad is a **5**, (or a **5-7-9** upper structure - see **Fig. 5.4.**) resolving to a **C** triad which is a **1** (or a **1-3-5** upper structure - see **Fig. 5.1.**). This figure is typically used within major chords built from the **1st** & **4th** degrees of a major key (i.e. C & F major chords in the key of C major) and built from the **b3rd** & **b6th** degrees of a minor key (i.e. C & F major chords in the key of A minor). Now a rhythmic example:-

Figure 12.10. '5 to 1' alternating triads on major chord - rhythmic example
(Cassette Tape Example 288)

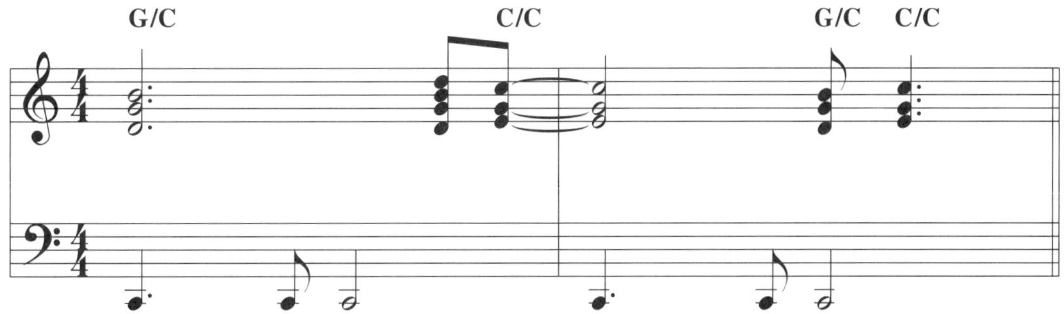

In the above (and subsequent) examples I have reflected all of the alternating triads in the chord symbols - however, don't forget that in many cases the leadsheet might only say (for the above example) two measures of C major - it would then be up to you to spontaneously apply the alternating triad concepts. Notice in this example

Pop-rock alternating triad concepts (contd)

that the right hand is anticipating beats **1** & **4** of the second measure, while the left hand (using pattern **#6** - see **Fig. 12.6.**) is landing on the primary beats **1** & **3** of each measure.

Figure 12.11. '4 to 1' alternating triads on major chord
(CASSETTE TAPE EXAMPLE 289)

With respect to the overall **C** chord, the upper **F** triad is a **4**, resolving to a **C** triad which is a **1** (or a **1-3-5** upper structure - see **Fig. 5.1.**). This figure is typically used within major chords built from the **1st** & **5th** degrees of a major key (i.e. C & G major chords in the key of C major) and built from the **b3rd** & **b7th** degrees of a minor key (i.e. C & G major chords in the key of A minor). Now a rhythmic example:-

Figure 12.12. '4 to 1' alternating triads on major chord - rhythmic example
(CASSETTE TAPE EXAMPLE 290)

Notice in this example that the right hand is anticipating beats **3** & **4** in the first measure, while the left hand (using pattern **#5** - see **Fig. 12.5.**) is providing all the 8th-note subdivisions using alternating octaves. Now we will look at a rhythmic example combining the previous '**5 to 1**' and '**4 to 1**' devices - i.e. using the **1**, **4** and **5** upper triads on the major chord (with left hand pattern **#2** - see **Fig. 12.2.**):-

Figure 12.13. Mixing 1, 4 and 5 alternating triads on major chord - rhythmic example
(CASSETTE TAPE EXAMPLE 291)

Pop-rock alternating triad concepts (contd)

Now we will continue looking at the different alternating triad 'formulae' as follows:-

Figure 12.14. '9 to 1' alternating triads on major chord
(Cassette Tape Example 292)

With respect to the overall F chord, the upper G triad is a 9 (or a 9-#11-13 upper structure - see **Fig. 5.7.**), resolving to an F triad which is a 1 (or a 1-3-5 upper structure - see **Fig. 5.1.**). This figure is typically used within major chords built from the **4th** degree of a major key (i.e. F major chord in the key of C major) and built from the **b6th** degree of a minor key (i.e. F major chord in the key of A minor). Now a rhythmic example:-

Figure 12.15. '9 to 1' alternating triads on major chord - rhythmic example
(Cassette Tape Example 293)

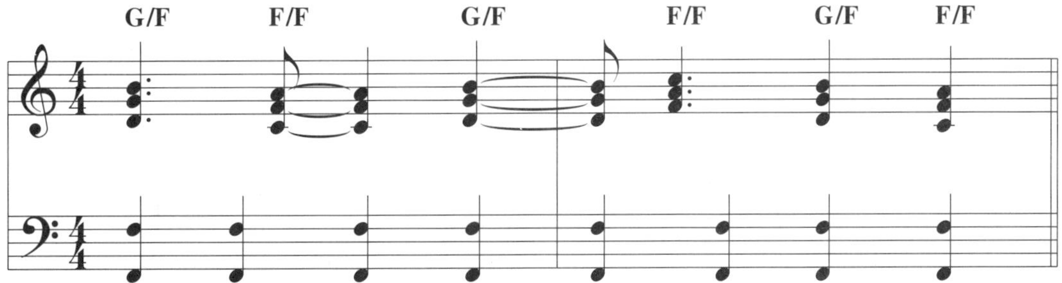

Notice in this example that the right hand is anticipating beat **3** in the first measure and beat **2** in the second measure, by an eighth note each time. The left hand is using pattern **#4** (see **Fig. 12.4.**), giving a strong downbeat using doubled octaves.

Figure 12.16. '9 to 5' alternating triads on major chord
(Cassette Tape Example 294)

With respect to the overall F chord, the upper G triad is a 9 (or a 9-#11-13 upper structure - see **Fig. 5.7.**), moving to a C triad which is a 5 (or a 5-7-9 upper structure - see **Fig. 5.4.**). This figure creates a more sophisticated sound vertically as both of the triad-over-root chords here contain some vertical tension i.e. we do not in this case resolve to a basic triad. This alternating triad combination is found within major chords built from the **4th** and **b7th** degrees of a major key (i.e. F & Bb major chords in the key of C major), and built from the **b6th** degree of a minor key (i.e. an F major chord in the key of A minor). Now a rhythmic example (on the following page):-

Pop-rock alternating triad concepts (contd)

Figure 12.17. '9 to 5' alternating triads on major chord - rhythmic example
(Cassette Tape Example 295)

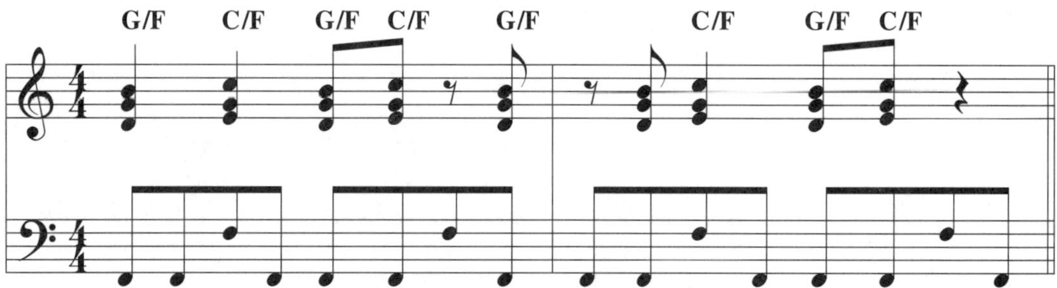

Notice in this example that the right hand is anticipating beat **4** in the first measure and beats **1** & **4** in the second measure. The left hand is using pattern **#8** (see **Fig. 12.8.**), giving a busy yet driving effect. Now we will look at a rhythmic example combining the previous '**5 to 1**' and '**9 to 5**' devices - i.e. using the **1**, **5** and **9** upper triads on the major chord (and left hand rhythm pattern **#3** - see **Fig. 12.3.**):-

Figure 12.18. Mixing 1, 5 and 9 alternating triads on major chord - rhythmic example
(Cassette Tape Example 296)

Now we will continue looking at the different alternating triad 'formulae' as follows:-

Figure 12.19. 'b7 to b3' alternating triads on minor chord
(Cassette Tape Example 297)

This device works within a **minor** or **minor 7th**-type chord. With respect to the overall **Ami** or **Ami7** chord, the upper **G** triad is a **b7** (or a **b7-9-11** upper structure - see **Fig. 5.2.**), resolving to a **C** triad which is a **b3** (or a **b3-5-b7** upper structure - see **Fig. 5.6.**). This figure is typically used within minor chords built from the **2nd** & **6th** degrees of a major key (i.e. Dmi7 & Ami7 in the key of C major), and built from the **1st** & **4th** degrees of a minor key (i.e. Ami7 & Dmi7 in the key of A minor). Now a rhythmic example:-

Pop-rock alternating triad concepts (contd)

Figure 12.20. 'b7 to b3' alternating triads on minor chord - rhythmic example
(CASSETTE TAPE EXAMPLE 298)

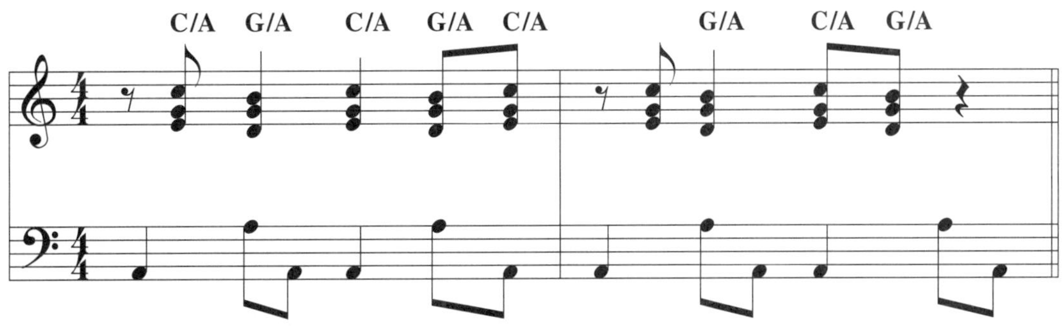

Notice in this example that the right hand is anticipating beats **1** & **4** in the second measure. The left hand is using pattern **#7** (see Fig. **12.7**.) giving good rhythmic 'forward motion' to the overall sound.

Figure 12.21. 'b7 to 1' alternating triads on dominant chord
(CASSETTE TAPE EXAMPLE 299)

This device works within a dominant chord or a basic triad form functioning as a '**five**' chord (i.e. built from the 5th degree) in a key. With respect to the overall **G** or **G7** chord, the upper **F** triad is a **b7** (or a **b7-9-11** upper structure - see **Fig. 5.2.**), resolving to a G triad which is a **1** (or a **1-3-5** upper structure - see **Fig. 5.1.**). The use of this device will alternately 'suspend' and 'unsuspend' the dominant chord. Now a rhythmic example:-

Figure 12.22. 'b7 to 1' alternating triads on dominant chord - rhythmic example
(CASSETTE TAPE EXAMPLE 300)

Notice in this example that the right hand is anticipating beat **4** in the first measure and beat **1** in the second measure. The left hand is using pattern **#1** (see **Fig. 12.1**.), providing a steady eighth-note pulse.

CHAPTER TWELVE

Pop-rock pentatonic scale intervals

The minor pentatonic scale (see **Fig. 1.67**. and accompanying text) is widely used in contemporary pop-rock styles. A useful application of the minor pentatonic scale in rhythmic 'comping' situations is to construct perfect 4th intervals from this scale, and then to place those intervals over different roots, creating various vertical relationships in the process. For example, if we were to take all of the perfect 4th intervals available within the C minor pentatonic scale and place them over the note C in the root, we would obtain the following:-

Figure 12.23. C minor pentatonic scale 4th intervals over C in bass voice
(Cassette Tape Example 301)

Notice the vertical functions of each 4th interval with respect to the root, are indicated above the staff, i.e. the first interval **F-Bb** is shown as an **11-b7** pair with respect to the note C as the root. These couplings could be used over chords such as **Cmi**, **Cmi7**, **C(no 3rd)** etc. With care and depending on the context, they may even be used over major and dominant chords to impart more of a 'blues' or minor pentatonic feeling.

Now we will take the same 4th interval couplings available within the C minor pentatonic scale, and look at the vertical relationships created when we place these intervals over different root note choices, as follows:-

Figure 12.24. C minor pentatonic scale 4th intervals over Eb in bass voice
(Cassette Tape Example 302)

These couplings could be used over such chords as **Eb**, **Eb6**, **Eb69**, **Eb(add9)**, **Ebma7** etc. (Again note the vertical functions indicated above the staff).

Figure 12.25. C minor pentatonic scale 4th intervals over F in bass voice
(Cassette Tape Example 303)

These couplings could be used over such chords as **Fmi**, **Fmi7**, **Fsus**, **F(no 3rd)**, **Fmi7sus**, **F7sus** etc. With care they might even be used over F dominant or major chords, again generating more of a 'blues' impression.

Pop-rock pentatonic scale intervals (contd)

Figure 12.26. C minor pentatonic scale 4th intervals over G in bass voice

(CASSETTE TAPE EXAMPLE 304)

These couplings could be used over such chords as **Gmi**, **Gmi7**, **Gmi7sus** etc., however the **#5** (Eb here) may need careful handling, being an out-of-chord tone. Again with care these may also be used over G dominant/suspended chords.

Figure 12.27. C minor pentatonic scale 4th intervals over Ab in bass voice

(CASSETTE TAPE EXAMPLE 305)

These couplings could be used over such chords as **Ab**, **Ab6**, **Ab69**, **Ab(add9)**, **Abma7** etc.

Figure 12.28. C minor pentatonic scale 4th intervals over Bb in bass voice

(CASSETTE TAPE EXAMPLE 306)

These couplings could be used over such chords as **Bb(no 3rd)**, **Bbsus**, **Bb7sus** etc. Again with care they might be used over Bb dominant or major chords, depending upon the context.

We will now look at a rhythmic comping example combining together all of the above root note choices below the fourth intervals in a C minor pentatonic scale. As we have noted in the individual examples, in some cases out-of-chord tones are produced. In a solo keyboard context this is generally not a problem, as all of the vertical relationships generated between the interval couplings and the various chord roots, are tonally acceptable - however in an ensemble situation you would need to co-ordinate with other chord-playing instruments (i.e. guitar) to avoid any voicing clashes. Here now is the eight-measure comping example:-

Pop-rock pentatonic scale intervals (contd)

Figure 12.29. Pop-rock comping example using right-hand 4th interval couplings from C minor pentatonic scale *(CASSETTE TAPE EXAMPLE 307)*

We can analyze each measure above for the use of right-hand fourth interval couplings as follows:-

Pop-rock pentatonic scale intervals (contd)

- Measure 1 Here we are using the pentatonic 4th couplings over the **Cmi7** chord as in **Fig. 12.23.** In addition to the tones implied by the chord symbol, we are adding an **11th** (F) as part of the **1-11** coupling. The 11th is normally a safe and effective addition to minor 7th-type chords.

- Measure 2 Here we are using the pentatonic 4th couplings over the **Eb** chord as in **Fig. 12.24.** In addition to the tones implied by the chord symbol, we are adding the **6th** and **9th** of the chord as a result of using the **3-6**, **6-9** and **9-5** couplings. The 9th is normally a safe addition to the major chord in most situations. The 6th however can sometimes sound 'dated' and should be used with care - here it works well because the 6th of the Eb chord is C, which is the tonic of the key being used.

- Measures 3 & 4 Here we are using the pentatonic 4th couplings over the **Ab** chord as in **Fig. 12.27**. In addition to the tones implied by the chord symbol, we are adding the **6th**, **7th** & **9th** of the chord as a result of using the **3-6**, **9-5**, **6-9** and **7-3** couplings. Care needs to be taken when using major 7ths in rock styles - sometimes this interval may be too angular or dissonant - here it works well because the 7th of the Ab chord is G, which is the 5th scale degree (and therefore an important and prominent tone) of the key. In addition we are using the 7th as a passing tone on the '**& of 1**' in both measures. Refer to measure 2 comments regarding the use of the 6th & 9th on the major chord.

- Measure 5 Here we are using the pentatonic 4th couplings over the **Bbsus** chord as in **Fig. 12.28**. In addition to the tones implied by the chord symbol, we are adding the **6th** and **9th** of the chord as a result of using the **6-9** and **9-5** couplings. Again the 6th & 9th here are available extensions which reinforce the overall key of the song.

- Measure 6 Here we are using the pentatonic 4th couplings over the **F7sus** chord as in **Fig. 12.25**. In addition to the tones implied by the chord symbol, we are adding the **9th** of the chord as a result of using the **9-5** coupling. Again the 9th is a safe extension to use here.

- Measure 7 Here we are again using the pentatonic 4th couplings over the **Cmi7** chord as in **Fig. 12.23.** In addition to the tones implied by the chord symbol, we are adding the **11th** as a result of using the **1-11** & **11-b7** couplings. See measure 1 comments.

- Measure 8 Here we are using the pentatonic 4th couplings over the **Gmi7** chord as in **Fig. 12.26**. In addition to the tones implied by the chord symbol, we are adding the **11th** and **#5th** of the chord as a result of using the **11-b7** and **b3-#5** couplings. The 11th is generally safe on minor chords (see measure 1 comments) but the raised 5th needs to be used with care and will conflict if an unaltered (perfect) 5th is also being used. This conflict does not occur in the example, and the use of the #5th (Eb) further reinforces the key being used.

Now on the following page we have the practice directions for the areas covered so far in this chapter:-

CHAPTER TWELVE

PRACTICE DIRECTIONS:-

- ***Practice the pop-rock left hand patterns as in Figs. 12.1. - 12.8.***
- ***Practice the alternating triad examples on major, minor and dominant chords as in Figs. 12.9. - 12.22.***
  (For extra practice, try transposing these examples into different keys!)
- ***Practice the pentatonic 4th intervals over individual chords as in Figs. 12.23. - 12.28.***
- ***Practice the pentatonic 4th interval comping example as in Fig. 12.29.***
  (This is another good example for transposing practice!)

Pop-rock chord chart interpretation

In the next section we will look at a series of chord charts and illustrate different comping solutions to the charts in pop-rock and hard rock styles. In those solutions which use the left hand patterns in **Figs. 12.1. - 12.5.** (see comments at the bottom of p.186) we will also present a 'swing 8ths' as well as a 'straight 8ths' treatment. The right hand devices used to interpret the chord charts will be:-

- Alternating triad concepts (see **Figs. 12.9.** - **12.22.** and accompanying text in this chapter), inverted and voiceled according to the guidelines in **Chapter 4**.
- Pentatonic 4th interval couplings (see **Figs. 12.23.** - **12.29.** and accompanying text in this chapter).
- 'Double-4th' chord shapes (see **Chapter 10**).
- Arpeggiated triads (see **Figs. 11.23.** - **11.27.** and text in **Chapter 11**).
- 'Parallel' interval couplings within triads (see **Fig. 11.16.** and text in **Chapter 11**).
- '**9 to 1**' resolutions within triads (see **Chapter 8**).
- '**4 to 3**' resolutions within triads (see **Chapter 9**).

We will first look at a simple four-measure chord chart or 'leadsheet' as follows:-

Figure 12.30. Chord chart example #1

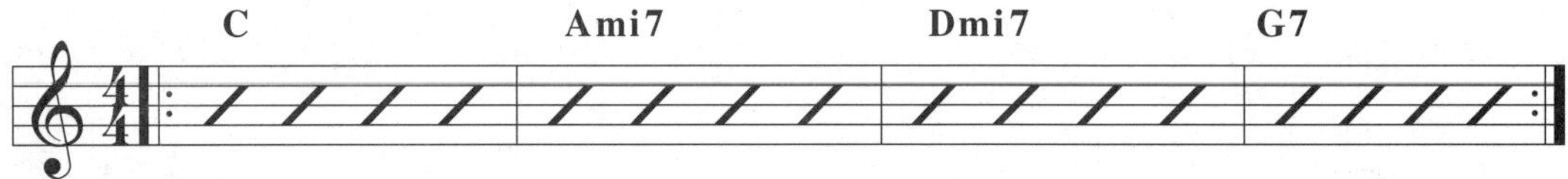

We will interpret this typical 1 - 6 - 2 - 5 progression with alternating triads as follows:-

Pop-rock chord chart interpretation (contd)

Figure 12.31. Pop-rock comping solution for chord chart #1 (Fig. 12.30.)
(CASSETTE TAPE EXAMPLE 308 - 'STRAIGHT 8THS')
(CASSETTE TAPE EXAMPLE 309 - 'SWING 8THS')

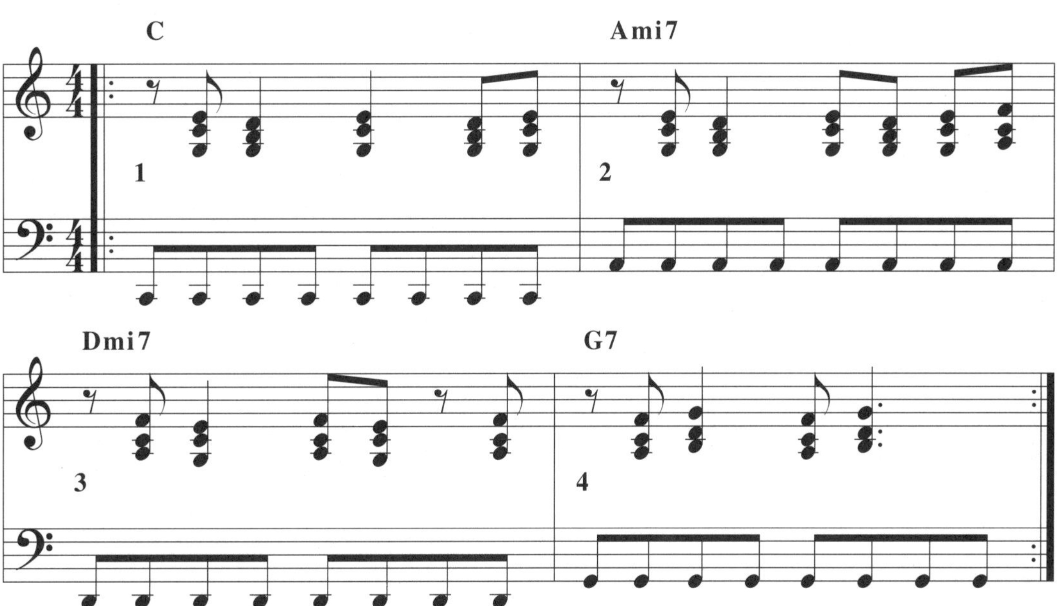

In this example we are using a basic eighth-note subdivision in the left hand (see **Fig. 12.1**.). We can analyze the right-hand devices used in each measure as follows:-

- Measure 1 On the **C** chord we are using '**5 to 1**' alternating triads (see **Fig. 12.9**.). The C triad on the '**& of 4**' is anticipating beat **1** of measure 2 and therefore harmonically should be considered as part of the following Ami7 chord.

- Measure 2 On the **Ami7** chord we are using '**b7 to b3**' alternating triads (see **Fig. 12.19**.). The F triad on the '**& of 4**' is anticipating beat **1** of measure 3 and therefore harmonically should be considered as part of the following Dmi7 chord.

- Measure 3 On the **Dmi7** chord we are again using '**b7 to b3**' alternating triads (see **Fig. 12.19**.). The F triad on the '**& of 4**' is anticipating beat **1** of measure 4 and therefore harmonically should be considered as part of the following G7 chord. Also note that the C triad on the '**& of 3**' is anticipating beat **4** of the measure.

- Measure 4 On the **G7** chord we are using '**b7 to 1**' alternating triads (see **Fig. 12. 21**.). The G triad on the '**& of 3**' is anticipating beat **4** of the measure. Note that the use of these triads over the dominant means that we are alternating between a suspended (F/G) and unsuspended (G/G) chord.

Also observe that we are using all inversions of the upper triads as necessary, and that the voiceleading between triads is very typically in a circle-of-fifths or circle-of-fourths fashion. A good command of the principles and exercises in **Chapters 4** and **5** is the key to being spontaneous in your application of alternating triads! Note also that the upper triads used were collectively the 1, 4 & 5 (C, F & G) of the key (C major) - this will typically be the case in simpler applications. Now we'll look at the second chord chart example as follows:-

Pop-rock chord chart interpretation (contd)

Figure 12.32. Chord chart example #2

This progression suggests a more 'modal' context - all of the chords are within a '**C Mixolydian**' scale source restriction (see **Fig. 1.42**. and accompanying text). The first solution features a dotted quarter-eighth note bass pattern (see **Fig. 12.6**.), and the right hand is mixing some arpeggiation and 'parallel' interval couplings in with the alternating triads as follows:-

Figure 12.33. Pop-rock comping solution a) for chord chart #2 (Fig. 12.32.)
(Cassette Tape Example 310 - 'Straight 8ths')

Again we will analyze each measure as follows:-

- Measure 1 On the **C** chord we start out by using '**5 to 1**' alternating triads (see **Fig. 12.9**.), with the C triad on the '**& of 2**' anticipating beat **3**. Starting on the '**& of 3**' we then arpeggiate the **1** triad (C) - this creates eighth-note 'pickups' into the following measure.

- Measure 2 On the **Ami7** chord we start with 'parallel' interval couplings within a C triad, one of the '**b7 to b3**' alternating triads (C & G) used on this chord. (The C triad is also a **b3-5-b7** upper structure on the Ami7 chord - see **Fig. 5.6**.). We first saw the 'parallel' interval concept used within an upper triad, in **Fig. 11.16**. Later in the measure on the '**& of 3**' (anticipating beat **4**) and the '**& of 4**', we continue to use the '**b7 to b3**' alternating triads (see **Fig. 12.19**.).

Pop-rock chord chart interpretation (contd)

- Measure 3 On the **Bb** chord we start out by using '**5 to 1**' alternating triads (see **Fig. 12.9.**), with the Bb triad on the '**& of 2**' anticipating beat **3**. Starting on the '**& of 3**' we then arpeggiate the **1** triad (Bb) - this again creates eighth-note 'pickups' into the following measure.

- Measure 4 On the **Gmi7** chord we are again using 'parallel' interval couplings within the **b3-5-b7** upper structure Bb triad, in a similar manner to measure 2. Again we then use the '**b7 to b3**' alternating triads (see **Fig. 12.19.**) on the '**& of 3**' (anticipating beat **4**) and the '**& of 4**'.

The second version of this chart now has an eighth-note alternating octave pattern in the left hand (see **Fig. 12.5.**) and features '**9 to 1**' resolutions within upper triads in the right hand as follows:-

Figure 12.34. Pop-rock comping solution b) for chord chart #2 (Fig. 12.32.)
(CASSETTE TAPE EXAMPLE 311 - 'STRAIGHT 8THS')
(CASSETTE TAPE EXAMPLE 312 - 'SWING 8THS')

Again we will analyze each measure as follows:-

- Measure 1 On the **C** chord we are using a '**9 to 1**' resolution within the **1-3-5** basic C triad upper structure (see **Fig. 8.12.**). For extra 'weight' the note G has been doubled.

- Measure 2 On the **Ami7** chord we are using a '**9 to 1**' resolution within the **b3-5-b7** upper structure C triad (see **Figs. 5.6. & 8.14.**). Again we are doubling the top note G.

- Measure 3 On the **Bb** chord we are using a '**9 to 1**' resolution within the **1-3-5** basic Bb triad upper structure (see **Fig. 8.12.**). For extra 'weight' the note F has been doubled.

- Measure 4 On the **Gmi7** chord we are using a '**9 to 1**' resolution within the **b3-5-b7** upper structure Bb triad (see **Figs. 5.6.** & **8.14.**) Again we are doubling the top note F.

Pop-rock chord chart interpretation (contd)

We will now interpret the next chord charts using some 'harder' rock styles - this involves using more 'root-5th' couplings in the right hand, together with pentatonic 4th intervals, 'double-4th' chords and '**9 to 1**' resolutions. The root-5th interval in the right hand can be considered as an inversion of the **5-1** pentatonic 4th coupling (see earlier text in this chapter). 'Double-4th' chords of particular interest in harder rock styles are the **9-5-1** on major chords (see **Fig. 10.7**.) and the **5-1-11** and **11-b7-b3** on minor chords (see **Figs. 10.3**. & **10.5**.). Resolving from 9ths on major chords and 11ths on minor chords is also a useful device. Here is the next chord chart:-

Figure 12.35. Chord chart example #3

Firstly we will use a basic root-5th approach in the right hand, together with a steady eighth-note pulse in the left hand (see **Fig. 12.1**.) as follows:-

Figure 12.36. Pop-rock comping solution a) for chord chart #3 (Fig. 12.35.)
(Cassette Tape Example 313 - 'Straight 8ths')
(Cassette Tape Example 314 - 'Swing 8ths')

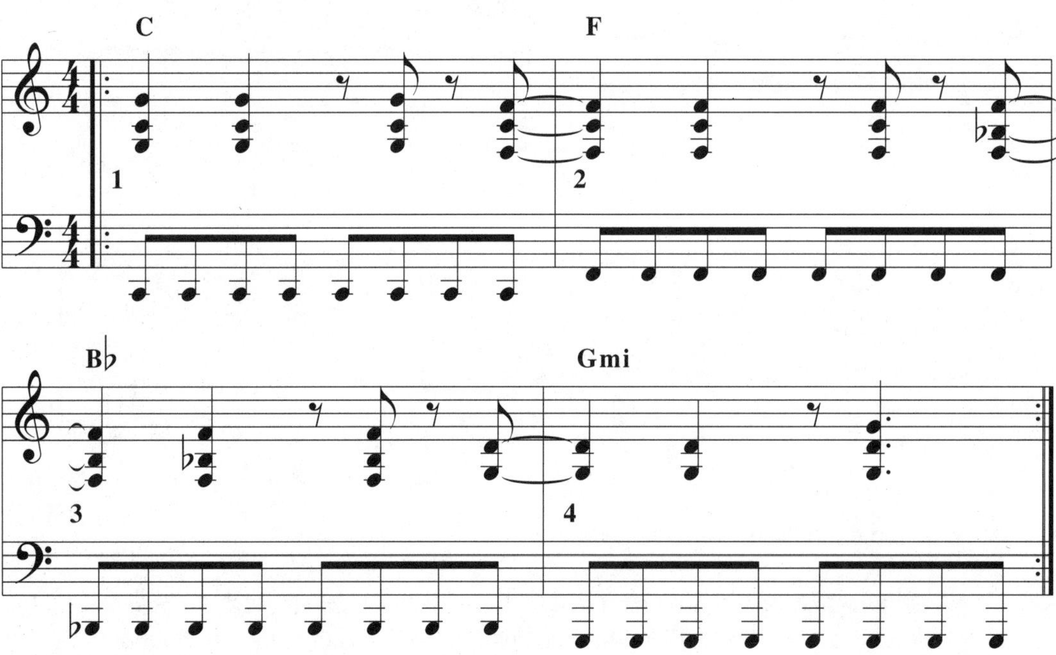

On each measure we are playing the root-5th of the chord in the right hand - this gives a very 'hollow' and guitar-like effect suited to basic rock styles. Notice also we are anticipating beat **1** of measures **2**, **3** and **4** in the right hand, against the left hand part which is covering all the downbeats - a common rhythmic treatment. The next version of these chords adds the use of 'double-4th' shape ideas to the basic root-5th couplings in the right hand, while the left hand plays a steady quarter-note pulse (see **Fig. 12.3**.) as follows:-

Pop-rock chord chart interpretation (contd)

Figure 12.37. Pop-rock comping solution b) for chord chart #3 (Fig. 12.35.)
(Cassette Tape Example 315 - 'Straight 8ths')
(Cassette Tape Example 316 - 'Swing 8ths')

We can analyze each measure here as follows:-

- Measure 1 On the **C** chord, all of the notes (except the anticipation on the '**& of 4**') are within the **9-5-1** double-4th structure (see **Fig. 10.7.**). The root (C) on beat **1** is moving to the 9th (D) on beats **2** & **3**, resolving back to the root on the '**& of 3**'.

- Measure 2 On the **F** chord, all of the notes are again within the **9-5-1** double-4th structure (see **Fig. 10.7.**). The 9th (G) on beat **3** is resolving to the root (F) on the '**& of 3**'.

- Measure 3 On the **Bb** chord, all of the notes are again within the **9-5-1** double-4th structure (see **Fig. 10.7.**). The root (Bb) on beat **1** is moving to the 9th (C) on beats **2** & **3**, resolving back to the root on the '**& of 3**'.

- Measure 4 On the **Gmi** chord, all of the notes are within the **5-1-11** double-4th structure (see **Fig. 10.3.**). The 11th (C) on beat **3** is moving to the 5th (D) on the '**& of 3**'.

The next version of this chart now arpeggiates double-4th structures in the right hand, while the left hand is using eighth-note doubled octaves (see **Fig. 12.2.**) as shown on the following page:-

Pop-rock chord chart interpretation (contd)

Figure 12.38. Pop-rock comping solution c) for chord chart #3 (Fig. 12.35.)
(Cassette Tape Example 317 - 'Straight 8ths')
(Cassette Tape Example 318 - 'Swing 8ths')

Again we can analyze each measure as follows:-

- Measure 1 On the **C** chord we are arpeggiating the **9-5-1** double-4th structure (see **Fig. 10.7.**), with the 5th of the chord (G) anticipating beat **3**. The use of the successive 5th intervals here (i.e. G to D and C to G) gives an effective modern sound.

- Measure 2 On the **F** chord we are again arpeggiating the **9-5-1** double-4th structure (see **Fig. 10.7.**), with the root of the chord (F) anticipating beat **3**. Again note that beat **1** of this measure is anticipated in the previous measure, using the note G which is plural to both chords (i.e. G is the 5th of the C chord and the 9th of the F chord).

- Measure 3 On the **Bb** chord we are again arpeggiating the **9-5-1** double-4th structure (see **Fig. 10.7.**), with the 5th of the chord (F) anticipating beat **3**.

- Measure 4 On the **Gmi** chord we are arpeggiating the **11-b7-b3** double-4th structure (see **Fig. 10.5.**), with the 7th of the chord (F) anticipating beat **3**. Similar right-hand anticipation is being used between measures 3 & 4 as between measures 1 & 2 - this time the note C (which is anticipating beat **1** of measure **4**) is both the 9th of the preceeding chord (Bb) and the 11th of the following chord (Gmi).

Now we will look at another chord chart example as follows:-

Figure 12.39. Chord chart example #4

Pop-rock chord chart interpretation (contd)

We will first of all interpret this chart with simple root-5th couplings in the right hand, together with a steady eighth-note pulse in the left hand (see **Fig. 12.1**.) as follows:-

Figure 12.40. Pop-rock comping solution a) for chord chart #4 (Fig. 12.39.)
(Cassette Tape Example 319 - 'Straight 8ths')
(Cassette Tape Example 320 - 'Swing 8ths')

In the above example note that in the right hand we are anticipating beat **3** in measures **1** & **3** and beat **4** in measures **2** & **4**. As an alternative interpretation we will now use pentatonic 4th interval couplings in the right hand, together with a quarter-eighth octave pattern in the left hand (see **Fig. 12.7**.). As previously discussed, the use of these 4th couplings can result in out-of-chord tones and/or imply different chord qualities - here they imply that the C chord has become a Cmi or Cmi7-type chord, and that the F chord has become an Fsus or F7sus-type chord. This 'bending' of the chord quality will often work in rock styles as long as other potentially conflicting chord tones are not used in conjunction with the pentatonic 4th couplings. As we said before, this can often impart a 'blues' or minor pentatonic feeling to a progression, as in the following example:-

Figure 12.41. Pop-rock comping solution b) for chord chart #4 (Fig. 12.39.)
(Cassette Tape Example 321 - 'Straight 8ths')

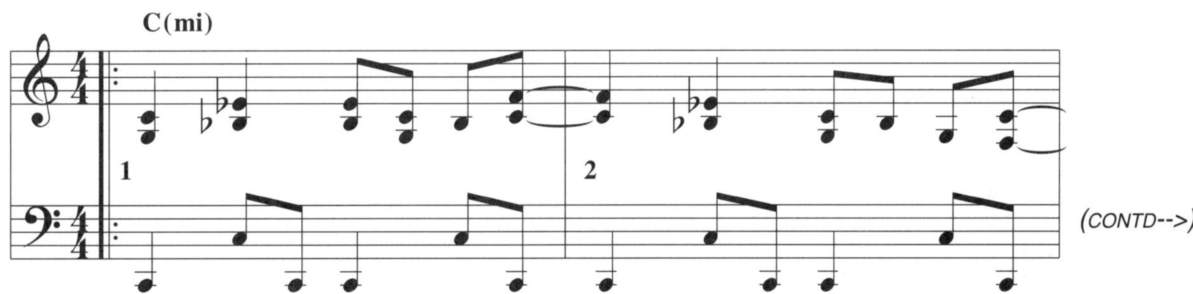

(CONTD-->)

Pop-rock chord chart interpretation (contd)

Figure 12.41. (contd)

We can analyze each measure as follows:-

- Measure 1 On the **C** chord we are using **5-1**, **b7-b3**, and **1-11** pentatonic 4th couplings (see **Fig. 12.23.**). In addition the b7th (Bb) is used on beat **4** as a passing tone. The **1-11** coupling used on the '**& of 4**' is anticipating beat **1** of the next measure.

- Measure 2 Continuing on the **C** chord, we are using same 4th couplings as for measure 1. In addition the 5th (G) & b7th (Bb) are used as passing tones, on the '**& of 3**' and beat **4** respectively. The F-C interval on the '**& of 4**' is anticipating beat **1** of measure **3** and therefore harmonically should be considered as part of the following F chord.

- Measure 3 On the **F** chord we are using **5-1** and **11-b7** pentatonic 4th couplings (see **Fig. 12.25.**). The measure begins with a root-5th interval (F-C) that could be considered as an inverted **5-1** 4th coupling. In addition the 5th and root are used as passing tones, on the '**& of 3**' and beat **4**.

- Measure 4 Continuing on the **F** chord, in addition to the previous 4th couplings we are also using a **1-11** interval on the '**& of 3**', anticipating beat **4**.

Now we will consider an eight-measure leadsheet example containing 'punches' i.e. anticipations in the harmonic rhythm. In the earlier examples we have frequently used eighth-note anticipations in the right hand as a stylistic device, however the left hand has generally been covering the downbeats (consistent with the harmonic rhythm of the chart). There will be situations however where the chord rhythm itself features eighth-note anticipations, as on the following chart example using rhythmic notation symbols (review rhythmic notation in **Chapter 2** as necessary):-

Figure 12.42. Chord chart example #5

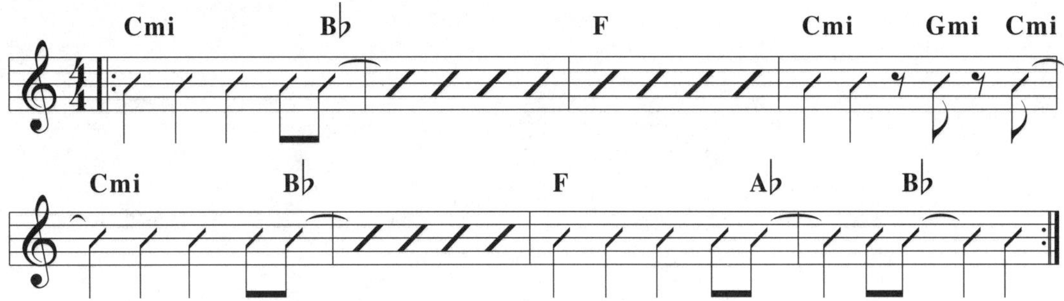

Pop-rock chord chart interpretation (contd)

We will now interpret this chart using a mixture of alternating triads, 4th couplings, and '**9 to 1**' & '**4 to 3**' resolutions in the right hand, together with a quarter-eighth octave left hand pattern (see **Fig. 12.7.**) as follows:-

Figure 12.43. Pop-rock comping solution for chord chart #5 (Fig. 12.42.)
(Cassette Tape Example 322 - 'Straight 8ths')

Again we will analyze the right hand devices used in each measure as follows:-

Pop-rock chord chart interpretation (contd)

- Measure 1 On the **Cmi** chord we are using **b7-b3** alternating triads (see **Fig. 12.19**.), with the 7th of the chord (Bb) being used as a passing tone on beat **4**. The right and left hands are both landing on the '**& of 4**' with the **Bb** chord, anticipating the following downbeat as required by the chart.

- Measure 2 Continuing on the **Bb** chord, we are using a '**9 to 1**' resolution within the basic triad (see **Fig. 8.12**.), with the 5th of the chord (F) being used as a passing tone on the '**& of 1**' and on beat **4**. The F triad on the '**& of 4**' is anticipating beat **1** of measure 3 and therefore harmonically should be considered as part of the following F chord.

- Measure 3 On the **F** chord we are using **4-1** alternating triads (see **Fig. 12.11**.), with the root of the chord (F) being used as a passing tone on the '**& of 1**' and on beat **4**. The Eb triad on the '**& of 4**' is anticipating beat **1** of measure 4 and therefore harmonically should be considered as part of the following Cmi chord.

- Measure 4 On the **Cmi** chord we are again using **b7-b3** alternating triads (see **Fig. 12.19**.), with the 7th of the chord (Bb) as a passing tone on the '**& of 2**' leading into a **5-1** 4th coupling on beat **3**. The following **Gmi** chord then begins on the '**& of 3**' (anticipating beat **4**) as required by the chord chart, and within this chord we are again using **b7-b3** alternating triads, with an incomplete Bb triad (Bb & D) on beat **4**. Again the Eb triad on the '**& of 4**' is anticipating beat **1** of measure 5 and therefore harmonically should be considered as part of the following Cmi chord.

- Measures 5-6 Similar comments as for measures **1-2**.

- Measure 7 Similar comments as for measure **3** regarding the **F** chord. The right and left hands are both landing on the '**& of 4**' with the **Ab** chord, anticipating the following downbeat.

- Measure 8 The **Bb** chord begins on the '**& of 2**' (anticipating beat **3**) as required by the chord chart, and we are using a '**4 to 3**' resolution within the basic triad (see **Chapter 9**). The final G-C interval is in fact a **5-1** 4th coupling on the Cmi chord - anticipating the downbeat at the top of the chart when the repeat is taken.

We will now examine an additional rhythmic possibility when interpreting a pop-rock chart in 'swing 8ths' - the use of the **middle** (2nd) subdivision within the implied 8th-note triplet. When interpreting some of the previous pop-rock charts in a 'swing 8ths' style, we have only been using the 1st & 3rd subdivisions of each 8th-note triplet (review **Figs. 2.30. & 2.31.** as necessary). As we saw in **Chapter 2**, the use of the 'middle' or 2nd triplet subdivision now requires a triplet sign in the music, assuming we wish to stay in 4/4 time. Any patterns we now generate using this 'middle' subdivision will **not** have a 'straight 8ths' equivalent i.e. we will be unable to re-interpret them back in a 'straight 8ths' style. Here is the next chord chart, to be interpreted in the manner described above:-

Figure 12.44. Chord chart example #6

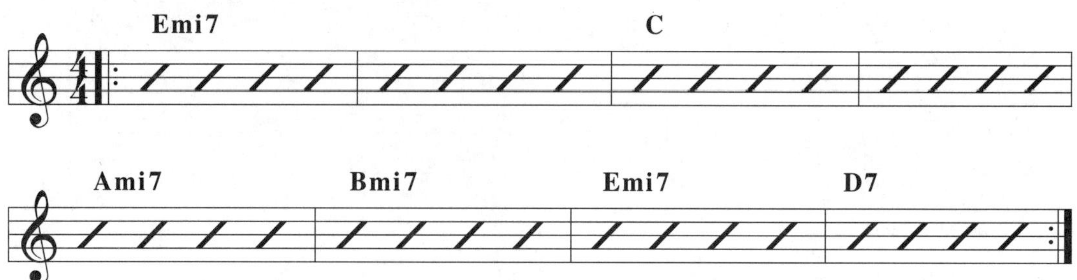

Pop-rock chord chart interpretation (contd)

Notice the 'swing eighths' symbol at the top of the chart (two eighth notes = quarter-eighth note triplet) - this tells the player that a 'swing eighths' subdivision is required (again review rhythmic subdivision concepts in **Chapter 2** as necessary). This chart can now be interpreted as follows:-

Figure 12.45. Pop-rock comping solution for chord chart #6 (Fig. 12.44.)
(Cassette Tape Example 323 - 'Swing 8ths')

Pop-rock chord chart interpretation (contd)

Again note in the previous example that whenever the **second** subdivision of an eighth-note triplet is used in the right hand part, then a triplet sign is needed - this is happening on beats **1** & **4** of measures 1 - 7 and beats **1** & **3** of measure 8. Here the right hand triad is playing in the rhythmic space between the left hand roots. In all other places within the right hand part, and throughout the left hand part, we are just using eighth notes without triplet signs - each pair of eighth notes is then interpreted as the first & third 'events' within an eighth-note triplet, as a result of the 'swing eighths' symbol placed above the chart as discussed. Each measure can be further analyzed as follows:-

- Measures 1-2	On the **Emi7** chord we are using '**b7 to b3**' alternating triads (see **Fig. 12.19**.), with the **b7** triad (D major - can also be called a **b7-9-11** upper structure - see **Fig. 5.2.**) anticipating beat **3**. Also within beat **4** we have a '**9 to 1**' resolution within this upper triad.
- Measures 3-4	On the **C** chord we are using '**9 to 5**' alternating triads (see **Fig. 12.16**.), which are the same triads (D & G) as were used over the Emi7 chord in measures 1 & 2. Here the **9** triad (D major - can also be called a **9-#11-13** upper structure - see **Fig. 5.7.**) is anticipating beat **3**, and again within beat **4** we have a '**9 to 1**' resolution within this upper triad.
- Measure 5	On the **Ami7** chord we are again using '**b7 to b3**' alternating triads (see **Fig. 12.19**.), with the **b7** triad (G) anticipating beat **3**. Also within beat **4** we have a '**9 to 1**' resolution within the **b3** triad (C major - can also be called a **b3-5-b7** upper structure - see **Fig. 5.6.**). We first saw this resolution within the **b3-5-b7** upper structure triad in **Fig. 8.14**.
Measure 6	On the **Bmi7** chord we are again using '**b7 to b3**' alternating triads (see **Fig. 12.19**.), with the **b7** triad (A) anticipating beat **3**. Also within beat **4** we have a '**9 to 1**' resolution within the **b3** triad (D major - again can be called a **b3-5-b7** upper structure).
- Measure 7	Similar comments as for measure **1**.
- Measure 8	On the **D7** chord we are using **b7-1** alternating triads (see **Fig. 12.21**.) Note that the use of the **b7** triad (C) over D in the first half of the measure creates a dominant suspension (see **Fig. 5.2**.), resolving to a basic D triad in the second half of the measure.

PRACTICE DIRECTIONS:-

- ***Practice the various pop-rock comping examples based on the chord charts provided, as in Figs. 12.30. - 12.45., in particular noting the rhythmic and harmonic devices used to interpret each chart as indicated.***
  *Don't forget to practice the examples in both '**straight 8ths**' & '**swing 8ths**' where applicable!*
  (For extra practice - try transposing the examples into different keys!)
- ***Work on applying these patterns and concepts to other tunes of your choice, and to the practice progressions at the end of this chapter.***

Pop-rock melody

Although the pop-rock style does not perhaps lend itself quite so well to solo piano melody treatment as for example the pop ballad style (see **Chapter 11**), there may be occasions where you need to reflect the melody or manipulate the top-note voiceleading in a certain manner, in the right-hand part. As you can see in the pop-rock 'comping' examples studied so far, the right hand part is frequently based on three-note 'shapes' (triads, double-4ths etc.) and interval couplings i.e. 4ths. It would be useful therefore to see how we could use these devices **below a melody or desired top-note** in the right hand. We will analyze this on the basic chord types encountered in this style; major, minor and dominant/suspended. First we will look at all of the melody or top-note options available on a **C** major chord, together with the various shapes and couplings which could be used to support those top notes, as follows:-

Figure 12.46. Top-note harmonization options on C major chord
(CASSETTE TAPE EXAMPLE 324)

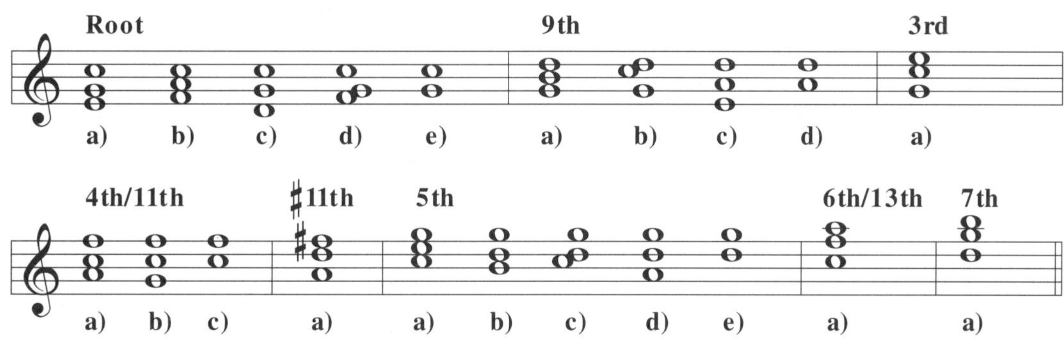

The text above the staff (**Root**, **9th** etc.) refers to the melody or top-note being supported. For example, in the first measure the note C (the root of a C major chord) is the top note on each structure. The versions **a)** - **e)** are five different ways in which the top note could be supported in the right hand. We will now analyze these melody support options on the major chord as follows:-

Root in melody

a) This is the basic **C** triad (also known as a **1-3-5** upper structure - see **Fig. 5.1.**), inverted to accommodate the melody. Normally a safe option, except in some harder rock idioms where the 3rd of the chord is undesirable (in which case options **c)** or **e)** might be preferred).

b) This is an **F** triad below melody, which might be used as part of a '**4 to 1**' alternating triad pattern (see **Fig. 12.11.**) as F is the **4** triad of C.

c) This is a **9-5-1** double-4th structure (see **Fig. 10.7.**) - this has a hollow and powerful sound and is often a good alternative to a triad i.e. option **a)**.

d) This is an inverted **5-1-11** double-4th structure (see **Fig. 10.3.**) creating a suspended quality - depending on the context the 4th/11th (F) may resolve to the 3rd of the chord (see **Chapter 9**).

e) This is a **5-1** pentatonic 4th interval coupling (see **Fig. 12.23.** etc.) - very suitable for most rock styles. Optionally the top note may be doubled an octave lower.

9th in melody

a) This is a **G** triad below melody, which might be used as part of a '**5 to 1**' (see **Fig. 12.9.**) or '**9 to 5**' (see **Fig. 12.16.**) alternating triad pattern, as G is the **5** triad of C. The G triad can also be considered as the **5-7-9** upper structure triad of the overall C major chord (see **Fig. 5.4.**).

Pop-rock melody (contd)

Analysis of Figure 12.46. contd

9th in melody contd	*b)*	This is an inverted 9-5-1 double-4th structure (see **Fig. 10.7.**) - again a frequent choice in these styles.
	c)	This is a 3-6-9 double-4th structure (see **Fig. 10.6.**) - this sophisticated sound works best on chords built from the **b3rd**, **b6th** or **b7th** degrees of a minor key.
	d)	This is a 6-9 pentatonic 4th coupling (see **Fig. 12.24.** etc.), which again works best on chords built from the **b3rd**, **b6th** or **b7th** degrees of a minor key.
3rd in melody	*a)*	This is the basic C triad (again a 1-3-5 upper structure) inverted below melody.
4th/11th in melody	*a)*	This is an inverted F triad below melody, which again might be used as part of a '4 to 1' alternating triad pattern (see **Fig. 12.11.**) as F is the 4 triad of C.
	b)	This is a 5-1-11 double-4th structure (see **Fig. 10.3.**) again creating a suspension.
	c)	This is a 1-11 pentatonic 4th coupling (see **Fig. 12.23.** etc.) - a safe choice.
#11th in melody	*a)*	This is an inverted D triad below melody, which might be used as part of a '9 to 1' (see **Fig. 12.14.**) or '9 to 5' (see **Fig. 12.16.**) alternating triad pattern, as D is the 9 triad of C (and is also a 9-#11-13 upper structure - see **Fig. 5.7.**).
5th in melody	*a)*	This is the basic C triad (and the 1-3-5 upper structure) below the melody. Again if we need to avoid the 3rd of the chord, then option c) might be preferred.
	b)	This is a G triad below melody, which might be used as part of a '5 to 1' (see **Fig. 12.9.**) or '9 to 5' (see **Fig. 12.16.**) alternating triad pattern, as G is the 5 triad of C (and is also the 5-7-9 upper structure - see **Fig. 5.4.**).
	c)	This is an inverted 9-5-1 double-4th structure (see **Fig. 10.7.**) - very effective.
	d)	This is a 6-9-5 double-4th structure (see **Fig. 10.11.**) - this device works best on chords built from the **b3rd**, **4th**, **b6th** or **b7th** degrees of a minor key.
	e)	This is a 9-5 pentatonic 4th coupling (see **Fig. 12.24.** etc.) - again a safe choice.
6th/13th in melody	*a)*	This is an inverted F triad below melody, which again might be used as part of a '4 to 1' alternating triad pattern (see **Fig. 12.11.**) as F is the 4 triad of C.
7th in melody	*a)*	This is an inverted G triad below melody, which might be used as part of a '5 to 1' (see **Fig. 12.9.**) or 9 to 5 (see **Fig. 12.16.**) alternating triad pattern, as G is the 5 triad of C (and again is also the 5-7-9 upper structure triad).

Now we will assess the melody harmonization options on a minor or minor 7th-type chord as follows:-

Figure 12.47. Top-note harmonization options on A minor chord
(Cassette Tape Example 325)

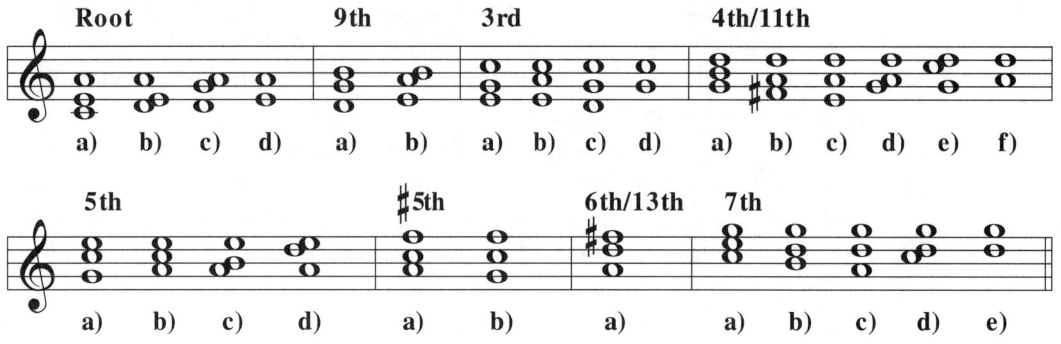

Root a) b) c) d) 9th a) b) 3rd a) b) c) d) 4th/11th a) b) c) d) e) f)

5th a) b) c) d) #5th a) b) 6th/13th a) 7th a) b) c) d) e)

Pop-rock melody (contd)

We will now analyze these melody harmonization options on the minor chord as follows:-

Root in melody

a) This is the basic **Ami** triad inverted to accommodate the melody (a **1-b3-5** upper structure - see **Fig. 5.8.**). This is normally a safe option.

b) This is an inverted **5-1-11** double-4th structure (see **Fig. 10.3.**) - although a suspended quality is implied, the addition of the 11th to the minor chord does not normally cause any conflicts with other chord tones.

c) This is an inverted **1-11-b7** double-4th structure (see **Fig. 10.8.**) - similar comments as for b) above, now with the addition of the 7th of the chord.

d) This is a **5-1** pentatonic 4th coupling (see **Fig. 12.23.** etc.) - again very suitable for most rock styles.

9th in melody

a) This is an inverted **G** triad below melody, which might be used as part of a **'b7 to b3'** alternating triad pattern (see **Fig. 12.19.**) as G is the **b7** triad of the Ami chord (and is also the **b7-9-11** upper structure triad - see **Fig. 5.2.**).

b) This is an inverted **9-5-1** double-4th structure (see **Fig. 10.7.**) giving good support to the 9th in the melody - again this structure is very useful in rock styles.

3rd in melody

a) This is an inverted **C** triad below melody, which might be used as part of a **'b7 to b3'** alternating triad pattern (see **Fig. 12.19.**) as C is the **b3** triad of the Ami chord (and is also the **b3-5-b7** upper structure triad - see **Fig. 5.6.**).

b) This is the basic **Ami** triad (see **Fig. 5.8.**) inverted to accommodate the melody.

c) This is an **11-b7-b3** double-4th structure (see **Fig. 10.5.**) - a very useful solution with the added 11th again usually not causing any conflicts.

d) This is a **b7-b3** pentatonic 4th coupling (see **Fig. 12.23.** etc.) - a safe choice.

4th/11th in melody

a) This is a **G** triad below melody, which might be used as part of a **'b7 to b3'** alternating triad pattern (see **Fig. 12.19.**) as G is the **b7** triad of the Ami chord (and again is also the **b7-9-11** upper structure - see **Fig. 5.2.**).

b) This is an inverted **D** triad below melody, which is a **4** triad with respect to the overall Ami chord. Widely used in jazz contexts (implying a Dorian mode - see **Chapter 1**), this structure may not be diatonic to (i.e. contained within) the key of the song, and therefore needs to be used with care in contemporary styles.

c) This is a **5-1-11** double-4th structure (see **Fig. 10.3.**), a very useful sound.

d) This is an inverted **1-11-b7** double-4th structure (see **Fig. 10.8.**), similar to the previous shape, now with the addition of the 7th of the chord.

e) This is an inverted **11-b7-b3** double-4th structure (see **Fig. 10.5.**), more definitive than the previous double-4th variations due to the 3rd of the chord being present.

f) This is a **1-11** pentatonic 4th coupling (see Fig. **12.23.** etc.) - again a useful choice below the 11th.

5th in melody

a) This is an inverted **C** triad below melody, which might be used as part of a **'b7 to b3'** alternating triad pattern (see **Fig. 12.19.**) as C is the **b3** triad of the Ami chord (and again is also the **b3-5-b7** upper structure - see **Fig. 5.6.**).

b) This is the basic **Ami** triad (in root position - see **Fig. 5.8.**) below the melody.

c) This is an inverted **9-5-1** double-4th structure (see **Fig. 10.7.**). As discussed, this shape works well in rock styles, however on minor chords you may want to ensure that the **b3** (C in this case) is not being played by another instrument in this range - this will potentially sound angular with the 9th of this shape.

Pop-rock melody (contd)

Analysis of Fig 12.47. contd

5th in melody contd ***d)*** This is an inverted **5-1-11** double 4th structure (see **Fig. 10.3.**), a useful sound.

#5th in melody ***a)*** This is an inverted **F** triad below melody, which is a **b6** triad with respect to the overall minor chord. This triad may be useful in situations where the minor chord is built from the **3rd** or **6th** degrees of a major key, or the **1st** or **5th** degrees of a minor key.

b) This is a **b7-b3-#5** double-4th structure (see **Fig. 10.10.**), useful in similar situations to **a)** above.

6th/13th in melody ***a)*** This is an inverted **D** triad below melody, which is a **4** triad with respect to the overall Ami chord. (See earlier comments on the **4** triad on minor chords).

7th in melody ***a)*** This is an inverted **C** triad below melody, which might be used as part of a **'b7 to b3'** alternating triad pattern (see **Fig. 12.19.**) as C is the **b3** triad of Ami.

b) This is an inverted **G** triad below melody, which might also be used as part of a **'b7 to b3'** alternating triad pattern (see **Fig. 12.19.**) as G is the **b7** triad of Ami.

c) This is a **1-11-b7** double-4th structure (see **Fig. 10.8.**), again a useful choice.

d) This is an inverted **11-b7-b3** double-4th structure, more definitive than **c)** above due to the 3rd of the chord being present.

e) This is an **11-b7** pentatonic 4th coupling (see **Fig. 12.23.** etc.) - a safe choice.

Now we will look at the melody harmonization options on a dominant or suspended dominant as follows:-

Figure 12.48. Top-note harmonization options on G seventh chord
(Cassette Tape Example 326)

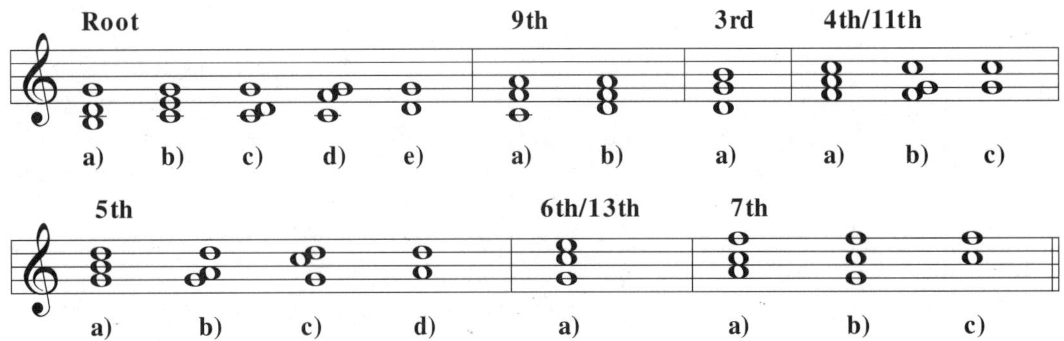

Again we will analyze the melody harmonization options as follows:-

Root in melody ***a)*** This is the basic **G** triad (a **1-3-5** upper structure - see **Fig. 5.1.**) inverted to accommodate the melody. A safe option unless a suspended quality is desired.

b) This is an inverted **C** triad below melody, which might be used as part of a **'4 to 1'** alternating triad pattern (see **Fig. 12.11.**) as C is the **4** triad of G.

c) This is an inverted **5-1-11** double-4th structure (see **Fig. 10.3.**), in this context implying a suspension of the G or G7 chord.

d) This is an inverted **1-11-b7** double-4th structure (see **Fig. 10.8.**), in this case a more definitive suspension with the 7th of the chord present.

Pop-rock melody (contd)

Analysis of Fig. 12.48. contd

Root in melody contd	***e)***	This is a **5-1** pentatonic 4th coupling (see **Fig. 12.23**. etc.), a safe choice.
9th in melody	***a)***	This is an inverted **F** triad below melody, which might be used as part of a **'b7 to 1'** alternating triad pattern (see **Fig. 12.21**.) - in this case the F triad creates a dominant suspension (and is a **b7-9-11** upper structure - see **Fig. 5.2**.).
	b)	A less definitive form of **a)** above, using the **5mi** triad (Dmi) below melody.
3rd in melody	***a)***	This is the basic **G** triad (see **Fig. 5.1.**) inverted to accommodate the melody.
4th/11th in melody	***a)***	This is an **F** triad below melody, which again might be used as part of a **'b7 to 1'** alternating triad pattern (see **Fig. 12.21**.) - again the F triad creates a dominant suspension (and is a **b7-9-11** upper structure - see **Fig. 5.2**.).
	b)	This is an inverted **1-11-b7** double-4th structure (see **Fig. 10.8**.), again creating a suspended dominant quality.
	c)	This is a **1-11** pentatonic 4th coupling (see **Fig. 12.23**. etc.), again a good basic choice below the 11th.
5th in melody	***a)***	This is the basic **G** triad (in root position - see **Fig. 5.1.**) below the melody.
	b)	This is an inverted **9-5-1** double-4th structure (see **Fig. 10.7**.), in this case a neutral and non-definitive solution.
	c)	This is an inverted **5-1-11** double-4th structure (see **Fig. 10.3**.), giving a basic suspended quality.
	d)	This is a **9-5** pentatonic 4th coupling (see **Fig. 12.24**. etc), again a neutral sound.
6th/13th in melody	***a)***	This is an inverted **C** triad below melody, which might be used as part of a **'4 to 1'** alternating triad pattern (see **Fig. 12.11**.) as C is the **4** triad of G.
7th in melody	***a)***	This is an inverted **F** triad below melody, which again might be used as part of a **'b7 to 1'** alternating triad pattern (see **Fig. 12.21**.) - again the F triad creates a dominant suspension (and is a **b7-9-11** upper structure - see **Fig. 5.2**.).
	b)	This is a **1-11-b7** double-4th structure (see **Fig. 10.8**.), again creating a suspended dominant quality.
	c)	This is an **11-b7** pentatonic 4th coupling (see **Fig. 12.25**. etc.), a variation on the above suspension.

Although particularly useful in pop-rock styles, the right-hand 'shapes' are also used in other contemporary styles such as **New age**, **R'n'B ballad** & **R'n'B/Funk** - as we shall see later! We will now see how some of these right-hand devices work when interpreting a pop-rock melody leadsheet, as follows:-

Figure 12.49. Pop-rock melody leadsheet example

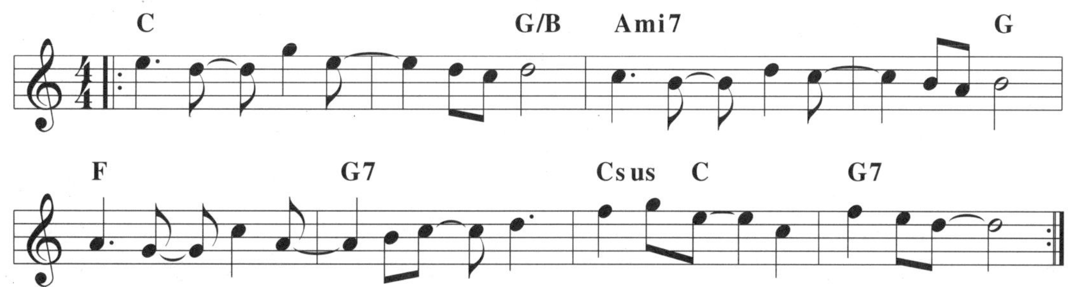

Pop-rock melody (contd)

We will now look at an interpretation of this melody leadsheet, using the right-hand devices previously described in **Figs. 12.46. - 12.48.** and accompanying text. There are many ways in which this could have been done - in the solution presented, the right hand is mainly using triads below melody, with some double-4th shapes, 4th couplings, and resolutions. The left hand meanwhile is maintaining a steady eighth-note pulse, as follows:-

Figure 12.50. Pop-rock melody treatment solution for Fig. 12.49. leadsheet

(Cassette Tape Example 327 - 'Straight 8ths')
(Cassette Tape Example 328 - 'Swing 8ths')

Notice that the chord symbols now reflect the alternating triad choices which have been made to support the melody - compare the chord symbols to the leadsheet in **Fig. 12.49.** Again we can analyze each measure:-

Pop-rock melody (contd)

Measure 1 The melody notes within the C chord are being harmonized by different inversions of the '5 to 1' alternating triads - see text accompanying **Fig. 12.46**. for harmonization choices.

Measure 2 The melody note D within the G/B chord on beat **3** is being harmonized by an inverted 9-5-1 double-4th structure. Here the 9-5-1 of a major chord inverted over the 3rd in the bass, gives an effective modern sound (see **Fig. 10.10.**, and **Fig. 12.48.** 5th measure).

Measure 3 The melody notes within the Ami7 chord are being harmonized by different inversions of the 'b7 to b3' alternating triads - see text accompanying **Fig. 12.47**. for individual harmonization choices.

Measure 4 The melody note B within the G chord is being harmonized using a '9 to 1' resolution within the basic triad (see **Fig. 8.12.**).

Measure 5 The melody notes within the F chord are being harmonized by different inversions of the '5 to 1' alternating triads - see text accompanying **Fig. 12.46**. for harmonization choices.

Measure 6 The melody notes within the G7 chord are being harmonized by different inversions of the 'b7 to 1' alternating triads - see text accompanying **Fig. 12.48**. for individual harmonization choices.

Measure 7 The melody notes within the C chord are being harmonized by different inversions of the '4 to 1' and '5 to 1' alternating triads - again see text accompanying **Fig. 12.46**. Also a 5-1 4th coupling is being used on beat **4**.

Measure 8 The melody notes within the G7 chord are being harmonized by different inversions of the 'b7 to 1' and '4 to 1' alternating triads - again see text accompanying **Fig. 12.48**.

PRACTICE DIRECTIONS:-

- ***Practice the pop-rock melody harmonization options on major, minor and dominant chords as shown in Figs. 12.46. - 12.48.***
  (For extra practice - try transposing these examples into different keys!)
- ***Practice the pop-rock melody solution as in Fig. 12.50.***
- ***Work on applying these concepts to other tunes of your choice, and to the practice tunes at the end of this chapter.***

Figure 12.51. Practice leadsheet #1 (chords only - for 'comping' practice)

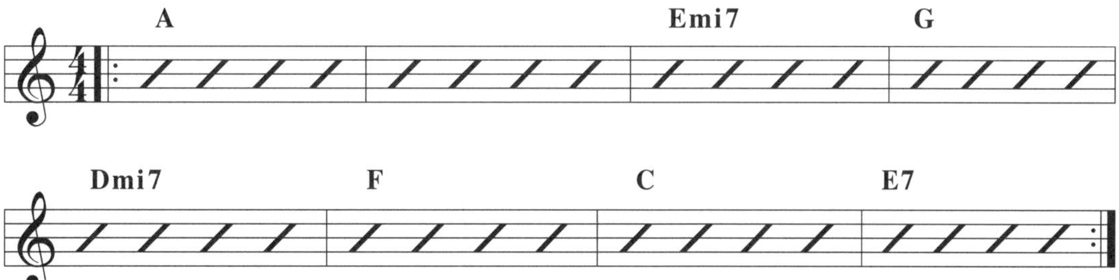

Pop-rock practice examples

Figure 12.52. Practice leadsheet #2 (chords only - for 'comping' practice)

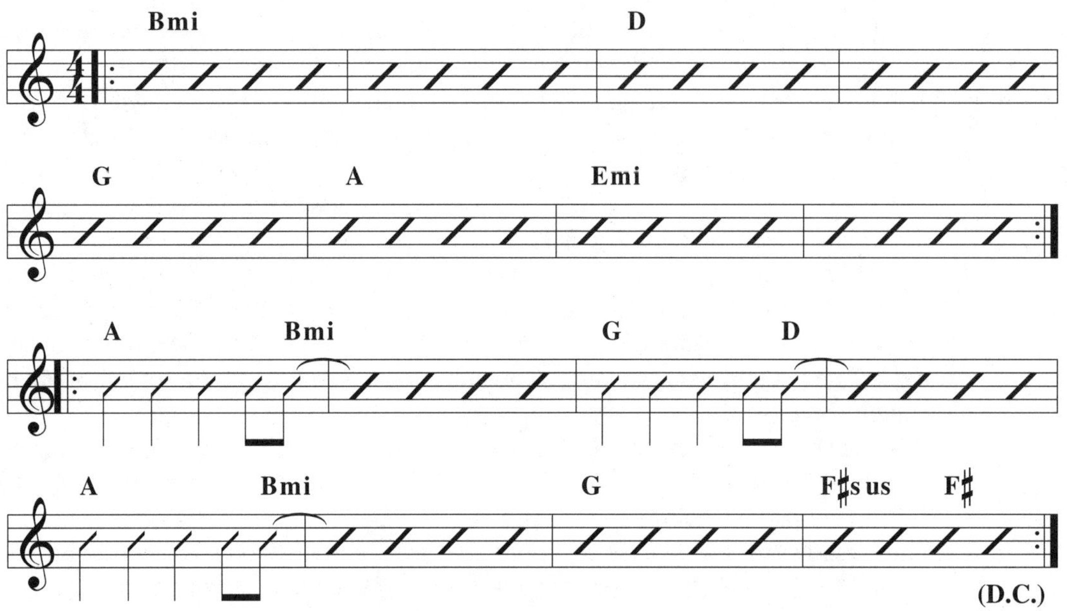

Figure 12.53. Practice leadsheet #3 (chords only - for 'comping' practice in a shuffle style)

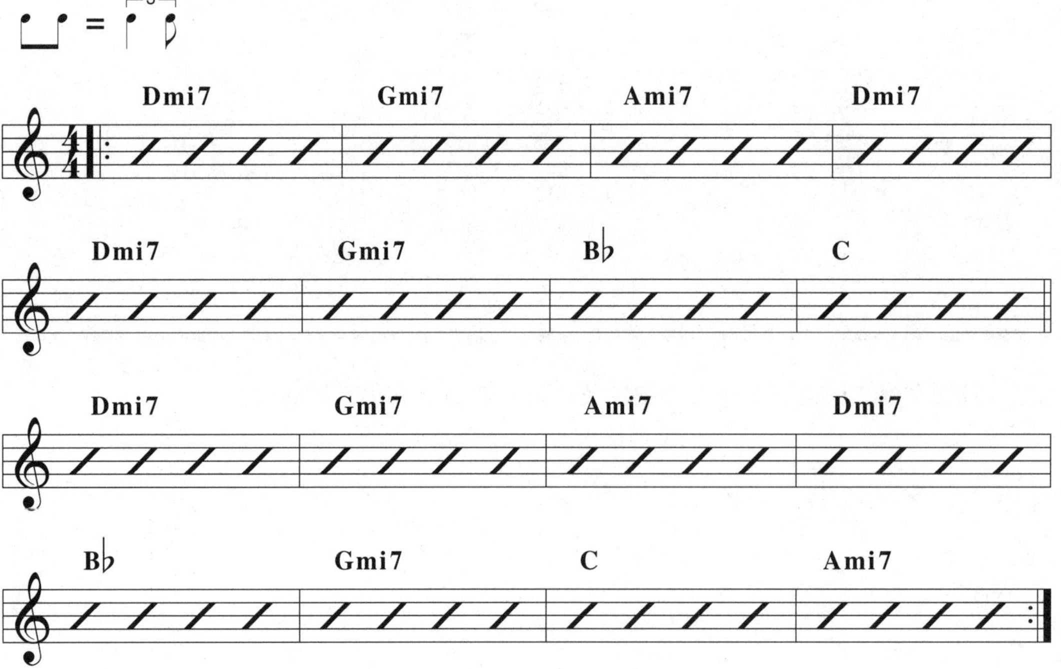

Pop-rock practice examples (contd)

Figure 12.54. Practice leadsheet #4 (melody & chords, for melody treatment or 'comping' practice)

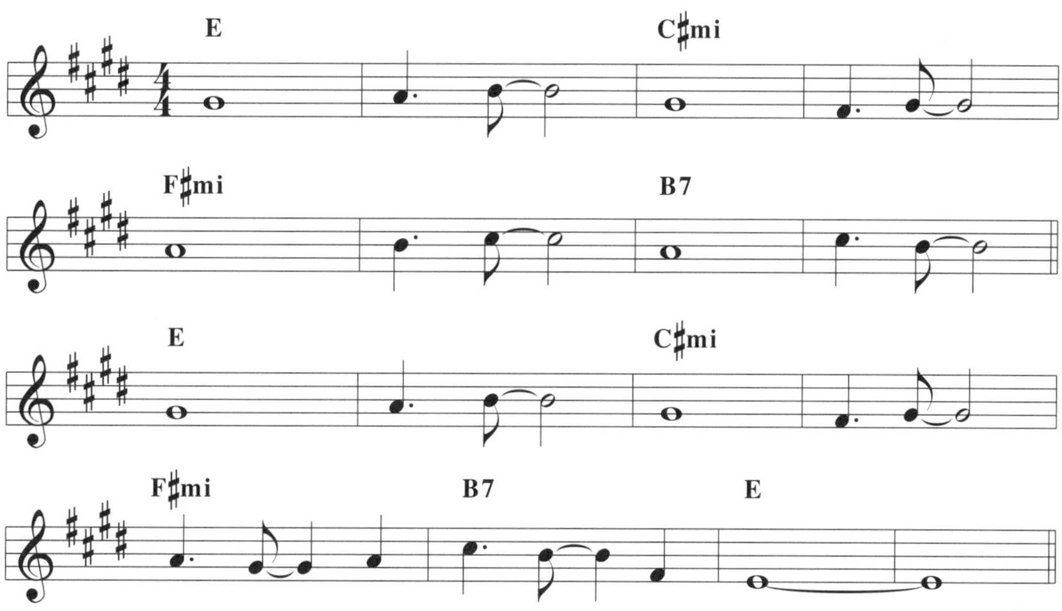

Figure 12.55. Practice leadsheet #5 (melody & chords, for melody treatment or 'comping' practice)

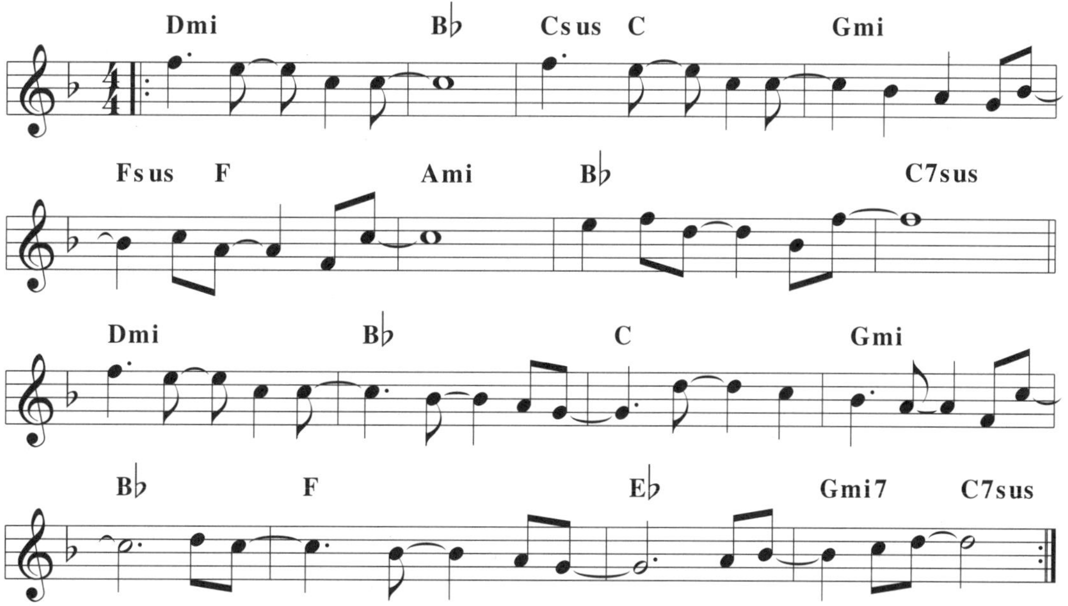

--- NOTES ---

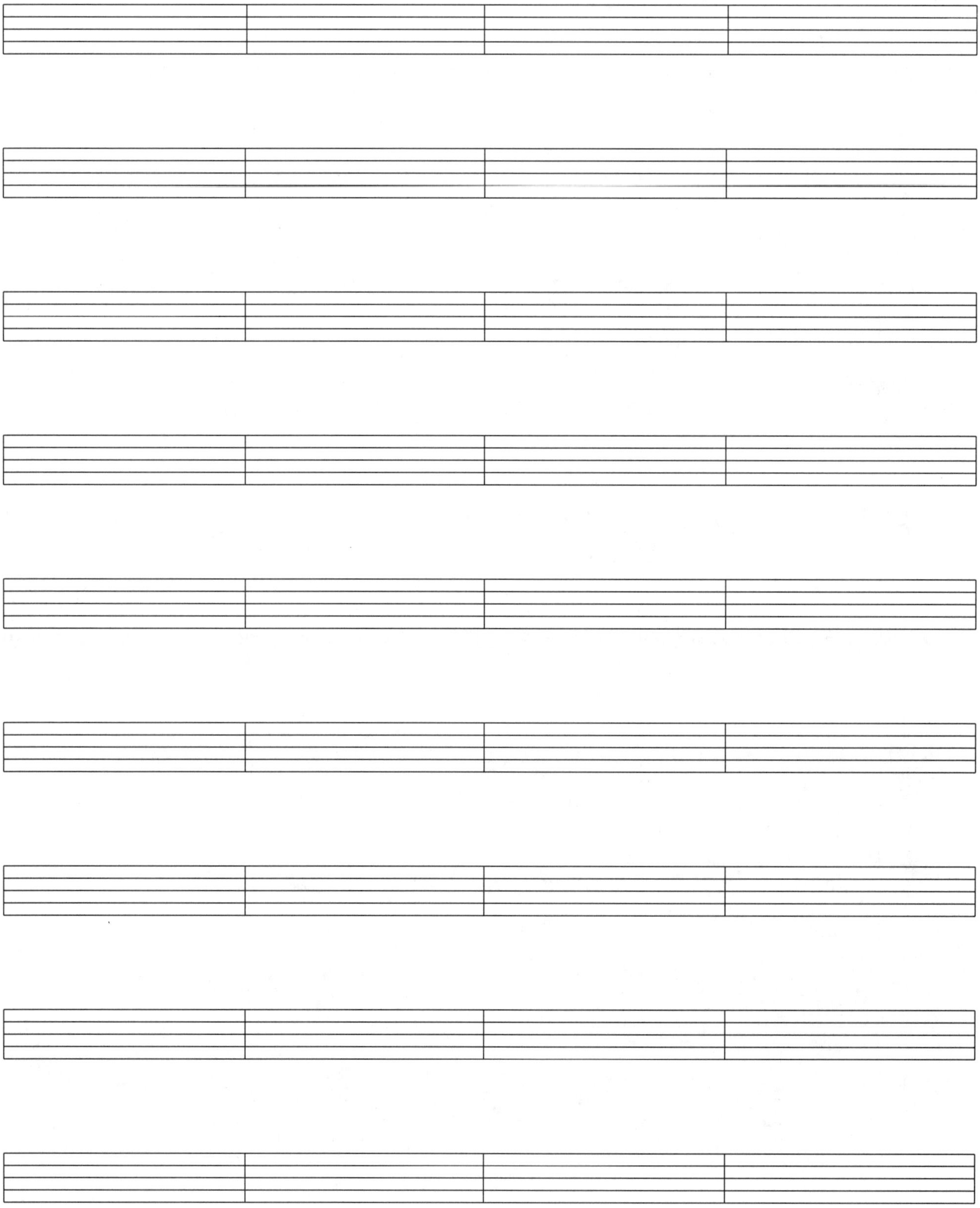

CHAPTER THIRTEEN

New Age

Introduction

We will now turn our attention to the style of music known as 'New Age'. This is perhaps a hard category to define, not least because the term 'New Age' is also applied to lifestyles and attitudes as well as to a music style! I have no intention here of addressing any of the philosophical implications of this - for which in any case I am probably not qualified! - instead I would simply like to offer some technical observations about how as keyboard players we can manipulate our playing to infuse the appropriate 'New Age' elements which will then hopefully be recognized by our audience! We can start out by making some broad stylistic observations regarding 'New Age' music:-

- Tempos are generally slow to medium.
- Both eighth-note and sixteenth-note rhythmic subdivisions are used (generally in a 'straight' rather than 'swing' interpretation), without a lot of anticipations in the chord rhythms (see **Chapter 2**).
- Harmony is generally diatonic to a major or minor key, with an emphasis on major, minor and suspended dominant chord forms. Frequent use of upper extensions on these chords as follows:-
    - 7th, 9th, #11th & 13th (6th) on major chords
    - b7th, 9th & 11th on minor and suspended dominant chords.
- Use of inversions in the bass voice (i.e. major & minor chords inverted over the 3rd & 5th).
- Use of 'open' voicing structures as follows:-
    - double-4th structures (see **Chapter 10**)
    - 4th interval couplings (see **Chapter 12 Figs. 12.23**. - **12.28**.)
    - '4th clusters' and 'half step & 5th' structures as detailed in this chapter.
- Melodies are frequently sparse and repetitive. Often a pentatonic scale source is used, to eliminate the leading half-steps in the major scale (see **Chapter 1 Fig. 1.52**.)
- Frequent use of the 'arpeggiated left hand' for piano, mainly using basic chord tones (Root, 3rd & 5th - see **Chapter 11 Figs. 11.11**. & **11.12**.) in the lower register, and then adding extensions as described above as the left hand moves higher up the keyboard (around Middle C).

As you can see from the above description, there are some technical similarities between this style and the '**Pop Ballad**' style studied in **Chapter 11**. The techniques presented in this chapter build upon (and could be considered as a supplement to) the information in the 'Pop Ballad' chapter. In this 'New Age' chapter we will for example discuss some additional devices to place below the melody in the right hand which are appropriate in 'New Age' settings - you will recall that in **Chapter 11** we have already studied such 'melody support' concepts as triads, 3rd/6th intervals, octaves & filled-in octaves, arpeggios etc. - these can of course also work in 'new age' situations and you need to be familiar with them. Also in this chapter we will present a number of different arpeggiated left hand patterns based on the principles described above - this builds on the more basic left hand arpeggio concepts again developed in **Chapter 11**. To summarize - to get the best out of this 'New Age' chapter, you need to have already familiarized yourself with the **Chapter 11** 'Pop Ballad' concepts!

There are a lot of artists who apply these stylistic elements to their work, not all of whom would be considered as falling into the 'New Age' category! The work of George Winston, with its sparse repetitive melodies and arpeggiated textures, has no doubt been influential. More recent artists of note include the electronic stylings of Patrick O'Hearn, the lush romanticism of Yanni and the classical & jazz influenced Liz Story. Also hybrid categories like 'New-Age-Jazz' have emerged, fusing some of the above elements with more sophisticated

CHAPTER THIRTEEN

Introduction (contd)

melodies and harmonies. A percentage of the work by artists such as David Benoit and Rippingtons (more typically associated with modern jazz) would definitely fall into this 'hybrid' category. A lot of 'New Age' music is instrumental-based (i.e. without vocals) and so the main focus of this chapter will be towards melody treatment - however I have also included some accompaniment or 'comping' methods and examples. Don't forget that (as for Pop Ballad styles) you will need to **depress the sustain pedal for the duration of each chord!**

Left hand arpeggiated patterns

Now we will look at some left hand patterns, using eighth- and sixteenth-note arpeggios on different chord types. First of all we will look at some eighth-note patterns for major and minor chords in root position:-

Figure 13.1. Left hand 8th note patterns, for use on root-position major and minor chords
(Cassette Tape Examples 329-340)

Left hand arpeggiated patterns (contd)

A general point to keep in mind with these left hand patterns is that any upper extensions applied (chord tones other than the root, 3rd & 5th) need to be no lower than around **E below middle C**. This is because these extensions will sound 'muddy' in the low register and will detract from the definition of the chord. Normally only the basic chord tones (typically arranged in an 'open triad' structure - see **Figs. 11.11.** & **11.12.**) are found in this lower register. This therefore means that a particular left hand pattern may work better in some keys than others, i.e. in those keys which permit the chord tones and any extensions to be allocated within the above range limits. For example, pattern **#11** above for the **A** major chord, plays the **6-9-5** double 4th structure (see **Fig. 10.11.**) on beat **3**. The tones outside the basic triad here (i.e. the **6th** and **9th**) are the F# and B below middle C, above the lower register previously described. However, if we were to transpose this pattern down a perfect 5th to D major, then the **6-9-5** would begin with the B which is a ninth below middle C - well below the 'E below middle C' guide-line suggested above, and therefore sounding very muddy - try it for yourself! For space reasons I have not listed every pattern in every suitable key/range - but by following the above 'register' guidelines (and working through

Left hand arpeggiated patterns (contd)

the subsequent examples in this chapter) you will develop the ability to use and adapt the left hand patterns to fit in the correct range. In any case there are a great many patterns available for each chord type and inversion - the ones provided in the book are only examples to get you started, and you are of course encouraged to experiment with and to develop new pattern ideas based on the above criteria. Now we will analyze the patterns presented in **Figure 13.1**:-

Pattern #1 This is a basic **1-5-9-3** pattern on the major chord, and a **1-5-9-b3** pattern on the minor chord.

Pattern #2 Variations on the above. On the major chord this is a **1-5-6-3** pattern - 6ths (along with 9ths) are frequently added to major chords. On the minor chord, this is a **1-5-b7-b3** pattern - 7ths (along with 9ths & 11ths) are frequently added to minor chords. As in pattern **#1**, beat **3** is anticipated.

Pattern #3 Another variation, this time landing on beat **3** using a **1-5-1-5-9** pattern on the major and minor chords. A neutral, 'hollow' sound results from the omission of the 3rd of these chords.

Pattern #4 Similar to **#3**, using a **1-5-9-5-3** pattern on the major chord, and **1-5-9-5-b3** on the minor chord.

Pattern #5 Another variation - a **1-5-9-6-3** pattern on the major chord, and **1-5-9-b7-b3** on the minor chord.

Pattern #6 A more continuous arpeggiated pattern, using **1**, **5**, **9** & **3** on the major chord and **1**, **5**, **9** & **b3** on the minor chord.

Pattern #7 A variation on the above continuous pattern, now using **1**, **5**, **9**, **6** & **3** on the major chord and **1**, **5**, **9**, **b7** & **b3** on the minor chord.

Pattern #8 Another variation on pattern **#6** using the same chord tones overall.

Pattern #9 A **1-5-9-1** pattern followed by a **9-3-5** 'whole-step-4th cluster' on the major chord, and by a **9-b3-5** 'half-step-4th' cluster on the minor chord, on beat **3.** See further explanation in this chapter (**Figs. 13.9. - 13.18.**) regarding these right hand 'cluster' voicings.

Pattern #10 A pattern using 6th couplings (**3-1**, **11-9**, **5-3** on major; **b3-1**, **11-9**, **5-b3** on minor) leading into beat **3**, together with a **1-5** 5th interval on beat **4.** See discussions of 6th couplings in **Chapter 11**.

Pattern #11 A **1-5-9-1** pattern followed by a **6-9-5** double 4th structure (see **Fig. 10.11.**) on the major chord, and followed by a **5-1-11** double 4th structure (see **Fig. 10.3.**) on the minor chord. In each case the double 4th falls on beat **3**.

Pattern #12 A variation using the same double 4th structures as above, now with a **1-5-3-1** pattern on the major chord and a **1-5-b3-1** pattern on the minor chord, during beats **1** & **2.**

Now we will look at some left hand patterns for major and minor chords inverted over the 3rd in the root voice - a common harmonic device in this style. Again I have illustrated major and minor chord patterns side-by-side - not that you need to treat each line as a 'progression' from left to right! - I just did it this way to save space!

Figure 13.2. Left hand 8th note patterns, for use on major and minor chords inverted over the 3rd in the bass voice *(Cassette Tape Examples 341-347)*

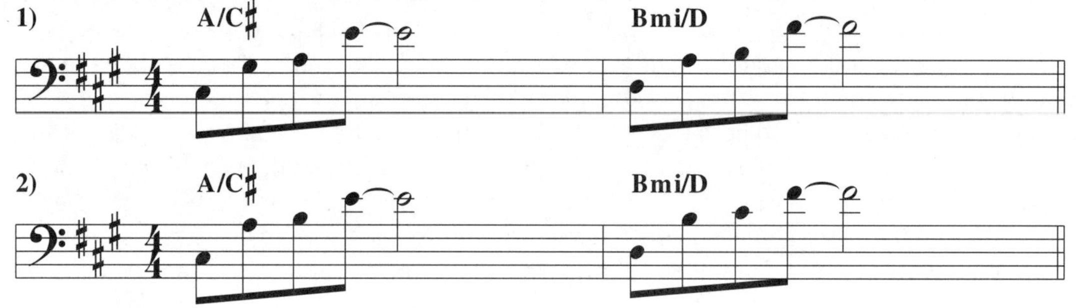

Left hand arpeggiated patterns (contd)

Figure 13.2. contd

We wil analyze these patterns with the 3rd of the chord in the bass voice, as follows:-

Pattern #1 A **3-7-1-5** pattern on the major chord, and a **b3-b7-1-5** pattern on the minor chord, anticipating beat **3**. A stylistic and effective choice especially on the major chord - best however to avoid playing the root of the major chord in the right hand, if the 7th is being used in the left hand.

Pattern #2 A variation on the above, using a **3-1-9-5** pattern on the major chord (a less dissonant alternative to pattern **#1**) and a **b3-1-9-5** pattern on the minor chord (adding the 9th above the 3rd here creates a more sophisticated sound).

Pattern #3 Another variation on pattern **#1**, this time adding the **9th** on the '**& of 3**' and the **3rd** of the major chord (**b3rd** of the minor chord) on beat **4**.

Pattern #4 This is a **3-1-5-9-3** pattern on the major chord, and a **b3-1-5-9-b3** pattern on the minor chord, anticipating beats **3** & **4**.

Pattern #5 A more continuous arpeggiated pattern, using **3**, **1**, **5** & **9** on the major chord and **b3**, **1**, **5** & **b7** on the minor chord.

Pattern #6 A variation on the above, this time using **3**, **7**, **1**, **5** & **9** on the major chord and **b3**, **b7**, **1**, **5** & **9** on the minor chord.

Pattern #7 A **3-1-9-3** pattern followed by a **6-9-5** double 4th structure (see **Fig. 10.11.**) on the major chord, and a **b3-1-9-b3** pattern followed by a **5-1-11** double 4th structure (see **Fig. 10.3.**) on the minor chord. In both cases the double 4th fall on beat **3**.

Left hand arpeggiated patterns (contd)

Continuing with eighth-note subdivisions, we will now look at left hand patterns for major and minor chords inverted over the 5th, as follows:-

Figure 13.3. Left hand 8th note patterns, for use on major and minor chords inverted over the 5th in the bass voice *(Cassette Tape Examples 348-353)*

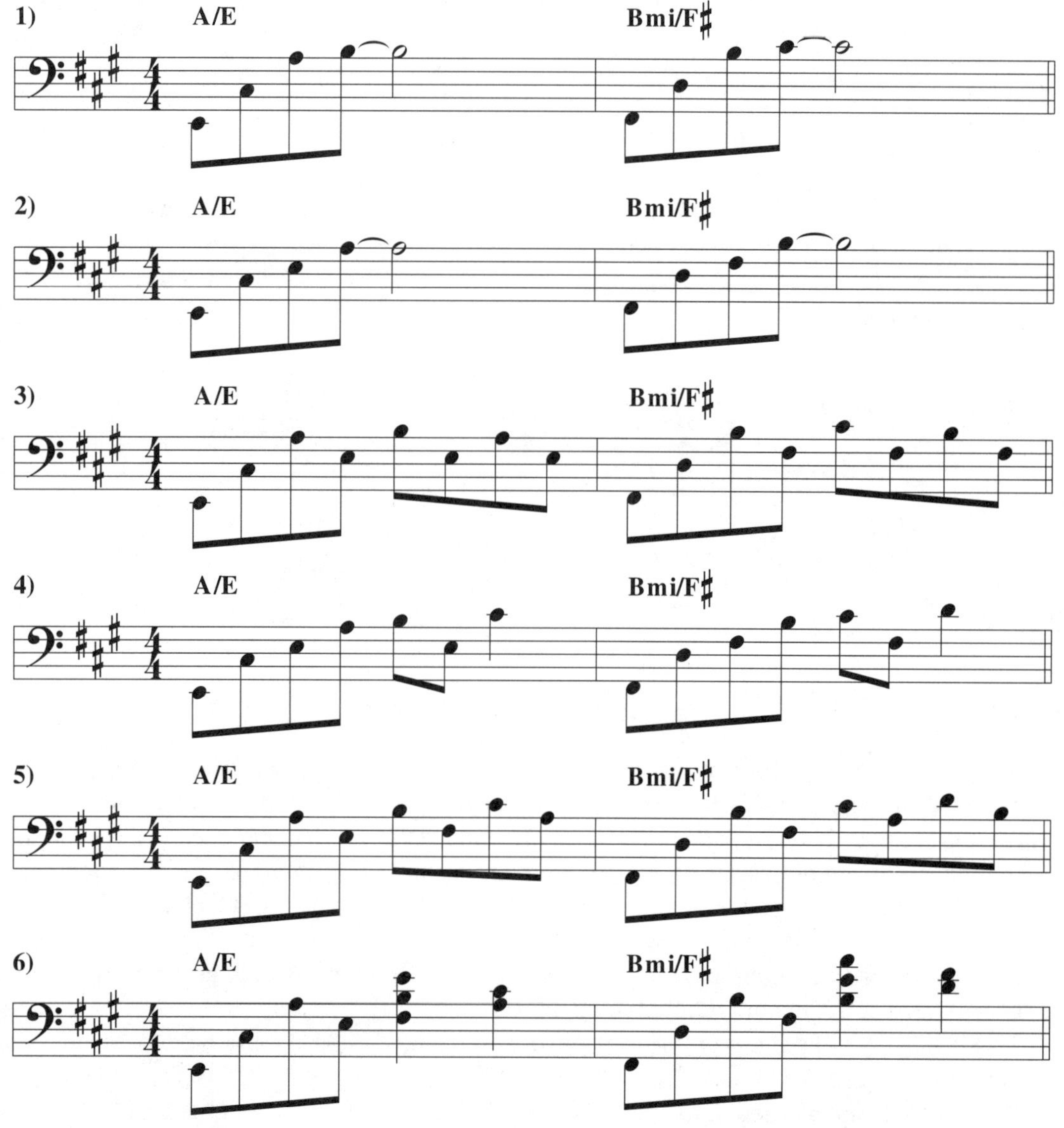

We will analyze these patterns with the 5th of the chord in the bass voice, as follows:-

Pattern #1 A **5-3-1-9** pattern on the major chord, and **5-b3-1-9** on the minor chord, anticipating beat **3**.

Pattern #2 A variation of the above using basic triad tones only, with a **5-3-5-1** pattern on the major chord and a **5-b3-5-1** pattern on the minor chord.

Pattern #3 A more continuous arpeggiated pattern, using **5**, **3**, **1** & **9** (on major) and **5**, **b3**, **1** & **9** (on minor).

Left hand arpeggiated patterns (contd)

Pattern #4 A variation of pattern **#3**, ending on the **3rd** of the major chord (**b3rd** of minor chord) on beat **4**.

Pattern #5 Another continuous arpeggiated pattern, this time using **5**, **3**, **1**, **9** & **6** on the major chord and **5**, **b3**, **1**, **9** & **b7** on the minor chord.

Pattern #6 On the major chord, we have a **5-3-1-5** pattern during beats **1** & **2**, a **6-9-5** double 4th structure (see **Fig. 10.11.**) on beat **3**, and a **1-3** 3rd interval coupling on beat **4**. On the minor chord we use a **5-b3-1-5** pattern followed by a **1-11-b7** double 4th structure (see **Fig. 10.8.**) on beat **3**, and a **b3-5** 3rd interval coupling on beat **4**.

Apart from major and minor chords (with any necessary extensions as indicated), the other popular chord type in this style is the **suspended dominant** i.e. a dominant chord which has the **4th** (**11th**) in place of the **3rd** (see **Figs. 1.78.**, **1.89.**, **5.2.**, **7.2.** & **7.4.** for illustrations of suspended dominant chords). These structures are also plural to an incomplete minor 11th (i.e. without the 3rd) chord. Here now are some left hand eighth-note patterns illustrated on this type of suspended chord:-

Figure 13.4. Left hand 8th note patterns, for use on suspended dominant (or incomplete minor 11th) chords *(Cassette Tape Examples 354-360)*

Left hand arpeggiated patterns (contd)

We will analyze these patterns for suspended dominant chords as follows:-

Pattern #1 A **1-11-5-b7** pattern, anticipating beat **3**. This is basically an arpeggiated '**7sus**' chord from bottom to top - see **Fig. 1.78**.

Pattern #2 A small variation on the above, now using a **1-5-11-b7** pattern.

Pattern #3 This pattern begins with the **1** & **5** during beat **1**, and then uses **11-b7** and **5-1** 4th couplings (see **Fig. 12.25**.) on beat **2** and on the '**& of 2**', anticipating beat **3**.

Pattern #4 A busier **1-5-b7-9-11-b7** pattern, with the **9th** anticipating beat **3**.

Pattern #5 A variation on the above, with a **9-11** 3rd coupling now anticipating beat **3**.

Pattern #6 A more continuous arpeggiated pattern, using the **1**, **5**, **b7** & **11** of the chord.

Pattern #7 A **1-5-9** pattern followed by an inverted **1-11-b7** double 4th structure (see **Fig. 10.8**.), anticipating beat **3**.

Now we will turn our attention to some sixteenth-note left hand patterns on major, minor and suspended dominant chords. These may now feature sixteenth-note anticipations of beats **2**, **3** or **4** (see discussion in the text accompanying **Fig. 2.44**.). Generally however in sixteenth-note new age styles, the main chord rhythms are still falling on the downbeats, and any anticipations function as rhythmic embellishments within the duration of the chord. Again when applying these patterns, bear in mind the comments made regarding the appropriate registers for basic chord tones and extensions, as outlined in the text following **Fig. 13.1**. We will now look at some 16th-note patterns for major and minor chords in root position:-

Figure 13.5. Left hand 16th note patterns, for use on root position major and minor chords
(Cassette Tape Examples 361-367)

Left hand arpeggiated patterns (contd)

Figure 13.5. contd

We will analyze these patterns on root-position major and minor chords as follows:-

Pattern #1 A **1-5-9-3-5** pattern followed by a **6-9-5** double 4th structure (see **Fig. 10.11**.) on the major chord, and a **1-5-9-b3-5** pattern followed by an **11-b7-b3** double 4th structure (see **Fig. 10.5**.) on the minor chord. In both cases the **3rd** (or **b3rd**) is anticipating beat **2**, and the double 4th is anticipating beat **3**.

Pattern #2 A busier arpeggiated pattern using 1, 5, 9, 3 & 6 on the major chord and 1, 5, 9, **b3**, **b7** & 11 on the minor chord. Beats **2**, **3** & **4** are being anticipated.

Pattern #3 A **1-5-3** pattern followed by **9-5**, **3-6** & **5-1** 4th couplings on the major chord (see **Fig. 12.24**.), and a **1-5-b3** pattern followed by **9-5**, **11-b7** & **5-1** 4th couplings on the minor chord (see **Fig. 12.25**.). In each case the 4th couplings are anticipating beats **2** & **3**.

Pattern #4 A more continuous arpeggiated pattern leading to an anticipation of beat **3**, using the 1, 5, 3, 9 & 6 of the major chord and 1, 5, **b3**, 9, **b7** & 11 on the minor chord.

Pattern #5 A variation on the above, now using a **3-6-9** double 4th structure (see **Fig. 10.6**.) and a **5-1** 4th coupling (see **Fig. 12.24**.) on the major chord, and using an **11-b7-b3** double 4th structure (see **Fig. 10.5**.) and a **5-1** 4th coupling (see **Fig. 12.25**.) on the minor chord. In each case the 4th coupling is anticipating beat **3**.

Pattern #6 Another busier pattern, this time starting with an 8th note and using 1, 5, 3, 9 & 6 on the major chord and 1, 5, **b3**, 9 & 11 on the minor chord. Again beats **2**, **3** & **4** are being anticipated.

Pattern #7 A sparser version of pattern **#1**. A **1-5-3-5** pattern is followed by a **6-9** 4th coupling (see **Fig. 12.24**.) on the major chord, and a **1-5-b3-5** pattern is followed by an **11-b7** 4th coupling (see **Fig. 12.23**.) on the minor chord. In both cases beats **2** & **3** are being anticipated.

Now we will look at some 16th-note left hand patterns for major and minor chords inverted over the 3rd in the bass voice, as follows:-

Left hand arpeggiated patterns (contd)

Figure 13.6. Left hand 16th note patterns, for use on major and minor chords inverted over the 3rd in the bass voice *(CASSETTE TAPE EXAMPLES 368-372)*

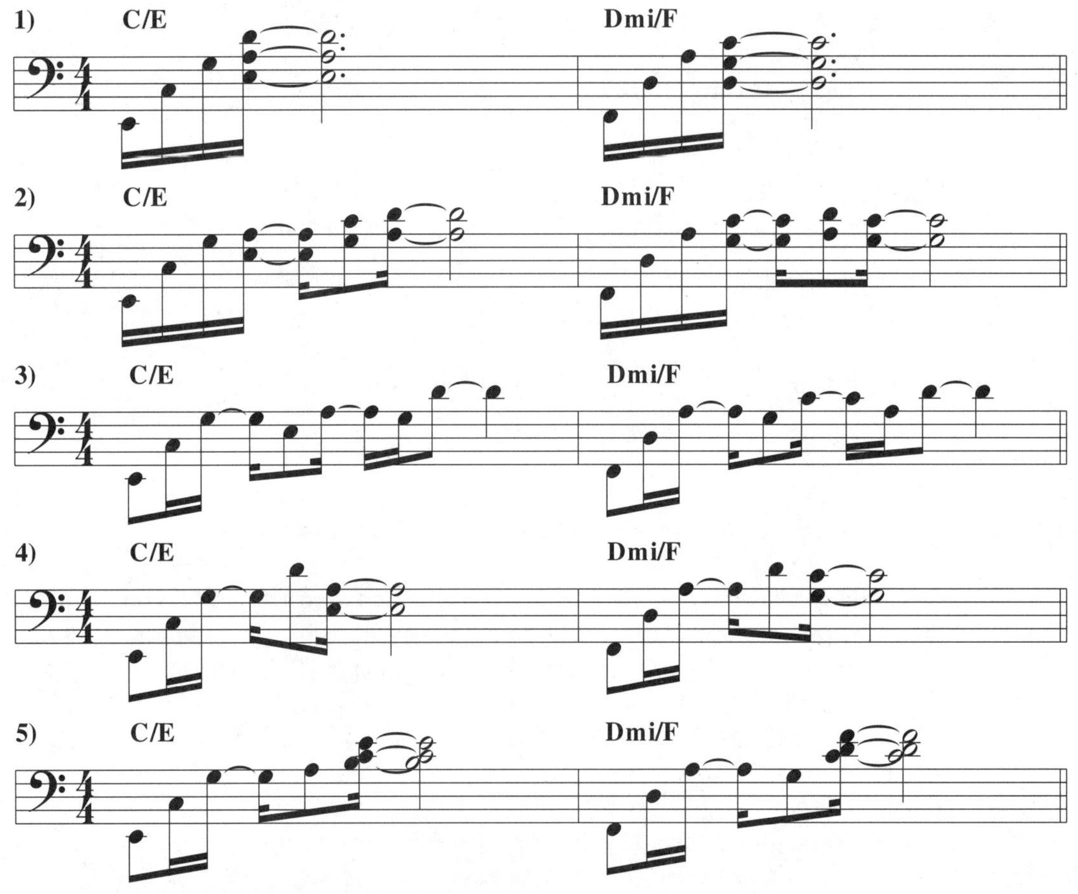

We will analyze these patterns with the 3rd of the chord in the bass voice, as follows:-

Pattern #1 A **3-1-5** pattern followed by a **3-6-9** double 4th structure (see **Fig. 10.6.**) on the major chord, and a **b3-1-5** pattern followed by a **1-11-b7** double 4th structure (see **Fig. 10.8.**) on the minor chord. In both cases the double 4th is anticipating beat **3**.

Pattern #2 A **3-1-5** pattern followed by **3-6**, **5-1** & **6-9** 4th couplings on the major chord (see **Fig. 12.24.**) and a **b3-1-5** pattern followed by **11-b7**, **5-1** & **11-b7** 4th couplings (see **Fig. 12.23.**) on the minor chord. The 4th couplings are anticipating beats **2** & **3**.

Pattern #3 A busier pattern, starting with an 8th note and using **3**, **1**, **5**, **6** & **9** on the major chord and **b3**, **1**, **5**, **11** & **b7** on the minor chord. Beats **2**, **3** & **4** are being anticipated.

Pattern #4 A **3-1-5-9** pattern followed by a **3-6** 4th coupling (see **Fig. 12.24.**) on the major chord, and a **b3-1-5-1** pattern followed by an **11-b7** 4th coupling (see **Fig. 12.23.**) on the minor chord. In both cases beats **2** & **3** are being anticipated.

Pattern #5 A **3-1-5-6** pattern followed by a **7-1-3** 'half-step-4th' cluster on the major chord, and a **b3-1-5-11** pattern followed by a **b7-1-b3** 'whole-step-4th' cluster on the minor chord. As discussed later in this chapter (in **Figs. 13.9. - 13.18.**), the 'half-step-4th' cluster has a span of a 4th interval with

Left hand arpeggiated patterns (contd)

a half-step at the bottom, while a 'whole-step-4th' cluster has a span of a 4th interval with a whole-step at the bottom. In each case the 5th of the chord is anticipating beat **2** and the 'cluster' is anticipating beat **3**.

Now we will look at some 16th-note left hand patterns for major and minor chords inverted over the 5th in the bass voice, as follows:-

Figure 13.7. Left hand 16th note patterns, for use on major and minor chords inverted over the 5th in the bass voice *(Cassette Tape Examples 373-376)*

We will analyze these patterns with the 5th of the chord in the bass voice, as follows:-

Pattern #1 A **5-3-1-7-5** pattern followed by a **6-9** 4th coupling on the major chord (see **Fig. 12.24.**) and a **5-b3-1-b7-5** pattern followed by an **11-b7** 4th coupling (see **Fig. 12.23.**) on the minor chord. The 7th after the root here on the major chord (with the sustain pedal depressed) causes a dissonant quality due to the half-step interval used. Beats **1** & **2** are being anticipated.

Pattern #2 A **5-3-1** pattern followed by a **6-9-5** double 4th structure (see **Fig. 10.11.**) on the major chord, and a **5-b3-1** pattern followed by an **11-b7-b3** double 4th structure (see **Fig. 10.5.**) on the minor chord. The double 4th is anticipating beat **2**.

Pattern #3 A variation on pattern **#1**, starting with an 8th note and without the 4th coupling at the end.

Pattern #4 Another variation of the above, this time ending on a **9-3-5** 'whole-step-4th' cluster on the major chord, and ending on a **9-b3-5** 'half-step-4th' cluster on the minor chord. (See later discussion in this chapter regarding these clusters). Again beats **2** & **3** are being anticipated.

Left hand arpeggiated patterns (contd)

Now we will look at some 16th-note patterns for suspended dominant (or incomplete minor) chords:-

Figure 13.8. Left hand 16th note patterns, for use on suspended dominant (or incomplete minor 11th) chords *(Cassette Tape Examples 377-381)*

We will analyze these patterns for suspended dominant chords as follows:-

Pattern #1 A **1-5-9-b7-11** pattern followed by a **5-1** 4th coupling (see **Fig. 12.25.**). Beats **2** & **3** are being anticipated.

Pattern #2 A **1-5-1-11-5** pattern followed by an inverted **1-11-b7** double 4th structure (see **Fig. 10.8.**). Again beats **2** & **3** are being anticipated.

Pattern #3 A syncopated **1-11-b7-5-1** pattern, starting with an 8th note and again anticipating beats **2** & **3**.

Pattern #4 A more continuous arpeggiated pattern, using the **1**, **5**, **b7** & **11** of the chord. Beats **2**, **3** & **4** are being anticipated.

Pattern #5 A **1-5-9-13-b7-11** pattern, followed by a **5-1** 4th coupling (see **Fig. 12.25.**). The addition of the **13th** to the dominant suspension gives a more sophisticated sound. Beats **2**, **3** & **4** are again being anticipated.

Left hand arpeggiated patterns (contd)

Practice directions:-

- ***Practice the new age 8th-note left hand patterns on major*** *(root position and inverted),* ***minor*** *(root position and inverted)* ***and suspended dominant chords as in Figs. 13.1. - 13.4.***
- ***Practice the new age 16th-note left hand patterns on major*** *(root position and inverted),* ***minor*** *(root position and inverted)* ***and suspended dominant chords as in Figs. 13.5. - 13.8.***
- ***Experiment with adapting these patterns to different keys, ensuring that basic chord tones and extensions are kept in the appropriate registers as detailed in the text following Fig. 13.1.***

(Don't forget to depress the sustain pedal for the duration of each chord - and of course to release the pedal between chord changes!)

Right hand 'clusters'

As well as the previously studied right hand devices (triads, double 4ths, interval couplings etc.) there are some additional structures to look at which are of particular use in new age styles. We will first look at a couple of note configurations which I have termed '**whole-step-4th**' and '**half-step-4th**' clusters. I use the term 'cluster' here because we have three pitches together within a short interval span (a perfect 4th), creating a dense and to some degree dissonant quality. These are sophisticated sounds which can be very stylistic, as follows:-

Figure 13.9. 'Whole-step-4th' cluster example
(Cassette Tape Example 382)

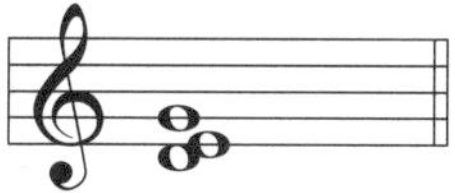

Here we use the term '**whole-step-4th**' cluster because:-
- the overall span from bottom to top is a perfect **4th** interval
- the interval between the bottom two notes is a **whole-step**.

Compare this to **Fig. 8.1**. and you'll see that this structure looks like the **9th**, **3rd** & **5th** of a major chord (without the '**9 to 1**' resolution).

Figure 13.10. 'Half-step-4th' cluster example
(Cassette Tape Example 383)

Here we use the term '**half-step-4th**' cluster because:-
- the overall span from bottom to top is a perfect **4th** interval
- the interval between the bottom two notes is a **half-step**.

Compare this to **Fig. 8.21**. and you'll see that this structure looks like the **9th**, **b3rd** & **5th** of a minor chord (again without the '**9 to 1**' resolution).

Right hand 'clusters' (contd)

We will now see what happens when we place these clusters over different roots in the bass voice. This process has some parallels in the previous text concerning '**9 to 1 resolutions within triad-over-root chords**' and you are encouraged to refer back to **Chapter 8** as necessary. Placing these 'clusters' over different roots creates interesting and sophisticated vertical sounds which are of great value in new age (and new-age-jazz) styles. First we will start with the 'whole-step-4th' cluster (see **Fig. 13.9.**) over different roots as follows:-

Figure 13.11. D-E-G 'whole-step-4th' cluster with C in bass voice
(Cassette Tape Example 384)

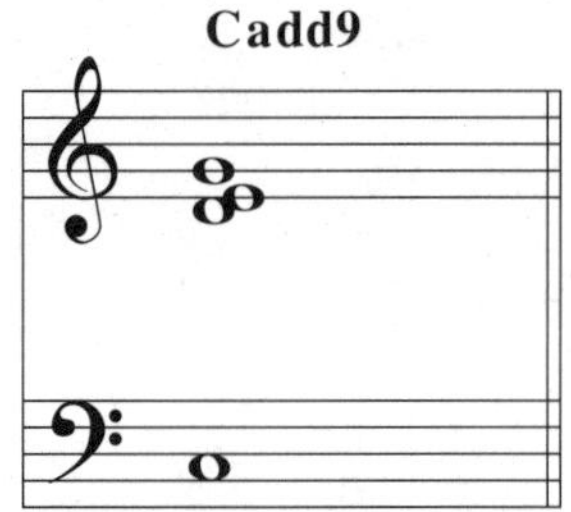

This creates a **major chord** with an added **9th** (see **Figs. 1.93.** & **8.12.**). The top note is the **5th** of the chord - so this structure could be used under the 5th in the melody on a major chord, or to place the 5th on top for voiceleading purposes. When using this voicing, we will refer to it as a **9-3-5** upper structure, as (with respect to the C in the bass) we are using the 9th, 3rd & 5th of the overall major chord. This structure could also be inverted over the 3rd of the chord in the bass voice (see **Fig. 13.14.**), or (less frequently) over the 5th.

Figure 13.12. D-E-G 'whole-step-4th' cluster with A in bass voice
(Cassette Tape Example 385)

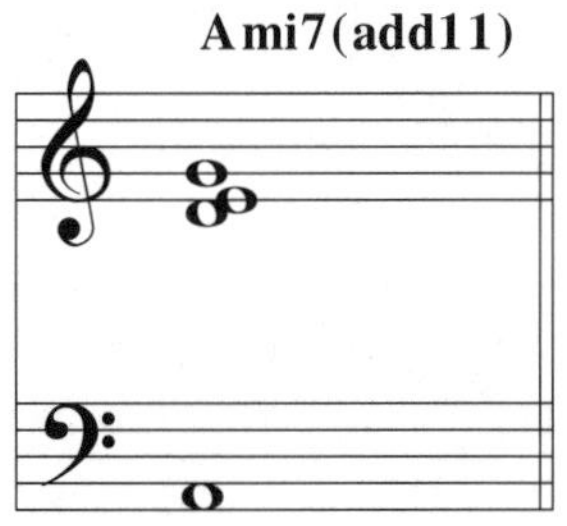

This creates a **minor 7th** chord with an added **11th** (see **Fig. 8.14.**), or a **suspended dominant 7th** chord (see **Fig. 1.78.**). The top note is the **7th** of the chord - so this structure could be used under the 7th in the melody on a minor or suspended dominant chord, or to place the 7th on top for voiceleading purposes. When using this voicing, we will refer to it as an **11-5-b7** upper structure, as (with respect to the A in the bass) we are using the 11th, 5th & b7th of the overall minor or suspended dominant chord.

Figure 13.13. D-E-G 'whole-step-4th' cluster with F in bass voice
(Cassette Tape Example 386)

This creates a **major 69** chord with an added **7th** (see **Fig. 8.16.**). (A major quality is implied even though the 3rd is not present). The top note is the **9th** of the chord - so this structure could be used under the 9th in the melody on a major chord, or to place the 9th on top for voiceleading purposes. When using this voicing, we will refer to it as a **6-7-9** upper structure, as (with respect to the F in the bass) we are using the 6th, 7th & 9th of the overall major chord.

Right hand 'clusters' (contd)

Figure 13.14. D-E-G 'whole-step-4th' cluster with E in bass voice

(Cassette tape Example 387)

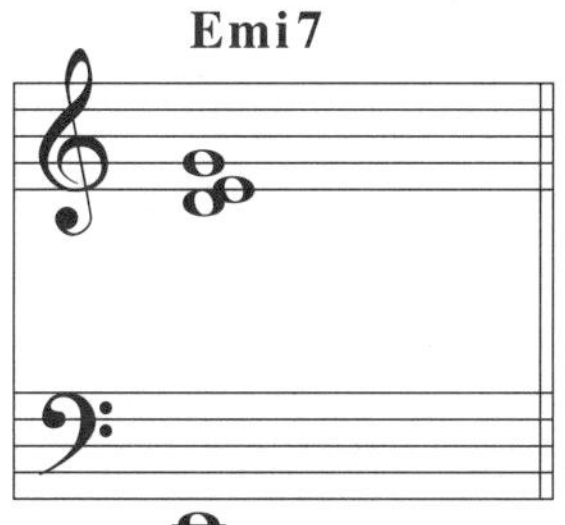

This will frequently be heard as a **minor 7th** chord - in which case it can be used under the b3rd in the top voice on this chord. In this context we will refer to it as a **b7-1-b3** upper structure, as (with respect to the E in the bass) we are using the b7th, root & b3rd of the overall minor chord. Another interpretation is as an incomplete **major (add9)** chord inverted the 3rd (**Cadd9/E** in this example) which could then be used under the 5th in the top voice. In this context we will refer to it as a **9-3-5** upper structure (see **Fig. 13.11.**) inverted over the 3rd (E in this case).

Now we will place the 'half-step-4th' cluster (see **Fig. 13.10.**) over some different roots as follows:-

Figure 13.15. D-Eb-G 'half-step-4th' cluster with C in bass voice

(Cassette tape Example 388)

This creates a **minor chord** with an added **9th** (see **Figs. 1.94.** & **8.30.**) The top note is the **5th** of the chord - so this structure could be used under the 5th in the melody on a minor chord, or to place the 5th on top for voiceleading purposes. When using this voicing, we will refer to it as a **9-b3-5** upper structure, as (with respect to the C in the bass) we are using the 9th, b3rd & 5th of the overall minor chord.

Figure 13.16. D-Eb-G 'half-step-4th' cluster with Ab in bass voice

(Cassette tape Example 389)

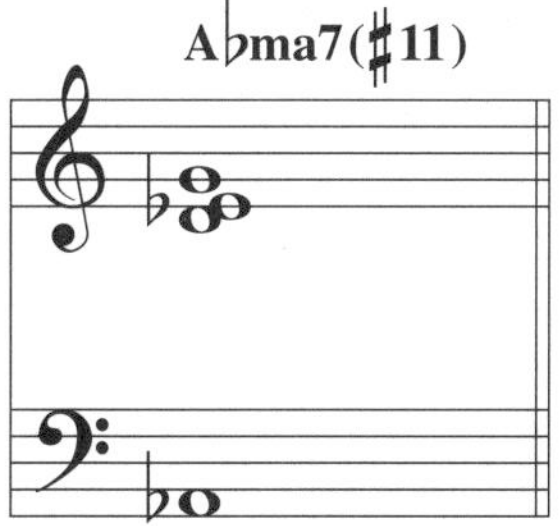

This creates a **major 7th** chord with a raised **11th** (see **Fig. 8.32.**) The top note is the **7th** of the chord - so this structure could be used under the 7th in the melody on a major chord (with care as this is a rather angular sound!) or to place the 7th on top for voiceleading purposes. When using this voicing, we will refer to it as a **#11-5-7** upper structure, as (with respect to the Ab in the bass) we are using the #11th, 5th & 7th of the overall major chord.

Figure 13.17. D-Eb-G 'half-step-4th' cluster with F in bass voice

(Cassette tape Example 390)

This creates an incomplete **13th** chord which could assume any of the chord symbol implications shown, depending on the context (see **Fig. 8.34.**). The top note is the **9th** of the chord - so this structure could be used under the 9th in the melody on a minor/dominant/suspended chord, or to place the 9th on top for voiceleading purposes.When using this voicing, we will refer to it as a **13-b7-9** upper structure, as (with respect to the F in the bass) we are using the 13th, b7th & 9th of the overall 13th chord.

Right hand 'clusters' (contd)

Figure 13.18. D-Eb-G 'half-step-4th' cluster with Eb in bass voice
(Cassette Tape Example 391)

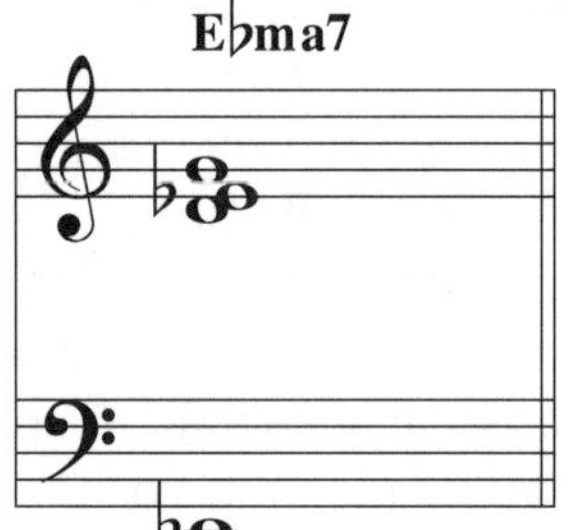

This creates a **major 7th** chord - the upper structure represents the 7th, root and 3rd (from bottom to top) of the major chord. This is a 'definitive' sound as the important tones of the 7th chord (i.e. the 3rd & 7th) are present. The top note is the **3rd** of the chord - so this structure could be used under the 3rd in the melody on a major chord, or to place the 3rd on top for voiceleading purposes. When using this voicing, we will refer to it as a **7-1-3** upper structure, as (with respect to the Eb in the bass) we are using the 7th, root & 3rd of the overall major chord.

Right hand 'half-step & 5th' structures

Another very useful right hand device in new age styles (as well as jazz-influenced idioms such as R'n'B/ Funk) is what I call the '**half-step & 5th**' structure. Basically this is a perfect 5th interval stacked on top of a half-step, as follows:-

Figure 13.19. 'Half-step & 5th' structure example
(Cassette Tape Example 392)

As you can see, the bottom interval (B up to C) is a half-step, and the top interval (C up to G) is a perfect 5th. This creates an angular and stylistic quality.

Now we will see what happens when we place this 'half-step & 5th' structure over some different roots, as follows:-

Figure 13.20. B-C-G 'Half-step & 5th' structure with A in bass voice
(Cassette Tape Example 393)

This creates a **minor 9th** chord (technically, without the 5th - which is not a critical definitve note on this chord). This is a very popular new age-type voicing for the minor chord. The top note is the **7th** of the chord - so this is typically used under the 7th in the melody on the minor chord, or to place the 7th on top for voiceleading purposes. When using this voicing, we will refer to it as a **9-b3-b7** upper structure, as (with respect to the A in the bass) we are using the 9th, b3rd & b7th of the overall minor chord.

Right hand 'half-step & 5th' structures

Figure 13.21. B-C-G 'half-step & 5th' structure with F in bass voice
(Cassette Tape Example 394)

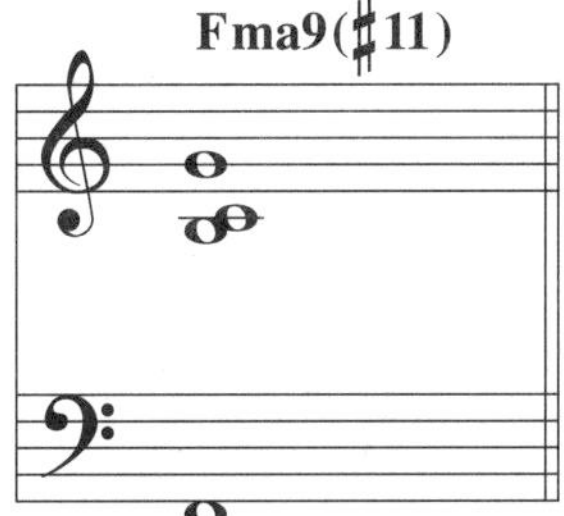

This creates an incomplete **major 9th** chord with a raised **11th**. (The 3rd and 7th of the chord are not present). The result is a sophisticated and 'tense' vertical quality. The top note is the **9th** of the chord - so this could be used under the 9th in the melody on a major chord, or to place the 9th on top for voiceleading purposes. When using this voicing, we will refer to it as a **#11-5-9** upper structure, as (with respect to the F in the bass) we are using the #11th, 5th & 9th of the overall major chord.

Figure 13.22. B-C-G 'half-step & 5th' structure with E in bass voice
(Cassette Tape Example 395)

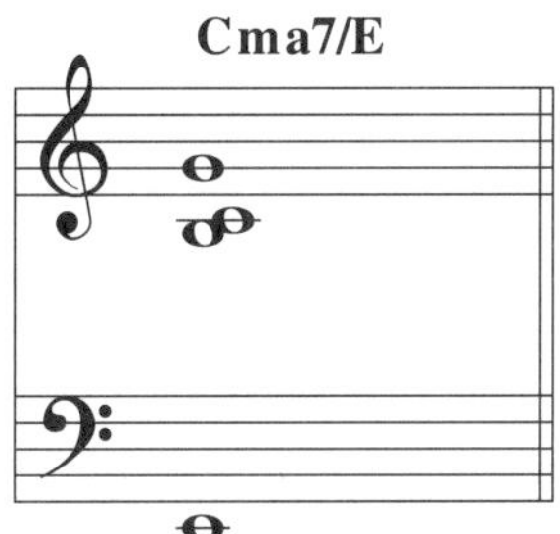

This creates a **major 7th** chord, inverted over the **3rd** - another very popular voicing in this style (see the various left hand patterns inverting major and minor chords over the 3rd, earlier in this chapter). The top note is the **5th** of the chord - so this could be used under the 5th in the melody on an (inverted) major chord, or to place the 5th on top for voiceleading purposes. When using this voicing, we will refer to it as a **7-1-5** upper structure (see **Fig. 13.24.**) inverted over the 3rd - in this example we have the 7th, root & 5th of an inverted Cma7 chord.

Figure 13.23. B-C-G 'half-step & 5th' structure with D in bass voice
(Cassette Tape Example 396)

This creates an incomplete **suspended dominant 13th** chord. (The 5th and the 9th of the chord are not present). In a small number of cases, an incomplete **minor 13th** chord quality may also be implied. The top note is the **11th** of the chord - so this could be used under the 11th in the melody on a suspended dominant chord, or to place the 11th on top for voiceleading purposes. When using this voicing, we will refer to it as a **13-b7-11** upper structure, as (with respect to the D in the bass) we are using the 13th, b7th & 11th of the overall suspended or minor chord.

Figure 13.24. B-C-G 'half-step & 5th' structure with C in bass voice
(Cassette Tape Example 397)

This creates an incomplete **major 7th** chord. (The 3rd of the chord is not present). The top note is the **5th** of the chord - so this could be used under the 5th in the melody on the major chord, or to place the 5th on top for voiceleading purposes. When using this voicing, we will refer to it as a **7-1-5** upper structure, as (with respect to the C in the bass) we are using the 7th, root & 5th of the overall major chord. This structure can also be inverted over the 3rd (see **Fig. 13.22.**) or 5th of the chord.

<u>*PRACTICE DIRECTIONS:-*</u>

- ***Practice the new age 'whole-step-4th cluster over root' examples as in Figs. 13.11. - 13.14.***
- ***Practice the new age 'half-step-4th cluster over root' examples as in Figs. 13.15. - 13.18.***
- ***Practice the new age 'half-step-&-5th over root' examples as in Figs. 13.19. - 13.24.***

*It is very desirable to familiarize yourself with these vertical structures **in all keys!** You should take each one round the circle-of-5ths and/or circle-of-4ths, as was done for the triad-over-root chords in **Chapter 5** and the 4-part-over-root chords in **Chapter 7**.*

New age accompaniment

We will now turn our attention to some accompaniment examples in a new age style. In the introduction to this chapter we said that new age can be played with both 8th-note and 16th-note rhythmic subdivisions. We will look at a simple chord chart example and illustrate some different 8th- and 16th-note 'comping' interpretations. The chord chart here contains a simple **1 - 6 - 4 - 5** progression as follows:-

Figure 13.25. New age chord chart example #1

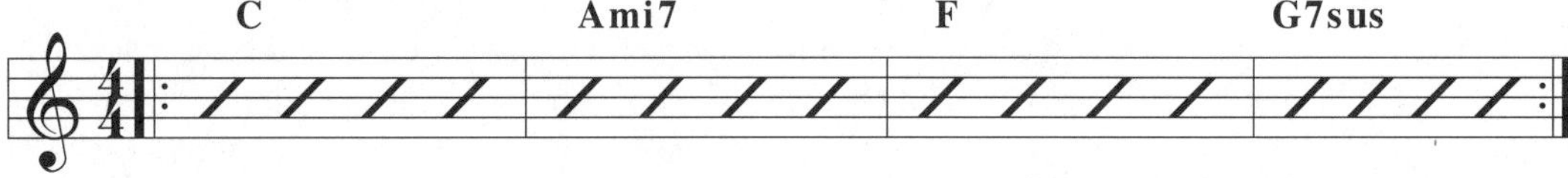

Our first 8th-note 'comping' version of these chords uses arpeggiated left hand patterns with double-4th structures in the right hand, as follows (again don't forget to use the sustain pedal for the duration of each chord):-

Figure 13.26. New age comping solution a) for chord chart #1 (Fig. 13.25.)
(CASSETTE TAPE EXAMPLE 398)

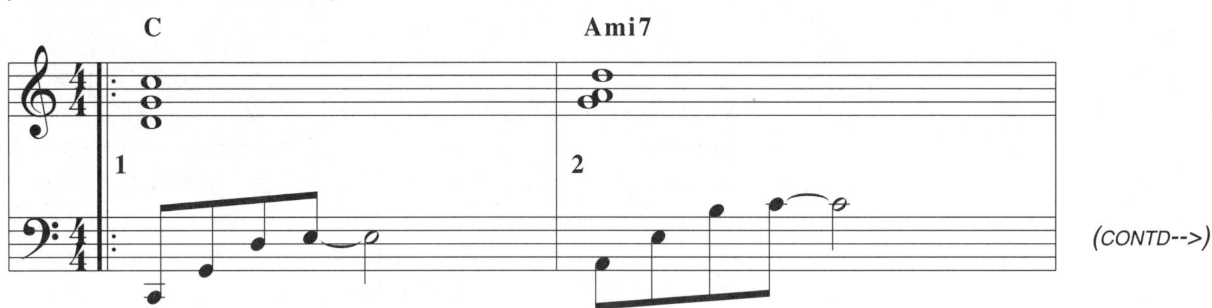

(CONTD-->)

New age accompaniment (contd)

Figure 13.26. contd

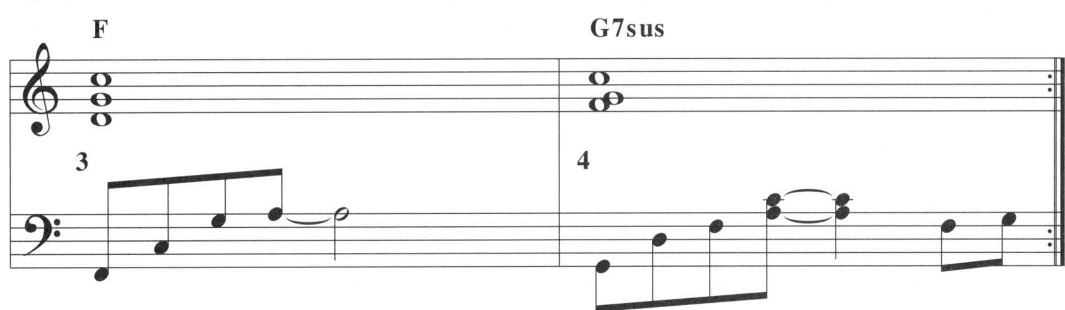

We can analyze the above example as follows:-

- Measure 1 The left hand is playing a **1-5-9-3** pattern on the **C** chord, anticipating beat **3** (see **Fig. 13.1. pattern #1 1st half**). The right hand is playing a **9-5-1** double 4th structure (see **Fig. 10.7.**).

- Measure 2 The left hand is playing a **1-5-9-b3** pattern on the **Ami7** chord, again anticipating beat **3** (see **Fig. 13.1. pattern #1 2nd half**). The right hand is playing an inverted **1-11-b7** double 4th structure (see **Fig. 10.8.**).

- Measure 3 The left hand is playing a **1-5-9-3** pattern on the **F** chord, again anticipating beat **3** (see **Fig. 13.1. pattern #1 1st half**). The right hand is playing a **6-9-5** double 4th structure (see **Fig. 10.11.**).

- Measure 4 The left hand is playing a **1-5-b7** pattern followed by a **9-11** 3rd interval coupling on the **G7sus** chord, anticipating beat **3** (see **Fig. 13.4. pattern #5**). The right hand is playing an inverted **1-11-b7** double 4th structure (see **Fig. 10.8.**).

Now the next 8th-note 'comping' version uses arpeggiated double 4th structures in the right hand:-

Figure 13.27. New age comping solution b) for chord chart #1 (Fig. 13.25.)
(Cassette Tape Example 399)

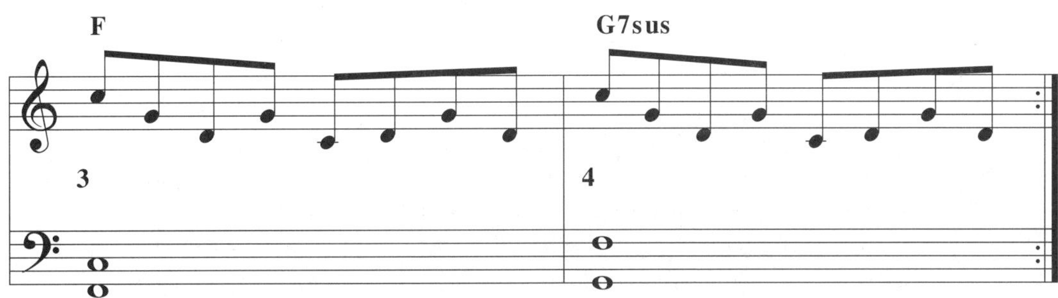

New age accompaniment (contd)

Again we can analyze the previous example as follows:-

- Measure 1 The right hand is arpeggiating inversions of a **9-5-1** double 4th structure (see **Fig. 10.7.**) on the **C** chord. The left hand is using a simple root-5th interval coupling.

- Measure 2 The right hand is arpeggiating inversions of an **11-b7-b3** double 4th structure (see **Fig. 10.5.**) on the **Ami7** chord. The left hand is using a simple root-b7th interval coupling. (Left hand 'root-b7ths' are very useful in this register on minor and dominant-type chords).

- Measure 3 The right hand is arpeggiating inversions of a **6-9-5** double 4th structure (see **Fig. 10.11.**) on the **F** chord. The left hand is using a simple root-5th interval coupling.

- Measure 4 The right hand is arpeggiating inversions of a **5-1-11** double 4th structure (see **Fig. 10.3.**) on the **G7sus** chord. The left hand is again using a root-b7th interval coupling.

Now we will look at the first of two 16th-note subdivision 'comping' solutions for the same chord sequence. As with the first 8th-note solution (see **Fig. 13.26.**), we will use arpeggiated left hand patterns, this time with a 'constant' or repeated double 4th structure in the right hand, as follows:-

Figure 13.28. New age comping solution c) for chord chart #1 (Fig. 13.25.)
(Cassette Tape Example 400)

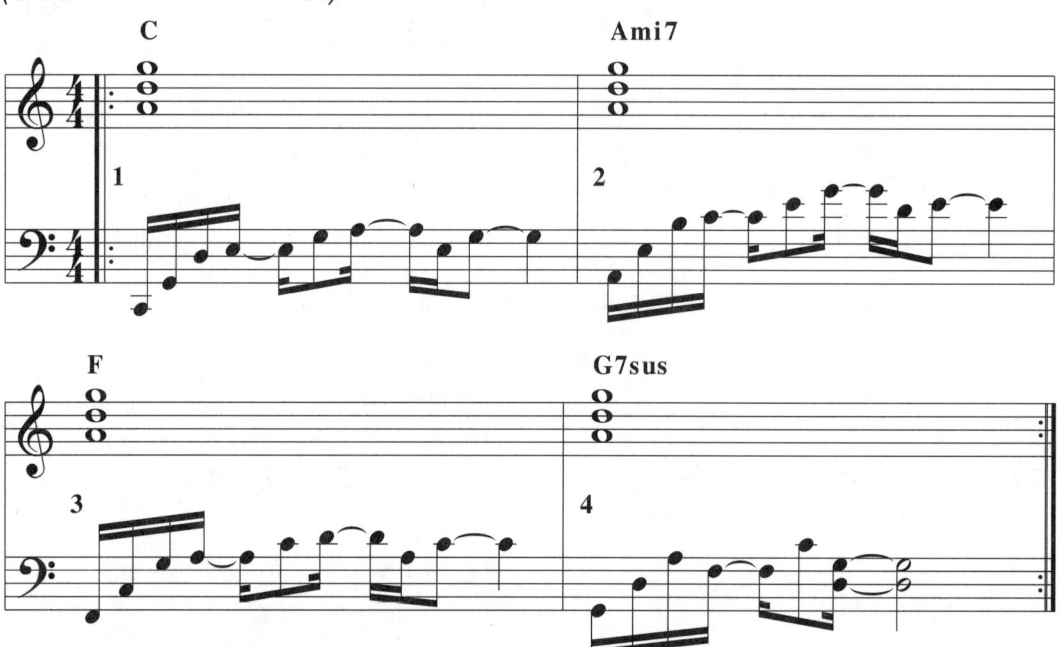

We can analyze the above example as follows:-

- Measure 1 The left hand is playing a syncopated pattern using the **1**, **5**, **9**, **3** & **6** of the **C** chord (see **Fig. 13.5. pattern #2 1st half**). The right hand is playing a **6-9-5** double 4th structure (see **Fig. 10.11.**).

- Measure 2 The left hand is playing a similar pattern on the **Ami7**, this time using the **1**, **5**, **9**, **b3**, **b7** & **11** of the chord (see **Fig. 13.5. pattern #2 2nd half**). The right hand is repeating the **A-D-G** double 4th, which on this chord becomes a **1-11-b7** structure (see **Fig. 10.8.**).

New age accompaniment (contd)

- Measure 3 The left hand is using the same pattern on the F chord as was used for the C chord in measure **1** (see **Fig. 13.5. pattern #2 1st half**). The right hand is repeating the **A-D-G** double 4th, which on this chord becomes a **3-6-9** structure (see **Fig. 10.6.**).

- Measure 4 The left hand is using a **1-5-9-b7-11** pattern followed by a **5-1** 4th coupling (see **Fig. 13.8. pattern #1**). The right hand is repeating the **A-D-G** double 4th, which on this chord becomes a **9-5-1** structure (see **Fig. 10.7.**). The **9-5-1** double 4th here will generally work on (or at least not contradict) the suspended dominant chord, if the **7th** & **11th** (the other critical tones of the suspended dominant apart from the root) are also provided - this is the case in measure 4 as the left hand pattern is providing these chord tones.

Now the next 16th-note 'comping' version uses syncopated arpeggios in both hands, as follows:-

Figure 13.29. New age comping solution d) for chord chart #1 (Fig. 13.25.)
(Cassette Tape Example 401)

We can analyze the above example as follows:-

- Measure 1 The right hand is arpeggiating a combination of **9-5-1** (see **Fig. 10.7.**) and **3-6-9** (see **Fig. 10.6.**) double 4th structures on the **C** chord, anticipating beats **2** & **3**. The left hand is using a simple **1-5-1** pattern, with the same anticipations.

- Measure 2 The right hand is repeating the same notes and rhythms from measure **1**, which now become a combination of **11-b7-b3** (see **Fig. 10.5.**) and **5-1-11** (see **Fig. 10.3.**) double 4th structures on the **Ami7** chord. The left hand is using a simple **1-5-b7** pattern, again anticipating beats **2** & **3**.

- Measure 3 The right hand is again repeating the same notes and rhythms, which now become a combination of **6-9-5** (see **Fig. 10.11.**) and **7-3-6** (see **Fig. 10.9.**) double 4th structures on the **F** chord. The left hand is using a simple **1-5-3** open triad pattern (see **Fig. 11.11.**).

New age accompaniment (contd)

Analysis of Fig. 13.29. contd

- Measure 4

The right hand is again repeating the same notes and rhythms, which now become a combination of **5-1-11** (see **Fig. 10. 3.**) and **6-9-5** (see **Fig. 10.11.**) double 4th structures on the **G7sus** chord. In fact the note E here is more correctly termed a 13th than a 6th on the dominant chord, and generally needs the support of the 7th of the chord to work. This is provided by the left hand, which is using a simple **1-b7-9** pattern.

New age melody

We will now look at the interpretation of some leadsheets (melody and chord symbols) in a new age style. Typically (although not always) the melody will be slow moving, repetitive and motivic. Here is our first leadsheet example, using inversions in the bass voice and an 8th-note rhythmic subdivision:-

Figure 13.30. New age leadsheet example #1

The simplest new age treatment is play the melody as (unsupported) single notes in the right hand, with arpeggiated patterns in the left hand, as follows:-

Figure 13.31. New age melody solution a) for leadsheet #1 (Fig. 13.30.)
(Cassette Tape Example 402)

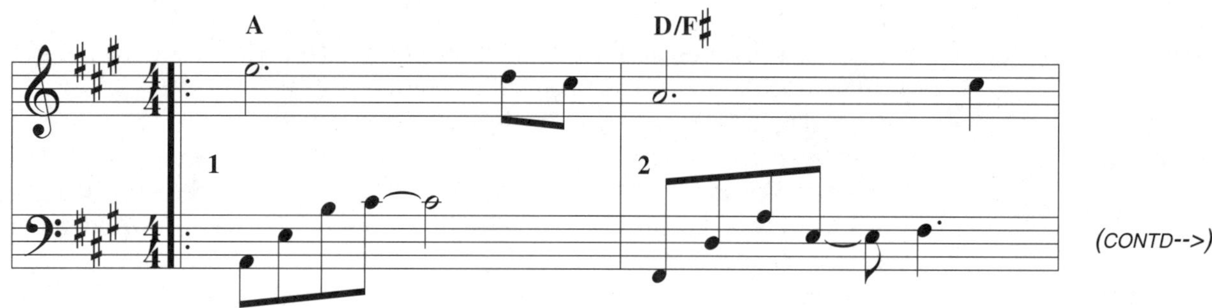

(CONTD-->)

New age melody (contd)

Figure 13.31. (contd)

We can analyze each left hand arpeggio pattern in this example as follows:-

- Measure 1	A **1-5-9-3** pattern on the **A** chord (see **Fig. 13.1. pattern #1 1st half**), anticipating beat **3**.
- Measure 2	A **3-1-5-9-3** pattern on the **D/F#** chord (see **Fig. 13.2. pattern #4 1st half**), anticipating beats **3** & **4**.
- Measure 3	As for measure **1**, this time on a **G** chord.
- Measure 4	As for measure **2**, this time on a **C/E** chord.
- Measure 5	As for measure **1**, this time on an **F** chord.
- Measure 6	A **5-3-1-9** pattern on the **A/E** chord (see **Fig. 13.3. pattern #1 1st half**), anticipating beat **3**.
- Measure 7	A more continuous arpeggiated pattern using the **1**, **5**, **3**, **9** & **6** of the **D** chord - a variation on **Fig. 13.1. patterns #6 - #8 (1st half)**.
- Measure 8	A **1-5-9-1** pattern followed by a **9-3-5** 'whole-step-4th cluster' (see **Fig. 13.1. pattern #9 1st half** & **Fig. 13.11.**) on beat **3**, on the **D** chord.

New age melody (contd)

Now we will look at the next version of this melody, using the same left hand patterns but with different structures under the melody in the right hand. These include double-4ths, 'half-step-&-5th' structures, 'whole-step-4th' clusters and triads, as follows:-

Figure 13.32. New age melody solution b) for leadsheet #1 (Fig. 13.30.)
(CASSETTE TAPE EXAMPLE 403)

Now we will analyze the right hand structures used in the above example as follows:-

- Measure 1 A **6-9-5** double 4th structure (see **Fig. 10.11**.) is being used under the 5th in the melody (E) on the **A** chord.

New age melody (contd)

- Measure 2	A **7-1-5** 'half-step-&-5th' structure (inverted over the 3rd in the bass voice - see **Fig. 13.22.**) is being used under the 5th in the melody (A) on the **D/F#** chord.
- Measure 3	A **9-3-5** 'whole-step-4th' cluster (see **Fig. 13.11.**) is being used under the 5th in the melody (D) on the **G** chord.
- Measure 4	An inverted **9-5-1** double 4th structure (also inverted over the 3rd in the bass voice - see **Fig. 10.10.**) is being used under the 5th in the melody (G) on the **C/E** chord.
- Measure 5	An inverted **7-3-6** double 4th structure (see **Fig. 10.9.**) is being used under the 3rd in the melody (A) on the **F** chord.
- Measure 6	A **1-3-5** upper structure (a 1st inversion A triad, inverted over the 5th in the bass voice - see **Fig. 5.5.**) is being used below the root in the melody (A) on the **A/E** chord.
- Measure 7	A **5-7-9** upper structure (a 2nd inversion A triad - see **Fig. 5.4.**) is being used below the 7th in the melody (C#) on the **D** chord.
- Measure 8	As for measure **1**, under the 5th in the melody (A) on the **D** chord.

Now we will look at another version, this time using right hand arpeggios to support the melody. This is similar to the pop ballad treatment in **Fig. 11.40.**, except that we are now also using structures other than triads:-

Figure 13.33. New age melody solution c) for leadsheet #1 (Fig.13.30.)
(Cassette Tape Example 404)

(CONTD-->)

New age melody (contd)

Figure 13.33. (contd)

Notice that the left hand this time is playing a simple dotted quarter-eighth pattern using the roots of the chords (or inversions), as first shown in the pop ballad example **Fig. 11.3.** We are using arpeggiated tones below the melody in the right hand, in the 'rhythmic spaces' between the melody notes i.e. on the 8th-note subdivisions not being used by the melody, in a similar manner to the pop ballad melody treatment illustrated in **Fig. 11.40.**, except that we are now using some of the new age right hand devices (double-4ths, clusters etc.) in the right hand arpeggios. These are analyzed as follows:-

- ***Measure 1*** An arpeggiated 9-5-1 double 4th structure (see **Fig. 10.7.**) on the A chord.
- ***Measure 2*** An arpeggiated combination of a 7-1-5 'half-step-&-5th' structure (inverted over the 3rd in the bass voice - see **Fig. 13.22.**) and a 9-3-5 'whole-step-4th' cluster (again inverted over the 3rd in the bass voice - see **Fig. 13.14.**) on the D/F# chord.
- ***Measure 3*** As for measure **1**, on the G chord.
- ***Measure 4*** As for measure **2**, on the C/E chord.
- ***Measure 5*** As for measure **1**, on the F chord.
- ***Measure 6*** An arpeggiated 9-3-5 'whole-step-4th' cluster (over the 5th in the bass) on the A/E chord.
- ***Measure 7*** An arpeggiated 9-3-5 'whole-step-4th' cluster on the D chord, adding the root on beat **4**.
- ***Measure 8*** An arpeggiated 3-6-9 double 4th structure (see **Fig. 10.6.**) on the D chord.

Now we will look at another new age leadsheet using 8th-note subdivisions, this time with some suspensions in the harmony, as follows:-

Figure 13.34. New age leadsheet example #2

Our focus for this example will be on different left hand arpeggiated treatments, supporting a single note melody in the right hand. Here is the first version using this setting:-

New age melody (contd)

Figure 13.35. New age melody solution a) for leadsheet #2 (Fig. 13.34.)
(CASSETTE TAPE EXAMPLE 405)

We will analyze the left hand arpeggiated patterns used as follows:-

- Measures 1-2 A **1-11-5-b7** pattern on the **E7sus** chord (see **Fig. 13.4. pattern #1**), anticipating beat **3**.

- Measures 3-4 As for measures **1-2**, on the **D7sus** chord.

- Measure 5 A **3-7-1-5** pattern on the **Bb/D** chord (see **Fig. 13.2. pattern #1 1st half**), again anticipating beat **3**.

- Measure 6 A **1-5-6-3** pattern on the **C** chord (see **Fig. 13.1. pattern #2 1st half**), anticipating beat **3**.

- Measure 7 A **3-1-5-9-3** pattern on the **D/F#** chord (see **Fig. 13.2. pattern #4 1st half**), anticipating beats **3** & **4**.

New age melody (contd)

Analysis of Fig. 13.35. contd.

- Measure 8 A **1-5-b7** pattern followed by a **9-11** 3rd coupling on the **A7sus** chord (see **Fig. 13.4. pattern #5**), again anticipating beat **3**.

The next version of this chart now uses different left hand patterns, still combined with a single note melody in the right hand as follows:-

Figure 13.36. New age melody solution b) for leadsheet #2 (Fig. 13.34.)
(Cassette Tape Example 406)

Again we will analyze the different left hand arpeggiated patterns used, as follows:-

New age melody (contd)

- Measure 1	A **1-5-b7** pattern followed by a **9-11** 3rd coupling on the **E7sus** chord (see **Fig. 13.4. pattern #5**), anticipating beat **3**.
- Measure 2	A pattern beginning with the **1** & **5**, and then **11-b7** & **5-1** 4th couplings, on the **E7sus** chord (see **Fig. 13.4. pattern #3**), again anticipating beat **3**.
- Measures 3-4	As for measures **1-2**, on the **D7sus** chord.
- Measure 5	A **3-1-5-9-3** pattern on the **Bb/D** chord (see **Fig. 13.2. pattern #4 1st half**), anticipating beats **3** & **4**.
- Measure 6	A **1-5-9-3** pattern on the **C** chord (see **Fig. 13.1. pattern #1 1st half**), anticipating beat **3**.
- Measure 7	A more continuous pattern using the **3**, **1**, **5** & **9** of the **D/F#** chord (see **Fig. 13.2. pattern #5 1st half**).
- Measure 8	A **1-5-9** pattern followed by an inverted **1-11-b7** double 4th structure on the **A7sus** chord (see **Fig. 13.4. pattern #7**), again anticipating beat **3**.

Now we will look at a leadsheet using 16th-note subdivisions as well as inversions in the bass voice:-

Figure 13.37. New age leadsheet example #3

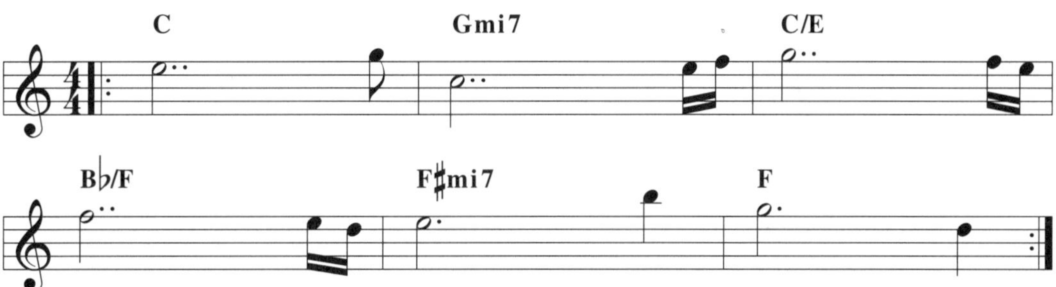

We will first interpret this with single notes in the right hand and arpeggiated patterns in the left hand:-

Figure 13.38. New age melody solution a) for leadsheet #3 (Fig. 13.37.)
(Cassette Tape Example 407)

(CONTD-->)

New age melody (contd)

Figure 13.38. contd.

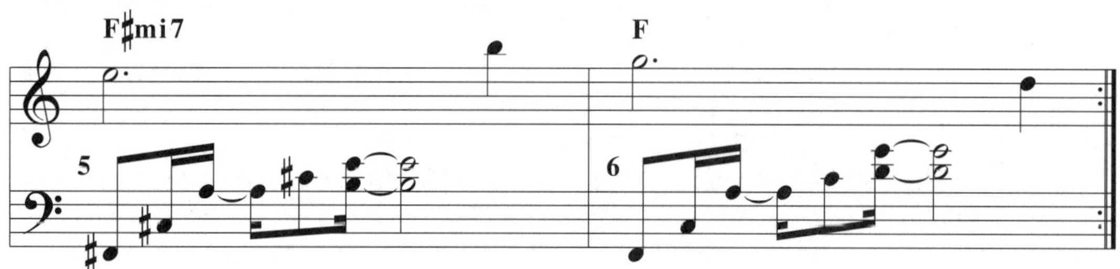

We will analyze the different 16th-note arpeggiated left hand patterns as follows:-

- Measure 1 A pattern using the 1, 5, 3, 9 & 6 on the C chord (see **Fig. 13.5. pattern #6 1st half**). Beats **2**, **3** & **4** are being anticipated.

- Measure 2 A pattern using the 1, 5, b3, 9 & 11 on the Gmi7 chord (see **Fig. 13.5. pattern #6 2nd half)**, with the same anticipations as measure **1**.

- Measure 3 A **3-1-5-6** pattern followed by a **7-1-3** 'half-step-4th' cluster on the **C/E** chord (see **Fig. 13.6. pattern #5 1st half**), anticipating beats **2** & **3**.

- Measure 4 A **5-3-1-7** pattern followed by a **9-3-5** 'whole-step-4th' cluster on the **Bb/F** chord (see **Fig. 13.7. pattern #4 1st half**), with the same anticipations as measure **3**.

- Measure 5 A **1-5-b3-5** pattern followed by an **11-b7** 4th coupling on the **F#mi7** chord (see **Fig. 13.5. pattern #7 2nd half**), with the same anticipations as measure **3**.

- Measure 6 A **1-5-3-5** pattern followed by a **6-9** 4th coupling on the **F** chord (see **Fig. 13.5. pattern #7 1st half**), with the same anticipations as measure **3**.

In the next version of this melody, we use the same left hand patterns but with different structures under the melody in the right hand (i.e. double 4ths, clusters etc.) as follows:-

Figure 13.39. New age melody solution b) for leadsheet #3 (Fig. 13.37.)

(CASSETTE TAPE EXAMPLE 408)

C Gmi7

1 2

C/E B♭/F

3 4

(CONTD-->)

New age melody (contd)

Figure 13.39. (contd)

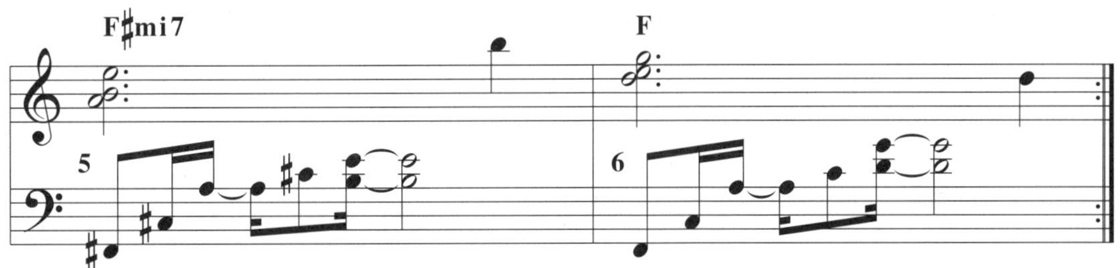

Now we will analyze the right hand structures used in the above example as follows:-

- ***Measure 1*** — An inverted **7-3-6** double 4th structure (see **Fig. 10.9.**) is being used under the 3rd in the melody (E) on the **C** chord.
- ***Measure 2*** — An inverted **1-11-b7** double 4th structure (see **Fig. 10.8.**) is being used under the 11th in the melody (C) on the **Gmi7** chord.
- ***Measure 3*** — A **7-1-5** 'half-step-&-5th' structure (inverted over the 3rd in the bass voice - see **Fig. 13.22.**) is being used under the 5th in the melody (G) on the **C/E** chord.
- ***Measure 4*** — A **7-1-5** 'half-step-&-5th' structure (this time inverted over the 5th in the bass) is being used under the 5th in the melody (F) on the **Bb/F** chord (see **Fig. 13.24.** comments).
- ***Measure 5*** — An inverted **11-b7-b3** double 4th structure (see **Fig. 10.5.**) is being used under the 7th in the melody (E) on the **F#mi7** chord.
- ***Measure 6*** — A **6-7-9** 'whole-step-4th' cluster (see **Fig. 13.13.**) is being used under the 9th in the melody (G) on the **F** chord.

Now we will look at a longer leadsheet example again using 16th-note subdivisions. The first 8 measures (**A** section) constitute the introduction, with chord symbols and 'slashes' provided on the chart. In the 8th measure a melodic 'pickup' occurs into the main melody (beginning at the **B** section, measure 9). Notice the repetitive nature of the melodic motif during this section - just repeating the notes C, D & G (scale source can be C major or C pentatonic). The next motif starts at the **C** section (measure 17), and consists of a repeated four-measure phrase followed by a two-measure 'tag', repeating back to the **B** section, as follows:-

Figure 13.40. New age leadsheet example #4

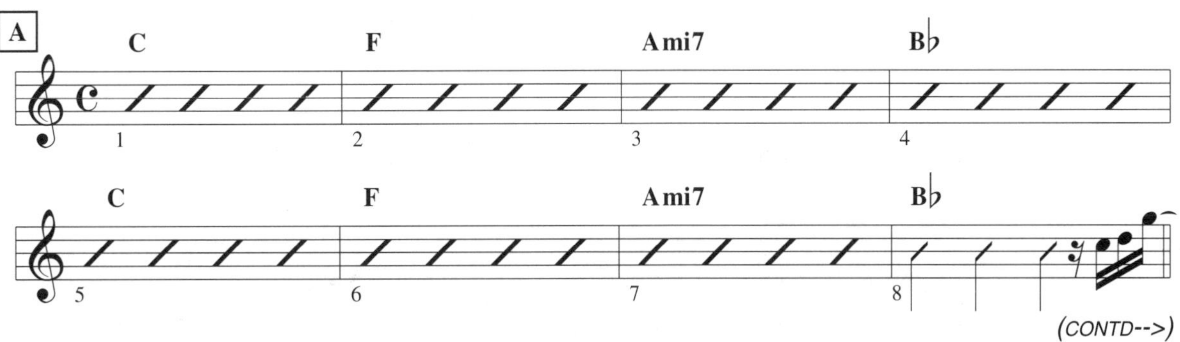

(CONTD-->)

New age melody (contd)

Figure 13.40. contd

We will now interpret this leadsheet using 16th-note arpeggiated left hand patterns, and right hand devices such as single notes, couplings, triads and double 4th structures as follows:-

Figure 13.41. New age melody solution for leadsheet #4 (Fig. 13.40.)

(CASSETTE TAPE EXAMPLE 409)

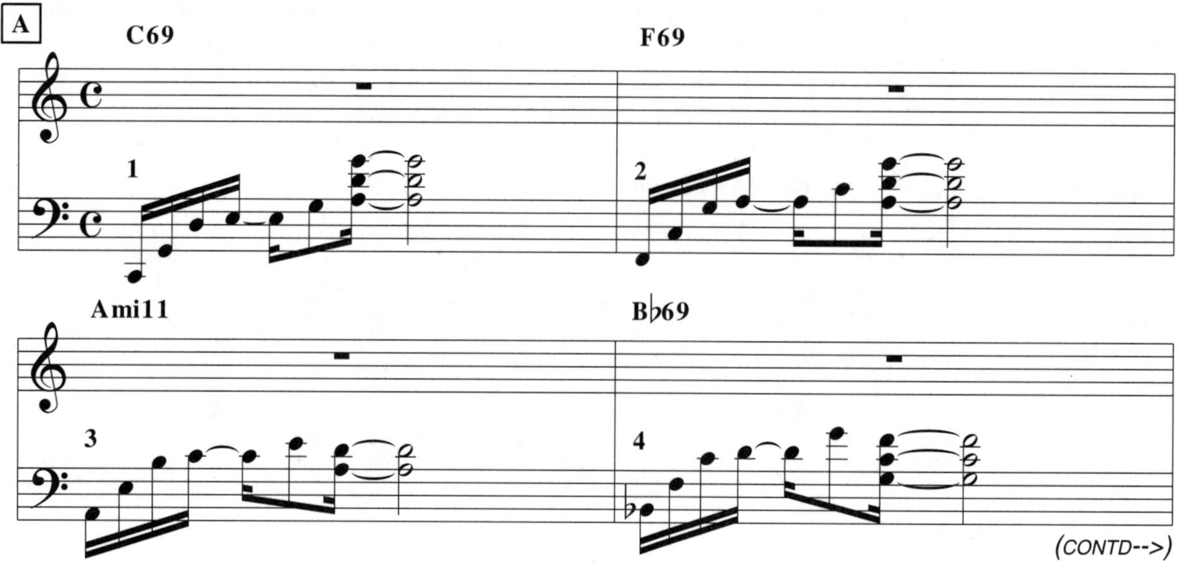

(CONTD-->)

New age melody (contd)

Figure 13.41. (contd)

(CONTD-->)

New age melody (contd)

Figure 13.41. (contd)

(CONTD-->)

New age melody (contd)

Figure 13.41. (contd)

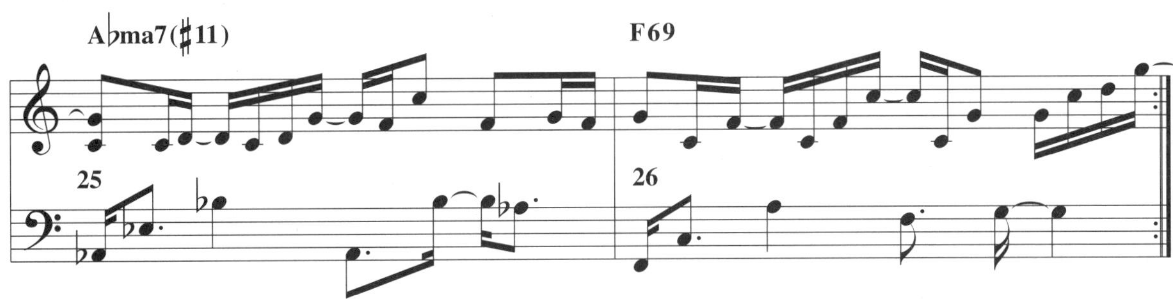

For the purposes of illustration, the chord symbols on the above version have been 'upgraded' (compared to the original leadsheet in **Fig. 13.40.**) to take into account the extensions added by the left hand patterns and any structures used to support the melody in the right hand. We can make some general observations about the devices used in this arrangement as follows:-

'A' section (measures 1-8)

Here the left hand is defining the harmony and rhythm, with 16th-note arpeggiated patterns. Measure 1 on the original **C** chord is using **Fig. 13.5. pattern #1 1st half**, upgrading the chord to a **C69** overall. Variations on this left hand pattern are used in measures 2 & **4** (creating **F69** & **Bb69** respectively), keeping the final double 4th structure in the same register (see comments accompanying **Fig. 13.1.**). Measure 2 on the original **Ami7** chord is using a variation on **Fig. 13.1. pattern #1 2nd half**, ending on a **1-11** 4th coupling again in the same 'middle' register, upgrading the chord to an **Ami11** overall. The left hand patterns used in measure 1-4 are repeated in measures 5-8, leading into a melodic 'pickup' in measure 8.

'B' section (measures 9-16)

Here the left hand is using the same patterns as for the **A** section (measures 1-8). The right hand is generally using single notes in the melody, except for measures 12 & 16 where 6th couplings have been used to support the melody (see **Fig. 11.35.** and accompanying text).

'C' section (measures 17-26)

Here the chord rhythm has increased to 2 chords per measure. The left hand is generally using **1-5-9-3** patterns and variations on the major and minor chords, similar to **Fig. 13.1. pattern #1**, but divided in half rhythmically i.e. using 16th notes over 2 beats rather than 8th notes over 4 beats. This process upgrades the original major and minor chords to **'add9'** at least. The **G#dim7** (review the chord spelling for the diminished 7th chord in **Fig. 1.81.** as necessary) in measures 19 & 23 is using a **1-bb7-b3-1** pattern in each case, with the right hand now using 3rd interval couplings below melody (see **Fig. 11.37.** and accompanying text). The original **Ami7** and **F** chords in measures 20 & 24 (upgraded to **Ami11** & **F69** respectively) last for 1 beat each, during which the left hand is using a **1-5-3** (or **b3**) pattern. The melody note B on the **F69** chord has been supported with an inverted **G** triad, which is a **9-#11-13** upper structure on this chord (see **Fig. 5.7.**) - a good choice below the **#11th** of the overall chord in the melody. The melody note G on the **C/E** chord has been supported with an inverted **9-5-1** double 4th structure (inverted over the 3rd in the bass voice - see **Fig. 10.10.**), creating **Cadd9/E** overall. Note that in measures 20 & 24 these right hand structures anticipate beats **2** & **3**, while the left hand still lands on the downbeats - as well as sometimes occurring in 16th-note new age styles, this is a

New age melody (contd)

Analysis of Fig. 13.41. contd.

'C' section contd staple rhythmic ingredient in R'n'B ballad styles (see **Fig. 2.44.** and **Chapter 14**). In measures 25 & 26, both hands are contributing to a busy arpeggiated texture, using the **1**, **5**, **9**, **3**, **#11**, **6** & **7** on the original **Ab** chord, and using the **1**, **5**, **3**, **9** & **6** on the original **F** chord.

PRACTICE DIRECTIONS:-

- ***Practice the new age 8th-note and 16th-note 'comping' examples as in Figs. 13.26. - 13.29.***
  *Also - work on adapting these patterns for use in different keys - refer to comments regarding register placement of basic chord tones and extensions (following **Fig. 13.1.**) as necessary.*
- ***Practice the new age 8th note melody treatment examples as in Figs. 13.31. - 13.33. and 13.35. - 13.36.***
- ***Practice the new age 16th note melody treatment examples as in Figs. 13.38. - 13.39. and 13.41.***
- ***Work on applying these concepts to other tunes of your choice, and to the practice leadsheets at the end of this chapter.***

Figure 13.42. Practice leadsheet #1 (chords only - for 'comping' practice)
(EIGHTH-NOTE SUBDIVISION)

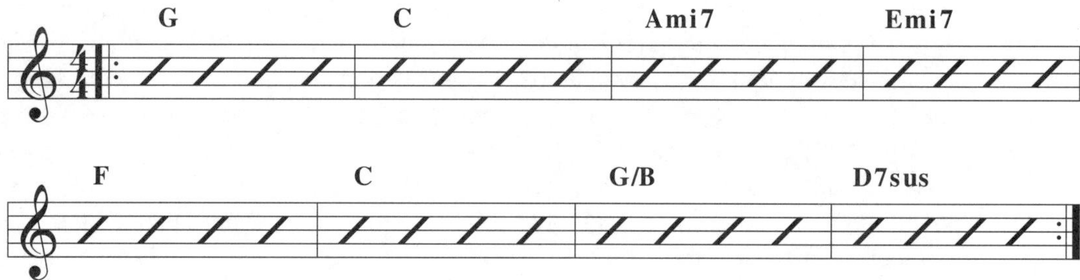

New age practice examples

Figure 13.43. Practice leadsheet #2 (chords only - for 'comping' practice)
(SIXTEENTH-NOTE SUBDIVISION)

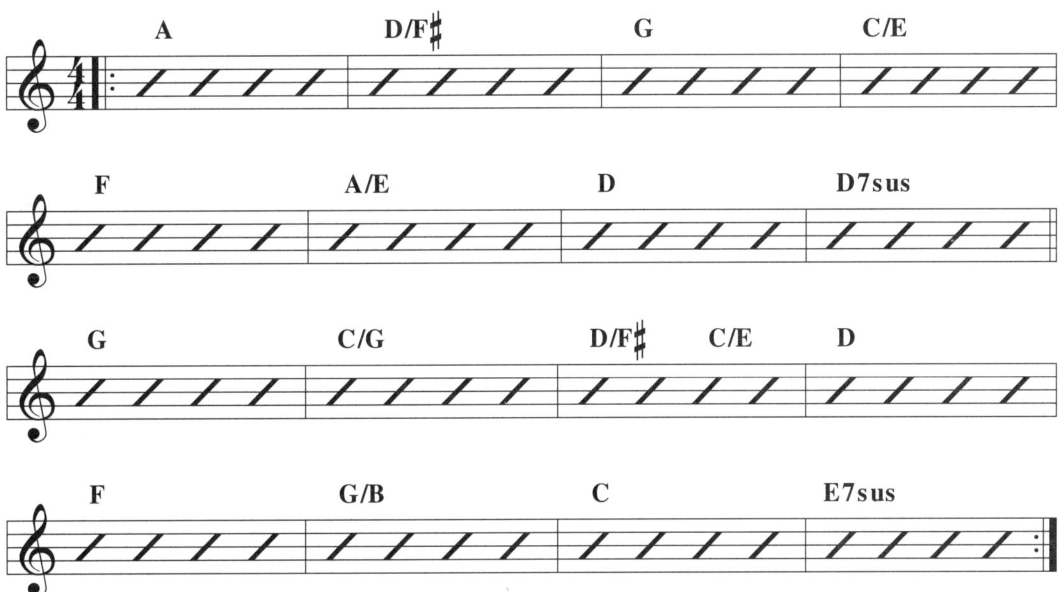

Figure 13.44. Practice leadsheet #3 (melody & chords, for melody treatment or 'comping' practice)
(EIGHTH-NOTE SUBDIVISION)

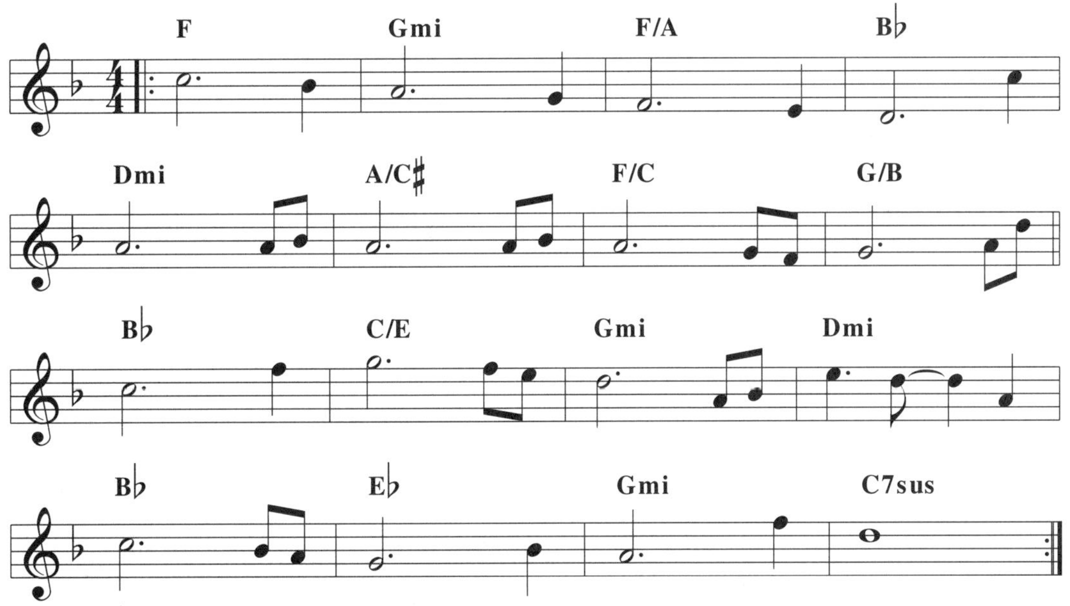

New age practice examples (contd)

Figure 13.45. Practice leadsheet #4 (melody & chords, for melody treatment or 'comping' practice)
(SIXTEENTH-NOTE SUBDIVISION)

Figure 13.46. Practice leadsheet #5 (melody & chords, for melody treatment or 'comping' practice)
(SIXTEENTH-NOTE SUBDIVISION)

R'n'B Ballad

Introduction

The next contemporary style to be examined is R'n'B ballad. This is a category of popular music featuring slow to medium tempos and sixteenth-note subdivisions/anticipations. In the introduction to the chapter on Pop ballad (see **Chapter 11**), we drew the distinction between ballads built around an eighth-note subdivision (referred to in this book as **Pop Ballads**), and ballads built around a sixteenth-note subdivision and using sixteenth-note anticipations (referred to in this book as **R'n'B Ballads**). As mentioned before, this is largely a technical distinction which we will use to select the correct rhythmic and harmonic devices for a particular ballad. A large percentage of the slower-tempo output from today's contemporary artists would therefore fall into this R'n'B ballad category as defined here - examples include tunes by Anita Baker, Whitney Houston, Luther Vandross, George Benson, Michael Bolton and many others - in fact the majority of ballads making it into the charts these days are using sixteenth note subdivisions/anticipations, including some by artists perhaps not readily associated with R'n'B idioms - tunes by pop and rock artists such as Elton John, Foreigner, Richard Marx etc. come to mind. For our purposes then we will use the term **R'n'B ballad** as a 'catch-all' category for ballads containing sixteenth-note subdivisions and anticipations.

From a harmony standpoint, in an R'n'B ballad style the right hand will be using the following devices:-

- Triad-over-root chords (see **Chapter 5**) and 4-part-over-root chords (see **Chapter 7**). We will continue to refer to these as 'upper structures' within the overall chord, as we have in previous 'style' chapters.
- '**9 to 1**' resolutions within (upper structure) triads - see **Chapter 8**.
- '**4 to 3**' resolutions within (upper structure) triads - see **Chapter 9**.
- Double 4th structures - see **Chapter 10**.
- Alternating triad concepts - see **Chapter 12** (Pop/Rock).
- 4th clusters - see **Chapter 13** (New Age).

The left hand will mainly be using single-note patterns built around basic chord tones, in a supportive role. Left hand arpeggios will also be used (refer to left hand arpeggio material in **Chapters 11** & **13** as necessary). In the Pop ballad text (**Chapter 11**) we covered basic left & right hand co-ordination using upper structure triads in the right hand with simple arpeggio patterns in the left hand - this chapter will build on these concepts by using larger chord forms and more rhythmic subdivisions - to get the best out of this chapter therefore you need to be well acquainted with the material in **Chapter 11** as well as of course with the earlier harmonic material mentioned above! Again (as with the previously described Pop ballad and New Age styles) you will generally need to depress the sustain pedal for the duration of each chord.

R'n'B ballad rhythmic concepts

As mentioned above, this style is built around the 16th-note rhythmic subdivision (and generally uses 'straight' rather than 'swing' 16ths). A rhythmic 'interplay' between the hands is set up, giving forward motion to the arrangement. Often the right hand will be anticipating the downbeat by a 16th-note, whereas the left hand is still typically landing on the downbeat (unless the chord rhythm is itself anticipated). You need to be familiar with 16th-note counting and anticipation concepts - refer to the text accompanying **Fig. 2.42**. & **Fig. 2.44.** as required.

R'n'B ballad rhythmic concepts (contd)

We will now look at some typical rhythmic patterns in this styles for the left and right hand. These are presented in rhythmic notation (see text accompanying **Figs. 2.25. - 2.28.**). Often one of the following rhythmic 'interplay' situations is occurring:-

- The right hand is anticipating a downbeat by a 16th-note, but the left hand is landing on the same downbeat. This will typically occur on the 'primary beats' **1** & **3**, although it could happen on any downbeat. The right hand might play one, two or three 16th-note 'pickups' into this anticipation, either by arpeggiating the relevant 'upper structure' or by using a connecting line from the major scale of the key signature.
- The right hand is landing on a downbeat, and the left hand is providing a 16th-note 'pickup' into the same downbeat. This works most effectively into beats **2** & **4** (the 'backbeats').
- The right hand is generally emphasizing the 'weak' 16th notes within the beat i.e. the 2nd & 4th subdivisions (as we count 16th-note rhythms as '1 e & a 2 e & a' etc. we refer to these 'weak' 16ths as the '**e**' and the '**a**' of the beat - see **Fig. 2.42.**), as we can see in the following R'n'B ballad rhythm patterns:-

Figure 14.1. Rhythmic pattern #1

(Cassette Tape Example 410)

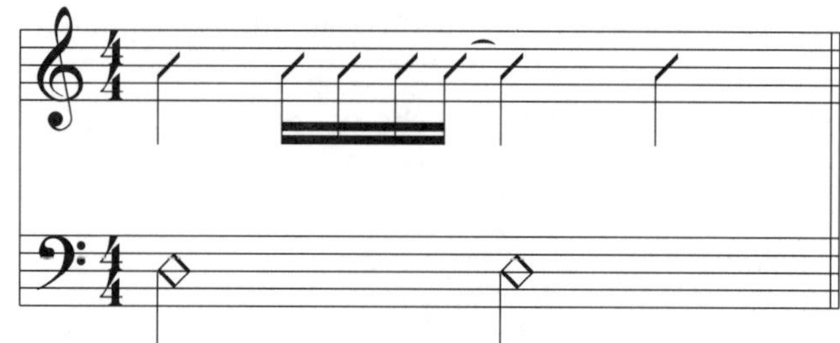

A basic R'n'B ballad pattern. The left hand is landing on the primary beats **1** & **3**. The right hand is subdividing in 16th notes throughout beat **2**, ending on an anticipation of beat **3**. Otherwise the right hand is landing on the remaining downbeats (**1**, **2** & **4**).

Figure 14.2. Rhythmic pattern #2

(Cassette Tape Example 411)

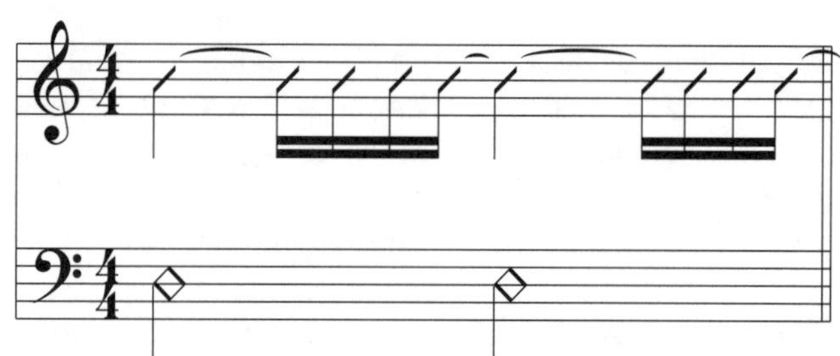

The right hand is now anticipating beats **1** & **3**, with 2 16th-note pickups into each anticipation (the right hand does not now land on beats **2** or **4**). The left hand is still landing on the primary beats **1** & **3**.

Figure 14.3. Rhythmic pattern #3

(Cassette Tape Example 412)

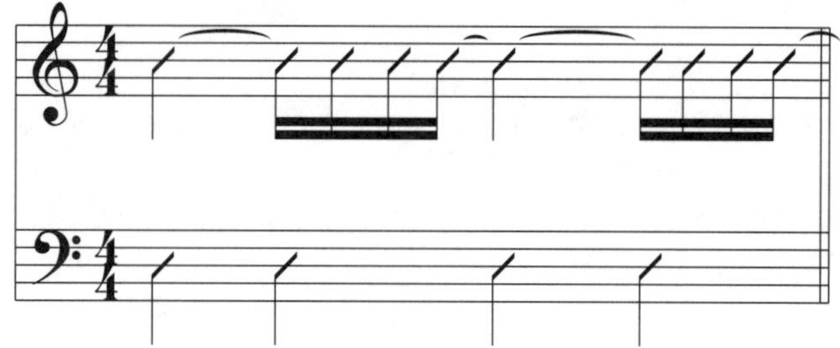

A variation on the above pattern, with the left hand now providing a steady quarter-note pulse.

R'n'B ballad rhythmic concepts (contd)

Figure 14.4. Rhythmic pattern #4
(Cassette Tape Example 413)

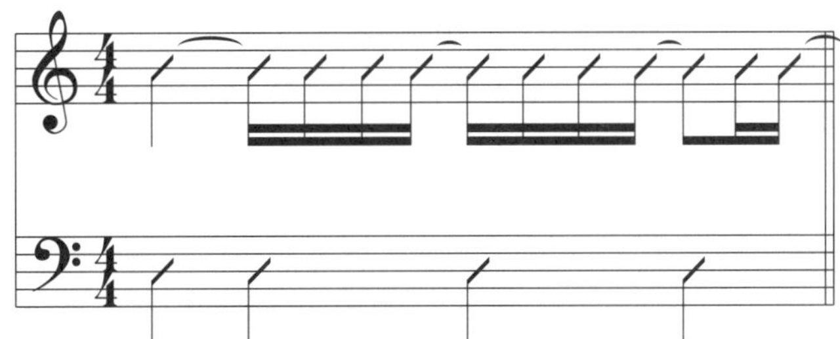

A busier version of the previous pattern, with the right hand now anticipating beats **2** & **3**, and beat **1** of the following measure. 16th-note pickups are played into each anticipation.

Figure 14.5. Rhythmic pattern #5
(Cassette Tape Example 414)

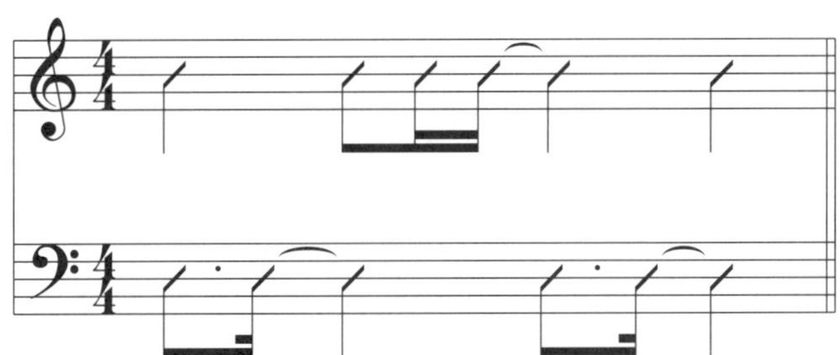

Now the left hand is landing a 16th-note ahead of beats **2** & **4**. These effectively function as pickups into these beats, as the right hand is landing on **2** & **4** (the 'backbeats'). The right hand is also anticipating beat **3**, with a 16th-note pickup.

Figure 14.6. Rhythmic pattern #6
(Cassette Tape Example 415)

A busier version of the above pattern, with the right hand landing on beat **2** and playing extra 16th-note pickups into the anticipation of beat **3**. Also the right hand is landing on the 2nd & 4th subdivisions of beat **4** (i.e. on the '**e**' and '**a**'), creating a syncopated effect.

Figure 14.7. Rhythmic pattern #7
(Cassette Tape Example 416)

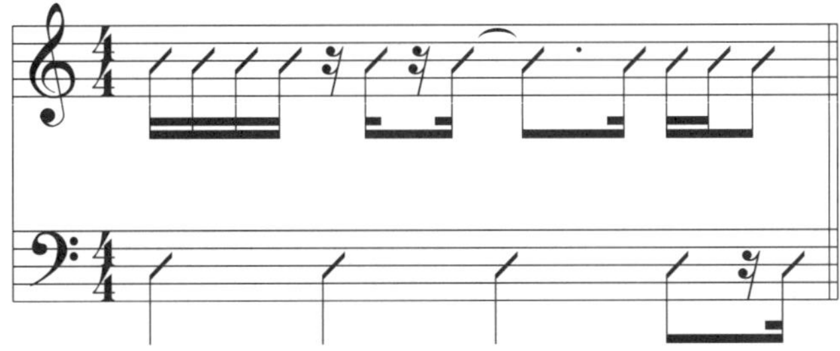

Now the left hand has returned to a quarter note pulse, adding a pickup into beat **1** of the following measure. The busier right hand part is anticipating beats **2** & **3**, additionally landing on the '**e**' of beat **2**.

R'n'B ballad rhythmic concepts (contd)

Figure 14.8. Rhythmic pattern #8
(Cassette Tape Example 417)

Now the right hand is anticipating beats **2** & **3**, and beat **1** of the next measure. The left hand is landing a 16th-note ahead of beat **4**, functioning again as a pickup into the right hand part. The right hand is adding 16th-note pickups into the anticipation of beat **3** (& beat **1**).

R'n'B ballad harmonic concepts

In addition to the various harmonic devices mentioned in the introduction to this chapter, it is typical in R'n'B ballad styles to 'enlarge' the chord forms shown on a leadsheet i.e. to turn a 3-part triad into a 4-part 7th chord, or to turn a 4-part 7th chord into a 5-part 9th chord etc. Although enlarging the chords in this way is not unique to the R'n'B ballad style, it is particularly relevant here as the 4-part-over-root chords (see **Chapter 7**) often used in this style, are 'enlarged' versions of simpler 3- & 4-part chord symbols on a leadsheet. When the chords are upgraded in this way, the root of the chord will generally be confined to the left hand part, with the right hand using an appropriate 'upper structure' triad or 4-part chord. In order to decide when and how basic chords are to be upgraded, the following points should be borne in mind:-

- Any extensions added should generally be diatonic to the key of the song. For example, in the key of C if we upgrade a **Dmi7** chord to **Dmi9**, we add the note E which is within a C major scale. However if we upgrade an **Emi7** to **Emi9**, we add the note F# which is not within a C major scale - this may be inappropriate in more commercial R'n'B styles (although it would generally be acceptable in 'jazzier' styles).
- Any extensions added should be compatible with the melody (if that is a consideration) or with the voiceleading intention. However - do not add upper extensions simply for voiceleading purposes - in commercial styles we generally need to find the vertical structures most appropriate for the situation, and then voicelead (i.e. invert the upper structures) as best as possible within those restrictions.

Subject to the above comments, we will now see how the various chords common in this style can be upgraded/extended (refer to chord-spelling review information in **Chapter 1** as necessary):-

Figure 14.9. Upgrading a major triad to a major (add9) chord *(also see Fig. 1.93.)*
(Cassette Tape Example 418)

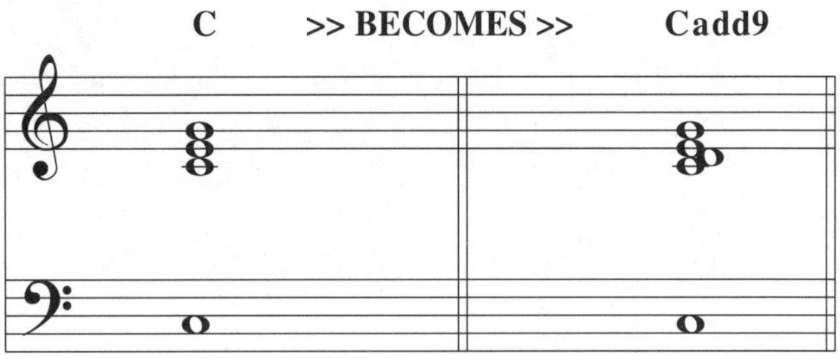

C >> BECOMES >> Cadd9

We encountered the **major (add9)** chord when using '**9 to 1**' resolutions (see **Fig. 8.12.**). Also one use of the 'whole-step-4th' cluster was to create a major (add9) chord (see **Fig. 13.11.**).

R'n'B ballad harmonic concepts (contd)

Figure 14.10. Upgrading a minor triad to a minor (add9) chord *(also see Fig. 1.94.)*
(Cassette Tape Example 419)

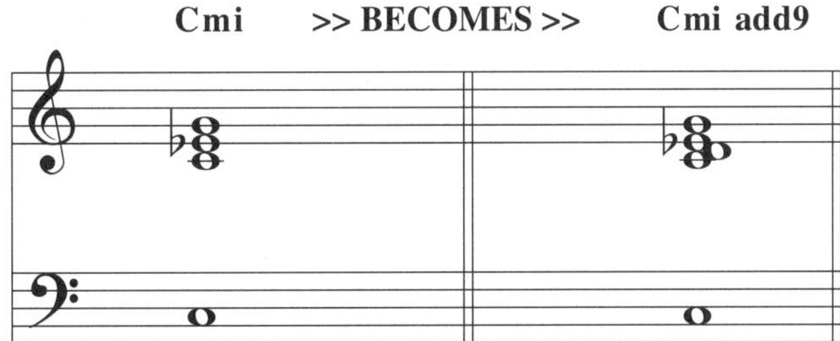

We encountered the **minor (add9)** chord when using '**9 to 1**' resolutions (see **Fig. 8.30.**). Also one use of the 'half-step-4th' cluster was to create a minor (add9) chord (see **Fig. 13.15.**).

Figure 14.11. Upgrading a major 7th chord to a major 9th chord *(also see Fig. 1.86.)*
(Cassette Tape Example 420)

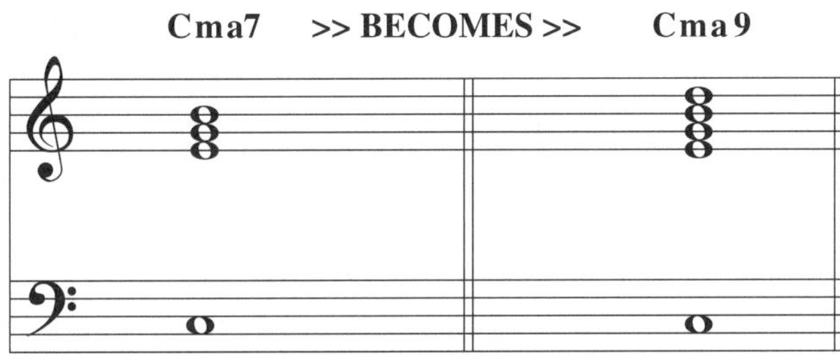

Notice that as with most of the 4- & 5-part overall structures illustrated, the root is only in the left hand and is not present in the right hand part. Looking at the left-hand measure, we saw this voicing for a **Cma7** in our study of minor-triad-over-root chords (see **Fig. 5.12.**), where we referred to it as a '**3-5-7**' upper structure on the chord - the upper **Emi** triad is built from the **3rd** of the **Cma7**. Looking at the right-hand measure, we saw this voicing for a **Cma9** in our study of 4-part-over-root chords (see **Fig. 7.3.**), where we referred to it as a '**3-5-7-9**' upper structure on the chord - the upper **Emi7** shape is again built from the **3rd** of the **Cma9**. Again as with most of these triad- or 4-part-over-root chords presented, we will invert the upper structures as necessary to accomodate melody or voiceleading considerations. With care and considering the context, we can also upgrade the **major triad** or **major (add9**) chords shown in **Fig. 14.9.**, to the **major 7th** or **major 9th** forms shown above.

Figure 14.12. Upgrading a minor 7th chord to a minor 9th chord *(also see Fig. 1.87.)*
(Cassette Tape Example 421)

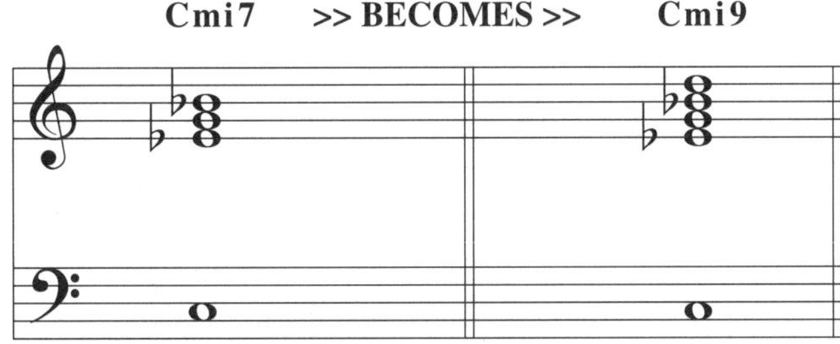

Looking at the left-hand measure, we saw this voicing for a **Cmi7** chord in our study of major-triad-over-root chords (see **Fig. 5.6.**), where we referred to it as a '**b3-5-b7**' upper structure on the chord - the upper **Eb** triad is built from the **b3rd** of the **Cmi7**. Looking at the right hand measure, we saw this voicing for a **Cmi9** chord in our study of 4-part-over-root chords (see **Fig. 7.1.**), where we referred to it as a '**b3-5-b7-9**' upper structure on the chord - the upper **Ebma7** shape is again built from the **b3rd** of the **Cmi9**. With care and considering the context, we can also upgrade the **minor triad** or **minor (add9)** chords in **Fig. 14.10.**, to the **minor 7th** or **minor 9th** forms shown above.

R'n'B ballad harmonic concepts (contd)

Figure 14.13. Upgrading a dominant 7th suspension to a dominant 9th suspension (or 11th chord) *(also see Fig. 1.89.) (Cassette Tape Example 422)*

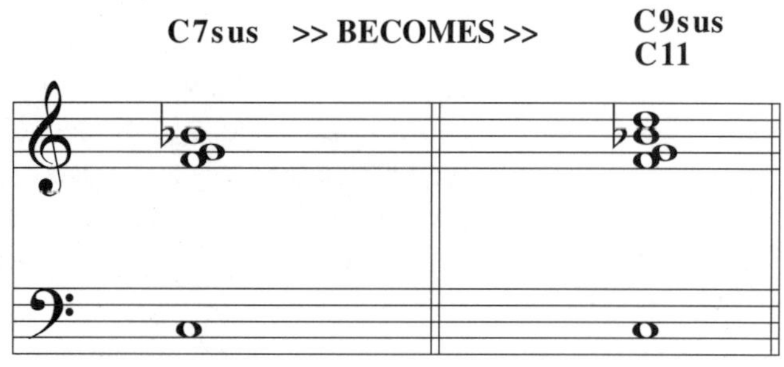

Note that the chord symbols **C9sus** and **C11** amount to the same thing - both chord symbols imply the presence of the **root**, **4th** (**11th**), **5th**, **b7th** & **9th** in the chord. Looking at the left-hand measure, we saw this voicing for a **C7sus** chord in **Fig. 13.12.**, where we referred to it as an **11-5-b7** 'whole-step-4th' cluster voicing on the chord. Looking at the right hand measure, we saw this voicing for a **C9sus** or **C11** chord in our study of 4-part-over-root chords (see **Fig. 7.4.**), where we referred to it as a '**5-b7-9-11**' upper structure on the chord - the **Gmi7** upper shape (in 3rd inversion here) is built from the **5th** of the **C9sus** or **C11**.

Figure 14.14. Upgrading a dominant 9th suspension (or 11th chord) to a dominant 13th suspension *(Cassette Tape Example 423)*

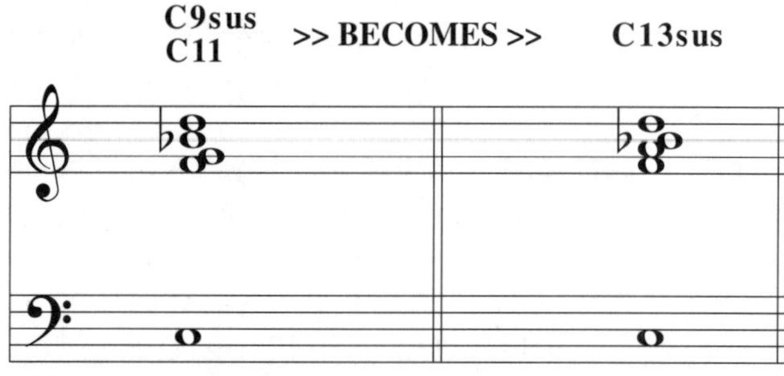

(See above comments regarding the **C9sus** or **C11** chord, in the left-hand measure). Looking at the right-hand measure, we saw this voicing for a **C13sus** chord in our study of 4-part-over-root chords (see **Fig. 7.2.**), where we referred to it as a '**b7-9-11-13**' upper structure. This chord 'upgrading' replaces the 5th (a basic chord tone) with the 13th (an upper extension), creating a more sophisticated sound. Depending on the context, the **C7sus** chord shown in **Fig. 14.13.** can also be upgraded to the **C13sus** chord shown above.

Figure 14.15. Upgrading a dominant 7th chord to a dominant 9th chord *(also see Fig. 1.88.) (Cassette Tape Example 424)*

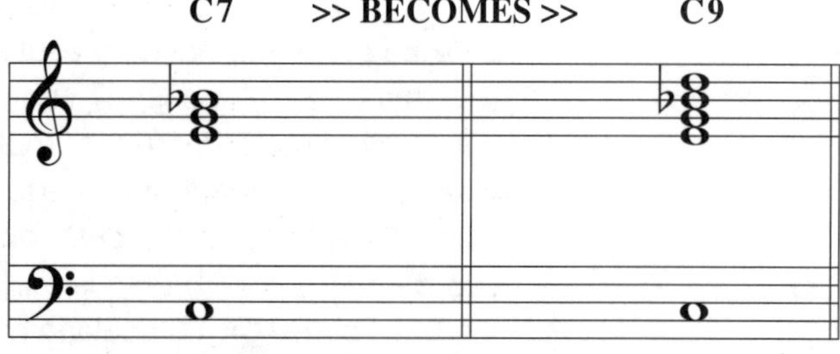

As previously discussed, the suspended version of the dominant chord is widely found in contemporary styles - however if the more 'leading' sound of the regular dominant chord is required, then it is often desirable to add a 9th to the chord as shown here. This helps make the rather stark and basic dominant 7th chord sound a little more interesting! We can refer to this voicing on the **C9** chord as a '**3-5-b7-9**' upper structure - note that the right hand is playing a '**mi7(b5)**' shape. Regular (that is **un**suspended) dominant chords are widely used in jazz, blues and gospel styles but these days are found less frequently in commercial pop, rock and R'n'B styles.

<u>PRACTICE DIRECTIONS:-</u>

- ***Practice the rhythmic patterns shown in Figures 14.1. - 14.8.*** *This is really a hand-cordination drill, and can be practiced by playing one note in each hand, or by 'tapping' rhythmically on any surface. You may optionally practice these patterns with hands separately as needed.*
- ***Play through the 'chord upgrading' examples shown in Figures 14.9. - 14.15.*** *Most of these are based on the triad-over-root and 4-part-over-root examples in* ***Chapters 5 & 7*** *- review these as necessary. Ideally you should play each upper structure inversion on each chord example, in all keys!*

R'n'B ballad accompaniment

As with the other styles addressed in this book, we need to look at ways to accompany or 'comp' our way through an R'n'B ballad leadsheet or chord chart. In the Pop ballad text (**Chapter 11**), we started out by determining the harmonic structure of the right hand part i.e. which 'upper structure' to play on each chord, and then how to invert the resulting structures to achieve good voiceleading from left to right. This is also a good starting approach for R'n'B ballad styles, and additionally we are likely to be expanding the chord forms as detailed in **Figs. 14.9.** - **14.15**. We will then further vary the right hand part by using the devices outlined in the introduction (double 4ths, clusters etc.) as desired. We will begin with a leadsheet example as follows:-

Figure 14.16. Chord chart example #1

Again as with the initial Pop ballad examples (see **Chapter 11**), we will illustrate some right hand upper structure voiceleading solutions for this progression, beginning with the following:-

Figure 14.17. Upper structure voiceleading for chord chart #1 (Fig. 14.16.) - first example
(CASSETTE TAPE EXAMPLE 425)

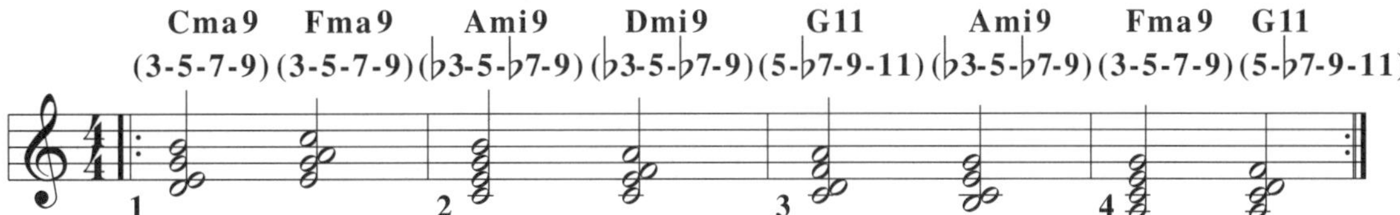

R'n'B ballad accompaniment (contd)

Again bear in mind that these upper structure voicings shown do not by themselves define the chord - they need to be placed over the roots of the original chords in the bass register to create the chord symbols seen in **Fig. 14.17.** (as in the earlier Pop ballad voiceleading, for example **Fig. 11.2.**). Also notice in **Fig. 14.17.** that the chord symbols are modified from those originally shown in **Fig. 14.16.** This is to reflect the 'upgrading' which has been done to these chords. Now we will analyze the upper structures and voiceleading as follows:-

- Measure 1

- On the original **Cma7** chord we are using a **3-5-7-9** upper structure, upgrading the chord to a **Cma9** overall (see **Fig. 14.11.**). The upper structure is a 3rd inversion **Emi7** shape - review **Fig. 6.7.** concerning 'minor 7th' inversions and **Fig. 7.3.** concerning the 'minor-7th-over-root' chord as necessary.
- On the original **Fma7** chord we are again using a **3-5-7-9** upper structure, upgrading the chord to an **Fma9** overall (see **Fig. 14.11.**). The upper structure is a 2nd inversion **Ami7** shape, chosen to voicelead from the 3rd inversion **Emi7** shape used on the previous chord. Note that this upper structure voiceleading is of a circle-of-fifths nature (see **Figs. 6.14.** and **7.13.**), voiceled on this occasion to achieve an ascending top-line.

- Measure 2

- On the original **Ami7** chord we are using a **b3-5-b7-9** upper structure, upgrading the chord to an **Ami9** overall (see **Fig. 14.12.**). The upper structure is a root position **Cma7** shape, voiceleading from the previous chord - review **Fig. 6.4.** concerning 'major 7th' inversions and **Fig. 7.1.** concerning the major-7th-over-root chord as necessary.
- On the original **Dmi7** chord we are again using a **b3-5-b7-9** upper structure, upgrading the chord to a **Dmi9** overall (see **Fig. 14.12.**). The upper structure is a 2nd inversion **Fma7** shape, voiceleading from the previous **Cma7** upper structure - again using a circle-of-fifths type of voiceleading (see **Figs. 6.10.** and **7.5.**).

- Measure 3

- On the original **G7sus** chord we are using a **5-b7-9-11** upper structure, upgrading the chord to a **G11** overall (see **Fig. 14.13.**). The upper structure is a 3rd inversion **Dmi7** shape, voiceleading from the previous chord - review **Fig. 7.4.** as necessary.
- On the original **Ami7** chord, similar comments as for the Ami7 chord in measure 2. Now the upper **Cma7** shape is in 3rd inversion, creating a descending top-line.

- Measure 4

- On the original **Fma7** chord, similar comments as for the Fma7 chord in measure 1. Now the upper **Ami7** shape is in root position, voiceleading from the previous chord.
- On the original **G7sus** chord, similar comments as for the G7sus chord in measure 3. Now the upper **Dmi7** shape is in 2nd inversion, continuing the descending voiceleading.

The first comping pattern uses the above voiceleading and rhythm pattern #1 (**Fig. 14.1.**) as follows:-

Figure 14.18. R'n'B ballad comping solution a) for chord chart #1 (Fig. 14.16.) using upper structure voiceleading example #1 (Fig. 14.17.) and rhythm pattern #1 (Fig. 14.1.)

(Cassette Tape Example 426)

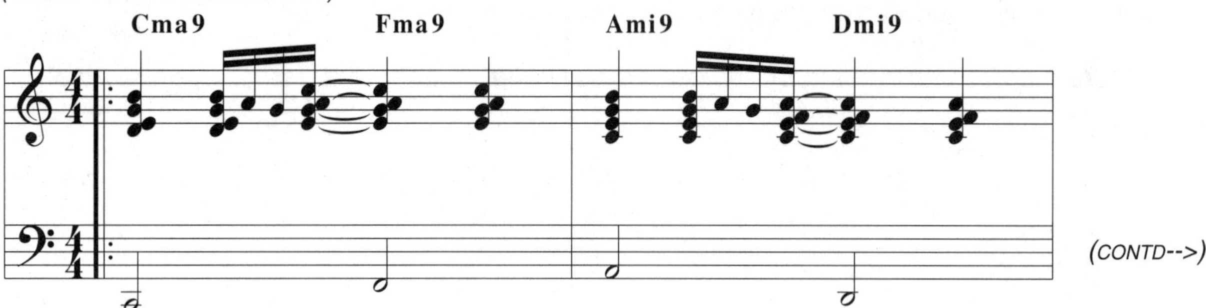

(CONTD-->)

R'n'B ballad accompaniment (contd)

Figure 14.18. (contd)

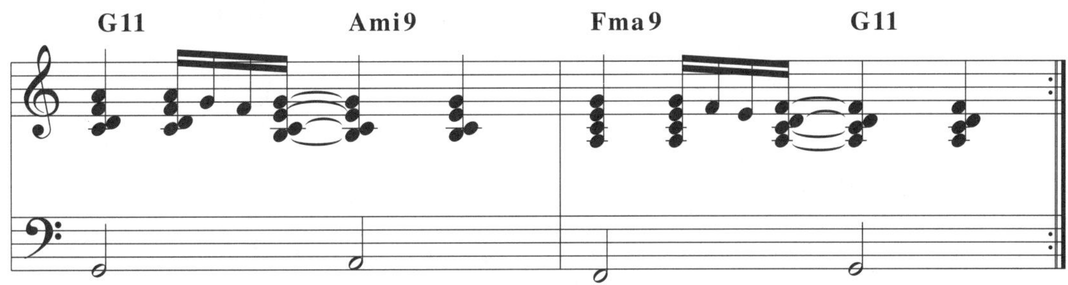

It's important to understand that a **combination** of the **rhythm pattern** in **Fig. 14.1.** and the **upper voice-leading** in **Fig. 14.17.** has created the above comping example! Connecting tones from the major scale of the key signature (C major - see text prior to **Fig. 14.1.**) are used between the upper structure landing points (the 1st and 4th 16th-note subdivisions of beat **2**) as rhythmic 'pickups'. The left hand is providing harmonic support, playing the roots of the chords at the points of chord change (beats **1** & **3** in this case). Now we will consider another voiceleading variation, and see the effect it would have on this comping pattern:-

Figure 14.19. Upper structure voiceleading for chord chart #1 (Fig. 14.16.) - 2nd example
(Cassette Tape Example 427)

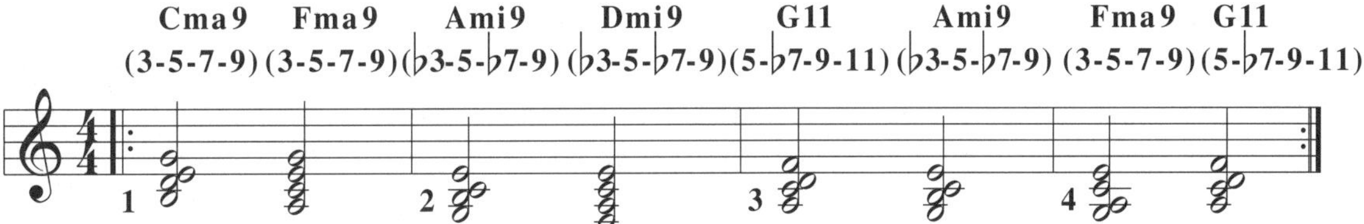

Notice that the upper structures used are exactly the same as in the first voiceleading example, but now the inversions have been changed to accommodate a different voiceleading intention, as follows:-

- Measure 1	- On the **Cma7** chord (upgraded to **Cma9**), the upper **Emi7** shape is in 2nd inversion.
	- On the **Fma7** chord (upgraded to **Fma9**), the upper **Ami7** shape is in root position.
- Measure 2	- On the **Ami7** chord (upgraded to **Ami9**), the upper **Cma7** shape is in 2nd inversion.
	- On the **Dmi7** chord (upgraded to **Dmi9**), the upper **Fma7** shape is in root position.
- Measure 3	- On the **G7sus** chord (upgraded to **G11**), the upper **Dmi7** shape is in 2nd inversion.
	- On the **Ami7** chord (upgraded to **Ami9**), the upper **Cma7** shape is in 2nd inversion.
- Measure 4	- On the **Fma7** chord (upgraded to **Fma9**), the upper **Ami7** shape is in 3rd inversion.
	- On the **G7sus** chord (upgraded to **G11**), the upper **Dmi7** shape is in 2nd inversion.

Notice that the top-note voiceleading is fairly smooth - mainly moving by commontone or scalewise step, with a minor 3rd interval occurring between measures **1** & **2**. We will now amend the comping pattern shown in **Fig. 14.18.**, to use the 2nd version of the upper structure voiceleading (**Fig. 14.19.**), as follows:-

R'n'B ballad accompaniment (contd)

Figure 14.20. R'n'B ballad comping solution b) for chord chart #1 (Fig. 14.16.) using upper structure voiceleading example #2 (Fig. 14.19.) and rhythm pattern #1 (Fig. 14.1.)
(Cassette Tape Example 428)

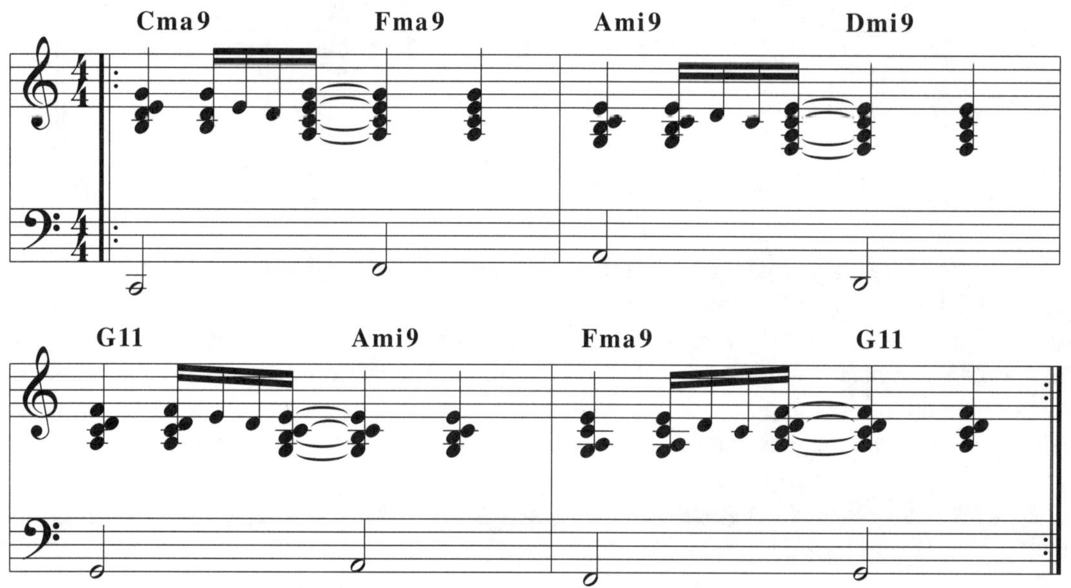

Again notice that scalewise connecting tones are used on the rhythmic pickups during beat **2** of each measure. Now we will look at the next leadsheet example, featuring a one-chord-per-measure chord rhythm (as opposed to the previous example, with two chords per measure):-

Figure 14.21. Chord chart example #2

In this situation with a slower chord rhythm, we may optionally choose to vary the upper structure inversion within the duration of each chord - while not giving us the smoothest voiceleading from left to right, this will add some interest and forward motion to the arrangement. For now we will use **3-5-7-9** upper structures on all of these **major 7th** chords, upgrading them to **major 9th** chords overall (see **Fig. 14.11.**). We will place an inversion of the appropriate upper structure on each primary beat (**1** & **3**), as in the following example:-

Figure 14.22. Upper structure voiceleading for chord chart #2 (Fig. 14.21.) - first example
(Cassette Tape Example 429)

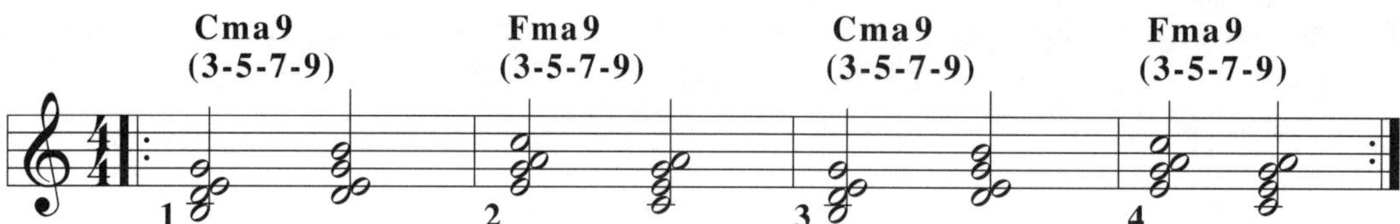

R'n'B ballad accompaniment (contd)

Again notice that the chord symbols have been modified to reflect the 'upgrading' which has occurred in the harmony. We can analyze the **3-5-7-9** upper structures used on these major chords as follows:-

- Measure 1	On the original **Cma7** chord, the upper **Emi7** shape is being used in 2nd inversion and then in 3rd inversion.
- Measure 2	On the original **Fma7** chord, the upper **Ami7** shape is being used in 2nd inversion and then in 1st inversion.
- Measures 3-4	As for measures **1-2**.

The first comping solution for this chart features the above upper structure voiceleading, used within rhythm pattern **#4** (**Fig. 14.4.**) as follows:-

Figure 14.23. R'n'B ballad comping solution a) for chord chart #2 (Fig. 14.21.) using upper structure voiceleading example #1 (Fig. 14.22.) and rhythm pattern #4 (Fig. 14.4.)
(CASSETTE TAPE EXAMPLE 430)

This is a busier rhythmic pattern, with 16th-note pickups into the anticipations of beats **3**, **4** & **1** in the right hand. Again the inverted upper structures used in the right hand are anticipating the downbeats played by the left hand (this time playing a simple quarter-note alternating octave pattern). The single notes used on the 16th-note pickups in the right hand, are arpeggiated tones from the upper structure being used and/or scalewise connecting tones from the major scale of the key signature (in this case C major). Now we will look at a further voiceleading variation of the upper structures used over this chord sequence, again using two different inversions of each upper structure within the duration of each chord, as follows:-

R'n'B ballad accompaniment (contd)

Figure 14.24. Upper structure voiceleading for chord chart #2 (Fig. 14.21.) - 2nd example
(Cassette Tape Example 431)

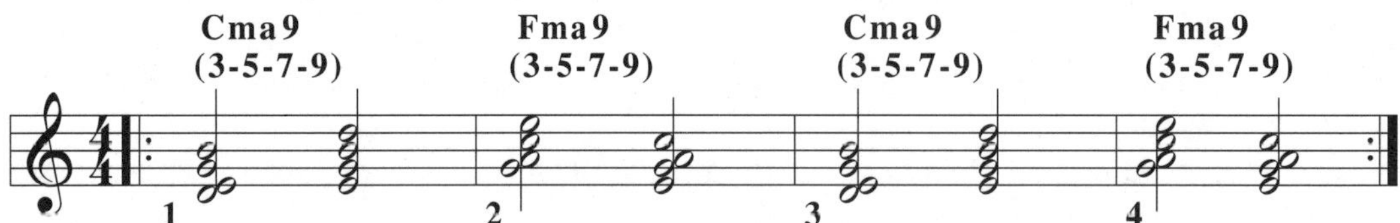

Again we are using **3-5-7-9** upper structures on all of the major chords, using inversions as follows:-

- Measure 1 On the original **Cma7** chord, the upper **Emi7** shape is being used in 3rd inverison and then in root position.

- Measure 2 On the original **Fma7** chord, the upper **Ami7** shape is being used in 3rd inversion and then in 2nd inversion.

- Measures 3-4 As for measures **1**-**2**.

The second comping solution for this chart features the above upper structure voiceleading, again used within rhythm pattern **#4** (**Fig. 14.4.**) as follows:-

Figure 14.25. R'n'B ballad comping solution b) for chord chart #2 (Fig. 14.21.) using upper structure voiceleading example #2 (Fig. 14.24.) and rhythm pattern #4 (Fig. 14.4.)
(Cassette Tape Example 432)

The harmonic and rhythmic aspects above are similar to **Fig. 14.23.**, but now using the modified upper structure inversions and voiceleading. Now for our next leadsheet, for which we will use some different harmonic and rhythmic concepts:-

R'n'B ballad accompaniment (contd)

Figure 14.26. Chord chart example #3

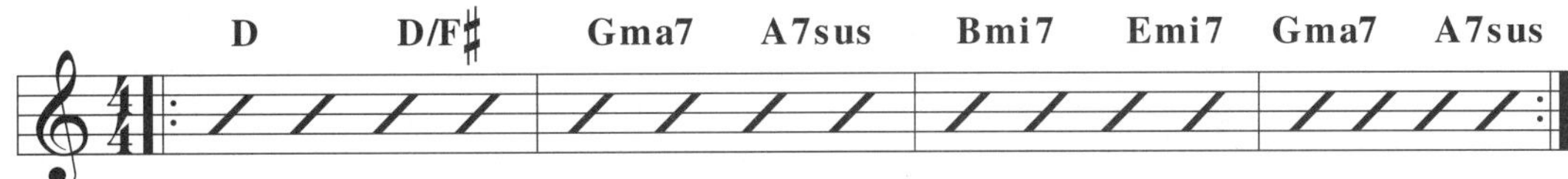

We will base the comping solution for this on rhythm pattern **#5** (**Fig. 14.5.**), and include the following harmonic devices in the right hand part:-

- '**9 to 1**' resolutions within upper structure triads (see **Chapter 8**).
- Triad-over-root and 4-part-over-root chords (see **Chapters 5** & **7**).

Figure 14.27. R'n'B ballad comping solution for chord chart #3 (Fig. 14.26.) using rhythm pattern #5 (Fig. 14.5.)
(Cassette Tape Example 433)

We can analyze the various devices used in this example as follows:-

- Measure 1

- On the **D** chord, we are using a '**9 to 1**' resolution within a 2nd inversion **1-3-5** upper structure i.e. the basic D triad (see **Figs. 8.12.** & **8.17.**) in the right hand. The left hand is playing the root in octaves, providing a pickup into beat **2**.
- On the **D/F#** chord, the first right hand voicing is landing on the last 16th note of beat **2**, anticipating the left hand which is landing on beat **3**. The right hand is using a **5-1** interval coupling (with the 5th doubled), an effective choice when the 3rd of the chord is in the bass voice. The left hand is using a **3-1-3** arpeggiated pattern, landing on beats **3** & **4**.

CHAPTER FOURTEEN

R'n'B ballad accompaniment (contd)

Analysis of Fig. 14.27. contd

- Measure 2

- On the **Gma7** chord, we are using a '**9 to 1**' resolution within a 2nd inversion **5-7-9** upper structure (a **D** triad) in the right hand. This gives a transparent, modern sound and is a popular variation on the major or major 7th chord - see **Figs. 5.4., 8.16.** & **8.19.** The left hand is again playing the root in octaves, providing a pickup into beat **2**.
- On the **A7sus** chord, we are using a **5-b7-9-11** upper structure (an **Emi7** shape) in the right hand, first in 2nd inversion (anticipating beat **3**) and then in 3rd inversion (on beat **4**). This upgrades the chord to an **A9sus** or **A11** overall (see **Figs. 7.4.** & **14.13.**). The left hand is playing a **1-5-1** arpeggiated pattern, landing on beats **3** & **4**.

- Measure 3

- On the **Bmi7** chord, we are using a '**9 to 1**' resolution within a root positioon **b3-5-b7** upper structure (again a **D** triad) in the right hand (see **Figs. 5.6., 8.14.** & **8.18.**). The left hand is playing a **1-b7** pattern (an effective choice in this register on minor 7th, dominant and suspended dominant chords), providing a pickup into beat **2**.
- On the **Emi7** chord, we are again using a '**9 to 1**' resolution within a 2nd inversion **b3-5-b7** upper structure (a **G** triad) in the right hand - see above comments. The left hand is playing a **1-5-b3** 'open triad' pattern (see **Fig. 11.12.**), landing on beats **3** & **4**.

- Measure 4

- On the **Gma7** chord, we are using a '**9 to 1**' resolution within a root position **5-7-9** upper structure (a **D** triad) in the right hand (see measure **2** comments), this time anticipating beat **1**. The left hand is again playing the root in octaves, providing a pickup into beat **2**.
- On the **A7sus** chord, we are using a **b7-9-11** upper structure (a **G** triad - see **Fig. 5.2.**) in 2nd inversion anticipating beat **3**, followed by a **5-b7-9-11** upper structure (an **Emi7** shape - see **Figs. 7.4.** & **14.13.**) in 2nd inversion on beat **4**, in the right hand. This again has the overall effect of upgrading the chord to an **A9sus** or **A11**. The left hand is using a **1-5-b7** arpeggiated pattern, landing on beats **3** & **4**.

Now we will move on to our next leadsheet example, containing an often-encountered **1 - 6 - 4 - 5sus** chord progression (illustrated here in the key of E), as follows:-

Figure 14.28. Chord chart example #4

To interpret this leadsheet we will use rhythm pattern **#7** (**Fig. 14.7.**), and include the following harmonic devices in the right hand part:-

- Alternating triad concepts, originally discussed in the text on Pop-Rock (**Chapter 12**) but also very applicable in R'n'B styles - review the examples in **Figs. 12.9. - 12.22.** as necessary.
- 'Parallel 5th' intervals derived from double 4th structures. There are two 5th intervals which can be derived from the inversions of a double 4th structure (for example in **Fig. 10.14.** the 5th interval **F-C** can be derived from the 1st inversion of the **C-F-Bb** double 4th, and the 5th interval **Bb-F** can be derived from the 2nd inversion). These 5th intervals can then be used as right hand embellishments in situations where we have determined that the original double 4th structure can be used (see **Chapter 10**).

R'n'B ballad accompaniment (contd)

Figure 14.29. R'n'B ballad comping solution for chord chart #4 (Fig. 14.28.) using rhythm pattern #7 (Fig. 14.7.)
(CASSETTE TAPE EXAMPLE 434)

Again we can analyze the various devices used in this example as follows:-

- Measure 1

On the **E** chord, the right hand part is based upon a '**5 to 1**' alternating triad pattern, which in this case uses **B** (the 5) and **E** (the 1) major triads, over E in the root voice (see **Fig. 12.9.**). During beat **1** the right hand is arpeggiating the '1' triad (E), and then plays the alternating triads using the 'weak' 16th note subdivisions (see text prior to **Fig. 14.1.**). The first E triad is on the last 16th of beat **1** (or the '**a**' of **1**) anticipating beat **2**; the B triad is on the 2nd 16th of beat **2** (or the '**e**' of **2**) anticipating the '**& of 2**'; and the 2nd E triad is on the last 16th of beat **2** (or the '**a**' of **2**) anticipating beat **3**. During beat **4** the right hand is playing 5th intervals (**5-9** & **1-5**) derived from inversions of a **9-5-1** double 4th structure (see **Fig. 10.7.** and text following **Fig. 14.28.**). The left hand is playing the root of the chord in alternating octaves, an effective rhythmic counterpoint to the busy rhythmic anticipations in the right hand part. On the last 16th of beat **4** (or the '**a**' of **4**) the D# is a pickup and melodic connecting tone into the root of the next chord (C#). This is sometimes referred to as a '**descending 7th**' bass line, as the note used to connect the two chord roots (i.e. D# is connecting between E & C#) is the 7th of the first chord (i.e. D# is the 7th of E major).

- Measure 2

The notes and rhythms in the right hand part are the same as for measure 1, but now on a **C#mi7** chord the alternating triads are a '**b7 to b3**' pattern (see **Fig. 12.19.**). The 5th intervals during beat **4** now represent **b7-11** and **b3-b7** couplings on this chord, derived from inversions of an **11-b7-b3** double 4th structure (see **Fig. 10.5.**) which the **F#-B-E** double 4th has now become. The left hand is again using a descending 7th during beat **4**.

R'n'B ballad accompaniment (contd)

Analysis of Fig. 14.29. contd

- Measure 3 Again the notes and rhythms in the right hand part are the same as for measure 1, but now on an **Ama7** chord the alternating triads are a '**9 to 5**' pattern (see **Fig. 12.16.**). The 5th intervals during beat **4** now represent **9-6** & **5-9** couplings on this chord, derived from inversions of a **6-9-5** double 4th structure (see **Fig. 10.11.**) which the **F#-B-E** double 4th has now become. The left hand part is similar to measures 1 & 2, now using the 3rd of Ama7 chord (C#) as a connecting tone on the last 16th of beat **4**, into the root of the next chord (B).

- Measure 4 On the **B7sus** chord, the right hand part is rhythmically similar to the previous measures, except for the quarter note on beat **4**. Harmonically, during beat **1** we are using a **b7-9-11-13** upper structure, upgrading the chord to a **B13sus** overall (see **Fig. 14.14.**). The upper structure is a root position **Ama7** shape (see **Fig. 7.2.**), and this is being arpeggiated during beat **1**. In order to be consistent with the top-note voiceleading used in the previous measures, we have used a **5-b7-9** upper structure (a 1st inversion **F#mi** triad - see **Fig. 5.10.**) on the 2nd 16th of beat **2** - this is consistent with the suspended dominant chord and gives us the top line of **G# - F# - G#** on the rhythmic anticipations, as in the previous measures (we return to the upper Ama7 shape on the last 16th of beat **2**, anticipating beat **3**). On beat **4** a **5-b7-9-11** upper structure (a 2nd inversion **F#mi7** shape - see **Fig. 7.4.**) is being used. The left hand is providing a pickup into beat **4**, again playing the roots of the chord in alternating octaves.

As we have seen in these examples, the right hand hand routinely anticipates the left hand (by a 16th note) in this style, even though the chord rhythms shown on the leadsheet will generally fall on downbeats. However there will be times when the leadsheet will require specific anticipations in the chord rhythm, as in the following example:-

Figure 14.30. Chord chart example #5

Notice the rhythmic notation in the 3rd measure - this is specifically telling us to place the Eb/G chord on the 2nd 16th of beat **2** (or the '**e**' of **2**), which we will hear as an anticipation of the '**& of 2**'. In these situations it is normally best for the left and right hands to play 'concerted' i.e. to both land on this point, to better define the anticipation required. As well as showing this technique, the following interpretation of this leadsheet also includes some additional harmonic devices in the right hand part:-

- '**9 to 1**' and '**4 to 3**' resolutions within upper structure triads (see **Chapters 8** & **9**).
- Double 4th structures (see **Chapter 10**).
- 4th 'clusters' (see **Chapter 13**).

We will use these devices within a rhythmic framework based on pattern **#8** (**Fig. 14.8.**) as follows:-

R'n'B ballad accompaniment (contd)

Figure 14.31. R'n'B ballad comping solution for chord chart #5 (Fig. 14.30.) using rhythm based on pattern #8 (Fig. 14.8.)

(Cassette Tape Example 435)

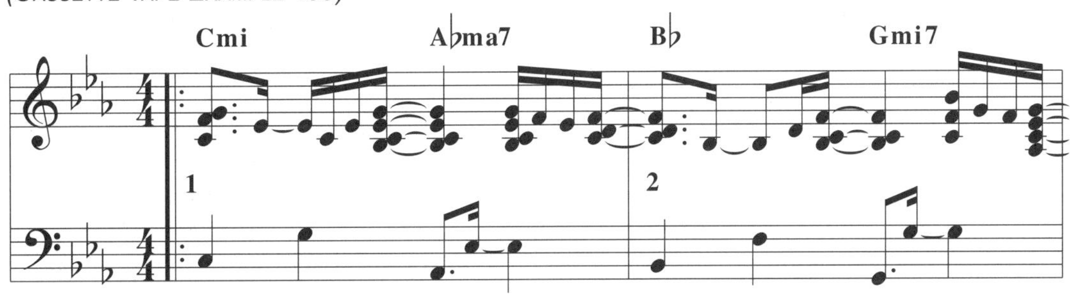

Again we will analyze the various devices used in this example as follows:-

- Measure 1

- On the **Cmi** chord, we are using a '**4 to 3**' resolution within a root position **1-b3-5** upper structure i.e. the basic Cmi triad (see **Figs. 5.8. & 9.2.**) in the right hand. The resolution to the b3rd of the chord, is anticipating beat **2**. During beat **2** the right hand is arpeggiating tones from the Cmi triad. The left hand is using a simple root-5th pattern, landing on beats **1** & **2**.
- On the **Abma7** chord, we are using a **3-5-7-9** upper structure (a **Cmi7** shape, in 3rd inversion), in the right hand, anticipating beat **3**. This upgrades the chord to an **Abma9** overall (see **Figs. 7.3.** & **14.11.**). This structure is repeated on beat **4**, followed by some scalewise connecting tones (the 6th & 5th of the chord) leading into the anticipation of the next chord. The left hand is again playing a root-5th pattern, this time with the 5th landing on the last 16th of beat **3**, acting as a pickup into beat **4**.

- Measure 2

- On the **Bb** chord, we are using a '**9 to 1**' resolution within a root position **1-3-5** upper structure i.e. the basic Bb triad (see **Figs. 5.1.**, **8.12.** & **14.9.**) in the right hand. The 'shape' used on the anticipation of beat **1**, can also be considered as a **9-3-5** 'whole-step-4th' cluster (see **Fig. 13.11.**). The resolution to the root of the chord, is anticipating beat **2**. During beat **2** the connecting tone into the next anticipation (D) also comes from the Bb triad. The left hand is again using a root-5th pattern, landing on beats **1** & **2**.
- On the **Gmi7** chord, we are using an inverted **11-b7-b3** double 4th structure (see **Fig. 10.5.**), anticipating beat **3**. The same double 4th is used in root position on beat **4**, followed by scalewise connecting tones (the root & 7th of the chord) leading into the next anticipation. The left hand is playing the root, providing a pickup into beat **4**.

R'n'B ballad accompaniment (contd)

Analysis of Fig. 14.31. contd

- Measure 3

- On the **Fmi7** chord, we are using a **b3-5-b7-9** upper structure (an **Abma7** shape, in root position) in the right hand, anticipating beat **1**. This upgrades the chord to an **Fmi9** overall (see **Figs. 7.1.** & **14.12.**). The following connecting tones C & F, are the 5th & root respectively of the overall chord. The left hand is playing the root of the chord in an octave pattern, and the F on the '**& of 1**' in the left hand together with the C on the last 16th of beat **1** in the right hand, function as two 16th note pickups into beat **2**.
- On the **Eb/G** chord, we are using a root position **9-5-1** double 4th structure in the right hand (inverted over the 3rd of the chord - see **Fig. 10.10.**). The left hand is playing G in the bass voice, as required by the chord symbol. Both left and right hands are landing on the 2nd 16th of beat **2**, obtaining the rhythmic 'punch' indicated on the chart.
- On the **Ab** chord, we are using a **9-3-5** 'whole-step-4th' cluster (see **Figs. 13.11.** & **14.9.**) on beat **3** in the right hand, followed by a **3-5-7-9** upper structure (a **Cmi7** shape, in 3rd inversion) on beat **4**. This again upgrades the chord to an **Abma9** - see measure 1 comments. Connecting tones into the next chord are also as for measure 1. As a variation, the left hand is playing a root-7th pattern, providing a pickup into beat **4**.

- Measure 4

- On the **Bb7sus** chord, we are using a **5-b7-9** upper structure (a 1st inversion **Fmi** triad - see **Fig. 5.10.**) in the right hand, anticipating beat **1**. This triad is again used on beat **2**, followed by a connecting tone (Eb - the 4th/11th of the chord) into the following chord. The left hand is playing a root-5th pattern, providing a pickup into beat **2**.
- On the **G/B** chord, the sum total of the left and right hand notes on beat **3** is an open **G** triad inverted over the 3rd (see **Fig. 11.11.**). The right hand is playing the top part of this structure (root & 5th), anticipating beat **3**. During beat **4** we have some scalewise tones moving in contrary motion, leading back to the first chord. These represent the 7th & b9th of the chord on beat **4**, resolving to the root on the '**& of 4**'.

We will now look at the next leadsheet, which again features some different chord rhythms (number of chords per meeasure):-

Figure 14.32. Chord chart example #6

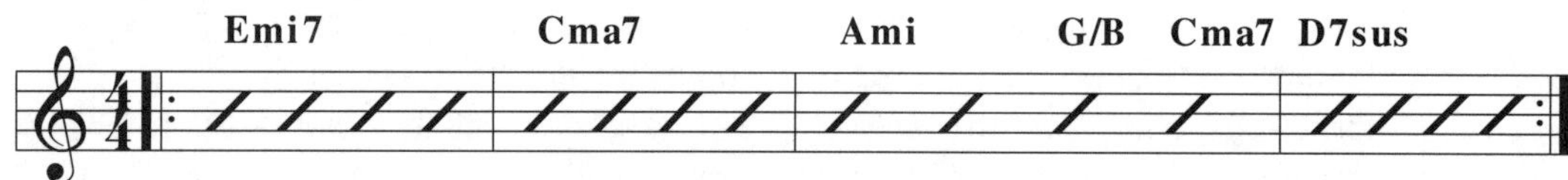

We will interpret this leadsheet with a repeated right hand sequence using double 4ths and alternating triads over the first 3 measures, with some upper structure variations in the 4th measure. We will also be using 3- and 4-part upper structures on chords, and resolutions within upper triads. Rhythmically we will now use the busier pattern #6 (**Fig. 14.6.**), featuring a syncopated phrase during beat **4** (effectively a double anticipation) as follows:-

R'n'B ballad accompaniment (contd)

Figure 14.33. R'n'B ballad comping solution for chord chart #6 (Fig. 14.32.) using rhythm pattern #6 (Fig. 14.6.)
(CASSETTE TAPE EXAMPLE 436)

Again we will analyze the various devices used in this example as follows:-

- Measure 1 - On the **Emi7** chord, we are using an inverted **5-1-11** double 4th structure (see **Fig. 10.3.**) in the right hand. This is also arpeggiated during beat **2**, leading into a **b3-5-b7** upper structure (a root position **G** triad) on the last 16th of beat **2**, anticipating beat **3**. During beat **4** we are using a '**b7 to b3**' alternating triad pattern (see **Fig. 12.19.**), with a 1st inversion **G** triad on beat **4** followed by a 2nd inversion **D** triad on the 2nd 16th of beat **4** (heard as an anticipation of the '**& of 4**'). These triads can also be thought of as as **b3-5-b7** and **b7-9-11** upper structures on the overall **Emi7** chord, respectively. The left hand is playing the root in alternating octaves, providing pickups into beats **2** & **4**.

- Measure 2 - On the **Cma7** chord, the right hand notes and rhythms are the same as for measure 1, except for the anticipation of beat **1** in the right hand. Here the **B-E-A** inverted double 4th has now become a **7-3-6** structure with respect to the Cma7 chord (see **Fig. 10.9.**). The **G** triad anticipating beat **3** has now become a **5-7-9** upper structure on this chord, and the alternating **G** & **D** triads during beat **4** represent a '**9 to 5**' pattern (see **Fig. 12.16.**). These triads can also be thought of as **5-7-9** and **9-#11-13** upper structures on the overall Cma7 chord, respectively.

- Measure 3 - Again in this measure the right hand notes and rhythms are the same as for measure 1 (except for the anticipation of beat **1**). On the **Ami** chord, the inverted **B-E-A** double 4th has now become a non-definitive **9-5-1** structure (see **Fig. 10.7.**). The G triad anticipating beat **3** has now become a **1-3-5** upper structure (inverted over the 3rd - see **Fig. 5.3.**) on the **G/B** chord.

R'n'B ballad accompaniment (contd)

Analysis of Fig. 14.33. contd

- Measure 3 contd - On the **Cma7** chord on beat **4**, the **G** and **D** triads again represent a '**9 to 5**' alternating pattern - see measure 2 comments. The left hand is also playing the root (C) on beat **4**.

- Measure 4 - On the **D7sus** chord, we are using a **b7-9-11-13** upper structure (a 3rd inversion **Cma7** shape) in the right hand, anticipating beat **1**. This upgrades the chord to a **D13sus** overall (see **Figs. 7.2., 14.13. & 14.14.**). During beat **2** we are arpeggiating the 13th, 7th & 11th of the chord from this upper structure - this subset of notes can also be considered as a **13-b7-11** 'half-step-&-5th' structure (see **Fig. 13.23.**). A **b7-9-11** upper structure (a 2nd inversion **C** triad - see **Fig. 5.2.**) is also being used on this chord, on the last 16th of beat **2** (anticipating beat **3**). A '**9 to 1**' resolution is occurring within this upper triad on beat **4** (see **Fig. 8.2.**). The left hand is again playing the root of the chord in an alternating octave pattern, providing pickups into beats **2** & **4**.

Now we will look at an eight-measure leadsheet, and see how the various rhythmic patterns and harmonic devices can be used to build the energy of the arrangement:-

Figure 14.34. Chord chart example #7

This progression uses a bass 'pedal' i.e. the same bass note repeats, for the first three and a half measures - in this case the tonic of the key (A) is used in the bass, with the 1, 4 & 5 triads of the key used over this bass tone to create triad-over-root chords (see **Chapter 5**). We saw an example of using the 1, 4 & 5 triads over the tonic, in the text on Pop-Rock (see **Fig. 12.13.**). In this type of situation, to preserve the required 'triad-over-root' sound it is generally not necessary to enlarge the chord form as described in **Figs. 14.9. - 14.15.**, although added 9ths and/or resolutions within the upper triads (as in **Chapters 8** & **9**) are sometimes desirable. In the following interpretation of the above leadsheet, we have not expanded upon the upper structures required by these 'slash' chord symbols, except for adding a 9th on the A chord in the first two measures. In the remainder of the chart, we use upper triads and 4-part structures, double 4ths and 4th 'clusters' as follows:-

Figure 14.35. R'n'B ballad comping solution for chord chart #7 (Fig. 14. 34.)
(CASSETTE TAPE EXAMPLE 437)

(CONTD-->)

R'n'B ballad accompaniment (contd)

Figure 14.35. contd.

In this example, we are using rhythm pattern **#2** (**Fig. 14.2.**) in the first two measures, starting with a fairly low energy level, with roots of the chords on the primary beats (**1** & **3**) in the left hand. Then in measures 3 & 4 the energy increases a little with the use of rhythm pattern **#3** (**Fig. 14.3.**), the left hand now playing quarter notes. Measures 5 - 8 are based upon rhythm pattern **#6** (**Fig. 14.6.**), again raising the energy level with more anticipations in the right hand, and left hand pickups into beats **2** & **4**. We will further analyze the devices used in each measure as follows:-

- Measure 1

- On the **A** chord, we are using a **9-3-5** 'whole-step-4th' cluster (see **Fig. 13.11.**) in the right hand, upgrading the chord to an **Aadd9** (see **Fig. 14.9.**). During beat **2**, tones from this structure are being arpeggiated, leading into the anticipation of the next chord. The left hand is playing the root of the chord on beat **1**.
- On the **D/A** chord, we are using a (2nd inversion) **D** triad in the right hand, anticipating beat **3** - see comments prior to **Fig. 14.35**. Scalewise connecting tones (the 9th and root of the upper triad) are used to lead into the anticipation of the next chord. The left hand is playing the bass note required by the chord symbol (A) on beat **3**. This chord can also be viewed as a **1-3-5** upper structure, inverted over the 5th - see **Fig. 5.5.**

R'n'B ballad accompaniment (contd)

Analysis of Fig. 14.35. contd.

- Measure 2

- On the **E/A** chord, we are using a (1st inversion) **E** triad in the right hand, anticipating beat **1** - see comments prior to **Fig. 14.35**. Scalewise connecting tones (B & D, the 2nd & 4th degrees of the **A major** scale) are used to lead into the anticipation of the next chord. Again the left hand is playing the bass note required by the chord symbol (A) on beat **3**. This chord can also be viewed as a **5-7-9** upper structure - see **Fig. 5.4.**
- On the **A** chord, we are again using a **9-3-5** 'whole-step-4th' cluster - see measure 1 comments. During beat **4** the tones from this structure (plus the root) are being arpeggiated. The left hand is again playing the root of the chord on beat **3**.

- Measure 3

- On the **A** chord, we are now using a 1st inversion **1-3-5** upper structure (the basic **A** triad). The left hand is playing a root-5th pattern, now landing on beats **1** & **2**.
- On the **D/A** chord, we are now using a root position **D** triad in the right hand, anticipating beat **3**. The left hand is playing a root-6th pattern (with respect to A in the bass voice), landing on beats **3** & **4**. The F# in the left hand on beat **4** is also the 3rd of the upper triad. Again this is a variation on a **1-3-5** structure over the 5th - see **Fig. 5.5.**

- Measure 4

- On the **E/A** chord, we are now using a 2nd inversion **E** triad in the right hand, anticipating beat **1**. The left hand is playing a root-7th pattern (with respect to A in the bass voice), landing on beats **1** & **2**. The G# in the left hand on beat **2** is also the 3rd of the upper triad. Again this is a variation on a **5-7-9** upper structure - see **Fig. 5.4.**
- On the **C#sus** chord, we are using an inverted **5-1-11** double 4th structure (see **Fig. 10.3.**) in the right hand, anticipating beat **3**. The left hand is playing the root of the chord on beat **3**.
- On the **C#/F** chord, we are using a **1-5-1** structure in the right hand, giving an open sound against the 3rd of the chord in the bass voice. Both left and right hands are landing on beat **3**, with the right hand playing a connecting tone (B) during beat **4**.

- Measure 5

- On the **F#mi7** chord, we are using a **b3-5-b7** upper structure (a 2nd inversion **A** triad) in the right hand on beats **1** & **2**, followed by scalewise connecting tones (the 4th/11th and the 3rd of the chord) leading into the anticipation of the next chord. The left hand is playing the root of the chord in octaves, providing a pickup into beat **2**.
- On the **C#mi/E** chord, we are using a **1-5-1** structure in the right hand, anticipating beat **3** and landing on beat **4**. The connecting tone B is played on the 2nd 16th of beat **4**, leading into the anticipation of the next chord. The left hand is playing the bass voice required by the chord symbol (E), landing on beat **3** and with a pickup into beat **4**.

- Measure 6

- On the **Dma7** chord, we are using a **3-5-7-9** upper structure (a 2nd inversion **F#mi7** shape) in the right hand, anticipating beat **1**. This upgrades the chord to a **Dma9** overall (see **Figs. 7.3.** & **14.11.**). Again scalewise connecting tones (the #11th & 3rd of the chord) are used to lead into the anticipation of the next chord. The left hand is again playing the root of the chord, landing on beat **1** and with a pickup into beat **2**.
- On the **A/C#** chord, we are again using a **1-5-1** structure in the right hand (over the 3rd of the chord in the bass), anticipating beat **3**. The connecting tone G# is played on the 2nd 16th of beat **4**, leading into the anticipation of the next chord. The left hand is playing the bass voice required by the chord symbol (C#), landing on beat **3** and with a pickup into beat **4**.

R'n'B ballad accompaniment (contd)

Analysis of Fig. 14.35. contd.

- Measure 7

- On the **Bmi7** chord, we are using a **b3-5-b7** upper structure (a 2nd inversion **D** triad) in the right hand, anticipating beat **1** and landing on beat **2**. Again scalewise connecting tones (the 4th/11th and 3rd of the chord) are used during beat **2** to lead into the anticipation of the next chord. The left hand is again playing the root of the chord, landing on beat **1** and with a pickup into beat **2**.
- On the **G** chord, we are using a **9-3-5** 'whole-step-4th' cluster (see **Fig. 13.11.**) in the right hand, anticipating beat **2**. This upgrades the chord to a **Gadd9** (see **Fig. 14.9.**). A similar rhythmic figure is used during beat **4**, as for measures 5 & 6. The notes used here (a **9-5** coupling on beat **4**, and the **3rd** of the chord on the 2nd 16th of beat **4**) are taken from the same cluster voicing (i.e. the **9-3-5**). The left hand is using a root-5th pattern, landing on beat **3** and with a pickup into beat **4**.

- Measure 8

- On the **Esus** chord, we are using an inverted **5-1-11** double 4th structure (see **Fig. 10.3.**) in the right hand, anticipating beat **1**. The **11-1** coupling and remaining arpeggiated tones during beat **2**, are also taken from the same double 4th structure (i.e. the **5-1-11**). The left hand is again playing the root of the chord, landing on beat **1** and with a pickup into beat **2**.
- On the **E** chord, we are using a first inversion **1-3-5** upper structure (the basic **E** triad) in the right hand on beat **3**. The left hand is playing a **1-5-1** pattern, landing on beats **3** & **4** and with a pickup into beat **4**.

PRACTICE DIRECTIONS:-

- ***Practice the upper structure voiceleading and comping examples for chord charts #1 & #2, as in Figs. 14.16. - 14.25.***
- ***Practice the comping examples for chord charts #3 - #7, as in Figs. 14.26. - 14.35.***
  (For extra practice - try transposing these into different keys!)
- ***Work on applying these concepts to other tunes of your choice, and to the practice leadsheets at the end of this chapter.***

CHAPTER FOURTEEN

R'n'B ballad melody

We will now turn our attention to performing a melody treatment in an R'n'B ballad style. Generally these melodies will feature 16th note subdivisions and anticipations. Indeed the melody is often subject to interpretation and rephrasing - I have seen sheet music for R'n'B ballads where the melody has been transcribed with rather tortuous 16th note (and sometimes 32nd note!) rhythms, and this can be evidence of a fussy or 'literal' transcription of a spontaneous performance - in these situations, don't be afraid to rephrase or simplify as your ear dictates.

The general approach here (once the overall melodic rhythm has been established), is to place various structures below the melody in the right hand, at least on the points of chord change or anticipations thereof. The left hand continues to provide rhythmic and harmonic support, typically with open triad arpeggios (see **Figs. 11.11. & 11.12.**) rythmically rephrased to use 16th note subdivisions and anticipations. We analyzed various right hand melody support options including triads, 4th couplings and double 4th structures on major, minor and suspended chords in the Pop-Rock chapter (see text accompanying **Figs. 12.46. - 12.48.**) - these structures will also work under R'n'B melodies and you need to be familiar with them. Additionally we will make use of the following devices below the melody in the right hand:-

- Four-part 'major 7th' & 'minor 7th' shapes (within 4-part-over-root chords) - see **Chapters 6** & **7**, and **Figs. 14.11. - 14.14.**
- '**9 to 1**' & '**4 to 3**' resolutions within upper structure triads - see **Chapters 8** & **9**.
- 'Whole-step-4th' and 'half-step-4th' clusters - see **Figs. 13.9. - 13.18.**
- 'Half-step-&-5th' structures - see **Figs. 13.19. - 13.24.**
- Interval couplings below melody (i.e. 6ths & 3rds) - see **Figs. 11.35. - 11.37.**

Now we will look at our first melody leadsheet as follows:-

Figure 14.36. Leadsheet (with melody) example #1

In the following interpretation of this example, the left hand is landing on all the downbeats and providing pickups into beats **2** & **4**. The right hand structures are frequently anticipating beat **3** (and on one occasion beat **1**) as indicated by the melodic rhythm, as follows:-

R'n'B ballad melody (contd)

Figure 14.37. R'n'B ballad melody solution for leadsheet example #1 (Fig. 14.36.)
(Cassette Tape Example 438)

We will analyze the various devices used in the above melody treatment as follows:-

- Measure 1

- A **9-3-5** 'whole-step-4th' cluster (see **Fig. 13.11.**) is being used in the right hand on beat **1** under the 5th in the melody (A) on the **D** chord, upgrading the chord to a **Dadd9**. The left hand is playing a **1-5-3** open triad arpeggio pattern.
- A **7-1-5** 'half-step-&-5th' structure (over the 3rd in the bass voice - see **Fig. 13.22.**) is being used in the right hand on the last 16th of beat **2**, anticipating beat **3** according to the melodic rhythm shown on the chart. This is under the 5th in the melody (A) on the **D/F#** chord, effectively upgrading the chord to **Dma7/F#**. The left hand is playing a **3-1-5** open triad arpeggio pattern.
- A **9-5-1** double 4th structure (over the 3rd in the bass voice, still heard from beat **3** - see **Fig. 10.10.**) is being used in the right hand on beat 4 under the melody note D.

- Measure 2

- A '**9 to 1**' resolution within a **1-3-5** upper structure (a 2nd inversion basic **G** triad) is being used in the right hand from beats **1** to **2**, under the 3rd in the melody (B) on the **G** chord (see **Fig. 8.12.**). The left hand is again playing a **1-5-3** open triad arpeggio pattern.
- An **11-5-b7** 'whole-step-4th' cluster (see **Fig. 13.12.**) is being used in the right hand on the last 16th of beat **2**, anticipating beat **3** according to the melodic rhythm shown on the chart. This is under the 7th in the melody (A) on the **Bmi7** chord, effectively upgrading the chord to a **Bmi7(add11)** or **Bmi7(11)**. This in turn resolves to a **b3-5-b7** upper structure (a root position **D** triad) again below the melody note A, on beat **4**. This movement can be considered as a '**9 to 1**' resolution within this upper triad (see **Fig. 8.14.**). The left hand is playing a **1-5-b7** arpeggio pattern.

R'n'B ballad melody (contd)

Analysis of Fig. 14.37. contd.

- Measure 3

- A **b3-5-b7** upper structure (an **A** triad) is being used in the right hand on beats **1** & **2** on the **F#mi7** chord, first in 2nd inversion under the 5th (C#) in the melody, and then in root position under the 7th (E) in the melody. The left hand is playing a **1-b7-b3** pattern.
- A **9-3-5** 'whole-step-4th' cluster (see **Fig. 13.11.**) is being used in the right hand on the last 16th of beat **2**, anticipating beat **3** according to the melodic rhythm. This is under the 5th in the melody (D) on the **G** chord, upgrading the chord to a **Gadd9**. This in turn resolves to a **1-3-5** upper structure (a root position **G** triad) on beat **4**, again constituting a '**9 to 1**' resolution within this upper triad. The left hand is again playing a **1-5-3** open triad arpeggio pattern.

- Measure 4

- This chord is a **D** triad inverted over the 5th. In this context a **1-3-5** upper structure (a 2nd inversion **D** triad - see **Fig. 5.5.**) is being used on the last 16th of beat **4** in the previous measure, anticipating beat **1** in this measure. This is under the melody note D. On beat **2** the melody note A is supported wth a 3rd interval coupling, in turn part of the previous D triad. The left hand is playing a **5-3-1** open triad arpeggio pattern.
- A **5-b7-9-11** upper structure (a 3rd inversion **Emi7** shape - see **Fig. 7.4.**) is being used in the right hand on beat **3** under the 9th in the melody (B) on the **A7sus** chord, upgrading the chord to an **A11** or **A9sus** (see **Fig. 14.13.**). The left hand is playing a **1-b7-9** pattern.
- An **11-5-b7** 'whole-step-4th' cluster (see **Fig. 13.12.**) is being used in the right hand on beat **4**, under the 7th in the melody (G) on the **A7sus** chord. This structure is in turn part of the previous (inverted) **5-b7-9-11** structure on this chord.

We will now look at a longer melody leadsheet example (containing some harmonic anticipations), and see how these various rhythmic and harmonic devices can be used to build the energy of the arrangement:-

Figure 14.38. Leadsheet (with melody) example #2

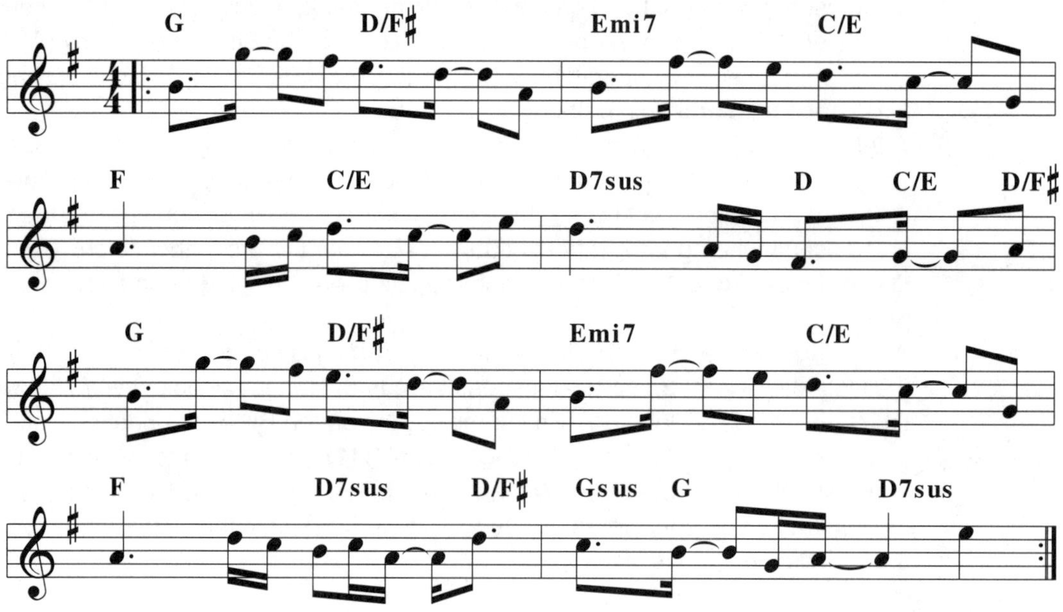

G D/F♯ Emi7 C/E

F C/E D7sus D C/E D/F♯

G D/F♯ Emi7 C/E

F D7sus D/F♯ Gsus G D7sus

R'n'B ballad melody (contd)

In the following interpretation of this example, we can decide to have a lower energy level for the first four measures, and then to build up the energy level for the last four measures. The lower energy level in the first four measures is achieved by using a single-note melody in the right hand (i.e. without any supporting structures) and by using closed-voiced arpeggio patterns (i.e. with an overall span of less than an octave) in the left hand, in the middle-to-lower register on the keyboard. In the second half of the chart, we will use the various right hand melody support devices as previously discussed, together with open triads extending into the lower register from the left hand (review the discussion on left hand arpeggio placement in the text following **Fig. 13.1.** as necessary). This will have the effect of increasing the energy level of the arrangement. The left hand arpeggio patterns are mostly using all of the 16th subdivisions in beats **1** & **3**, while anticipating beats **2** & **4**, as follows:-

Figure 14.39. R'n'B ballad melody solution for leadsheet example #2 (Fig. 14.38.)
(Cassette Tape Example 439)

(contd-->)

R'n'B ballad melody (contd)

Figure 14.39. contd.

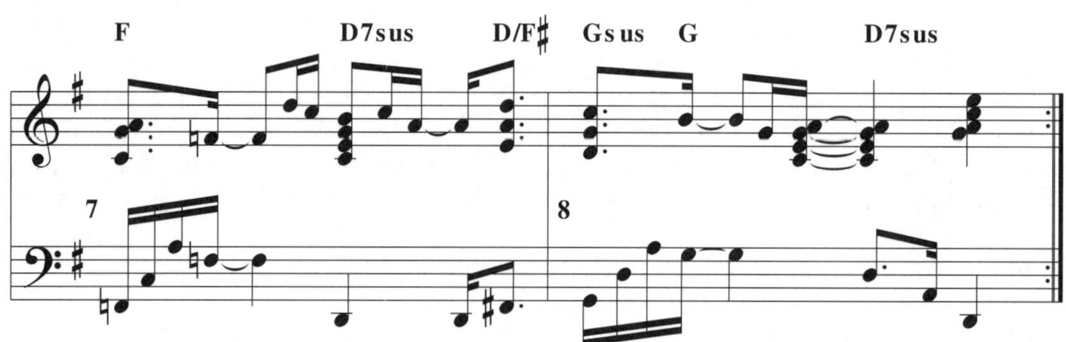

Again we will analyze the various devices used in this example as follows:-

- Measure 1
- On the **G** chord, the left hand is playing a **1-9-3-5** pattern.
- On the **D/F#** chord, the left hand is playing a **3-5-9-1** pattern.

- Measure 2
- On the **Emi7** chord, the left hand is playing a **1-b3-5-b7** pattern.
- On the **C/E** chord, the left hand is again playing a **3-5-9-1** pattern.

- Measure 3
- On the **F** chord, the left hand is agian playing a **1-9-3-5** pattern.
- On the **C/E** chord, the left hand is again playing a **3-5-9-1** pattern.

- Measure 4
- On the **D7sus** chord, the left hand is playing a **1-11-5-b7** pattern.
- A '**9 to 1**' resolution within a **1-3-5** upper structure (a 2nd inversion **D** triad), is being used in the right hand on beat **3**, under the 3rd in the melody (F#) on the **D** chord. The left hand is also playing the root of the chord (D) on beat **3**.
- A **5-1-5** structure on the **C/E** chord, is being used in the right hand on the last 16th of beat **3**, anticipating beat **4** according to the melodic rhythm. As discussed before, this is an effective structure to use over the 3rd of the chord in the bass voice. This is being used below the 5th in the melody (G) on this chord. The left hand is similarly playing the bass voice required by the chord symbol (E) on the last 16th of beat **3**, thereby ensuring that both hands are 'concerted' in their anticipation of beat **4**, as required by the chord rhythm on the leadsheet.
- Another **5-1-5** structure (this time on the **D/F#** chord) is being used in the right hand on the '**& of 4**' according to the melodic rhythm, below the 5th in the melody (A) on this chord. The left hand is playing the bass voice required by the chord symbol (F#) on the '**& of 4**', again resulting in a concerted effect with the two hands on this chord change. The notes D, E & F# used in this bass line also represent a diatonic 'walkup' back to the tonic of the next chord - see **Chapter 16** for more information on 'walkups'.

- Measure 5
- A '**9 to 1**' resolution within a **1-3-5** upper structure (a 2nd inversion **G** triad) is being used in the right hand on beat **1**, under the 3rd in the melody (B) on the **G** chord. Under the remaining melody notes within this chord, diatonic 6th interval couplings have been used (see **Fig. 11.35.**). The left hand is playing a **1-5-3-1** open triad arpeggio pattern.
- On beat **3** and the last 16th of beat **3**, the 5th of the chord (A) is used as an interval coupling below the melody, creating 5th and 4th intervals respectively. The left hand is playing a **3-1-5-3** open triad arpeggio pattern.

R'n'B ballad melody (contd)

Analysis of Fig. 14.39. contd

- Measure 5 contd

- A **9-3-5** 'whole-step-4th' cluster (inverted over the 3rd in the bass voice - see **Fig. 13.14.**) is being used in the right hand on the '**& of 4**', under the 5th in the melody (A) on the **D/F#** chord.

- Measure 6

- A **9-b3-5** 'half-step-4th' cluster (see **Fig. 13.15.**) is being used on in the right hand on beat **1**, under the 5th in the melody (B) on the **Emi7** chord. Under the remaining melody notes within this chord, diatonic 6th interval couplings have been used (see **Fig. 11.35.**). The left hand is playing a **1-5-b3-5** arpeggio pattern.
- The root and 5th of the upper **C** triad, have been used to support the melody notes D and C on the **C/E** chord. The **1-5-9** structure which results on beat **3** could be considered as an inverted/rearranged double 4th structure. On the last 16th of beat **3**, this moves to a **1-5-1** structure, again an effective choice over the 3rd in the bass voice. The left hand is playing a **3-1-5-3** arpeggio pattern.
- A **9-3-5** 'half-step-4th' cluster (inverted over the 3rd in the bass voice - see **Fig. 13.14.**) is being used in the right hand on the '**& of 4**', under the 5th in the melody (G) on the **C/E** chord.

- Measure 7

- A '**9 to 1**' resolution within a **1-3-5** upper structure (a 2nd inversion **F** triad) is being used in the right hand on beat **1**, under the 3rd in the melody (A) on the **F** chord. The left hand is playing a **1-5-3-1** open triad arpeggio pattern.
- A **b7-9-11-13** upper structure (a root position **Cma7** shape - see **Fig. 7.2.**) is being used in the right hand on beat **3** under the 13th in the melody (B) on the **D7sus** chord. This upgrades the chord to a **D13sus** overall (see **Fig. 14.14.**). The left hand is playing the root of the chord (D) on beats **3** & **4**, the latter functioning as a pickup into the following anticipation (the D/F# chord).
- A **9-5-1** double 4th structure (inverted over the 3rd in the bass voice - see **Fig. 10.10.**) is being used in the right hand on the 2nd 16th of beat **4**, under the melody note D on the **D/F#** chord. This is felt as an anticipation of the '**& of 4**', and is played together with the F# in the bass voice as required by the chord rhythm on the chart.

- Measure 8

- A '**4 to 3**' resolution within a **1-3-5** upper structure (a 2nd inversion **G** triad - see **Fig. 9.1.**) is being used in the right hand on beat **1** under the 11th in the melody (C) on the **Gsus** chord. The resolution to the 3rd in the melody (B) occurs on the last 16th of beat **1.** The voicing on beat **1** can also be considered as a **5-1-11** double 4th structure (see **Fig. 10.3.**). The left hand is playing a **1-5-9-1** arpeggio pattern.
- A **5-b7-9-11** upper structure (an **Ami7** shape - see **Fig. 7.4.**) is being used in the right hand on the **D7sus** chord, first in 1st inversion under the 5th (A) in the melody on the last 16th of beat **2**, and then in 3rd inversion under the 9th in the melody (E) on beat **4**. This upgrades the chord to an **A9sus** or **A11** overall (see **Fig. 14.13.**). The left hand is playing a **1-5-1** pattern, landing on beats **3** & **4** and with a pickup into beat **4**.

R'n'B ballad melody (contd)

PRACTICE DIRECTIONS:-

- *Practice the R'n'B ballad melody treatment examples for leadsheets #1 & #2, as in Figs. 14.37. & 14.39.*
- *Work on applying these concepts to other tunes of your choice, and to the practice leadsheets at the end of this chapter.*

Figure 14.40. Practice leadsheet #1 (chords only - for 'comping' practice)

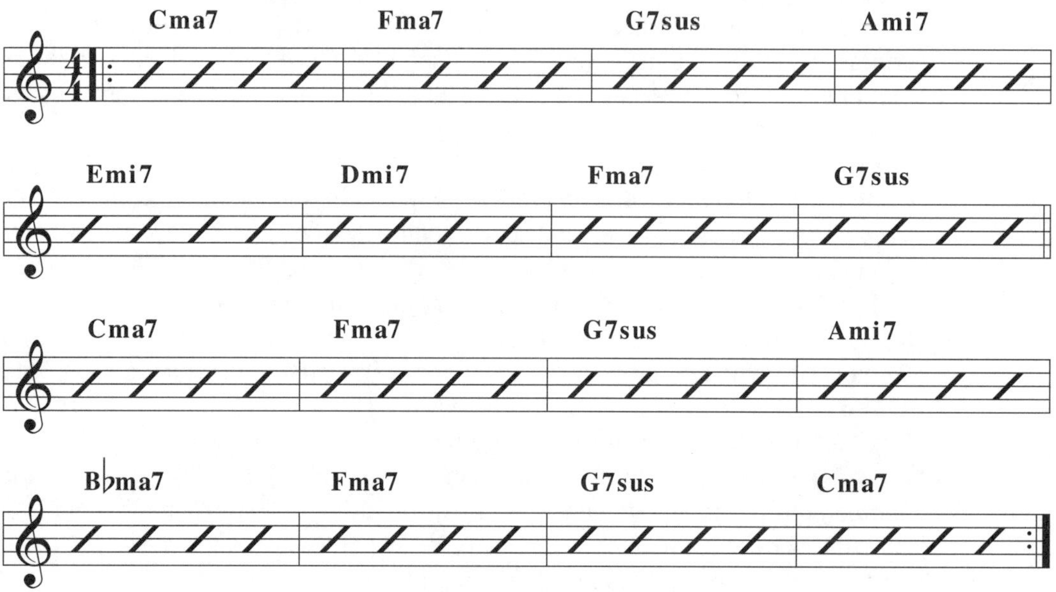

R'n'B ballad practice examples

Figure 14.41. Practice leadsheet #2 (chords only - for 'comping' practice)

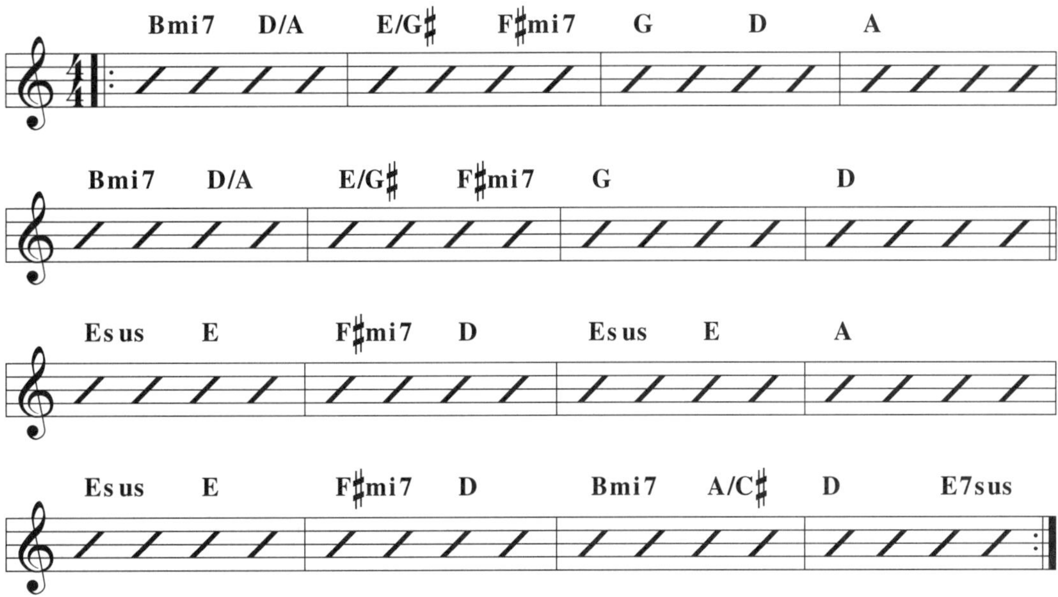

Figure 14.42. Practice leadsheet #3 (chords only - for 'comping' practice)

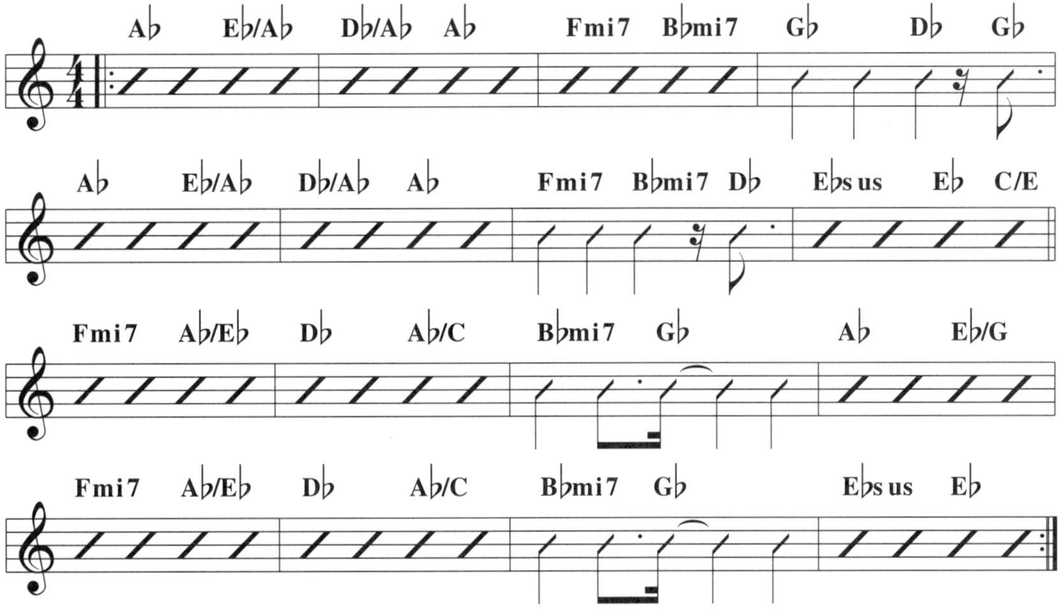

R'n'B ballad practice examples (contd)

Figure 14.43. Practice leadsheet #4 (melody & chords, for melody treatment or 'comping' practice)

Figure 14.44. Practice leadsheet #5 (melody & chords, for melody treatment or 'comping' practice)

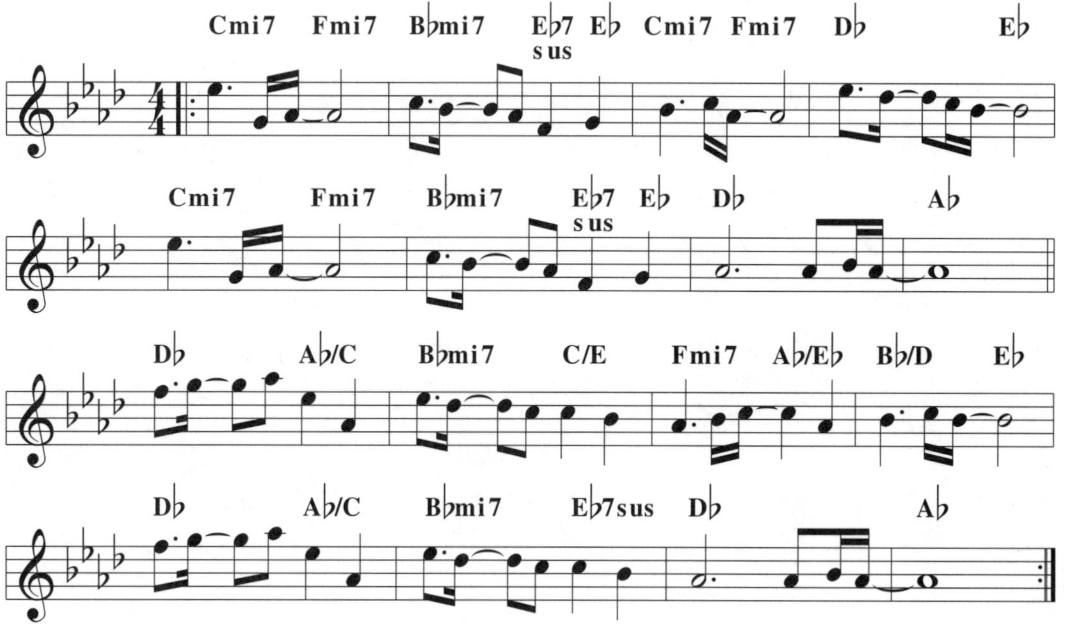

CHAPTER FIFTEEN

R'n'B/Funk

Introduction

Following on from the previous chapter on R'n'B ballad, we will now focus on **R'n'B/Funk** styles. From a rhythmic point of view, we will still be making use of 16th note subdivisions and anticipations, but now at faster tempos and with greater emphasis on syncopations. Everybody seems to have their own idea about what sounds 'funky' to them - for our purposes here we will be manipulating 16th note rhythms and emphasizing anticipations (at medium-to-fast tempos) in order to achieve a 'funky' effect. Funk grooves can be played in 'straight' 16ths and 'swing' 16ths (see **Figs. 2.37. - 2.38.** and accompanying text), and we will address both rhythmic treatments of this style. This chapter deals with basic R'n'B/funk comping grooves (involving some sustained/legato phrasing, suitable for piano) as well as more percussive 'two-handed funk patterns' (involving a staccato rhythmic conversation between the left and right hands, suitable for clavinet-style sounds as well as for piano). These type of keyboard stylings are featured on tunes by artists as diverse as the Chick Corea Elektric Band and Paula Abdul! Noted keyboard experts in this style include George Duke, Max Middleton, Michael Ruff, Mike Lindup (of Level 42) and Jeff Lorber, who in addition to being a jazz & funk artist is also a session ace on many of today's dance hits.

From a harmony standpoint, in an R'n'B/Funk style the right hand devices will include those used in the R'n'B ballad text (see **Chapter 14**). The overall right hand options can be summarized as follows:-

- Triad-over-root chords (see **Chapter 5**) and 4-part-over-root chords (see **Chapter 7**). Chord symbols may be 'upgraded' to larger forms, as seen in **Chapter 14 Figs. 14.9. - 14.15.**
- '**9 to 1**' resolutions within (upper structure) triads - see **Chapter 8**.
- '**4 to 3**' resolutions within (upper structure) triads - see **Chapter 9**.
- Double 4th structures - see **Chapter 10**.
- 4th interval couplings - see **Chapter 12** (Pop/Rock).
- Alternating triad concepts - see **Chapter 12** (Pop/Rock).
- 4th clusters - see **Chapter 13** (New Age).
- 'Half-step-&-5th' structures (see **Chapter 14** - R'n'B Ballad) and 'whole-step-&-5th' structures (see later text in this chapter).

The left hand part will almost always consist of single notes (frequently using root, 5th or 7th of the chord, although other tones from the relevant scale source are also available), used in either a supportive role or in a rhythmic conversation with the right hand part. Also in these funk styles, the sustain pedal is generally not used - in contrast with some of the styles previously studied (pop ballad, new age, R'n'B ballad) where the sustain pedal is generally used for the duration of each chord.

As mentioned above, R'n'B/funk styles use both 'straight 16ths' and 'swing 16ths' rhythmic treatments. The 'swing 16ths' funk style (also sometimes referred to as 'hip-hop' or 'funk shuffle') has become very popular in recent years, on the charts and in the dance clubs. Most of the rhythmic and comping patterns presented in this chapter can be played using both 'straight 16ths' and 'swing 16ths' interpretations, and we will demonstrate and practice these examples both ways - subjectively the difference between these rhythmic treatments becomes easier to hear in patterns containing more 16th-note subdivisions. We'll additionally look at some patterns specifically designed for a 'swing 16ths' interpretation, making use of an additional subdivision (the 2nd 16th note within a 16th note triplet) made available by this rhythmic treatment.

Basic R'n'B/funk comping - rhythmic concepts

We will first of all look at the construction of basic comping patterns in funk styles. Rhythmically the left hand is normally playing on beats **1** & **3**, except in situations where beat **3** is being anticipated (typically by a 16th note - review text accompanying **Fig. 2.44**. as necessary). The left hand can also be playing on, and providing 16th note pickups into, any of the downbeats (**1**, **2**, **3** or **4**). The right hand can play a more sustained role against the left hand rhythms, although some 16th note subdivisions & anticipations can be used. Here are some rhythm patterns (for left and right hands) to get us started in this style - don't forget that the difference between 'straight 16ths' and 'swing 16ths' treatments may not seem so apparent in the first few patterns which don't have a lot of 16th note subdivisions!

Figure 15.1. Basic comping rhythmic phrase #1
(Cassette Tape Example 440 - 'Straight 16ths')
(Cassette Tape Example 441 - 'Swing 16ths')

Here the right hand is sustained through the whole measure, while the left hand is playing on beats **1** & **3** (and with a 16th note pickup into beat **3**).

Figure 15.2. Basic comping rhythmic phrase #2
(Cassette Tape Example 442 - 'Straight 16ths')
(Cassette Tape Example 443 - 'Swing 16ths')

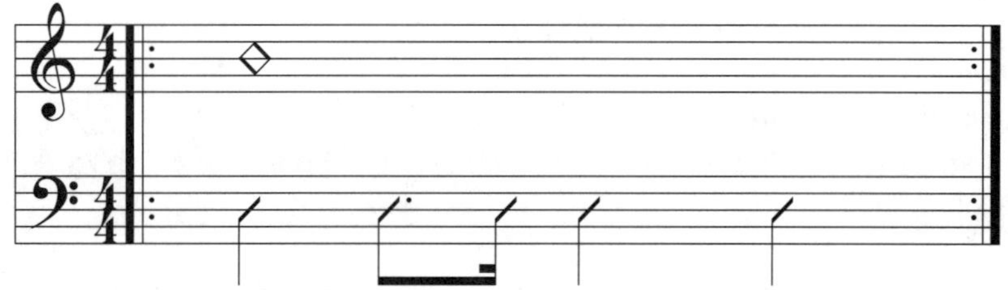

A variation on pattern **#1**, with the left hand now playing on all the downbeats (**1**, **2**, **3** & **4**) as well as the pickup into beat **3**.

Figure 15.3. Basic comping rhythmic phrase #3
(Cassette Tape Example 444 - 'Straight 16ths')
(Cassette Tape Example 445 - 'Swing 16ths')

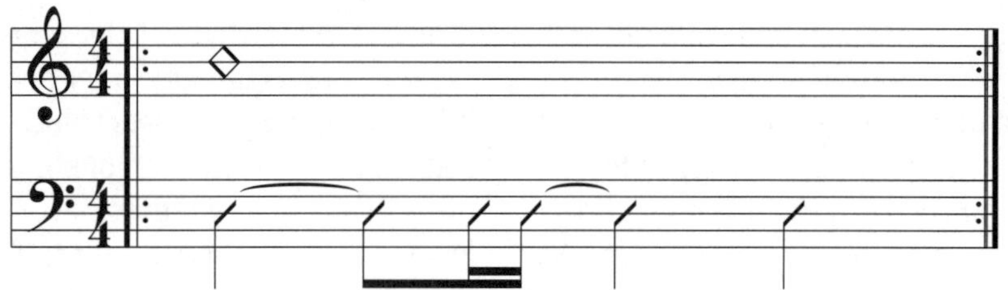

A variation on pattern **#2**, this time with the left hand landing on the 2nd & 3rd 16ths of beat **2**, anticipating beat **3** (with a pickup into the anticipation).

Basic R'n'B/funk comping - rhythmic concepts (contd)

Figure 15.4. Basic comping rhythmic phrase #4

(Cassette Tape Example 446 - 'Straight 16ths')
(Cassette Tape Example 447 - 'Swing 16ths')

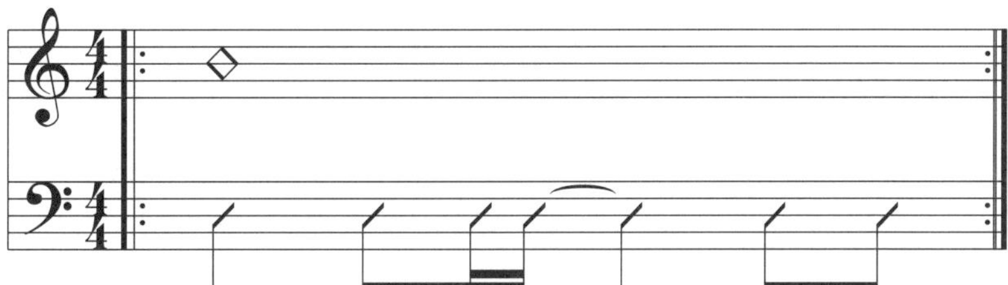

A small variation on pattern **#3**, this time with an extra left hand event on the '**& of 4**'.

Figure 15.5. Basic comping rhythmic phrase #5

(Cassette Tape Example 448 - 'Straight 16ths')
(Cassette Tape Example 449 - 'Swing 16ths')

Now the right hand is anticipating beats **2** & **3** (by a 16th and 8th note respectively). The successive right hand attacks are separated by three quarters of a beat - a typical rhythmic device.

Figure 15.6. Basic comping rhythmic phrase #6

(Cassette Tape Example 450 - 'Straight 16ths')
(Cassette Tape Example 451 - 'Swing 16ths')

A variation on pattern **#5**, now with the left hand landing on all the downbeats (**1**, **2**, **3** & **4**).

Figure 15.7. Basic comping rhythmic phrase #7

(Cassette Tape Example 452 - 'Straight 16ths')
(Cassette Tape Example 453 - 'Swing 16ths')

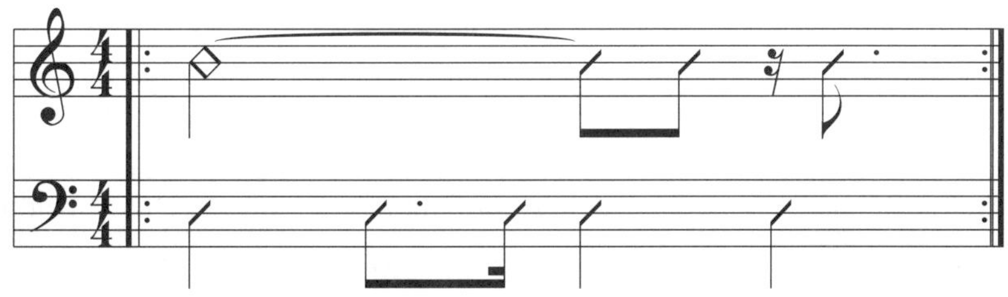

Same left hand rhythm as pattern **#2**, now with the right hand additionally landing either side of beat **4** (on the '**& of 3**' and the 2nd 16th of beat **4**).

Basic R'n'B/funk comping - rhythmic concepts (contd)

Figure 15.8. Basic comping rhythmic phrase #8
(Cassette Tape Example 454 - 'Straight 16ths')
(Cassette Tape Example 455 - 'Swing 16ths')

A variation on pattern **#7**, now with the left hand adding 16th note pickups into beats **4** & **1** (on the repeat).

Figure 15.9. Basic comping rhythmic phrase #9
(Cassette Tape Example 456 - 'Straight 16ths')
(Cassette Tape Example 457 - 'Swing 16ths')

Another variation, this time combining the same right hand phrase (from patterns **#7** & **#8**) with the left hand anticipation of beat **3** (as in pattern **#3**).

Figure 15.10. Basic comping rhythmic phrase #10
(Cassette Tape Example 458 - 'Straight 16ths')
(Cassette Tape Example 459 - 'Swing 16ths')

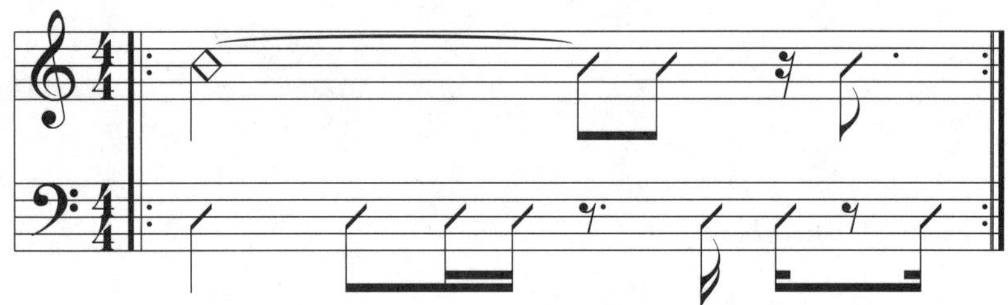

A variation on pattern **#9**, with the left hand adding pickups into beats **4** & **1** (on the repeat).

Feel free to experiment with these rhythms to create your own ideas! Now we will present each of the above rhythms within a funk comping example. Harmonically the left hand is normally playing basic chord tones (i.e. root & 5th) as supportive single notes, with some neighbouring or scale tones as 'pickups'. The right hand is typically using chordal 'upper structures' to create triad-over-root chords (see **Chapter 5**) or 4-part-over-root chords (see **Chapter 7**). The triad-over-root chords can also be used in the context of 'alternating triads', a technique we first applied in **Chapter 12** (Pop-Rock). Sometimes double-4th structures (see **Chapter 10**) and resolutions within triads (see **Chapters 8** & **9**) can also be used in the right hand. Here now are the two-measure comping examples using the above rhythmic phrases:-

Basic R'n'B/funk comping patterns

Figure 15.11. Basic funk comping pattern #1 (using rhythm pattern #1 - Fig. 15.1.)
(Cassette Tape Example 460 - 'Straight 16ths')
(Cassette Tape Example 461 - 'Swing 16ths')

- On the **Cmi9** chord, the right hand is using a **b3-5-b7-9** upper structure (a 2nd inversion **Ebma7** shape - see **Fig. 7.1.**). The left hand is playing the root of the chord.
- On the **Fmi9** chord, the right hand is again using a **b3-5-b7-9** upper structure (a root position **Abma7** shape). The left hand is playing the root, with the 5th as a pickup into beat **3**.

Figure 15.12. Basic funk comping pattern #2 (using rhythm pattern #2 - Fig. 15.2.)
(Cassette Tape Example 462 - 'Straight 16ths')
(Cassette Tape Example 463 - 'Swing 16ths')

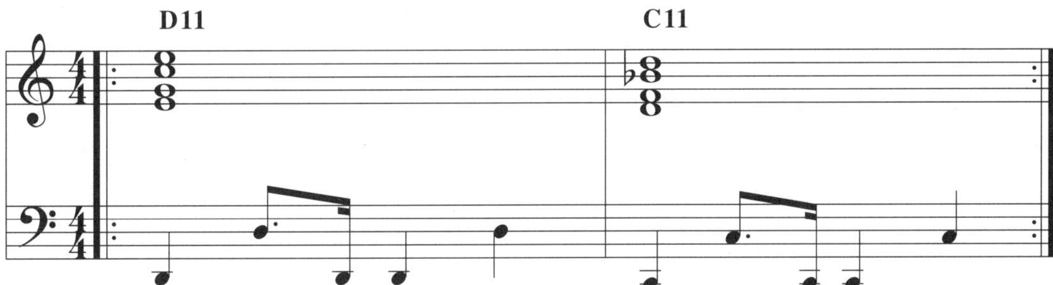

- On the **D11** chord, the right hand is using a **b7-9-11** upper structure (a 2nd inversion **C** triad, with the top note doubled - see **Fig. 5.2.**). The left hand is playing the root of the chord in an octave pattern.
- On the **C11** chord, the right hand is again using a **b7-9-11** upper structure (a 2nd inversion **Bb** triad, with the top note doubled). The left hand is continuing the octave pattern using the root of the chord.

Figure 15.13. Basic funk comping pattern #3 (using rhythm pattern #3 - Fig. 15.3.)
(Cassette Tape Example 464 - 'Straight 16ths')
(Cassette Tape Example 465 - 'Swing 16ths')

Basic R'n'B/funk comping patterns (contd)

(Analysis of Fig. 15.13.)

- On the **Emi11** chord, the right hand is using an **11-b7-b3** double 4th structure (see **Fig. 10.5.**). The left hand is using the root and 5th of the chord.
- On the **D69** chord, the right hand is using a **6-9-5** double 4th structure (see **Fig. 10.11.**). The left hand is continuing the root-&-5th pattern.

Figure 15.14. Basic funk comping pattern #4 (using rhythm pattern #4 - Fig. 15.4.)
(Cassette Tape Example 466 - 'Straight 16ths')
(Cassette Tape Example 467 - 'Swing 16ths')

- On the **Cma9** chord, the right hand is using a **3-5-7-9** upper structure (a 2nd inversion **Emi7** shape - see **Fig. 7.3.**). The left hand is playing the root on beat **1** and on the anticipation of beat **3**, with the 5th on beat **2** and the 6th on the '**& of 2**' (acting as a pickup into the anticipation). The connecting tones E & F are used during beat **4** to lead into the next chord.
- On the **Gmi9** chord, the right hand is using a **b3-5-b7-9** upper structure (a 3rd inversion **Bbma7** shape - see **Fig. 7.1.**). The left hand concept is similar to the first measure, this time using the b7th on the '**& of 2**' and the connecting tones Bb & B during beat **4** (leading back to the first measure).

Figure 15.15. Basic funk comping pattern #5 (using rhythm pattern #5 - Fig. 15.5.)
(Cassette Tape Example 468 - 'Straight 16ths')
(Cassette Tape Example 469 - 'Swing 16ths')

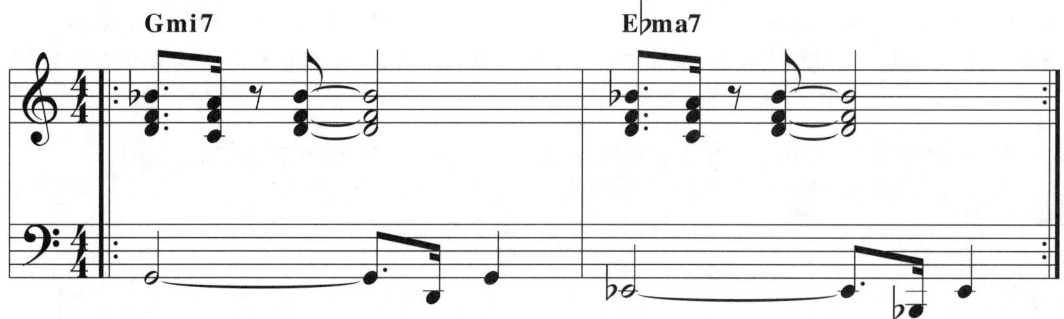

- On the **Gmi7** chord, the right hand is using '**b7 to b3**' alternating triads (see **Fig. 12.19.**). The left hand is playing the root of the chord, with the 5th as a pickup into beat **4**.
- On the **Ebma7** chord, the right hand is using '**9 to 5**' alternating triads (see **Fig. 12.16.**). The left hand is continuing the previous root-&-5th pattern.

Basic R'n'B/funk comping patterns (contd)

Figure 15.16. Basic funk comping pattern #6 (using rhythm pattern #6 - Fig. 15.6.)
(Cassette Tape Example 470 - 'Straight 16ths')
(Cassette Tape Example 471 - 'Swing 16ths')

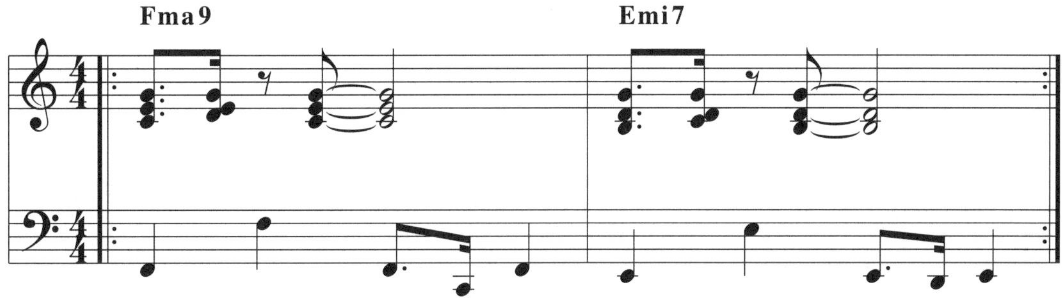

- On the **Fma9** chord, the right hand is using a '**9 to 1**' resolution within a **5-7-9** upper structure (a root position **C** triad - see **Fig. 8.16.**). The left hand is playing the root of the chord, with the 5th as a pickup into beat **4**
- On the **Emi7** chord, the right hand is using a '**4 to 3**' resolution within a **b3-5-b7** upper structure (a first inversion **G** triad - see **Fig. 9.7.**). The left hand concept is similar to the first measure, this time with the 7th used as a pickup into beat **4**.

Figure 15.17. Basic funk comping pattern #7 (using rhythm pattern #7- Fig. 15.7.)
(Cassette Tape Example 472 - 'Straight 16ths')
(Cassette Tape Example 473 - 'Swing 16ths')

- On the **Dmi7** chord, the right hand is using '**b7 to b3**' alternating triads (see **Fig. 12.19.**) The left hand is playing the root, in an octave pattern.
- On the **Bbma9** chord, the right hand is using '**9 to 5**' alternating triads (see **Fig. 12.16.**). The left hand is continuing the octave pattern.

Basic R'n'B/funk comping patterns (contd)

Figure 15.18. Basic funk comping pattern #8 (using rhythm pattern #8 - Fig. 15.8.)

(Cassette Tape Example 474 - 'Straight 16ths')
(Cassette Tape Example 475 - 'Swing 16ths')

- On the **Dmi9** chord, the right hand is using a **b3-5-b7-9** upper structure (a 2nd inversion **Fma7** shape - see **Fig. 7.1.**). The left hand is playing the root in octaves, with the 5th on beat **4**.
- On the **C13sus** chord, the right hand is using a **b7-9-11-13** upper structure (a root position **Bbma7** shape - see **Fig. 7.2.**). The left hand pattern is similar to the first measure.

Figure 15.19. Basic funk comping pattern #9 (using rhythm pattern #9 - Fig. 15.9.)

(Cassette Tape Example 476 - 'Straight 16ths')
(Cassette Tape Example 477 - 'Swing 16ths')

- On the **Emi7** chord, the right hand is using a **b3-5-b7** upper structure (a first inversion **G** triad - see **Fig. 5.6.**). The left hand is playing the root of the chord in an octave pattern, during the first 2 beats of the first measure.
- On the **Gma7** chord, the right hand is using a **5-7-9** upper structure (a 2nd inversion **D** triad - see **Fig. 5.4.**). The left hand is playing the root of the chord on beat **4** of the first measure.
- On the **Ami7** chord, the right hand is again using a **b3-5-b7** upper structure (a 2nd inversion **C** triad - see **Fig. 5.6.**). The left hand is again playing the root of the chord in an octave pattern, during the first two beats of the second measure.
- On the **Bmi7** chord, the right hand is again using a **b3-5-b7** upper structure (a 2nd inversion **D** triad). The left hand is playing the root of the chord on beat **4** of the second measure.

Basic R'n'B/funk comping patterns (contd)

Figure 15.20. Basic funk comping pattern #10 (using rhythm pattern #10 - Fig. 15.10.)

(Cassette Tape Example 478 - 'Straight 16ths')
(Cassette Tape Example 479 - 'Swing 16ths')

(This example is similar to the funk pattern used for triad-over-root practice in **Fig. 5.29.**).

- On the **Ami7** chord, the right hand is using '**b7 to b3**' alternating triads (see **Fig. 12.19.**). The left hand is playing the root in an octave pattern, with the 5th on beat **4**.
- On the **Dmi7** chord, the right hand is using a **b3-5-b7** upper structure (a 2nd inversion **F** triad - see **Fig. 5.6.**). The left hand is continuing the previous octave pattern.
- On the **G7** chord, the right hand is using '**b7 to 1**' alternating triads (see **Fig. 12.21.**). The left hand is using a root-&-5th pattern (with the root anticipating beat **3**).

Now we will apply these funk comping concepts to some leadsheet examples. Here is the first chord chart, to be interpreted in a funk comping style:-

Figure 15.21. Chord chart example #1

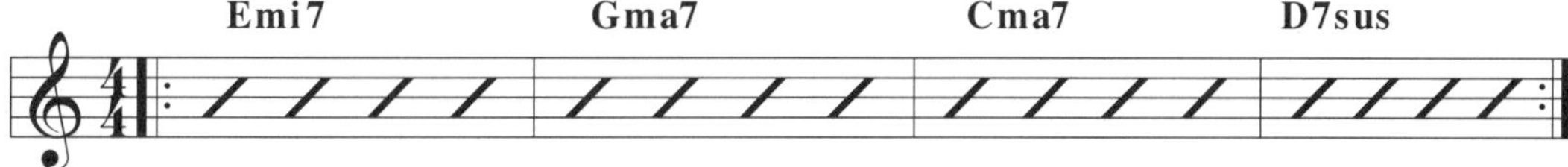

We will use upper structure triad-over-root and 4-part-over-root chords in the following version:-

Figure 15.22. Funk comping solution for chord chart #1 (Fig. 15.21.)

(Cassette Tape Example 480 - 'Straight 16ths')
(Cassette Tape Example 481 - 'Swing 16ths')

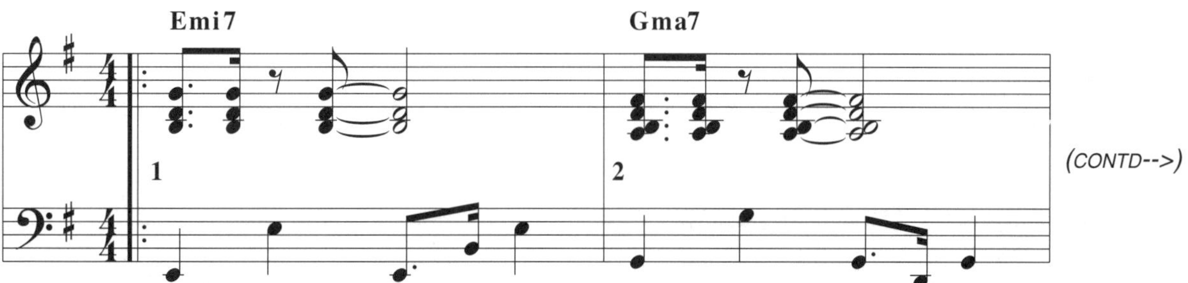

Basic R'n'B/funk comping patterns (contd)

Figure 15.22. (contd)

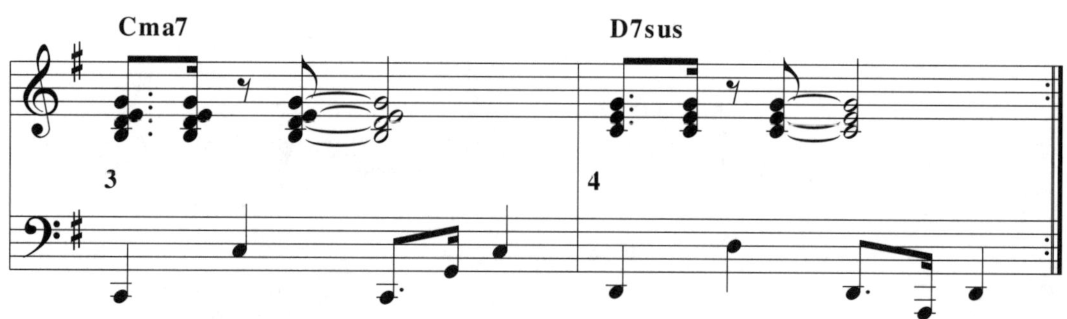

Rhythmically this is based on pattern **#6** (see **Figs. 15.6.** & **15.16.**). The left hand is playing the roots of the chords on the downbeats in an octave pattern, with the 5th of the chord as a pickup into beat **4** of each measure. Note that in this example (and in the following 'basic comping' examples) that some of the chord symbols have again been 'upgraded' i.e. extensions have been added, by using appropriate 4-part upper shapes. We first saw this process at work in **Chapter 14** (R'n'B Ballad - review **Figs. 14.9. - 14.15.** as necessary). The right hand part in the previous example can be harmonically analyzed as follows:-

- Measure 1 - On the **Emi7** chord, the right hand is using a **b3-5-b7** upper structure (a 1st inversion **G** triad - see **Fig. 5.6.**).

- Measure 2 - On the **Gma7** chord, the right hand is using a **3-5-7-9** upper structure (a 3rd inversion **Bmi7** shape - see **Fig. 7.3.**). This is upgrading the chord to a **Gma9** overall (see **Fig. 14.11.**).

- Measure 3 - On the **Cma7** chord, the right hand is again using a **3-5-7-9** upper structure (this time a 2nd inversion **Emi7** shape). This is upgrading the chord to a **Cma9** overall (see **Fig. 14.11.**).

- Measure 4 - On the **D7sus** chord, the right hand is using a **b7-9-11** upper structure (a root position **C** triad) - see **Fig. 5.2.**). This is upgrading the chord to a **D9sus** or **D11** overall.

Now we will look at a further leadsheet example as follows:-

Figure 15.23. Chord chart example #2

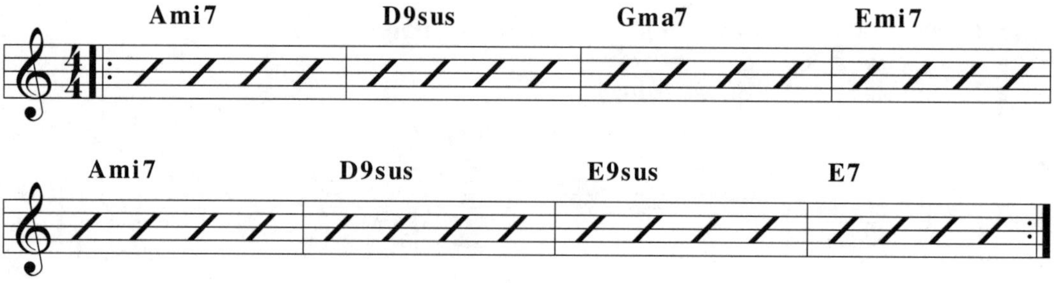

The interpretation of this chart now uses 4-part-over-root chord structures as follows:-

Basic R'n'B/funk comping patterns (contd)

Figure 15.24. Funk comping solution for chord chart #2 (Fig. 15.23.)
(Cassette Tape Example 482 - 'Straight 16ths')
(Cassette Tape Example 483 - 'Swing 16ths')

Rhythmically this is based on pattern **#8** (see **Figs. 15.8. & 15.18.**) in the odd-numbered measures, and pattern **#10** (see **Figs. 15.10. & 15.20.**) in the even-numbered measures. Again the left hand is playing the roots in an octave pattern, with the 5th of each chord on beat **4**. The right hand part can be analyzed as follows:-

Basic R'n'B/funk comping patterns (contd)

(Analysis of Fig. 15.24.)

- Measure 1 - On the **Ami7** chord, the right hand is using a **b3-5-b7-9** upper structure (a root position **Cma7** shape - see **Fig. 7.1.**). This is upgrading the chord to an **Ami9** overall (see **Fig. 14.12.**).

- Measure 2 - On the **D9sus** chord, the right hand is using a **b7-9-11-13** upper structure (again a root position **Cma7** shape - see **Fig. 7.2.**). This is upgrading the chord to a **D13sus** overall (see **Fig. 14.14.**).

- Measure 3 - On the **Gma7** chord, the right hand is using a **3-5-7-9** upper structure (a root position **Bmi7** shape - see **Fig. 7.3.**). This is upgrading the chord to an **Gma9** overall (see **Fig. 14.11.**).

- Measure 4 - On the **Emi7** chord, the right hand is using a **b3-5-b7-9** upper structure (a 2nd inversion **Gma7** shape - see **Fig. 7.1.**). This is upgrading the chord to an **Emi9** overall (see **Fig. 14.12.**).

- Measure 5 - As for measure 1.

- Measure 6 - On the **D9sus** chord, the right hand is using a **5-b7-9-11** upper structure (a 1st inversion **Ami7** shape - see **Fig. 7.4.**).

- Measure 7 - On the **E9sus** chord, the right hand is again using a **5-b7-9-11** upper structure (this time a root position **Bmi7** shape - see **Fig. 7.4.**).

- Measure 8 - On the **E7** chord, the right hand is using a **3-5-b7-9** upper structure (a 2nd inversion **G#mi7(b5)** shape - review **Fig. 1.83.** as necessary for the spelling of this chord shape). We saw in **Fig. 14.15.** that this structure can be built from the 3rd of a dominant chord, in this case upgrading the chord to an **E9** overall.

Now we will look at the final leadsheet example in this section, as follows:-

Figure 15.25. Chord chart example #3

The interpretation of this chart now uses upper structure 'half-step-4th' and 'whole-step-4th' clusters (see **Figs. 13.13. - 13.18.**) as follows:-

Figure 15.26. Funk comping solution for chord chart #3 (Fig. 15.25.)
(Cassette Tape Example 484 - 'Straight 16ths')
(Cassette Tape Example 485 - 'Swing 16ths')

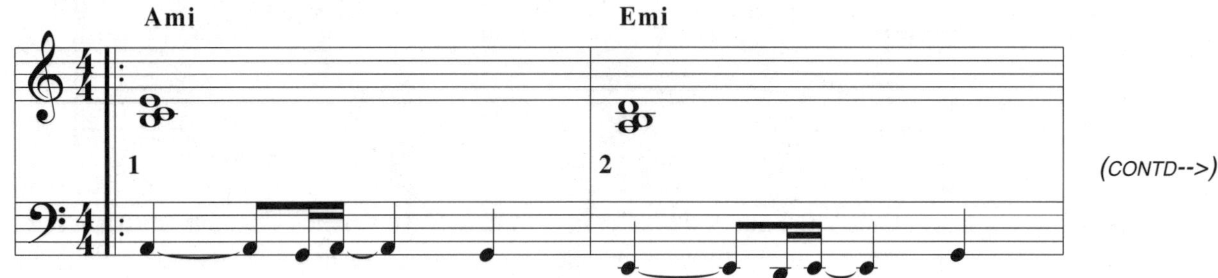

(CONTD-->)

Basic R'n'B/funk comping patterns (contd)

Figure 15.26. (contd)

Rhthmically this is based on pattern **#3** (see **Figs. 15.3.** & **15.13.**). The left hand is playing the chord roots on beat **1** and on the anticipation of beat **3**, with the 7th and 3rd (11th on the Gsus) also being used as embellishment tones. The right hand part can be harmonically analyzed as follows:-

- Measure 1 - On the **Ami** chord, the right hand is using a **9-b3-5** 'half-step-4th' cluster (see **Fig. 13.15.**). This upgrades the chord to an **Ami(add9)** overall.

- Measure 2 - On the **Emi** chord, the right hand is using an **11-5-b7** 'whole-step-4th' cluster (see **Fig. 13.12.**). This upgrades the chord to an **Emi7sus** or **Emi7(add11)** overall.

- Measure 3 - On the **F** chord, the right hand is using a **9-3-5** 'whole-step-4th' cluster (see **Fig. 13.11.**). This upgrades the chord to an **F(add9)** overall.

- Measure 4 - On the **Gsus** chord, the right hand is using an **11-5-b7** 'whole-step-4th' cluster (see **Fig. 13.12.**). This upgrades the chord to a **G7sus** overall.

PRACTICE DIRECTIONS:-

- ***Practice the basic left- and right-hand comping rhythm patterns shown in Figs. 15.1. - 15.10.***
  You can play a single repeated note in each hand to practice these rhythms. Start at a slow tempo and gradually increase as desired.
- ***Practice the comping pattern examples based on these rhythms, as shown in Figs. 15.11. - 15.20.***
  For extra practice - try playing these in different keys!
- ***Practice the comping solutions for chord charts #1, #2 and #3, as in Figs. 15.21. - 15.26.***
- ***Work on applying these concepts to tunes of your choice, and to the practice leadsheets at the end of this chapter.***

CHAPTER FIFTEEN

Two-handed 'staccato' funk comping - rhythmic concepts

Now we will focus on some more rhythmically complex funk grooves, involving a staccato rhythmic conversation between the left and right hands. By 'staccato' we mean the notes are generally of short duration (and are often accented). This style contrasts with the preceding section on 'basic comping', where the left hand was typically more 'supportive' of the right hand, and where either hand could play a more sustained role. The first stage in deriving these more percussive two-handed patterns is to consider the rhythmic requirements, as follows:-

- Creation of an initial right-hand rhythmic phrase.
- Creation of a complementary left-hand 'counter-rhythm' to match the right hand phrase.

We will start here by considering one-measure right hand rhythmic phrases. There are sixteen different places within a measure where a rhythmic attack could occur (see **Fig. 2.37.**) - so there are a very large number of rhythmic permutations available using sixteenth notes! We will do our best here to analyze the components of effective funk rhythms, however this is largely an 'ear' process and you are encouraged to experiment. Here are some observations regarding the initial **right-hand rhythmic phrase:-**

- Don't overdo the number of subdivisions! Leave space between the rhythmic attacks (as this is where later the left hand rhythms will occur). The right-hand rhythmic examples in this section generally have between five and nine rhythmic attacks in the measure (out of a possible 16). Also the right hand will rarely use all the subdivisions in any one beat, or use more than 2 consecutive subdivisions (although when the left hand part is added in, the resulting subdivisions may be more continuous).
- Try to achieve a balance between anticipated and non-anticipated 16th notes in the right hand rhythm. (Review text prior to **Fig. 2.44.** for definition of 16th note anticipations as necessary). For our purposes here, we will refer to the '**strong 16ths**' as landing on beat **1**, the '**& of 1**', beat **2**, the '**& of 2**' etc. in other words those places which would be available **within an eighth-note subdivision**, and we will refer to the 'weak' 16ths as landing on the '**e of 1**', the '**a of 1**', the '**e of 2**', the '**a of 2**' etc. in other words on the 2nd and 4th subdivisions within the beat (review 16th note counting in **Fig. 2.42.** as necessary). So using this terminology, an attack on a 'weak 16th' followed by an attack on a 'strong 16th' would function as a pickup (into the 'strong 16th'), and an attack on a 'weak 16th' followed by a rest or tied across the next subdivision, would function as an **anticipation**. Most of the right hand rhythms in this section use an approximately equal number of 'strong' and 'weak' 16ths - however, feel free to experiment with this!

Once the right hand rhythmic phrase has been established, the left hand rhythm is then generated. Again we can make the following observation regarding the **left hand rhythmic phrase:-**

- The left hand is generally landing on the downbeat of each chord change (typically using the root of the chord), unless the chord rhythm is itself anticipated. Within the duration of the chord however, there is considerable rhythmic freedom regarding the left hand placement.
- Generally the objective is to play in the 'rhythmic spaces' within the right hand part, creating a rhythmic conversation between the hands. It is rare therefore for the two hands to be playing 'concerted' or together (unlike any other contemporary style studied so far). One exception to this may be at the point of chord change and/or harmonic anticipation, where the hands may be playing on the same subdivision.
- A busy left hand part may 'fill up' all the rhythmic spaces left in the right hand part - however this is not always appropriate and may 'dilute' the effect of any anticipations in the right hand part. Again the left hand part normally uses between five and nine subdivisions per measure (out of a possible 16).

We will now see these concepts at work, with the following right-hand and left-hand rhythmic phrases:-

Two-handed 'staccato' funk comping - rhythmic concepts (contd)

Figure 15.27. Right hand rhythmic phrase #1

(Cassette Tape Example 486 - 'Straight 16ths')
(Cassette Tape Example 487 - 'Swing 16ths')

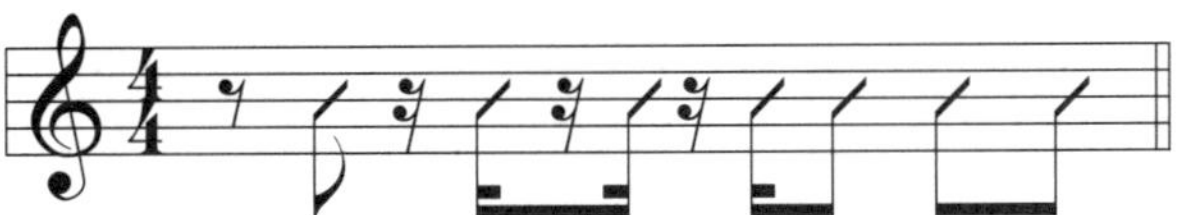

This rhythm contains a good mix of 'strong' and 'weak' 16ths. 'Weak' 16ths within beat **2** are followed by rests, producing anticipations of the '**& of 2**' and beat **3**. The attack on the 2nd 16th of beat **3** is effectively a pickup into the '**& of 3**'. Now we will match a left hand rhythm to this as follows:-

Figure 15.28. Two-handed rhythmic phrase #1

(Cassette Tape Example 488 - 'Straight 16ths')
(Cassette tape Example 489 - 'Swing 16ths')

In this case all of the left hand additions were in the rhythmic spaces within the right hand part. Notice in beats **2**, **3** & **4** that the left hand is supplying the remaining two subdivisions of each beat which are **not** used in the right hand part. In beat **2**, the right hand is using the 'weak' 16ths (2nd & 4th of the beat) and the left hand is playing the 'strong' 16ths (1st & 3rd of the beat) in between. These roles are reversed during beat **4**.

Figure 15.29. Right hand rhythmic phrase #2

(Cassette Tape Example 490 - 'Straight 16ths')
(Cassette Tape Example 491 - 'Swing 16ths')

A syncopated effect is created here by the successive use of 16th note pairs, on the 3rd & 4th 16ths of beat **2**, the 2nd & 3rd 16ths of beat **3** and the 1st & 2nd 16ths of beat **4**. Again beat **3** is being anticipated. Again we will add a left hand rhythm to this as follows:-

Figure 15.30. Two handed rhythmic phrase #2

(Cassette Tape Example 492 - 'Straight 16ths')
(Cassette Tape Example 493 - 'Swing 16ths')

In this busy example, all of the rhythmic spaces in the right hand part have been used in the left hand. Notice the 'mirror image' rhythm during beats **1** & **2** - the right hand is landing on the 2nd 16th of beat **1**, with the left hand taking the remaining subdivisions in beat **1** - the roles however are reversed during beat **2**. In beats **3** & **4**, the left and right hands are taking 2 subdivisions each.

Two-handed 'staccato' funk comping - rhythmic concepts (contd)

Figure 15.31. Right hand rhythmic phrase #3
(Cassette Tape Example 494 - 'Straight 16ths')
(Cassette Tape Example 495 - 'Swing 16ths')

During beats **1** & **2** we are using the 'strong' 16ths here, which helps to accentuate the impact of the 'weak' 16th in beat **3** (the 4th 16th of beat **3** is anticipating beat **4**). This also gives the left hand a chance to emphasize any 'weak' 16th notes in the first half of the measure, as desired. Now the left hand is added as follows:-

Figure 15.32. Two handed rhythmic phrase #3
(Cassette Tape Example 496 - 'Straight 16ths')
(Cassette Tape Example 497 - 'Swing 16ths')

This sparse left hand part effectively complements the right hand rhythm, defining the first downbeat and using a single attack in beats **3** & **4**. The attack on the '**& of 3**' further accentuates the anticipation of beat **4** in the right hand, acting as a pickup.

Figure 15.33. Right hand rhythmic phrase #4
(Cassette Tape Example 498 - 'Straight 16ths')
(Cassette Tape Example 499 - 'Swing 16ths')

Here we have a 'weak 16th' being used in beat **1** (the 2nd 16th of beat **1**, functioning as an anticipation of the '**& of 1**'). During beats **2** & **3** the 'strong 16ths' are used, leading into an anticipation of beat **4**. Now the left hand is added:-

Figure 15.34. Two handed rhythmic phrase #4
(Cassette Tape Example 500 - 'Straight 16ths')
(Cassette Tape Example 501 - 'Swing 16ths')

Here the left hand is using all of the remaining subdivisions of beat **1** (including the downbeat). The 'weak 16th' used in beat **2** (on the last 16th subdivision) is an effective pickup into the attack on beat **3** being played by the right hand.

Two-handed 'staccato' funk comping - rhythmic concepts (contd)

Figure 15.35. Right hand rhythmic phrase #5
(Cassette Tape Example 502 - 'Straight 16ths')
(Cassette Tape Example 503 - 'Swing 16ths')

Note the 16th-8th-16th phrase in beat **2** - using both 'weak 16ths' in beat **2** (anticipating beat **3**) is effective here. This series of 'weak 16ths' continues into beat **3**, with the 2nd 16th of beat **3** acting as a pickup into the **'& of 3'**. Now the left hand is added as follows:-

Figure 15.36. Two handed rhythmic phrase #5
(Cassette Tape Example 504 - 'Straight 16ths')
(Cassette Tape Example 505 - 'Swing 16ths')

Here the left hand is landing with the right hand on beat **1**, which might typically occur at the point of chord change and/ or harmonic anticipation. The left hand is again using all of the 'rhythmic spaces' left by the right hand part - note the different allocation of the subdivisions between the hands during beats **2**, **3** and **4**.

Figure 15.37. Right hand rhythmic phrase #6
(Cassette Tape Example 506 - 'Straight 16ths')
(Cassette Tape Example 507 - 'Swing 16ths')

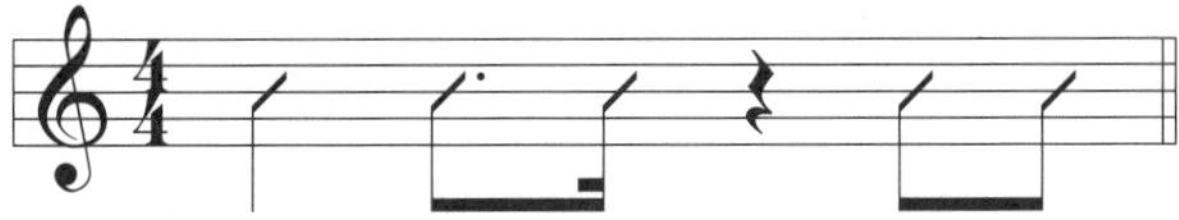

This comparatively sparse right hand pattern is using 'strong 16ths' except for the last 16th of beat **2**, anticipating beat **3**. Now the left hand is added as follows:-

Figure 15.38. Two handed rhytyhmic phrase #6
(Cassette Tape Example 508 - 'Straight 16ths')
(Cassette Tape Example 509 - 'Swing 16ths')

The resulting rhythm here is still fairly sparse (only 5 attacks in each hand). There are some interesting contrasts in rhythmic 'density' - while in beat **2** the added left hand part results in all the subdivisions being used during this beat, the only attack during beat **3** is on the last 16th in the left hand (functioning as a pickup into the right hand attack on beat **4**). Like the previous pattern, the left hand is joining the right hand on the first attack (beat **1**).

Two-handed 'staccato' funk comping - rhythmic concepts (contd)

Figure 15.39. Right hand rhythmic phrase #7
(Cassette Tape Example 510 - 'Straight 16ths')
(Cassette Tape Example 511 - 'Swing 16ths')

A busier right hand rhythm, with 9 attacks being used. The 16th-16th-8th figure used in beat **1** is reversed in beat **2**, leading to an anticipation of beat **3**. Now the left hand is added as follows:-

Figure 15.40. Two handed rhythmic phrase #7
(Cassette Tape Example 512 - 'Straight 16ths')
(Cassette Tape Example 513 - 'Swing 16ths')

With the addition of the left hand, all of the rhythmic subdivisions are being used except for beat **3**, where the only subdivision used is the left hand landing on the last 16th (picking up into beat **4**).

As you can see, this is only a selection from the huge number of possibilities available - use the principles outlined to experiment with your own rhythmic ideas! In the following text we will now use these rhythmic ideas as part of a step-by-step technique to create two-handed funk patterns on the keyboard.

Two-handed 'staccato' funk comping patterns

We will now take a tour through the following process to create a two-handed funk pattern from 'scratch':-

1) Create a right hand rhythmic phrase (see above examples).
2) Create a melodic (or top-note) motif, to be played by the right hand using the previously created rhythm pattern. The motif will normally be derived from one of the following scales, depending upon the chord quality in force:-
    - Minor pentatonic (see **Fig. 1.67.**)
    - Blues (see **Fig. 1.68.**)
    - Modal i.e. Dorian, Mixolydian (see **Figs. 1.32. - 1.45.**).
3) Where appropriate, add couplings/structures below the top note motif in the right hand, according to the discipline of the chord symbol in force. All the various devices listed in the introduction to this chapter are available i.e. triads, 4-part chords, triad resolutions, double 4ths, clusters etc.
4) Add a single note part in the left hand. Rhythmically this will be according to the principles laid down in the earlier text on 'Two-handed staccato funk comping - rhythmic concepts' - generally using the left hand in a rhythmic conversation with the right hand part. Harmonically this part often consists of the root, 5th or 7th of the chord, although other scale source tones are also available.

Two-handed 'staccato' funk comping patterns (contd)

Let's see how this process works! We'll first take a right hand rhythmic pattern - say pattern **#1** from the preceding section in this chapter (repeated for your convenience here):-

Figure 15.41. (15.27.) Right hand rhythmic phrase #1
(Cassette Tape Example 486 - 'Straight 16ths')
(Cassette Tape Example 487 - 'Swing 16ths')

Now we move to the second stage which is to create a right hand motif based around this rhythm, from an appropriate scale source. The first scale we will use is a minor pentatonic scale (see **Fig. 1.65.**), a frequently used choice in funk styles. If we for example take a C minor pentatonic scale (which would be appropriate over a **Cmi** or **Cmi7** chord for example), some of the various motif choices based on the above rhythm are as follows:-

Figure 15.42. Right hand C minor pentatonic phrase a), based on rhythmic phrase #1 (Fig. 15.41.)
(Cassette Tape Example 514 - 'Straight 16ths')
(Cassette Tape Example 515 - 'Swing 16ths')

Figure 15.43. Right hand C minor pentatonic phrase b), based on rhythmic phrase #1 (Fig. 15.41.)
(Cassette Tape Example 516 - 'Straight 16ths')
(Cassette Tape Example 517 - 'Swing 16ths')

Figure 15.44. Right hand C minor pentatonic phrase c), based on rhythmic phrase #1 (Fig. 15.41.)
(Cassette Tape Example 518 - 'Straight 16ths')
(Cassette Tape Example 519 - 'Swing 16ths')

As you can see, these are only a few of the huge number of possibilities available from the minor pentatonic scale, and as usual you are encouraged to experiment! Now we will take the last motif above (**Fig. 15.44.**) and take it to the next stage which is to place various structures below the top note in the right hand. One solution using 4th interval couplings is shown at the top of the next page:-

Two-handed 'staccato' funk comping patterns (contd)

Figure 15.45. Right hand structures below top-note version a), based on Fig. 15.44. motif
(Cassette Tape Example 520 - 'Straight 16ths')
(Cassette Tape Example 521 - 'Swing 16ths')

Here we are using 4th couplings below the top notes of **Eb**, **F**, **Eb** and **Bb** in the motif (see **Fig. 12.23.** and accompanying text for explanation of 4th interval couplings from a C minor pentatonic scale, suitable for a **Cmi** or **Cmi7** chord). The **F-Bb** coupling on the 2nd 16th of beat **3** is about the lowest point we would want to place this interval, as it will become 'muddy' if used much lower on the keyboard. The 4th couplings from left to right would represent **b7-b3**, **1-11**, **b7-b3**, **11-b7**, **11-b7** and **b7-b3** pairs with respect to a **Cmi7** chord (again review **Fig. 12.23.** as necessary). Now we will look at another upper voicing variation below the same top note line, this time using some double 4th structures as follows:-

Figure 15.46. Right hand structures below top note version b), based on Fig. 15.44. motif
(Cassette Tape Example 522 - 'Straight 16ths')
(Cassette Tape Example 523 - 'Swing 16ths')

Here we have expanded the first three 4th couplings used above into double 4th structures, again a typical right hand choice in funk styles. From left to right the double 4ths represent **11-b7-b3**, **5-1-11** and **11-b7-b3** structures with respect to a **Cmi7** chord (see **Figs. 10.3. & 10.5.**). Again the **F-Bb-Eb** double 4th here on the '**& of 1**' and the last 16th of beat **2**, is about the lowest point we would want to use this structure on the keyboard. Now we will take another top note motif (C minor pentatonic phrase '**b**' - see **Fig. 15.43.**) and apply right hand structures below, as follows:-

Figure 15.47. Right hand structures below top note version a), based on Fig. 15.43. motif
(Cassette Tape Example 524 - 'Straight 16ths')
(Cassette Tape Example 525 - 'Swing 16ths')

Now in addition to the 4th couplings in the right hand, we have some 'whole-step-4th' and 'half-step-4th' clusters being used. With respect to an overall **Cmi7** chord, we have an **11-5-b7** 'whole-step-4th' cluster on the '**& of 1**' (see **Fig. 13.12.**), a **9-b3-5** 'half-step-4th' cluster on the 2nd 16th of beat **2** (see **Fig. 13.15.**) and a **b7-1-b3** 'whole-step-4th' cluster on the last 16th of beat **2** (see **Fig. 13.14.**). Now for another upper structure variation on the C minor pentatonic motif in **Fig. 15.43**:-

Two-handed 'staccato' funk comping patterns (contd)

Figure 15.48. Right hand structures below top note version b), based on Fig. 15.43. motif

(Cassette Tape Example 526 - 'Straight 16ths')
(Cassette Tape Example 527 - 'Swing 16ths')

Now instead of the clusters in the right hand, we have some structures made up of a fifth interval stacked on top of a second interval. One structure of this nature we have already seen is the 'half-step-&-5th' (see **Figs. 13.19. - 13.24.**). It is also possible to stack a perfect 5th interval on top of a whole-step, and we will henceforth refer to this as a 'whole-step-&-5th' structure. Here is a summary of the useful vertical relationships created when 'half-step-&-5th' and 'whole-step-&-5th' structures are placed over roots in the bass voice:-

Figure 15.49. Summary of 'half-step-&-5th' structures placed over roots in the bass voice

(Cassette Tape Example 528)

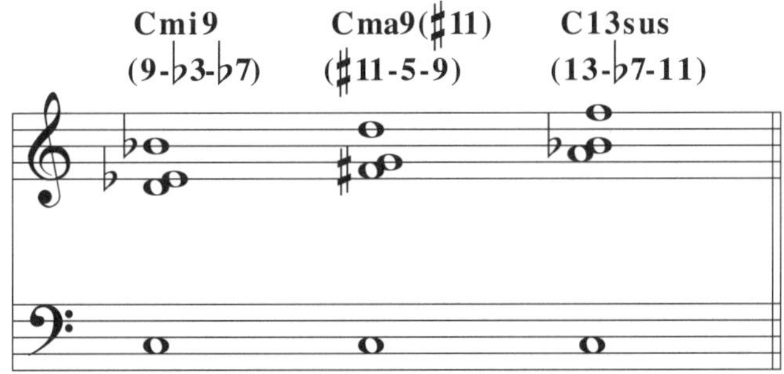

These equate to the examples in **Figs. 13.20.**, **13.21.** & **13.23**. The other vertical uses of this structure shown in **Chapter 13** are less useful in funk styles.

Figure 15.50. Summary of 'whole-step-&-5th' structures placed over roots in the bass voice

(Cassette Tape Example 529)

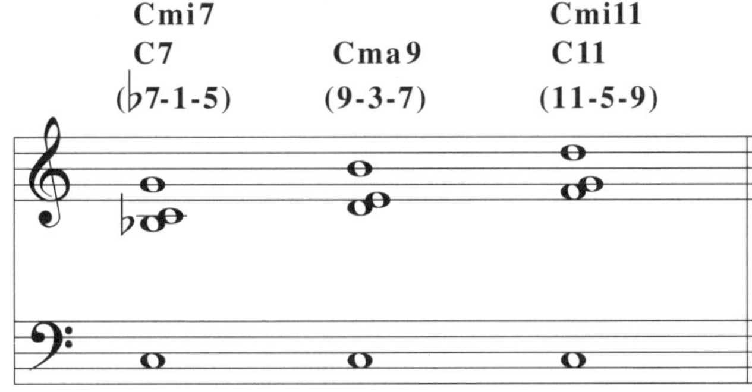

Here are the most useful combinations of the 'whole-step-&-5th' structure with a root in the bass voice. The first combination can be used on a minor or dominant chord, while the last combination can be used on a minor or suspended chord.

Returning to analyze **Fig. 15.48.**, with respect to an overall **Cmi7** chord we have a **9-b3-b7** 'half-step-&-5th' structure on the '**& of 1**' (see **Figs. 13.20.** & **15.49.**) and a **b7-1-5** 'whole-step-&-5th' structure on the 2nd 16th of beat **2** (see **Fig. 15.50.** above).

Two-handed 'staccato' funk comping patterns (contd)

Now we will address the final part of the process - adding a single-note left hand part in the rhythmic 'spaces' in between the right hand part. Review the text prior to **Fig. 15.27.** as necessary regarding the rhythmic placement of this left hand part. In the examples so far, we have been using C minor pentatonic as a scale source - so in the following two-handed examples the left hand part is also chosen from the same source. As we said before, the root of the chord is normally played in the left hand at the point of chord change and/or harmonic anticipation - however the remaining left hand rhythmic attacks within the duration of the chord, can often be assigned on a somewhat arbitrary basis to the different scale source tones available, with arguably a preference for roots, 5ths and 7ths of chords in many cases. Here now are some patterns for left and right hands, based on the two-handed rhythmic phrase **#1** (**Fig. 15.28.**, incorporating the right hand rhythmic phrase **#1** in **Fig. 15.27.**) and using the right hand upper structures (4th couplings in this case) shown in **Fig. 15.45**:-

Figure 15.51. Addition of left hand part a) to Fig. 15.45. right hand structures (4th couplings) creating a funk comping pattern using two-handed rhythmic phrase #1 (Fig. 15.28.)

(Cassette Tape Example 530 - 'Straight 16ths')
(Cassette Tape Example 531 - 'Swing 16ths')

Here (with respect to an overall **Cmi7** chord, or C minor pentatonic scale) the left hand from left to right is using the **1**, **1**, **b7**, **5**, **b7**, **b7**, & **1**.

Figure 15.52. Addition of left hand part b) to Fig. 15.45. right hand structures (4th couplings) creating a funk comping pattern using two-handed rhythmic phrase #1 (Fig. 15.28.)

(Cassette Tape Example 532 - 'Straight 16ths')
(Cassette Tape Example 533 - 'Swing 16ths')

Here the left hand is still starting with the **1**, but then is following with the **1**, **5**, **b7**, **b3**, **4** & **5** of the chord/scale.

Figure 15.53. Addition of left hand part c) to Fig. 15.45. right hand structures (4th couplings) creating a funk comping pattern using two-handed rhythmic phrase #1 (Fig. 15.28.)

(Cassette Tape Example 534 - 'Straight 16ths')
(Cassette Tape Example 535 - 'Swing 16ths')

Now the left hand is again starting with the **1**, followed by the **1**, **5**, **b3**, **5**, **4** & **1** of the chord/scale. Note this time that the left hand is operating in the same register as the right hand - an effective 'funk' technique.

[I'd like to gratefully acknowledge my good friend (and outstanding San Francisco Bay area keyboardist) Don Turney, for his contribution of the comping pattern in Fig. 15.51. - MH]

Two-handed 'staccato' funk comping patterns (contd)

As you can see, even within this rhythmic and scale framework, there are many left hand note choices which can be made. Now we will take another rhythmic pattern and go through the various stages in order to create a two-handed funk groove. This time we will start with rhythmic pattern **#4** (again repeated here for your convenience):-

Figure 15.54. (15.33.) Right hand rhythmic phrase #4
(Cassette Tape Example 498 - 'Straight 16ths')
(Cassette Tape Example 499 - 'Swing 16ths')

Now again we will create a right hand motif around this rhythm, this time using a C Dorian mode (see **Fig. 1.39.**). This mode could be used as a scale source for a **Cmi7** chord. Some of the numerous top-note motif choices from this scale (based on the above rhythm) are as follows:-

Figure 15.55. Right hand C Dorian phrase a), based on rhythmic phrase #4 (Fig. 15.54.)
(Cassette Tape Example 536 - 'Straight 16ths')
(Cassette Tape Example 537 - 'Swing 16ths')

Figure 15.56. Right hand C Dorian phrase b), based on rhythmic phrase #4 (Fig. 15.54.)
(Cassette Tape Example 538 - 'Straight 16ths')
(Cassette Tape Example 539 - 'Swing 16ths')

Figure 15.57. Right hand C Dorian phrase c), based on rhythmic phrase #4 (Fig. 15.54.)
(Cassette Tape Example 540 - 'Straight 16ths')
(Cassette Tape Example 541 - 'Swing 16ths')

Now we will take one of these C Dorian motifs (**Fig. 15.55.** above) and place upper structures below the top note in the right hand. Triads and 4-part-structures (see **Chapters 4** & **6**) are often effectively used below the top note of both Dorian and Mixolydian motifs in funk styles. As the C Dorian mode is a displaced version of a Bb major scale (see **Fig. 1.39.**), then all diatonic triads (see **Fig. 3.4.**) and 4-part chords (see **Fig. 3.35.**) from Bb major, should work harmonically on a C Dorian mode. These 'modal triads' are typically used in 1st or 2nd inversion - see following summary of triads available within a C Dorian mode:-

Two-handed 'staccato' funk comping patterns (contd)

Figure 15.58. 1st inversion triad choices available in a C Dorian mode
(CASSETTE TAPE EXAMPLE 542)

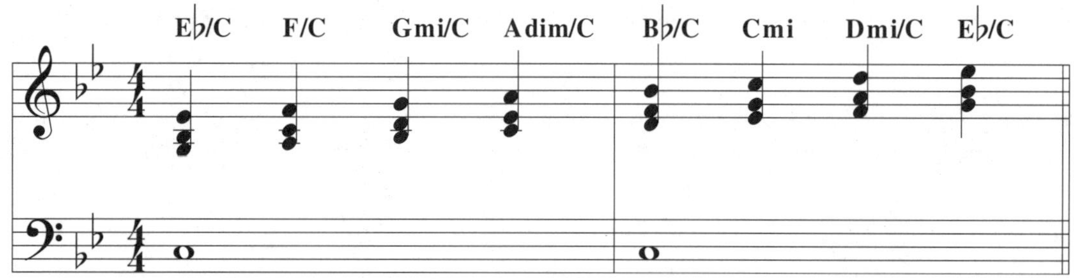

Figure 15.59. 2nd inversion triads choices available in a C Dorian mode
(CASSETTE TAPE EXAMPLE 543)

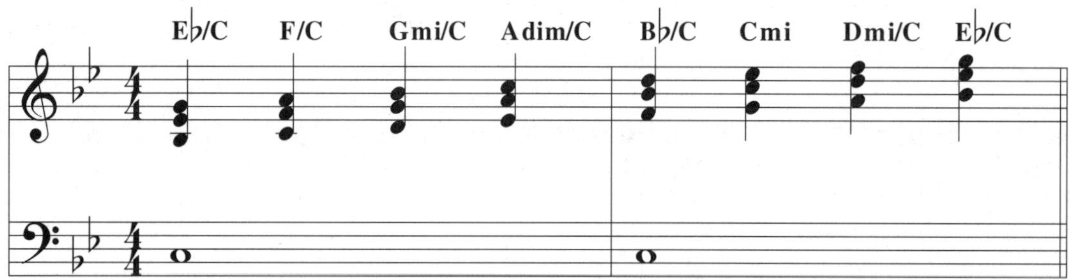

All root position, 1st inversion and 2nd inversion Dorian triads are available - however, most of the time 2nd and 1st inversions will be preferred. Now we will use C Dorian triads below the top note motif in **Fig. 15.55.** as follows:-

Figure 15.60. Right hand structures below top note version a), based on Fig. 15.55. motif
(CASSETTE TAPE EXAMPLE 544 - 'STRAIGHT 16THS')
(CASSETTE TAPE EXAMPLE 545 - 'SWING 16THS')

Here from left to right we have 2nd inversion **Eb**, 2nd inversion **F**, root position **Eb**, 2nd inversion **F**, and 2nd inversion **Eb** triads. The **Eb** and **F** triads are the **b3 - 4** with respect to C Dorian (and the implied **Cmi7** chord) - a frequent choice in this type of modal setting. Now for a solution using 4-part upper structures:-

Figure 15.61. Right hand structures below top note version b), based on Fig. 15.55. motif
(CASSETTE TAPE EXAMPLE 546 - 'STRAIGHT 16THS')
(CASSETTE TAPE EXAMPLE 547 - 'SWING 16THS')

Two-handed 'staccato' funk comping patterns (contd)

On the previous example (**Fig. 15.61.**) from left to right we have 2nd inversion **Ebma7**, 3rd inversion **Dmi7**, 3rd inversion **Ebma7**, 3rd inversion **Dmi7**, and 2nd inversion **Ebma7** structures. Again all of these 4-part chords are available over a C Dorian mode (review diatonic 4-part chords from the relative major of Bb, in **Fig. 3.35.** as necessary). Now we will demonstrate some left hand parts which can be added to the upper structures in **Fig. 15.60.** to complete a two-handed C Dorian funk groove. These solutions will be based on the two-handed rhythmic phrase **#4** (**Fig. 15.34.**, incorporating the right hand rhythmic phrase **#4** in **Fig. 15.33.**):-

Figure 15.62. Addition of left hand part a) to Fig. 15.60. right hand structures (Dorian triads) creating a funk comping pattern using two-handed rhythmic phrase #4 (Fig. 15.34.)
(Cassette Tape Example 548 - 'Straight 16ths')
(Cassette Tape Example 549 - 'Swing 16ths')

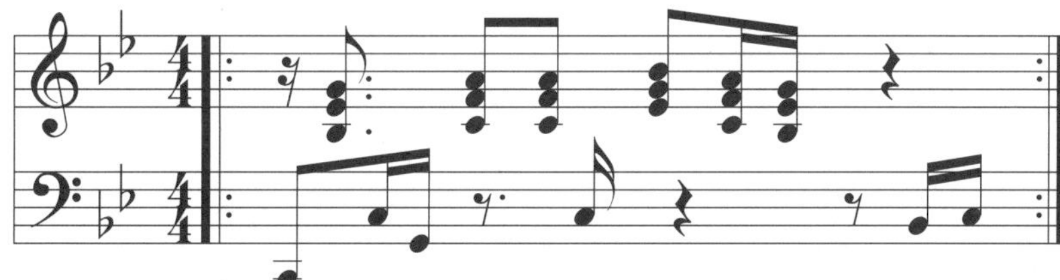

Here (with respect to an overall **Cmi7** chord, or C Dorian mode) the left hand from left to right is using the **1**, **1**, **5**, **1**, **b7** & **1**.

Figure 15.63. Addition of left hand part b) to Fig. 15.60. right hand structures (Dorian triads) creating a funk comping pattern using two-handed rhythmic phrase #4 (Fig. 15.34.)
(Cassette Tape Example 550 - 'Straight 16ths')
(Cassette Tape Example 551 - 'Swing 16ths')

Here the left hand is again starting with the **1**, **5** and **1**, but is then following with the **9** (up in the right hand register), **b7** and **5**, of the chord/scale.

Practice directions:-

- ***Practice the right hand and two-handed funk rhythm patterns shown in Figs. 15.27. - 15.40.***
  You can play a single repeated note in each hand to practice these rhythms. Start at a slow tempo and gradually increase as desired. Also - experiment with your own rhythms!
- ***Practice all of the various 'stages' in creating the sample two-handed funk grooves, as in Figs. 15.41. - 15.63.***
  Use these as a springboard for your own ideas and experimentation!
  Don't forget to practice all examples in both straight and swing 16ths!

Two-handed 'staccato' funk comping patterns (contd)

We will now look at some further examples of the **four-stage process** (summarized in the text prior to **Fig. 15.41.**) involved in creating two-handed funk patterns, as follows:-

Figure 15.64. Funk pattern creation process example A
Stage 1 - Creating a right hand rhythmic phrase (from rhythm pattern #6 - Fig. 15.37)
(CASSETTE TAPE EXAMPLE 506 - 'STRAIGHT 16THS')
(CASSETTE TAPE EXAMPLE 507 - 'SWING 16THS')

Figure 15.65. Funk pattern creation process example A
Stage 2 - Creating a top-note motif for the right hand, based on the rhythm used in Stage 1
(CASSETTE tape EXAMPLE 552 - 'STRAIGHT 16THS')
(CASSETTE tape EXAMPLE 553 - 'SWING 16THS')

This example is again based on the C Dorian mode as a scale source.

Figure 15.66. Funk pattern creation process example A
Stage 3 - Creating structures below the top note motif in the right hand
(CASSETTE TAPE EXAMPLE 554 - 'STRAIGHT 16THS')
(CASSETTE TAPE EXAMPLE 555 - 'SWING 16THS')

Here from left to right we have 1st inversion **Eb**, 2nd inversion **Bb**, 1st & 2nd inversion **Eb**, and root position **Bb** triads. These are all available within a C Dorian mode (see **Figs. 15.58. & 15.59.**). Also the **Bb** & **Eb** triads could be considered as '**b7 to b3**' alternating triads (see **Fig. 12.19.**) over an implied **Cmi7** chord.

Figure 15.67. Funk pattern creation process example A
Stage 4 - Adding a single-note left hand part in the 'rhythmic spaces'
(CASSETTE TAPE EXAMPLE 556 - 'STRAIGHT 16THS')
(CASSETTE TAPE EXAMPLE 557 - 'SWING 16THS')

Here the interaction of the left and right hand parts is based on the two-handed rhythm pattern **#6** (see **Fig. 15.38.**). From left to right, the left hand is using the **1**, **1**, **5**, **1** & **5** with respect to a C Dorian mode (and the implied **Cmi7** chord).

Two-handed 'staccato' funk comping patterns (contd)

Now in the next example of the creation process, we will make use of an upper motif and triads built from a C Mixolydian mode (see **Fig. 1.42.**). This mode would typically be used as a scale source for a dominant chord i.e. **C7** or **C7sus** in this case. As the C Mixolydian mode is a displaced version of an F major scale, then all diatonic triads (see **Fig. 3.3.**) and 4-part chords (see **Fig. 3.34.**) from F major, should work harmonically on a C Mixolydian mode. In a similar manner to the construction of inverted Dorian triads as in **Figs. 15.58.** & **15.59.**, we can construct triads from a C Mixolydian mode as follows:-

Figure 15.68. 1st inversion triad choices available in a C Mixolydian mode
(Cassette Tape Example 558)

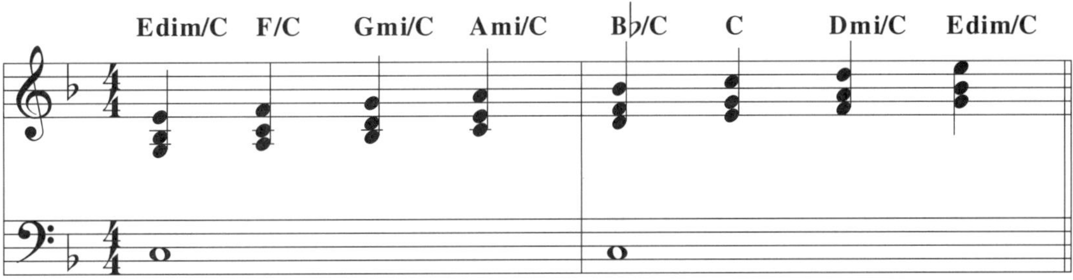

Figure 15.69. 2nd inversion triad choices available in a C Mixolydian mode
(Cassette Tape Example 559)

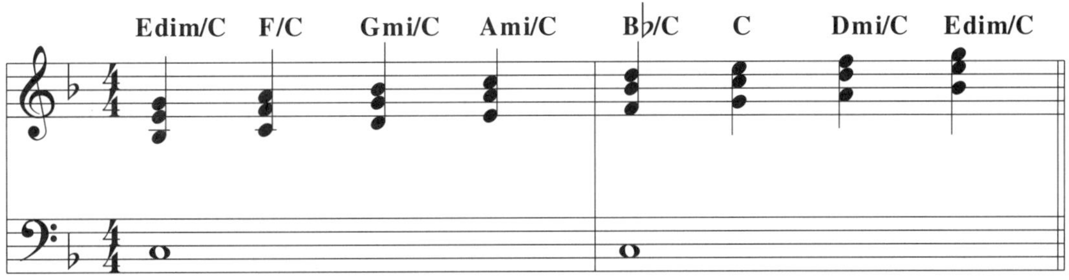

Mixolydian triads are also extensively used as a right hand device in gospel styles - see **Chapters 17** & **18**. As with the Dorian triads, generally 2nd and 1st inversions will be preferred. These will be used as we develop the next funk groove, starting with a right hand rhythm as follows:-

Figure 15.70. Funk pattern creation process example B
Stage 1 - Creating a right hand rhythmic phrase (from rhythm pattern #5 - Fig. 15.35.)
(Cassette Tape Example 502 - 'Straight 16ths')
(Cassette Tape Example 503 - 'Swing 16ths')

Two-handed 'staccato' funk comping patterns (contd)

Figure 15.71. Funk pattern creation process example B
Stage 2 - Creating a top-note motif for the right hand, based on the rhythm used in stage 1
(CASSETTE TAPE EXAMPLE 560 - 'STRAIGHT 16THS')
(CASSETTE TAPE EXAMPLE 561 - 'SWING 16THS')

This motif is selected from a C Mixolydian mode.

Figure 15.72. Funk pattern creation process example B
Stage 3 - Creating structures below the top-note motif in the right hand
(CASSETTE TAPE EXAMPLE 562 - 'STRAIGHT 16THS')
(CASSETTE TAPE EXAMPLE 563 - 'SWING 16THS')

Here from left to right we have **E dim**, **F**, **Gmi**, **F** and **E dim** triads, all in 2nd inversion. These triads are from the C Mixolydian mode (see **Fig. 15.69.**), and collectively imply a **C7** chord.

Figure 15.73. Funk pattern creation process example B
Stage 4 - Adding a single-note left hand part in the 'rhythmic spaces'
(CASSETTE TAPE EXAMPLE 564 - 'STRAIGHT 16THS')
(CASSETTE TAPE EXAMPLE 565 - 'SWING 16THS')

Here the interaction of the left and right hand parts is based on the two-handed rhythm pattern **#5** (**see Fig. 15.36.**). From left to right, the left hand is using the **1**, **b7**, **1**, **1**, **b7**, **5**, **b7** & **1** with respect to a C Mixolydian mode (and the implied **C7** chord).

Now for the next example of this process, this time using 'half-step-&-5th', 'whole-step-&-5th' and 4th couplings below a C Dorian motif:-

Figure 15.74. Funk pattern creation process example C
Stage 1 - Creating a right hand rhythmic phrase (from rhythm pattern #2 - Fig. 15.29.)
(CASSETTE TAPE EXAMPLE 490 - 'STRAIGHT 16THS')
(CASSETTE TAPE EXAMPLE 491 - 'SWING 16THS')

Two-handed 'staccato' funk comping patterns (contd)

Figure 15.75. Funk pattern creation process example C
Stage 2 - Creating a top-note motif for the right hand, based on the rhythm used in stage 1
(CASSETTE TAPE EXAMPLE 566 - 'STRAIGHT 16THS')
(CASSETTE TAPE EXAMPLE 567 - 'SWING 16THS')

This motif is selected from a C Dorian mode.

Figure 15.76. Funk pattern creation process example C
Stage 3 - Creating structures below the top-note motif in the right hand
(CASSETTE TAPE EXAMPLE 568 - 'STRAIGHT 16THS')
(CASSETTE TAPE EXAMPLE 569 - 'SWING 16THS')

With respect to an implied Cmi7 chord overall, on the 2nd 16th of beat **1** we have a **9-b3-b7** 'half-step-&-5th' structure (see **Figs. 13.20.** & **15.49.**), and on beat **2** we have a **b7-1-5** 'whole-step-&-5th' structure (see **Fig. 15.50.**). For the remainder of the phrase we are using **b7-b3**, **1-11**, **11-b7** and **5-1** 4th couplings (see earlier example **Fig. 15.45.** and also **Fig. 12.23.**).

Figure 15.77. Funk pattern creation process example C
Stage 4 - Adding a single-note left hand part in the 'rhythmic spaces'
(CASSETTE TAPE EXAMPLE 570 - 'STRAIGHT 16THS')
(CASSETTE TAPE EXAMPLE 571 - 'SWING 16THS')

Here the interaction of the left and right hand parts is based on the two-handed rhythm pattern **#2** (see **Fig. 15.30.**). From left to right, the left hand is using the 1, b7, 5, 11(4), b7, 5, b3 & b7 with respect to a C Dorian mode (and the implied Cmi7 chord).

For the next example of the pattern creation process, we will use a motif based on the C Blues scale (see **Fig. 1.68.**). As we said in **Chapter 1**, the blues scale can be considered as a minor pentatonic scale (see **Fig. 1.67.**) with the addition of a half-step 'connector' between the 3rd and 4th scale degrees - also referred to as a b5 or 'flat 5th' with respect to the tonic of the scale. The 'blues' quality imparted by this altered scale degree can be very useful in rock, funk and gospel styles. We will see how this is used in a funk pattern on the following page:-

Two-handed 'staccato' funk comping patterns (contd)

Figure 15.78. Funk pattern creation process example D
Stage 1 - Creating a right hand rhythmic phrase (from rhythm pattern #7 - Fig. 15.39.)
(CASSETTE TAPE EXAMPLE 510 - 'STRAIGHT 16THS')
(CASSETTE TAPE EXAMPLE 511 - 'SWING 16THS')

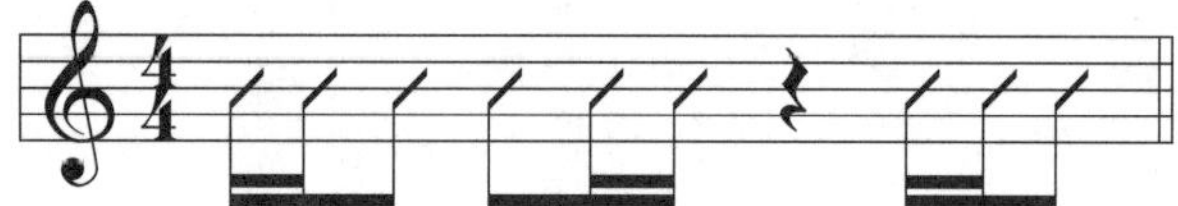

Figure 15.79. Funk pattern creation process example D
Stage 2 - Creating a top-note motif for the right hand, based on the rhythm used in stage 1
(CASSETTE TAPE EXAMPLE 572 - 'STRAIGHT 16THS')
(CASSETTE TAPE EXAMPLE 573 - 'SWING 16THS')

This motif is selected from a C Blues scale.

Figure 15.80. Funk pattern creation process example D
Stage 3 - Creating structures below the top-note motif in the right hand
(CASSETTE TAPE EXAMPLE 574 - 'STRAIGHT 16THS')
(CASSETTE TAPE EXAMPLE 575 - 'SWING 16THS')

With respect to an implied **Cmi7** chord overall, we have **5-1**, **1-11** & **b7-b3** 4th couplings (see **Fig. 12.23.**), on beat **1** and the 2nd & 3rd 16ths of beat **2** respectively. Note that we also have a 4th coupling under the **b5** on beat **2** - technically creating a **b9-b5** coupling with respect to the implied **Cmi7** chord - these out-of-chord tones 'pass through' and resolve to the following **1-11** coupling. On beat **4** we have an **11-b7-b3** double 4th structure (see **Fig. 10.5.**) again with respect to a **Cmi7** chord.

Figure 15.81. Funk pattern creation process example D
Stage 4 - Adding a single-note left hand part in the 'rhythmic spaces'
(CASSETTE TAPE EXAMPLE 576 - 'STRAIGHT 16THS')
(CASSETTE TAPE EXAMPLE 577 - 'SWING 16THS')

Here the interaction of the left and right hand parts is based on the two-handed rhythm pattern **#7** (see **Fig. 15.40.**). From left to right, the left hand is using the **1**, **1**, **b7**, **4(11)**, **5** & **b7** with respect to a C Dorian mode (and the implied **Cmi7** chord). Note that again the left and right hands are in the same range, at the end of beat **1** and during beat **2** - an effective technique.

Two-handed 'staccato' funk comping patterns (contd)

We will now look at a learning device which I believe is useful in developing these funk patterns. This is what I call the 'rhythmic shell', consisting of a short two-handed comping phrase (typically occupying between 1 & 2 beats of a single measure) which can be 'looped' or repeated (in a practice environment, playing along with a metronome or drum machine is suggested). As you repeat this rhythmic fragment, you can work on using the remaining space in the 'rhythmic shell' (i.e. the remainder of the measure) for additional comping embellishments, working towards a point where this can be spontaneously improvised. Here is the first example of this concept:-

Figure 15.82. Rhythmic shell example A
(Cassette Tape Example 578 - 'Straight 16ths')
(Cassette Tape Example 579 - 'Swing 16ths')

The top-note motif here can be derived from a C Dorian or C Blues scale. With respect to the implied **Cmi7** chord, the right hand is using **11-b7-b3** and **5-1-11** double 4th structures (see **Figs. 10.5.** & **10.3.** respectively), anticipating beat **3**. The left hand is using the **1**, **1** & **5** with respect to the implied **Cmi7**, providing a pickup into beat **2**. Notice that nothing is occurring in this pattern during beats **3** & **4**. If we chose to, there are various ways we could use this space in the 'rhythmic shell', as follows:-

Figure 15.83. Rhythmic shell example A - variation #1
(Cassette Tape Example 580 - 'Straight 16ths')
(Cassette Tape Example 581 - 'Swing 16ths')

Here a 16th note run using the C minor pentatonic scale is being used during beat **4**, leading back to the beginning (beat **1**). The added notes are the **b3**, **1**, **b7** & **5** with respect to a C minor pentatonic scale (and the implied **Cmi7** chord).

Figure 15.84. Rhythmic shell example A - variation #2
(Cassette Tape Example 582 - 'Straight 16ths')
(Cassette Tape Example 583 - 'Swing 16ths')

Similar to the above variation #1, now with the addition of the note C on the last 16th of beat **3** in the left hand. This functions as a pickup into the right hand phrase beginning on beat **4**.

Two-handed 'staccato' funk comping patterns (contd)

Figure 15.85. Rhythmic shell example A - variation #3
(Cassette Tape Example 584 - 'Straight 16ths')
(Cassette Tape Example 585 - 'Swing 16ths')

Now a pair of 4th couplings have been added. With respect to an implied **Cmi7** chord, we have a **b7-b3** coupling on the '**& of 3**' and a **5-1** coupling on the 2nd 16th of beat **4** (see **Fig. 12.23.**).

Figure 15.86. Rhythmic shell example A - variation #4
(Cassette Tape Example 586 - 'Straight 16ths')
(Cassette Tape Example 587 - 'Swing 16ths')

Similar to the above variation #3, now with the addition of the notes C & G (the root & 5th of the implied **Cmi7** chord) on the 2nd 16th of beat **3** and the last 16th of beat **4**, functioning as pickups into the '**& of 3**' and back to beat **1**, respectively.

Figure 15.87. Rhythmic shell example A - variation #5
(Cassette Tape Example 588 - 'Straight 16ths')
(Cassette Tape Example 589 - 'Swing 16ths')

Now the left and right hands are rhythmically alternating during beats **3** & **4**. With respect to an implied **Cmi7** chord, the right hand is playing an **11-b7** 4th coupling on the '**& of 3**' (see **Fig. 12.23.**), the **5** on the last 16th of beat **3**, the **4(11)** on beat **4**, the **11-b7** coupling on the '**& of 4**', and the **5** on the last 16th of beat **4**, leading back into beat **1**. The left hand meanwhile is fitting into the rhythmic spaces, with the **b3** on the 2nd 16th of beat **3** and the **1** on the 2nd 16th of beat **4**.

The next variation of this 'rhythmic shell' uses a mixture of double 4ths (root position and inverted) and triads in the right hand, as follows:-

Two-handed 'staccato' funk comping patterns (contd)

Figure 15.88. Rhythmic shell example A - variation #6

(CASSETTE TAPE EXAMPLE 590 - 'STRAIGHT 16THS')
(CASSETTE TAPE EXAMPLE 591 - 'SWING 16THS')

With respect to the implied **Cmi7** chord, in the right hand we now have a **1-11-b7** double 4th structure (see **Fig. 10.8.**) on the '**& of 3**' and (inverted) on beat **4**, and a 2nd inversion **Eb** triad (a **b3-5-b7** upper structure of the **Cmi7** chord) on the last 16th of beat **4**. Again the left hand is using the 'rhythmic spaces', playing the **4(11)**, **5** & **5** (with respect to the implied **Cmi7** chord) on the 2nd and 4th 16ths of beat **3** and the '**& of 4**', respectively.

CASSETTE TAPE EXAMPLE 592 CONTAINS RHYTHMIC SHELL EXAMPLE A FOLLOWED BY VARIATIONS 1-6 (FIGS. 15.82. - 15.88.) IN A CONTINUOUS SERIES, PLAYED IN 'STRAIGHT 16THS'.
CASSETTE TAPE EXAMPLE 593 CONTAINS RHYTHMIC SHELL EXAMPLE A FOLLOWED BY VARIATIONS 1-6 (FIGS. 15.82. - 15.88.) IN A CONTINUOUS SERIES, PLAYED IN 'SWING 16THS'.

Now we will look at a new rhythmic shell example, this time only using the first beat of a one measure phrase, leaving the rest of the measure open for improvisation and embellishment:-

Figure 15.89. Rhythmic shell example B

(CASSETTE TAPE EXAMPLE 594 - 'STRAIGHT 16THS')
(CASSETTE TAPE EXAMPLE 595 - 'SWING 16THS')

The top-note motif here can again be derived from a C Blues or C Dorian scale. With respect to the implied **Cmi7** chord, the right hand is using **b7-b3** and **5-1** 4th couplings (see **Fig. 12.23.**), on beat **1**, the '**& of 1**' and the last 16th of beat **1**, anticipating beat **2**. The left hand is playing the root of the implied **Cmi7** chord in octaves, on beat **1** and the 2nd 16th of beat **1**.

In the above 'rhythmic shell', beats **2**, **3** and **4** currently contain rests. Again we will consider a number of variations on this phrase in which this rhythmic space is used in various ways, as follows:-

Two-handed 'staccato' funk comping patterns (contd)

Figure 15.90. Rhythmic shell example B - variation #1

(Cassette Tape Example 596 - 'Straight 16ths')
(Cassette Tape Example 597 - 'Swing 16ths')

With respect to the implied **Cmi7** chord, the added **Eb** and **Bb** triads in the right hand can be considered as '**b7 to b3**' alternating triads (see **Fig. 12.19.**). These triads are also available within a C Dorian mode (see **Figs. 15.58.** & **15.59.**). We have a 2nd inversion **Eb** triad on the '**& of 2**', a root position **Bb** triad on the '**& of 3**', a 1st inversion **Eb** triad on beat **4** and a 2nd inversion **Bb** triad on the '**& of 4**'. Note that the successive pairs of **Eb** & **Bb** triads are voice-led in a circle-of-4ths manner (see **Figs. 4.18.** & **4.17.**). This additional right hand part is landing on the 'strong 16ths' (see 'Two-handed staccato funk comping - rhythmic concepts' text earlier in this chapter), allowing the left hand to provide pickups (using the 'weak' 16th notes) in the rhythmic spaces. With respect to the implied **Cmi7** chord, the left hand is playing the **b7** on the 2nd 16th of beat **2**, the **5** on the last 16th of beat **3** and the **4(11)** on the 2nd 16th of beat **4**.

Figure 15.91. Rhythmic shell example B - variation #2

(Cassette Tape Example 598 - 'Straight 16ths')
(Cassette Tape Example 599 - 'Swing 16ths')

With respect to the implied **Cmi7** chord, during the last half of beat **2** we are using a '**9 to 1**' resolution within a **b3-5-b7** upper structure (a 2nd inversion **Eb** triad - see **Fig. 8.14.**). The **Eb** triad is also available within a C Dorian mode (see **Figs. 15.58.** & **15.59.**). This resolution is also occurring (using a 1st inversion **Eb** triad) during the last half of beat **3**. The 7th (of the **Cmi7** chord) is also being used on beats **3** & **4**. During the last half of beat **4**, **11-b7** and **5-1** 4th couplings (see **Fig. 12.23.**) are being used, leading back to beat **1**. The left hand is again using the rhythmic spaces (the 2nd 16th of beats **2**, **3** & **4**), using the **5**, **4(11)** & **b3** of the implied **Cmi7** respectively.

The next variation contains single notes alternating between the left and right hands, continuously during beats **3** and **4** of the pattern. Again the right hand is landing on the 'strong 16ths', with the left hand filling in between, as follows:-

Two-handed 'staccato' funk comping patterns (contd)

Figure 15.92. Rhythmic shell example B - variation #3

(Cassette Tape Example 600 - 'Straight 16ths')
(Cassette Tape Example 601 - 'Swing 16ths')

All of the single notes added in this variation are available from the C minor pentatonic scale. From left to right, with respect to the implied **Cmi7** chord the right hand is playing the **1**, **b7** & **5** during beat **2**, and the **4(11)**, **b7**, **5** & **4(11)** on the 'strong 16ths' during beats **3** & **4**. The left hand is fitting in the rhythmic spaces, using the **b3**, **b7**, **1** & **5** of the implied **Cmi7** chord on the 'weak 16ths' during beats **3** & **4**. In this busy variation, all of the 16th note subdivisions from the 2nd 16th of beat **2** onwards, are being used by single notes in either the right or left hands.

Figure 15.93. Rhythmic shell example B - variation #4

(Cassette Tape Example 602 - 'Straight 16ths')
(Cassette Tape Example 603 - 'Swing 16ths')

With respect to the implied **Cmi7** chord, the right hand notes added at the end of beat **2** are collectively an inverted **11-b7-b3** double 4th structure (see **Fig. 10.5.**), with the **b3** & **b7** landing on the '**& of 2**' and the **4(11)** landing on the last 16th of beat **2**. 'Splitting up' the right hand double 4th like this, is a very useful device in this (and other) styles. Similarly, we have an inverted **1-11-b7** double 4th structure (see **Fig. 10.8.**) in the right hand during beat **3** (with the **11** & **b7** landing on the 2nd 16th of beat **3** and the **1** landing on the '**& of 3**') and during the last half of beat **4** (with the **1** & **11** landing on the '**& of 4**' and the **b7** landing on the last 16th of beat **4**). In between we have (again with respect to the implied **Cmi7** chord) a 'split' **b3-5-b7** upper structure (a 1st inversion **Eb** triad) on the first 2 16ths of beat **4**. The left hand is again making use of the rhythmic spaces in the right hand part (with the exception of the '**& of 4**' where both hands are playing together), playing the **5** on the 2nd 16th of beat **2**, the **b3** on beat **3**, the **4(11)** on the last 16th of beat **3**, and the **5** (the note G, together with the F & C in the right hand, momentarily implying a **G7sus** chord) on the '**& of 4**'.

Cassette Tape Example 604 contains rhythmic shell example B followed by variations 1-4 (Figs. 15.89. - 15.93.) in a continuous series, played in 'Straight 16ths'.
Cassette Tape Example 605 contains rhythmic shell example B followed by variations 1-4 (Figs. 15.89. - 15.93.) in a continuous series, played in 'Swing 16ths'.

Two-handed 'staccato' funk comping patterns (contd)

PRACTICE DIRECTIONS:-

- ***Practice the funk pattern creation process examples A - D as in Figs. 15.64. - 15.81.***
  Experiment with your own variations at each stage of the process.
  For extra practice - try transposing these patterns into different keys!
- ***Practice the 'rhythmic shell' examples and variations as in Figs. 15.82. - 15.93.***
  Experiment with your own variations on these 'rhythmic shells', and create your own 'rhythmic shells' for further practice.
  As before - try transposing these into different keys!

Don't forget to practice all examples in straight and swing 16ths!

We will now begin to look at some other harmonic devices which can be used to create funk patterns. We have already seen that the use of double 4th structures is an effective right hand technique. We will next look at some more chromatic applications of this idea, where a double 4th used does not appear to be related to the overall chord in force, but then resolves by half step into a more diatonic structure, with respect to the chord being used. Root-position double 4th structures tend to work best for this purpose (review **Fig. 10.14.** as necessary). Our first example of this technique is as follows:-

Figure 15.94. Comping pattern example #1 using an 'out-of-chord' chromatic double 4th structure
(CASSETTE TAPE EXAMPLE 606 - 'STRAIGHT 16THS')
(CASSETTE TAPE EXAMPLE 607 - 'SWING 16THS')

In this example (with respect to an implied **Cmi7** chord) we have an **11-b7-b3** double 4th structure (see **Fig. 10.5.**) in the right hand, on the '**& of 2**'. The **Ab-Db-Gb** double 4th on beat **3** is technically a **b6-b9-b5** with respect to a **Cmi7** - this of course is totally 'outside' the chord, but resolves to a **5-1-11** double 4th (see **Fig. 10.3.**) on the last 16th of beat **2**. This creates an interesting 'tension-release' effect. The top note of the chromatic structure (the **b5**) can also be derived from the **C Blues** scale - see pattern creation process example **D** (**Figs. 15.78. - 15.81.**). Again with respect to an implied **Cmi7** chord, the right hand is using an **11-b7** 4th coupling (see **Fig. 12.23.**) on the '**& of 4**', and the **5** on the last 16th of beat **4**. The left hand is using the **1**, **1** & **b3** during beat **1** (on the 1st, 2nd and 4th 16ths respectively), and the **4(11)** on the 2nd 16th of beat **4**.

Two-handed 'staccato' funk comping patterns (contd)

Figure 15.95. Comping pattern example #2 using 'out of chord' chromatic double 4th structures
(Cassette Tape Example 608 - 'Straight 16ths')
(Cassette Tape Example 609 - 'Swing 16ths')

This is a further variation on the previous example in **Fig. 15.94.**, now with the right hand using additional double 4th structures on the '**& of 3**' and the 2nd 16th of beat **4**. The **F#-B-E** double 4th on the '**& of 3**' is technically a **#11-7-3** with respect to the overall **Cmi7** chord - again this is 'outside' the chord, but resolves to an **11-b7-b3** double 4th (see **Fig. 10.5.**) on the 2nd 16th of beat **4**. The left hand meanwhile is using the **4(11)** on the 2nd 16th of beat **3**, the **1** on beat **4**, and the **5** on the last 16th of beat **4**. These function as pickups, into the last 2 double 4ths and back to beat **1** respectively.

The next funk comping example features a 'split' version of the 'half-step-&-5th' structure (see **Figs. 13.20. - 13.24.** and **Fig. 15.49.**), going back and forth between the upper 5th interval and the tone a half-step below, as follows:-

Figure 15.96. Comping pattern using split 'half-step-&-5th' right hand structures
(Cassette Tape Example 610 - 'Straight 16ths')
(Cassette Tape Example 611 - 'Swing 16ths')

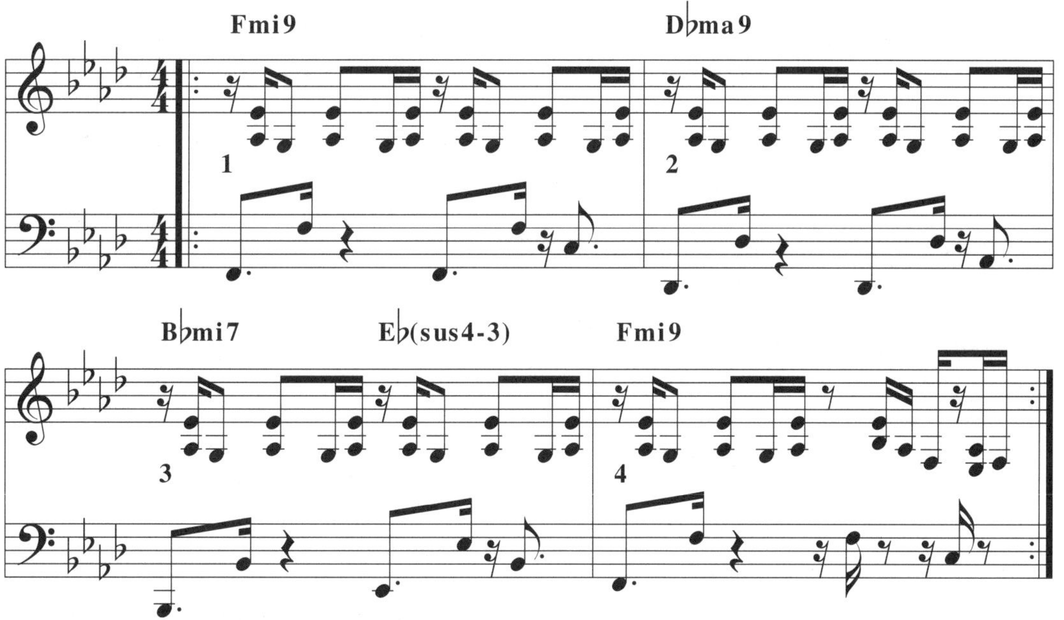

Note that the 'half-step-&-5th' structure **G-Ab-Eb** is 'split' as described above, and then used throughout the right hand part in this example. We can analyze the devices used here as follows:-

Two-handed 'staccato' funk comping patterns (contd)

(Analysis of Fig. 15.96.)

- Measure 1 With respect to the **Fmi9** chord, the right hand is using a **9-b3-b7** 'half-step-&-5th' structure (see **Figs. 13.20.** & **15.49.**), alternating back and forth between the upper 5th interval **Ab-Eb** (the **b3-b7** of the chord) and the lower note **G** (the **9** of the chord). The rhythmically syncopated right hand part is anticipating beats **1** & **3**. The left hand is playing the root of the chord in octaves on the primary beats (**1** & **3**), providing pickups into beats **2** & **4**, and playing the **5th** of the chord (C) on the 2nd 16th of beat **4**. The left hand is filling most of the rhythmic spaces in the right hand part, creating a busy effect overall.

- Measure 2 The same **G-Ab-Eb** 'half-step-&-5th' now becomes a **#11-5-9** structure with respect to the **Dbma9** chord (see **Figs. 13.21.** & **15.49.**). Rhythmic and pattern concepts are the same as for measure **1**, with the left hand now playing the root and 5th of **Dbma9.**

- Measure 3 The same **G-Ab-Eb** 'half-step-&-5th' now becomes a **13-b7-11** structure with respect to the **Bbmi7** chord (see **Figs. 13.23.** & **15.49.**), and is also technically a **3-11-1** with respect to the **Eb(sus4-3)** chord - this chord symbol indicates a resolution from the 4th (11th) to the 3rd on the chord, which is being provided by this right hand figure. (Review **Chapter 9** regarding suspended 4th resolutions as necessary). Again the rhythmic and pattern concepts are the same as for measure **1**, with the left hand using the root of the **Bbmi7** chord during the first half of the measure, and the root & 5th of the **Eb** chord during the second half of the measure.

- Measure 4 The first half of this measure is a repeat of the first 2 beats of measure **1**, on the **Fmi9** chord. During the last half of beat **3** the right hand is 'splitting' an inverted **11-b7-b3** double 4th structure (see **Fig. 10.5.**), with the **11-b7** coupling landing on the '**& of 3**' and the **b3** landing on the last 16th of beat **3**. Also during the last half of beat **4** the right hand is 'splitting' a **b7-1-b3** 'whole-step-4th' cluster (see **Fig. 13.14.**), with the **b7-b3** coupling landing on the '**& of 4**' and the **1** landing on the last 16th of beat **4**, leading back into beat **1**. The left hand is using the rhythmic spaces here, with the root and 5th of the chord on the 2nd 16th of beats **3** and **4** respectively.

The next series of examples deals with some right hand devices derived from the blues scale. We will first look at a series of what I call 'cross-over' licks based on the C Blues scale as follows:-

Figure 15.97. 'Cross-over' licks derived from the C Blues scale
(Cassette Tape Example 612)

Suggested right hand fingering for this phrase is for the thumb to play all the single notes on the upbeats ('**& of 1**', '**& of 2**' etc.) and for the 2nd finger to play the bottom note of all the couplings on the downbeats. As you play this, you can see why the term 'cross-over' is used, as the 2nd finger keeps 'crossing over' the thumb. The top note of each coupling is played by the 4th or 5th finger. Harmonically, a cycle repeats every 3 beats:-

Two-handed 'staccato' funk comping patterns (contd)

First beat:- On beat **1** the right hand is playing a **b5-1** coupling (Gb & C) with respect to the C Blues scale. This then moves to the **4** (F) on the '**& of 1**'.

Second beat:- On beat **2** the right hand is playing a **b3-b7** coupling (Eb & Bb) with respect to the C Blues scale. This then moves to the **1** (C) on the '**& of 2**'.

Third beat:- On beat **3** the right hand is playing a **b7-b3** coupling (Bb & Eb) with respect to the C Blues scale. This then moves to the **5** (G) on the '**& of 3**'.

The above series of events then repeats an octave lower, over the next three beats and so on. This pattern can be started at any point and can of course be varied rhythmically. Here is an example of a funk pattern using these 'cross-over' phrases from a C Blues scale, over a **Cmi7** chord:-

Figure 15.98. Comping pattern using C blues scale 'cross-over' licks
(Cassette Tape Example 613 - 'Straight 16ths')
(Cassette Tape Example 614 - 'Swing 16ths')

This pattern is similar to the Dorian triad funk groove presented in **Fig. 15.62.** & **15.63.**, using the Eb & F triads over the tonic of C in the bass voice. 'Cross-over' licks from the C blues scale are used in each measure, from the '**& of 3**' into beat **4**. The notes used in this part of the first measure are equivalent to beats **1-3** of the 2nd measure of **Fig. 15.97.**, this time using a 16th note subdivision. Similarly, the notes used in the corresponding part of the 2nd measure above are equivalent to beat **4** of the first measure, through beat **2** of the 2nd measure, of the example in **Fig. 15.97**. again using 16th notes.

Now we will look at some blues scale related licks using grace notes, which are very useful in R'n'B/Funk styles. This type of grace note embellishment is related to the 'hammer' frequently used in country idioms (see **Chapter 16**). Normally this process involves selecting a 'target' tone (typically the **5**, **b5** or **1** of the blues scale) and then approaching this target with an adjacent scale tone played very quickly or in a 'grace note' fashion. At the same time, an interval coupling is created above the target tone, typically creating a 3rd or 4th interval. (In country styles this added top note is often referred to as a 'drone' - see **Chapter 16**). Afterwards, the note next to the target tone (used for the grace note) is frequently repeated, as in the following examples:-

Figure 15.99. 'Grace note' licks derived from the C blues scale
(Cassette Tape Example 615)

1 ♭3 4 ♭5 5 ♭7
1/5 4 (4) · 1/♭5 4 (4) · ♭7/5 4 (4) · ♭7/♭5 4 (4) · 4/1 ♭7 (♭7) · ♭3/1 ♭7 (♭7)

Two-handed 'staccato' funk comping patterns (contd)

In the previous example (**Fig. 15.99.**), to the left of the double bar the notes and scale degrees of a **C Blues** scale are repeated for your convenience. (Note that the scale degrees are numbered according to the **intervals** between the tonic and the various scale tones). These are followed by six 'grace note' phrases, with descriptive numbers applied as follows:-

- The first number (in parentheses) is the scale degree of the C blues scale being used as the grace note. For the first phrase, the number **4** in parentheses signifies that the tone which is a 4th interval above the tonic (i.e. F - see above comments) is the grace note being used.
- Immediately following, the two numbers in a column are the scale degrees of the C blues scale being used as an interval coupling, the lowest note being the target note 'approached' by the grace note. In the first phrase, the target tone is the **5** (G) and the 'drone' note added above is the **1** (C), creating a 4th interval coupling.
- Immediately following, the single number to the right and in between the previous coupling, is the original grace note, now being repeated. In the first phrase, the grace note was the **4** (F), which is now repeated.

The same analysis works for all six phrases, and you are encouraged to work through these! The blues scale is rather unique as its melodically strong and 'funky' character enables it to be used over a great many different chords - in fact the horizontal strength of this scale can often compensate for the fact that its use may apparently result in 'out-of-chord' tones arising, with respect to the harmony in force. The above phrases (and others) will generally work in situations where the blues scale itself is appropriate. A complete dissertation on blues harmony is beyond the scope of this chapter - however, here is a brief guide to the possible chords over which a C blues scale (and related licks/embellishments) might be used:-

Figure 15.100. Chords over which the C blues scale may be used *(subject to above comments)*

The root notes over which a C blues scale may be played, are shown above together with the chord qualities which will best work with the scale. Normally at least one 'out-of-chord' tone (or 'alteration' to a dominant chord) will result from the use of the blues scale over each of these chords - again depending on style and rhythmic placement, these 'out-of-chord' tones will frequently be acceptable as discussed above.

Using this information, if a tune was in the **key** of **C minor** and included chords from the table above, we should be able to use phrases based on the C Blues scale, over these other chords. In other words we are using the **blues scale of the key** (i.e. **C** Blues, in the key of **C** minor) over the different chords in the song. Some of the C blues scale 'grace note' licks (see **Fig. 15.99.**) are used over some of the above chords in the funk pattern example on the following page:-

FOR FURTHER INFORMATION ON USING BLUES SCALES OVER DIFFERENT CHORDS, PLEASE REFER TO CHAPTER 9 OF OUR CONTEMPORARY MUSIC THEORY LEVEL 2 BOOK (SEE PAGE IX IN THIS BOOK).

Two-handed 'staccato' funk comping patterns (contd)

Figure 15.101. Comping pattern using C blues scale 'grace note' licks

(Cassette Tape Example 616 - 'Straight 16ths')
(Cassette Tape Example 617 - 'Swing 16ths')

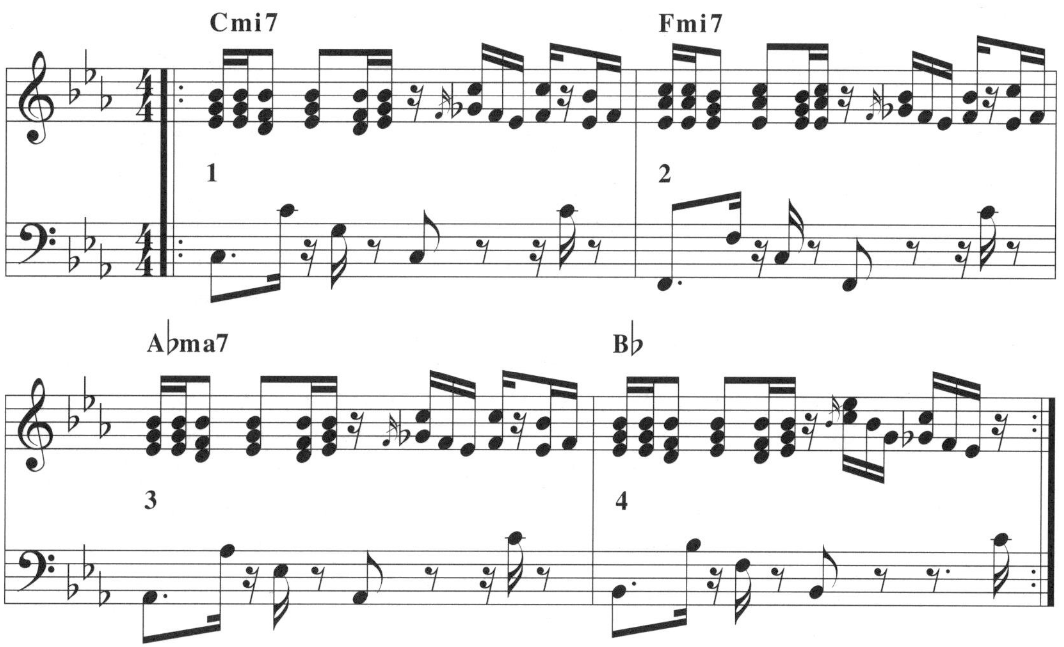

We can analyze the above example as follows:-

- Measure 1

On the **Cmi7** chord in the right hand, we are using **b7 to b3** alternating triads (see **Fig. 12.19.**) during the first 2 beats - in this case the **b3** is a root position **Eb** triad, while the **b7** is a 1st inversion **Bb** triad. During beat **3** we are using the 2nd 'grace note' lick shown in **Fig. 15.99.** (see accompanying text for description). With respect to the **Cmi7** chord, the target tone approached by the grace note is the **b5** (Gb - an 'out-of-chord' tone), on the 2nd 16th of beat **3**, while the 'drone' note added on top to create the interval coupling, is the **1** (C). During the last half of beat **4** we have a 'split' inverted **11-b7-b3** double 4th structure (see **Fig. 10.5.**), with the **b3-b7** coupling landing on the '**& of 4**' and the **11** landing on the last 16th of beat **4**. The left hand is playing a pattern using the root and 5th of the chord in the rhythmic spaces, with the rhythmic interaction between the hands during the first 2 beats being based upon the first half of the 'two-handed rhythmic phrase' **#7** (see **Fig. 15.40.**).

- Measure 2

On the **Fmi7** chord in the right hand, we are again using **b7 to b3** alternating triads (see **Fig. 12.19.**) during the first 2 beats - in this case the **b3** is a 2nd inversion **Ab** triad, while the **b7** is a root-position **Eb** triad. During beat **3** we are using the 4th 'grace note' lick shown in **Fig. 15.99**. With respect to the **Fmi7** chord, the target tone approached by the grace note is the **b9** (Gb - an 'out-of-chord' tone), again on the 2nd 16th of beat **3**, while the 'drone' added on top to create the interval coupling, is the **11** (Bb). During the last half of beat **4** we have a 'split' **b7-1-5** 'whole-step-&-5th' structure (see **Fig. 15.50.**), with

CHAPTER FIFTEEN

Two-handed 'staccato' funk comping patterns (contd)

Analysis of Fig. 15.101. contd.

- Measure 2 contd. the **b7-5** coupling landing on the '**& of 4**' and the **1** landing on the last 16th of beat **4**. The left hand is again playing the root and 5th of the chord, similar rhythmically to measure 1.

- Measure 3 On the **Abma7** chord in the right hand, we are using '**9 to 5**' alternating triads (see **Fig. 12.16.**) during the first 2 beats - in this case the **5** is a root position **Eb** triad, while the **9** is a 1st inversion **Bb** triad. These triads are same as for the corresponding part of measure 1. Again during beat **3** we are using the 2nd 'grace note' lick shown in **Fig. 15.99**. With respect to the **Abma7** chord, the target tone approached by the grace note is the **b7** (Gb - an 'out-of-chord' tone), on the 2nd 16th of beat **3**, while the 'drone' note added on top is the **3** (C). During the last half of beat **4** we have a 'split' inverted **6-9-5** double 4th structure (see **Fig. 10.11.**), with the **5-9** coupling landing on the '**& of 4**' and the **6** landing on the last 16th of beat **4**. Again the right hand notes used here are the same as for measure 1. The left hand is playing the root and 5th of the chord (and the 3rd on the 2nd 16th of beat 4), again rhythmically similar to the previous measures.

- Measure 4 On the **Bb** chord in the right hand, we are using '**4 to 1**' alternating triads (see **Fig. 12.11.**) during the first 2 beats - in this case the **4** is a root position **Eb** triad, while the **1** is a 1st inversion **Bb** triad (same triads again as in measures 1 & 3). During beat **3** we are using the sixth 'grace note' lick shown in **Fig. 15.99**. With respect to the Bb chord, the target tone approached by the grace note is the **9** (C), while the 'drone' note added on top is the **11** (Eb). During the rest of this measure, a 'cross-over' phrase is used, based on the 2nd half of the 1st measure of **Fig. 15.97**. Again the left hand is based around the root & 5th of the **Bb** chord, with the 'C' on the last 16th of beat **4** acting as a pickup back into beat **1**.

Now we will look at some more leadsheets and see how we can construct two-handed 'staccato' funk patterns based on the chords and rhythms shown. We start with the following four measure example:-

Figure 15.102. Chord chart example #4

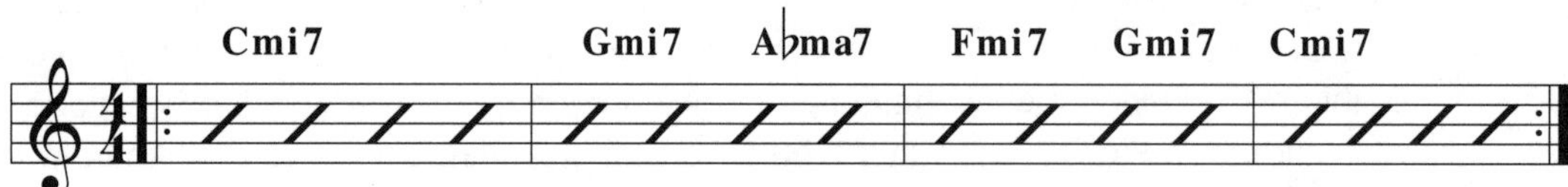

When interpreting this leadsheet, the following right hand devices will be used:-

- alternating triads ('**b7 to b3**' and '**9 to 5**')
- double 4th structures (root position and inversions)
- 4th interval couplings
- '**9 to 1**' resolutions within upper structure triads
- blues scale 'cross-over' phrases

See example on following page:-

Two-handed 'staccato' funk comping patterns (contd)

Figure 15.103. Funk comping solution for chord chart #4 (Fig. 15.102.)
(Cassette Tape Example 618 - 'Straight 16ths')
(Cassette Tape Example 619 - 'Swing 16ths')

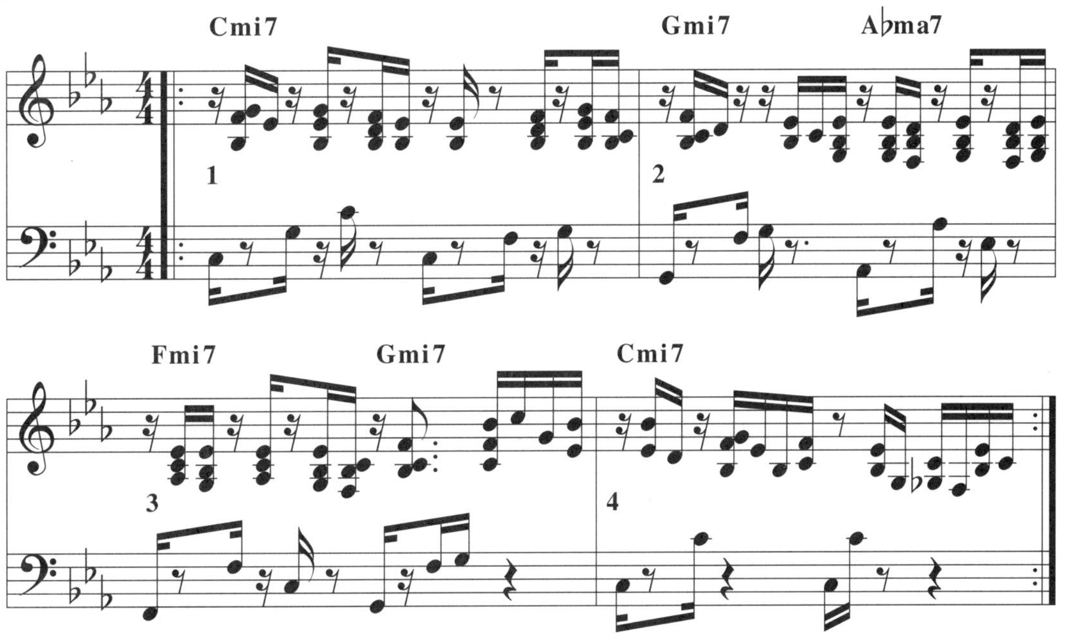

We can analyze the various devices used in this example as follows:-

- Measure 1 - On the **Cmi7** chord the following right hand devices are used:-

- a '**9 to 1**' resolution is occurring within a **b3-5-b7** upper structure (a 2nd inversion **Eb** triad) on the 2nd & 3rd 16ths of beat **1** (see **Fig. 8.14.**).
- '**b7 to b3**' alternating triads are being used (**see Fig. 12.19.**) - the **b3** is a 2nd inversion **Eb** triad (on beat **2** and the '**& of 4**') and the **b7** is a root position **Bb** triad (on the '**& of 2**' and beat **4**).
- '**b7-b3**' 4th interval couplings (see **Fig. 12.23.**) are being used, on the last 16th of beat **2** and the 2nd 16th of beat **3**.
- an inverted **1-11-b7** double 4th structure (see **Fig. 10.8.**) is being used on the last 16th of beat **4** - however this is heard as an anticipation of the next chord.

The left hand pattern is using the **1**, **4(11)** and **5** of the chord, landing on beats **1** & **3** and otherwise making use of the 'weak 16th' subdivisions as pickups.

- Measure 2 - On the **Gmi7** chord the following right hand devices are used:-

- an inverted **11-b7-b3** double 4th structure (see **Fig. 10.5.**) is being used on the 2nd 16th of beat **1** (and also anticipating beat **1**), followed by the 5th of the chord on the '**& of 1**'. This could also be considered as a '**9 to 3**' movement within the the upper **Bb** triad.
- a **Bb-Eb** 4th coupling is being used on beat **2**. Technically a **b3-#5** coupling (see **Fig. 12.26.**), the 'out-of-chord' Eb is a reference back to the key of C minor, and is leading into the subsequent anticipation of the **Abma7** chord (on the last 16th of beat **2**).

Two-handed 'staccato' funk comping patterns (contd)

Analysis of Fig. 15.103. contd.

- Measure 2 (contd) - On the **Abma7** chord the following right hand devices are used:-

- '**9 to 5**' alternating triads are being used (see **Fig. 12.16.**) - the **5** is a 1st inversion **Eb** triad (on the last 16th of beat **2**, the 2nd 16th of beat **3**, beat **4** and the last 16th of beat **4**), and the **9** is a 2nd inversion **Bb** triad (on the '**& of 3**' and the '**& of 4**').

The left hand meanwhile is using the root & 7th of the **Gmi7** chord, and the root & 5th of the **Abma7** chord, rhythmically similar to measure 1 (except for landing on beat **2**).

- Measure 3 - On the **Fmi7** chord the following right hand devices are used:-

- '**b7 to b3**' alternating triads are being used (see **Fig. 12.19.**) - the **b3** is a root position **Ab** triad (on the 2nd 16th of beat **2**, and beat **3**), and the **b7** is a 1st inversion **Eb** triad (on the '**& of 1**' and the '**& of 2**').
- an inverted **5-1-11** double 4th structure (see **Fig. 10.3.**) is being used on the last 16th of beat **2** - however this is heard as an anticipation of the next chord.

- On the **Gmi7** chord the following right hand devices are used:-

- root position and inverted **11-b7-b3** double 4th structures (see **Fig. 10.5.**) are being used (anticipating beat **3**, on the 2nd 16th of beat **3** and on beat **4**).

The left hand meanwhile is using the root & 5th of the **Fmi7** chord, and the root & 7th of the **Gmi7** chord, again landing on beats **1** & **3** and providing pickups into beat **4**.

- Measure 4 - On the **Cmi7** chord the following right hand devices are used:-

- a 'split' **9-b3-b7** 'half-step-&-5th' structure (see **Figs. 13.20.**, **15.49.** & **15.96.**) is being used, with the **b3-b7** coupling anticipating beat **1** and landing on the 2nd 16th of beat **1**, and the **9** landing on the '**& of 1**'.
- a '**9 to 1**' resolution is occurring within a **b3-5-b7** upper structure (a 2nd inversion **Eb** triad) on the 1st & 2nd 16ths of beat **2**.
- a 'split' inverted **1-11-b7** double 4th structure (see **Fig. 10.8.**) is being used, with the **b7** landing on the '**& of 2**' and the **1-11** coupling landing on the last 16th of beat **2**.
- during beats **3** & **4** 'cross-over' phrases from the C blues scale are being used (see **Fig. 15.97.**).

The left hand meanwhile is playing the root of the **Cmi7** chord in an octave pattern, again landing on beats **1** & **3**.

The next leadsheet is an eight measure example which uses some 16th note anticipations in the chord rhythms, as follows:-

Figure 15.104. Chord chart example #5

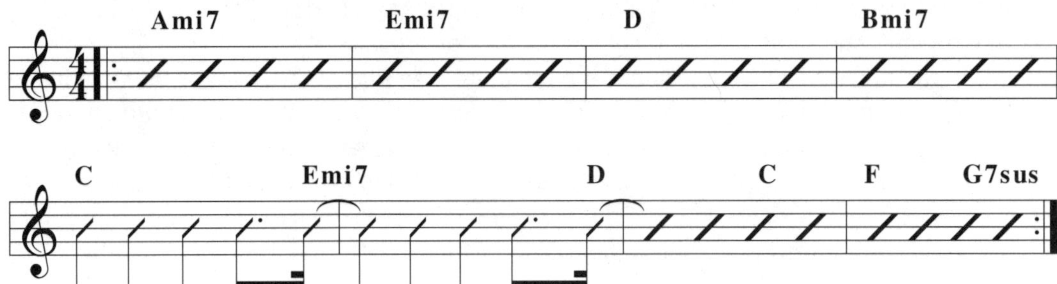

Two-handed 'staccato' funk comping patterns (contd)

In the following interpretation of this leadsheet, the first four measures feature a sparser rhythmic feel, which then builds in the next four measures as more rhythmic subdivisions are used. Various right hand devices such as alternating triads, resolutions within triads, double 4ths, 4-part upper structures, blues scale phrases, 4th clusters etc. are used as follows:-

Figure 15.105. Funk comping solution for chord chart #5 (Fig. 15.104.)

(Cassette Tape Example 620 - 'Straight 16ths')
(Cassette Tape Example 621 - 'Swing 16ths')

Two-handed 'staccato' funk comping patterns (contd)

Again we can analyze the devices used in the previous example (**Fig. 15.105.**) as follows:-

- Measure 1 - On the **Ami7** chord the following right hand devices are used:-
- a **b3-5-b7** upper structure (a 2nd inversion **C** triad - see **Fig. 5.6.**), on the 2nd 16th of beat **1** and the 1st & 4th 16ths of beat **2** (anticipating beat **3**).
- a '**9 to 1**' resolution within the same **b3-5-b7** upper structure (see **Fig. 8.14.**), during the last half of beat **4**.
- a **9-b3-b7** 'half-step-&-5th' structure (see **Figs. 13.20.** & **15.49.**), on the '**& of 2**'.

The left hand is playing a sparse pattern using the root and 5th of the chord.

- Measure 2 - On the **Emi7** chord the following right hand devices are used:-
- an **11-b7-b3** double 4th structure (see **Fig. 10.5.**), on the 2nd 16th of beat **1** and the 1st & 4th 16ths of beat **2**, rhythmically based upon measure 1.
- a **5-1-11** double 4th structure (see **Fig. 10.3.**), on the '**& of 2**'.
- a '**9 to 1**' resolution within a **1-b3-5** upper structure (a 2nd inversion **Emi** triad - see **Fig. 8.30.**), during the last half of beat **4**.

The left hand is the same rhythmically as measure 1, playing the root in octaves.

- Measure 3 - On the **D** chord the following right hand devices are used:-
- '**4 to 1**' alternating triads (see **Fig. 12.11.**). In this case the **1** (a 2nd inversion **D** triad) is landing on the 2nd 16th of beat **1** and the 1st & 4th 16ths of beat **2**, while the **4** (a 1st inversion **G** triad) is landing on the '**& of 2**'.
- a '**9 to 1**' resolution within a **1-3-5** upper structure (a 2nd inversion **D** triad - see **Fig. 8.12.**), during the last half of beat **4**.

The left hand is again using a similar rhythmic idea as the previous measures, this time adding the root (D) on the 2nd 16th of beat **4**.

- Measure 4 - On the **Bmi7** chord the following right hand devices are used:-
- '**b7 to b3**' alternating triads (see **Fig. 12.19.**). In this case the **b3** (a 2nd inversion **D** triad) is landing on the 2nd 16th of beat **1** and the 1st & 4th 16ths of beat **2**, while the **b7** (a root position **A** triad) is landing on the '**& of 2**'.
- a 'grace note' lick derived from the B blues scale, during beat **3**. This is a based on a transposed version of the 4th phrase shown in **Fig. 15.99.** (using the C blues scale).
- **1-11** & **b7-b3** 4th couplings (see **Fig. 12.23.**), on the 1st & 2nd 16ths of beat **4**.
- the **C** triad on the last 16th of beat **4**, is an anticipation of the next chord.

The left hand is resting apart from playing the root in octaves during beat **1**.

- Measure 5 - On the **C** chord the following right hand devices are used:-
- '**9 to 1**' alternating triads (see **Fig. 12.14.**). In this case the **1** (a **C** triad) is used in 2nd inversion on the 2nd 16th of beat **1** and the last 16th of beat **2**, and in root position on beat **2**, while the **9** (a 2nd inversion **D** triad) is landing on the '**& of 1**' and the '**& of 2**'.
- a 'grace note' lick derived from the E blues scale, during beat **3**. This is based on a transposed version of the 2nd phrase shown in **Fig. 15.99.** (using the C blues scale).
- the **Emi** triad on the the last 16th of beat **4**, is an anticipation of the next chord.

The left hand is now rhythmically busier using the root & 5th, landing on beats **1** & **3** and some 'weak 16ths' in the rhythmic spaces. During beat **4** a short run (using notes from the E minor pentatonic scale) is functioning as a pickup into the note E, landing on the last 16th of beat **4** (and anticipating beat **1**). Both left and right hands are therefore anticipating the next **Emi7** chord, as required by the harmonic rhythm on the leadsheet (see **Fig. 15.104.**)

Two-handed 'staccato' funk comping patterns (contd)

Analysis of Fig. 15.105. contd.

- Measure 6 - On the **Emi7** chord the following right hand devices are used:-

- '**b7 to b3**' alternating triads (see **Fig. 12.19.**). In this case the **b7** (a 2nd inversion **D** triad) is landing on the '**& of 1**' and the '**& of 2**', while the **b3** (a 1st inversion **G** triad) is landing on beat **2**.
- a **1-b3-5** upper structure (a 1st inversion **Emi** triad - see **Fig. 5.8.**) is being used on the 2nd 16th of beat **1**, and the last 16th of beat **2**.
- the same 'grace note' lick during beat **3** as in the previous measure, now over the **Emi7** chord - see measure 5 comments.
- the **D** triad on the last 16th of beat **4**, is an anticipation of the next chord.

Again the left hand is using the root and 5th of the chord in the rhythmic spaces, landing on beat **3**. During beat **4** a short run is functioning as a pickup into the note D, landing on the last 16th of beat **4** (and anticipating beat **1**). Both left and right hands are therefore anticipating the next **D** chord, as required by the harmonic rhythm on the leadsheet (see **Fig. 15.104.**).

- Measure 7 - On the **D** chord the following right hand devices are used:-

- a '**9 to 1**' resolution within a **1-3-5** upper structure (a 2nd inversion **D** triad - see **Fig. 8.12.**), during beat **1**.
- **6-9** & **5-1** 4th couplings (see **Fig. 12.24.**), on beat **2** and the '**& of 2**'.
- the **C** triad on the last 16th of beat **2**, is an anticipation of the next chord.

The left hand is playing the root on the last 16th of beat **1**, and the 5th on the 2nd 16th of beat **2**.

- On the **C** chord the following right hand devices are used:-

- a '**9 to 1**' resolution within a **1-3-5** upper structure (a 2nd inversion **C** triad - see **Fig. 8.12.**), during beat **3**.
- **5-1** & **6-9** 4th couplings (see **Fig. 12.24.**), on beat **4** and the '**& of 4**'.
- the **G-A-C** 'whole-step-4th' cluster on the last 16th of beat **4**, is an anticipation of the next chord.

The left hand is again using the root on beat **3** and the last 16th of beat **3**, and the 5th on the 2nd 16th of beat **4**.

- Measure 8 - On the **F** chord the following right hand devices are used:-

- a **9-3-5** 'whole-step-4th' cluster (see **Fig. 13.11.**), on the 2nd 16th of beat **1** (and anticipating beat **1**).
- a **3-5-7-9** upper structure (a 3rd inversion **Ami7** 4-part shape - see **Fig. 7.3.**) on beat **2**, followed by the 6th (D) & 5th (C) of the chord as single notes.
- the inverted **Dmi7** shape on the last 16th of beat **2**, is an anticipation of the next chord.

The left hand is playing the root on beat **1** and the '**& of 1**', and the 5th on the last 16th of beat **1**.

- On the **G7sus** chord the following right hand devices are used:-

- a **5-b7-9-11** upper structure (a 3rd inversion **Dmi7** 4-part shape - see **Fig. 7.4.**) on the 2nd 16th of beat **3** (and anticipating beat **3**).
- a **b7-9-11** upper structure (a 1st inversion **F** triad - see **Fig. 5.2.**), followed by the 13th (E), 11th (C) and 5th (D) of the chord as single notes, leading back to the first chord.

The left hand is playing the root on beat **3** and the '**& of 3**', and the 5th on the last 16th of beat **3**.

Two-handed 'staccato' funk comping patterns (contd)

We will now look at some leadsheet examples to be specifically interpreted using a '**swing 16ths**' feel (with a 16th note triplet subdivision). We discussed the 'straight 16ths' vs. 'swing 16ths' issue in the introduction to this chapter (and in **Chapter 2**), and all of the pattern examples in this chapter so far have been applicable for both types of 16th subdivision. However, the 'swing 16ths' style does offer some additional rhythmic possibilities if all three subdivisions within a 16th note triplet are used - as opposed to just the first and third 16ths within a 16th note triplet, which would be the typical way to interpret 'swing 16ths' (review **Figs. 2.37. - 2.39.** as necessary). It is wise not to 'overdo' the use of all 3 triplet subdivisions within a 16th note triplet - however, used sparingly as a rhythmic embellishment device it can be effective in a 'swing 16ths' comping groove. With this in mind, we will now look at the following leadsheet, to be interpreted in a 'swing 16ths' funk style:-

Figure 15.106. Chord chart example #6

We will now consider two different interpretations of this leadsheet, using the above 16th note triplet devices. Note that whereas all the previous comping examples in this chapter can be interpreted in both 'straight' and 'swing' 16ths (because each pattern contains no more than two rhythmic attacks per half-a-beat, so the choice is between splitting the 8th note 50/50 for 'straight 16ths', or 66/33 for 'swing 16ths'), the following patterns **cannot be played in 'straight 16ths'** because there are three rhythmic attacks per half-a-beat in some cases, i.e. when all subdivisions within a 16th note triplet are used. The first 'comping' version of this chart is as follows:-

Figure 15.107. Funk comping solution a) for chord chart #6 (Fig. 15.106.), using 16th note triplets
(Cassette Tape Example 622 - 'Swing 16ths')

(Note the 'swing 16ths' symbol at the top of the chart - see **Fig. 2.38.**)

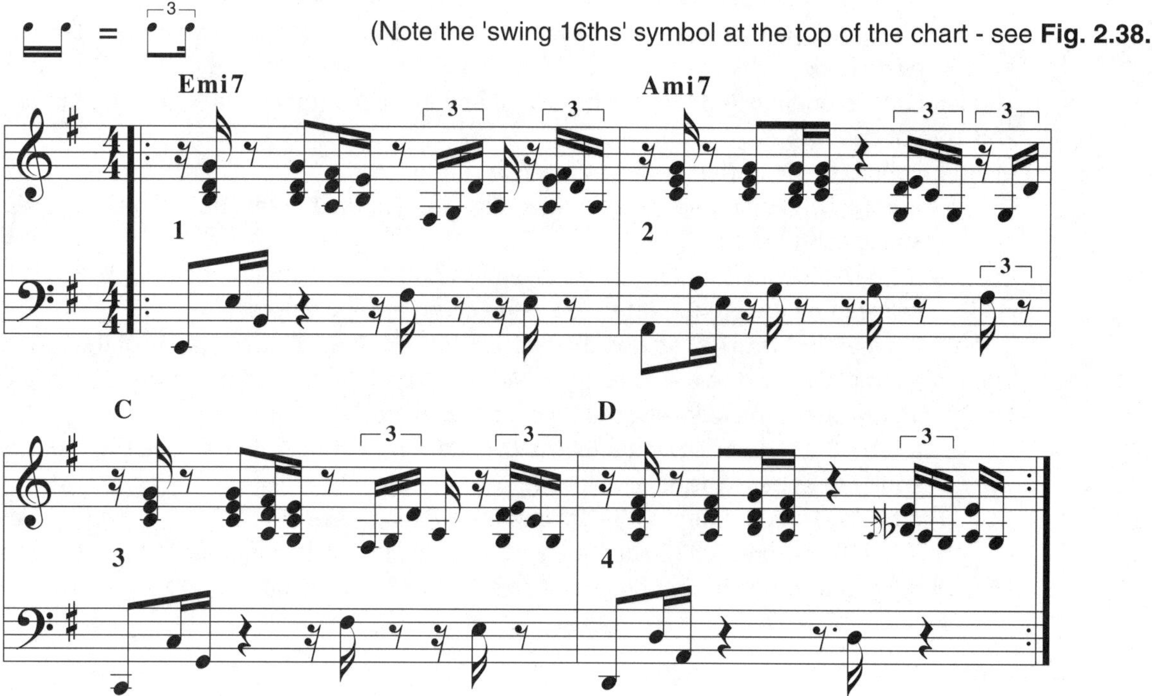

Two-handed 'staccato' funk comping patterns (contd)

We can analyze the devices used in the previous example (**Fig. 15.107.**) as follows:-

- Measure 1 - On the **Emi7** chord the following right hand devices are used:-

- '**b7 to b3**' alternating triads (see **Fig. 12.19.**). In this case the **b3** (a 1st inversion **G** triad) is landing on the 2nd 16th of beat **1**, and on beat **2**, while the **b7** (a 2nd inversion **D** triad) is landing on the '**& of 2**'.
- a **5-1** 4th coupling (see **Fig. 12.23.**), landing on the last 16th of beat **2**.
- an arpeggiated **9-b3-b7** 'half-step-&-5th' structure (see **Figs. 13.20.** & **15.49.**), using all 3 triplet subdivisions in the last half of beat **3**.
- a '**9 to 1**' resolution within a **b7-9-11** upper structure (a 2nd inversion **D** triad) is occurring during the last half of beat **4**. The **D** triad is also one of the 'alternating triads' described above.
- the 11th of the chord (A) is also used as a passing tone on beat **4**, and on the final triplet subdivision at the end of beat **4**.

The left hand is playing the root and 5th of the chord during beat **1**, and the 9th and root on the 2nd 16ths of beats **3** & **4** respectively. During the second half of the measure, the left hand is in the same register as the right hand - in particular during beat **3** where the F# on the 2nd 16th of beat **3** in the left hand, is immediately followed by the same note at the beginning of the 16th note triplet in the right hand. This creates a useful rhythmic effect when played staccato (short and accented).

- Measure 2 - On the **Ami7** chord the following right hand devices are used:-

- '**b7 to b3**' alternating triads (see **Fig. 12.19.**). In this case the **b3** (a root position **C** triad) is landing on the 2nd 16th of beat **1**, and on the 1st & 4th 16ths of beat **2**, while the **b7** (a 1st inversion **G** triad) is landing on the '**& of 2**'.
- a '**9 to 1**' resolution within a **b3-5-b7** upper structure (a 2nd inversion **C** triad) is occurring during the first half of beat **4**. The **C** triad is also one of the 'alternating triads' described above.
- the left and right hands together during the last half of beat **4** are creating a **13-b7-11** 'half-step-&-5th' structure (see **Figs. 13.23.** & **15.49.**), using all 3 triplet subdivisions in the last half of beat **4**.

The left hand is also playing the root and 5th of the chord during beat **1**, and the 7th (G) on the 2nd 16th of beat **2**, and the last 16th of beat **3**.

- Measure 3 - On the **C** chord the following right hand devices are used:-

- '**9 to 1**' alternating triads (see **Fig. 12.14.**). In this case the **1** (a **C** triad) is used in root position on the 2nd 16th of beat **1**, and on beat **2**, and in 2nd inversion on the last 16th of beat **2**, while the **9** (a 2nd inversion **D** triad) is landing on the '**& of 2**'.
- an arpeggiated **#11-5-9** 'half-step-&-5th' structure (see **Figs. 13.21.** & **15.49.**), using all 3 triplet subdivisions in the last half of beat **3**. The notes used (**F#-G-D**) are a repetition from the previous measures.
- a '**9 to 1**' resolution within a **1-3-5** upper structure (a 2nd inversion **C** triad) is occurring during the last half of beat **4**. The **C** triad is also one of the 'alternating triads' described above.
- the 6th/13th of the chord (A) is also used as a passing tone on beat **4**, and the 5th of the chord (G) is used on the final triplet subdivision at the end of beat **4**.

Two-handed 'staccato' funk comping patterns (contd)

Analysis of Fig. 15.107. contd.

- Measure 3 (contd) The left hand is again playing the root and 5th of the chord during beat **1**, and the #11th and 3rd on the 2nd 16ths of beats **3** & **4** respectively. During the second half of the measure, the pitches used and the rhythmic interaction with the right hand, are the same as for the first measure - see previous left hand comments for measure 1.

- Measure 4 - On the **D** chord the following right hand devices are used:-

- '**4 to 1**' alternating triads (see **Fig. 12.11.**). In this case the **1** (a 2nd inversion **D** triad) is landing on the 2nd 16th of beat **1**, and on the 1st & 4th 16ths of beat **2**, while the **4** (a 1st inversion **G** triad) is landing on the '**& of 2**'.
- a 'grace note' lick derived from the E blues scale, during beat **4**. This is based on a transposed version of the 2nd phrase shown in **Fig. 15.99.** (using the C blues scale).

The left hand is again playing the root and 5th during beat **1**, and the root on the last 16th of beat **3**, as a pickup into the right hand phrase during beat **4** described above.

Now we will look at another comping interpretation of the leadsheet shown in **Fig. 15.106**. This version still uses a 'swing 16ths' feel, this time using a busier level of 16th note triplet subdivisions, as follows:-

Figure 15.108. Funk comping solution b) for chord chart #6 (fig. 15.106.), using 16th note triplets
(Cassette Tape Example 623 - 'Swing 16ths')

Again we will analyze the various devices used in this example as follows:-

Two-handed 'staccato' funk comping patterns (contd)

- Measure 1 - On the **Emi7** chord the following right hand devices are used:-

- an **11-b7-b3** double 4th structure (see **Fig. 10.5.**), on the middle subdivision of the 16th note triplet during the first half of beat **1**, and on the last 16th of beat **1**.
- a **5-1-11** double 4th structure (see **Fig. 10.3.**), on the '**& of 1**'.
- 4th couplings (see **Fig. 12.23.**) as follows:-
  - **11-b7** on the middle subdivision of the 16th note triplet during the first half of beat **3**.
  - **5-1** on the '**& of 3**' and on beat **4**.
  - **1-11** at the beginning of the 16th note triplet during the last half of beat **4**.
  - **b7-b3** at the end of the 16th note triplet during the last half of beat **4**.
- the 7th & 5th of the chord are also used as passing tones in the triplets during beat **4**.

The left hand is playing the root of the chord on the 1st & 3rd subdivisions of the 16th note triplets at the beginning of beats **1** & **3** respectively. During these triplets, the combination of the two hands results in the use of all the triplet subdivisions. The left hand is also using the 5th & 11th of the chord as passing tone pickups into beats **3** & **4** respectively.

- Measure 2 - On the **Ami7** chord the following right hand devices are used:-

- a **1-11-b7** double 4th structure (see **Fig. 10.8.**), on the middle subdivision of the 16th note triplet during the first half of beat **1**, and on the last 16th of beat **1**.
- a **9-5-1** double 4th structure (see **Fig. 10.7.**), on the '**& of 1**'.
- 4th couplings (see **Fig. 12.23.**) as follows:-
  - **b7-b3** on the middle subdivision of the 16th note triplet during the first half of beat **3**.
  - **1-11** on the '**& of 3**' and on beat **4**.
  - **11-b7** at the beginning of the 16th note triplet during the last half of beat **4**.
- a **b3-5** 3rd interval coupling at the end of the 16th note triplet during the last half of beat **4**.
- the 3rd & root of the chord are also used as passing tones in the triplets during beat **4**.

The left hand is using the root, 5th & 7th of the chord, rhythmically similar to measure 1.

- Measure 3 - On the **C** chord the following right hand devices are used:-

- a **6-9-5** double 4th structure (see **Fig. 10.11.**), on the middle subdivision of the 16th note triplet during the first half of beat **1**, and on the last 16th of beat **1**.
- a **7-3-6** double 4th structure (see **Fig. 10.9.**), on the '**& of 1**'.
- '**9 to 5**' alternating triads (see **Fig. 12.16.**). In this case the **5** (a 1st inversion **G** triad) is landing on the middle subdivision of the 16th note triplet during the first half of beat **3**, while the **9** (a 2nd inversion **D** triad) is landing on the '**& of 3**'.
- a '**9 to 1**' resolution within a **1-3-5** upper structure (a 2nd inversion **C** triad), within the triplet during the first half of beat **4**.
- a **9-5** 4th coupling (see **Fig. 12.24.**) at the beginning of the 16th note triplet during the last half of beat **4**.
- a **1-3** 3rd interval coupling at the end of the 16th note triplet during the last half of beat **4**.
- the 5th & root of the chord are also used as passing tones in the triplets during beat **4**.

The left hand is using the root & 5th of the chord, rhythmically similar to the previous measures.

Two-handed 'staccato' funk comping patterns (contd)

Analysis of Fig. 15.108. contd.

- Measure 4 - On the D chord the following right hand devices are used:-

- a **5-1-11** double 4th structure (see **Fig. 10.3.**), on the middle subdivision of the 16th note triplet during the first half of beat **1**, and on the '**& of 1**'.
- a **1-3-5** upper structure (a 2nd inversion **D** triad), on the last 16th of beat **1**. (This movement during beat **1** can also be considered as a '**4 to 1**' resolution within the D triad - see **Chapter 9**).
- '**b7 to 1**' alternating triads (see **Fig. 12.21.**) as follows:-
  - the **b7** (2nd inversion **C** triad) on the middle subdivision of the 16th note triplet during the first half of beat **3**, and on the '**& of 3**'.
  - the 1 (2nd inversion **D** triad) on the middle subdivision of the 16th note triplet during the first half of beat **4**, and on the first subdivision of the 16th note triplet during the last half of beat **4**.
- the 9th & root of the chord are also used as passing tones in the triplets during beat **4**.

The left hand is again playing the root & 5th of the chord, now additionally landing on beat **4** and the last subdivision of the 16th note triplet during the first half of beat **4** (as a pickup into the last half of beat **4**.).

PRACTICE DIRECTIONS:-

- ***Practice the funk comping patterns using the 'chromatic' double 4ths, and 'half-step-&-5th' structures, as in Figs. 15.94. - 15.96.***
  As usual you are encouraged to experiment with variations of these patterns, and to transpose them into different keys!
- ***Practice the blues scale 'cross-over' licks and 'grace note' licks as in Figs. 15.97. & 15.99., and work on transposing these to other keys.***
- ***Practice the comping examples using the above blues scale devices, as in Figs. 15.98. & 15.101.***
- ***Practice the comping examples for chord charts #4 and #5 (as in Figs. 15.102. - 15.105.) using straight and swing 16th treatments.***
- ***Practice the comping examples for chord chart #6 (as in Figs. 15.106. - 15.108.) using a swing 16th treatment*** *(these examples contain 16th note triplets).*
- ***Work on applying these concepts to tunes of your choice, and to the practice leadsheets at the end of this chapter.***

Funk comping practice examples

(Don't forget to practice all examples in straight and swing 16ths!)

Figure 15.109. Practice leadsheet #1

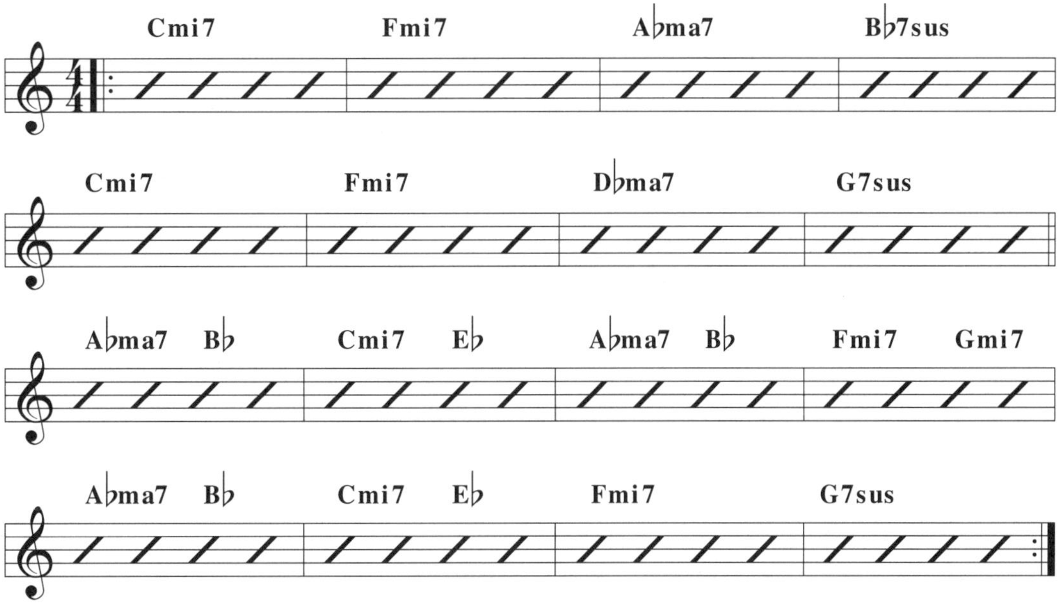

Figure 15.110. Practice leadsheet #2

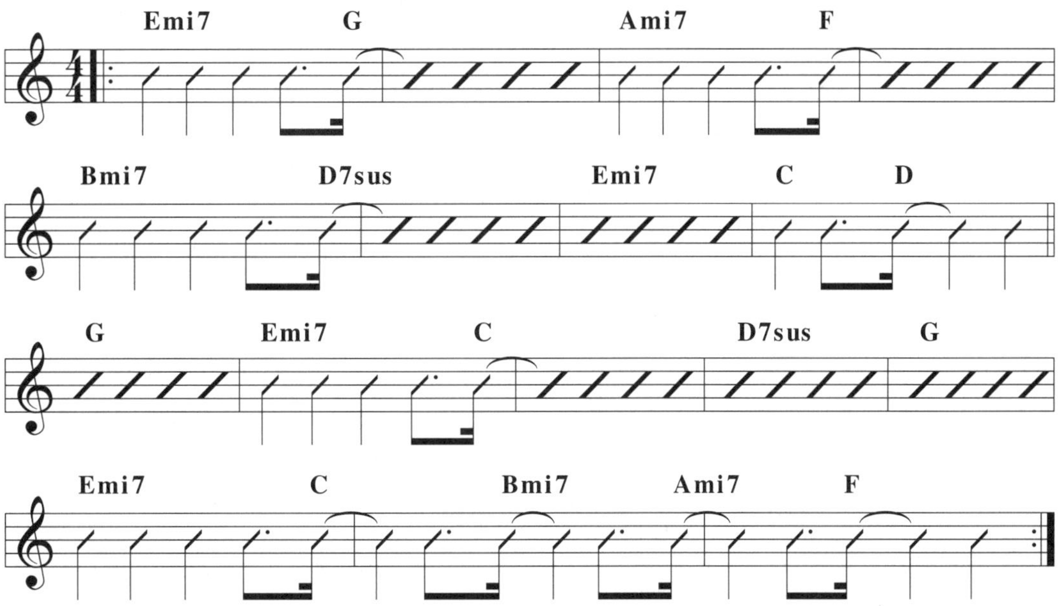

Funk comping practice examples (contd)

Figure 15.111. Practice leadsheet #3

(PRACTICE HINT - ON THESE DOMINANT CHORDS, TRY USING MIXOLYDIAN TRIADS IN THE RIGHT HAND - SEE *FIGS. 15.68. - 15.73.*)

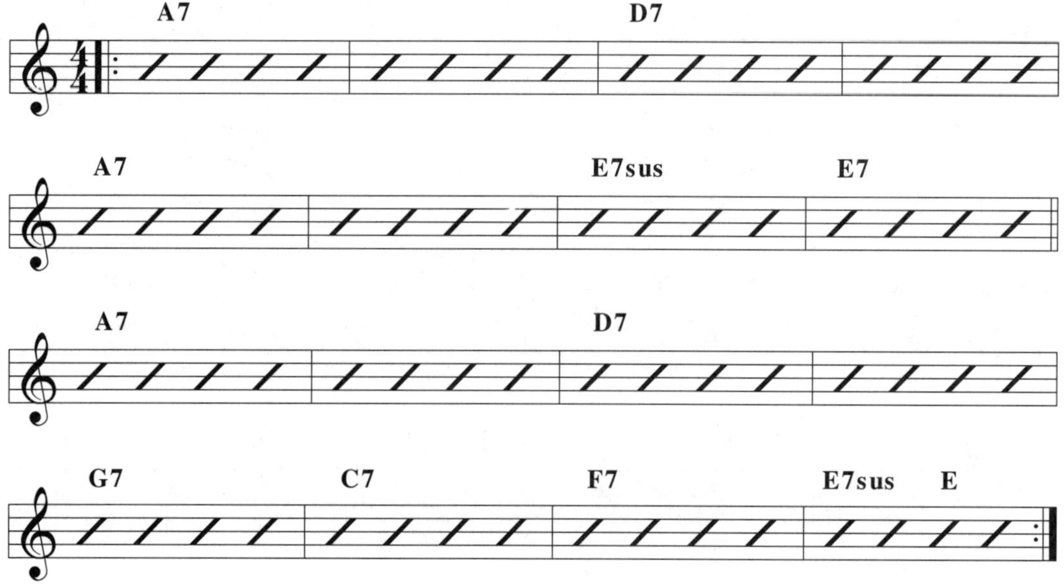

Figure 15.112. Practice leadsheet #4

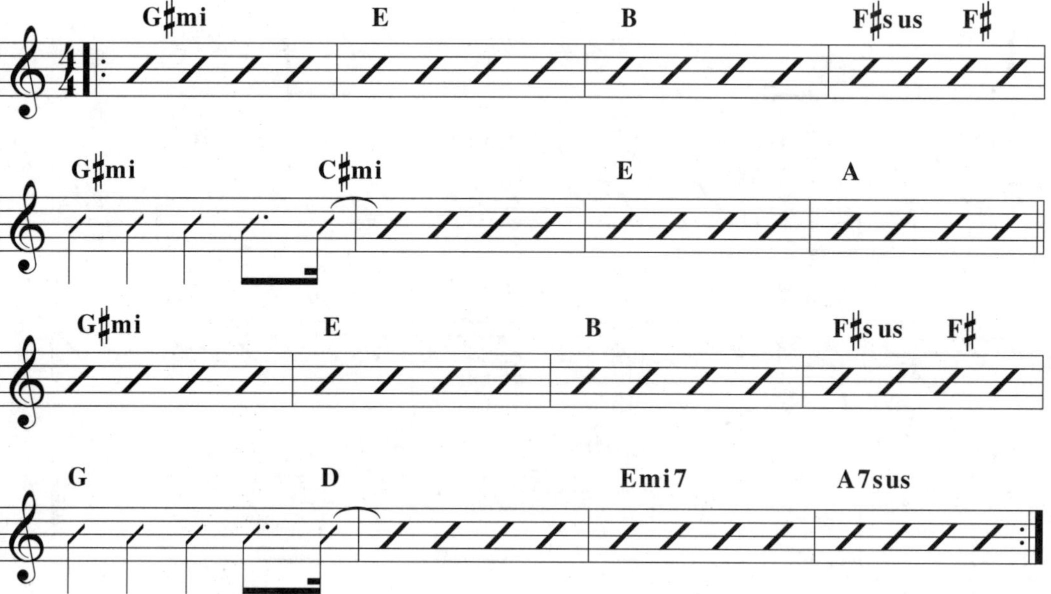

CHAPTER SIXTEEN

Country & Country-Rock

Introduction

The next styles to be studied are contemporary country and country-rock. Arguably an important ancestor of modern rock styles (along with blues and gospel), country music continues to be very popular. Many people are familiar with the work of 'mainstream' contemporary country artists such as Garth Brooks, George Strait, Judds etc. to name but a few. However, the considerable influence of country stylings on other contemporary idioms (and artists not typically regarded as being in the 'country' category) is often overlooked. For example, in the 70s and 80s the rock band The Eagles drew heavily on country influences. The keyboard work of Bruce Hornsby is an excellent example of country devices being brought into the pop & rock mainstream. Even modern jazz keyboardists like David Benoit make use of the country devices (i.e. the 'hammers' and 'drones' as detailed in this chapter) first popularized by the pianist Floyd Kramer. The British rock band Dire Straits is very influenced by country styles - and the list goes on!

Country styles generally use an eighth-note subdivision, with either straight or rolled eighth treatments (review **Chapter 2** as necessary). Basic mainstream country is frequently limited to triad chord forms, although more evolved country styles may use seventh (4-part) and/or ninth (5-part) chords. Right hand devices typically include the following:-

- Basic triads, or triad-over-root chords (see **Chapter 5**) in more evolved forms.
- Specific country devices as presented in this chapter:-
    - 'Drones'
    - 'Hammers'
    - 'Walkups'
- Embellishments based on pentatonic scales (see **Chapter 1**).
- Some '**9 to 1**' resolutions (within triads) and '4th clusters' in more evolved forms.

In this chapter we will look at accompaniment ('comping') and melody treatments, and use the above devices in both situations. Rhythmically the right hand normally has most of the 'subdivision responsibility' (i.e. providing the eighth-note subdivisions) in this style, and sometimes the right hand part may use eighth-note anticipations (as in pop-rock styles). The left hand is generally playing a supportive role, based around the root & 5th of the chord on the 'primary beats' (**1** & **3**) with some variations.

Left hand patterns

Now we will look at some typical left hand patterns for country styles. A basic starting point is to use the root of the chord on beat **1**, and the 5th of the chord on beat **3**. Sometimes the root of the chord may be repeated on beat **3**, for example if a chord change is occurring in the following measure. Also it is possible to add eighth-note pickups into beats **1** and/or **3**. These ideas are now demonstrated in the following examples, based upon an **A major** chord:-

Left hand patterns (contd)

Figure 16.1. Country left hand pattern #1
(Cassette Tape Example 624)

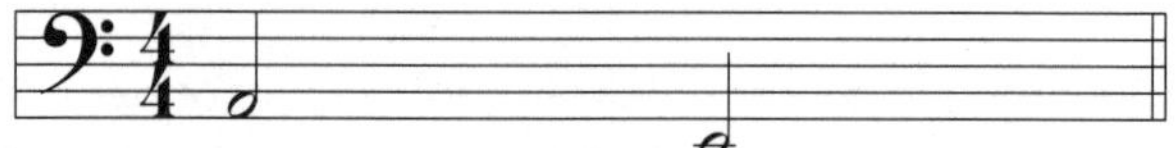

The basic country left hand pattern. Root of the chord on beat **1**, 5th of the chord on beat **3**.

Figure 16.2. Country left hand pattern #2
(Cassette Tape Example 625)

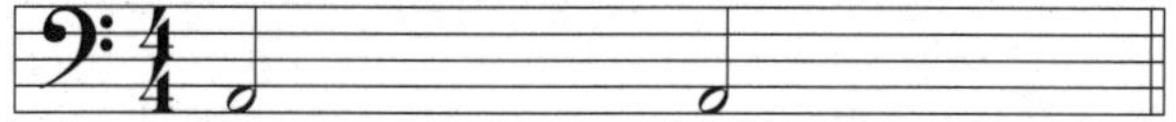

As above, now with the root repeated on beat **3**.

Figure 16.3. Country left hand pattern #3
(Cassette Tape Example 626)

Based on pattern **#1**, now with the root as an 8th-note pickup into beat **3**.

Figure 16.4. Country left hand pattern #4
(Cassette Tape Example 627)

Based on pattern **#2**, now with the 5th of the chord as an 8th-note pickup into beat **3**.

Figure 16.5. Country left hand pattern #5
(Cassette Tape Example 628)

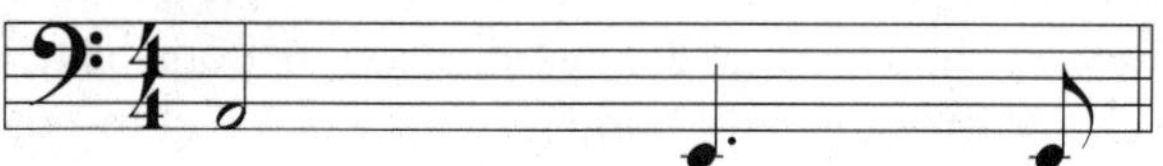

Based on pattern **#1**, now with the 5th of the chord as an 8th-note pickup into beat **1** of the following measure.

Figure 16.6. Country left hand pattern #6
(Cassette Tape Example 629)

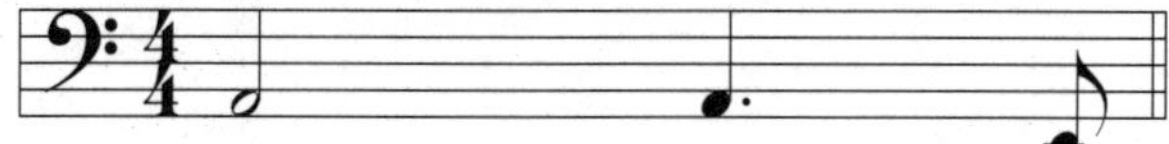

Based on pattern **#2**, now with the 5th of the chord as an 8th-note pickup into beat **1** of the following measure.

Left hand patterns (contd)

Figure 16.7. Country left hand pattern #7
(Cassette Tape Example 630)

A combination of patterns **#3** & **#5**, with 8th-note pickups into beat **3**, and beat **1** of the following measure.

Figure 16.8. Country left hand pattern #8
(Cassette Tape Example 631)

A variation on pattern **#7**, with the root on beats **1** & **3**, and the 8th-note pickups using the 5th of the chord.

Figure 16.9. Country left hand pattern #9
(Cassette Tape Example 632)

A busier variation of pattern **#7**, with the 5th of the chord additionally placed on the '**& of 3**'.

Constructing country patterns

We will now look at the construction of some basic two-handed country patterns, to be used for accompaniment or 'comping' purposes. In this section we will see how to interpret country chord charts, and how to integrate the various devices ('hammers', 'drones', 'walkups' etc.) into the patterns. The basic nucleus of a simple country comping pattern is to play a chord voicing (typically a triad) on beats **2** & **4** of the measure (the backbeats) and to play the root & 5th of the chord on beats **1** & **3** respectively in the left hand (as shown in **Fig. 16.1.**), as follows:-

Figure 16.10. Basic 1-measure comping pattern
(Cassette Tape Example 633)

From this simple beginning, we can now add some 8th-note subdivisions to create a useful result. This is most easily done by doubling the top note of the triad (in this case the note A, as the triad is arbitrarily in first inversion) one octave lower, on all of the 'upbeats' i.e. the '**& of 1**', '**& of 2**' etc. as follows:-

Constructing country patterns (contd)

Figure 16.11. Comping pattern variation #1 - upper triad in 1st inversion

(Cassette Tape Example 634 - 'Straight 8ths')
(Cassette Tape Example 635 - 'Swing 8ths')

As you practice this, make sure that the thumb of the right hand **stays on the A below middle C** - resist the temptation to use the thumb on the upper triad - use the remaining fingers in the right hand for this. Now that we have some 8th-note subdivisions, the manner in which we treat them (either 'straight' or 'swing') becomes an issue - we will be working on comping patterns using straight and swing 8ths treatments as appropriate. As previously mentioned, the original starting point for this pattern (see **Fig. 16.10.**) used the A triad in first inversion. We have already seen from our work on other styles, that the choice of right-hand triad inversions is typically driven by voiceleading considerations i.e. the need to provide smooth voiceleading 'from left to right' in a given chord progression. It seems likely therefore that we would need to adapt the 8th-note subdivision treatment shown in **Fig. 16.11.**, to any inversion of the right hand triad being used (i.e. not only for first inversion). The same principle of doubling the top note of the right hand triad an octave lower on the 'upbeats' will apply regardless of the right hand triad inversion, as in the following examples:-

Figure 16.12. Comping pattern variation #2 - upper triad in 2nd inversion

(Cassette Tape Example 636 - 'Straight 8ths')
(Cassette Tape Example 637 - 'Swing 8ths')

Here the top note of the upper triad (C#) is being doubled by the thumb of the right hand, on all of the 'upbeats'.

Figure 16.13. Comping pattern variation #3 - upper triad in root position

(Cassette Tape Example 638 - 'Straight 8ths')
(Cassette Tape Example 639 - 'Swing 8ths')

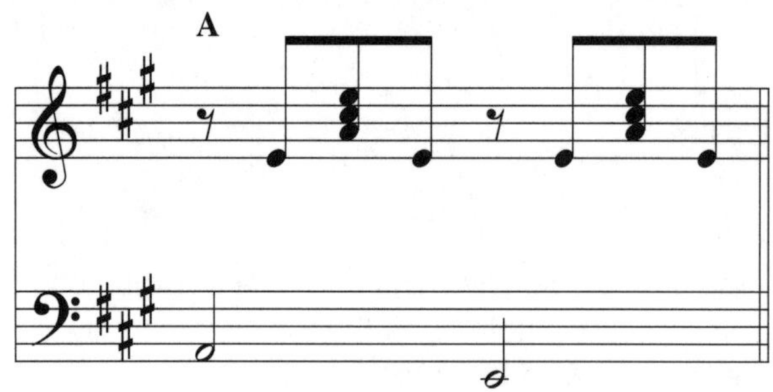

Here the top note of the upper triad (E) is being doubled by the thumb of the right hand, again on all of the 'upbeats'.

Constructing country patterns (contd)

We will now apply these comping pattern ideas to a country leadsheet. Here is a simple 8-measure progression using the 1, 4 & 5 triads of a major key - a typical harmonic concept in more 'mainstream' country situations:-

Figure 16.14. Chord chart example #1

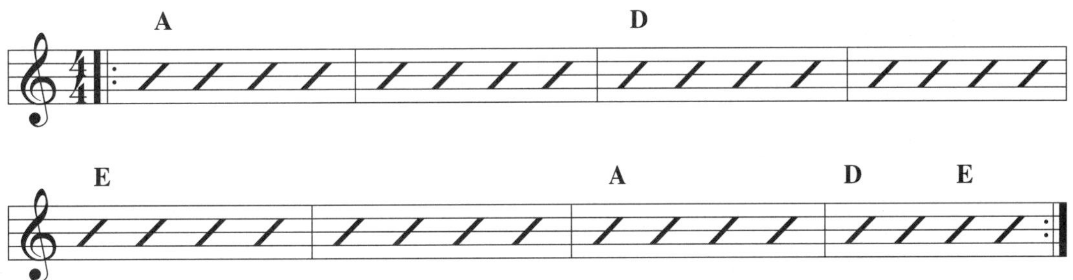

To interpret this progression, we will use basic **1-3-5** upper structure triads (see **Fig. 5.1.**) in the right hand i.e. we will not be using other extensions higher than the 5th on these chords. This is normal in basic country idioms, although later we will see how to imply larger chord forms in a country style. In a similar manner as was first done for Pop Ballad styles (review **Chapter 11** and **Figs. 11.1. & 11.2.** as necessary), we will first choose some upper triad inversions which will voicelead (i.e. move smoothly between chord changes) from 'left to right'. One of many possible voiceleading solutions (using **1-3-5** upper structure triads) is shown as follows:-

Figure 16.15. Upper structure voiceleading for chord chart #1 (Fig. 16.14.)
(Cassette Tape Example 640)

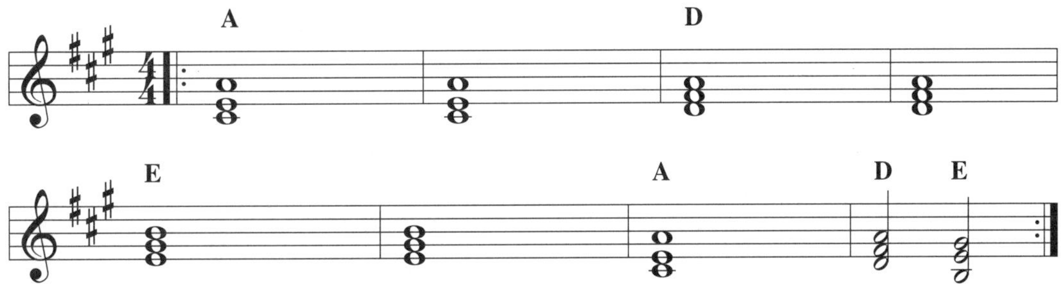

This voiceleading will now form the basis for the following comping solution:-

Figure 16.16. Country comping solution a) for chord chart #1 (Fig. 16.14.)
(Cassette Tape Example 641 - 'Straight 8ths')
(Cassette Tape Example 642 - 'Swing 8ths')

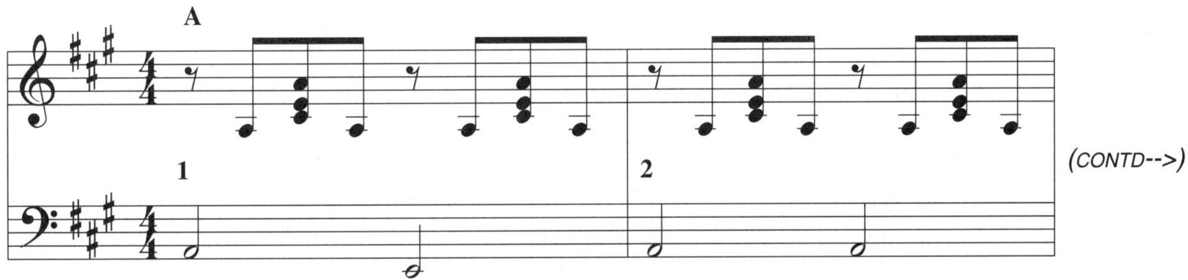

(contd-->)

Constructing country patterns (contd)

Figure 16.16. (contd)

We can analyze the right hand devices in the above comping example as follows:-

- Measures 1 & 2 On the **A** chord, the upper triad is in 1st inversion, with the root (A) on top. This top note is doubled by the right hand thumb an octave lower on the 'upbeats', as in **Fig. 16.11**.

- Measures 3 & 4 On the **D** chord, the upper triad is in root position, with the 5th (A) on top. This top note is doubled by the right hand thumb an octave lower on the 'upbeats', as in **Fig. 16.13**.

- Measures 5 & 6 On the **E** chord, the upper triad is in root position, with the 5th (B) on top. This top note is doubled by the right hand thumb an octave lower on the 'upbeats', as in **Fig. 16.13**.

- Measure 7 On the **A** chord, the upper triad is in 1st inversion, with the root (A) on top. This top note is doubled by the right hand thumb an octave lower on the 'upbeats', as in **Fig. 16.11**.

- Measure 8 On the **D** chord, the upper triad is in root position, with the 5th (A) on top. This top note is doubled by the right hand thumb an octave lower on the 'upbeats', as in **Fig. 16.13**.
On the **E** chord, the upper triad is in 2nd inversion, with the 3rd (G#) on top. This top note is doubled by the right hand thumb an octave lower on the 'upbeats', as in **Fig. 16.12**.

Again it's important to emphasize that this comping solution is based on the upper structure voiceleading shown in **Fig. 16.15.** - be sure to compare the right hand part from **Fig. 16.16.** above, with **Fig. 16.15.** as required.

Constructing country patterns (contd)

We can also analyze the left hand patterns in the previous example (**Fig. 16.16.**) as follows:-

- Measure 1 On the **A** chord, we are using the root (A) on beat **1** and the 5th (E) on beat **3**, as in **Fig. 16.1**. This frequently occurs when the same chord continues into the following measure (the **A** chord continues into measure 2).

- Measure 2 On the **A** chord, we are using the root (A) on beats **1** & **3**, as in **Fig. 16.2**. This frequently occurs in a measure leading up to a chord change (we are about to change to a **D** chord in measure 3).

- Measure 3 On the **D** chord, we are using a root & 5th pattern similar to the **A** chord in measure 1.

- Measure 4 On the **D** chord, we are using the root on beats **1** & **3**, as for the **A** chord in measure 2.

- Measure 5 On the **E** chord, we are using a root & 5th pattern similar to the **A** chord in measure 1.

- Measure 6 On the **E** chord, we are using the root on beats **1** & **3**, as for the **A** chord in measure 2.

- Measure 7 On the **A** chord, we are using the root (A) on beat **1** and the 5th (E) on beat **3**, as in measure 1. As a variation, here we are not repeating the root in the left hand on beat **3** prior to a chord change (as we did in measures 2, 4 & 6) - the 5th of the chord (E) on beat **3**, voiceleads well into the next chord (**D**).

- Measure 8 Here we have a change of chord rhythm - 2 chords per measure. The root of the first chord (**D**) is on beat **1**, and the root of the 2nd chord (**E**) is on beat **3**.

Now we will look at some variations of this comping solution. One way to impart more 'forward motion' is to add some 8th-note pickups in the left hand part (as in **Figs. 16.3. - 16.9.**). Here now is the next version of this progression, using these left hand variations:-

Figure 16.17. Country comping solution b) for chord chart #1 (Fig. 16.14.)
(Cassette Tape Example 643 - 'Straight 8ths')
(Cassette Tape Example 644 - 'Swing 8ths')

(CONTD-->)

Constructing country patterns (contd)

Figure 16.17. (contd)

The right hand part above is the same as in **Fig. 16.16**. We can analyze the left hand patterns as follows:-

- Measure 1 On the **A** chord, we are using left hand pattern **#3** as in **Fig. 16.3.**, with the 8th-note pickup into the 5th of the chord on beat **3**.

- Measure 2 On the **A** chord, we are using left hand pattern **#4** as in **Fig. 16.4.**, with the 8th-note pickup into the root of the chord on beat **3**.

- Measure 3 On the **D** chord, we are using left hand pattern **#3** as in **Fig. 16.3.**, with the 8th-note pickup into the 5th of the chord on beat **3**.

- Measure 4 On the **D** chord, we are using left hand pattern **#4** as in **Fig. 16.4.**, with the 8th-note pickup into the root of the chord on beat **3**.

- Measure 5 On the **E** chord, we are using left hand pattern **#3** as in **Fig. 16.3.**, with the 8th-note pickup into the 5th of the chord on beat **3**.

- Measure 6 On the **E** chord, we are using left hand pattern **#4** as in **Fig. 16.4.**, with the 8th-note pickup into the root of the chord on beat **3**.

- Measure 7 On the **A** chord, we are using left hand pattern **#3** as in **Fig. 16.3.**, with the 8th-note pickup into the 5th of the chord on beat **3**.

- Measure 8 Here again on this 2-chord measure, the root of the 1st chord (**D**) is on beat **1**, with an 8th-note pickup into the root of the 2nd chord (**E**) on beat **3**.

Now we will look at another left hand variation, this time using 'walkups' - scalewise connecting tones between chord roots. These typically connect successive chords with roots a perfect 4th interval apart (ascending or descending). In this simple application of the 'walkup' idea, the right hand part remains unchanged - however later we will see more sophisticated 'walkup' devices using a correspondingly amended right hand part. Here now is the same comping pattern, amended to include left hand 'walkups':-

Constructing country patterns (contd)

Figure 16.18. Country comping solution c) for chord chart #1 (Fig. 16.14.)
(Cassette Tape Example 645 - 'Straight 8ths')
(Cassette Tape Example 646 - 'Swing 8ths')

The only differences between this version and the previous version shown in **Fig. 16.17**. are in measures 2, 6 & 7 in the left hand part where the 'walkups' are occurring. The left hand part for these measures can be analyzed as follows:-

Constructing country patterns (contd)

Analysis of Fig. 16.18.

- Measure 2 This is the last measure on the **A** chord, prior to the **D** chord occurring in measure 3. The roots of these two chords are a perfect 4th interval apart, ideal for a 'walkup' to be used. We use the tones in the major scale of the key signature (A major) to connect between the roots of these chords. In this case, connecting from A up to D within an A major scale would produce the notes A, B, C#, & D. Rhythmically these pitches are given quarter-note durations in measure 2, as follows:-

- the root of the chord (A) is typically played on beats **1** & **2**. Sometimes (as here) there is an octave interval between the chord roots played on beats **1** & **2** - to facilitate the register placement of the walkup line.
- the next connecting tone from the scale (in this case B) is played on beat **3**.
- the last connecting tone from the scale (in this case C#) is played on beat **4**, leading into the root of the next chord (D).

- Measure 6 This is the last measure on the **E** chord, prior to the **A** chord occurring in measure 7. Again the roots of these two chords are a perfect 4th interval apart. Using the A major scale to connect between the roots of these chords, produces the notes E, F#, G# and A. These tones are then used in a similar manner to the walkup occurring in measure 2.

- Measure 7 Again here we are moving from an **A** chord to a **D** chord, as described for measure 2.

Now we will look at some arpeggiated right-hand techniques available for building country patterns. This concept is sometimes used on the keyboard to simulate a 'bluegrass' guitar-picking style. The right hand arpeggio part uses an 8th-note rhythmic subdivision, and anticipation of downbeats (i.e. beat **3**) is common. As with the previous comping pattern and variations, it is desirable to start with a concept of how the right hand upper triad structures are to be voiceled, which then forms a basis for the accompaniment created. In this case we are still working from chord chart **#1** (**Fig. 16.14.**) and using the upper structure voiceleading as in **Fig. 16.15.** - review these as necessary. The left hand is using the half-note pattern first seen in **Fig. 16.16.**, in the following arpeggiated comping pattern:-

Figure 16.19. Country comping solution d) for chord chart #1 (Fig. 16.14.)
(Cassette Tape Example 647 - 'Straight 8ths')
(Cassette Tape Example 648 - 'Swing 8ths')

(contd-->)

Constructing country patterns (contd)

Figure 16.19. (contd)

Note that in each measure the basic **1-3-5** upper triad is arpeggiated, beginning on the '**& of 1**' and anticipating beat **3**. Also in each measure, the directional contour or 'shape' of the arpeggiated line is similar. There are many different solutions for this type of line (even using just the basic 1-3-5 tones of each chord), and of course you are encouraged to experiment! Again the last measure represents a variation in the pattern as there are two chords in this measure. We first saw the use of right hand arpeggios based on upper structure triads in **Chapter 11** - review **Figs. 11.22. & 11.23.** as necessary.

Also in **Chapter 11** we saw a right-hand device known as 'parallel intervals' - playing the two outer tones of a root position or inverted triad together, creating a 5th or 6th interval - see **Fig. 11.16.** and accompanying text. This is also a useful variation within an arpeggiated country pattern. In the following example, an interval coupling (either the **3-1**, **1-5** or **5-3** of the chord) is being used on beat **2**, within an arpeggiated pattern now ending with a quarter note on beat **4** (except for the last measure):-

Constructing country patterns (contd)

Figure 16.20. Country comping solution e) for chord chart #1 (Fig. 16.14.)
(Cassette Tape Example 649 - 'Straight 8ths')
(Cassette Tape Example 650 - 'Swing 8ths')

Again note the relationship between the patterns used here and the upper triads originally selected for voiceleading purposes on this progression, in **Fig. 16.15**. As in the previous example, the arpeggiated line has an anticipation of beat **3**.

Constructing country patterns (contd)

PRACTICE DIRECTIONS:-

- ***Practice the country left hand patterns as in Figs. 16.1. - 16.9.***
- ***Practice the basic two-handed country pattern and inversion variations as in Figs. 16.10. - 16.13.***
- ***Practice the various comping pattern solutions for chord chart #1, as in Figs. 16.16. - 16.20.***
- *For extra practice - work on transposing these patterns into different keys!*
- *Don't forget to practice all patterns in both straight and swing 8ths!*

Now we will take a closer look at the 'walkup' idea first shown in **Fig. 16.18**. In that example, the 'walkup' was occurring in the left hand part, without affecting the right hand part. However, for a more stylistic result we can alter the right hand part to complement the left hand 'walkup' (or 'walkdown'). The various stages in this process are now illustrated, beginning with a bass line linking two chords with roots a perfect 4th interval apart, as follows:-

Figure 16.21. Walkup example stage #1 - bass line only
(CASSETTE TAPE EXAMPLE 651)

This is similar to the bass walkups used in **Fig. 16.18.** - review as necessary. Next we will add a 'moving 10th' line above the bass part, in the right hand. (A 10th interval is an octave plus a 3rd). The 'moving 10th' line will always be a **diatonic 10th** above the bass part i.e. we will stay within the major scale implied by the chord:-

Figure 16.22. Walkup example stage #2 - adding 'moving 10th' line in right hand
(CASSETTE TAPE EXAMPLE 652)

Constructing country patterns (contd)

Technically we can observe that the 10th intervals used on the C & F chords (i.e. on the first 2 beats of the first measure, and in the second measure) are major 10th intervals i.e. an octave plus a major 3rd, whereas the 10th intervals used on the walkup in between the chords (i.e. on the 3rd & 4th beats of the first measure) are minor 10th intervals i.e. an octave plus a minor 3rd.

The next stage is to add a 'drone' note above the moving 10th line in the right hand. A 'drone' is a note repeated against other moving lines or harmonies. In country music, the most typical 'drone' notes are the root or 5th of the chord (with sometimes the 3rd or 7th being used). In a normal walkup situation, the root of the first chord (in this case C) is used as the 'drone', as follows:-

Figure 16.23. Walkup example stage #3 - adding a 'drone' note in the right hand
(Cassette Tape Example 653)

The next stage is to add some 8th-note rhythmic subdivisions. When discussing our first basic country pattern in **Fig. 16.10.**, we found that doubling the top note of the upper structure an octave below on the upbeats was a useful approach (as in **Fig. 16.11.**). We can use a similar concept on the above example, this time doubling the drone note an octave below on the upbeats in the right hand (and using an 8th note rest at the start of the first measure, as in the previous examples), creating a rhythmic pattern as follows:-

Figure 16.24. Walkup example stage #4 - creating a rhythmic pattern using 8th notes
(Cassette Tape Example 654 - 'Straight 8ths')
(Cassette Tape Example 655 - 'Swing 8ths')

We can now go through the same process to illustrate a 'walkdown', again typically occurring between chords with roots a perfect 4th interval apart, this time a descending 4th interval. Again we can begin with the bass line as follows:-

Constructing country patterns (contd)

Figure 16.25. Walkdown example stage #1 - bass line only
(Cassette Tape Example 656)

F C

We now add a diatonic moving 10th line in the right hand (a reverse of **Fig. 16.22.**):-

Figure 16.26. Walkdown example stage #2 - adding 'moving 10th' line in right hand
(Cassette Tape Example 657)

Next we add the drone note in the right hand. In a typical walkdown situation, the drone note is the 5th of the first chord, which becomes the root of the second chord (as opposed to the walkup in **Fig. 16.23.**, where the drone was the root of the first chord and became the 5th of the second chord). This example is a reverse of **Fig. 16.23.**:-

Figure 16.27. Walkdown example stage #3 - adding a 'drone' note in the right hand
(Cassette Tape Example 658)

Again the final stage is to double the drone note creating an 8th-note subdivision, reversing **Fig. 16.24.** as follows:-

Constructing country patterns (contd)

Figure 16.28. Walkdown example stage #4 - creating a rhythmic pattern using 8th notes

(CASSETTE TAPE EXAMPLE 659 - 'STRAIGHT 8THS')
(CASSETTE TAPE EXAMPLE 660 - 'SWING 8THS')

Note that the walkup is typically used to connect chords moving in a circle-of-5ths sequence (as in the 'C to F' progression in **Figs. 16.21. - 16.24.**) and that the walkdown is typically used to connect chords moving in a circle-of-4ths sequence (as in the 'F to C' progression in **Figs. 16.25. - 16.28.**). I have devised some exercises taking the walkup pattern around the complete circle-of-fifths, and the walkdown pattern around the complete circle-of-4ths - playing them will familiarize you with these concepts in all keys:-

Figure 16.29. Walkup pattern around the circle-of-5ths

(CASSETTE TAPE EXAMPLE 661 - 'STRAIGHT 8THS')
(CASSETTE TAPE EXAMPLE 662 - 'SWING 8THS')

(CONTD-->)

Constructing country patterns

Figure 16.29. (contd)

Note that in this walkup pattern, that the drone note used on beats **2**, **3** & **4** of the measure is the root of the chord currently in force - which then becomes the 5th of the next chord on beat **1** of the following measure. Now the reverse exercise, taking the walkdown pattern around the complete circle-of-4ths:-

Figure 16.30. Walkdown pattern around the circle-of-4ths

(Cassette Tape Example 663 - 'Straight 8ths')
(Cassette Tape Example 664 - 'Swing 8ths')

(contd-->)

Constructing country patterns (contd)

Figure 16.30. (contd)

Note that in this walkdown pattern, that the drone note used on beats **2**, **3** & **4** of the measure is now the 5th of the chord currently in force - which then becomes the root of the next chord on beat **1** of the following measure. Now we will see how to apply these two-handed walkup/walkdown ideas in a chord progression. Here is another simple chord chart using the **1**, **4** & **5** chords in the key of A major:-

Figure 16.31. Chord chart example #2

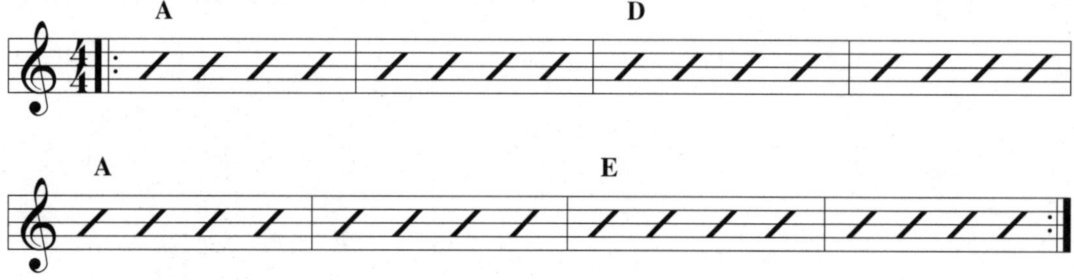

We will now interpret this chord chart in a similar manner to **Fig. 16.16.**, but with the addition of the two-handed walkup/walkdown devices:-

Constructing country patterns (contd)

Figure 16.32. Country comping solution for chord chart #2 (Fig. 16.31.)
(Cassette Tape Example 665 - 'Straight 8ths')
(Cassette Tape Example 666 - 'Swing 8ths')

Note the walkup/walkdown devices in the above example - up from the **A** chord to the **D** chord in measures 2-3, down from the **D** chord to the **A** chord in measures 4-5, down from the **A** chord to the **E** chord in measures 6-7, and up from the **E** chord to the **A** chord from measure 8, assuming a repeat back to the first measure. (Refer to **Figs. 16.24.**, **16.28.**, **16.29.** & **16.30.** as necessary).

Constructing country patterns (contd)

PRACTICE DIRECTIONS:-

- ***Practice the walkup/walkdown creation process examples as in Figs. 16.21. - 16.28.***
- ***Practice the walkup pattern around the circle-of-5ths as in Fig. 16.29.***
- ***Practice the walkdown pattern around the circle-of-4ths as in Fig. 16.30.***
- ***Practice the comping solution for chord chart #2 (with walkups & walkdowns) as in Fig. 16.32., and work on transposing this to other keys.***

Again don't forget to practice all patterns in straight and swing 8ths!

We will now look at various embellishments possible using pentatonic scales (see **Figs. 1.52. - 1.66.**). These devices are used extensively in country and country-rock styles. We will first see how to combine a drone (a repeated or sustained note) with a device known as a 'hammer', within a pentatonic scale framework. The 'hammer' occurs when an adjacent scalewise step (normally a major 2nd interval, ascending or descending) is played against a repeated or sustained note (the 'drone'). The following example reviews the C pentatonic scale, and shows the hammer/drone combinations available within the scale:-

Figure 16.33. C pentatonic scale with hammer/drone combinations

(CASSETTE TAPE EXAMPLE 667)

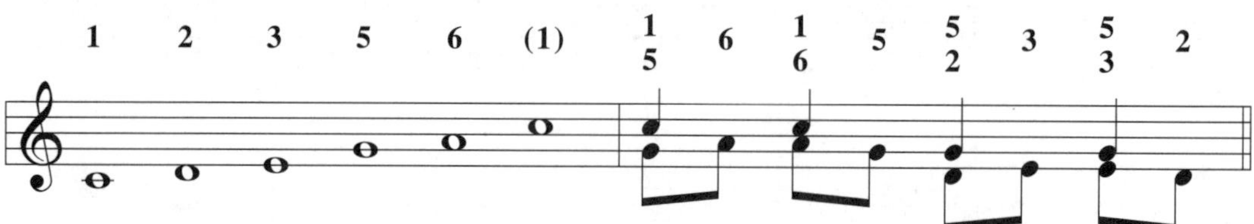

In the first measure above, the C pentatonic scale is reviewed - the numbers above the staff correspond to the scale degrees of a C major scale - we saw in **Fig. 1.52.** that the pentatonic scale can be derived by removing the 4th & 7th degrees from the corresponding major scale. In the second measure, the upward stems are the drone notes (either the '**1**' or '**5**' of the scale) and the downward stems are the 'hammers'. These movements can be summarized as follows:-

- movement (up or down) between the 5th & 6th scale degrees (in this case G & A) with the 1st degree above as a drone (in this case C)
- movement (up or down) between the 2nd & 3rd scale degrees (in this case D & E) with the 5th degree above as a drone (in this case G).

Constructing country patterns (contd)

From an interval standpoint, the devices in the second measure of **Fig. 16.33.** are alternating between perfect 4th (i.e. G up to C, D up to G) and minor 3rd (i.e. A up to C, E up to G) intervals. Rhythmically these hammers can be notated in various ways, and in any case are often interpreted without strict adherence to the written rhythm. Here is a two-measure phrase using hammers and drones within a C pentatonic scale, notated different ways as follows:-

Figure 16.34. C pentatonic phrase using hammers & drones (8th notes)
(Cassette Tape Example 668)

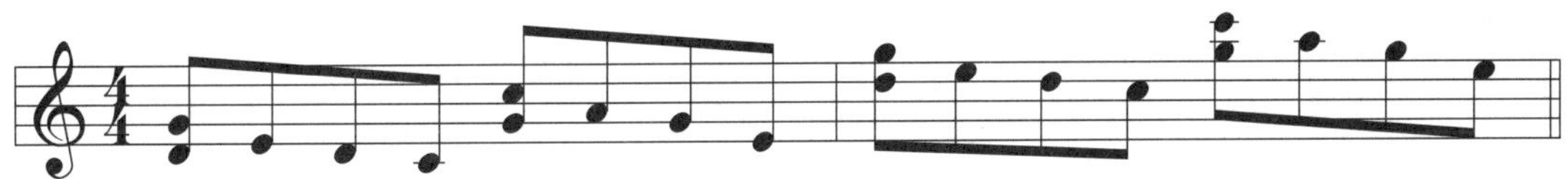

Figure 16.35. C pentatonic phrase using hammers & drones (16th-dotted 8th notes)
(Cassette Tape Example 669)

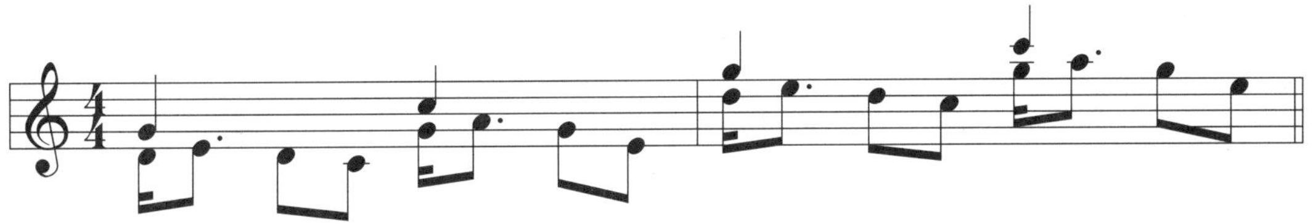

Figure 16.36. C pentatonic phrase using hammers & drones (grace notes)
(Cassette Tape Example 670)

These examples can be summarized as follows:-

- in **Fig. 16.34.**, everything is written as 8th notes and there is only one system (i.e. not two 'parallel' systems as in **Fig. 16.35.**) on the staff. However, in actual interpretation the drone notes (G & C in this case) may well last for a whole beat, or even two beats in some cases i.e. continuing to sound while the lower 'hammer' tones are being played. Also the first 8th note of each 'pair' may well be interpreted 'short' i.e. as a 16th note or grace note as in the subsequent examples.
- in **Fig. 16.35.**, the hammers are now written as '16th-dotted 8th' pairs, on beats **1** & **3**. Again in this situation the 16th note may well be interpreted 'short' i.e. more like a grace note (as in the last example).
- in **Fig. 16.36.**, the first note of each hammer is now written as a grace note. Interpreting the hammers this way can create a more 'immediate' and 'punchy' result.

As you can see, there are a number of different notation and interpretation possibilities and you are encouraged to experiment. I think it is very useful to be able to play these hammer/drone phrases in all keys, which the following exercise gives you the opportunity to do! As you can see it is notated in 8th notes (like **Fig. 16.34.** above), however you should feel free to vary the rhythmic interpretation (as in **Figs. 16.35.** & **16.36.**):-

Constructing country patterns (contd)

Figure 16.37. Pentatonic phrase exercise using hammers & drones, around the circle-of-5ths
(Cassette Tape Example 671)

Now we will consider how we can apply this type of pentatonic scale phrase over different chords. A good rule-of-thumb is that if a major triad will work as an upper structure on a given chord, then the corresponding pentatonic scale can be used as a source of embellishments over that chord. (The concept of upper structure triads has been used extensively in the preceding styles chapters). On the following page are some specific examples:-

Constructing country patterns (contd)

- A C major triad can be considered as a **1-3-5** upper structure of a **C major** chord (as first seen in **Fig. 5.1.**), therefore the C pentatonic scale can be used as a source of embellishments over this chord. With respect to the overall C major chord, the C pentatonic scale represents the root, 9th, 3rd, 5th and 6th (13th) of the chord. Another way to conceptualize this is to say that we can 'build a pentatonic scale from the **root** of a major chord'.
- A C major triad can be considered as a **b3-5-b7** upper structure of a **Ami** or **Ami7** chord (as first seen in **Fig. 5.6.**), therefore the C pentatonic scale can be used as a source of embellishments over this chord. With respect to the overall A minor chord, the C pentatonic scale represents the b3rd, 4th(11th), 5th, b7th and root of the chord. Another way to conceptualize this is to say that we can 'build a pentatonic scale from the **b3rd** of a minor chord'.
- A C major triad can be considered as a **5-7-9** upper structure of an **F**, **Fma7** or **Fma9** chord (as first seen in **Fig. 5.4.**), therefore the C pentatonic scale can be used as a source of embellishments over this chord. With respect to the overall F major chord, the C pentatonic scale represents the 5th, 6th(13th), 7th, 9th & 3rd of the chord. Another way to conceptualize this is to say that we can 'build a pentatonic scale from the **5th** of a major chord'.
- A C major triad can be considered as a **b7-9-11** upper structure of a **Dmi**, **Dmi7/9/11**, **D7/9sus** or **D11** chord (as first seen in **Fig. 5.2.**), therefore the C pentatonic scale can be used as a source of embellishments over this chord. With respect to the overall D minor or suspended chord, the C pentatonic scale represents the b7th, root, 9th, 4th(11th) & 5th of the chord. Another way to conceptualize this is to say that we can 'build a pentatonic scale from the **b7th** of a minor or suspended chord'.
- A C major triad can be considered as a **9-#11-13** upper structure of a **Bb** or **Bbma7/9/#11/13** chord (as first seen in **Fig. 5.7.**), therefore the C pentatonic scale can be used as a source of embellishments over this chord (however the #11th should be used with care). With respect to the overall Bb major chord, the C pentatonic scale represents the 9th, 3rd, #11th, 6th(13th) & 7th of the chord. Another way to conceptualize this is to say that we can 'build a pentatonic scale from the **9th** of a major chord'.

Here is an example of the original C pentatonic phrase in **Fig. 16.34.** being used over all of the above chords, as outlined above:-

Figure 16.38. C pentatonic phrase with hammers & drones, used over different chords
(Cassette Tape Example 672)

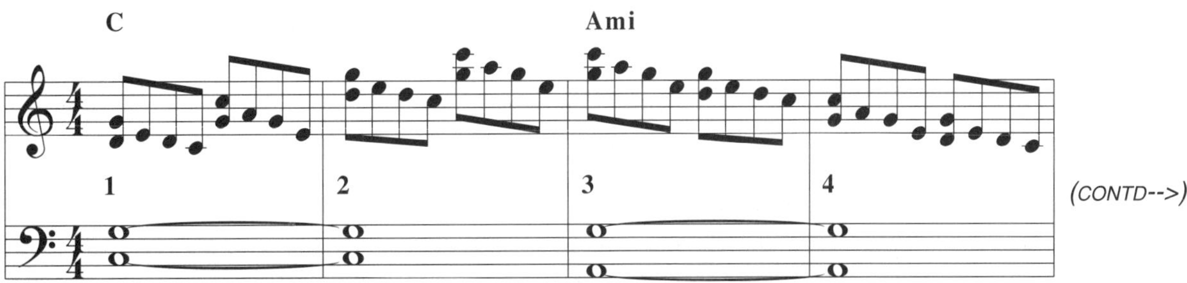

(CONTD-->)

For further information on using pentatonic scales over different chords, please refer to Chapter 9 of our Contemporary Music Theory Level 2 book (see page ix in this book).

Constructing country patterns (contd)

Figure 16.38. (contd)

As we progress through the above chords, you can hear that the vertical impressions become more sophisticated. This is due to the increasing number of higher extensions/tension tones in the C pentatonic scale, with respect to each successive chord. This type of pentatonic 'superimposition' is typical of artists such as Bruce Hornsby for example. In the above exercise, the usage of the C pentatonic scale can be summarized as follows:-

- Measures 1-2	The C pentatonic scale has been built from the **root** of the **C** chord.
- Measures 3-4	The C pentatonic scale has been built from the **b3rd** of the **Ami** chord.
- Measures 5-6	The C pentatonic scale has been built from the **5th** of the **F** chord.
- Measures 7-8	The C pentatonic scale has been built from the **b7th** of the **Dmi** chord.
- Measures 9-10	The C pentatonic scale has been built from the **9th** of the **Bb** chord.
- Measures 11-12	As for measures 1-2.

I have constructed a final pentatonic exercise which combines the ideas in **Fig. 16.37.** (pentatonic scale phrase around the circle-of-5ths) with **Fig. 16.38.** above (using the pentatonic scale over different chords). In the following example, the pattern in **Fig. 16.37.** has now been placed over various chord roots - each pentatonic scale is now built from either the root, 3rd, 5th, 7th or 9th of a chord. (This means there were five choices of chord for each pentatonic scale - feel free to vary the exercise by experimenting with the different chord choices for each scale!). The chord symbols indicate which pentatonic scale is being used, and which root is being placed below - as explained in the text prior to **Fig. 16.38.**, this will create various 'composite' chord relationships overall:-

Constructing country patterns (contd)

Figure 16.39. Pentatonic phrase exercise using hammers and drones, around the circle-of-5ths, using different chord roots for each scale (CASSETTE TAPE EXAMPLE 673)

(CONTD-->)

Constructing country patterns (contd)

Figure 16.39. (contd)

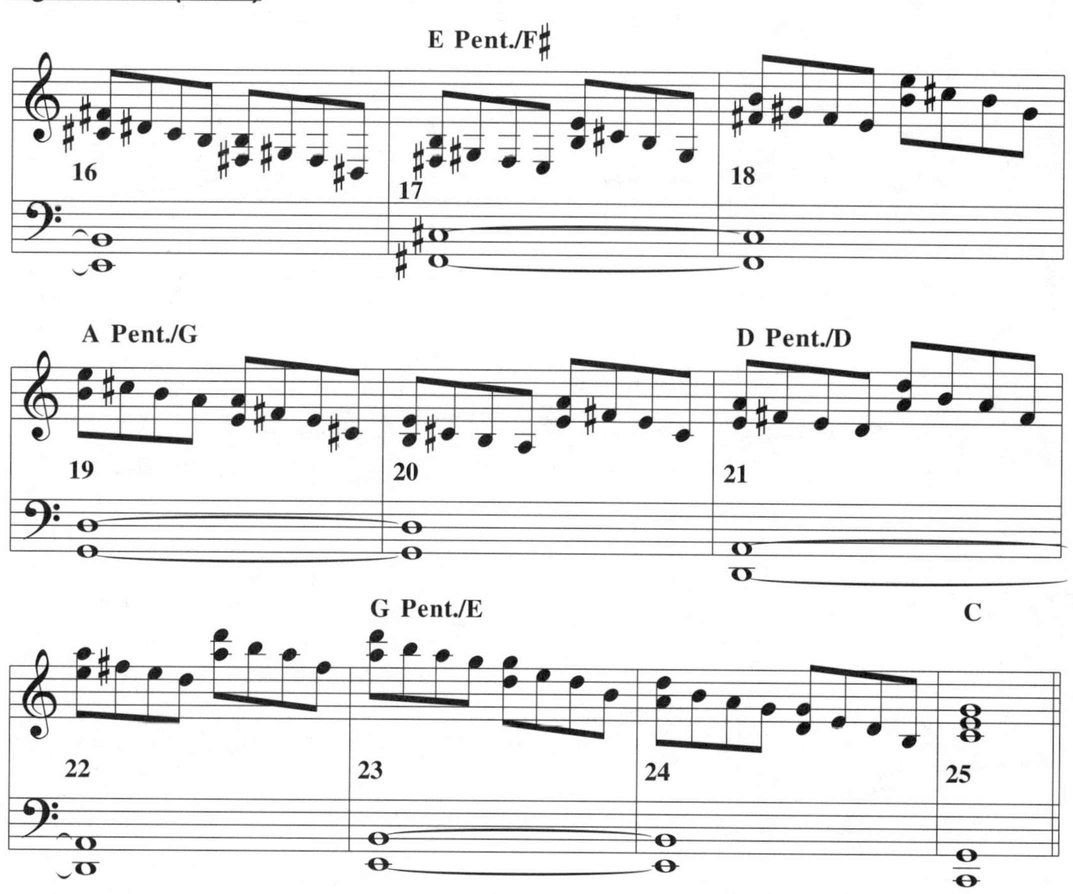

The pentatonic scale usage in the above example can be summarized as follows:-

- Measures 1-2	The **C** pentatonic scale has been built from the **root** of a **C** chord.
- Measures 3-4	The **F** pentatonic scale has been built from the **b3rd** of a **Dmi** chord.
- Measures 5-6	The **Bb** pentatonic scale has been built from the **5th** of an **Eb** chord.
- Measures 7-8	The **Eb** pentatonic scale has been built from the **b7th** of an **Fmi** or **Fsus** chord.
- Measures 9-10	The **Ab** pentatonic scale has been built from the **9th** of a **Gb** chord.
- Measures 11-12	The **Db** pentatonic scale has been built from the **root** of a **Db** chord.
- Measures 13-14	The **Gb** pentatonic scale has been built from the **b3rd** of an **Ebmi** chord.
- Measures 15-16	The **B** pentatonic scale has been built from the **5th** of an **E** chord.
- Measures 17-18	The **E** pentatonic scale has been built from the **b7th** of an **F#mi** or **F#sus** chord.
- Measures 19-20	The **A** pentatonic scale has been built from the **9th** of a **G** chord.
- Measures 21-22	The **D** pentatonic scale has been built from the **root** of a **D** chord.
- Measures 23-24	The **G** pentatonic scale has been built from the **b3rd** of an **Emi** chord.

Again, bear in mind that upper chord extensions will be added to these major or minor chords by 'super-imposing' pentatonic scales on top - these extensions are summarized in the text prior to **Fig. 16.38**.

Constructing country patterns (contd)

PRACTICE DIRECTIONS:-

- ***Practice the C pentatonic hammer & drone phrases as in Figs. 16.33. - 16.36.***
- ***Practice the pentatonic phrase exercise in all pentatonic scales around the circle-of-5ths as in Fig. 16.37.***
- ***Practice the C pentatonic phrase over the different chord roots, as in Fig. 16.38.***
- ***Practice the pentatonic phrase exercise in all pentatonic scales around the circle-of-5ths over the different chord roots, as in Fig. 16.39.***

Now we will see how to combine these 'hammers & drones' with the previous walkup ideas, in order to create an accompaniment pattern. Here is another basic country progression, this time in the key of C:-

Figure 16.40. Chord chart example #3

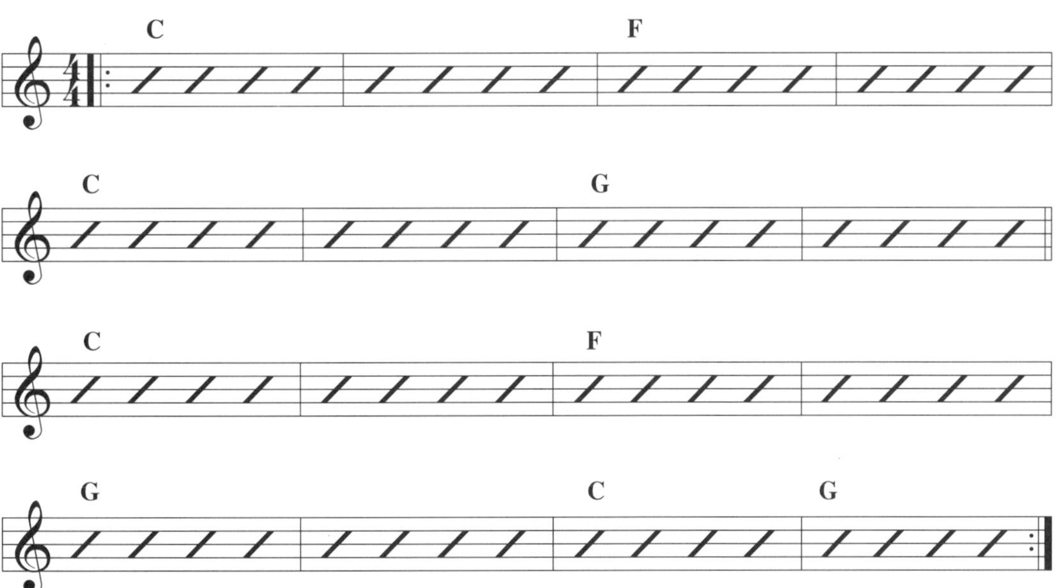

We will now interpret this chart, using 'hammer & drone' embellishments from the pentatonic scale **built from the root of each major chord** (the simplest and safest option in more basic styles), as follows:-

Constructing country patterns (contd)

Figure 16.41. Country comping solution a) for chord chart #3 (Fig. 16.40.)
(CASSETTE TAPE EXAMPLE 674 - 'STRAIGHT 8THS')
(CASSETTE TAPE EXAMPLE 675 - 'SWING 8THS')

Note that we have used a combination of hammers, drones and walkups in the above example. The hammers have been written as 16th notes - as discussed, the first 16th of each 'pair' might typically be played shorter i.e. more like a grace note. The above example can be analyzed as follows:-

Constructing country patterns (contd)

- Measures 1-2 On the **C** chord we are using 'hammer & drone' embellishments from the **C pentatonic** scale in the right hand. The drone note is the 5th of the chord (G), and the hammer is occurring between the 9th (D) and the 3rd (E), as first seen in **Fig. 16.33**. The 9th is also resolving to the root of the chord at the end of the measure. The left hand is using half-note patterns - 'root-5th' in measure 1 (as in **Fig. 16.1.**) and 'root-root' in measure 2 (as in **Fig. 16.2.**).

- Measures 3-4 On the **F** chord we are using 'hammer & drone' embellishments from the **F pentatonic** scale in the right hand. The drone note is the root of the chord (F), and the hammer is occurring between the 5th (C) and the 6th (D). The 3rd of the chord (A) is also being used in the pattern. The left hand is again using half-note patterns - 'root-5th' in measure 3 (as in **Fig. 16.1.**) and 'root-root' in measure 4 (as in **Fig. 16.2.**).

- Measures 5-6 As for measures 1-2.

- Measure 7 On the **G** chord we are using 'hammer & drone' embellishments from the **G pentatonic** scale in the right hand. The drone note is the 5th of the chord (D), and the hammer is occurring between the 9th (A) and the 3rd (B). The 9th is also resolving to the root of the chord at the end of the measure. The left hand is again using a 'root-5th' half-note pattern (as in **Fig. 16.1.**).

- Measure 8 Here we have a walkup (using quarter notes) from the **G** chord to the **C** chord (see **Fig. 16.23**. and accompanying text).

- Measure 9-12 As for measures 1-4.

- Measure 13 On the **G** chord we are again using 'hammer & drone' embellishments from the **G pentatonic** scale in the right hand. This time the drone note is the root of the chord (G), and the hammer is occurring between the 5th (D) and the 6th (E). The 3rd of the chord is also used at the end of the measure. The left hand is again using a 'root-5th' half-note pattern (as in **Fig. 16.1.**).

- Measure 14 As for measure 8.

- Measure 15 The embellishments at the beginning of this measure are the same as for measure 1. The figure during beat **4** can be found in both the **C** & **G** pentatonic scales, as is functioning as an anticipation of the next chord. With respect to the following **G** chord, during beat **4** the drone note is the root of the chord (G), and the hammer is occurring between the 5th (D) and the 6th (E). The left hand is using a 'root-root' half-note pattern (as in **Fig. 16.2.**).

- Measure 16 As for measure 8 (with right hand anticipating first beat, as discussed above).

Now we will look at another approach to comping over this progression, again using pentatonic scales and walkups. This approach involves arpeggiating the pentatonic scale tones in the right hand, emulating a 'guitar picking' or 'bluegrass' style. Now instead of limiting ourselves to just the root, 3rd & 5th of the chord (as we did in the arpeggiated example in **Fig. 16.19.**), we will now use all of the tones of the pentatonic scale built from **the root of the chord** (i.e., including the 6th and 9th of the chord in the arpeggiated pattern - review the first measure of **Fig. 16.33.** as necessary). We could even use this idea to construct patterns using pentatonic scales built from other parts of the chord i.e. from the 3rd, 5th, 7th or 9th as shown in **Figs. 16.38.** & **16.39.** - although this would be less common in 'traditional' bluegrass idioms. Here now is the second comping version of this progression, using this 'arpeggiated pentatonic scale' concept:-

Constructing country patterns (contd)

Figure 16.42. Country comping solution b) for chord chart #3 (Fig. 16.40.)
(CASSETTE TAPE EXAMPLE 676 - 'STRAIGHT 8THS')
(CASSETTE TAPE EXAMPLE 677 - 'SWING 8THS')

Notice that in the right hand, beat **1** of every even-numbered measure is anticipated by an 8th-note (landing on the '**& of 4**' of the previous odd-numbered measure). This type of anticipation is very typical in this arpeggiated country comping style. We will analyze each measure using pentatonic 'scale degree numbers' as in **Fig. 16.33.** - these will equate to the different chord tones/extensions, as each pentatonic scale has been built from the root of a (major) chord:-

Constructing country patterns (contd)

Analysis of Fig. 16.42.

- Measures 1-2 On the **C** chord, the right hand part is derived from the **C pentatonic** scale. From left to right in measure 1, the **C** pentatonic scale degrees used are **1**, **2**, **3**, **1**, **5**, **1** & **6** (see **Fig. 16.33.**). In measure 2 the scale degrees are **6** (tied), **1**, **5** & **1**. The 7th of the chord (B) is also used as a passing tone on beat **4** of the 2nd measure. The left hand is playing the root and 5th of the chord in measure 1, and the root and 3rd in measure 2 (using half notes).

- Measures 3-4 On the **F** chord, the right hand part is derived from the **F pentatonic** scale (see **Fig. 1.53.**). From left to right in measure 3, the **F** pentatonic scale degrees used are **3**, **5**, **6**, **3**, **1**, **3** & **2**. In measure 4 the scale degrees are **2** (tied), **3**, **1**, **5** & **6**. The left hand is playing the root and 5th of the chord in measure 3, and the root on beat **1** of measure 4, followed by the passing tones A & B (as quarter notes) leading back to the note C in measure 5. These bass notes on beats **3** & **4** of measure 4 create a minor 10th interval below the notes C & D in the right hand - a small 'walkup'-style embellishment.

- Measure 5-6 Similar to measures 1-2 in the use of the **C pentatonic** scale over the **C** chord. Measure 6 has a walkdown phrase (over beats **3** & **4**) similar to the walkup in measure 4 - this time the intervals of B up to D, and A up to C, create descending minor 10th intervals.

- Measure 7 On the **G** chord, the right hand part is derived from the **G pentatonic** scale (see **Fig. 1.60**). From left to right in measure 7, the **G** pentatonic scale degrees used are **3**, **5**, **6**, **3**, **2**, **3** & **1**. The left hand is again playing a root-&-5th pattern using half notes.

- Measure 8 Here we have a walkup (with moving 10th line and drone note, using quarter notes) from the **G** chord up to the **C** chord in measure 9 (see **Fig. 16.23.** and accompanying text).

- Measures 9-10 As for measures 1-2.

- Measures 11-12 As for measures 3-4, except that the bass notes on beats **3** & **4** of measure 12 are now E & F, scalewise connections into the following **G** chord in measure 13.

- Measures 13-14 As for measures 7-8.

- Measure 15 Similar to measure 1 in the use of the **C pentatonic** scale over the **C** chord, except for using the C pentatonic scale degrees **6** & **5** during beat **4**. The left hand is again using the connecting tones E & F on beats **3** & **4** to lead into the following **G** chord - as was done between measures 12 & 13.

- Measure 16 A walkup from the **G** chord to the **C** chord, in a similar manner to measures 8 & 14.

Now we will look at another chord chart, this time to be interpreted in a swing 8ths style only (i.e. not straight 8ths). We saw in **Chapter 2** that eighth-note rhythms can be played in either 'straight 8ths' or 'swing 8ths', and both approaches have been available on the comping examples so far in this chapter. Playing in a 'swing 8ths' style effectively means **using the 1st & 3rd events of each implied 8th-note triplet** (see **Figs. 2.30.**, **2.31.** & accompanying text if you need to review this). However, in country styles we sometimes want to use all three events within an 8th-note triplet (requiring a triplet sign in 4/4 time - see **Fig. 2.32.**). As soon as we see this usage of the 8th-note triplet in the music, we know that the 'swing 8ths' style is required, and that the 'straight 8ths' interpretation will not work. Here now is the next chord chart, to be interpreted in a 'swing 8ths' manner (including 8th-note triplets with all of the subdivisions used):-

Constructing country patterns (contd)

Figure 16.43. Chord chart example #4

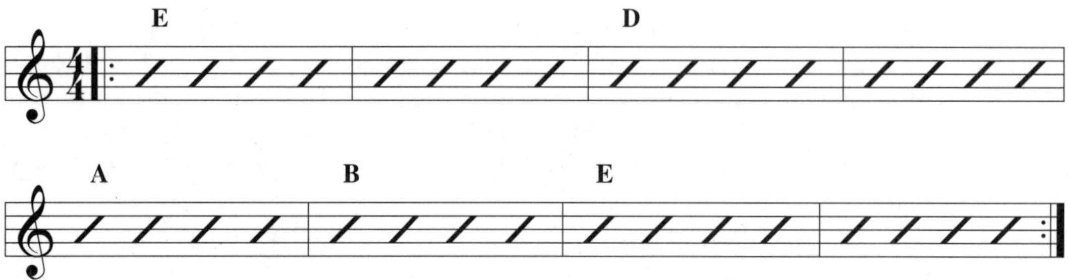

This chord chart is now interpreted as follows:-

Figure 16.44. Country comping solution for chord chart #4 (Fig. 16.43.)
(Cassette Tape Example 678 - 'Swing 8ths')

(Note the 'swing 8ths' symbol at the top of the chart - see **Fig. 2.30.**)

(CONTD-->)

Constructing country patterns (contd)

Figure 16.44. (contd)

The above example can be analyzed as follows:-

- ***Measure 1*** On the **E** chord, in the right hand we begin with the original comping pattern (see measures 5-6 of **Fig. 16.16.**) during beats **1** & **2**, using a basic **1-3-5** upper structure (an E triad) in root position, with the top note (B) doubled an octave lower on the upbeats. During beat **4** we have a 'hammer & drone' embellishment using the **E pentatonic** scale (see **Fig. 1.63.**). Here the drone note is the 5th of the chord (B), and the hammer is occurring between the 9th (F#) and 3rd (G#) - review **Figs. 16.33.** & **16.37.** as necessary. Again the first 16th note (F#) may typically be played shorter i.e. more like a grace note. The final **F#-B** interval coupling on the '**& of 4**' is also anticipating beat **1** of the following measure. The left hand is using a root-&-5th pattern with an 8th note pickup into beat **3**, as in **Fig. 16.3**.
- ***Measure 2*** Continuing on the **E** chord, this measure is similar to measure 1, except that the **E pentatonic** 'hammer & drone' phrase during beat **4** is now using all 3 subdivisions of the final eighth note triplet. In this situation, the first 16th note (F#) is even more likely to be interpreted as a grace note. The left hand is now adding a connecting tone (C#) on beat **4**, leading to the D chord in the following measure.
- ***Measure 3*** On the **D** chord, in the right hand we are again using the original comping pattern during beats **1** & **2**, using a basic **1-3-5** upper structure (a D triad) in root position, with the top note (A) doubled an octave lower on the upbeats. During beat **4** we have a 'hammer & drone' embellishment using the **D pentatonic** scale (see **Fig. 1.61.**). Here the drone note is the 5th of the chord (A), and the hammer is occurring between the 9th (E) and 3rd (F#). The final **E-A** interval coupling on the '**& of 4**' is also anticipating beat **1** of the following measure. The left hand is again using a root-&-5th pattern with an 8th note pickup into beat **3**, as in **Fig. 16.3**. (This whole measure is the same as measure 1, but transposed down a whole-step).
- ***Measure 4*** In this measure we have a walkdown occurring between the **D** chord and the following **A** chord - these chord roots are a perfect 4th interval apart (see **Figs. 16.28.** & **16.30.**).
- ***Measure 5*** On the **A** chord, in the right hand we are using a **3-1** (3rd & root) interval coupling on beat **1** - the logical finish to the previous walkdown figure (again review **Figs. 16.28.** & **16.30.** as necessary). The root (A) is also used on the '**& of 1**' to continue the subdivision pattern. During beats **2** & **4** we are using 'hammer & drone' embellishments using the **A pentatonic** scale (see **Fig. 1.62.**). During beat **2**, the drone note is the root of the chord (A), and the hammer is occurring between the 5th (E) and 6th (F#). These tones are also

Constructing country patterns (contd)

Analysis of Fig. 16.44. contd.

- Measure 5 contd plural to the D pentatonic scale (used in measure 3). The **E-A** coupling on the '**& of 2**' is anticipating beat **3**. The 'hammer & drone' figure in beat **4** is using all of the 8th-note triplet subdivisions. This could be considered as a 'double drone', as both the 5th (E) and the root (A) are held throughout beat **4**. (This could also be considered as a **9-5-1** double 4th structure - see **Fig. 10.7.**). The hammer is occurring between the 9th (B) and the 3rd (C#), with the root (A) being played on the final 8th-note of the triplet. The left hand is again using a root-&-5th pattern based on **Fig. 16.3.**, with the addition of the root on beat **4** to lead into the next chord.

- Measure 6 In this measure we have a walkup occurring between the **B** chord and the following **E** chord. This is a rhythmic variation of the walkups in **Figs. 16.24.** & **16.29.**, with the interval coupling now oocupying the first & 3rd events of the 8th-note triplets during beats **2**, **3** & **4**. (This rhythm would in fact be a useful practice variation for **Fig. 16.29.**).

- Measure 7 On the **E** chord, in the right hand we are using 'hammer & drone' embellishments from the **E pentatonic** scale. During beats **1** & **2**, the drone note is the 5th of the chord (B) and the hammer is occurring between the 9th (F#) and the 3rd (G#). During beats **3** & **4**, the drone note is the root of the chord (E) and the hammer is occurring between the 5th (B) and the 6th (C#), anticipating beat **1** of the following measure. The left hand is again using a root-&-5th pattern based on **Fig. 16.3.**

- Measure 8 This is a variation on the previous walkup idea, and implies a **B7** chord (leading back to the first **E** chord) during beats **2** - **4**. After playing the note E on beat **1**, the left hand is ascending chromatically from the 5th (B) to the 7th (D#) of an E major scale, using 8th-note subdivisions from beat **2** to beat **4**. The right hand part is still based around the E triad during beat **1**, but starting on beat **2** we are using a series of descending 6th intervals, beginning with the root (B) of the implied B7 on top, and ending with the 5th (F#). This has a chromatic and colorful effect in conjuction with the ascending bass line.

Now we will look at another chord chart to be interpreted using 8th-note triplets, this time using some larger chord forms (i.e. 7th & 9th chords). We saw in Figure **16.38.** that a pentatonic scale could be built from the **root**, **5th** or **9th** of a major chord, and from the **b3rd** or **b7th** of a minor chord (review text prior to **Fig. 16.38.** as necessary). When interpreting the next chart, we will use 'hammer & drone' figures from pentatonic scales built from some of these chord tones. For example:-

- on an **Ami7** chord we can derive embellishments from a C pentatonic scale - C is the **b3rd** of the **Ami7**.
- on an **Fma9** chord we can derive embellishments from a C pentatonic scale - C is the **5th** of the **Fma9**.
- etc.

As we saw earlier, this is a good way to interpret larger chord forms (7th, 9th chords etc.) as the pentatonic scale generates upper extensions on the chord. This can also be used even for basic major & minor triad chord forms on a chart, if it is desired to add upper extensions for a more sophisticated sound. Here is the next chord chart, to be interpreted as described above:-

Constructing country patterns (contd)

Figure 16.45. Chord chart example #5

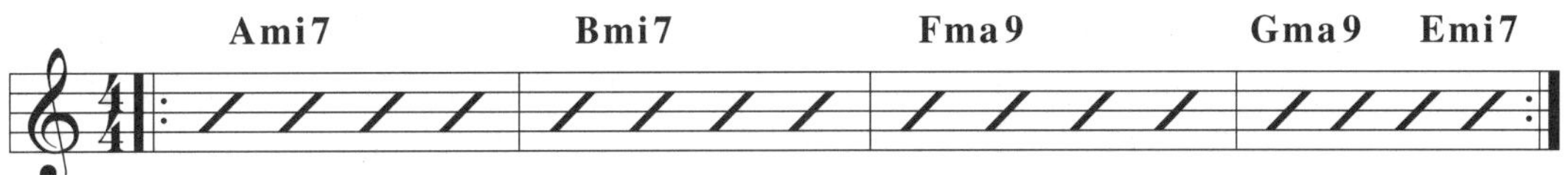

This (more sophisticated) chord progression is now interpreted as follows:-

Figure 16.46. Country comping solution for chord chart #5 (Fig. 16.45.)
(Cassette Tape Example 679 - 'Swing 8ths')

The above example can be analyzed as follows:-

- Measure 1

On the **Ami7** chord, in the right hand we are using 'hammer & drone' embellishments derived from a **C pentatonic** scale (C is the **b3rd** of Ami7). Analyzing the C pentatonic scale degrees, the **5** is the drone, and the hammer is occurring between **2** & **3**, with the **1** also being used (see **Fig. 16.33.**). With repect to the overall **Ami7**, the drone note is the 7th of the chord (G), and the hammer is occuring between the 11th (D) and 5th (E), with the 3rd (C) also being used. During beat **4**, the first 2 events of the 8th-note triplet are a continuation of the 'hammer & drone' figure, and the last subdivision is used for a 2nd inversion D triad. This is a **b3-5-b7** upper structure triad on the following **Bmi7** chord (see **Fig. 5.6.**) and functions as an anticipation of that chord. The left hand is playing the root on beats **1** & **3**, with the 5th of the chord as an 8th-note pickup into beat **3** (see **Fig. 16.4.**).

Constructing country patterns (contd)

Analysis of Fig. 16.46. contd.

- Measure 2 On the **Bmi7** chord, in the right hand the **b3-5-b7** upper structure (a 2nd inversion D triad) is held over from the anticipation at the end of measure 1. The first 2 events within the final 8th-note triplet represent a '**9 to 1**' resolution within this 2nd inversion D triad upper structure (see **Fig. 8.14.**), with the 5th of the triad (7th of the overall **Bmi7** chord) also being used on the final subdivision. The left hand is using a root-&-5th pattern as in **Fig. 16.3.**

- Measure 3 The notes in the right hand are the same as for measure 1, but now with respect to the overall **Fma9** chord we are using different chord tones/extensions. We are again using the 'hammer & drone' embellishments from the C pentatonic scale, which this time is built from the 5th of the **Fma9** chord. With respect to this chord, the drone note is now the 9th (G), and the hammer is occurring between the 6th (D) and 7th (E), with the 5th (C) also being used. Again this figure is continued into the 8th-note triplet on beat **4**, with the final D triad this time representing a **5-7-9** upper structure anticipating the following **Gma9** chord. The left hand pattern is similar to measure 1 (see **Fig. 16.4.**).

- Measure 4 On the **Gma9** chord, in the right hand the **5-7-9** upper structure (a 2nd inversion D triad) is held over from the anticipation at the end of measure 3. (We first built this voicing in **Fig. 5.4.**). At the end of beat **2** leading into beat **3**, we have a 'hammer & drone' figure derived from a **G pentatonic** scale (see **Fig. 1.60.**). This scale can be considered as being built from the root of the **Gma9** chord, and from the 3rd of the **Emi7** chord. During the last half of beat **2**, the drone note is the 5th of the **Gma9** chord (D), and the hammer is occurring between the 9th (A) and the 3rd (B). This then moves back to the **A-D** 4th coupling on beat **3**, which by then has become the 11th & 7th on the **Emi7** chord. During beat **4**, another 'hammer & drone' figure (using an 8th-note triplet) has been derived from a **D pentatonic** scale (see Fig. **1.61.**). Here the scale has been built from the 7th of the chord (D is the **7th** of **Emi7**). Analyzing the D pentatonic scale degrees, the **5** is the drone, and the hammer is occurring between **2** & **3**, with the **1** also being used. With respect to the overall **Emi7**, the drone note is the 11th of the chord (A), and the hammer is occurring between the root (E) and 9th (F#), with the 7th (D) also being used. The left hand is playing the roots of the chords on beats **1** & **3**, with the connecting tone F# used as a pickup into beat **3**.

We will next look at a chord chart to be interpreted in a modern country-rock 'Bruce Hornsby'-type style. In addition to building pentatonic scales from various chord tones as in the previous example, we will now add other right-hand devices such as 4th clusters (first seen in **Figs. 13.9. - 13.18.**) and 4-part-over-root chords (see **Chapter 7**), as well as left hand arpeggios (first seen in **Figs. 11.11. & 11.12.**). This will be done using a medium-to-fast tempo and a 'straight 8ths' rhythmic subdivision. On the following page is the next chord chart, to be interpreted as described above:-

Constructing country patterns (contd)

Figure 16.47. Chord chart example #6

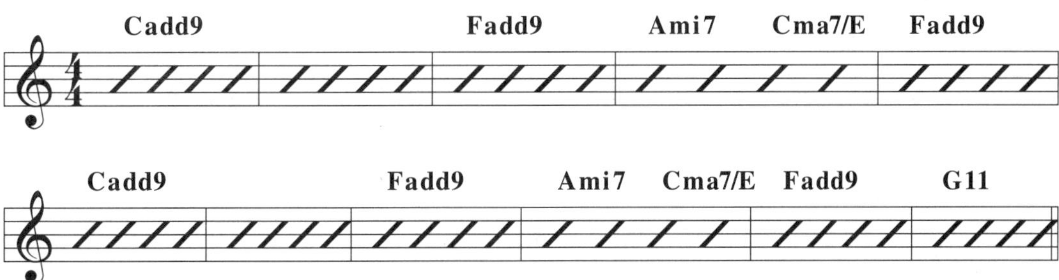

Note that the phrase lengths above are also non-traditional - a five-measure phrase followed by a six-measure phrase. We will interpret this chart as follows:-

Figure 16.48. Country comping/melody solution for chord chart #6 (Fig. 16.47.)
(Cassette Tape Example 680 - 'Straight 8ths')

(CONTD-->)

Constructing country patterns (contd)

Figure 16.48. (contd)

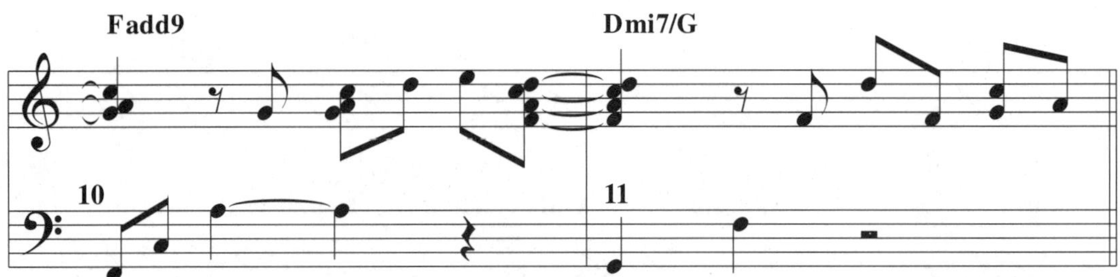

I used the phrase "comping/melody solution" in the previous example heading, as this more elaborate interpretation has a melodic quality, and could function as a stand-alone melody or instrumental section. Notice that in this case the hammers have been notated as grace notes (see **Fig. 16.36.**). We can analyze the above example as follows:-

- Measure 1

On the **Cadd9** chord, in the right hand we are using 'hammer & drone' embellishments derived from a **C pentatonic** scale. During beats **2** & **3** the drone note is the 5th of the chord (G), with the hammer occurring between the 9th (D) and 3rd (E). During beat **4**, the drone note is the root (C), with the hammer occurring between the 5th (G) and 6th (A). The final **G-C** 4th coupling is also anticipating beat **1** of the next measure. The left hand is playing a **1-5-3** open triad arpeggio pattern (first seen in **Fig. 11.11.**), ending on beat **2**.

- Measure 2

Continuing on the **Cadd9** chord, we are now arpeggiating various tones from the C pentatonic scale over this chord in the right hand. From left to right the C pentatonic scale degree numbers are **5** & **1** (on the last 2 16ths of beat **2**), **5**, **5**, **2** & **1**. Another angle on this figure is that it is an arpeggiated **9-5-1** double 4th structure on the **Cadd9** chord (see **Fig. 10.7.**). The left hand pattern is a variation of measure 1, this time combining the root & 5th together on beat **1**.

- Measure 3

On the **Fadd9** chord, in the right hand the **G-A** coupling on beat **1** can be considered as an incomplete **9-3-5** 'whole-step-4th' cluster (see **Fig. 13.11.**), with the 5th of the chord on the '**& of 4**' of the previous measure, and the 9th & 3rd together on beat **1** (of measure 3). From beat **2** onwards, we are again using 'hammer & drone' embellishments derived from a **C pentatonic** scale (this scale is now built from the **5th** of the overall **Fadd9** chord). The drone during beats **2** & **3** is now the 9th of the chord (with the hammers between the 6th & 7th), and the drone during beat **4** is now the 5th of the chord (with the hammers between the 9th & 3rd). Again the final **G-C** 4th coupling is anticipating beat **1** of the next measure. The left hand is again using a **1-5-3** open triad arpeggio pattern, similar to measure 1.

- Measure 4

In the right hand the **C pentatonic** 'hammer & drone' figure is continuing over the **Ami7** chord (the C pentatonic scale is now built from the **b3rd** of the **Ami7** chord). During beats **3** & **4**, we are arpeggiating a **7-1-5** 'half-step-&-5th' structure (over the 3rd in the bass voice - see **Fig. 13.22.**) on the **Cma7/E** chord, ending with a **9-3-5** 'whole-step-4th' cluster (with respect to the following **Fadd9** chord - see **Fig. 13.11.**) on the '**& of 4**', anticipating beat **1** of the next measure. The left hand is playing the root & 5th of the **Ami7** chord during beats **1** & **2**, and the root of the **Cma7/E** chord on beat **3**.

Constructing country patterns (contd)

Analysis of Fig. 16.48. contd.

- Measure 5 On the **Fadd9** chord, in the right hand the **9-3-5** 'whole-step-4th' cluster is held over from the anticipation at the end of measure 4. In the last half of the measure the phrase is constructed from melodic 6th intervals (E up to C, D up to B etc.) from the major scale of the key signature (i.e. C major), ending with the connecting tone A into the next measure. The left hand is again using a **1-5-3** open triad arpeggio pattern.

- Measure 6 On the **Cadd9** chord, in the right hand we are using another **9-3-5** 'whole-step-4th' cluster on beat **1**. During the rest of the measure there is a similar 'hammer & drone' figure to measure 1, transposed up an octave.

- Measures 7-9 Similar to measures 2-4, with the right hand part transposed up an octave (and a simplified left hand part in measure 9).

- Measure 10 On the **Fadd9** chord, in the right hand the **9-3-5** 'whole-step-4th' cluster is held over from the anticipation at the end of measure 9, and is repeated on beat **3**. With respect to the following **Dmi7/G** chord, we are using an inverted **5-b7-9-11** upper structure (a 1st inversion Dmi7 shape - see **Fig. 7.4.**) on the '**& of 4**' anticipating beat **1** of the following measure. The left hand is again using a **1-5-3** open triad arpeggio pattern.

- Measure 11 On the **Dmi7/G** chord, the **5-b7-9-11** upper structure is held over from the anticipation at the end of measure 10. During beats **2** & **3** we are using melodic 6th intervals (similar to measure 5) and during beat **4** the figure is derived from an F (or C) pentatonic scale. The left hand is playing the root & 7th of the chord on beats **1** & **2**.

PRACTICE DIRECTIONS:-

- ***Practice the comping example using 'hammer & drone' figures as in Fig. 16.41.***
- ***Practice the comping example using the 'bluegrass' pentatonic scale arpeggios as in Fig. 16.42.***
- ***Practice the comping example using swing 8ths and triplet walkups as in Fig. 16.44.***
  (For extra practice - try these examples in different keys!)
- ***Practice the comping examples using larger chord forms and shape concepts as in Figs. 16.46. & 16.48.***
- ***Work on applying these concepts to tunes of your choice, and to the practice charts at the end of this chapter.***

CHAPTER SIXTEEN

Country melody

We will now turn our attention to the treatment of melodies in a contemporary country style. We will make use of the 'hammer & drone' concepts previously discussed, but this time as devices to support the melody. The stages involved in this process are described as follows:-

1) Placing a drone note above the melody

Country is one style in which a harmony or coupling note (in this case the 'drone') can be placed above the melody, instead of below as is typically the case in other styles. Normally the root or 5th of the chord (whichever is the nearest) is chosen as a drone note above the melody, although it is possible to use other chord tones (i.e. 3rds, 7ths) in some cases.

2) Embellishing the melody with hammers

The best places to do this are when the melody is moving in whole steps (against the added drone note above) - particularly when the interval between the melody and the drone alternates between a perfect 4th and a minor 3rd interval (review **Fig. 16.33.** as necessary).

3) Adding a rhythmic left hand pattern

Similar concept as for the previous patterns - see **Figs. 16.1. - 16.9.** and subsequent comping examples.

We will now examine this process in detail by taking an example through these various stages. We will start with a melody leadsheet as follows:-

Figure 16.49. Leadsheet (with melody) example
(Cassette Tape Example 681 - 'Straight 8ths' - melody only)
(Cassette Tape Example 682 - 'Swing 8ths' - melody only)

We will now add drone notes above the melody as follows:-

Country melody (contd)

Figure 16.50. Adding drone notes above melody on leadsheet example (Fig. 16.49.)
(Cassette Tape Example 683 - 'Straight 8ths')
(Cassette Tape Example 684 - 'Swing 8ths')

Generally the criteria for choosing the drone note above the melody are as follows:-

- the nearest chord tone (preferably the root or 5th) to the melody, which is still above the melody for the duration of the chord change (unless different drones are chosen at different points during the chord)
- a tone which will result in perfect 4th & minor 3rd intervals when combined with the melody
- a tone which voiceleads well from the previous measure and/or into the next measure.

With these comments in mind, the addition of drones to the above melody can be analyzed as follows:-

- Measure 1 On the **C** chord, the drone note added is C (the root of the chord). This results in perfect 4th intervals on beats **1** & **3**, and a minor 3rd on the '**& of 2**'. The melody and drone in this measure can all be derived from the **C pentatonic** scale.

- Measure 2 On the **F** chord, the drone note added is F (the root of the chord) except for the G on the '**& of 4**' which is an anticipation of the next chord. Adding the drone note F results in perfect 4th intervals on the '**& of 1**' and beats **2** & **3**, and minor 3rds on beats **1** & **4**. The melody and drone in this measure (except for the '**& of 4**') can all be derived from the **F pentatonic** scale.

- Measure 3 On the **G** chord, the drone note added is G (the root of the chord) starting with the anticipation on the '**& of 4**' of the previous measure. Adding the drone note G results in perfect 4th intervals on the '**& of 1**', beats **2** & **3**, and the '**& of 4**', and minor 3rds on beat **1** (anticipated) and beat **4**. The melody and drone in this measure can all be derived from the **G pentatonic** scale.

- Measure 4 On the **C** chord, the drone note added is C (the root of the chord). This results in a perfect 4th interval on the '**& of 1**', and a minor 3rd on beat **2**. The melody and drone in this measure can all be derived from the **C pentatonic** scale.

- Measure 5 On the **F** chord, the drone note added is C (the 5th of the chord). This results in perfect 4th intervals on beat **2** and the '**& of 3**', and a minor 3rd on the '**& of 2**'. The hollow-sounding perfect 5th intervals on beat **1** and the '**& of 4**' are also useful. The melody and drone in this measure can all be derived from the **F pentatonic** scale.

Country melody (contd)

Analysis of Fig. 16.50. contd.

- Measure 6 On the **Ami** chord, the drone note added is the **b3rd** of the chord (C). We choose the **b3rd** instead of the root or 5th in this instance beacause:-

- the **b3rd** (C) is the nearest chord tone above the melody
- the note C voiceleads well between the drones used in measures 5 & 7 (C & D respectively)
- the note C combines with the melody to create perfect 4th & minor 3rd intervals.

A minor 3rd interval is created on beat **2**, and a perfect 4th on the '**& of 2**'. The melody and drone in this measure can all be derived from the C pentatonic scale (which in turn is built from the **b3rd** of the **Ami** chord).

- Measure 7 On the **D** chord, the drone note added is the root of the chord (D). This again creates a minor 3rd interval on beat **2**, and a perfect 4th on the '**& of 2**'. The melody and drone in this measure can all be derived from the **D pentatonic** scale.

- Measure 8 On the **G** chord, the drone note added is the 5th of the chord (D). This results in perfect fourth intervals on beat **2** and the '**& of 3**', and a minor 3rd on the '**& of 2**'. The melody and drone in this measure can all be derived from the **G pentatonic** scale.

Now the next stage is to embellish the melody with hammers. As previously mentioned, we are looking for places where the melody moves by whole step, which in conjunction with the added drone creates alternating perfect 4th & minor 3rd intervals. Here is the previous melody with drones, now with hammers added:-

Figure 16.51. Adding hammers to melody (with drone notes) on leadsheet example (Fig. 16.49.)
(Cassette Tape Example 685 - 'Straight 8ths')
(Cassette Tape Example 686 - 'Swing 8ths')

Again the first 16th note of each hammer may typically be interpreted shorter rhythmically i.e. more like a grace note. We can analyze these added hammers as follows:-

Country melody (contd)

Analysis of Fig. 16.51.

- Measure 1 On the **C** chord, the hammer has been added on the '**& of 2**'. With respect to the implied **C pentatonic** scale, we are hammering between scale degrees **5** & **6** (with the **1** as the drone). Review **Fig. 16.33.** as necessary.

- Measure 2 On the **F** chord, hammers have been added on beats **1** & **4**, and additionally on the '**& of 4**' anticipating the following measure. With respect to the implied **F pentatonic** scale (and the implied **G pentatonic** scale on the '**& of 4**') we are again hammering between scale degrees **5** & **6**, with the **1** as the drone.

- Measure 3 On the **G** chord, the hammer has been added on beat **4** (in addition to the anticipation on the '**& of 4**' of the previous measure). With respect to the implied **G pentatonic** scale, we are again hammering between scale degrees **5** & **6**, with the **1** as the drone.

- Measure 4 Similar to measure 1, on the **C** chord.

- Measure 5 On the **F** chord, hammers have been added on the '**& of 2**' and on beat **4**. With respect to the implied **F pentatonic** scale, we are hammering between scale degrees **2** & **3**, with the **5** as the drone.

- Measure 6 On the **Ami** chord, a hammer has been added on beat **2**. With respect to the implied **C pentatonic** scale (buillt from the **b3rd** of the **Ami** chord), the hammer is occurring between scale degrees **5** & **6**, with the **1** as the drone.

- Measure 7 On the **D** chord, a hammer has again been added on beat **2**. With respect to the implied **D pentatonic** scale, the hammer is occurring between scale degrees **5** & **6**, with the **1** as the drone.

- Measure 8 On the **G** chord, hammers have been added on the '**& of 2**' and on the '**& of 3**'. With respect to the implied **G pentatonic** scale, we are hammering between scale degrees **2** & **3**, with the **1** as the drone.

The final stage in this melody treatment process is to add a suitable left hand pattern below the right hand. One of many possible solutions is presented below:-

Figure 16.52. Adding left hand part to 'hammered' melody, on leadsheet example (Fig. 16.49.)
(Cassette Tape Example 687 - 'Straight 8ths')
(Cassette Tape Example 688 - 'Swing 8ths')

(CONTD-->)

Country melody (contd)

Figure 16.52. (contd)

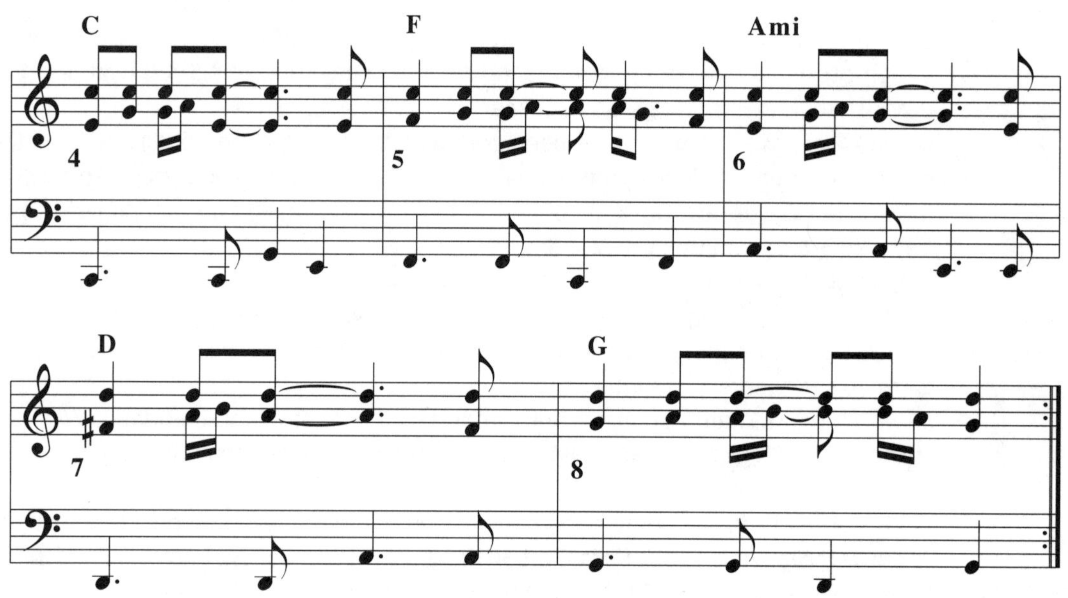

In the above example, the right hand part is the same as in **Fig. 16.51**. The left hand part can be analyzed as follows:-

- Measure 1	On the **C** chord, the left hand is using a root-&-5th pattern based on **Fig. 16.3.**, adding the 3rd of the chord (E) on beat **4** to lead into the root of the next chord (F).
- Measure 2	On the **F** chord, the left hand is again using a root-&-5th pattern based on **Fig. 16.3.**, now adding the root of the chord (F) on beat **4** to lead into the root of the next chord (G).
- Measure 3	As for measure 2, on the **G** chord.
- Measures 4-5	As for measures 1-2.
- Measure 6	On the **Ami** chord, the left hand is using a root-&-5th pattern as in **Fig. 16.7**.
- Measure 7	On the **D** chord, the left hand is again using a root-&-5th pattern as in **Fig. 16.7**.
- Measure 8	On the **G** chord, the left hand is again using a root-&-5th pattern based on **Fig. 16.3.** (as in measure 3).

This left hand pattern (with frequent use of dotted quarter-eighth pairs) gives good definition and forward motion to the arrangement. Again you are encouraged to experiment with different left hand variations.

PRACTICE DIRECTIONS:-

- *Practice the country melody treatment examples as in Figs. 16.49. - 16.52.*
- *Work on applying these melody treatment concepts to tunes of your choice, and to the practice leadsheets at the end of this chapter.*

Country practice examples

Figure 16.53. Practice leadsheet #1 (chords only - for 'comping' practice)

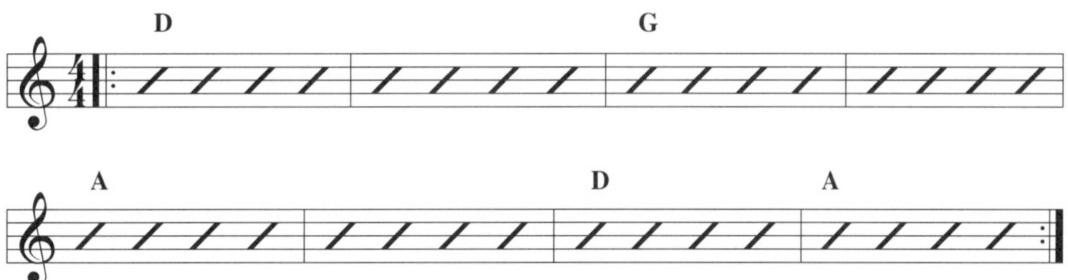

Figure 16.54. Practice leadsheet #2 (chords only - for 'comping' practice)

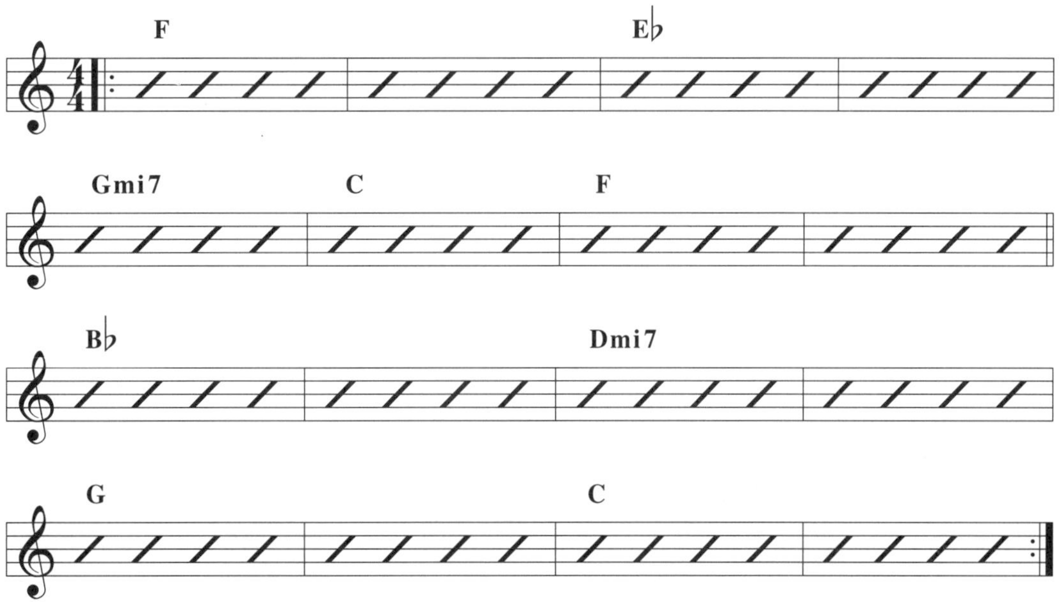

Country practice examples (contd)

Figure 16.55. Practice leadsheet #3 (chords only - for 'comping' practice)

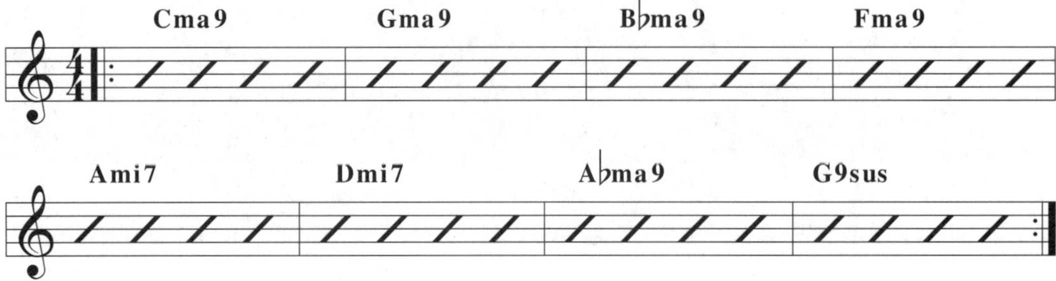

Figure 16.56. Practice leadsheet #4 (melody & chords, for melody treatment or 'comping' practice)

Figure 16.57. Practice leadsheet #5 (melody & chords, for melody treatment or 'comping' practice)

Slow Gospel

Introduction

The final style to be studied in this book is contemporary gospel. Many people think of this style in the context of the church and religious music. Here perhaps it would be productive to draw a distinction between the 'authentic' gospel music (using harmonic and rhythmic concepts analyzed in this chapter) and a lot of today's 'Contemporary Christian' music which essentially seems to use some of the musical idioms already covered (ballads, pop/rock, R'n'B/funk) along with religious lyrics. Keyboard players who draw heavily on gospel stylings include Leon Russell, Dr. John and especially Richard Tee (for a great example of the influence of gospel on contemporary pop music, check out Richard Tee's keyboard work on the Peter Gabriel tune "Don't Give Up").

Gospel styles typically feature an eighth-note triplet subdivision at slow-to-medium tempos (dealt with in this chapter under the heading '**Slow Gospel**'), and a 'straight' 16th note subdivision at faster tempos (dealt with in the next chapter under the heading '**Fast Gospel**'). Within both of these rhythmic frameworks, the harmonic devices used in gospel styles are typically as follows:-

- Triad or four-part 'upper structure' chord shapes (see **Chapters 5** & **7**). Generally there is an emphasis on 'dominant' harmony i.e. using/implying dominant 7th & 9th chords (see **Figs. 1.77.**, **1.88.** & **14.15.**), except where basic triad forms are used.
- Triads built from Mixolydian modes, especially in second inversion (first seen in **Fig. 15.69.**).
- 'Hammer' and 'drone' devices (first seen in **Fig. 16.33.**).
- Specific gospel devices as presented in this chapter:-
    - Chromatic walkups
    - 'Backcycling' (successive circle-of-fourths triad movement)
    - Unison and octave runs (built from pentatonic or mixolydian scales)
    - 'Dominant approach' chords.

In this chapter we will examine both accompaniment ('comping') and melody treatments using slow gospel rhythmic settings. In slow gospel, the left hand has a supportive role, playing roots (often in octaves and using the full range of the keyboard) or basic chord tones, or interval couplings such as root-5th or root-b7th. By contrast, in fast gospel (as we will see in **Chapter 18**) the left hand provides the rhythmic drive, typically using eighth-note octave patterns (sometimes interspersed with 16th notes). The role of the left hand in providing chromatic walkups in octaves, is also fundamental to both slow and fast gospel styles.

Slow gospel rhythmic concepts

Slow gospel is typically played using an eighth-note triplet subdivision, and with three beats or 'pulses' per measure. There are two ways in which this can be notated:-

- In **3/4** time, using triplet signs for the eighth-note triplets as required.
- In **9/8** time, which 'exposes' all of the (triplet) subdivisions - no triplet signs are needed.

[I'D LIKE TO GRATEFULLY ACKNOWLEDGE THE INFLUENCE OF MY FORMER FACULTY COLLEAGUE AT THE GROVE SCHOOL OF MUSIC, ROBBIE GILLMAN, IN THE WRITING OF THESE CHAPTERS ON GOSPEL STYLES - MH]

Slow gospel rhythmic concepts (contd)

Either way there are nine rhythmic subdivisions available in each measure. In the following examples, these subdivisions are notated using both **3/4** and **9/8** time signatures:-

Figure 17.1. Slow gospel rhythmic subdivisions in 3/4 time
(CASSETTE TAPE EXAMPLE 689)

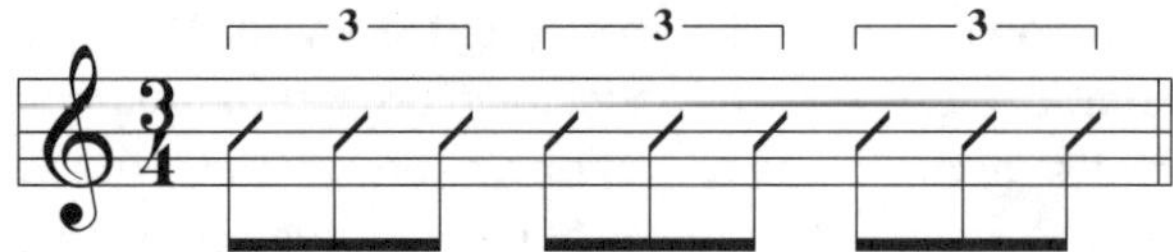

Figure 17.2. Slow gospel rhythmic subdivisions in 9/8 time
(CASSETTE TAPE EXAMPLE 689)

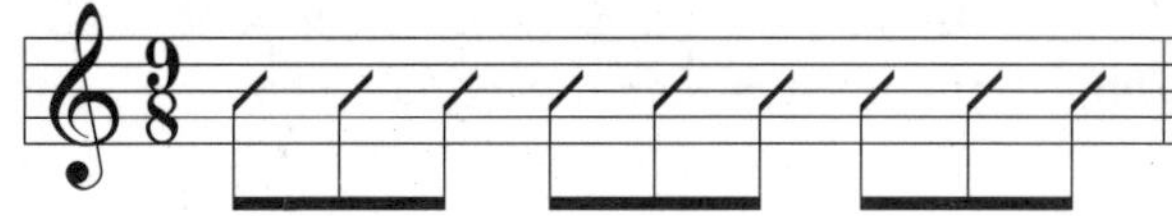

The notation differences here between **3/4** and **9/8** time are similar to those between **4/4** and **12/8** time as explained in **Figs. 2.32. - 2.33.** and accompanying text - review as necessary. In **9/8** time we will not need any triplet signs - however we are still feeling three beats or 'pulses' per measure, each of which would require a dotted quarter note - some people find this rather 'unfriendly' to read! At least in **3/4** time the beat is shown as a quarter note - but the downside is the need to write triplets each time the beat is subdivided (which is quite frequently in slow gospel). Here now is a 'shuffle' rhythm frequently used in this style (using the first and third events of each triplet subdivision), again notated in both **3/4** & **9/8** time:-

Figure 17.3. Slow gospel 'shuffle' rhythm in 3/4 time
(CASSETTE TAPE EXAMPLE 690)

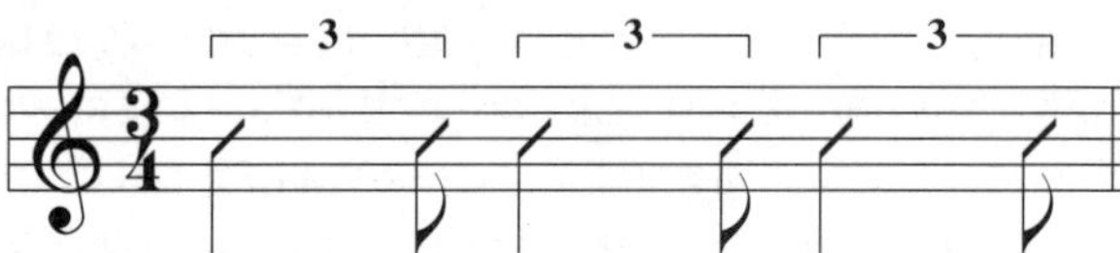

Figure 17.4. Slow gospel 'shuffle' rhythm in 9/8 time
(CASSETTE TAPE EXAMPLE 690)

In the remainder of this 'slow gospel' text, the patterns are notated in **3/4** time (using eighth-note triplet signs as necessary), which reflects the notation of the majority of music I have seen in this style - however, bear in mind that the **9/8** time signature is a valid alternative. In any case the term "**9/8 feel**" is often used to describe the slow gospel rhythmic framework. Within the nine subdivisions possible within a measure, there are a great many permutations for left and right hand rhythms, which we will begin to explore in the patterns that follow.

Constructing slow gospel patterns

The first harmonic device to be considered is the construction of triads from the Mixolydian mode, an idea first presented in **Figs. 15.68. - 15.69**. This is very appropriate for gospel styles, as the Mixolydian mode is a basic scale source for dominant chords, a staple ingredient of gospel harmonies. All inversions of Mixolydian triads can be used, although second inversion is often preferred. The following examples show the (first and second inversion) triads available from a G Mixolydian mode, which could be used in the context of a G7 (dominant 7th) chord:-

Figure 17.5. 1st inversion triads available within a G Mixolydian mode
(Cassette Tape Example 691)

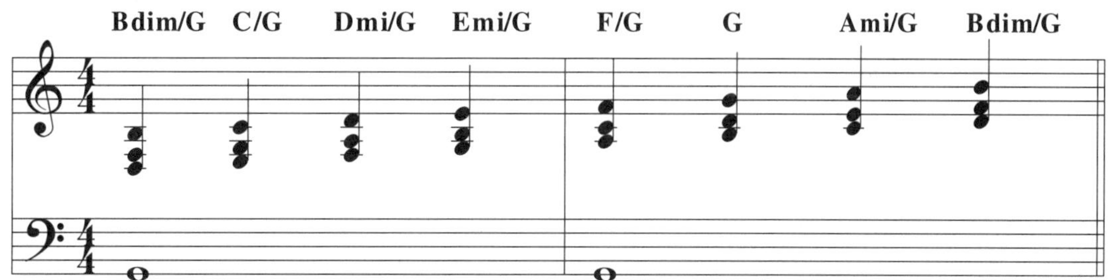

Figure 17.6. 2nd inversion triads available within a G Mixolydian mode
(Cassette Tape Example 692)

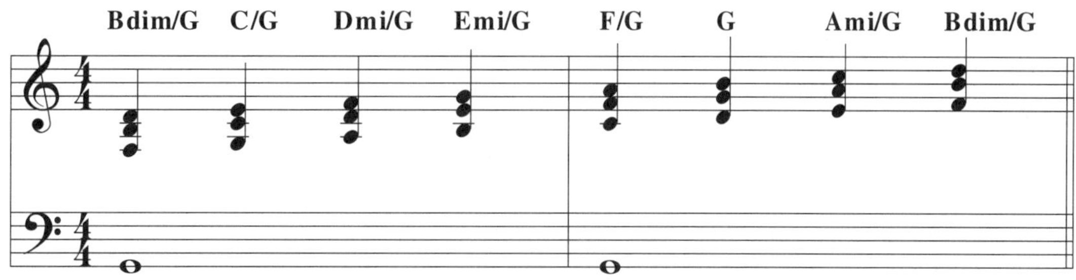

We will now make use of the above 2nd inversion G Mixolydian triads to construct our first pattern, on a **G7** chord:-

Figure 17.7. Slow gospel pattern #1 - Mixolydian triads
(Cassette Tape Example 693)

Constructing slow gospel patterns (contd)

In the previous example, rhythmically we are landing with both hands on beats **1** & **3** in the first measure, with an eighth note 'pickup' (on the last triplet subdivision of beat **3**) into the downbeat of the second measure. These are typical landing points in basic gospel patterns. Note the rest shown on the second triplet subdivision of beat **3** in the first measure, in both hands - implying a short duration for the chord on beat **3** - a useful stylistic effect. Harmonically we are using a second inversion B diminished triad (the first 'shape' shown in **Fig. 17.6.**) over the G in the bass on beat **1** of both measures, to create a **G7** chord overall (review **Fig. 1.77.** for dominant chord spelling as necessary). On the last triplet subdivision of beat **3** in the first measure, we are using a second inversion C triad (the second 'shape' shown in **Fig. 17.6.**), again over G in the bass. This movement back and forth between the B diminished and C major triads (over G in the bass voice) - two frequently used triads from the Mixolydian possibilities shown in **Fig. 17.6.** - is typical of gospel (and blues) stylings. Now we will see a variation on this pattern, adding left hand interval couplings as follows:-

Figure 17.8. Slow gospel pattern #2 - Mixolydian triads with left hand couplings
(Cassette Tape Example 694)

Now the left hand is playing the root and 5th of the chord on beats **1** & **3** of the first measure, and beat **1** of the second measure. On the last triplet subdivision of beat **3** in the first measure (under the C triad), the left hand is playing a root-6th interval (these notes G & E are also the outer tones of the inverted C triad in the right hand). The movement between the root-5th and root-6th intervals in the left hand gives effective support to the Mixolydian triad movements in the right hand. The above concepts can also be rhythmically varied as follows:-

Figure 17.9. Slow gospel pattern #3 - rhythmic variation on pattern #2 (Fig. 17.8.)
(Cassette Tape Example 695)

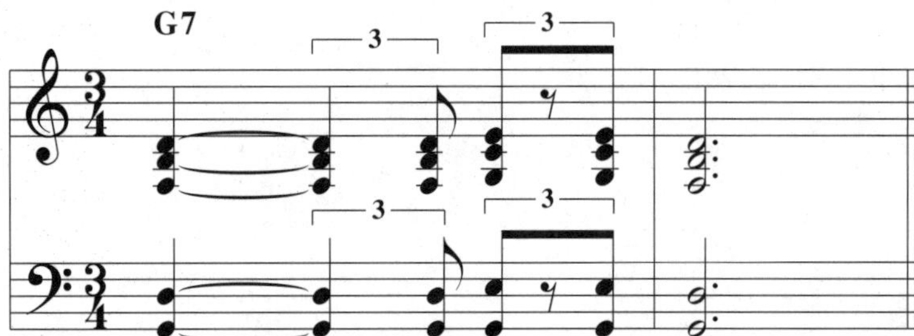

Now the upper B diminished triad (over the root-5th of the **G7** chord) is repeated on the last triplet subdivision of beat **2**, leading into the C triad (over the root-6th interval) on the first and third triplets within beat **3**. Now a harmonic variation on this latest rhythm, additionally using a D minor triad from the G Mixolydian scale, over a root-b7th interval in the left hand:-

Constructing slow gospel patterns (contd)

Figure 17.10. Slow gospel pattern #4 - harmonic variation on pattern #3 (Fig. 17.9.)
(Cassette Tape Example 696)

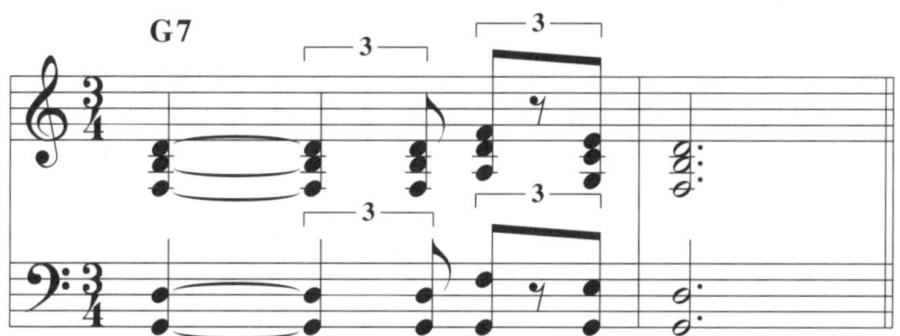

This is the same as **Fig. 17.9.**, except for the D minor triad in the right hand, and the G-F root-b7th coupling in the left hand, on beat **3** in the first measure. The (second inversion) D minor triad is again derived from the G Mixolydian mode (the third 'shape' shown in **Fig. 17.6.**). The root-b7th interval uses the same top note (F) as the upper D minor triad, and in general is a good choice in this register on dominant or mixolydian chord forms. The above pattern, using three important Mixolydian triads (B dimnished, C major and D minor over a **G7** chord) and left hand interval couplings (**5th**, **6th** & **b7th** intervals) is I think sufficiently important to be practiced and learnt in all 12 keys! Here is an example of how this pattern could modulate in a circle-of-fifths sequence through all the keys:-

Figure 17.11. Slow gospel Mixolydian triad pattern, through all 12 keys
(Cassette Tape Example 697)

(CONTD-->)

Constructing slow gospel patterns (contd)

Figure 17.11. (contd)

An important embellishment typically applied when using Mixolydian triads, is to add grace notes which are a half-step below the middle note of the (inverted) triad. This works well when the middle note is either the **5th**, **13th** (**6th**), **9th** or **3rd** with respect to the overall implied dominant chord. This sits 'under the hands' especially well when using a G Mixolydian mode, as in each case the grace note can be added by 'sliding off' a black note to an adjacent white note with the same finger. Here now are the grace notes applied within G Mixolydian triads:-

Constructing slow gospel patterns (contd)

Figure 17.12. 1st inversion triads available within a G Mixolydian mode, with grace notes
(Cassette Tape Example 698)

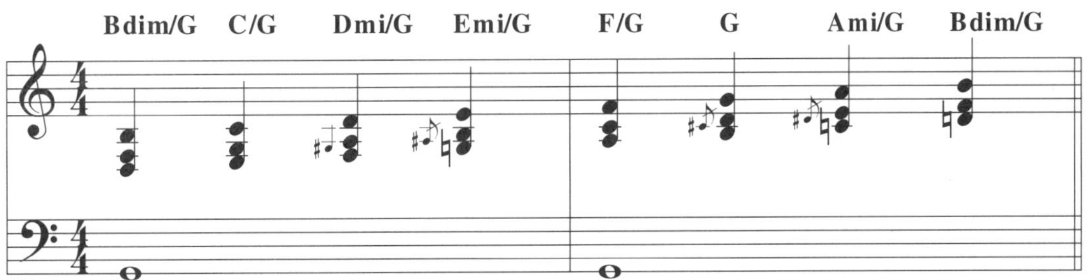

Figure 17.13. 2nd inversion triads available within a G Mixolydian mode, with grace notes
(Cassette Tape Example 699)

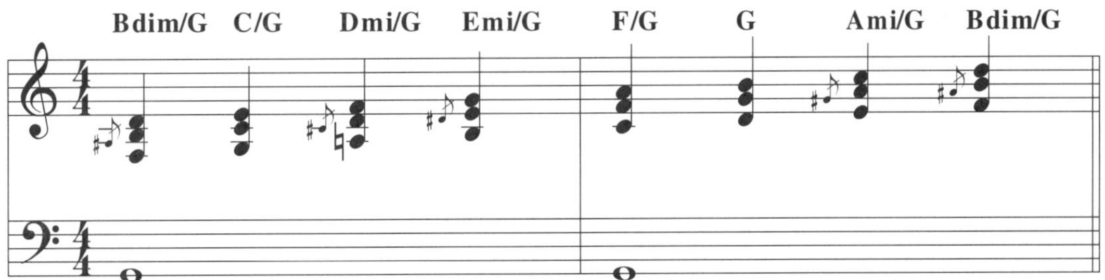

On the first inversion examples above (**Fig. 17.12.**), the grace notes are added as follows:-

- on the 3rd chord in the 1st measure, the G# is a grace note into A (the **9th** of the overall **G7** chord).
- on the 4th chord in the 1st measure, the A# is a grace note into B (the **3rd** of the overall **G7** chord).
- on the 2nd chord in the 2nd measure, the C# is a grace note into D (the **5th** of the overall **G7** chord).
- on the 3rd chord in the 2nd measure, the D# is a grace note into E (the **13th** of the overall **G7** chord).

On the second inversion examples above (**Fig. 17.13.**), the grace notes are added as follows:-

- on the 1st chord in the 1st measure, and the 4th chord in the 2nd measure, the A# is a grace note into B (the **3rd** of the overall **G7** chord).
- on the 3rd chord in the 1st measure, the C# is a grace note into D (the **5th** of the overall **G7** chord).
- on the 4th chord in the 1st measure, the D# is a grace note into E (the **13th** of the overall **G7** chord).
- on the 3rd chord in the 2nd measure, the G# is a grace note into A (the **9th** of the overall **G7** chord).

In each case the grace note is a half-step below the appropriate chord tone of the overall dominant chord, which in turn is the **middle note** of the upper Mixolydian triad. Now we will amend some of the earlier patterns to include grace notes. First we will take the pattern shown in **Fig. 17.8.** (pattern **#2**) and add grace notes as follows:-

Constructing slow gospel patterns (contd)

Figure 17.14. Slow gospel pattern #5 - adding grace notes to pattern #2 (Fig. 17.8.)
(CASSETTE TAPE EXAMPLE 700)

Notice that in both measures we have used the grace note A# (leading into the 3rd of the **G7** chord), as seen in the first 'shape' shown in **Fig. 17.13.** This has a very 'bluesy' and authentic effect. Now we will add grace notes to the pattern in **Fig. 17.10.** (pattern **#4**) as follows:-

Figure 17.15. Slow gospel pattern #6 - adding grace notes to pattern #4 (Fig. 17.10.)
(CASSETTE TAPE EXAMPLE 701)

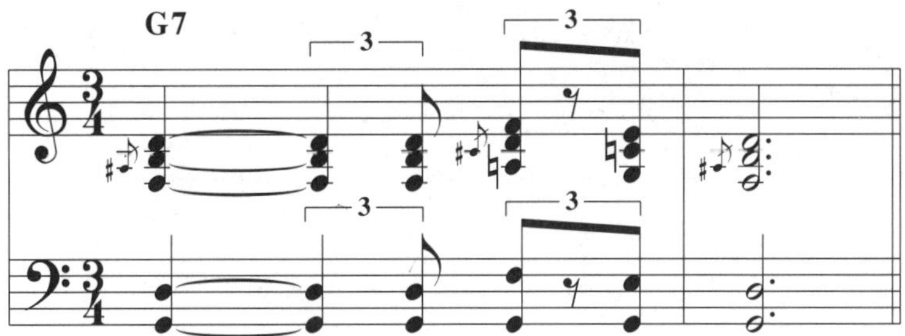

Now in addition to the grace note A# (again leading into the 3rd of the **G7** chord) we also have the C# just before beat **3** in the first measure (leading into the 5th of the **G7** chord), as seen in the third 'shape' shown in **Fig. 17.13.** Using the '**b3**' and '**b5**' of the dominant chord as grace notes, is extremely typical in this style. It would be a good idea for you to apply these grace notes to the original Mixolydian triad example around the circle-of-fifths as shown in **Fig. 17.11.** The following example adds the grace notes to this exercise, in the first two keys to get you started:-

Figure 17.16. Slow gospel Mixolydian triad pattern, with added grace notes
(CASSETTE TAPE EXAMPLE 702)

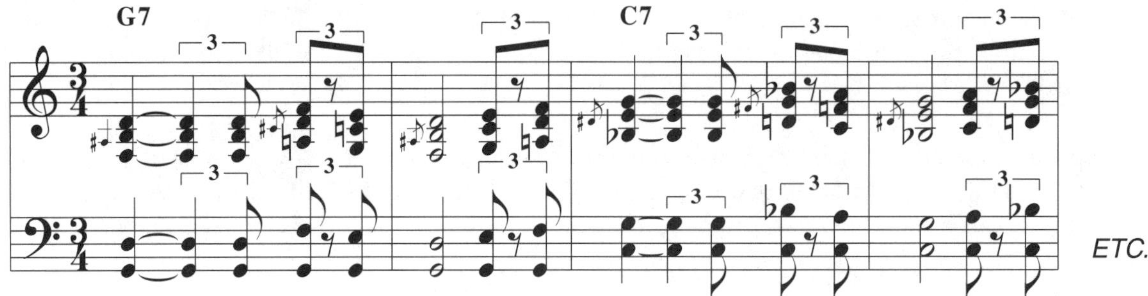

Constructing slow gospel patterns (contd)

Now we will deal with another frequently used gospel harmonic device known as '**backcycling**'. This involves triad progressions which 'jump' either one, two or three stages around the circle-of-fifths, and then work their way back sequentially using the circle-of-fourths (review our definitions of circle-of-fifths and circle-of-fourths at the end of **Chapter 1** as necessary). In this chapter I will use the terms **single**, **double** & **triple** backcycle to describe the various possibilities. A **single** backcycle would involve moving **one** stage around the circle-of-fifths, and then moving immediately back again around the circle-of-fourths, as in the following example (note names are major triad chord symbols):-

Start on:-	G
Jump **one** stage around circle-of-5ths, to:-	C
Move back around the circle-of-4ths, to:-	G
Resulting progression:-	**G - C - G**

A **double** backcycle would involve jumping **two** stages around the circle-of-fifths, and then moving sequentially back (one stage at a time) around the circle-of-fourths, as in the following example:-

Start on:-	**G**
Jump **two** stages around circle-of-5ths, to	**F**
Move sequentially back	
around the circle-of-4ths, first to:-	**C**
and then back to:-	**G**
Resulting progression:-	**G - F - C - G**

A **triple** backcycle would involve jumping **three** stages around the circle-of-fifths, and again moving sequentially back (one stage at a time) around the circle-of-fourths, as in the following example:-

Start on:-	**G**
Jump **three** stages around circle-of-5ths, to	**Bb**
Move sequentially back	
around the circle-of-4ths, first to:-	**F**
and then to:-	**C**
and then finally back to:-	**G**
Resulting progression:-	**G - Bb - F - C - G**

When the right hand is using these backcycling concepts the left hand is typically doing one of the following :-

1) Playing the roots corresponding to the upper triads. This may be done to harmonically embellish an existing progression, or it may be built in to the harmony of a tune from the outset. Indeed this harmonic device (major triad progressions moving around the circle-of-4ths) is often found in rock and pop styles.

2) Pedalling (staying on) the root of the original chord. In this context the 'backcycled' triads are passing shapes, with the left hand still defining the root of the chord as shown on the leadsheet.

3) Playing diatonic (within the key) or chromatic (ascending half-step) walkups against the triads, leading into the next chord change. This can result in some rather dissonant vertical sounds, which nonetheless work because of the 'linear' strength of the triads and the bass line used.

Constructing slow gospel patterns (contd)

Now we will look at some gospel pattern examples using backcycling. The next pattern uses a **single** backcycle over a **G7** chord, with the lowest voice staying on G throughout:-

Figure 17.17. Slow gospel pattern #7 - single backcycle (root staying on G)
(Cassette Tape Example 703)

In this example, the upper triad sequence **G - C - G** represents a **single** backcycle (the **C** triad occurs on beat **3**). Note that the left hand interval becomes a 6th (G-E) under the C triad, similar to pattern **#3** (**Fig. 17.9.**).

This type of single backcycle (over the root of the original chord) is safe to apply in most situations, and is routinely used in gospel styles. Now the same pattern, this time moving the lowest voice in a manner corresponding to the (backcycled) triads:-

Figure 17.18. Slow gospel pattern #8 - single backcycle (root moving G - C - G)
(Cassette Tape Example 704)

In this example, the left hand is now playing C during beat **3**, to correspond with the **C** triad in the right hand part required by the **single** backcycle.

Another way to look at this is to observe that both the left and right hands are now backcycling i.e. the left hand is playing the roots of the triads used in the right hand. Now we will look at a double backcycle, first with the lowest voice staying the same throughout (but with varying left hand intervals) as follows:-

Figure 17.19. Slow gospel pattern #9 - double backcycle (root staying on G)
(Cassette Tape Example 705)

In this example, the upper triad sequence **G - F - C - G** represents a **double** backcycle (the **F** triad lands on beat **3**, and the **C** triad last on the last subdivision of beat **3**). Note the various left hand intervals (5th, b7th, 6th), as in pattern **#4** (**Fig. 17.10.**).

Constructing slow gospel patterns (contd)

Now we will again amend the previous pattern to move the bass line corresponding to the upper triads:-

Figure 17.20. Slow gospel pattern #10 - double backcycle (root moving G - F - C - G)
(Cassette Tape Example 706)

In this example, the left hand is now playing F on beat **3**, and C on the last subdivision of beat **3**, to correspond with the right hand part required by the **double** backcycle.

Now we will look at a triple backcyle, first with the lowest voice staying the same throughout:-

Figure 17.21. Slow gospel pattern #11 - triple backcycle (root staying on G)
(Cassette Tape Example 707)

In this example, the upper triad sequence **G - Bb - F - C - G** represents a **triple** backcycle (the **Bb** triad lands on the last subdivision of beat **2**, the **F** triad lands on beat **3**, and the **C** triad lands on the last subdivision of beat **3**). The left hand intervals are the same as for patterns **#4** & **#9** (**Figs. 17.10.** & **17.19.**).

As before we will amend the above pattern to move the bass line corresponding to the upper triads:-

Figure 17.22. Slow gospel pattern #12 - triple backcycle (root moving G - Bb - F - C - G)
(Cassette Tape Example 708)

In this example, the left hand is now playing Bb on the last subdivision of beat **2**, F on beat **3**, and C on the last subdivision of beat **3**, to correspond with the right hand part required by the **triple** backcycle.

Clearly the double, and especially the triple, backcycles do rather 'stretch' the chord and the key (i.e. they introduce chromatic tones to the key and/or alterations to the chord) and therefore need to be used with care!

Constructing slow gospel patterns (contd)

Now we will take the two main harmonic techniques discussed so far (Mixolydian triads and backcycling) and use them to construct accompaniments for the following leadsheet:-

Figure 17.23. Slow gospel chord chart example #1

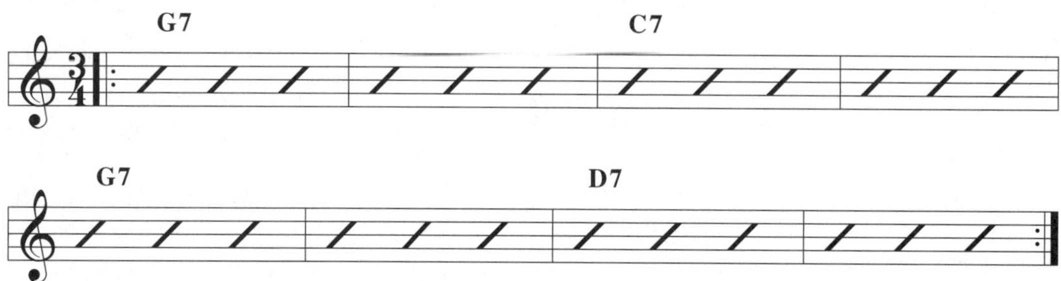

This type of **1 - 4 - 1 - 5** progression using dominant chords is typical in basic gospel styles. We will first interpret this progression using Mixolydian triads as follows:-

Figure 17.24. Slow gospel comping solution a) for chord chart #1 (Fig. 17.23.) - Mixolydian triads
(CASSETTE TAPE EXAMPLE 709)

All the upper triads are in second inversion in this example, which can be further analyzed as follows:-

- Measure 1 On the **G7** chord, the right hand is playing a B diminished triad on beat **1**, a D minor triad on beat **3** and a C major triad on the last subdivision of beat **3**. These are all **G Mixolydian** triads (see **Fig. 17.6.**). The lowest voice in the left hand is repeating the note G, with the upper voice changing to reflect the top notes in the upper triads (resulting in root-5th, root-b7th and root-6th intervals in the left hand).

Constructing slow gospel patterns (contd)

Analysis of Fig. 17.24. contd.

- Measure 2 Continuing on the **G7** chord, the right hand is playing a B diminished triad on beat **1**, a C major triad on beat **2**, and a D minor triad on beat **3**. Again all of these are **G Mixolydian** triads. The left hand is using root-5th, root-6th and root-b7th intervals to correspond with the top notes of the right hand triads.

- Measure 3 On the **C7** chord, the right hand is playing an E diminished triad on beat **1** and on the last subdivision of beat **2**, a G minor triad on beat **3**, and an F major triad on the last subdivision of beat **3**. These are all **C Mixolydian** triads (we are building triads from C Mixolydian over a C7 chord, in the same way as we built triads from G Mixolydian over a G7 chord) - see **Fig. 17.11.** measures 3 to 4. The left hand is again using root-5th, root-6th and root-b7th intervals (this time with C as the lowest voice) to support the upper triads.

- Measure 4 Continuing on the **C7** chord, the right hand is playing an E diminished triad on beat **1**, a D minor triad on beat **2**, and a C major triad on beat **3**. Again all of these are **C Mixolydian** triads. The left hand uses a root-5th coupling on beat **1**, and repeats the root on the last subdivision of beat **2**, acting as a 'pickup' into the chord played on beat **3** in the right hand.

- Measure 5 On the **G7** chord, the right hand is playing a B diminished triad on beats **1** & **3**, and a C major triad on the last subdivision of beat **3**. These are **G Mixolydian** triads. The left hand is using root-5th and root-6th intervals (with G as the lowest voice) to support these triads.

- Measure 6 Continuing on the **G7** chord, the right hand is playing a B diminished triad on beat **1**, an A minor triad on beat **2**, and a G major triad on beat **3**. Again all of these are **G Mixolydian** triads. The left hand uses a root-5th coupling on beat **1**, and repeats the root on the last subdivision of beat **2**, acting as a pickup into the chord played on beat **3** in the right hand.

- Measure 7 On the **D7** chord, the right hand is playing an F# diminished triad on beats **1** & **3**, and a G major triad on the last subdivision of beat **3**. These are **D Mixolydian** triads - see **Fig. 17.11.** measures 23 to 24. The left hand is using root-5th and root-6th intervals (with D as the lowest voice) to support the upper triads.

- Measure 8 Continuing on the **D7** chord, the right hand is playing an A minor triad on beat **1**, a B minor triad on beat **2**, and a C major triad on beat **3**. Again all of these are **D Mixolydian** triads. The left hand uses a root-b7th coupling on beat **1**, and repeats the root as a pickup into beat **3**.

Now we will look at another interpretation of the same leadsheet, this time using backcycling techniques:-

Figure 17.25. Slow gospel comping solution b) for chord chart #1 (Fig. 17.23.) - backcycling
(Cassette Tape Example 710)

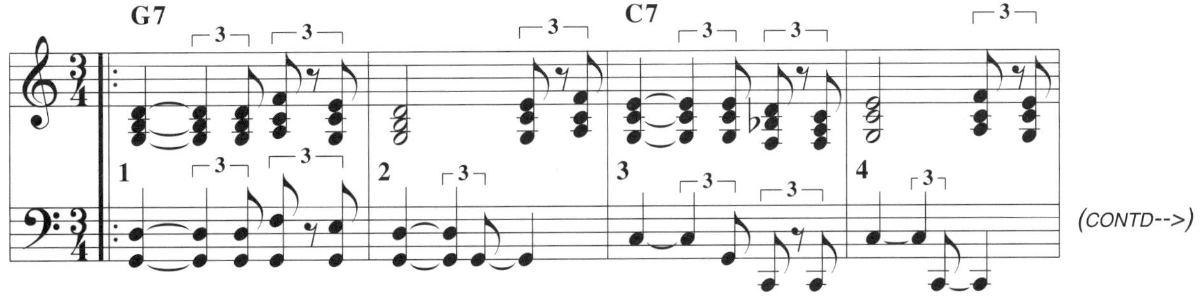

Constructing slow gospel patterns (contd)

Figure 17.25. (contd)

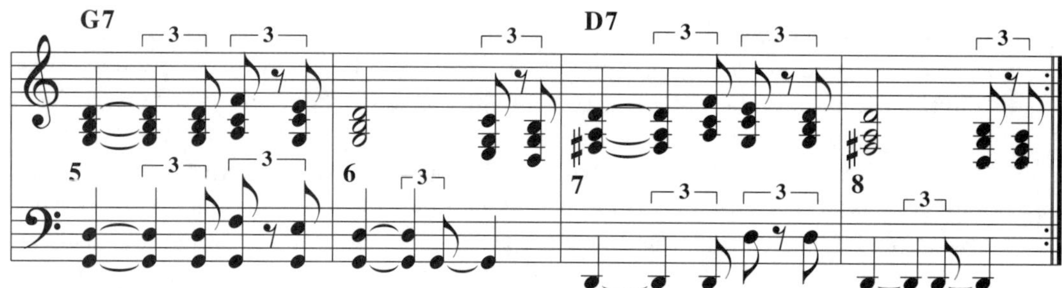

Throughout this backcycling example, the roots of the chords are maintained in the left hand, and the backcycled triads are functioning as harmonic embellishments or passing chords, over these roots (review text prior to **Fig. 17.17.** as necessary).

IMPORTANT TIP:- Notice in all these backcycling examples (**Figs. 17.17. - 17.22.** and the preceding **Fig. 17.25.**) that the upper triads will 'voicelead' from left to right - therefore **familiarity with major triad circle-of-4ths voiceleading in all positions is crucial!** Ensure that you have the voiceleading routines in **Figs. 4.16. - 4.18.** under your fingers!

The preceding example can be further analyzed as follows:-

- Measure 1 On the **G7** chord, the right hand is playing a root position G triad on beat **1** and on the last subdivision of beat **2**, a 1st inversion F triad on beat **3**, and a 2nd inversion C triad on the last subdivision of beat **3**. This represents a **double backcycle** on the G7 chord (see **Fig. 17.19.**). The left hand is using root-5th, root-b7th and root-6th intervals to correspond with the top notes of the upper triads.

- Measure 2 Continuing on the **G7** chord, the right hand is playing a root position G triad on beat **1**, a 2nd inversion C triad on beat **3**, and a 1st inversion F triad on the last subdivision of beat **3**. Normally the F triad would precede the C triad on a backcycle over the G7 chord - on this occasion they are 'switched around' in order to set up the following C7 chord - the C & F triads here (followed by the C triad on beat **1** of measure 3) are effectively a backcycle on the following C7 chord, played in the previous measure as a harmonic anticipation. The left hand uses a root-5th coupling on beat **1**, and repeats the root as a pickup into beat **3**.

- Measure 3 On the **C7** chord, the right hand is playing a 2nd inversion C triad on beat **1** and on the last subdivision of beat **2**, a 2nd inversion Bb triad on beat **3**, and a root postion F triad on the last subdivision of beat **3**. This represents a **double backcycle** on the C7 chord. The left hand is playing the root of the chord on beats **1** & **3** and the last subdivision of beat **3**, with the 5th as a connecting tone on the last subdivision of beat **2**.

- Measure 4 Continuing on the **C7** chord, the right hand is playing a 2nd inversion C triad on beat **1** and on the last subdivision of beat **3**, and a 1st inversion F triad on beat **3**. This represents a **single backcycle** on the C7 chord (see **Fig. 17.17.**). The left hand is playing the root on beat **1** and as a pickup into beat **3**.

Constructing slow gospel patterns (contd)

Analysis of Fig. 17.25. contd.

- Measure 5 As for measure 1, on the **G7** chord.

- Measure 6 Continuing on the **G7** chord, the right hand is playing a root position G triad on beat **1**, a 1st inversion C triad on beat **3**, and a 2nd inversion G triad on the last subdivision of beat **3**. This represents a **single backcycle** on the G7 chord. The left hand root-5th coupling followed by the root, is the same as in measure 2.

- Measure 7 On the **D7** chord, the right hand is playing a 1st inversion D triad on beat **1**, a 1st inversion F triad on the last subdivision of beat **2**, a 2nd inversion C triad on beat **3**, and a root position G triad on the last subdivision of beat **3**. This represents a **triple backcycle** on the D7 chord (review triple backcycle example over a G7 chord in **Fig. 17.21.** as necessary). The left hand is playing the root, on beats **1** & **3** and on the last subdivisions of beats **2** and **3**.

- Measure 8 Continuing on the **D7** chord, the right hand is playing a 1st inversion D triad on beat **1**, a 2nd inversion G triad on beat **3**, and a root position D triad on the last subdivision of beat **3**. This represents a **single backcycle** on the D7 chord. The left hand is playing the root on beat **1** and on the pickup into beat **3**.

PRACTICE DIRECTIONS:-

- ***Practice the Mixolydian triad pattern examples #1 - #4 over a G7 chord (as in Figs. 17.7. - 17.10.) and the 12-key Mixolydian triad pattern (as in Fig. 17.11.).***
- ***Practice the Mixolydian triad pattern examples #5 & #6 using grace notes (as in Figs. 17.14. - 17.15.), and work on applying grace notes to the 12-key pattern in Fig. 17.11.*** *(First 2 keys shown in Fig. 17.16.).*
- ***Practice the backcycling pattern examples #7 - #12 over a G7 chord (as in Figs. 17.17. - 17.22.).***
- ***Practice the comping solutions for chord chart #1:-***
    - ***using Mixolydian triads as in Fig. 17.24.***
    - ***using backcycling as in Fig. 17.25.***

For extra practice - these comping solutions for the basic 1 - 4 - 1 - 5 progression shown on chord chart ***#1*** *(**Fig. 17.23.**) could usefully be transposed into other keys!*

Constructing slow gospel patterns (contd)

We will now look at some further uses of backcycling devices. In the previous example, backcycling has been used to provide 'passing' triads in the right hand, while the left hand is still providing the root of the original chord as required by the chart. Another approach discussed in the text prior to **Fig. 17.17.**, was to also play the roots of the (backcycled) triads in the left hand - this effectively 'reharmonizes' the original progression by adding new chords. We will apply this concept, using single and double backcycling, to the following leadsheet:-

Figure 17.26. Slow gospel chord chart example #2

Firstly we will apply a basic triad solution to this chart with no backcycling, as follows:-

Figure 17.27. Slow gospel comping solution for chord chart #2 (Fig. 17.26.)
(Cassette Tape Example 711)

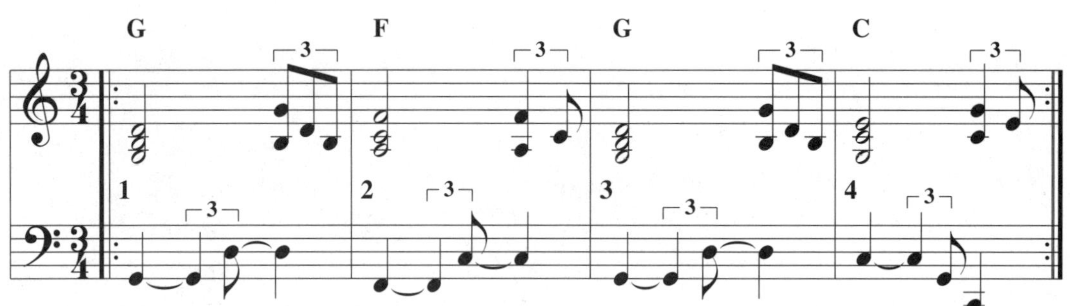

In each measure above, the right hand is playing the basic **1-3-5** triad of each chord, with no other added tones. During beat **3**, the outer 2 notes of the triad inversion are played, followed by either 1 or 2 arpeggiated chord tones. (We first saw this type of 'parallel interval' arpeggio embellishment in **Fig. 11.16.**). The left hand is using a root-&-5th pattern on each chord, landing on beat **1** and providing a pickup into the right hand couplings on beat **3** of each measure. This is a very simple pattern, which however might well be suitable for more basic gospel situations. Now we will embellish the above progression by adding a single backcycle before the 'target' chords in measures 2, 3 & 4. By 'target' here we mean that these chords (the F, G & C chords in measures 2 - 4) will each be approached in a circle-of-4ths manner i.e. a new chord will be inserted at the end of each preceding measure which will then resolve by circle-of-4ths to the target chord. This is probably best understood by looking at an example - here is our previous chord chart (**Fig. 17.26.**) with the added backcycle into measures 2, 3 & 4:-

Figure 17.28. Slow gospel chord chart #2 variation a) - single backcycle into measures 2 - 4

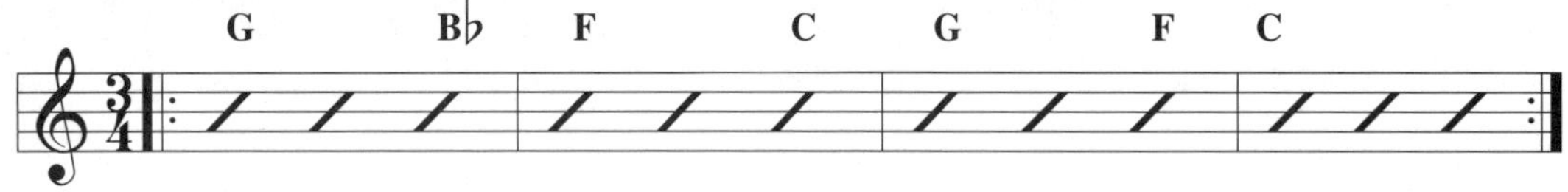

Constructing slow gospel patterns (contd)

Note the following differences between the chart in **Fig. 17.28.** (with the single backcycles added) and the chart in **Fig. 17.26.** (the original progression):-

- Prior to the **F** chord in the 2nd measure, a **Bb** chord has been added (on beat **3** of the previous measure). This is a **single backcycle** into the F chord (Bb to F is a circle-of-4ths movement).
- Prior to the **G** chord in the 3rd measure, a **C** chord has been added (on beat **3** of the previous measure). This is a **single backcycle** into the G chord (C to G is a circle-of-4ths movement).
- Prior to the **C** chord in the 4th measure, an **F** chord has been added (on beat **3** of the previous measure). This is a **single backcycle** into the C chord (F to C is a circle-of-4ths movement).

Each backcycle addition takes one beat away from the previous chord, in comparison to the original chart as in **Fig. 17.26**. (If you're still not sure what is meant by circle-of-4ths movements, review the text at the end of **Chapter 1** as necessary!). Now we will look at some interpretations of this embellished chart (**Fig. 17.28.**). First a more basic version as follows:-

Figure 17.29. Slow gospel comping solution a) for chord chart #2 variation a) (Fig. 17.28.)
(Cassette Tape Example 712)

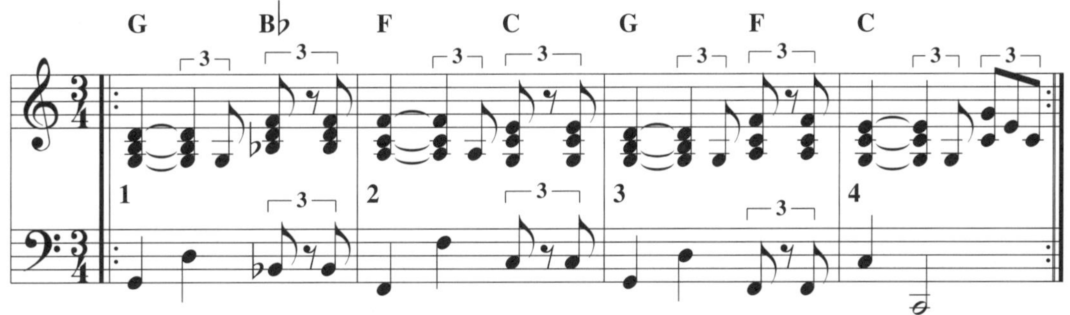

Within each chord in the above example (including the backcycle additions), the right hand is using the basic **1-3-5** triad. Each added backcycle chord is using the 1st & 3rd subdivisions of beat **3** (in measures 1-3) or playing an arpeggio during beat **3** (as in measure 4). Meanwhile the left hand is landing on all the downbeats as well as the last subdivision of beat **3** in each measure (except for the last measure where only beats **1** & **2** are used), playing the root of the chord in each case (except for the 5ths on beat **2** in measures 1 & 3). Note again that on each occasion when a backcycled triad leads into a target chord (i.e. **Bb to F**, **C to G**, **F to C**) that the voiceleading is according to our previously established circle-of-4ths triad movement rules as in **Fig. 4.18**.

Now we will look at a more complex solution to the same chart variation, this time using grace notes as well as some 'hammer and drone' and pentatonic scale concepts first seen in our work on Country styles (see **Fig. 16.33.** and accompanying text). In **Figs. 17.12.** & **17.13.** we saw that grace notes used in gospel styles are typically a half-step below either the 3rd, 5th, 9th or 13th(6th) of a chord - this is characteristic of the 'bluesy' and chromatic flavor of gospel. The addition of these chromatic grace notes to the 'hammer and drone' techniques within pentatonic scales (as studied in our work on Country) is an effective combination both in gospel styles and when a more blues/gospel flavor is needed for a country tune. Here is the second solution to the embellished chord chart in **Fig. 17.28.**, using this combination of harmonic devices:-

Constructing slow gospel patterns (contd)

Figure 17.30. Slow gospel comping solution b) for chord chart #2 variation a) (Fig. 17.28.)
(Cassette Tape Example 713)

We can analyze this version as follows:-

- Measure 1 - On the **G** chord, the right hand is playing a root position G triad on beat **1**, with an A# grace note leading into B (the 3rd of the chord) - we first saw this **b3 - 3** grace note phrase in **Fig. 17.12**. The right hand is also playing the root of the chord (G) as a pickup into beat **3**. The left hand is playing the root on beat **1** and the 5th on beat **2**.

- On the **Bb** chord, during beat **3** in the right hand we are using 'hammer and drone' embellishments from the **Bb pentatonic** scale (see **Figs. 1.54. & 16.37.**). The drone note is the 5th of the chord (F), played over the 3rd (D), 9th (C) and root (Bb) of the chord. Also on beat **3** a C# grace note is leading into D (the 3rd of the chord) resulting in another **b3 - 3** movement. The left hand is playing the root of the chord on beat **3** and on the last subdivision of beat **3**.

- Measure 2 - On the **F** chord, the right hand is playing a 1st inversion F triad on beat **1**, with a G# grace note leading into A (another **b3 - 3** movement). The right hand is also playing the 3rd of the chord (A) as a pickup into beat **3**. The left hand is again playing the root on beat **1** and the 5th on beat **2**.

- On the **C** chord, during beat **3** in the right hand we are using 'hammer and drone' embellishments from the **C pentatonic** scale (see **Fig. 16.33.**). The drone note is the 5th of the chord (G), played over the 3rd (E), 9th (D) and root (C) of the chord. Also on beat **3** a D# grace note is leading into E, again resulting in a **b3 - 3** movement on this chord. The left hand is playing the root of the chord on beat **3** and on the last subdivision of beat **3**.

Constructing slow gospel patterns (contd)

Analysis of Fig. 17.30. contd.

- Measure 3 - On the **G** chord, the right hand is playing a 1st inversion G triad on beat **1**, with an A# grace note leading into B (another **b3 - 3** movement). The right hand is also playing the root of the chord (G) as a pickup into beat **3**. The left hand is again playing the root on beat **1** and the 5th on beat **2**.

- On the **F** chord, during beat **3** in the right hand we are using 'hammer and drone' embellish- from the **F pentatonic** scale (see **Figs. 1.53. & 16.37.**). The drone note is the root of the chord (F), played over the 6th (D), 5th (C) and 3rd (A) of the chord. Also on beat **3** a C# grace note is leading into D, resulting in a **b6 - 6** movement on this chord. The left hand is playing the root of the chord on beat **3** and on the last subdivision of beat **3**.

- Measure 4 - On the **C** chord, the right hand is playing a 2nd inversion C triad on beat **1**, a 1st inversion F triad on beat **3**, and back to a 2nd inversion C triad on the last subdivision of beat **3**. This represents a **single backcycle** on the C chord. Also on beat 3 a G# grace note is leading into A, creating a momentary **b3 - 3** movement on the upper F triad. The left hand is playing the root in an octave pattern, on beats **1** & **2**, on the last subdivision of beat **2** and on the 2nd subdivision of beat **3** (rhythmically in between the backcycled triads in the right hand during beat **3**).

Now we will further embellish the original leadsheet by adding a double backcycle before each chord in measures 2, 3 & 4, as follows:-

Figure 17.31. Slow gospel chord chart #2 variation b) - double backcycle into measures 2 - 4

Note that in this case the double backcycle is occurring on the first and last subdivisions of beat **3** in the first 3 measures, prior to each target chord. Again compare this chart to the original in **Fig. 17.26.**, and to the single backcycle version in **Fig. 17.28.** The added chords can be analyzed as follows:-

- Prior to the **F** chord in the 2nd measure, **Eb** and **Bb** chords have been added (during beat **3** of the previous measure). This is a **double backcycle** into the F chord (Eb to Bb to F is two successive circle-of-4ths movements).
- Prior to the **G** chord in the 3rd measure, **F** and **C** chords have been added (during beat **3** of the previous measure). This is a **double backcycle** into the G chord (F to C to G is two successive circle-of-4ths movements).
- Prior to the **C** chord in the 4th measure, **Bb** and **F** chords have been added (during beat **3** of the previous measure). This is a **double backcycle** into the C chord (Bb to F to C is two successive circle-of-4ths movements).

Each double backcycle takes one beat away from the previous chord, in comparison to the original chart (**Fig. 17.26.**). Now we will interpret this latest chart variation using grace notes, hammers and drones as follows:-

Constructing slow gospel patterns (contd)

Figure 17.32. Slow gospel comping solution for chord chart #2 variation b) (Fig. 17.30.)
(Cassette Tape Example 714)

The double backcycling here produces a colorful, modulatory sound - however, it will be be too harmonically 'busy' for some applications, and therefore needs to be used with care and in the right context. This example can be further analyzed as follows:-

- Measure 1

- On the **G** chord, the right hand is playing a 1st inversion G triad on beat **1** (doubling the top note), with an A# grace note leading into B (a **b3 - 3** movement on the chord). During beat **2** the root of the chord (G) is used as a drone, with a scale run from the 3rd to the 5th (B, C, D) moving underneath. The left hand is playing the root in octaves, on beat **1** and on the pickup into beat **2**.
- On the **Eb** chord, the right hand is playing a 2nd inversion Eb triad (with the top note doubled) on beat **3**, with the left hand playing the root.
- On the **Bb** chord, the right hand is playing a root position Bb triad (with the top note doubled) on the last subdivision of beat **3**, with the left hand again playing the root.

- Measure 2

- On the **F** chord, the right hand is playing a 1st inversion F triad on beat **1** (doubling the top note), with a G# grace note leading into A (a **b3 - 3** movement on the chord). During beat **2** the root of the chord (F) is used as a drone, with a scale run from the 3rd to the 5th (A, Bb, C) moving underneath. The first inversion triad (with the top note doubled) is repeated on beat **3**. The left hand is playing the root in octaves, on beat **1,** the pickup into beat **2**, and beat **3**.
- On the **C** chord, the right hand is playing a 2nd inversion C triad on the last subdivision of beat **3**, with the left hand again playing the root.

Constructing slow gospel patterns (contd)

Analysis of Figure 17.32. contd.

- Measure 3 - On the **G** chord, the right hand is playing a root position G triad on beat **1**, with an A# grace note leading into B (a **b3 - 3** movement on the chord). During beat **2** we are using 'hammer and drone' embellishments from the **G pentatonic** scale (see **Figs. 1.60.** & **16.37.**). The drone note is the 5th of the chord (D), played over the 3rd (B), 9th (A) and root (G) of the chord. Also on beat **2** an A# grace note is leading into B, creating another **b3 - 3** movement. The left hand is playing the root on beat **1** and on the pickup into beat **2**.

- On the **Bb** chord, the right hand is playing a root position Bb triad (with the top note doubled) on beat **3**, with the left hand playing the root.
- On the **F** chord, the right hand is playing a 1st inversion F triad (with the top note doubled) on the last subdivision of beat **3**, with the left hand again playing the root.

- Measure 4 - On the **C** chord, the right hand is playing a 2nd inversion C triad on beat **1**, and the root of the chord (C) as a pickup into beat **3**. During beat **3** we are using 'hammer and drone' embellishments from the **C pentatonic** scale (see **Fig. 16.33.**). The drone note is the 5th of the chord (G), played over the 3rd (E), 9th (D) and root (C) of the chord. Also on beat **3** a D# grace note is is leading into E (the 3rd of the chord) resulting in another **b3 - 3** movement. The left hand is playing the root on beats **1** & **2**.

Now we will begin to look at the numerous applications of 'walkups' in gospel styles. We have already encountered walkups when studying country devices (see **Figs. 16.23. - 16.30.** for example) - they were used to connect chords with roots a 4th interval apart (using diatonic scale movement). This type of walkup also occurs in gospel styles, along with more 'chromatic' walkups using half-step movements in the root voice together with Mixolydian or backcycled triads in the right hand. First we will look at an example of a diatonic walkup, connecting chords with roots a 4th interval apart:-

Figure 17.33. Slow gospel pattern #13 - diatonic walkup

(Cassette Tape Example 715)

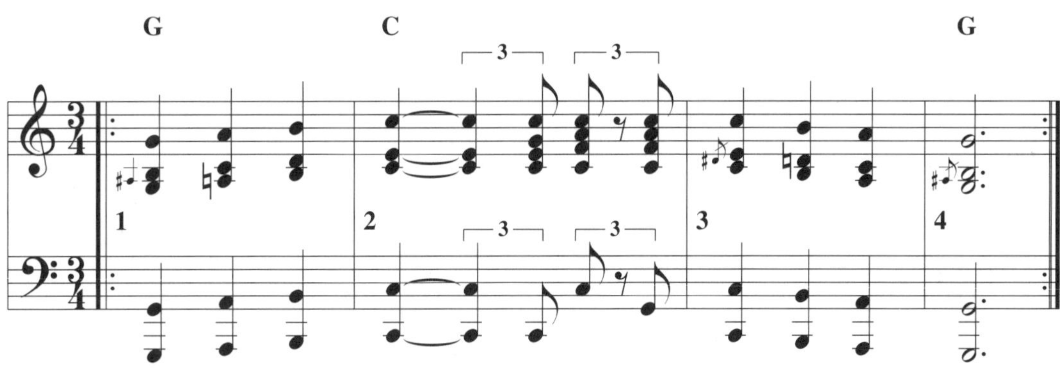

This example combines a diatonic walkup/walkdown with grace notes and a single backcycle. We can further analyze this example as follows:-

Constructing slow gospel patterns (contd)

Analysis of Fig. 17.33.

- Measure 1 - On the **G** chord, the top and bottom notes in the right hand, together with the octaves in the left hand, are the diatonic walkup tones G, A, & B on beats **1**, **2** & **3** respectively. Also the right hand is using a 'filled-in octave' (an octave with another note in between - we first saw this used in **Fig. 11.39.**). The notes inside the octave (B, C & D) are a diatonic 3rd interval above the walkup tones G, A & B. (This is similar to the addition of the 'diatonic 10th' in the country walkup - see **Fig. 16.22.**). The right hand is also using the grace note A# on beat **1**, leading into B (the 3rd of the chord) creating a **b3 - 3** movement.

- Measure 2 - On the **C** chord, the right hand is playing an incomplete C triad (root, 3rd, root) on beat **1**, continuing the previous ('filled-in octave') walkup pattern. This is followed by a 1st inversion C triad on the last subdivision of beat **2**, and a root position F triad on beat **3** and on the last subdivision of beat **3**, all with the top note doubled. This represents a **single backcycle** on the C chord. The left hand is using a root-&-5th pattern, rhythmically concerted with the right hand part.

- Measure 3 - Continuing on the **C** chord, the top and bottom notes in the right hand, together with the octaves in the left hand, are the diatonic walkdown tones C, B, & A on beats **1**, **2** & **3** respectively. Again the right hand is using 'filled-in octaves'. The notes inside the octave (E, D & C) are a diatonic 3rd interval above the walkdown tones C, B & A. The right hand is also using the grace note D# on beat **1**, leading into E (the 3rd of the chord) creating a **b3 - 3** movement.

- Measure 4 - On the **G** chord, the right hand is playing an incomplete G triad (root, 3rd, root) on beat **1**, continuing the previous ('filled-in octave') walkdown pattern. The grace note A# is also used on beat **1**, leading into B (see measure 1 comments). The left hand is also playing the root in octaves.

Now a variation on the previous example, with the top note staying the same (i.e. using a 'drone'):-

Figure 17.34. Slow gospel pattern #14 - diatonic walkup with drone note
(Cassette Tape Example 716)

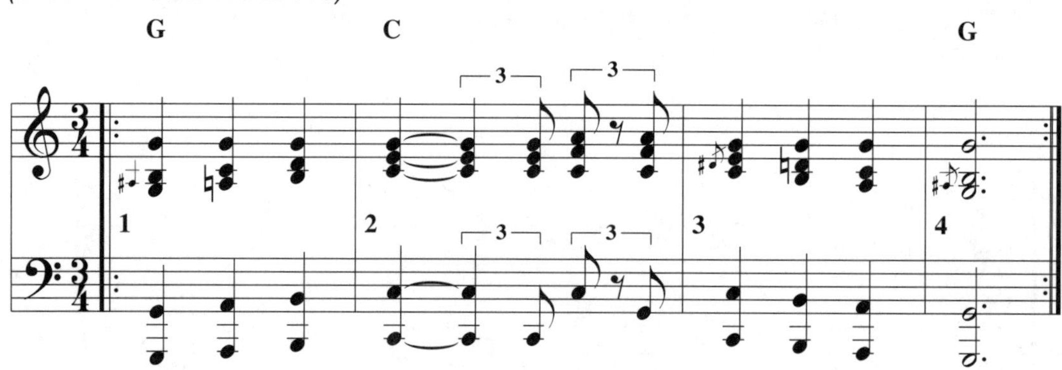

This is the same as the previous example (**Fig. 17. 33.**) except for the drone note of G being used across the walkup and walkdown. As we saw in the country examples (see **Figs. 16.23. & 16.27.**), the drone note is typically the root of the chord when walking **up**, and the 5th of the chord when walking **down**. (Here the drone note G is the root of the G chord in the 1st measure walkup, and the 5th of the C chord in the 3rd measure walkdown). The top note does move to A on beat **3** in measure 2 to allow the backcycle to occur. Now another version of the walkup/walkdown pattern in **Fig. 17.33.**, this time with some rhythmic variations:-

Constructing slow gospel patterns (contd)

Figure 17.35. Slow gospel pattern #15 - diatonic walkup (rhythmic variation)

(Cassette Tape Example 717)

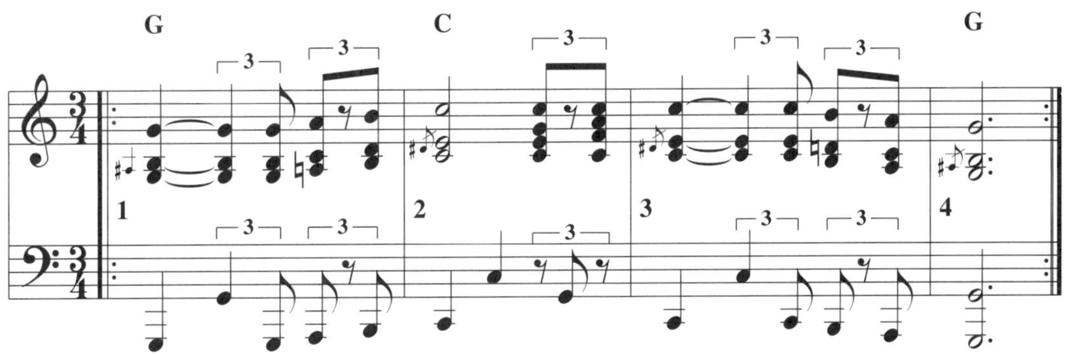

The harmonic aspects of the above example are as for the first walkup pattern (**Fig. 17.33.**), however we now have some rhythmic variations. Whereas the walkup & walkdown in measures 1 & 3 of **Fig. 17.33.** used quarter notes and occupied the whole measure, now in the corresponding measures of the above example the walkup & walkdown has been 'squeezed' into the last part of the measure i.e. from the last subdivision of beat **2** onwards, in measures 1 & 3. The left hand is also rhythmically alternating with the right hand during the backcycle on the **C** chord in measure 2.

The next series of walkup examples are of the more 'chromatic' variety, using ascending half-step lines in the left hand part. This left hand motion typically occurs between the 3rd & 5th of a key (using the sequence **3 - 4 - #4 - 5**) or between the 6th and tonic of the key (using the sequence **6 - #6 - 7 - 1**). The right hand then often plays Mixolydian and/or backcycled triads again these chromatic left hand lines. We will first look at some left hand examples, using these half-step lines:-

Figure 17.36. Slow gospel chromatic left hand pattern #1

(Cassette Tape Example 718)

Here with respect to G as the tonic, we are using the **6** (E) on the last subdivision of beat **2**, the **#6** or b7 (F) on beat **3**, and the **7** (F#) on the last subdivision of beat **4**, finishing back on the tonic in the next measure.

Figure 17.37. Slow gospel chromatic left hand pattern #2

(Cassette Tape Example 719)

A rhythmic variation on the above left hand pattern, with the walkup now using all 3 triplet subdivisions of beat **3**.

Constructing slow gospel patterns (contd)

Figure 17.38. Slow gospel chromatic left hand pattern #3
(CASSETTE TAPE EXAMPLE 720)

Now with respect to G as the tonic, we are using the **3** (B) on the last subdivision of beat **2**, the **4** (C) on beat **3**, and the **#4** (C#) on the last subdivision of beat **3**, finishing on the **5** (D) in the next measure.

Figure 17.39. Slow gospel chromatic left hand pattern #4
(CASSETTE TAPE EXAMPLE 721)

A rhythmic variation on the above left hand pattern, with the walkup now using all 3 triplet subdivisions of beat **3**.

Now we will begin to look at how to combine these left hand ideas with triads in the right hand. The following example uses G Mixolydian triads over a **G7** chord as follows:-

Figure 17.40. Slow gospel pattern #16 - chromatic walkup (Mixolydian triads over 1 - 6 - #6 - 7 - 1)
(CASSETTE TAPE EXAMPLE 722)

Rhythmically in this example, both hands are 'concerted' (together) in the first measure on beat **1**, the last subdivision of beat **2**, beat **3**, and the last subdivision of beat **3**, and in the second measure on beat **1**. Harmonically the right and left hands can be analyzed as follows:-

Right hand - From left to right we are using B diminished, E minor, D minor, C major and B diminished triads over the **G7** chord, all in 2nd inversion. These triads come from the **G Mixolydian mode** (see **Fig. 17.13.**). At the start of each measure, a C# grace note has been added, leading into D (the 5th of the G7 chord).

Left hand - The left hand is playing a **1 - 6 - #6 - 7 - 1** pattern (with respect to the **G7** chord) in octaves (see **Fig. 17.36.**), against the upper right hand triads.

Constructing slow gospel patterns (contd)

Notice that the previous example had a 'contrary motion' element, using descending Mixolydian triads in the right hand (approaching the B diminished triad, which over G in the left hand fully defines the **G7** chord) against an ascending chromatic idea in the left hand - this is very typical in gospel. Our main concern here is with the horizontal motion and direction of both the left and right hand parts - this will sometimes result in some dissonant vertical sounds i.e. the last chord in the first measure of **Fig. 17.40.** is a C triad over F# in the root. You would not want to 'sit on' this for any length of time! (at least not in mainstream commercial styles), but in the context of the pattern it 'passes through' because it is on a weak rhythmic subdivision and because the ear is attracted to the strong 'linear' nature of the left and right hand parts. However, if in certain contexts this vertical sound is judged to be too dissonant, it is often possible to adjust the upper triad to eliminate the 'minor 9th' interval between the two hands (in this case the right hand C triad contains the note G, which is a minor 9th above F# in the left hand - this interval is mainly responsible for the dissonance of this triad-over-root combination as a whole). The following example is the same as **Fig. 17.40.**, but with the right hand triad amended at the end of measure 1:-

Figure 17.41. Slow gospel pattern #17 - chromatic walkup (Mixolydian triads over 1 - 6 - #6 - 7 - 1) - with upper triad adjustment to avoid vertical dissonance *(Cassette Tape Example 723)*

The above example is the same as **Fig. 17.40.**, except for the **A minor** triad used in the right hand on the last subdivision of beat **3** in the first measure. The A minor triad is still within the G Mixolydian mode, but instead of in 1st or 2nd inversions (as in **Figs. 17.12. & 17.13.**) it is used here in root position. Over the F# in the left hand, a passing chord of **F#mi7(b5)** is created overall (review **Figs. 1.83.** and **5.13.** as necessary). This minor-triad-over-root solution (using an upper minor triad from the appropriate Mixolydian scale to create a **minor7th[b5]** chord overall) is a useful device when it is desired to limit vertical tension within chromatic walkups. Now we will look at another chromatic walkup pattern, this time using backcycled triads in the right hand over a **G7** chord:-

Figure 17.42. Slow gospel pattern #18 - chromatic walkup (backcycled triads over 1 - 6 - #6 - 7 - 1) *(Cassette Tape Example 724)*

Constructing slow gospel patterns (contd)

The rhythmic concept in the previous pattern is the same as for patterns **#16** & **#17** (**Figs. 17.40.** & **17.41.**). Harmonically the right and left hands can be analyzed as follows:-

Right hand - From left to right we are using a 1st inversion **G** triad, a 1st inversion **Bb** triad, a 2nd inversion **F** triad, a root position **C** triad, and back to a 1st inversion **G** triad in the 2nd measure. This collectively represents a **triple backcycle** on the overall **G7** chord (see **Fig. 17.21.**). At the start of each measure, an A# grace note has been added, leading into B (the 3rd of the G7 chord).

Left hand - The left hand is again playing a **1 - 6 - #6 - 7 - 1** pattern in octaves (see **Fig. 17.36.**).

Note that this pattern generates two dissonant triad-over-root combinations - the **Bb triad over E** on the last subdivision of beat **2**, and the **C triad over F#** on the last subdivision of beat **3** (in the first measure). Now we will look at a rhythmic variation of the previous pattern, as follows:-

Figure 17.43. Slow gospel pattern #19 - chromatic walkup (backcycled triads over 1 - 6 - #6 - 7 - 1) - rhythmic variation *(Cassette Tape Example 725)*

Rhythmically in this example, the chromatic walkup is now occurring during beat **3** of the first measure, using all of the triplet subdivisions (see **Fig. 17.37.**). Both hands are playing on beat **1** in the first & second measures, with the left hand also landing on beat **2** in the first measure. Harmonically the right and left hands can be analyzed as follows:-

Right hand - From left to right we are using a root position **G** triad, a root position **Bb** triad, a 1st inversion **F** triad (with the top note F held over from the previous Bb triad), a 2nd inversion **C** triad, and back to a root position **G** triad in the 2nd measure (with the bottom note G held over from the previous C triad). Again this collectively represents a '**triple backcycle**' on the **G7** chord. 'Holding' the commontone like this, between sucessive triads, is a convenient device when the backcycling rhythms are moving more quickly. (Review **Figs. 4.16. - 4.18.** showing commontones between triads voiceled in a circle-of-4ths manner, as necessary). Again an A# grace note has been added at the start of each measure, leading into B (the 3rd of the **G7** chord).

Left hand - The left hand is again playing a **1 - 6 - #6 - 7 - 1** pattern with respect to the overall **G7** chord.

Now we will look at some patterns using the **1 - 3 - 4 - #4 - 5** bass line (see **Figs. 17.38.** & **17.39.**). This is typically used to connect between a '**one**' chord and a '**five**' chord of a key, as in the following example:-

Constructing slow gospel patterns (contd)

Figure 17.44. Slow gospel pattern #20 - chromatic walkup (Mixolydian triads over 1 - 3 - 4 - #4 - 5)
(Cassette Tape Example 726)

Rhythmically the above pattern is the same as pattern **#18** (**Fig. 17.42.**) and other preceding patterns. Harmonically the right and left hands can be analyzed as follows:-

Right hand - From left to right we are using a 1st inversion G triad (with the top note doubled), and then 2nd inversion B diminished, A minor, G major and F# diminished triads. In the first measure the triads come from the **G Mixolydian** mode (see **Fig. 17.13.**). In the second measure, the F# diminished triad comes from a **D Mixolydian** mode (see **Fig. 17.11.** measures 23-24). Together with D in the bass voice, this upper 'shape' fully defines the **D7** chord. An A# grace note has been added on beat **1** of the first measure, leading into B (the 3rd of the **G7** chord), and a G# has been added on beat **3** of the first measure, leading into A (the 9th of the **G7** chord).

Left hand - The left hand is playing a **1 - 3 - 4 - #4 - 5** pattern, with respect to the **G7** chord (see **Fig. 17.38.**). The last note in the pattern (D) is also the root of the 2nd chord (**D7**).

Again here we have created a dissonant triad-over-root combination - the **G triad over C#** on the last subdivision of beat **3** in the first measure. If a more consonant vertical quality was desired here, an E minor triad (which is found in both the **G Mixolydian** and **D Mixolydian** modes) could be used, which over the C# in the bass would create a **C#mi7(b5)** chord - we first saw this technique used in **Fig. 17.41**. Here is the same pattern as in Figure **17.44.**, but with the above right hand triad amendment:-

Figure 17.45. Slow gospel pattern #21 - chromatic walkup (Mixolydian triads over 1 - 3 - 4 - #4 - 5) - with upper triad adjustment to avoid vertical dissonance *(Cassette Tape Example 727)*

Note the E minor triad used in the right hand at the end of the first measure.

Constructing slow gospel patterns (contd)

Now we will look at another example using triads from both the **G Mixolydian** and **D Mixolydian** modes:-

Figure 17.46. Slow gospel pattern #22 - chromatic walkup (Mixolydian triads over 1 - 3 - 4 - #4 - 5) - harmonic variation *(Cassette Tape Example 728)*

Rhythmically this example is the same as the previous pattern in the first measure. In the second measure the right hand is using all the downbeats (**1**, **2** & **3**), and the left hand is also landing on beat **1** as well as providing a pickup into beat **3**. Harmonically the right and left hands can be analyzed as follows:-

Right hand - From left to right in the 1st measure we are using a 1st inversion G major triad (with the top note doubled), and then 2nd inversion D minor, C major and B diminished triads. These all derive from a **G Mixolydian** mode (see **Figs. 17.12. & 17.13.**). In the second measure we are using 2nd inversion A minor, G major and F# diminished triads. These all derive from a **D Mixolydian** mode (see **Fig. 17.11.** measures 23-24). The following grace notes have been added:-

- an A# on beat **1** in the 1st measure, leading into B (the 3rd of the **G7** chord).
- a C# on the last subdivision of beat **2** in the 1st measure, leading into D (the 5th of the **G7** chord).
- a G# on beat **1** of the 2nd measure, leading into A (the 5th of the **D7** chord).

Left hand - The left hand is playing a **1 - 3 - 4 - #4 - 5** pattern in the first measure (with respect to the **G7** chord) and playing the root of the **D7** chord (on beat **1** and leading into beat **3**) in the 2nd measure.

Now we will look at a longer example incorporating both diatonic (within the key) and chromatic (moving by half-step) left hand walkup techniques, also featuring a rhythmically 'staggered' final walkup as follows:-

Figure 17.47. Slow gospel pattern #23 - diatonic and chromatic walkups
(Cassette Tape Example 729)

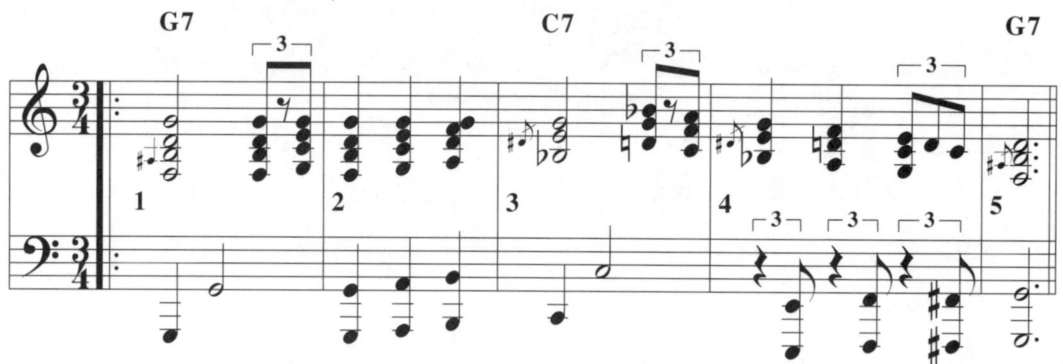

Constructing slow gospel patterns (contd)

We can analyze the previous example as follows:-

- Measure 1 - On the **G7** chord, in the right hand we are using a 4-part 'shape' which is a conbination of a 1st inversion G major triad (top 3 notes) with a 2nd inversion B diminished triad (bottom 3 notes), on beats **1** & **3**. These two triads both come from the **G Mixolydian** mode, and the structure as a whole is very effective in defining the G7 chord - however, don't worry if you can't stretch the 9th interval required - just use the top 3 notes. The right hand is also playing a root position C major triad (with the top note doubled) on the last subdivision of beat **3** - this could be thought of as a **single backcycle** on the G7 chord - also the C triad is found within a **G Mixolydian** mode. An A# grace note has been added on beat **1**, leading into B (the 3rd of the **G7** chord). The left hand is playing the root of the chord on beats **1** & **2**.

- Measure 2 - Continuing on the **G7** chord, we now have a diatonic walkup to the C7 chord similar to those in patterns **#13** & **#14** (**Figs. 17.33.** & **17.34.**). In the right hand, the note G on top is a 'drone' (the root of the G7 chord and the 5th of the next C7 chord). Underneath the drone, we are using 2nd inversion B diminished, C major and D minor triads, on beats **1**, **2** & **3** respectively. These triads again all originate from a **G Mixolydian** mode. The left hand is playing the diatonic walkup tones G, A & B in octaves on the downbeats, with the right hand part.

- Measure 3 - On the **C7** chord, the right hand is playing the 2nd inversion triads E diminished on beat **1**, G minor on beat **3**, and F major on the last subdivision of beat **3**. These triads are all from the **C Mixolydian** mode (see **Fig. 17.11.** measures 3-4). A D# grace note has been added on beat **1**, leading into E (the 3rd of the **C7** chord). The left hand is again playing the root of the chord on beats **1** & **2**.

- Measure 4 - Continuing on the **C7** chord, we now have a 'rhythmically staggered' walkup back into the G7 chord. The right hand is playing the 2nd inversion triads E diminished, D minor and C major, on beats **1**, **2** & **3** respectively. Also the single note embellishments D & C (which are in both of the scale sources **C Mixolydian** and **G Mixolydian**) have been added during the last 2 subdivisions of beat **3**, to lead into the following G7 chord. The grace note D# has again been added, in a similar way to the previous measure. Against this, the left hand is using the chromatic walkup tones E, F & F# in octaves on the last subdivision of beats **1**, **2** & **3**, in the rhythmic spaces between the right hand voicings. This bass line represents both a **3 - 4 - #4** (**- 5**) with respect to the **C7** chord, and a **6 - #6 - 7** (**- 1**) with respect to the **G7** chord following.

- Measure 5 - On the **G7** chord, the right hand is using a 2nd inversion B diminished triad (with the added grace note A# leading into B) from the **G Mixolydian** mode, on beat **1**. The left hand is playing the root of the chord in octaves, again on beat **1**.

PRACTICE DIRECTIONS:-

- Practice the backcycling 'reharmonization' examples as in Figs. 17.26. - 17.32.
- Practice the diatonic and chromatic walkup examples as in Figs. 17.33. - 17.47. (including patterns #13 - #23).
Again - these examples could usefully be transposed to other keys!

Constructing slow gospel patterns (contd)

Now we will turn to another favorite gospel technique, the use of '**parallel minor triads**'. This is the name I have given to the use of minor triads (normally in 2nd inversion) descending in successive half-steps. This can occur when two 'adjacent' minor triads within a Mixolydian mode, are connected by a chromatic minor triad in between. For example, in **Fig. 17.6.** showing the 2nd inversion triads available within a **G Mixolydian** mode, the two minor triads next to each other are D minor and E minor. Another way to arrive at these two triads is to know that the top notes (in 2nd inversion) will be the 7th and tonic of the overall Mixolydian mode (in this case, the note F is on top of the D minor triad and is the 7th degree in G Mixolydian, and G is on top of the E minor triad and is tonic of G Mixolydian). Once we derived these triads, they can then be 'connected' by using the chromatic minor triad in between, as in the following example:-

Figure 17.48. 'Parallel minor triad' example - connecting E minor with D minor (using Eb minor)
(CASSETTE TAPE EXAMPLE 730)

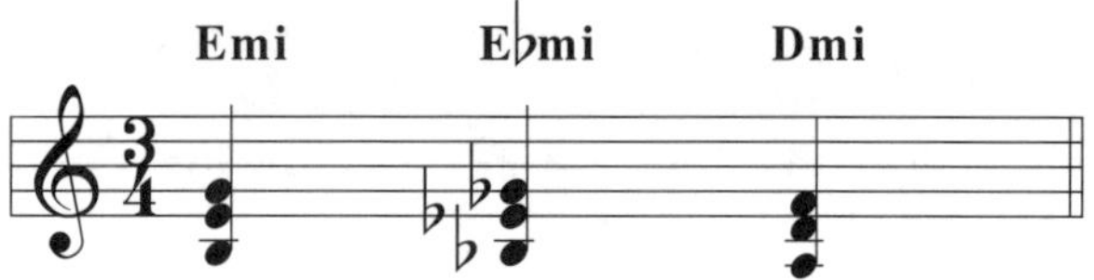

This chromatic minor triad idea can then be used within a G Mixolydian mode context over a G7 chord, as in the following example:-

Figure 17.49. Slow gospel pattern #24 - 'parallel' minor triads used within G Mixolydian
(CASSETTE TAPE EXAMPLE 731)

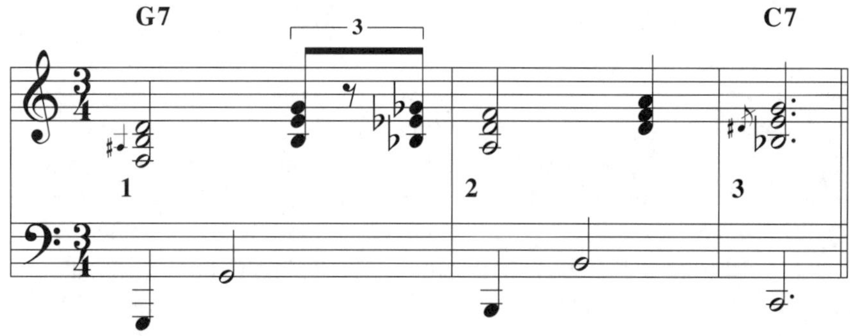

This example can be analyzed as follows:-

- Measure 1 - On the **G7** chord, the right hand is playing the 2nd inversion triads B diminished on beat **1**, and E minor on beat **3**. These triads are again from a **G Mixolydian** mode. The chromatic connecting triad of **Eb minor** is also used on the last subdivision of beat **3**, leading into the following D minor triad in the next measure (see **Fig. 17.48.** above). An A# grace note has been added on beat **1**, leading into B (the 3rd of the **G7** chord). The left hand is playing the root on beats **1** & **2**.

- Measure 2 - Continuing over the **G7** chord, the right hand is using 2nd inversion & root position D minor triads (again from a **G Mixolydian** mode), on beats **1** & **3** respectively. The left hand has moved up to B (on beats **1** & **2**) implying an inversion of the **G7**, or a **Bmi7(b5)** chord.

Constructing slow gospel patterns (contd)

Analysis of Fig. 17.49. contd.

- Measure 3 - On the **C7** chord, the right hand is playing a 2nd inversion E diminished triad on beat **1**, from the **C Mixolydian** mode. A D# grace note has also been added on beat **1**, leading into E (the 3rd of the C7 chord). The left hand is again playing the root on beat **1** of the measure.

Now we have a variation on the above pattern, this time using a chromatic walkup in the left hand between the root and 3rd of the G7 chord. This walkup could be termed a '**1 - 2 - #2 - 3**' pattern, as these are the scale degrees used to connect between these chord tones (on a **G7** the notes G - A - A# - B would be used). This is useful when leading into a dominant chord inverted over the 3rd, as in the following example:-

Figure 17.50. Slow gospel pattern #25 - 'parallel' minor triads used within G Mixolydian - with chromatic '1 - 2 - #2 - 3' walkup in left hand *(Cassette Tape Example 732)*

The right hand is the same as in pattern **#24** (**Fig. 17.49.**) except for the use of the 1st inversion G major triad at the beginning of the first measure. In the first measure the left hand is using a **1 - 2 - #2 - 3** pattern with respect to the **G7** chord, against the descending minor triads in the right hand. This left hand line (G, A, A# & B) is rhythmically 'concerted' with the right hand part, except for the pickup into beat **3** of the first measure. As in the previous example, the D minor triad in the second measure over B in the bass voice, implies an inverted **G7** chord over the 3rd, or a **Bmi7(b5)** chord. During the second measure the left hand is now playing the note B in octaves, landing on the last subdivisions of beats **2** & **3**.

The next example combines 'parallel minor triads' with diatonic and chromatic left hand walkups:-

Figure 17.51. Slow gospel pattern #26 - 'parallel' minor triads used within G Mixolydian - with chromatic ('1 - 6 - #6 - 7') and diatonic walkups in left hand *(Cassette Tape Example 733)*

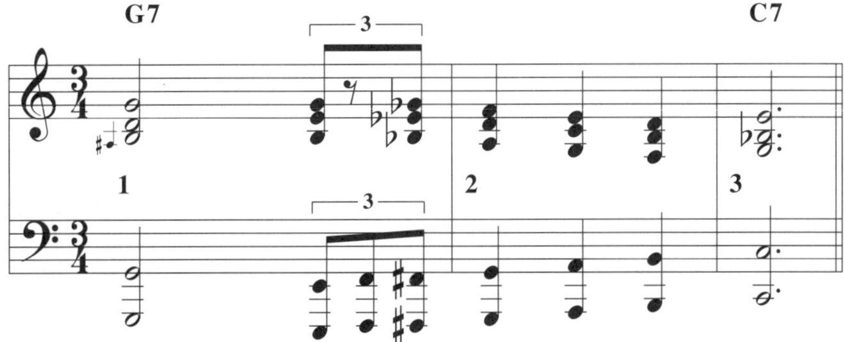

Constructing slow gospel patterns (contd)

The previous example (**Fig. 17.51.**) can be analyzed as follows:-

- Measure 1 - On the **G7** chord, the right hand is playing a 1st inversion G major triad on beat **1**, and the 2nd inversion triads E minor on beat **3** and Eb minor on the last subdivision of beat **3**. The G major and E minor triads are from the **G Mixolydian** mode, and the Eb minor triad is the 'chromatic connection' between the E minor triad and the following D minor triad (see **Fig. 17.48.**). An A# grace note has also been added on beat **1**, leading into B (the 3rd of the **G7** chord). The left hand is playing octaves and using a **1 - 6 - #6 - 7 - 1** pattern (see **Fig. 17.37.**), starting on beat **1** and then using all 3 subdivisions of beat **3**, leading into the next measure.

- Measure 2 - Continuing on the **G7** chord, the right hand is playing the 2nd inversion triads D minor, C major and B diminished, on beats **1**, **2** & **3** respectively. Against this in the left hand, we are using the diatonic walkup tones G, A & B in octaves again on the downbeats.

- Measure 3 - On the **C7** chord, the right hand is playing a 1st inversion E diminished triad (from the **C Mixolydian** mode) on beat **1**. The left hand is also playing the root in octaves on beat **1**.

Now we will examine another often-used gospel technique - the use of '**unison runs**' between left and right hands (i.e. playing the same notes in both left and right hands). Rhythmically this will typically use all 3 subdivisions of a beat (see **Fig. 17.1.**), or just the 1st and 3rd subdivisions (see **Fig. 17.3.**). Harmonically the note choices are normally made from pentatonic, mixolydian or blues scales, and can be used to imply a dominant-to-tonic (or 'five' to 'one') relationship, as in the following examples:-

Figure 17.52. Slow gospel pattern #27 - unison run example a)
(CASSETTE TAPE EXAMPLE 734)

Here rhythmically we are using the 1st & 3rd subdivisions of each beat, in the first measure (see **Fig. 17.3.**). The use of the note D on the first beat implies a potential **D7** harmony, leading to the following **G** chord. However, the **G pentatonic** scale (see **Fig. 1.60.**) built from the root of the second chord, is the scale source used for the unison run in the first measure. Now for a small variation on the above pattern:-

Figure 17.53. Slow gospel pattern #28 - unison run example b)
(CASSETTE TAPE EXAMPLE 735)

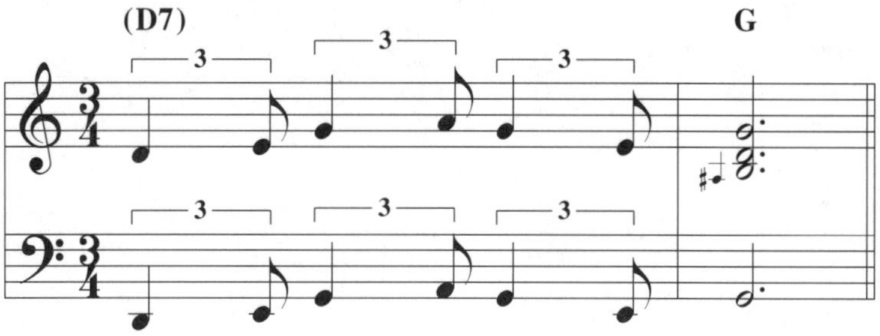

(D7) G

Similar to the above example, except for the note A on the last subdivision of beat **2** in the first measure, in both hands. This variation is still within the **G pentatonic** scale being used as the scale source for this 'run'.

Constructing slow gospel patterns (contd)

Figure 17.54. Slow gospel pattern #29 - unison run example c)
(CASSETTE TAPE EXAMPLE 736)

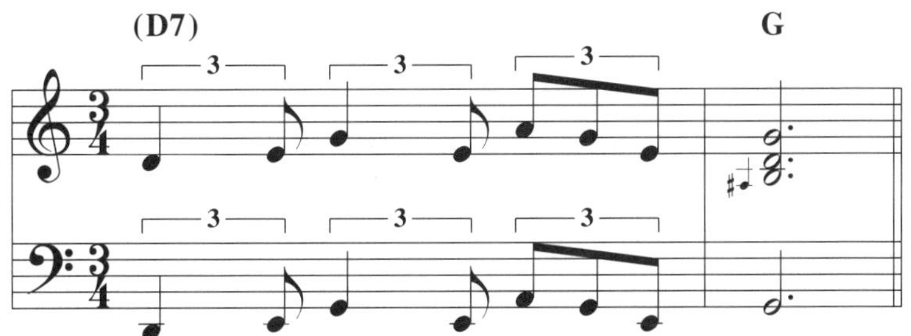

Another variation on pattern **#27** (**Fig. 17.52.**), this time using all three subdivisions of beat **3** in the first measure. The notes during beat **3** (A, G & E) are again from the **G pentatonic** scale.

Figure 17.55. Slow gospel pattern #30 - unison run example d)
(CASSETTE TAPE EXAMPLE 737)

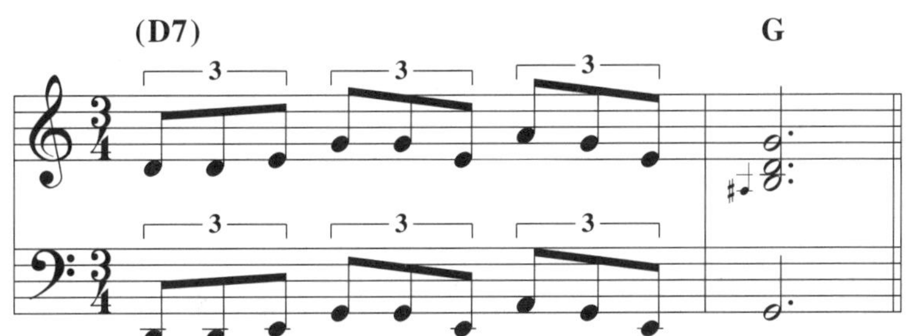

This run now uses all of the triplet subdivisions in the first measure. The notes played (D & E during beat **1**, G & E during beat **2**, and A, G & E during beat **3**) are again all from the **G pentatonic** scale.

Figure 17.56. Slow gospel pattern #31 - unison run example e)
(CASSETTE TAPE EXAMPLE 738)

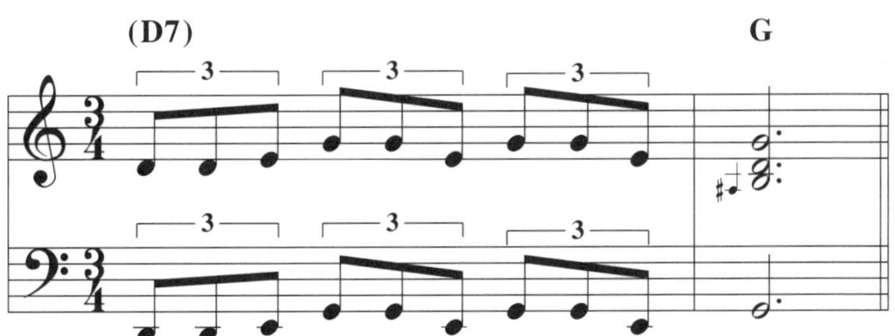

A small variation on the above pattern **#30** (**Fig. 17.55.**), with the note G being used on beat **3** in the first measure.

These are only a few of the numerous possibilities available, and as usual you are encouraged to experiment! Now we will consider the related concept of '**octave runs**' in either the left, right, or both hands. Again the source of these runs is normally either a pentatonic, blues or mixolydian scale (or a succession of half-steps) and if played in both hands is typically in 'unison' i.e. using the same pitch in both hands, in a similar manner to the above examples. Again normally these runs are used to 'connect' or to lead into a point of chord change. We will begin by looking at a right hand 'octave run' example as follows:-

Constructing slow gospel patterns (contd)

Figure 17.57. Slow gospel pattern #32 - octave run example a)
(CASSETTE TAPE EXAMPLE 739)

This example can be analyzed as follows:-

- Measure 1 - On the **G7** chord, the right hand is playing a combination of a 1st inversion G major triad and a 2nd inversion B diminished triad on beat **1**, the same as the start of pattern **#23** (**Fig. 17.47.**). During beats **2** & **3**, the right hand is playing an octave run using the entire **G pentatonic** scale (the notes G, A, B, D & E - see **Fig. 1.60.**), leading into the next chord. (Here the pentatonic scale has been built from the **root** of the G7 chord). The left hand is playing the root of the chord (in octaves) on beat **1**.

- Measure 2 - On the **C** chord, the right hand is using a root position C triad (with the top note doubled) on beat **1**. Note that the register of this voicing is an octave higher than the previous voicing on the **G7** chord - the pentatonic octave run in the previous measure provides an effective link and 'build' into the **C** chord. This type of quick register change is typical in gospel styles. Again the left hand is playing the root of the chord in octaves, on beat **1**.

Pentatonic octave runs can also be combined with chromatic half-steps, as in the following variation:-

Figure 17.58. Slow gospel pattern #33 - octave run example b)
(CASSETTE TAPE EXAMPLE 740)

This example can be analyzed as follows:-

Constructing slow gospel patterns (contd)

Analysis of Fig. 17.58. contd.

- Measure 1 - On the **G7** chord, the right hand voicing on beat **1** and the G pentatonic run during beat **3** are the same as for pattern **#32** (**Fig. 17.57.**). Now during the last 2 subdivisions of beat **2** we have an ascending octave run using A & A# - these notes are chromatically approaching the 3rd of the **G7** chord (B), in a similar way to the **1 - 2 - #2 - 3** line first seen in **Fig. 17.50.** The left hand is again playing the root in octaves.

- Measure 2 - On the **Emi7** chord, the right hand is playing a **b3-5-b7** upper structure triad (a 1st inversion G major triad with the top note doubled - see **Fig. 5.6.**). The left hand is again playing the root of the chord in octaves. As in pattern **#32** (**Fig. 17.57.**), this run has enabled a significant register change to occur between these two chords.

The next example combines a number of ideas we have looked at in recent patterns. The left and right hands can play unison runs in octaves, using chromatic half-steps as follows:-

Figure 17.59. Slow gospel pattern #34 - octave run example c)
(CASSETTE TAPE EXAMPLE 741)

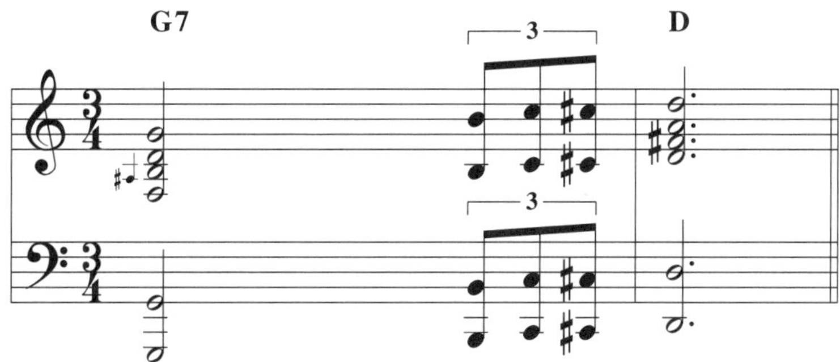

This example can be analyzed as follows:-

- Measure 1 - On the **G7** chord, the right hand is again playing a combination of a 1st inversion G major triad and a 2nd inversion B diminished triad on beat **1**, as in patterns **#23** & **#32** (**Figs. 17.47.** and **17.57.**). During beat **3** both hands are playing a **3 - 4 - #4** (leading to **5** in the next measure) pattern in octaves, with respect to the **G7** chord (see **Fig. 17.39.**).

- Measure 2 - On the **D** chord, the right hand is using a 1st inversion D triad (with the top note doubled) on beat **1**, together with the root in octaves in the left hand.

We have seen in these examples that the use of octave and/or unison runs can enable quick register changes to occur i.e. the register will change over a short period of time. Another device which facilitates this is the use of '**chord inversions**'. This involves using different inversions of the same chord (or of the same 'upper structure' on the chord) during the measure(s) prior to a chord change, to build the energy of the arrangement. The next examples demonstrate this technique:-

Constructing slow gospel patterns (contd)

Figure 17.60. Slow gospel pattern #35 - chord inversions example a)
(Cassette Tape Example 742)

This example can be analyzed as follows:-

- Measure 1 - On the **C** chord, the right hand is playing a 1st inversion C triad (with the top note doubled) on beats **1** & **3**, and a root position F triad (again with the top note doubled) on the last subdivision of beat **3**. This represents a **single backcycle** on the C chord. The left hand is playing the root of the chord on beats **1** & **2**. A D# grace note has been added on beat **1**, leading into E (the 3rd of the C chord).

- Measure 2 - Continuing on the C chord, the right hand is successively using 1st inversion, 2nd inversion, and root position C triads (all with top note doubled) on beats **1**, **2** & **3** respectively (review major triad inversions in **Fig. 4.3.** as necessary). Again the D# grace note has been added, in a similar manner to the first measure. The left hand is playing the root on beat **1** and the last subdivision of beat **2** (leading into beat **3**).

- Measure 3 - On the **G** chord, the right hand is playing a 1st inversion G triad (with the top note doubled) on beat **1**, together with an A# grace note leading into B (the 3rd of the chord). The left hand is again playing the root on beat **1**.

Again note the register change occurring during the second measure above, creating a build into the following chord. Now for another example, using inversions of a diminished seventh chord (review **Fig. 1.81.** as necessary):-

Figure 17.61. Slow gospel pattern #36 - chord inversions example b)
(Cassette Tape Example 743)

Constructing slow gospel patterns (contd)

The previous progression typically occurs in gospel styles as a **4**major - **#4**dim7 - **1**major/**5**. (Underlined numbers represent scale degrees with respect to the key). We can again analyze this example as follows:-

- Measure 1 - On the **C** chord, the right hand is playing a root position C triad (with the top note doubled) on beat **1** and on the last subdivisions of beats **2** & **3**. In between the right hand is playing a 2nd inversion F triad (again with the top note doubled) on beat **3**. This represents a **single backcycle** on the C chord. The left hand is playing the root on beats **1** & **2**.

- Measure 2 - On the **C#dim7** chord, the right hand is successively using 3rd inversion, root position, and 1st inversion C#dim7 4-part shapes (all with top note doubled) on beats **1**, **2** & **3** respectively. Note that the diminished 7th is unique among 4-part chord shapes in that the inversions do not change the internal intervals - we always have minor 3rds (three half-steps) between one chord tone and the next. The left hand is playing the root on beat **1** and the last subdivision of beat **2** (leading into beat **3**).

- Measure 3 - On the **G/D** chord, the right hand is playing a root position G triad (with the top note doubled) on beat **1**. The left hand is playing the 5th of the G chord (D) also on beat **1**, creating an inversion (see **Fig. 5.5.**). The bass line moving by half-steps throughout this progression (C - C# - D) is a common sound in gospel styles.

Now we will look at a final gospel harmonic device which is the use of a '**dominant approach**' chord. This harmonically embellishes a progression by adding a new dominant chord immediately before an existing chord in a gospel progression. This new dominant chord normally has a root which is a **half-step below** the chord being approached, and typically contains a **raised 5th** which then becomes a commontone between the new approach chord and the following chord. This commontone is then the (unaltered) 5th on the following chord, as follows:-

Figure 17.62. Dominant approach - harmonic example
(Cassette Tape Example 744)

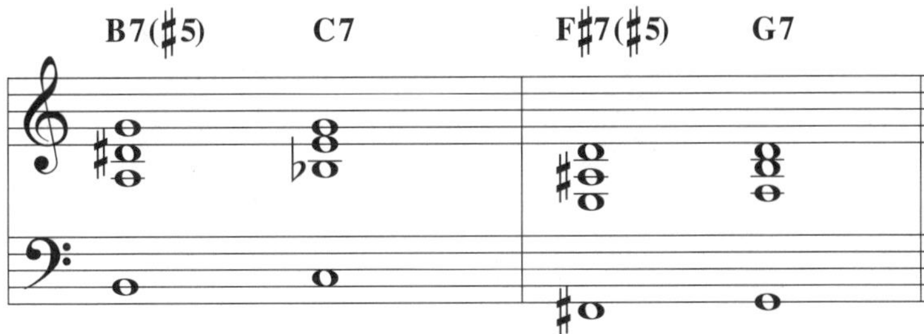

In the first measure above, the **C7** chord is being approached by the **B7(#5)** chord. (Review **Fig. 1.84.** as necessary regarding the spelling of the dominant 7th with raised 5th). Note the voicing on these chords which from bottom to top contains the **root** (in the left hand), **b7th**, **3rd** & **5th** (or **raised 5th**). This is a very common dominant voicing in jazz & blues as well as gospel styles. Note that the raised 5th on the B7(#5) - the note G - is also the 5th on the following C7 chord. In the second measure, a similar concept is occurring with the **G7** being approached by the **F#7(#5)** chord. Again the raised 5th on the F#7(#5) - the note D - is also the 5th on the following G7 chord. Rhythmically the dominant approach chord will often 'steal' the last beat from the measure prior to the chord being approached, as in the following pattern example:-

Constructing slow gospel patterns (contd)

Figure 17.63. Slow gospel pattern #37 - dominant approach example a)
(Cassette Tape Example 745)

We can analyze this pattern as follows:-

- Measure 1 - On the **G7** chord, the right hand is again playing a combination of a 1st inversion G major triad and a 2nd inversion B diminished triad (from the **G Mixolydian** mode), on beats **1** & **3** (including the grace note A# on beat **1**). The movement to a C triad on the last subdivision of beat **3**, could be thought of as a **single backcycle** on the G7 chord - also the C triad is found within a **G Mixolydian** mode. (See first measure of pattern **#23** - **Fig. 17.47.**). The left hand is playing the root in octaves on beat **1**, with the 5th (D) on the 2nd subdivision of beat **3** in the rhythmic space between the right hand voicings.

- Measure 2 - Continuing on the **G7** chord, the right hand voicing is the same as for the beginning of measure 1. The left hand is playing the root on beat **1** and on the last subdivision of beat **2**.
- On the **B7(#5)** chord, the right hand is playing (from bottom to top) a **b7-3-#5** voicing on this chord (see first measure of **Fig. 17.62.**) on beat **3**, **approaching the following C7 chord**. The left hand is playing the root of the chord on beat **3**.

- Measure 3 - On the **C7** chord, the right hand is playing a 2nd inversion E diminished triad (which is found in the **C Mixolydian** mode) on beat **1**, together with the D# grace note. The top note (G) is a commontone with the previous chord. The left hand is playing the root of the chord on beat **1**.

The next example uses a dominant approach chord within a chromatic walkup as follows:-

Figure 17.64. Slow gospel pattern #38 - dominant approach example b)
(Cassette Tape Example 746)

Constructing slow gospel patterns (contd)

The previous example can be analyzed as follows:-

- Measure 1 - On the **C7** chord, the right hand is playing the 2nd inversion triads G minor on beat **1**, F major on the last subdivision of beat **2**, E diminished on beat **3**, and D minor on the last subdivision of beat **3**. These are all derived from the **C Mixolydian** mode. Against this in the left hand, we are using a **1 - 6 - #6 - 7** (**- 1**) pattern, with respect to the **C7** chord (see **Fig. 17.36.**), with the same rhythm as the right hand part.

- Measure 2 - Continuing on the **C7** chord, the right hand is now playing the 2nd inversion triads C major on beat **1** and the last subdivision of beat **2**, and Bb major on beat **3**. Again these triads are from the **C Mixolydian** mode. Meanwhile the left hand has begun a **1 - 3 - 4 - #4 - 5** pattern (with respect to the **C7** chord - see **Fig. 17.38.**) again using the same rhythm as the right hand part, arriving on the note F below the Bb triad in the right hand on beat **3**.

- The **F#7(#5)** chord occurs on the last subdivision of beat **3**, and is an approach chord to the following **G7** chord - these two chords are being used over the last two bass notes in the chromatic bass run described above. Again we are using a **b7-3-#5** voicing on the F#7(#5) chord (see 2nd measure of **Fig. 17.62.**) - the raised 5th on the F#7(#5) is a commontone with the following chord and in this case is 'tied over' the barline.

- Measure 3 - On the **G7** chord, the right hand is playing a 2nd inversion B diminished triad (with the top note tied over), from the **G Mixolydian** mode. The left hand is playing the root of the chord on beat **1**.

PRACTICE DIRECTIONS:-

- ***Practice the 'parallel' minor triad examples as in Figs. 17.49. - 17.51.***
- ***Practice the 'unison run' examples as in Figs. 17.52. - 17.56.***
- ***Practice the 'octave run' examples as in Figs. 17.57. - 17.59.***
- ***Practice the 'chord inversions' examples as in Figs. 17.60. - 17.61.***
- ***Practice the 'dominant approach' examples as in Figs. 17.62. - 17.64.***

Again - transposing the patterns is an excellent source of additional practice!

Constructing slow gospel patterns (contd)

Now we will begin to use the previously demonstrated harmonic concepts in the interpretation of some gospel leadsheets, to generate an accompaniment or 'comping' solution. We started to look at this in **Figs. 17.23. - 17.25.**, where a simple chord chart was interpreted using either Mixolydian triads or backcycling, and in **Figs. 17.26. - 17.32.** where we used backcycling to harmonically embellish the progression. Now we will add the use of 'parallel' minor triads, octave and unison runs, chord inversions etc. for the following leadsheet:-

Figure 17.65. Slow gospel chord chart example #3

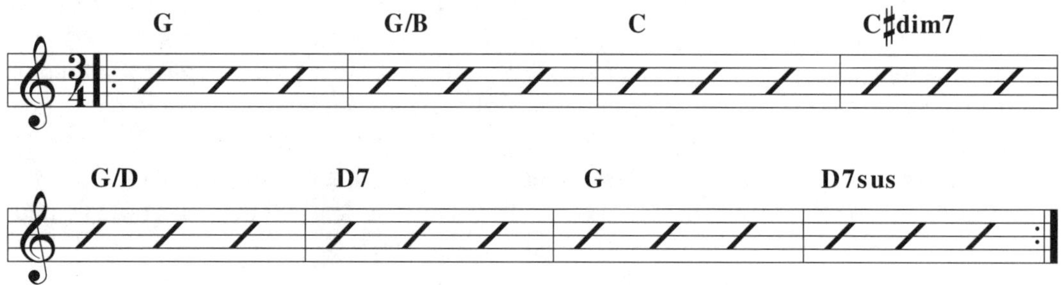

We will now interpret this leadsheet in a slow gospel 'comping' style as follows:-

Figure 17.66. Slow gospel comping solution for chord chart #3 (Fig. 17.65.)
(Cassette Tape Example 747)

(CONTD-->)

Constructing slow gospel patterns (contd)

Figure 17.66. contd.

We will analyze this comping solution as follows:-

- Measure 1 - On the **G** chord, the right hand is playing a 1st inversion G triad (with the top note doubled) on beats **1** & **3**, with an A# grace note on beat **1** leading into B (the 3rd of the chord). The root of the chord (G) is also used as a pickup into beat **3**. On the last subdivision of beat **3** we are using a root position C triad, again with the top note doubled - this represents a **single backcycle** on the **G** chord (see **Fig. 17.17.**). The left hand is playing the root of the chord on beats **1** & **2**, and in octaves on beat **3**. At this point the left hand is beginning a **1 - 2 - 3** diatonic walkup with respect to the **G** chord (see **Figs. 17.33. - 17.35.**), creating a momentary **Ami7** chord under the backcycled C triad on the last subdivision of beat **3**, leading to the following **G/B** chord.

- Measure 2 - On the **G/B** chord, the right hand voicing on beat **1** is the same as for the beginning of measure 1. During beats **2** & **3**, the right hand is playing an octave run using the entire **G pentatonic** scale (the notes G, A, B, D & E - see **Figs. 1.60.** & **17.57.**). In this case the pentatonic scale has been built from the root of the (inverted) **G** chord. The run is leading into the following **C** chord, building the energy level and quickly changing the right hand register. The left hand is playing the 3rd of the chord (B) on beat **1** in octaves, creating an inversion. This bass voice completes the **1 - 2 - 3** diatonic walkup (with respect to the **G** chord) which began in beat **3** of measure 1.

- Measure 3 - On the **C** chord, the right hand is playing a root position C triad (with the top note doubled) on beats **1**, **2** & **3**. The 5th of the chord (G) is used for an extra rhythmic subdivision leading into beat **3**, and the note A in octaves (found in both the **C Mixolydian** and **C Pentatonic** scales) is used on the last subdivision of beat **3** to connect into the next chord. The left hand is playing the root on beats **1** & **2**.

Constructing slow gospel patterns (contd)

Analysis of Fig. 17.66. contd.

- Measure 4 - On the **C#dim7** chord, the middle two notes of each right hand voicing (on beats **1**, **2** & **3**) are C# & E, the root & 3rd of the chord. Above and below this interval, the descending line of Bb, A & G is being played in octaves again on the downbeats. Over the C# in the root voice, this momentarily creates passing chords of **C#dim7**, **A/C#**, and **C#dim** respectively. The left hand is playing the root of the chord on beat **1** and on the last subdivision of beat **2**.

- Measure 5 - On the **G/D** chord, the right hand is playing a 2nd inversion G triad (with the top note doubled) on beat **1**, with a C# grace note leading into D (the 5th of the chord). At this point the left hand is playing the 5th of the chord (D) on beats **1** & **2**, creating an inversion. Starting on beat **3** and leading into the next measure, both hands are playing a **3 - 4 - #4 - 5** chromatic walkup pattern (with respect to the **G** chord) in octaves, using all the triplet subdivisions of beat **3** (see **Figs. 17.39.** & **17.59.**).

- Measure 6 - On the **D7** chord, all the triads used have 'doubled' top notes. The right hand is playing a 1st inversion D triad on beat **1**, followed by a 2nd inversion Bb minor triad on beat **2** and a 2nd inversion A minor triad on beat **3**. The Bb minor triad is a 'parallel' chromatic minor triad which is approaching the following A minor triad. Notice that the top note line here is **D - Db (C#) - C** which represents a chromatic half-step connection between the tonic (D) and 7th (C) of a **D Mixolydian** mode (see **Fig. 17.48.** and accompanying text, regarding the use of these 'parallel' minor triads). The A minor triad used on beat **3** is also from the **D Mixolydian** mode. Against these triads, the left hand is playing the diatonic walkup tones D, E & F# in octaves leading into the following G chord. This momentarily creates passing chords of **Bbmi/E** (a dissonant vertical sound) on beat **2** and **Ami/F#** or **F#mi7(b5)** on beat **3**.

- Measure 7 - On the **G** chord, the right hand voicing on beat **1** is the same as for the beginning of measure 5. At this point the left hand is playing the root on beats **1** & **2**. The right hand then repeats the 2nd inversion G triad (with the top note doubled) on beat **3**, followed by the connecting tones A & G (found in both the **G pentatonic** and **G Mixolydian** scales) in octaves on the remaining subdivisions of beat **3**. Against this in the left hand, starting on beat **3** we are using a **3 - 4 - #4 - 5** chromatic walkup pattern (with respect to the **G** chord) in octaves (see **Fig. 17.39.**). This again uses the remaining subdivisions of beat **3**.

- Measure 8 - On the **D7sus** chord, again all the triads used have 'doubled' top notes. The right hand is using root position, 2nd inversion and 1st inversion C triads on beats **1**, **2** & **3** respectively (we first saw this type of 'upper shape' inversion changes used in **Fig. 17.60.**). The use of the successive inversions again results in a rapid register change, this time in a descending direction. This time though, the C triad is a **b7-9-11** upper structure triad on the **D7sus** chord (we first saw this voicing for a suspended dominant chord in **Fig. 5.2.**). During beat **3** chord tones from this upper triad (G & E) are being arpeggiated. The left hand is playing the root in octaves on beat **1**, and in an octave pattern on the last subdivision of beat **2**, leading into beat **3**.

Now we will consider a comping solution for a longer leadsheet (16 measures), containing major triad chord symbols. Again we will use a mixture of harmonic devices, including backcycling, octave runs (using pentatonic scales), Mixolydian triads, diatonic and chromatic walkups etc. Here is the next leadsheet to be interpreted in a slow gospel comping style:-

Constructing slow gospel patterns (contd)

Figure 17.67. Slow gospel chord chart example #4

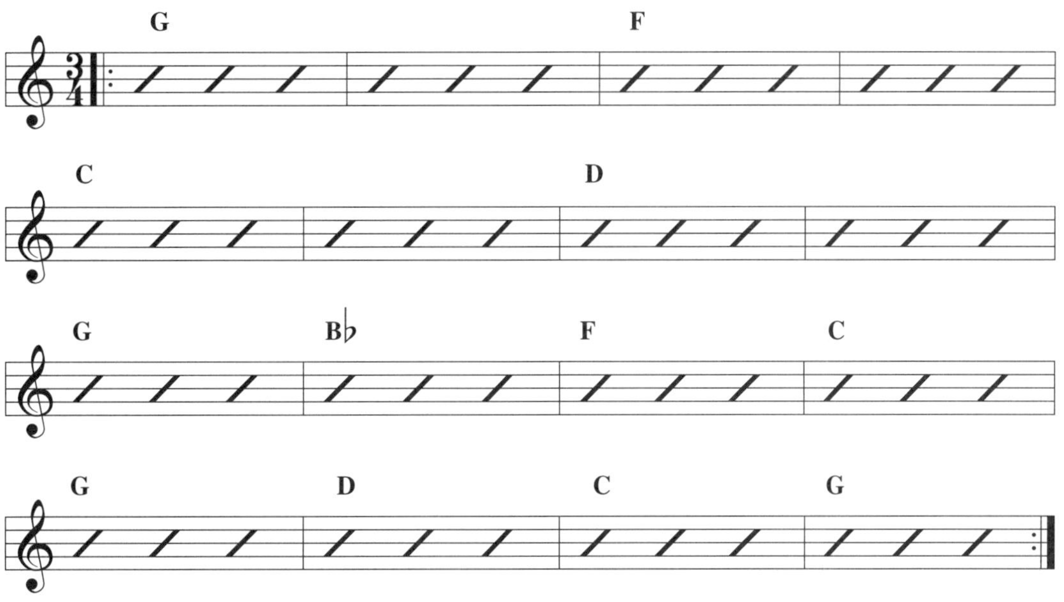

We will now interpret this chart as follows:-

Figure 17.68. Slow gospel comping solution for chord chart #4 (Fig. 17.67.)
(Cassette Tape Example 748)

(CONTD-->)

Constructing slow gospel patterns (contd)

Figure 17.68. contd.

Again this comping solution can be analyzed as follows:-

- Measure 1 - On the **G** chord, in the right hand we are using a **single backcycle** (moving between G & C major triads) against root-5th & root-6th couplings in the left hand, similar to **Fig. 17.17.** but with the top note doubled. An A# grace note has been added on beat **1**, leading into B (the 3rd of the chord).

- Measure 2 - Continuing on the **G** chord, the voicing on beat **1** is the same as for the previous measure. From the 2nd subdivision of beat **2** until the end of the measure, the right hand is playing an octave run using the entire **G pentatonic** scale (built from the root of the **G** chord - see **Figs. 1.60.** & **17.57.**), leading into the next chord.

Constructing slow gospel patterns (contd)

Analysis of Fig. 17.68. contd.

- Measure 3 - On the **F** chord, in the right hand we are again using a single backcycle (moving between F & Bb major triads) with the top note doubled, against root-5th & root-6th couplings in the left hand (see **Fig. 17.17.**). A G# grace note has been added on beat **1**, leading into A (the 3rd of the chord).

- Measure 4 - Continuing on the **F** chord, the voicing on beat **1** is the same as for the previous measure. During beat **3**, the right hand is playing a descending octave run using the diatonic connecting tones F, E & D to lead into the next chord.

- Measure 5 - On the **C** chord, in the right hand we are using a **double backcycle** (moving between C, Bb & F major triads, with doubled top notes - see **Fig. 17.19.**) against the left hand root-&-5th pattern.

- Measure 6 - Continuing on the **C** chord, the voicing on beat **1** is the same as for the previous measure. The right hand is repeating the 2nd inversion C triad (with top note doubled) on beat **3**, followed by the descending connecting tones D & C in octaves (which could be considered as coming from either the **C pentatonic** or **C Mixolydian** scales). The left hand is playing the root on beats **1** & **2**.

- Measure 7 - On the **D** chord, the right hand is playing 1st inversion D major triads on beat **1** (with the top note doubled) and on beat **3**, leading to the 2nd inversion Bb minor triad on the last subdivision of beat **3**. This is a 'parallel' chromatic minor triad (see **Figs. 17.48. - 17.51.**) leading to the A minor triad (from the **D Mixolydian** mode) in the following measure. Against this the left hand is using a **1 - 6 - #6 - 7 - 1** pattern (with respect to the the **D** chord - see **Fig. 17.36.**) which finishes on the note D at the beginning of the next measure.

- Measure 8 - Continuing on the **D** chord, the right hand is now using the 2nd inversion triads A minor, G major and F# diminished (from the **D Mixolydian** mode) on beats **1**, **2** & **3**. This is upgrading the original **D** chord symbol to a **D7** implication overall. Against this in the left hand the diatonic walkup tones D, E & F# are being used (similar to the left hand part in **Fig. 17.34.**).

- Measure 9 - On the **G** chord, the right hand is playing a 2nd inversion G triad on beat **1**, followed by another octave run using the tones from the **G pentatonic** scale during beats **2** & **3** - similar to measure 2, but now starting on the 5th of the chord (D) and ending on the 3rd (B). This facilitates an abrupt change of register into the following **Bb** chord. The left hand is playing the root of the chord on beats **1** & **2**.

- Measure 10 - On the **Bb** chord, in the right hand we are using a **single backcycle** (moving between Bb & Eb major triads, with the top notes doubled) during beats **1** & **2** and again during beat **3** - see **Fig. 17.17.** Against this the left hand is using a **1 - 3 - 4 - #4 - 5** pattern (with respect to the **Bb** chord - see **Fig. 17.38.**) which starts on beat **1**, rhythmically alternates with the upper backcycle during beats **3** & **4**, and finishes on the root of the **F** major chord in the following measure.

- Measure 11 - On the **F** chord, the right hand is playing a 2nd inversion F triad on beat **1**, with the left hand playing the root on beats **1** & **2**. During beat **3** the right hand is using a **single backcycle** (moving between F & Bb major triads), against a chromatically ascending left hand line. Overall the left hand is using a **1 - 3 - 4 - #4 - 5** pattern (with respect to the **F** chord - see **Fig. 17.38.**) which again starts on beat **1**, uses all of the subdivisions in beat **3**, and finishes on the root of the **C** chord in the following measure.

Constructing slow gospel patterns (contd)

Analysis of Fig. 17.68. contd.

- Measure 12 - On the **C** chord, in the right hand we are using a **double backcycle** (moving between C, Bb, F & C major triads, with doubled top notes except for the first C triad - see **Fig. 17.19.**). The grace note D# is also used on beat **1**, leading into E (the 3rd of the chord). Against this the left hand is again using a **1 - 3 - 4 - #4 - 5** pattern (with respect to the **C** chord - see **Fig. 17.42.**) rhythmically 'concerted' with the right hand part, creating the dissonant passing chords of **Bb/E** and **C/F#** on the last subdivisions of beats **2** & **3** respectively.

- Measure 13 - On the **G** chord, the right hand is playing a 1st inversion G triad (with the top note doubled), and 2nd inversion D minor and C major triads, on beats **1**, **2** & **3** respectively. These are derived from the **G Mixolydian** mode, and upgrade the chord to a **G7** implication overall. An A# grace note has been added on beat **1**, leading into B (the 3rd of the chord). Again the left hand is using a **1 - 3 - 4 - #4 - 5** pattern (with respect to the **G** chord), also landing on the downbeats and adding a pickup into the next measure. This momentarily creates the passing chords of **Dmi/B** or **Bmi7(b5)** on beat **2**, and **C** major on beat **3**. Note that the progression from measure 10 to measure 14 is itself a series of 'backcycles' i.e. moving by circle-of-4ths. In measures 10 to 13 we have used rhythmic variations of the chromatically ascending **1 - 3 - 4 - #4 - 5** bass line (see **Figs. 17.38.** & **17.39.**) to connect the left hand into the root of the next chord.

- Measure 14 - On the **D** chord, the right hand is playing a 1st inversion D triad on beat **1**, followed by an ascending octave run using the notes from the **G pentatonic** scale during beats **2** & **3**. The left hand is playing the root of the chord on beat **1**, and doubling the right hand pentatonic run during beats **2** & **3** (see **Figs. 17.52.** - **17.56.**, and **17.59.**, for examples of 'unison' runs between left and right hands).

- Measure 15 - On the **C** chord, we are playing a diatonic walkdown using a 'filled-in octave' concept - see measure 3 of **Fig. 17.33**. The left hand octaves, and the top & bottom notes in the right hand voicings, are using the diatonic walkdown tones C, B & A, with a diatonic 3rd interval being maintained above the bottom note in the right hand. A D# grace note has also been added on beat **1**, leading into E (the 3rd of the C chord).

- Measure 16 - On the **G** chord, the right hand is playing a 1st inversion G triad (with the top note doubled). Again an A# grace note has been added on beat **1**, leading into B (the 3rd of the chord). The left hand is playing the root of the chord in octaves, on beat **1**.

PRACTICE DIRECTIONS:-

- Practice the gospel comping solutions to leadsheets #3 and #4, as shown in Figs. 17.66. and 17.68.
- Work on applying these concepts to tunes of your choice, and to the practice charts at the end of this chapter.

Slow gospel melody

We will now focus on the treatment of melodies in a slow gospel style. All of the previously explained harmonic concepts will also apply here - the main difference is the manipulation of the upper right hand shape (typically a triad or 4-part chord) to ensure that the melody is on top. Often the melody may be played an octave higher than shown on the leadsheet, and doubled in octaves with the rest of the right hand shape in between these top and bottom notes. This will give the larger 'span of orchestration' (distance between lowest and highest note on the keyboard) and greater 'harmonic weight' (number of notes played simultaneously) typically needed in gospel styles. The melody may also be rephrased to accommodate upper voiceleading or backcycling ideas. We will now look at a 16-measure leadsheet with melody, to be interpreted in a slow gospel style:-

Figure 17.69. Slow gospel leadsheet (with melody) example

G D7 Emi7 C

G/B D♯dim7 Emi7 A7

C G/B F C C♯dim7

G/D D7 G

We will now interpret this gospel melody using the concepts explained above, as follows:-

Figure 17.70. Slow gospel melody treatment for leadsheet example (Fig. 17.69.)
(Cassette Tape Example 749)

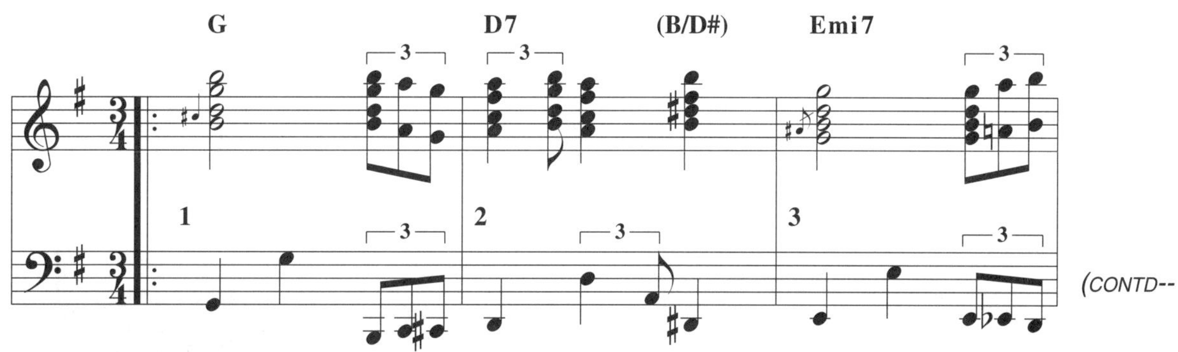

(CONTD--

Slow gospel melody (contd)

Figure 17.70. contd.

Slow gospel melody (contd)

In the previous example, the leadsheet melody was played an octave higher in the right hand, and most of the time was also doubled (i.e. the right hand was playing the melody in octaves, with the remainder of the voicing in between). We can further analyze this interpretation as follows:-

- Measure 1 - On the **G** chord, in the right hand a 2nd inversion G triad is being used under the 3rd of the chord (B) in the melody on beats **1** & **3**. The remaining melody notes A & G during beat **3** are played in octaves. The left hand is playing the root of the chord on beats **1** & **2**, which starts a **1 - 3 - 4 - #4 - 5** pattern (with respect to the **G** chord - see **Fig. 17.39.**), continuing through beat **3** into the next measure.

- Measure 2 - On the **D7** chord, in the right hand a 2nd inversion F# diminished triad is being used under the 5th of the chord (A) in the melody on beat **1**. The melody is embellished at this point with the note B on the last subdivision of beat **1** (supported by a 2nd inversion G major triad) and back to the note A on beat **2** (supported again with the 2nd inverison F# diminished triad). These triads all derive from the **D Mixolydian** mode, again built from the root of the **D7** chord. This figure is also rather similar to a **single backcycle** on the **D7** chord. The left hand is playing the root on beats **1** & **2**, with the 5th being played on the last subdivision of beat **2**. On beat **3**, a passing chord of **B/D#** has been introduced, below the note B in the melody. This effectively leads into the next chord (Emi7) - the root moves up by half-step (from D# to E), and the overall chord moves in a circle-of-5ths manner (from B to E minor).

- Measure 3 - On the **Emi7** chord, in the right hand a 1st inversion G triad is being used under the 3rd of the chord (G) in the melody on beats **1** & **3**. The G triad is a **b3-5-b7** upper structure on the overall **Emi7** chord - we first saw this voicing for a minor 7th chord in **Fig. 5.6.** An A# grace note has also been added on beat **1**, leading into B (the 3rd of the upper G triad, and the 5th of the overall **Emi7** chord). The remaining melody notes A & B during beat **3** are played in octaves. The left hand is playing the root on beats **1** & **2**, and during beat **3** is using the chromatically descending line E - Eb - D to connect into the root of the next chord (C).

- Measure 4 - On the **C** chord, in the right hand a 1st inversion C triad is being used under the root of the chord (C) in the melody on beat **1**. The melody is rhythmically embellished here with a **single backcycle**, moving to an F triad on the last subdivision of beat **1**, and back to the C triad on beat **2**. A 2nd inversion C triad is used under the 3rd of the chord (E) in the melody on beat **3**. The left hand is playing the root of the chord on beat **1** and on the last subdivision of beat **2**.

- Measure 5 - On the **G/B** chord, in the right hand a root position G triad is being used under the 5th of the chord (D) in the melody on beats **1** & **3**, with the remaining melody during beat **3** being played as single notes. The left hand is playing the 3rd of the chord (B) on beats **1** & **2**, creating an inversion. During beat **3** the left hand is playing the diatonic connecting tones B, C & D (which are the **3**, **4** & **5** with respect to **G** chord), leading into the root of the next chord (D#dim7) by half-step.

- Measure 6 - On the **D#dim7** chord, in the right hand a root position D#dim7 4-part shape is being used under the diminished 7th of the chord (C) on beat **1**. During beats **2** & **3** the melody is altered to accommodate the octave run using tones of the D#dim7 chord - from bottom to top the arpeggio is using C, D#, F#, A & C in octaves. This effectively leads into the melody note B on the following **Emi7** chord. The left hand is playing the root of the chord on beats **1** & **2**.

Slow gospel melody (contd)

Analysis of Fig. 17.70. contd.

- Measure 7 - On the **Emi7** chord, in the right hand a 2nd inversion G triad is being used under the 5th of the chord (B) in the melody, on beat **1** (and played again on beat **2**). The G triad is a **b3-5-b7** upper structure on the **Emi7** chord (see **Fig. 5.6.**). In between these two G triads, a C triad is being used on the last subdivision of beat **1**. This figure during beats **1** & **2** rather looks like a **single backcycle** on a **G** chord - but instead of G in the bass voice we have E, creating an **Emi7** overall. This technique (applying a backcycle to a **b3-5-b7** upper structure) allows us to use backcycling on chords with an overall minor or minor 7th quality - for this to work, the upper triads generally need to be diatonic to the key being used. In this case the G & C triads are contained within the key of G major. Note that the backcycle, and the single note line during beat **3**, are embellishments added to the main melody. The left hand is playing the root on beats **1** & **3**, with the 5th on the last subdivision of beat **2**.

- Measure 8 - On the **A7** chord, in the right hand the 2nd inversion triads G major, F# minor and E minor (all with top notes doubled) are being used under 9th (B), root (A) and 7th (G) of the chord respectively on beats **1**, **2** & **3**. These triads all derive from the **A Mixolydian** mode (again built from the root of the **A7** chord). A C# grace note has been added on beat **1** (leading into D) and an A# grace note has been added on beat **3** (leading into B). The left hand is playing the root on beat **1**, and is then rhythmically alternating with the right hand part during beats **2** & **3**, using the diatonic walkup tones A & B leading into the following chord (C major).

- Measure 9 - On the **C** chord, in the right hand a 2nd inversion C triad is being used under the 3rd of the chord (E) in the melody on beat **1**. The melody is embellished here with a **single backcycle** - moving to an F triad on the last subdivision of beat **1**, and back to the C triad on beat **2** (in a similar manner to measure 4). A root position C triad is used under the 5th of the chord (G) in the melody on beat **3**. The left hand is playing the root on beat **1** and leading into beat **3**.

- Measure 10 - On the **G/B** chord, in the right hand a root position G triad is being used under the 5th of the chord (D) in the melody on beat **1**. The melody is again embellished here with a **single backcycle** - moving to a C triad on the last subdivision of beat **1**, and back to the G triad on beat **2** (similar to the previous measure). Two A# grace notes have been added on beats **1** & **2**, leading into B (the 3rd of the chord). The melody phrase during beat **3** is derived from the G pentatonic scale and is therefore ideal for an octave run (see **Fig. 17.57.**). The left hand is playing the 3rd of the chord (an inversion) on beat **1** and on the last subdivision of beat **2**.

- Measure 11 - On the **F** chord, in the right hand a 2nd inverison F triad is being used under the 3rd of the chord (A) in the melody on beats **1** & **3**. The melody note is repeated an octave lower leading into beat **3**, to create more rhythmic subdivision. The **single backcycle** during beat **3** (with the 1st inversion Bb triad on top) is a natural consequence of the chromatic melody note Bb on the last subdivision of beat **3**. Against this in the left hand, we are using a **1 - 3 - 4 - #4 - 5** bass line (with respect to the **F** chord - see **Fig. 17.38.**) beginning on beat **2** and leading into the next measure. This momentarily creates the passing chords of **F/Bb**(A#) on beat **3**, and the dissonant **Bb/B** on the last subdivision of beat **3**.

- Measure 12 - On the **C** chord, in the right hand a 2nd inversion F triad is being used under the 6th of the chord (A) on beat **1**, moving to a root position C triad under the 5th (G) on beat **2**. This is a **single backcycle** on the **C** chord, and is suggested by the A to G (**6** to **5** on this chord) movement in the melody. At this point the left hand is playing the root on beats **1** & **2** and on the last subdivision of beat **2**.

Slow gospel melody (contd)

Analysis of Fig. 17.70. contd.

- Measure 12 (contd) - On the **C#dim7** chord on beat **3**, in the right hand a 2nd inversion C#dim7 4-part shape is being used under the 3rd of the chord (E) in the melody. The left hand is playing the root of the chord.

- Measure 13 - On the **G/D** chord, in the right hand a root position G triad is being used under the 5th of the chord (D) in the melody on beat **1**. An A# grace note has also been added on beat **1**, leading into B (the 3rd of the chord). At this point the left hand is playing the 5th of the chord on beats **1** & **2**, creating an inversion. During beat **3** the melodic phrase is derived from the G pentatonic scale (D, E & G), and as such is ideal for another octave run (see **Fig. 17.57.**), creating a change of register into the next chord. Against this, the left hand is playing a chromatically ascending run starting on the 3rd of the chord (B) on beat **3**, and continuing into the next measure. This could be considered a **3 - 4 - #4 - 5** figure with respect to the G chord.

- Measure 14 - On the **D7** chord, in the right hand the 2nd inversion triads A minor, G major and the first inversion triad A minor (all with top notes doubled) are being used under 7th (C), 13th (B) and 5th (A) of the chord respectively on beats **1**, **2** & **3**. These triads all come from the **D Mixolydian** mode (again built from the root of the **D7** chord). Against this, the left hand is using the diatonic walkup tones D, E & F# also on the downbeats.

- Measure 15 - On the **G** chord, in the right hand a 1st inversion G triad is being used under the root of the chord (G) in the melody on beat **1**. An A# grace note has also been added on beat **1**, leading into B (the 3rd of the chord). During the rest of the measure we are moving between G & C major triads in the right hand, creating a **single backcycle** on the G chord (see **Fig. 17.17.**). The left hand is using root-5th and root-6th interval couplings to support the upper backcycle.

- Measure 16 - Continuing on the **G** chord, the voicing in this measure is the same as for beat **1** of measure 15.

Practice directions:-

- Practice the slow gospel melody treatment presented in Fig. 17.70. and explained in the subsequent text.
- Work on applying these slow gospel melody concepts to other tunes of your choice, and to the practice charts at the end of this chapter.

CHAPTER SEVENTEEN

Slow gospel practice examples

Figure 17.71. Practice leadsheet #1 (chords only - for 'comping' practice)

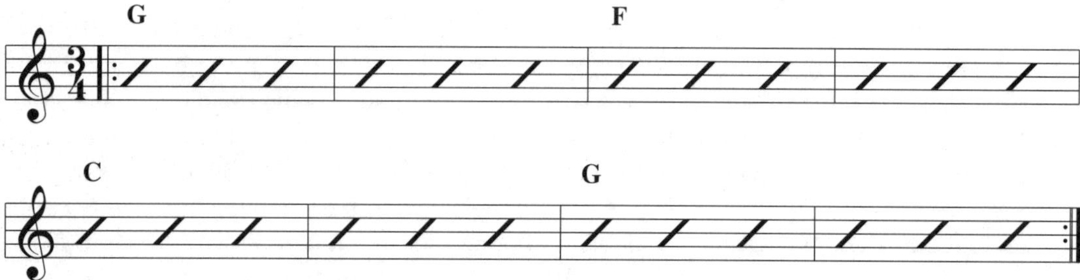

Figure 17.72. Practice leadsheet #2 (chords only - for 'comping' practice)

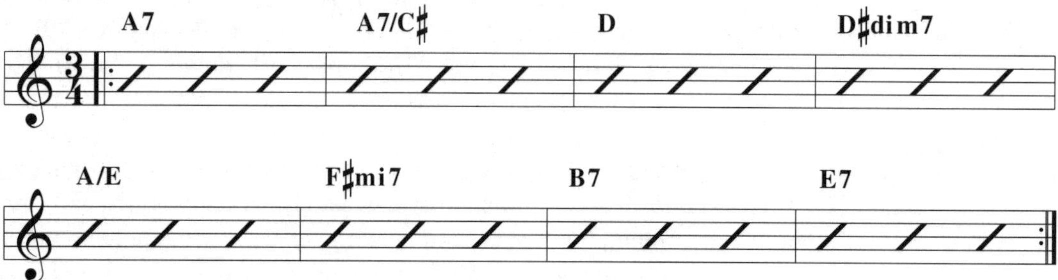

Figure 17.73. Practice leadsheet #3 (chords only - for 'comping' practice)

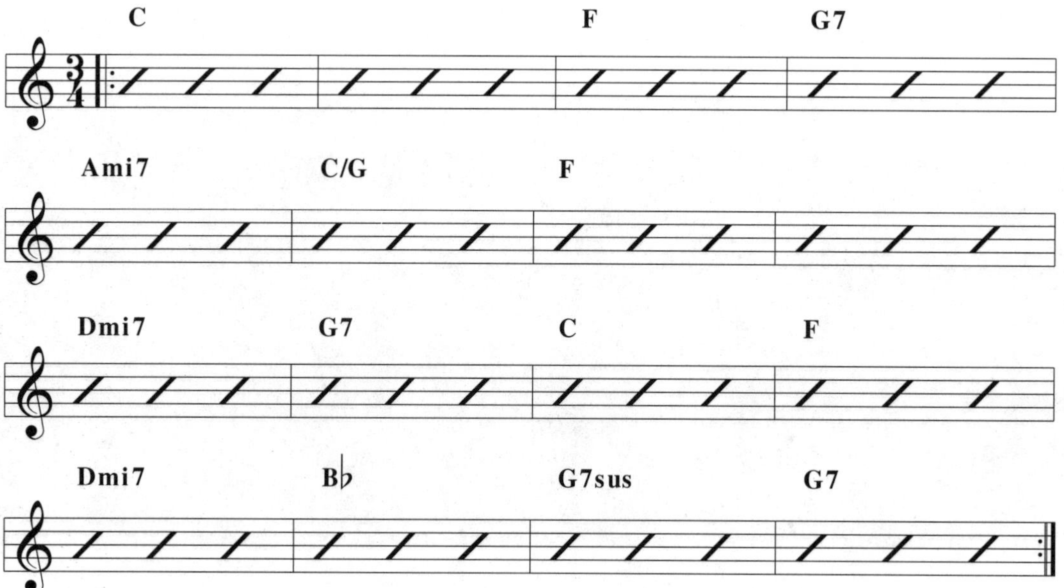

Slow gospel practice examples (contd)

Figure 17.74. Practice leadsheet #4 (chords only - for 'comping' practice)

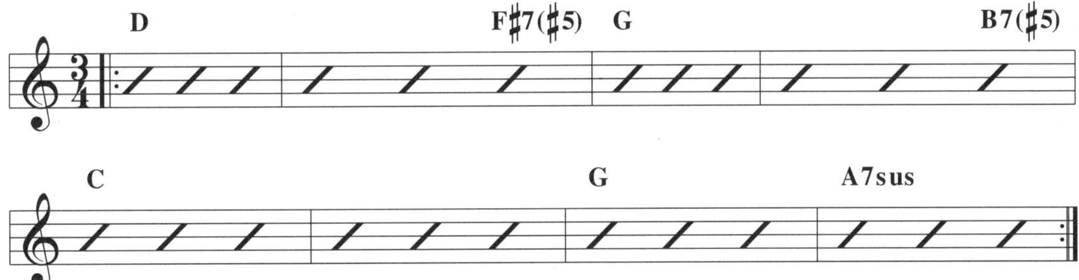

Figure 17.75. Practice leadsheet #5 (melody & chords, for melody treatment or 'comping' practice)

Figure 17.76. Practice leadsheet #6 (melody & chords, for melody treatment or 'comping' practice)

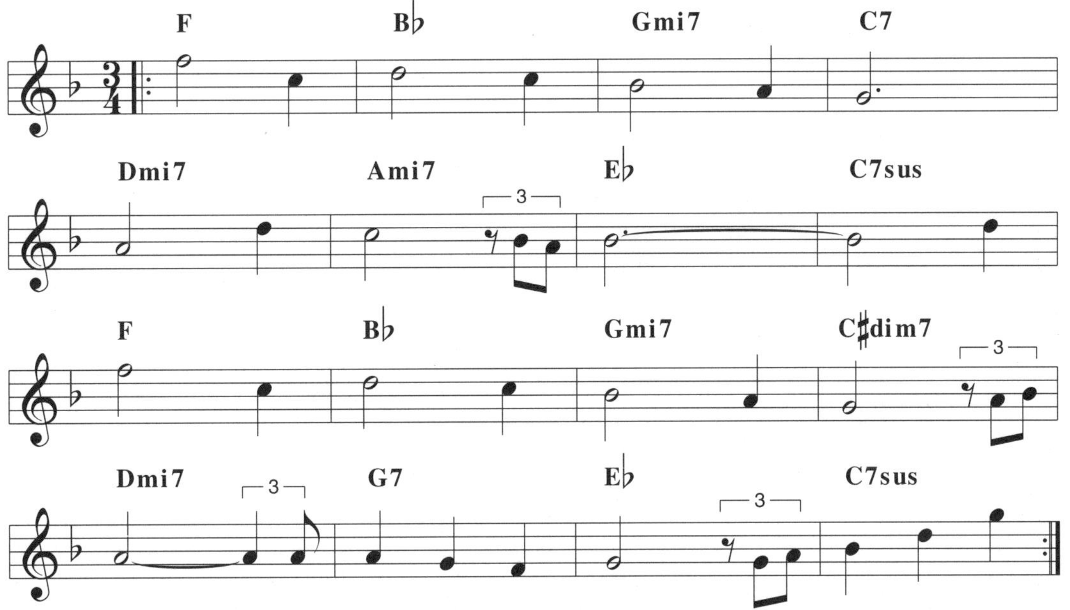

--- NOTES ---

CHAPTER EIGHTEEN

Fast Gospel

Introduction

We will now complete our work on gospel styles by studying '**Fast Gospel**'. Review the introduction to **Chapter 17** as necessary for general observations regarding gospel styles. All of the harmonic devices used in the previous chapter on '**Slow Gospel**' will also apply here, but in a different rhythmic context. In this chapter we will look at those gospel styles which use faster tempos and sixteenth note subdivisions (in **4/4** time). As an alternative to notating fast gospel in **4/4** time, we may also use '**Cut time**' - see following explanation in 'rhythmic concepts'. **Fast gospel patterns are generally created by combining a steady driving pulse in the left hand, with syncopated right hand upper structures (using anticipations).** Within this rhythmic framework, harmonic devices such as Mixolydian and backcycled triads, chromatic and diatonic walkups, unison and octave runs etc. (seen in the last chapter on Slow Gospel) will be used. At this point you should be familiar with these gospel harmonic concepts from our work in **Chapter 17** - review any areas as necessary! Again we generally have an emphasis on dominant harmony, frequently upgrading basic chord symbols to dominant 7th or 9th implications.

Fast gospel rhythmic notation concepts

As mentioned above, fast gospel can be notated in either **4/4** or '**Cut**' time (review **Figs. 2.17.** & **2.20.** as necessary), and you need to become familiar with each method. In each case the pattern will **sound the same** - it will just be **notated differently**! We can summarize the notation differences as follows:-

- In **4/4** time:- The beat or 'pulse' is felt on the **quarter** note. **Four** of these occur in each measure. The smallest written rhythmic subdivision generally used is the **sixteenth** note.
- In '**Cut**' time:- The beat or 'pulse' is felt on the **half** note. **Two** of these occur in each measure. The smallest written rhythmic subdivision generally used is the **eighth** note.

This leads to the following rule:- **Any one measure of 4/4 will become two measures in cut time**. Think of it like this - you have four beats or 'pulses' in a measure of **4/4** - but there are only two beats or 'pulses' in a measure of **cut** time - so to get four beats in cut time, you need two measures! Similarly, changing from cut time back to 4/4 time **divides** the number of measures by **2**. We will start out by showing some typical right hand fast gospel rhythmic phrases, notated both in 4/4 and cut time. These right hand phrases normally use anticipations, which are rhythmically notated as follows:-

- In **4/4** time:- Sixteenth note and eighth note anticipations are used.
- In '**Cut**' time:- Eighth note and quarter note anticipations are used.

(Review **Figs. 2.43. - 2.44.** regarding eighth note and sixteenth note anticipations, as necessary).

There is some potential confusion with regard to the counting of cut-time measures. In earlier **4/4** eighth note styles (pop ballad, pop-rock) we counted each measure '**1 & 2 & 3 & 4 &**', with the beat falling on **1**, **2**, **3** & **4**. We will count a measure of cut time in the same way (see following examples), but the beat will now fall on **1 & 3 only!** (i.e. not on the quarter note as we have been used to). When analyzing the rhythmic attacks in the following cut-time examples therefore, I have referred to a location in a cut-time measure as "1" instead of "beat 1", "2" instead of "beat 2", etc. I hope you will find this clearer to follow!

CHAPTER EIGHTEEN

Fast gospel rhythmic phrases for right hand

Now we will begin to look at right hand fast gospel rhythmic phrases as follows:-

Figure 18.1. Fast gospel right hand rhythmic phrase #1
(Cassette Tape Example 750)

a) - notated in 4/4 time

In **4/4** time, this pattern anticipates beat **2** (by a 16th note) and beats **3** & **4** (by 8th notes). The last attack on the 2nd 16th of beat **4**, anticipates the '**& of 4**'.

b) - notated in Cut time

In **cut** time, this pattern anticipates '**3**' of the 1st measure and '**4**' of the 2nd measure (by 8th notes). The attacks on '**4**' (1st measure) and '**2**' (2nd measure) could also be quarter note anticipations.

Figure 18.2. Fast gospel right hand rhythmic phrase #2 - variation of phrase #1
(Cassette Tape Example 751)

a) - notated in 4/4 time

In **4/4** time, this is the same as **Fig. 18.1. a)** except the fourth attack is now on the last 16th of beat **3** (anticipating beat **4** by a 16th note).

b) - notated in Cut time

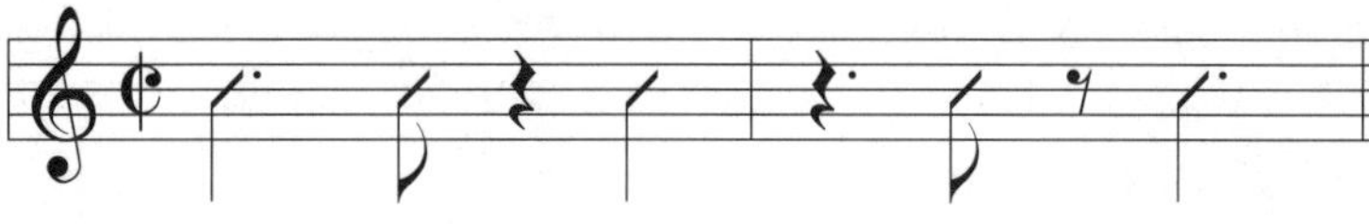

In **cut** time, this is the same as **Fig. 18.1. b)** except the first attack in the 2nd measure is now on the '**& of 2**' (anticipating '**3**' by an 8th note).

Figure 18.3. Fast gospel right hand rhythmic phrase #3
(Cassette Tape Example 752)

a) - notated in 4/4 time

In **4/4** time, this pattern anticipates beat **2** (by an 8th note) and beat **4** (by a 16th note). The attack on the 2nd 16th of beat **2**, anticipates the '**& of 2**'.

Fast gospel rhythmic phrases for right hand (contd)

Figure 18.3. contd
b) - notated in Cut time

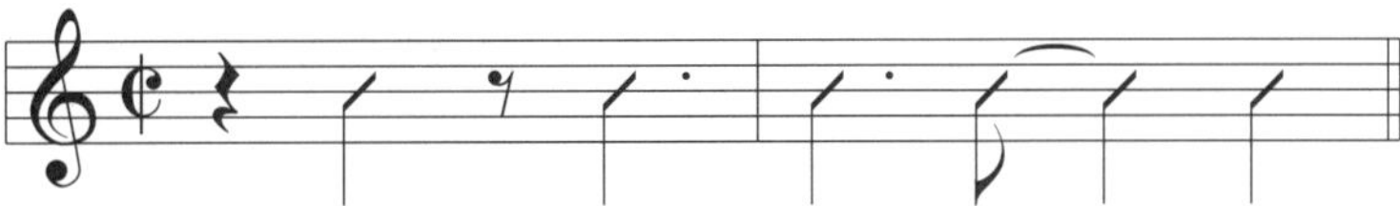

In **cut** time, this pattern anticipates '**4**' of the 1st measure and '**3**' of the 2nd measure (by 8th notes). The attack on '**2**' (1st measure) could also be a quarter note anticipation.

Figure 18.4. Fast gospel right hand rhythmic phrase #4 - variation of phrase #3
(Cassette Tape Example 753)

a) - notated in 4/4 time

In **4/4** time, this is the same as **Fig. 18.3. a)** except the last attack is now on the 2nd 16th of beat **4** (anticipating the '**& of 4**').

b) - notated in Cut time

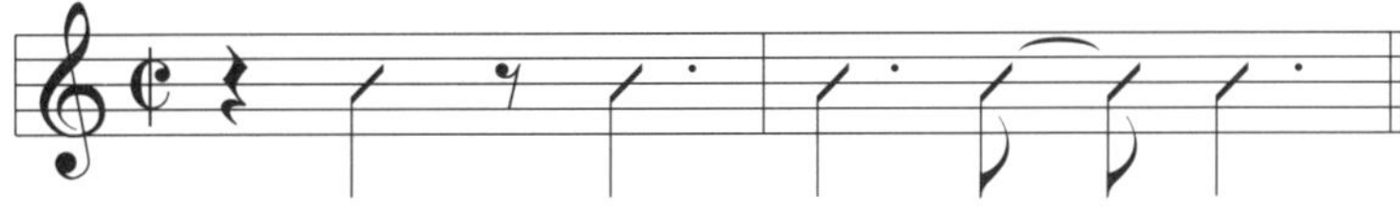

In **cut** time, this is the same as **Fig. 18.3. b)** except the last attack in the 2nd measure is now on the '**& of 3**' (anticipating '**4**').

Figure 18.5. Fast gospel right hand rhythmic phrase #5
(Cassette Tape Example 754)

a) - notated in 4/4 time

In **4/4** time, this pattern anticipates the '**& of 1**', beats **3** & **4**, and the '**& of 4**', all by 16th notes.

b) - notated in Cut time

In **cut** time, this pattern anticipates '**2**' of the 1st measure and '**1**', '**3**' & '**4**' of the 2nd measure, all by 8th notes.

Fast gospel rhythmic phrases for right hand (contd)

Figure 18.6. Fast gospel rhythmic phrase #6 - variation of phrase #5
(Cassette Tape Example 755)

a) - notated in 4/4 time

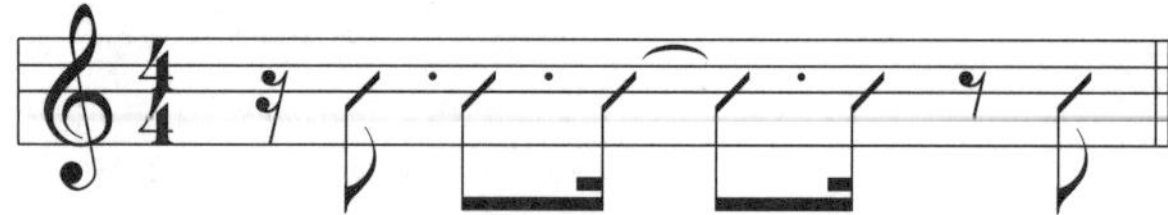

In **4/4** time, this is the same as **Fig. 18.5. a)** except the last attack is now on the '**& of 4**'.

b) - notated in Cut time

In **cut** time, this is the same as **Fig. 18.5. b)** except the last attack is now on '**4**' of the 2nd measure.

Figure 18.7. Fast gospel rhythmic phrase #7
(Cassette Tape Example 756)

a) - notated in 4/4 time

In **4/4** time, this pattern anticipates beat **2**, and the '**& of 4**' (by 16th notes).

b) - notated in Cut time

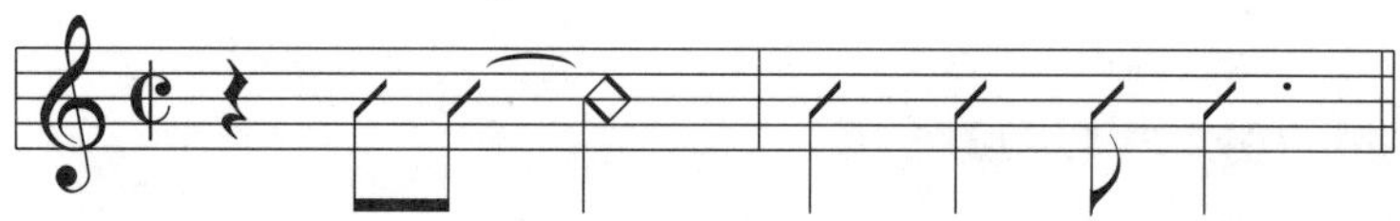

In **cut** time, this pattern anticipates '**3**' of the first measure and '**4**' of the 2nd measure.

Figure 18.8. Fast gospel rhythmic phrase #8 - variation of phrase #7
(Cassette Tape Example 757)

a) - notated in 4/4 time

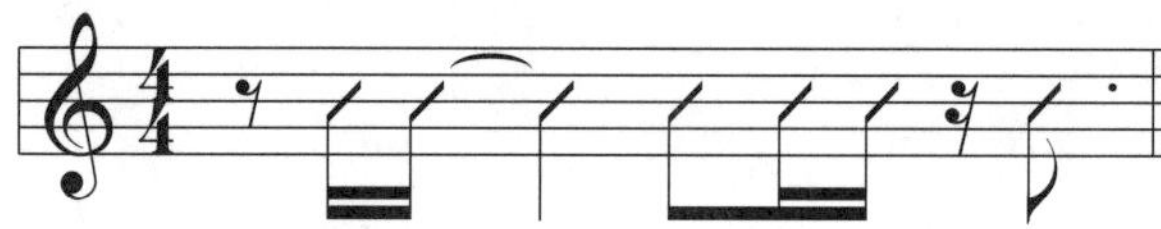

In **4/4** time, this is the same as **Fig. 18.7. a)** except the 5th attack is on the last 16th of beat **3** (anticipating beat **4**).

b) - notated in Cut time

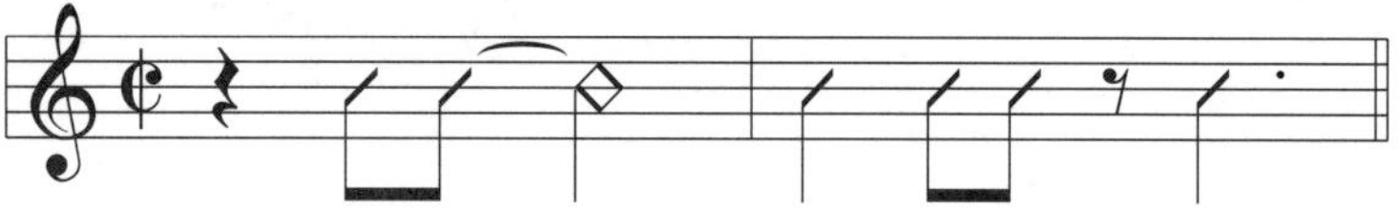

In cut time, this is the same as **Fig. 18.7. b)** except the 5th attack is now on the '**& of 2**' of the 2nd measure, anticipating '**3**'.

Fast gospel left hand patterns

As you can see, all of the previous right hand phrases contain rhythmic anticipations. Now we will look at some left hand bass patterns to go with the right hand phrases. The left hand bass part normally uses one note at a time (or in octaves), with a rhythmic emphasis on the downbeats (**1**, **2**, **3** & **4**) in **4/4 time**, or beats **1** & **3** in **cut time**. Often the root of the chord or basic chord tones are used, with the addition of diatonic or chromatic walkups between chord changes. The following left hand pattern examples will work with a **C Major** chord, and are again notated in both 4/4 and cut time:-

Figure 18.9. Fast gospel left hand pattern #1
(Cassette Tape Example 758)

a) - notated in 4/4 time

In **4/4** time, this basic pattern is playing the root on beats **1** & **3** and the 5th on beats **2** & **4**.

b) - notated in Cut time

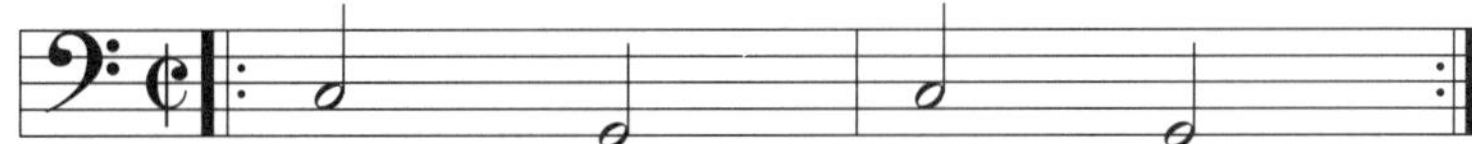

In **cut** time, this pattern places the root on '**1**', and the 5th on '**3**', of each measure.

Figure 18.10. Fast gospel left hand pattern #2
(Cassette Tape Example 759)

a) - notated in 4/4 time

In **4/4** time, this pattern is the same as **Fig. 18.9. a)** during the first 2 beats, and then uses an 8th note **1 - 5 - 6 - 5** pattern (with respect to the implied **C** chord) during beats **3** & **4**.

b) - notated in Cut time

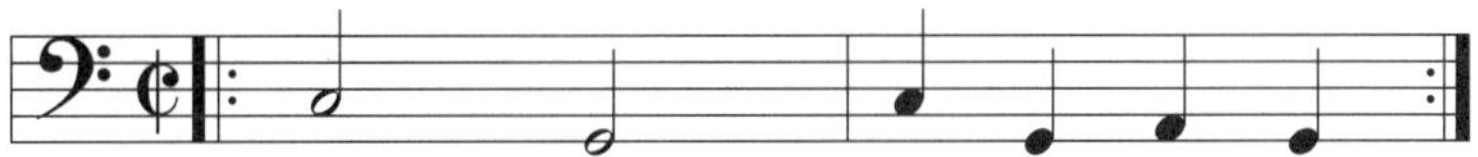

In **cut** time, this pattern is the same as **Fig. 18.9. b)** during the first measure, and then uses a quarter note **1 - 5 - 6 - 5** pattern during the 2nd measure.

Figure 18.11. Fast gospel left hand pattern #3
(Cassette Tape Example 760)

a) - notated in 4/4 time

In **4/4** time, this pattern is a variation on **Fig. 18.10. a)**, now using a **1 - 5 - 6 - 7** pattern during beats **3** & **4**.

Fast gospel left hand patterns (contd)

Figure 18.11. contd.
b) - notated in Cut time

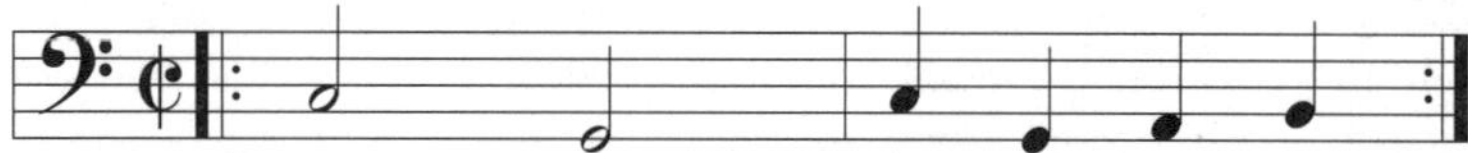

In **cut** time, this pattern is a variation of **Fig. 18.10. b)**, now using a **1 - 5 - 6 - 7** pattern during the 2nd measure.

Figure 18.12. Fast gospel left hand pattern #4
(Cassette Tape Example 761)

a) - notated in 4/4 time

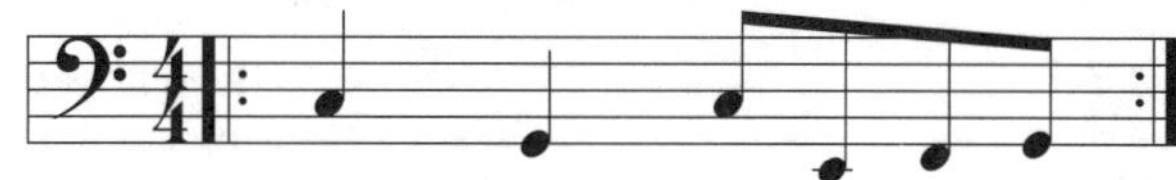

In **4/4** time, this is another variation on **Fig. 18.10. a)**, now using a **1 - 3 - 4 - 5** pattern during beats **3** & **4**.

b) - notated in Cut time

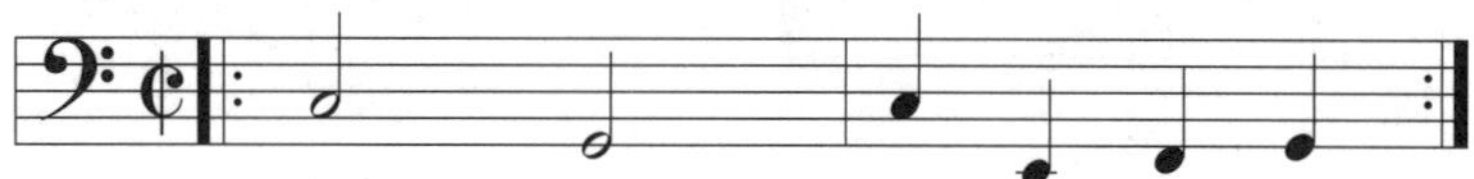

In **cut** time, this is another variation on **Fig. 18.10. b)**, now using a **1 - 3 - 4 - 5** pattern during the 2nd measure.

Figure 18.13. Fast gospel left hand pattern #5
(Cassette Tape Example 762)

a) - notated in 4/4 time

In **4/4** time, this is another variation on **Fig. 18.10. a)**, now using a **1 - 6 - #6 - 7** pattern during beats **3** & **4**.

b) - notated in Cut time

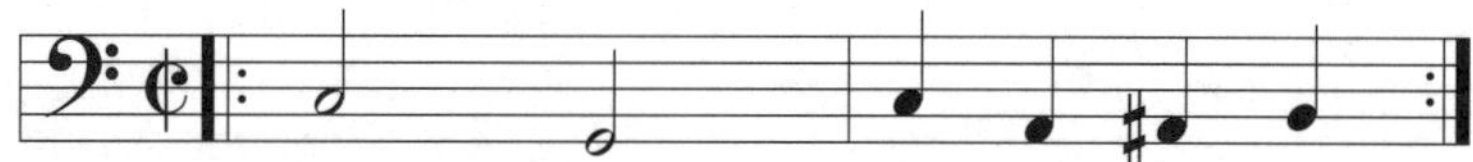

In **cut** time, this is another variation on **Fig. 18.10. b)**, now using a **1 - 6 - #6 - 7** pattern during the 2nd measure.

Figure 18.14. Fast gospel left hand pattern #6
(Cassette Tape Example 763)

a) - notated in 4/4 time

In **4/4** time, this rhythmically driving pattern is playing the root in 'alternating octaves' and using all of the 8th note subdivisions in the measure.

Fast gospel left hand patterns (contd)

Figure 18.14. contd.
b) - notated in Cut time

In **cut** time, this pattern is now using 'alternating octaves' on all of the quarter note subdivisions in each measure.

Figure 18.15. Fast gospel left hand pattern #7
(Cassette Tape Example 764)

a) - notated in 4/4 time

In **4/4** time, this is a variation on **Fig. 18.14. a)**, now using 2 16th notes (followed by an 8th note rest) during beat **4**. This would often be used to 'lead in' to a right hand attack on the '**& of 4**'.

b) - notated in Cut time

In **cut** time, this is a variation on **Fig. 18.14. b)**, now using 2 8th notes (followed by a quarter note rest) during the last half of the 2nd measure. This can lead into a right hand attack on '**4**' (in the 2nd measure).

Figure 18.16. Fast gospel left hand pattern #8
(Cassette Tape Example 765)

a) - notated in 4/4 time

In **4/4** time, this is another variation on **Fig. 18.14. a)**, now using 2 16th notes (followed by an 8th note rest) during beat **2**. This can lead in to a right hand attack on the '**& of 2**'.

b) - notated in Cut time

In **cut** time, this is another variation on **Fig. 18.14. b)**, now using 2 8th notes (followed by a quarter note rest) during the last half of the 1st measure. This can lead into a right hand attack on '**4**' (in the 1st measure).

CHAPTER EIGHTEEN

Constructing fast gospel patterns

We will now begin to construct fast gospel 'comping' patterns using both hands. The steps in this process can be summarized as follows:-

Left hand:- - Apply a pattern based on the examples in **Figs. 18.9. - 18.16.**, to the chord sequence required (also using walkups between chords as in the later examples).

Right hand:- - Choose a harmonic concept from the **Slow Gospel** chapter (i.e. Mixolydian triads, backcycling etc.), and apply it to the chord sequence required using the rhythmic phrases as in **Figs. 18.1. - 18.8.**

Now we will look at some examples of this process in action (again notating in both **4/4** and **cut** time):-

Figure 18.17. Fast gospel pattern #1
(Cassette Tape Example 766)

a) - notated in 4/4 time

In **4/4** time, the right hand is using rhythm **#1** (**Fig. 18.1. a)**) and the left hand is using pattern **#1** (**Fig. 18.9. a)**) applied to an **F** major chord. The right hand triads (F, Bb, Eb) are derived from a **double backcycle** on the **F** chord (see **Fig. 17.19.**).

b) - notated in Cut time

In **cut** time, the right hand rhythm and left hand pattern are now found in **Figs. 18.1. b)** and **18.9. b)** respectively. The right hand harmonic concepts are as noted for **Fig. 18.17. a**).

Figure 18.18. Fast gospel pattern #2
(Cassette Tape Example 767)

a) - notated in 4/4 time

In **4/4** time, the right hand is again using rhythm **#1** (**Fig. 18.1. a)**) and the left hand is using pattern **#8** (**Fig. 18.16. a)**) applied to a **C7** chord. The 2nd inversion right hand triads Edim, F & Gmi are all derived from the **C Mixolydian** mode (see **Fig. 17.11.** measures 3-4).

Constructing fast gospel patterns (contd)

Figure 18.18. contd.
b) - notated in Cut time

In **cut** time, the right hand rhythm and left hand pattern are now found in **Figs. 18.1. b)** and **18.16. b)** respectively. The right hand harmonic concepts are as noted for **Fig. 18.18. a)**.

Figure 18.19. Fast gospel pattern #3
(Cassette Tape Example 768)

a) - notated in 4/4 time

In **4/4** time, the right hand is using rhythm **#3** (**Fig.18.3. a)**) and the left hand is using pattern **#2** (**Fig. 18.10. a)**) applied to a **C7** chord. The 2nd inversion right hand triads C, Dmi & Edim are all derived from the **C Mixolydian** mode (see **Fig. 17.11.** measures 3-4).

b) - notated in Cut time

In **cut** time, the right hand rhythm and left hand pattern are now found in **Figs. 18.3. b)** and **18.10. b)** respectively. The right hand harmonic concepts are as noted for **Fig. 18.19. a)**.

Figure 18.20. Fast gospel pattern #4
(Cassette Tape Example 769)

a) - notated in 4/4 time

In **4/4** time, the right hand is using rhythm **#5** (**Fig. 18.5. a)**) and the left hand is using pattern **#6** (**Fig. 18.14. a)**). The right hand triads (C, F, Bb) are derived from a **double backcycle** on the **C** chord (see **Fig. 17.19.**).

Constructing fast gospel patterns (contd)

Figure 18.20. contd.
b) - notated in Cut time

In **cut** time, the right hand rhythm and left hand pattern are now found in **Figs. 18.5. b)** and **18.14. b)** respectively. The right hand harmonic concepts are as noted for **Fig. 18.20. a**).

Figure 18.21. Fast gospel pattern #5
(Cassette Tape Example 770)

a) - notated in 4/4 time

In **4/4** time, the right hand is using rhythm **#7** (**Fig. 18.7. a)**) and the left hand is using pattern **#4** (**Fig. 18.12. a)**). The right hand triads (C, F, Bb) are derived from a **double backcycle** on the **C** chord (see **Fig. 17.19.**).

b) - notated in Cut time

In **cut** time, the right hand rhythm and left hand pattern are now found in **Figs. 18.7. b)** and **18.12. b)** respectively. The right hand harmonic concepts are as noted for **Fig. 18.21. a**).

Constructing fast gospel patterns (contd)

Figure 18.22. Fast gospel pattern #6
(Cassette Tape Example 771)

a) - notated in 4/4 time

In **4/4** time, the right hand is using rhythm **#3** (**Fig. 18.3. a)**) and the left hand is using pattern **#7** (**Fig. 18.15. a)**) applied to an F major chord. The right hand triads (F & Bb) are derived from a **single backcycle** on the **F** chord (see **Fig. 17.17.**).

b) - notated in Cut time

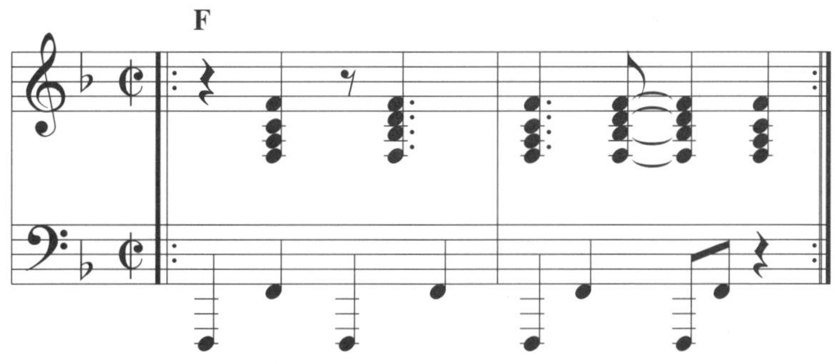

In **cut** time, the right hand rhythm and left hand pattern are now found in **Figs. 18.3. b)** and **18.15. b)** respectively. The right hand harmonic concepts are as noted for **Fig. 18.22. a**).

Practice directions:-

- ***Practice the fast gospel right hand rhythmic phrases shown in Figs. 18.1. - 18.8.***
  You can play a single note or chord in the right hand to practice these rhythms. Start at a slow tempo and gradually increase as desired. Also - experiment with your own rhythms!
- ***Practice the fast gospel left hand patterns shown in Figs. 18.9. - 18.16.***
- ***Practice the fast gospel patterns for both hands shown in Figs. 18.17. - 18.22.***

*Try thinking & counting in both **4/4** & **cut time** as you play the examples. Use these patterns as a springboard for your own ideas!*

Constructing fast gospel patterns (contd)

Now we will look at some fast gospel comping patterns using chromatic walkups in the left hand (see **Figs. 17.36.** - **17.47.** and accompanying text). This is a very effective technique, giving a pattern considerable energy and 'forward motion'. In the previous chapter we saw that the favorite places to apply chromatic walkups were between the **3rd** & **5th** of a chord (moving **3 - 4 - #4 - 5**) and between the **6th** and **root** of a chord (moving **6 - #6 - 7 - 1**), and this will also apply in a fast gospel setting. From now on I will save space by only showing each pattern in 4/4 time (i.e. not in cut time) - however it is always good practice to be thinking and counting in in both of these time signatures! Each of these walkup patterns contains two measures in 4/4 time, as follows:-

Figure 18.23. Fast gospel pattern #7 - chromatic walkup (Mixolydian triads over 1 - 3 - 4 - #4 - 5) *(Cassette Tape Example 772)*

In this example the left hand is playing the root in octaves in the first measure (see left hand pattern **#6** - **Fig. 18.14.**) and then walking up from the 3rd to the 5th (E, F, F#, G) of the **C7** chord in the second measure. In the right hand we are using 2nd inversion C, Dmi, C, Dmi & Edim triads in the first measure, using right hand rhythm **#3** (**Fig. 18.3.**), and 2nd inversion Gmi, F, Edim, Dmi & C triads in the second measure, using a rhythmic variation. In the second measure we momentarily create the passing chords **Gmi/E** or **Emi7(b5)** on beat **1**, **F** on beat **2**, **Edim/F#** or **F#7(b9)** on beat **3**, and **C/G** on the '**& of 4**'. All of these upper triads are derived from the **C Mixolydian** mode, built from the root of the **C7** chord. The grace note F# has also been added on beat **1** of the second measure, leading into G (the 5th of the chord). Now for a left hand rhythmic variation on this pattern:-

Figure 18.24. Fast gospel pattern #8 - chromatic walkup (Mixolydian triads over 1 - 3 - 4 - #4 - 5) - left hand rhythmic variation *(Cassette Tape Example 773)*

This is the same as the previous example, except that we are now using left hand pattern **#7** (**Fig. 18.15.**) resulting in two 16th notes in beat **4** of each measure - notice how this leads into the chord on the '**& of 4**' in the right hand, giving a syncopated 'kick' to the rhythmic phrase.

Constructing fast gospel patterns (contd)

Figure 18.25. Fast gospel pattern #9 - chromatic walkup (Mixolydian variation with drone note) *(Cassette Tape Example 774)*

In this example the left hand is again using pattern **#6** (**Fig. 18.14.**), except for the '**& of 3**' onwards in the second measure where a **6 - #6 - 7** (**- 1** on the repeat) line in octaves is being used, with respect to the **C7** chord. (See **Fig. 17.43.** for the similar idea in a slow gospel context). The right hand part is using a repeated top note or drone note - a device we encountered in country & funk styles, and also in a slow gospel walkup context in **Fig. 17.34.** The right hand is using a variation on rhythm pattern **#1** (**Fig. 18.1.**). The other notes below the drone note in the right hand (in the first measure and during beats **1** & **2** of the second measure) are again derived from the **C Mixolydian** mode - so you could think of this as using 1st inversion Mixolydian triads (C, Dmi, Edim etc.) but with the top note always being replaced by the drone note of C. During beats **3** & **4**, the right hand continues to use the drone note C, over a 'grace note' lick derived from the **C Blues** scale - see **Fig. 15.99.** and accompanying text.

Figure 18.26. Fast gospel pattern #10 - chromatic walkup (Mixolydian triads over 1 - 3 - 4 - #4 - 5) leading into chord change *(Cassette Tape Example 775)*

This example again uses the left hand line **1 - 3 - 4 - #4 - 5** (with respect to the **C7** chord) as in **Figs. 18.23.** & **18.24.**, except this time it has led us to a specific chord change (the **G7** in the second measure). The rhythm and octave doubling of the chromatic walkup is similar to **Fig. 18.25.** above. Either side of the walkup, the left hand is again playing the root using 8th note 'alternating' octaves (as in left hand pattern **#6** - **Fig. 18.14.**). The right hand is again using variations on rhythm pattern **#1** (**Fig. 18.1.**). The 2nd inversion triads in the first measure again all derive from the **C Mixolydian** mode. The grace note D# has been added on beat **1** (leading into E - the 3rd of the chord) and the grace note F# has been added on the '**& of 3**' (leading into G - the 5th of the chord). In the second measure the 2nd inversion triads Emi and Dmi (on beat **1** and the '**& of 2**' respectively) are derived from the **G Mixolydian** mode, and the Ebmi triad in between is a 'parallel' chromatic minor triad first seen

Constructing fast gospel patterns (contd)

Analysis of Fig. 18.26. contd.

in **Fig. 17.48.** in a slow gospel context. The grace note D# has been added on beat **1** of the second measure, leading into E (the 13th of the G7 chord). Now for an example combining backcycled and Mixolydian triads with chromatic walkups, as follows:-

Figure 18.27. Fast gospel pattern #11 - chromatic walkups (backcycled & Mixolydian triads)
(Cassette Tape Example 776)

This pattern uses two different chromatic walkup patterns to alternate between the C & F chords. These chromatic walkups could be considered as a 1 - 2 - #2 - 3 and a 6 - #6 - 7 (- 1) with respect to the C chord in the first measure, again using 8th note 'alternating ' octaves. Against this, in the right hand we are using a variation on a **triple backcycle** (see **Fig. 17.21.**) on the C chord, using C, Bb, Eb & Bb triads and moving back to the root & 5th of the C chord on the 2nd 16th of beat **4** - an effective sound over the 3rd in the bass voice, as we have seen in other styles. The grace note D# has been added on beat 1, leading into E (the 3rd of the chord) and the grace note F# has been added on the 2nd 16th of beat 4, leading into G (the 5th of the chord). In the second measure we are using a variation on a **double backcycle** on the F chord during the first 3 beats, using Bb, F, Eb & Bb triads. On the last beat the right hand is playing a D minor triad (from the **F Mixolydian** mode) to give a vertically consonant sound over the note B in the bass voice, momentarily creating a **Dmi/B** or **Bmi7(b5)** passing chord on beat **4** (all of the backcycle options on an F chord would be vertically dissonant over the note B in the bass voice).

As you can see from **Figs. 18.23. - 18.27.**, the use of Mixolydian triads is just as desirable and stylistic in fast gospel styles as it is in slow gospel. So - you guessed it! - I've given you a 12-key routine in a fast gospel setting using (2nd inversion) Mixolydian triads. This routine also includes the 'parallel' chromatic minor triad device first seen in **Figs. 17.48. - 17.51.** in slow gospel, and also used in **Fig. 18.26.** in fast gospel. To briefly review - the 'parallel' chromatic minor triad occurs between the two 2nd inversion minor triads within a Mixolydian mode which have 'top notes' of the tonic and 7th of the mode. For example - in **C Mixolydian**, the A minor triad in 2nd inversion has C (the tonic of the mode) as the top note, and the G minor triad in 2nd inversion has Bb (the 7th of the mode) as the top note. In this mode, these two minor triads can be 'connected' by the use of the Ab minor triad in between, as occurs in the 2nd measure of the following 12-key example. Also note in this example that the first measure on each chord uses rhythm pattern **#3** (**Fig. 18.3.**) in the right hand along with left hand pattern **#7** (**Fig. 18.15.**), and that the second measure on each chord uses rhythm pattern **#4** (**Fig. 18.4.**) along with left hand pattern **#6** (**Fig. 18.14.**), as follows:-

Constructing fast gospel patterns (contd)

Figure 18.28. Fast gospel Mixolydian triad pattern (with 'parallel' chromatic minor triads) through all 12 keys *(CASSETTE TAPE EXAMPLE 777)*

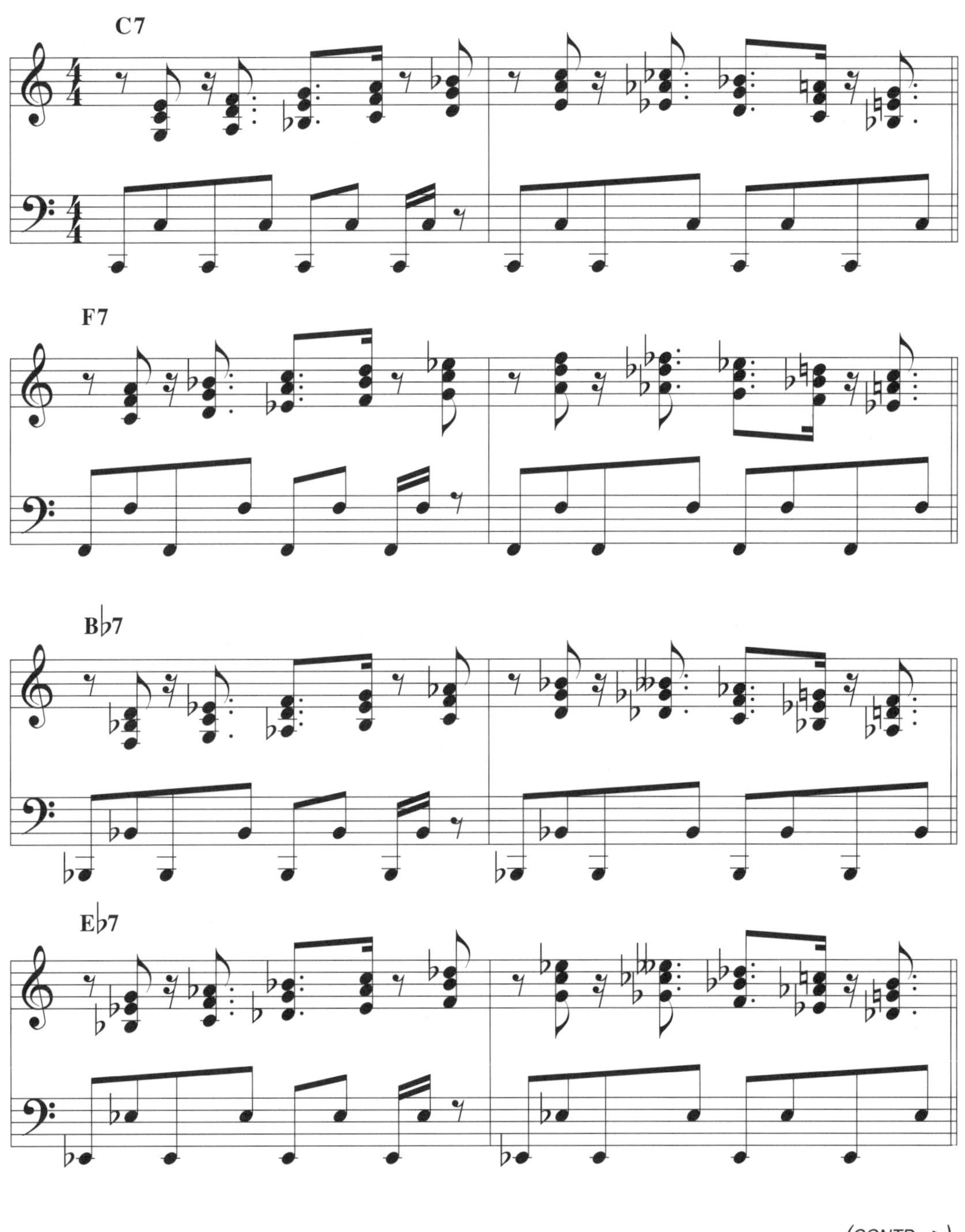

(CONTD-->)

Constructing fast gospel patterns (contd)

Figure 18.28. contd.

(CONTD-->)

Constructing fast gospel patterns (contd)

Figure 18.28. contd.

During each two-measure phrase, we are using 2nd inversion triads from the **Mixolydian mode** built from the root of the chord, except for the 2nd chord in the 2nd measure of each phrase which is the 'parallel' chromatic minor triad. Compare and contrast this routine with **Fig. 17.11.** (the equivalent 12-key pattern in slow gospel)!

Constructing fast gospel patterns (contd)

PRACTICE DIRECTIONS:-

- ***Practice the fast gospel chromatic walkup patterns as shown in Figs. 18.23. - 18.27.***
- ***Practice the fast gospel 12-key Mixolydian triad pattern (including 'parallel' chromatic minor triads) as shown in Fig. 18.28.***

*Practice tip - try applying **grace notes** into the Mixolydian triads on this fast gospel 12-key pattern, in a similar manner to the added grace notes shown in **Fig. 17.16.** (a variation on the slow gospel 12-key pattern in **Fig. 17.11.**).*

Now we will begin to apply all of these harmonic and rhythmic concepts, in order to 'comp' through a leadsheet in a fast gospel style. We will start with the following simple chart, using a familiar **1 - 4 - 5 - 1** progression in the key of C:-

Figure 18.29. Fast gospel chord chart example #1

We will interpret this chart using an 8th note octave pattern in the left hand, with backcycled triads in the right hand, as follows:-

Figure 18.30. Fast gospel comping solution for chord chart #1 (Fig. 18.29.)
(CASSETTE TAPE EXAMPLE 778)

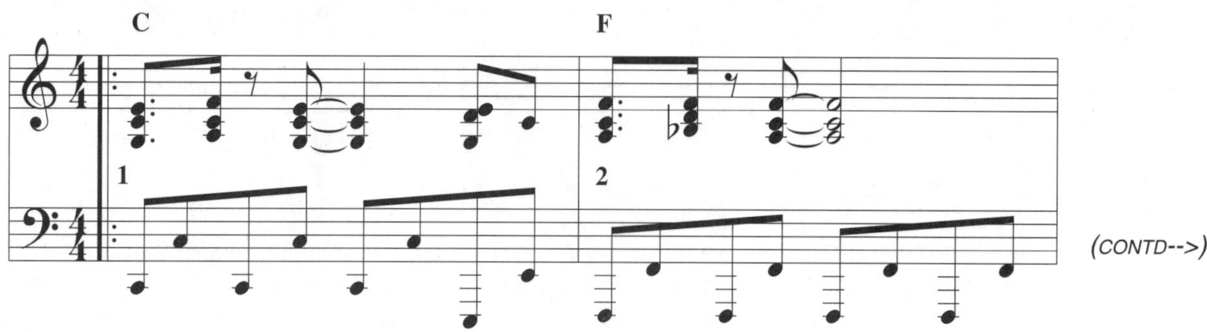

(CONTD-->)

Constructing fast gospel patterns (contd)

Figure 18.30. contd.

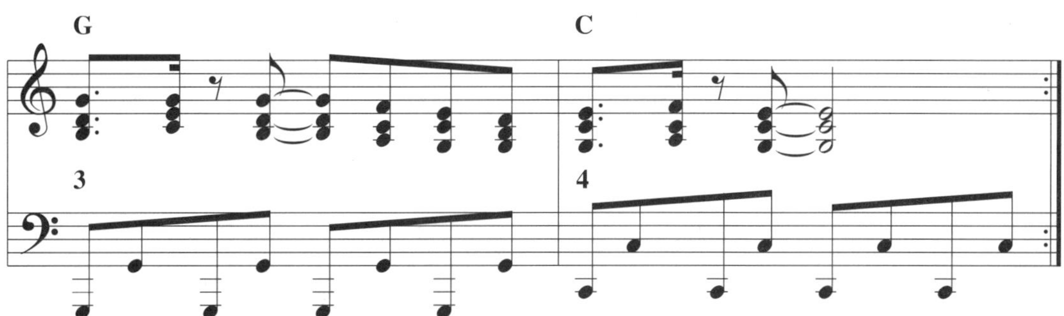

In this example the left hand is using an 8th note 'alternating' octave pattern first seen in **Fig. 18.14.**, playing the root of the chord in each measure (the 'E' during beat **4** of measure 1 is the 3rd of the C chord, and could be considered a short walkup into F, the root of the following chord). The rhythmic phrases in the right hand could all be considered as variations on **Fig. 18.1.** - anticipating beat **2** by a 16th note, and beat **3** by an 8th note. The harmonic devices used by the right hand in each measure can be analyzed as follows:-

- Measure 1 - On the **C** chord, a **single backcycle** is occurring (movement between the C & F upper triads - see **Fig. 17.17.**). During beat **4**, a **9 to 1** resolution is occurring within the upper 2nd inversion C triad (see **Fig. 8.12.**). This in combination with the root voice passing through E (see above comments) momentarily creates a passing chord of **Cadd9/E** during beat **4**.

- Measure 2 - On the **F** chord, another **single backcycle** is occurring (movement between F & Bb upper triads).

- Measure 3 - On the **G** chord, a **single backcycle** is occurring in the first half of the measure (movement between G & C upper triads) and a **double backcycle** is occurring in the second half of the measure (movement between G, F, C & G upper triads - see **Fig. 17.19.**).

- Measure 4 - On the C chord, another **single backcycle** is occurring, in a similar manner to measure 1.

Now for a more complex 8-measure chord progression, mixing major triad and dominant 7th chord symbols. (Don't forget however that basic triad symbols can be 'upgraded' to a dominant implication by the use of Mixolydian and/or backcycled triads, in this style).

Figure 18.31. Fast gospel chord chart example #2

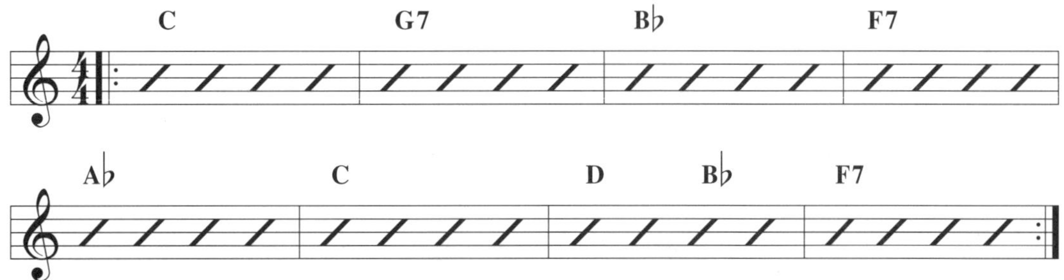

Constructing fast gospel patterns (contd)

We will now interpret the previous chart using Mixolydian, backcycled and 'parallel' minor triads in the right hand, with 8th & 16th note octave patterns and chromatic walkups in the left hand, as follows:-

Figure 18.32. Fast gospel comping solution for chord chart #2 (Fig. 18.31.)
(Cassette Tape Example 779)

Constructing fast gospel patterns (contd)

Rhythmically in the previous example, the right hand in measures 1 & 3 is using rhythmic phrase **#3** (see **Fig. 18.3.**), and in the remaining measures is using variations on rhythmic phrase **#1** (**Fig. 18.1.**). The left hand part is based upon pattern **#6** (**Fig. 18.14.**) in measures 1, 3 & 8; pattern **#8** (**Fig. 18.16.**) in measures 2, 4, 5 & 6; and pattern **#7** (**Fig. 18.15.**) in measure 7. Note the various places where two 16th notes in the left hand (beginning on a downbeat) are immediately followed by an 8th note in the right hand - a great syncopated effect first seen in **Figs. 18.18. & 18.22**. The previous example uses this rhythmic device during beat **2** of measures 2, 4, 5 & 6, and during beat **4** of measure 7. Also in the left hand, chromatic walkups are occurring from measure 5 into measure 6 and from measure 8 back to measure 1. These could be considered as **6 - #6 - 7 - 1** patterns with respect to the **C** chord being approached each time (see 2nd measure in **Fig. 18.25.**, and various **Chapter 17** examples). In addition, the harmonic devices used in the right hand of the previous example can be analyzed as follows:-

- Measure 1 - On the **C** chord, a **single** & **double backcycle** is occurring, with the successive use of the C, F, C, Bb, & F major triads (see **Figs. 17.17. & 17.19.**).

- Measure 2 - On the **G7** chord, the 2nd inversion triads Emi, Dmi, C, & Bdim are all derived from the use of the **G Mixolydian** mode (see last line of **Fig. 18.28.**). The Ebmi triad on the last 16th of beat **1**, is a parallel chromatic minor triad inserted between the Emi & Dmi triads (see **Figs. 18.26. & 17.48.**). On beat **1** the grace note D# has been added, leading into E (the 13th of the chord), and on beat **4** the grace note A# has been added, leading into B (the 3rd of the chord).

- Measure 3 - On the **Bb** chord, a **single** & **double backcycle** is occurring, with the successive use of the Bb, Eb, Bb, Ab, & Eb major triads, similar to measure 1 on the **C** chord.

- Measure 4 - On the **F7** chord, the 2nd inversion triads Dmi, Cmi, Bb, & Adim are all derived from the use of the **F Mixolydian** mode (see 2nd line of **Fig. 18.28.**). The Dbmi triad on the last 16th of beat **1**, is a parallel chromatic minor triad inserted between the Dmi & Cmi triads. On beat **1** the grace note C# has been added, leading into D (the 13th of the chord), and on beat **4** the grace note G# has been added, leading into A (the 3rd of the chord).

- Measure 5 - On the **Ab** chord, in the first half of the measure a **single backcycle** is occurring, with the use of the Ab, Db & Ab triads. In the second half of the measure, a 'drone" note of C is being used above a 'grace note' lick using the **C Blues** scale (see **Figs. 15.99. & 18.25.**).

- Measure 6 - On the **C** chord, the top 'drone' note of C is continuing, while the intervals used below are all derived from the **C Mixolydian** mode. (We first saw this 'drone note' variation on Mixolydian triads, in **Fig. 18.25.**). On beat **1** the grace note D# has been added, leading into E (the 3rd of the chord).

- Measure 7 - On the **D** chord, a **single backcycle** is occurring, with the use of the D, G & D triads.
- On the **Bb** chord, a **single backcycle** is occurring, with the use of the Bb, Eb & Bb triads. (Note the rhythmic alternation between the hands in this measure, from the '**& of 1**' until the '**& of 2**', and from the '**& of 3**' until the '**& of 4**'. The resulting rhythm when the two hands are combined, uses all of the 16th note subdivisions in these sections of the measure).

- Measure 8 - On the **F7** chord, the root position F triad and the 2nd inversion triads Adim, Gmi, F, Eb & Dmi are all derived from the **F Mixolydian** mode. Two G# grace notes have been added, on beat **1** and on the last 16th of beat **1**, both leading into A (the 3rd of the chord). In addition to the left hand chromatic walkup in the last part of the measure as described above, the left hand is also using the diatonic walkup tones F, G & A in octaves during beats **1 - 3**. The bass line as a whole in this measure is walking up (diatonically and then chromatically) from **F** back into the **C** chord.

Constructing fast gospel patterns (contd)

We will now look at a different harmonic application of fast gospel rhythms. It is sometimes desirable to interpret **pop-rock alternating triads** using a fast gospel rhythmic concept. (Review **Figs. 12.9. - 12.22.** as necessary regarding the various alternating triad combinations). This can be a stylistic requirement in more of a pop-gospel idiom for example. Take a moment to review the first chord chart and subsequent interpretation in the text on Pop-Rock (**Chapter 12 - Figs. 12.30. & 12.31.**). We will now look at the same chart, and apply the same alternating triads within a fast gospel rhythmic context:-

Figure 18.33. Fast gospel chord chart example #3 (also see Fig. 12.30.)

We will now interpret this chart as follows:-

Figure 18.34. Fast gospel comping solution for chord chart #3 (Fig. 18.33.) - using 'pop-rock' alternating triads (*Cassette Tape Example 780*)

In the above example, the right hand is using rhythmic phrase **#3** (see **Fig. 18.3.**) in measures 1 & 3, and rhythmic phrase **#4** (see **Fig. 18.4.**) in measures 2 & 4. The left hand is playing the root of each chord, and using pattern **#7** (see **Fig. 18.15.**) in measures 1 & 3, and pattern **#6** (see **Fig. 18.14.**) in measures 2 & 4. The harmonic devices used in the right hand part can be further analyzed as follows:-

Constructing fast gospel patterns (contd)

Analysis of Fig. 18.34.

- Measure 1 - On the **C** chord we are using '**5 to 1**' alternating triads (see **Figs. 12.9.** & **12.31.**), with the top note G doubled an octave below. The last C triad on the '**& of 4**' is an anticipation which harmonically 'belongs' to the following **Ami7** chord, as in the corresponding measure in **Fig. 12.31.**

- Measure 2 - On the **Ami7** chord we are using '**b7 to b3**' alternating triads (see **Figs. 12.19.** & **12.31.**), again with the top note doubled.

- Measure 3 - On the **Dmi7** chord we are again using '**b7 to b3**' alternating triads. The last F triad on the '**& of 4**' is again an anticipation which harmonically 'belongs' to the following **G7** chord, as in the corresponding measure in **Fig. 12.31.**

- Measure 4 - On the **G7** chord, the use of these upper triads actually means that we alternate between 'suspended' and 'unsuspended' versions of the chord - see **Fig. 12.21.** & **12.31**. We are using a combination of '**b7 to 1**' (see **Fig. 12.21.**) and '**4 to 1**' (see **Fig. 12.11.**) alternating triads. Another interpretation of these F, C & G triads over this chord is as a **double backcycle** (see **Fig. 17.19.**).

PRACTICE DIRECTIONS:-

- Practice the fast gospel comping solutions to leadsheets #1, #2 & #3, as shown in Figs. 18.30., 18.32. & 18.34.
- Work on applying these concepts to tunes of your choice, and to the practice leadsheets at the end of this chapter.

Fast gospel melody

Now we will examine the process involved in interpreting a melody in a fast gospel style. The subsequent examples demonstrate two 'stages' involved in a gospel melody treatment, described as follows:-

Stage 1:- Inverting triads to accommodate the melody on top. These may be basic triads indicated by the chord symbol, or they may be simple Mixolydian/backcycled/'alternating' triads. Adding a simple left hand pattern (for example the 8th note octaves in **Fig. 18.14.**).

Stage 2:- Rephrasing the top note melody by adding more Mixolydian triads, double and triple backcycles, 'parallel' minor triads, and drone & grace notes. Adding more 16th-notes in the left hand (as in **Figs. 18.15.** & **18.16.**) and diatonic/chromatic walkups between chord changes.

Fast gospel melody (contd)

These previous 'melody treatment' stages could be applied to a great many tunes, including some which would not be typically associated with a fast gospel interpretation! We will now try out this concept, using the well-known tune "**Happy Birthday**". Normally this tune is thought of in **3/4** time, and so we would have to rephrase the tune in **4/4** as a prerequisite to a fast gospel treatment, as follows:-

Figure 18.35. "Happy Birthday" leadsheet, rephrased in 4/4 time

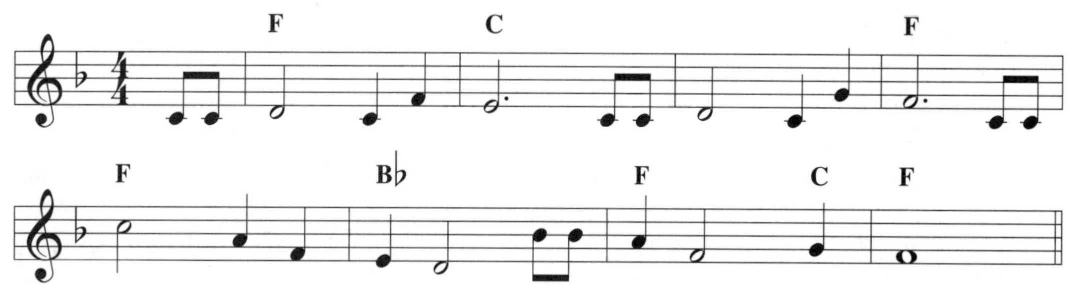

Note that the first measure shown above, appears incomplete (only containing two 8th notes). This is a melodic 'pickup', with the 8th notes beginning on beat **4** of the measure immediately prior to the first **F** chord. Now we will apply '**Stage 1**' of the fast gospel melody treatment, placing basic triads below melody in the right hand, over a simple left hand 8th note octave pattern:-

Figure 18.36. Fast gospel melody solution (Stage 1) for "Happy Birthday" chart (Fig. 18.35.)
(CASSETTE TAPE EXAMPLE 781)

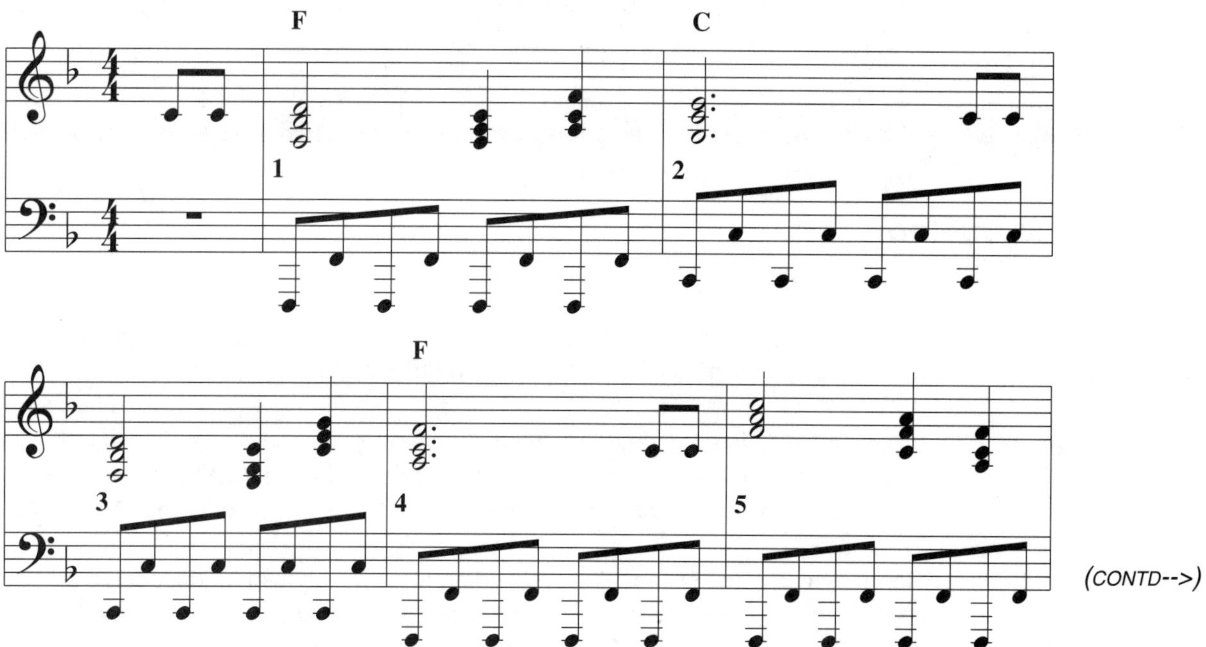

(CONTD-->)

Fast gospel melody (contd)

Fig. 18.36. (contd)

In this example, the left hand is playing the root of each chord using the 8th note octave pattern **#6** (**Fig. 18.14.**). The right hand part can be analyzed as follows:-

- Measure 1 - On the **F** chord, a 2nd inversion Bb triad is being used under the melody note D on beat **1**, moving to a root position F triad under the melody note C on beat **3**. These triads represent a **single backcycle** on the **F** chord - a good solution on this melodic interval which is moving between the 6th (D) and the 5th (C) on the F major chord. A 1st inversion F triad is being used under the root of the chord in the melody (F) on beat **4**.

- Measure 2 - On the **C** chord, a 2nd inversion C triad is being used under the 3rd of the chord in the melody on beat **1**. (This triad is a basic **1-3-5** upper structure on this chord). The melody during beat **4** is played as single notes.

- Measure 3 - Continuing on the **C** chord, a 2nd inversion Bb triad is being used under the melody note D on beat **1**, moving to a 1st inversion C triad under the melody note C on beat **3**. This could be considered as a '**b7 to 1**' alternating triad movement on the **C** chord (see **Fig. 12.21.**). This upgrades the chord to a dominant implication overall, which is appropriate as this chord is heading back to the **F** chord (in the next measure) in a 'five-to-one' manner. This triad movement is a good solution on this melodic interval which is moving between the 9th (D) and root (C) of a chord functioning as dominant. Another angle on this upper triad sequence is that both of the triads are found in the **C Mixolydian** mode, again reinforcing the dominant implication.

- Measure 4 - On the **F** chord, a 1st inversion F triad is being used under the root of the chord in the melody on beat **1**. (This triad is a basic **1-3-5** upper structure on this chord). The melody during beat **4** is played as single notes.

- Measure 5 - Continuing on the **F** chord, the F triad (again the basic **1-3-5** upper structure) is being used in root position under the 5th of the chord in the melody (C) on beat **1**, in 2nd inversion under the 3rd of the chord in the melody (A) on beat **3**, and in 1st inversion under the root of the chord in the melody (F) on beat **4**.

- Measure 6 - On the **Bb** chord, a 2nd inversion C triad is being used under the melody note E on beat **1**, moving to a 2nd inversion Bb triad under the melody note D on beat **2**. This could be considered as a '**9 to 1**' alternating triad movement on the **Bb** chord. As we saw in **Fig. 12.14.**, this figure might typically be used within major chords built from the 4th degree of a key (in this case Bb is the 4th degree of F major). This triad movement is a good solution on this melodic interval which

Fast gospel melody (contd)

Analysis of Fig. 18.36. contd.

- Measure 6 (contd) is moving between the #11th (E) and the 3rd (D) on the Bb major chord. A 1st inversion Bb triad (again the basic **1-3-5** upper structure) is being used under the root of the chord in the melody (Bb) on beat **4**, followed by the root on the '**& of 4**' as a single note.

- Measure 7
- On the **F** chord, the F triad (again the basic **1-3-5** upper structure) is being used in 2nd inversion under the 3rd of the chord in the melody (A) on beat **1**, and in 1st inversion under the root of the chord in the melody (F) on beat **2**.
- On the **C** chord, a root position C triad (again the basic **1-3-5** upper structure) is being used under the 5th of the chord in the melody (G) on beat **4**.

- Measure 8
- On the **F** chord, a 1st inversion F triad (again the basic **1-3-5** upper structure) is being used under the root of the chord in the melody (F) on beat **1**.

Now we will apply '**Stage 2**' of the fast gospel melody treatment, using more sophisticated Mixolydian triad and backcycling ideas, walkups, grace notes, left hand 16th note rhythms etc. as follows:-

Figure 18.37. Fast gospel melody solution (Stage 2) for "Happy Birthday" chart (Fig. 18.35.)
(Cassette Tape Example 782)

(CONTD-->)

Fast gospel melody (contd)

Figure 18.37. (contd)

In the above example, the left hand part is based on pattern **#6** (**Fig. 18.14.**) in measures 1, 3, and 5 - 8, with diatonic walkups used during measures 1, 6 & 7, and at the end of measure 5. Otherwise the left hand part is based on pattern **#8** (**Fig. 18.16.**) in measures 2 & 4. The right hand part now implies a rhythmic rephrasing of the melody, frequently based on variations of phrase **#1** (**Fig. 18.1.**). We can further analyze this example (and compare it to **Stage 1**) as follows:-

- Measure 1 - On the F chord, the right hand is still using a 2nd inversion Bb triad under the melody note D on beat **1**, now followed by a 1st inversion Eb triad on the last 16th of beat **1** (adding a top-note melodic embellishment of Eb). The 2nd inversion Bb triad is repeated on the '**& of 2**' (adding a top-note melodic embellishment of D). A root position F triad is still being used under the 5th of the chord (C) in the melody on beat **3**, now with an added grace note of G# leading into A (the 3rd of the chord). We are now using a root position Bb triad under the melody note F on beat **4**. Overall in the context of the F chord, these upper Bb, Eb, Bb & F triads represent a **double backcycle** on this chord (see **Fig. 17.19.**). The left hand is playing the diatonic walkup tones (in 'alternating' octaves) F, G, A, & Bb on the downbeats, approaching the root of the following **C** chord. This momentarily creates the passing chords **Bb/G** or **Gmi7** on the '**& of 2**', **F/A** on beat **3** and **Bb** on beat **4**.

- Measure 2 - On the **C** chord, the right hand is still using a 2nd inversion C triad under the 3rd of the chord in the melody (E) on beat **1**, now followed by three additional triads - a 2nd inversion Bb triad on the last 16th of beat **1**, a root position F triad on the '**& of 2**', and back to a 2nd inversion C triad on beat **3**. These triads are adding the top-note melodic embellishments of D, C & E

Fast gospel melody (contd)

Analysis of Fig. 18.37. contd.

- Measure 2 (contd) respectively, and represent a **double backcycle** on the **C** chord. The pair of 16th notes in the left hand starting on beat **2**, are leading into the F triad on the '**& of 2**' in the right hand. A G# grace note has also been added on the '**& of 2**', leading into A (the 3rd of the upper F triad). The melody during beat **4** is still played as single notes, as in **Stage 1**.

- Measure 3 - Continuing on the **C** chord, the right hand is still using a 2nd inversion Bb triad under the melody note D on beat **1**, now followed by three additional triads - a 1st inversion Eb triad on the '**& of 1**', another 2nd inversion Bb triad on the last 16th of beat **1**, and a root position F triad on the 2nd 16th of beat **2**. These triads are adding the top-note melodic embellishments of Eb, D & C respectively. The melody note C which was on beat **3** has now been anticipated by a 16th note (i.e. now placed on the last 16th of beat **2**) and is still supported by a 1st inversion C triad. Overall in the context of the C chord, the upper triads Eb, Bb, F & C represent a **triple backcycle** on this chord (see **Fig. 17.21.**). Note that the Bb, F & C triads (from the end of beat **1** to the end of beat **2**) are all on the 'weak 16ths', and rhythmically fit 'in between' the roots in the left hand part. A D# grace note has also been added on the last 16th of beat **2**, leading into E (the 3rd of the chord). We are now using a 2nd inversion Edim triad under the 5th of the chord (G) in the melody on beat **4** - this is derived from the **C Mixolydian mode** and defines a **C7** dominant chord at this point - upgrading the **C** chord to a **C7** is appropriate here as the chords in measures 3-4 (**C** to **F**) are functioning in a 'five-to-one' relationship.

- Measure 4 - On the **F** chord, the right hand is now using a 2nd inversion Dmi triad under the root of the chord in the melody (F) on beat **1**, now followed by four additional triads - a 2nd inversion Dbmi triad on the last 16th of beat **1**, a 2nd inversion Cmi triad on the '**& of 2**', a 2nd inversion Bb triad on the '**& of 3**', and a root position F triad under the original melody note C (the 5th of the chord) on beat **4**. The first three of these triads are adding the top-note melodic embellishments of Fb (E), Eb and D respectively. The upper Dmi, Cmi, Bb & F triads are all derived from the **F Mixolydian** mode (see second line of **Fig. 18.28.**), and as such give the chord a dominant implication overall. The Dbmi triad is a 'parallel' chromatic minor triad connecting the Dmi and Cmi triads (we first saw this idea in **Fig. 17.48.**). A C# grace note has been added on beat **1**, leading into D (the 13th of the implied F7 chord) and a G# grace note has been added on beat **4**, leading into A (the 3rd of the chord). The pair of 16th notes in the left hand starting on beat **2**, are leading into the Cmi triad on the '**& of 2**' in the right hand, in a similar manner to measure 2.

- Measure 5 - Continuing on the **F** chord, the right hand is still using a root position F triad under the 5th of the chord in the melody (C) on beat **1**, now with the top note doubled. Instead of the remaining F triad inversions in this measure as we had in **Stage 1**, now following the first F triad we are using a 2nd inversion Bb triad on the last 16th of beat **1** (with the top note doubled), another root position F triad on the '**& of 2**' (anticipating beat **3**, again with the top note doubled), a 2nd inversion F triad on the '**& of 3**', a root position Bb triad on beat **4**, and a 1st inversion F triad on the '**& of 4**'. These triads are adding the top-note melodic embellishments D & C during beats **1** & **2**, and rhythmically rephrasing the remaining melody notes (A & F) during beats **3** & **4**. The upper movement between the Bb & F triads represents a **single backcycle** on the F chord (see **Fig. 17.17.**). The left hand is using the diatonic walkup tones G & A in octaves during beat **4**, leading into the following **Bb** chord. This momentarily creates the passing chords of **Bb/G** or **Gmi7** on beat **4**, and **F/A** on the '**& of 4**'.

Fast gospel melody (contd)

Analysis of Fig. 18.37. contd.

- Measure 6 - On the **Bb** chord, the right hand is still using a 2nd inversion C triad under the melody note E on beat **1**, this time moving to a pair of 2nd inversion Bb triads on the last 16th of beat **1** and on the '**& of 2**', resulting in a repetition and rephrasing of the melody note D (the 3rd of the chord). Again this upper shape movement could be considered as a '**9 to 1**' alternating triad figure (see **Fig. 12.14.**). The root in the original melody during beat **4** has also been rhythmically rephrased, now supported by a 1st inversion Bb triad on the '**& of 3**' and a root position Eb triad on the 2nd 16th of beat **4** (both with top notes doubled). This could be considered as an incomplete **single backcycle** on the **Bb** chord i.e. upper triad movement from Bb to Eb, but without coming back to the Bb triad. Meanwhile the left hand is using the walkup tones D & Eb within the 'alternating' 8th note octave pattern, during beats **3** & **4**. This momentarily creates the passing chords of **Bb/D** during beat **3** and **Eb** during beat **4**.

- Measure 7 - On the **F** chord, the right hand is still using a 2nd inversion F triad (this time with the top note doubled) below the 3rd of the chord in the melody (A) on beat **1**. Again this is followed by a 1st inversion F triad under the root of the chord in the melody (F), this time on the last 16th of beat **1** (anticipating beat **2**). The melody note F is then supported by two root position Bb triads, on beat **3** and the last 16th of beat **3**. This could again be considered as an incomplete **single backcycle** on the **F** chord. Overall this top note sequence adds rhythmic rephrasing and repetition to this part of the melody. The left hand is using the diatonic walkup tones A & Bb during beats **2** & **3** (leading into the following C chord on beat **4**), momentarily creating an **F/A** chord during beat **2** and a **Bb** chord during beat **3**.

- On the **C** chord, the right hand is still using a root position C triad under the 5th of the chord in the melody (G), this time rephrased to fall on the 2nd 16th of beat **4**.

- Measure 8 - On the **F** chord, the right hand is still using a 1st inversion F triad under the root of the chord in the melody (F) on beat **1**. This top note is then used as a 'drone' over the structures used in the rest of the measure, in a similar manner to **Fig. 18.25**. The notes below the drone are derived from the **F Mixolydian** mode - the shapes on the last 16th of beat **1** and on the 2nd 16th of beat **2**, could be considered as altered versions of Adim & Gmi triads (from F Mixolydian) respectively - but with the top note replaced by the drone (F) in each case. Finally the Ab on the last 16th of beat **2** leads into the 3rd of the chord (A) under the drone on beat **3**.

PRACTICE DIRECTIONS:-

- Practice the fast gospel melody treatment stages #1 and #2, as shown in Figures 18.36. and 18.37.
- Work on applying these concepts to tunes of your choice, and to the practice leadsheets at the end of this chapter.

Fast gospel practice examples

Figure 18.38. Practice leadsheet #1 (chords only - for 'comping' practice)

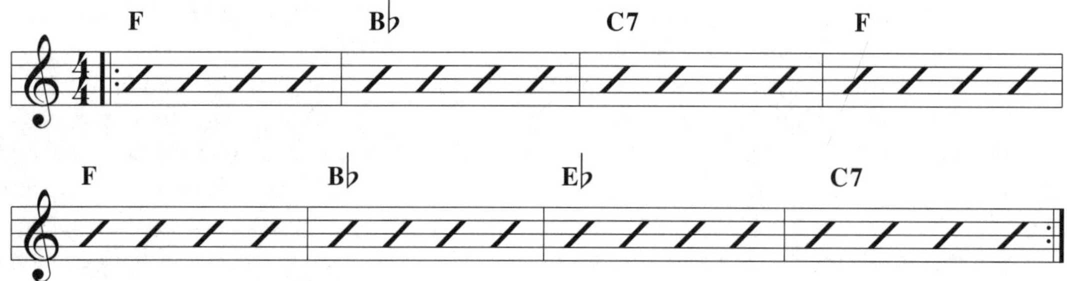

Figure 18.39. Practice leadsheet #2 (chords only - for 'comping' practice)

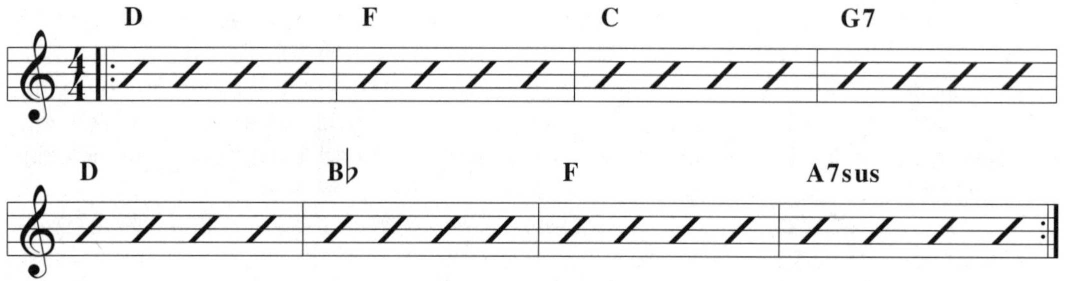

Figure 18.40. Practice leadsheet #3 (chords only - for 'comping' practice)

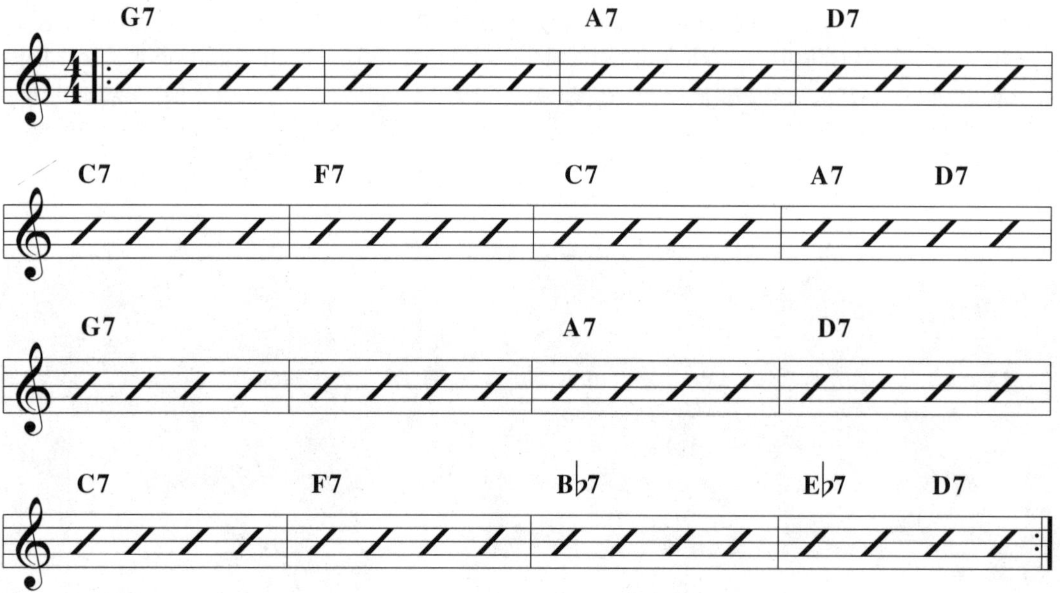

Fast gospel practice examples (contd)

Figure 18.41. Practice leadsheet #4 (chords only - for 'comping' practice)

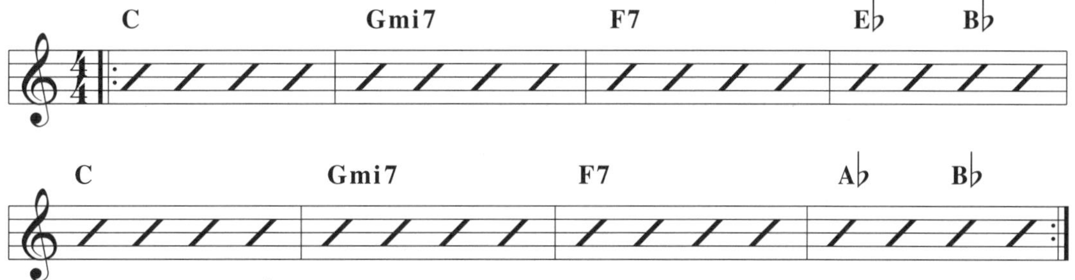

Figure 18.42. Practice leadsheet #5 (melody & chords, for melody treatment or 'comping' practice

Figure 18.43. Practice leadsheet #6 (melody & chords, for melody treatment or 'comping' practice

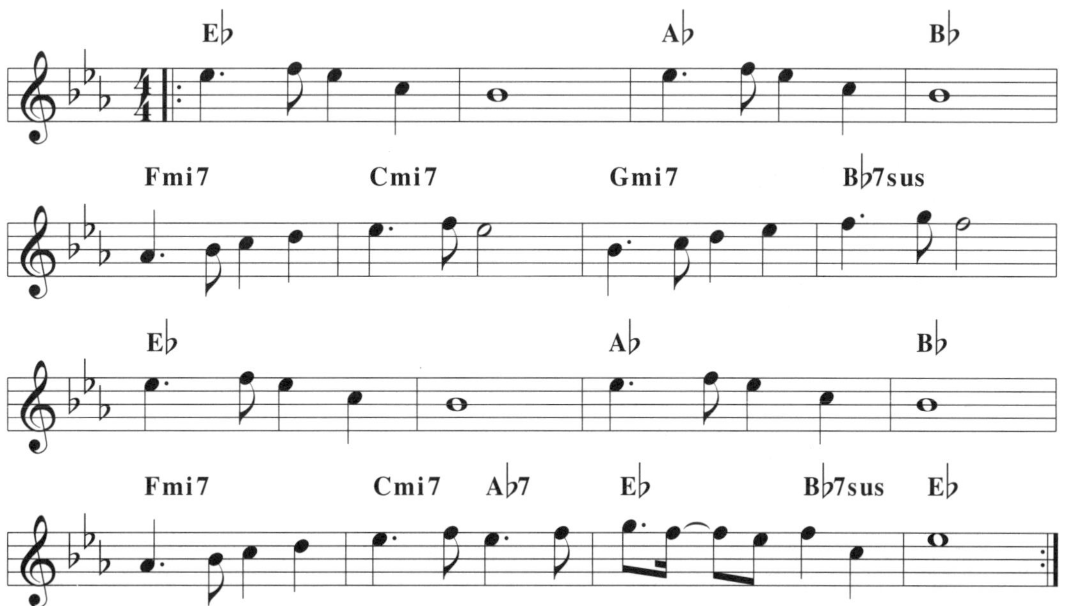

--- NOTES ---

Glossary of terms used in this book

Accidental — Collective term for prefixes such as sharps, flats, and natural signs placed to the left of music noteheads.

Accompaniment — Providing harmonic, rhythmic and stylistic support to a melody instrument or vocal. Also known as 'comping'.

Active — Generally used to describe certain scale degrees of a major scale/key which require resolution. For example, the pentatonic scale (see **Fig. 1.52.**) can be derived by removing the most 'active' scale degrees (4th & 7th) from a major scale. ***Contemporary Eartraining Levels 1 & 2*** (also from **HARRISON MUSIC EDUCATION SYSTEMS**) make extensive use of these 'active' and 'resting' scale degree concepts.

Add9 — Chord quality which results from the addition of the ninth to a basic major or minor triad. The use of the chord suffix '**add9**' implies a major triad with added 9th (see **Fig. 1.93.**). The use of the chord suffix '**mi(add9)**' implies a minor triad with added 9th (see **Fig. 1.94.**).

Aeolian (mode) — The mode created when a major scale is displaced to start on its 6th degree (see **Fig. 1.36.**) - also equivalent to a natural minor scale.

Alternating triads — The use of two or more triad shapes in the right hand in an 'alternating' manner over a constant bass note (see **Figs. 12.9. - 12.22.**). Used extensively in pop-rock and other contemporary styles.

'and of'*, as in '& of 1', '& of 2', etc.* — The rhythmic point in the measure which is halfway between successive down-beats i.e. the '& of 1' is halfway between beats 1 and 2 (assuming a 'straight-8ths' rhythmic interpretation is being applied) - see **Fig. 2.41.** Also known as an 'upbeat'.

Anticipations — Also known as 'pushes' or 'kicks'. Generally an **anticipation** occurs when a musical event is placed immediately before a downbeat, and then is sustained through or is followed by a rest on that downbeat. See text accompanying **Fig. 2.43.** for **8th-note** anticipations, and text accompanying **Fig. 2.44.** for **16th-note** anticipations.

Arpeggio, arpeggiate — An arpeggio is an arrangement of a chord or voicing played 'broken chord style' i.e. the notes played in succession rather than simultaneously. For example, **Fig. 3.19.** is an arpeggiated version of the voicings shown in **Fig. 3.17.**

Arrangement — In the context used in *Pop Piano Book*, the arrangement is the final interpretation at the keyboard of a chart or leadsheet, incorporating the appropriate voicings, rhythms and harmonic devices needed for the style being performed. The goal is to create the keyboard 'arrangement' as spontaneously as possible!

GLOSSARY

Attack	Used in the context of 'rhythmic attack', signifying the place(s) in a measure where a rhythmic event occurs i.e. "rhythmic attack on 1" means that a note or notes are beginning on beat 1.
Augmented triad	A triad consisting of two consecutive major third intervals - can also be derived by taking a major triad and raising the 5th by a half-step (see **Fig. 1.71.**).
Backbeats	Typically the beats of the measure that the drummer would emphasize with the snare drum in pop/rock/R'n'B styles - beats **2** & **4** in a 4/4 measure.
Backcycling	A chordal movement that jumps either one, two or three stages around the circle-of-fifths, and then moves back sequentially around the circle-of-fourths. Used especially in gospel (see **p397**) as well as rock styles.
Basic chord tones	Generally the root, third and fifth of the chord in question.
Bass clef	The bass clef staff contains the notes to be played on the keyboard with the left hand. (The first leger line above the staff represents Middle C).
Bass 'pedal'	A repeated bass note used below changing upper chords or voicings.
Bluegrass	A country style involving the use of fast, syncopated arpeggios (originating on the guitar).
Blues scale	A six-note scale containing the tonic, minor 3rd, perfect 4th, augmented 4th, perfect 5th and minor 7th intervals - see **Fig. 1.68.**
Chart	- See *Leadsheet, Chord chart.*
Chord	Term generally used to describe the harmony created when three or more pitches are used simultaneously, in a vertical 'stack'. Most contemporary pop styles are organized around 'chords' or stacks of pitches (as opposed to the 'linear' or horizontal approach of many classical and advanced jazz styles).
Chord chart	A basic chart of a tune which will indicate the 'road map' (number of measures in each section, where the repeats are, etc.), the chord symbols, and any necessary rhythmic figures.
Chord progression	A series of chords used in sequence (as indicated on a chord chart).
Chord quality	The vertical sound created by the chord i.e. major, minor, suspended etc.
Chord symbol	The symbol used on the chart to indicate the chord required. See **p12-17** for the definition of most common chord symbols.
Chord voicing	The specific pitches/intervals/'shapes' used to construct a solution for a chord in a particular style or situation. Many 'voicings' or solutions are possible for a given chord symbol, particularly in more evolved contemporary styles.

Chromatic Outside of, or not belonging to, the scale/key in question. For example:- "The note D# is chromatic to a C major scale". (Opposite of 'diatonic').

Chromatic walkup A left hand device used in gospel styles involving a succession of ascending half-steps in the bass voice (see **Figs. 17.36. - 17.39.** and subsequent **Chapter 17** examples).

Circle-of-fifths A succession of keys/scales/chords based on a series of '**five-to-one**' relationships - see **p18**.

Circle-of-fourths A succession of keys/scales/chords based on a series of '**four-to-one**' relationships - see **p18**.

Closed triad A triad voicing with a total span of less than one octave.

Clusters I have used this term in the *Pop Piano Book* to describe three-note voicing shapes with a total span of a fourth interval - see **Figs. 13.9.** and **13.10.**

Common time Another way to describe **4/4** time - see **Fig. 2.18.**

Commontone Term applied to any notes which are included in consecutive chords or voicings i.e. in **Fig. 4.13.** the Middle C is a commontone between the first 2 triads (**C** & **F**).

Comping - See *Accompaniment.*

Concerted Playing the notes of a chord or voicing together (i.e. simultaneously).

Consistent intervals A technique of applying the same interval (typically 3rds or 6ths) below the melody. For example, **Fig. 11.35.** contains 6th intervals below each melody note.

Consonant Used in the context of 'consonant interval' - creating a harmonious, smooth and pleasant sound - opposite of 'dissonant', implying harsh, edgy or clashing characteristics. Ultimately the concepts of consonance and dissonance are very subjective!

Contour A term used to describe the 'shape' created by the sequence of black and white keys in a scale - see **Fig. 3.1.** and accompanying text. (The term 'contour' can also be used to refer to the varying energy level or momentum of an arrangement - for example, **Fig. 11.29.** builds the 'contour' from beginning to end).

Contrary motion A situation resulting from the right and left hand parts of an arrangement moving in opposite directions (i.e. one up, one down) for any period of time.

Counting 'Counting' rhythms enables us to precisely outline the subdivisions involved. See **Fig. 2.41.** for **8th-note** counting and **Fig. 2.42.** for **16th-note** counting.

Country An American popular music style using 8th-note subdivisions and generally simple melodic/harmonic concepts - see **Chapter 16**.

Coupling Used in the context of 'interval coupling', implying the use of a harmonic interval (i.e. two notes played simultaneously) to support a melody or for accompaniment purposes. Typical intervals used in contemporary styles are thirds, fourths and sixths.

Cross-over *licks or phrases* This term refers to the 'cross-over' fingering style required for certain phrases across the range of the keyboard - see **Fig. 15.97.** and accompanying text.

Cut time Another name for the **2/2** time signature - two beats or pulses per measure, with the half note getting the beat. See **Fig. 2.20.** and discussion in **Chapter 18.**

Definitive A term applied to a chord or chord tone(s). A definitive voicing for a chord is one which clearly conveys the intended chord quality i.e. major, minor, dominant etc. For example, in distinguishing between major and minor triads, the 3rd of the triad is considered 'definitive' as this is controlling whether a major or minor chord quality is produced (i.e. depending on whether a major or minor third interval from the root, is present). Depending on the style and context, either definitive or non-definitive chord voicings may be appropriate.

Descending 7th A term used to describe a bass line connecting the roots of two chords which are a third interval apart, in a 'scalewise' manner. See **Fig. 14.29.**

Diatonic Belonging to, or part of, the scale/key in question. For example:- "The note E is diatonic to a C major scale". (Opposite of 'chromatic').

Diatonic intervals Intervals placed below a melody or desired top-line which belong to the key - see **Figs. 11.35. - 11.37.**

Diatonic triads Triads which belong to, or occur naturally within, the major scale/key in question. See **Fig. 1.74.** and **Chapter 3.**

Diatonic four-part chords Four-part chords which belong to, or occur naturally within, the major scale/key in question. See **Fig. 1.85.** and **Chapter 3.**

Diminished triad A triad consisting of two consecutive minor third intervals - can also be derived by taking a major triad and flatting the 3rd and 5th by half-step (see **Fig. 1.72.**).

Diminished 7th chord A four-part chord formed by adding a diminished 7th interval (equivalent to a major 6th interval) to a diminished triad. Intervals created are minor 3rd, diminished 5th, and diminished 7th with respect to the root (see **Fig. 1.81.**).

Dissonant Used in the context of 'dissonant interval' - having harsh, edgy or clashing characteristics. (Opposite of 'consonant').

Dominant approach chord The use of a dominant 7th chord as an added harmonic embellishment prior to another chord. The root of the dominant approach chord is typically a half-step below the root of the 'target' chord in gospel styles - see **Figs. 17.62. - 17.64.**

Dominant 7th chord	A four-part chord formed by adding a minor 7th interval to a major triad. Intervals created are major 3rd, perfect 5th and minor 7th with respect to the root (see **Fig. 1.77.**). The dominant 7th chord is built from the 5th degree of a major scale (see **Fig. 1.85.**) and generally needs to resolve back to the 'tonic' or **I** chord of the key.
Dominant 7th suspension, Dominant 7th suspended chord	A four part chord formed by adding a minor 7th interval to a suspended triad, or by taking a dominant 7th chord and altering the 3rd to a 4th (equivalent to an 11th). Intervals created are perfect 4th, perfect 5th and minor 7th with respect to the root (see **Fig. 1.78.**).
Dominant 9th chord	A five part chord formed by adding a major ninth interval to a dominant 7th chord. Intervals created are major 3rd, perfect 5th, minor 7th and major ninth with respect to the root (see **Fig. 1.88.**).
Dominant 9th suspension, Dominant 9th suspended chord	A five part chord formed by adding a major ninth interval to a suspended dominant 7th chord. Intervals created are perfect 4th, perfect 5th, minor 7th and major ninth with respect to the root (see **Figs. 1.89.** and **5.2.**).
Dominant 11th chord	Equivalent to the dominant 9th suspension - see **Fig. 14.13.**
Dominant 13th suspension	A six part chord (although the 5th is not essential and is frequently ommitted) formed by adding a major 13th interval (equivalent to an octave plus major sixth) to a dominant 11th or dominant 9th suspended chord. See **Figs. 7.2.** and **14.14.**
Dorian (mode)	The mode created when a major scale is displaced to start on its 2nd degree (see **Fig. 1.32.**).
Dorian triads	Triads built from a Dorian mode (see **Figs. 15.58.** & **15.59.**).
Dotted eighth note	A note with duration lasting for three-quarters of a beat (see **Fig. 2.7.**).
Dotted eighth note rest	A rest with duration lasting for three-quarters of a beat (see **Fig. 2.15.**).
Dotted half note	A note with duration lasting for three beats (see **Fig. 2.3.**).
Dotted half note rest	A rest with duration lasting for three beats (see **Fig. 2.11.**).
Dotted quarter note	A note with duration lasting for one-and-a-half beats (see **Fig. 2.5.**).
Dotted quarter note rest	A rest with duration lasting for one-and-a-half beats (see **Fig. 2.13.**).
Double, doubling	To 'double' a note within a chord is to add the same note either an octave above or below - see **Figs. 11.38.**, **11.43.** etc.
Double backcycle	A chordal movement that jumps two stages around the circle-of-fifths before moving back sequentially around the circle-of-fourths - see **p397**.

GLOSSARY

Double 4th	A three-note structure created by 'stacking' one perfect 4th interval on top of another - see **Fig. 10.1.**
Double-4th-over-root	These chord voicings are created by placing double 4th structures over various root notes - see **Figs. 10.2. - 10.11.**
Downbeat	The beats or 'pulses' within a 4/4 measure i.e. beats 1, 2, 3 & 4 - as opposed to 'upbeats' which occur in between the downbeats.
Drone	A repeated note sustained or played against another moving line. This device is used in various contemporary styles, especially country (see **Fig. 16.23.**).
Dynamics	Technically the degrees of loudness and softness in a musical performance. For example, the supporting tones below a melody generally need to be at a lower 'dynamic level' than the melody itself - see Pop Ballad example **Fig. 11.41.**
Eighth note	A note with duration lasting for one-half of a beat (see **Fig. 2.6.**).
Eighth note rest	A rest with duration lasting for one-half of a beat (see **Fig. 2.14.**).
Eighth note triplet	This is a rhythmic subdivision in which each eighth note occupies one-third of a beat (instead of the normal one-half of a beat) - see **Fig. 2.32.**
Extensions	Upper tones added to chords (beyond the basic root, 3rd and 5th of the chord).
Fake, Faking	The act of improvising an accompaniment or melody treatment, generally working from a leadsheet or 'fake book'.
Fake book	A book containing leadsheets of tunes rather than written-out arrangements. The musician is left to create their own arrangement based on the melody and chord symbols provided, and on their understanding of the harmony and style.
Fast gospel	An up-tempo, rhythmically driving gospel style described in **Chapter 18**.
Fifth (5th) interval	- A **perfect 5th** interval occurs between the tonic (1st degree) and the 5th degree of a major scale i.e. G is the 5th degree of C major, therefore C up to G is a perfect 5th interval. - A **diminished 5th** interval occurs when a perfect 5th interval is reduced by a half-step i.e. C up to G is a perfect 5th interval, therefore C up to Gb is a diminished 5th interval. - An **augmented 5th** interval occurs when a perfect 5th interval is increased by a half-step i.e. C up to G is a perfect 5th interval, therefore C up to G# is an augmented 5th interval.
Filled-in octave	A right-hand technique of 'doubling' the melody an octave lower, and then 'filling in' between the octave with an appropriate chord tone - see **Fig. 11.39.**

Fills — Single-note embellishments based on the chord/scale in force, generally leading into a point of chord change - see Pop Ballad example **Fig. 11.21.**

First inversion — A three- or four-part chord is in first inversion when the root has been transposed up an octave and has become the highest note - see **Figs. 4.3.** and **6.3.**

Flat — A flat sign prefixed to a note requires that note to be lowered in pitch by one half-step. May also form part of a key signature.

Four-four (4/4) time — A time signature with four beats or 'pulses' per measure, with the quarter note getting the beat (see **Fig. 2.17.**).

Four-part chords — Chords which have one extra tone in addition to the basic root, 3rd and 5th - typically the extra tone is a 6th or 7th. See **Figs. 1.75. - 1.85.** and **Chapter 6**.

Four-part-over-root chords — These chord voicings are created by using four-part chords as 'upper structures' over various root notes - see **Figs. 7.1. - 7.4.**

Fourth (4th) clusters — - See *Clusters.*

Fourth (4th) coupling — 'Harmonic' 4th intervals (i.e. both notes played simultaneously) derived from a scale source i.e. minor pentatonic scale - see **Figs. 12.23. - 12.28.**

Fourth (4th) interval
- A **perfect 4th** interval occurs between the tonic (1st degree) and the 4th degree of a major scale i.e. F is the 4th degree of C major, therefore C up to F is a perfect 4th interval.
- An **augmented 4th** interval occurs when a perfect 4th interval is increased by a half-step i.e. C up to F is a perfect 4th interval, therefore C up to F# is an augmented 4th interval.

Four-to-three (4 to 3) — A movement (between the 4th and the 3rd) which can occur in any inversion of a major or minor triad. The triad can in turn be part of a triad-over-root structure. See **Chapter 9**.

Funk (R'n'B/Funk) — A contemporary music style using medium-to-fast tempos and straight & swing 16th-note subdivisions with anticipations - see **Chapter 15**.

Gospel — A contemporary music style originating in the church and based around dominant/blues harmony.
- **Slow gospel** uses slow-to-medium tempos and an eighth-note triplet subdivision - see **Chapter 17**.
- **Fast gospel** uses faster tempos and a (straight) 16th-note subdivision with anticipations - see **Chapter 18**.

Grace note — An embellishment note of very short duration which is added before another note or chord (see the various **Chapter 17** & **18** examples). Normally shown in a smaller size on the staff.

Grace note licks I have used this term to describe right-hand phrases which incorporate grace-note embellishments within them - as in **Fig. 15.99.**

Half note A note with duration lasting for two beats (see **Fig. 2.2.**).

Half note rest A rest with duration lasting for two beats (see **Fig. 2.10.**).

Half-step The smallest unit of interval measurement in conventional Western tonal music. (Also known as a semitone). There are twelve half-steps in one octave.

Half-step-&-5th structure I have used this term in the *Pop Piano Book* to describe three-note voicing shapes with a half-step interval between the bottom two notes, and a perfect fifth interval between the top two notes (see **Fig. 13.19.**).

Half-step-4th cluster I have used this term in the *Pop Piano Book* to describe three-note voicing shapes with a half-step interval between the bottom two notes, and a perfect fourth interval between the lowest and highest notes (see **Fig. 13.10.**).

Hammer A hammer is a type of grace-note embellishment into a target or chord tone, typically moving by whole-step and accompanied by a drone (repeated or held note) above. Mainly associated with country styles (see **Fig. 16.33.**).

Harmonic minor One of the three minor scales in common usage. A harmonic minor scale can be derived by taking a major scale and flatting the 3rd and 6th degrees (see **Fig. 1.47.**) **OR** by raising the 7th degree with respect to the minor key signature in force (see **Fig. 1.50.**).

Hip-hop A style of modern urban dance music using a swing-sixteenth note rhythmic subdivision - see various **Chapter 15** references.

Interval The distance in pitch between two notes. (See individual glossary entries for the different types of intervals used in *Pop Piano Book*).

Inversion, inverted An inversion of a chord or voicing occurs when the normal sequence of notes from bottom to top is changed, typically by moving one or more notes up an octave. See **Fig. 4.3.** for a triad example and **Fig. 6.3.** for a four-part example.

Ionian (mode) The mode name given to a major scale which is NOT displaced, i.e. still starting on the normal tonic (see **Fig. 1.38.**).

Key Term used to indicate tonality of a piece of music i.e. the major or minor scale to be used as 'home base'. For example, a tune in the key of C major will use the C major scale (subject to any accidentals being used) and the note C will be heard as the tonic or 'home base'.

Key signature A group of sharps or flats placed at the beginning of a tune to indicate the key. (See **Figs. 1.2. - 1.16.** for major key signatures). Each key signature can also be used for a 'relative' minor key, built from the 6th of the major key - see **p8**.

Leading — This term refers to the resolution energy or momentum of chords or intervals i.e. to describe the dominant 7th as a leading chord means that it 'wants to' resolve back to a **I** or tonic chord.

Leadsheet — A written chart containing the melody and chord symbols for a tune. Also see *Fake Book.*

Legato — To play a phrase 'legato' means to play in a smooth and connected manner. (Opposite of 'staccato').

Lick — A previously-learned phrase or line inserted into a performance of a tune in a (hopefully!) spontaneous manner. See **Fig. 15.99.**

Locrian — The mode created when a major scale is displaced to start on its 7th degree (see **Fig. 1.37.**).

Lydian — The mode created when a major scale is displaced to start on its 4th degree (see **Fig. 1.34.**).

Lydian chord — I sometimes use this term to describe the **9-#11-13** traid-over-root combination shown in **Fig. 5.7.** All the notes in the **C/Bb** chord shown are found in a Bb Lydian mode, in particular the **#11** color tone (E in this example).

Major scale — A set of interval relationships (*whole-step, whole-step, half-step, whole-step, whole-step, whole-step & half-step*) constituting the basic tonality or 'reference point' for most Western music (see **Fig. 1.1.**).

Major triad — A three-note chord formed by taking the 1st, 3rd & 5th degrees of a major scale. Intervals created are major 3rd and perfect 5th, with respect to the root (see **Fig. 1.69.**).

Major 2nd (second) interval - See *Second Interval.*

Major 3rd (third) interval - See *Third Interval.*

Major 6th (sixth) — This term can be applied to a chord and an interval:-

- ***Major 6th chord*** — A four-note chord formed by adding a major 6th interval to a major triad. Intervals created are major 3rd, perfect 5th, and major 6th with respect to the root (see **Fig. 1.76.**).
- ***Major 6th interval*** - See *Sixth Interval.*

Major 69 (six-nine) chord — A five-note chord formed by adding a major ninth interval to a major 6th chord. Intervals created are major 3rd, perfect 5th, major 6th, and major 9th with respect to the root (see **Fig. 1.90.**).

Major 7th (seventh)

This term can be applied to a chord and an interval:-

Major 7th chord A four-note chord formed by adding a major 7th interval to a major triad. Intervals created are major 3rd, perfect 5th, and major 7th with respect to the root (see **Fig. 1.75.**).

Major 7th interval - See *Seventh Interval.*

Major 7th with altered 5th (b5 or #5) chord

These four-note chords are formed by taking a major 7th chord and altering the fifth (flatting or sharping) by half-step (see **Fig. 1.82.**).

Major 9th (ninth)

This term can be applied to a chord and an interval:-

Major 9th chord A five-note chord formed by adding a major 9th interval to a major seventh chord. Intervals created are major 3rd, perfect 5th, major 7th and major 9th with respect to the root (see **Fig. 1.86.**).

Major 9th interval - See *Ninth Interval.*

Major (add9) chord

This four-note chord is formed by adding a major 9th interval to a major triad (The use of this chord suffix implies that the 7th is omitted). See **Fig. 1.93.**

Major 13th chord

This major chord has all of the chord tones and available extensions - major 3rd, perfect 5th, major 7th, major 9th, augmented 11th and major 13th. (The augmented 11th interval is an octave plus an augmented 4th - the major 13th interval is an octave plus a major 6th). To 'voice' the chord with all these tones present, would generally be too 'dense' for most contemporary styles - however the **9-#11-13** upper structure described in **Fig. 5.7.** could represent an incomplete version of this chord.

Melodic minor scale

One of the three minor scales in common usage. A melodic minor scale can be derived by taking a major scale and flatting the 3rd degree (see **Fig. 1.46.**) **OR** by raising the 6th and 7th degrees with respect to the minor key signature in force (see **Fig. 1.51.**).

Minor pentatonic scale

Pentatonic scale starting from relative minor - see **Fig. 1.67.**

Minor scale

There are three minor scales in common usage - melodic, harmonic and natural. See **Figs. 1.46. - 1.51.** and individual glossary entries.

Minor triad

A three-note chord formed by:-

- taking a major triad and flatting the 3rd by half-step (see **Fig. 1.70.**).
- building a diatonic triad from either the 2nd, 3rd or 6th degrees of a major scale (see **Fig. 1.74.**).

Minor 2nd (second) interval - See *Second Interval.*

Minor 3rd (third) interval - See *Third Interval.*

Minor 6th (sixth) This term can be applied to a chord and an interval:-

Minor 6th chord A four-note chord formed by adding a major 6th interval to a minor triad. Intervals created are minor 3rd, perfect 5th, and major 6th with respect to the root (see **Fig. 1.80.**).

Minor 6th interval - See *Sixth Interval.*

Minor 69 (six-nine) chord A five-note chord formed by adding a major ninth interval to a minor 6th chord. Intervals created are minor 3rd, perfect 5th, major 6th, and major 9th with respect to the root (see **Fig. 1.92.**).

Minor 7th (seventh) This term can be applied to a chord and an interval:-

Minor 7th chord A four-note chord formed by adding a minor 7th interval to a minor triad. Intervals created are minor 3rd, perfect 5th, and minor 7th with respect to the root (see **Fig. 1.79.**).

Minor 7th interval - See *Seventh Interval.*

Minor 7th with altered 5th (b5 or #5) chord These four-note chords are formed by taking a minor 7th chord and altering the fifth (flatting or sharping) by half-step (see **Fig. 1.83.**).

Minor major 7th (seventh) chord A four-note chord formed by adding a major 7th interval to a minor triad. Intervals created are minor 3rd, perfect 5th, and major 7th with respect to the root (see **Fig. 1.80.**).

Minor 9th (ninth) This term can be applied to a chord and an interval:-

Minor 9th chord A five-note chord formed by adding a major 9th interval to a minor seventh chord. Intervals created are minor 3rd, perfect 5th, minor 7th and major 9th with respect to the root (see **Fig. 1.87.**).

Minor 9th interval - See *Ninth Interval.*

Minor (add9) chord This four-note chord is formed by adding a major 9th interval to a minor triad (The use of this chord suffix implies that the 7th is omitted). See **Fig. 1.94.**

Minor major 9th (ninth) chord — A five-note chord formed by adding a major 9th interval to a minor major 7th chord. Intervals created are minor 3rd, perfect 5th, major 7th and major 9th with respect to the root (see **Fig. 1.91.**).

Minor 11th chord — This six-note chord can be derived by adding a perfect 11th interval (perfect 4th plus one octave) to a minor 9th chord. In pop styles this chord is typically 'voiced' in an incomplete manner i.e. without all the chord tones present - see voicing solutions in **Figs. 5.2.**, **7.4.**, **10.5.**, **10.8.**, **13.12.** and **15.50.**

Mixolydian (mode) — The mode created when a major scale is displaced to start on its 5th degree (see **Fig. 1.35.**).

Mixolydian triads — Triads built from a Mixolydian mode (see **Figs. 15.68.**, **15.69.**, **17.5.** & **17.6.**).

Mode, modal scale — Terms used to describe a 'displaced' scale i.e. a scale starting from a note other than the normal tonic or first note of the scale. This concept is most frequently applied to major scales (see **Figs. 1.32. - 1.45.**), although it can be applied to any type of scale.

Modal triads — Triads built from a modal scale - see *Dorian triads, Mixolydian triads.*

Motif — A short melodic 'fragment' or phrase.

Moving 10th line — A pattern of consecutive 10th intervals moving in a scalewise manner, as used for walkups (see **Fig. 16.22.**) and walkdowns (see **Fig. 16.26.**) in country styles.

Muscle memory — I use this term when describing the spontaneous physical recognition and execution of 'shapes' and voicings - i.e. in order to immediately play a first inversion C major triad (without playing it in root position first) we need to have the shape in our 'muscle memory' - see discussion in **Chapter 4**.

Natural — A natural sign prefixed to a note cancels out a previously applied sharp or flat (either from an earlier accidental, or from a key signature).

Natural minor — One of the three minor scales in common usage. A natural minor scale can be derived by taking a major scale and flatting the 3rd, 6th and 7th degrees (see **Fig. 1.48.**) or by applying a minor key signature with no additional accidentals (see **Fig. 1.49.**).

Neighbour tone — An added embellishment note, typically a scalewise step either side of a melody or 'target' tone.

New Age — A contemporary instrumental music style using slow-to-medium tempos and (generally) diatonic harmony & repetitive melodies - see **Chapter 13**.

Nine-eight (9/8) time — A time signature with technically nine beats per measure with the eighth note getting the beat, although frequently an emphasis or pulse is felt every three eighth notes i.e. on the dotted quarter note (see **Fig. 2.23.**).

Nine-to-one (9 to 1) A movement (between the 9th and the root) which can occur in any inversion of a major or minor triad. The triad can in turn be part of a triad-over-root structure. See **Chapter 8**.

Ninth (9th) interval
- A **major 9th** interval can be derived by adding an octave to a major 2nd interval. A major 2nd interval occurs between the tonic (1st degree) and the 2nd degree of a major scale i.e. D is the 2nd degree of C major, so C up to D is a major 2nd interval - therefore C up to the D an octave above is a major ninth interval.
- A **minor 9th** interval occurs when a major 9th interval is reduced by a half-step i.e. C up to D (in the next octave) is a major 9th interval, therefore C up to the Db immediately below is a minor 9th interval.
- An **augmented 9th** interval occurs when a major 9th interval is increased by a half-step i.e. C up to D (in the next octave) is a major 9th interval, therefore C up to the D# immediately above is an augmented 9th interval.

Octave The interval created between notes with the same letter name. For example, the interval between middle C and the next C in either direction is one octave.

Octave runs Scalewise movements using octaves - frequently found in gospel styles (see **Figs. 17.57. - 17.59.**).

Open triad A triad voicing with a total span greater than one octave, typically due to one of the chord tones being transposed up or down by an octave (see **Figs. 11.11.** and **11.12.**).

Out-of-chord tone A melody note or embellishment tone which is not contained within the chord 'in force' at the time (see text accompanying **Fig. 11.34.**).

Pad Typically refers to a sustained chordal part of an arrangement.

Parallel 5ths I have used this term to describe perfect 5th intervals derived from a double 4th structure, played in succession - see example in **Fig. 14.29.**

Parallel interval I have used this term to describe the use of successive 5th and 6th intervals derived from inverted major and minor triads - see examples in **Fig. 11.16.**

Parallel minor triads I have used this term to describe the use of minor triads descending by half-steps, in a Mixolydian mode context in gospel styles - see **Figs. 17.48. - 17.51.**

Passing tone Similar to *out-of-chord tone*, a passing tone is not a basic chord tone but may be derived from the upper part of the chord or from the scale of the key signature. Typically a right hand embellishment 'passing' through towards a chord or 'target' tone in the melody or voiceleading.

Pentatonic scale A five-note scale which can be derived by taking the major scale and removing the 4th and 7th degrees (see **Fig. 1.52.**).

GLOSSARY

Pentatonic scale intervals I have used this term to describe the perfect 4th intervals available from minor pentatonic scales, as used in pop-rock styles (see **Figs. 12.23. - 12.29.**).

Phrygian (mode) The mode created when a major scale is displaced to start on its 3rd degree (see **Fig. 1.33.**).

Pickup A rhythmic event immediately prior to, and leading into, another rhythmic event landing on a downbeat or 'strong' rhythmic subdivision.

Pop Ballad A contemporary music style using slow-to-medium tempos with eighth-note subdivisions and simple harmonies - see **Chapter 11**.

Pop-Rock A contemporary music style using medium-to-fast tempos with a heavy 'driving' feel and eighth-note subdivisions/anticipations - see **Chapter 12**.

Primary beats Typically considered to be beats **1** & **3** in 4/4 time - the main points of rhythmic emphasis or 'important' beats.

Progression A series of chords used in succession in a tune or arrangement.

Punches - See *Anticipations.*

Quarter note A note with duration lasting for one beat (see **Fig. 2.4.**).

Quarter note rest A rest with duration lasting for one beat (see **Fig. 2.12.**).

Register Used to describe a general range of pitches on the keyboard i.e. 'lower register' refers to the lower notes on the keyboard - see discussion following **Fig. 13.1.**

Relative major This term can be used in two contexts:-

- in a **modal** context, the relative major scale is the major scale which has been displaced to create the mode in question - see discussion before **Fig. 1.39.**
- in a **key signature** context, the relative major is the key which shares the same key signature as the minor key in question. For example, **Ab major** is the relative major of **F minor** - see discussion following **Fig. 1.48.**

Relative minor The minor key which shares the same key signature as the major key in question. For example, **F minor** is the relative minor of **Ab major** - see discussion following **Fig. 1.48.**

Resolution A movement from active-to-resting or tension-to-release in music. See entries under *nine-to-one (9 to 1)* and *four-to-three (4 to 3)* movements. For more information on active-to-resting resolutions in music, refer to ***Contemporary Eartraining Levels 1 & 2*** from **HARRISON MUSIC EDUCATION SYSTEMS**.

Resting A point of release or resolution in music.

Rhythmic anticipations - See *Anticipations.*

Rhythmic attack - See *Attack.*

Rhythmic notation A style of music notation indicating the rhythmic figures required, without the actual notes being written out - see examples in **Figs. 2.25. - 2.28.**

Rhythmic shell I have used this term to describe a repeated comping 'framework' within which improvised ideas, fills etc. can be developed - see funk comping examples in **Figs. 15.82. - 15.93.**

Rhythmic subdivision This term is used to describe the smallest regularly-occurring rhythmic unit in a tune or arrangement - typically an 8th-note or 16th-note in contemporary styles (see discussion in **Chapter 2**).

R'n'B Ballad A contemporary music style using slow-to-medium tempos with sixteenth-note subdivisions and moderately sophisticated harmonies - see **Chapter 14**.

R'n'B/Funk A contemporary music style using medium-to-fast tempos with sixteenth-note subdivisions and rhythmic anticipations - see **Chapter 15**.

Root A term normally used in the context of a chord - the root of a chord is the fundamental tone of the chord, as contained in the chord symbol i.e. the root of a **Bmi** triad is the note **B**.

Root position A chord voicing in which the notes of the chord appear in their normal vertical sequence i.e. root, 3rd, 5th etc. (as opposed to an inversion, in which case this sequence is modified). A **root position** chord will therefore have the **root** on the bottom of the voicing.

Root-5th A basic chord voicing using the root and 5th of the chord, suitable for simpler rock styles - see **Figs. 12.36.** and **12.40.**

Scale A sequence of notes (typically considered in ascending order) governed by a specific interval relationship. For example, the major scale illustrated in **Fig. 1.1.** is created via the series of whole-steps and half-steps as indicated.

Scale source A scale from which a particular chord can be derived. For example, diatonic chords can be derived from modal scale sources - see discussion following **Fig. 1.85.**

Scalewise A movement occurring either up or down a scale by adjacent scale steps.

Second (2nd) interval - A **major 2nd** interval occurs between the tonic (1st degree) and the 2nd degree of a major scale i.e. D is the 2nd degree of C major, therefore C up to D is a major 2nd interval.

Second interval (contd)

- A **minor 2nd** interval occurs when a major 2nd interval is reduced by a half-step i.e. C up to D is a major 2nd interval, therefore C up to Db is a minor 2nd interval.
- An **augmented 2nd** interval occurs when a major 2nd interval is increased by a half-step i.e. C up to D is a major 2nd interval, therefore C up to D# is an augmented 2nd interval.

Second inversion

A three- or four-part chord is in second inversion when the root and third have been transposed up an octave, the third becoming the highest note - see **Figs. 4.3. and 6.3.**

Seventh (7th) interval

- A **major 7th** interval occurs between the tonic (1st degree) and the 7th degree of a major scale i.e. B is the 7th degree of C major, therefore C up to B is a major 7th interval.
- A **minor 7th** interval occurs when a major 7th interval is reduced by a half-step i.e. C up to B is a major 7th interval, therefore C up to Bb is a minor 7th interval.
- A **diminished 7th** interval occurs when a minor 7th interval is reduced by a half-step i.e. C up to Bb is a minor 7th interval, therefore C up to Bbb (B double-flat, equivalent to A) is a diminished 7th interval. This interval has the same span as a **major 6th** interval.

Shape

I have used this term to describe three- and four-note structures which have a specific interior interval relationship, enabling us to recognize and apply them to the keyboard. For example, the **double 4th** shape consists of two consecutive perfect 4th intervals (see **Fig. 10.1.**), the **whole-step-4th cluster** shape consists of a whole-step within a perfect 4th interval (see **Fig. 13.9.**) and so on.

Sharp

A sharp sign prefixed to a note requires that note to be raised in pitch by one half-step. May also form part of a key signature.

Shuffle

This term is frequently applied to rhythmic styles using a 'swing-8ths' rhythmic subdivision (see **Chapter 2**) - also the term 'funk shuffle' can be applied to styles using a 'swing-16ths' subdivision.

Single backcycle

A chordal movement that jumps one stage around the circle-of-fifths before moving back around the circle-of-fourths - see **p397**.

Sixteenth note

A note with duration lasting for one-quarter of a beat (see **Fig. 2.8.**).

Sixteenth note rest

A rest with duration lasting for one-quarter of a beat (see **Fig. 2.16.**).

Sixteenth note triplet

This is a rhythmic subdivision in which each sixteenth note occupies one-third of an eighth note (or one-sixth of a beat) instead of the normal one-half of an eighth note (or one-quarter of a beat). See **Figs. 2.38. and 2.39.**

Sixth (6th) interval

- A **major 6th** interval occurs between the tonic (1st degree) and the 6th degree of a major scale i.e. A is the 6th degree of C major, therefore C up to A is a major 6th interval.
- A **minor 6th** interval occurs when a major 6th interval is reduced by a half-step i.e. C up to A is a major 6th interval, therefore C up to Ab is a minor 6th interval.
- An **augmented 6th** interval occurs when a major 6th interval is increased by a half-step i.e. C up to A is a major 6th interval, therefore C up to A# is an augmented 6th interval.

Six-eight (6/8) time

A time signature with technically six beats per measure with the eighth note getting the beat, although frequently an emphasis or pulse is felt every three eighth notes i.e. on the dotted quarter note (see **Fig. 2.22.**).

Slash chords

This name is often given to chord symbols containing the '/' symbol i.e. C/F (see **Fig. 5.4.**), Cma7/D (see **Fig. 7.2.**) etc. The note on the right of the slash is the root or bottom voice of the chord.

Slow gospel

A slow-to-medium-tempo gospel style using eighth-note triplet subdivisions - see **Chapter 17.**

Split

I have used this term to describe the rhythmic 'staggering' or separation of a shape over different rhythmic attacks, rather than all of the notes in the shape being played simultaneously. For example, split double 4th shapes are used in **Fig. 15.93.** and split half-step-&-5th and whole-step-4th shapes are used in **Fig. 15.96.**

Staccato

A playing style in which the notes are 'detached' and are of short duration.

Straight eighths (8ths)

A rhythmic subdivision in which:-
- the smallest regularly-occuring rhythmic unit is an eighth-note
- each pair of eighth-notes are dividing the beat (quarter-note) exactly in half.

Straight sixteenths (16ths)

A rhythmic subdivision in which:-
- the smallest regularly-occuring rhythmic unit is a sixteenth-note
- each pair of sixteenth-notes are dividing the eighth-note exactly in half, and the beat (quarter-note) exactly into four quarters.

Strong 16ths

I have used this term to describe the places within a 16th-note subdivision rhythmic style which are also available within an 8th-note subdivision - i.e. beat 1, the '& of 1', beat 2, the '& of 2', etc. See explanation on **p302**.

Style

A set of parameters such as melody, harmony, rhythmic subdivision etc. which together create an identifiable type of contemporary music - see **Chapters 11 - 18**.

Sus, suspended
A suspended chord is one in which the 3rd is replaced by the 4th (i.e. the note which is a perfect 4th interval above the root of the chord). See **Figs. 1.73., 1.78.** See also *dominant 7th suspension, dominant 9th suspension, dominant 11th* etc.

Sustain pedal
A pedal on an acoustic piano which when pressed, causes the notes to 'sustain' i.e. to not be 'cut off' when the notes are released on the keyboard. On a digital piano or synthesizer, this effect is replicated electronically.

Swing eighths (8ths)
A rhythmic subdivision in which:-
- the smallest regularly-occuring rhythmic unit is an eighth-note triplet
- each pair of eighth-notes are dividing the beat (quarter-note) in a two-thirds/one-third fashion, unless all three subdivisions of the eighth-note triplet are being used. (See **Figs. 2.30. - 2.32.**).

Swing sixteenths (16ths)
A rhythmic subdivision in which:-
- the smallest regularly-occuring rhythmic unit is a sixteenth-note triplet
- each pair of sixteenth-notes are dividing the eighth-note in a two-thirds/one-third fashion, unless all three subdivisions of the sixteenth-note triplet are being used. (See **Figs. 2.38. - 2.39.**).

Syncopation
The placement of accents on parts of the measure not typically accented, for example by using *rhythmic anticipations.*

Target, target note
The eventual destination of a melodic embellishment or phrase, typically an important chord or scale tone - see examples in **Fig. 15.99.**

Tempo
The speed of an arrangement or performance. Often measured in beats-per-minute (or BPM).

Tenth (10th) interval
- A **major 10th** interval can be derived by adding an octave to a major 3rd interval. A major 3rd interval occurs between the tonic (1st degree) and the 3rd degree of a major scale i.e. E is the 3rd degree of C major, so C up to E is a major 3rd interval - therefore C up to the E an octave above is a major 10th interval.
- A **minor 10th** interval occurs when a major 10th interval is reduced by a half-step i.e. C up to E (in the next octave) is a major 10th interval, therefore C up to the Eb immediately below is a minor 10th interval.

See also *Moving 10th line.*

Third (3rd) interval
- A **major 3rd** interval occurs between the tonic (1st degree) and the 3rd degree of a major scale i.e. E is the 3rd degree of C major, therefore C up to E is a major 3rd interval.
- A **minor 3rd** interval occurs when a major 3rd interval is reduced by a half-step i.e. C up to E is a major 3rd interval, therefore C up to Eb is a minor 3rd interval.

Third inversion A four-part chord is in third inversion when the root, third and fifth have all been transposed up an octave (or when the 6th or 7th has been transposed down an octave). See **Fig. 6.3.**

Three-four (3/4) time A time signature with three beats or 'pulses' per measure, with the quarter note getting the beat (see **Fig. 2.21.**).

Transpose The movement of a note or group of notes either up or down by a specific pitch interval. For example, if we were to transpose the notes C, D & E up a perfect fifth, the resulting (transposed) notes would be G, A & B.

Treble clef The treble clef staff contains the notes to be played on the keyboard with the right hand. (The first leger line below the staff represents Middle C).

Triad A three-note chord using (in root position) consecutive third intervals (see **Figs. 1.69. - 1.72.**).

Triad below melody A harmonic device which places inverted triads below a desired melody or top-note (see **Fig. 11.34.**).

Triad-over-root chords A chord structure created by placing a major or minor triad over a root in the bass voice (see **Chapter 5**).

Triple backcycle A chordal movement that jumps three stages around the circle-of-fifths before moving back sequentially around the circle-of-fourths - see **p397**.

Triplet A triplet occurs when three notes occupy the rhythmic space normally taken by two notes. For example, in an eighth-note triplet the space taken by two eighth notes (i.e. one beat) is divided into three, and in a sixteenth-note triplet the space taken by two sixteenth notes (i.e. one-half of a beat) is divided into three.

Triplet subdivision Using the rhythmic subdivision as described above - also see *eighth-note triplet, sixteenth-note triplet.*

Twelve-eight (12/8) time A time signature with technically twelve beats per measure with the eighth note getting the beat, although frequently an emphasis or pulse is felt every three eighth notes i.e. on the dotted quarter note (see **Fig. 2.24.**).

Two-two (2/2) time - See *Cut time.*

Unison run A device using the same notes in both the right and left hands at the same time (separated by one or more octaves). Used frequently in gospel styles - see **Figs. 17.52. - 17.56.**

Unsuspended dominant A dominant chord in which the 3rd has not been replaced by the 4th (11th). See comments following **Fig. 14.15.**

GLOSSARY

Upbeat — This term is typically used to describe the subdivisions in a measure which are exactly half-way between the 'downbeats' i.e. beats 1, 2, 3 and 4 in 4/4 time. These half-way points would occur on the '& of 1', '& of 2' etc. - see **Fig. 2.41.**

Upgrading (chords) — I have used the term 'chord upgrading' to describe the additions of upper chordal extensions to basic symbols shown on a leadsheet. This is appropriate in (for example) an R'n'B ballad style - see **Figs. 14.9. - 14.15.**

Upper extensions — This term refers to the further tones available on a chord, beyond the basic triad form i.e. the 7th, 9th, 11th and 13th.

Upper structure — I have used this term to describe a shape or chord which is in turn used as the upper part of another chord, by placing it over another root in the bass voice. For example, a C triad over the note A in the bass is a **b3-5-b7** upper structure with respect to the overall Ami7 chord created - see **Fig. 5.6.**

Voicing — An interpretation of a chord symbol (for example from a leadsheet) using specific shapes and/or interval relationships. There are numerous such voicing 'solutions' for a given chord symbol - choice will depend on style and context.

Voiceleading — The movement from one chord voicing to the next in a smooth horizontal manner i.e. without unnecessary interval leaps. See **Figs. 4.2. and 6.2.**

Walkdown — The descending use of scalewise connecting tones between chord changes, typically used in country styles - see **Figs. 16.25. - 16.28.**

Walkup — The ascending use of scalewise connecting tones between chord changes, typically used in country styles - see **Figs. 16.21. - 16.24.**

Weak 16ths — I have used this term to describe the places within a 16th-note subdivision rhythmic style which are not available within an 8th-note subdivision - i.e. the 2nd & 4th 16th-notes within each beat. See explanation on **p302**.

Whole note — A note with duration lasting for four beats (see **Fig. 2.1.**).

Whole note rest — A rest with duration lasting for four beats (see **Fig. 2.9.**).

Whole-step — An interval measurement equivalent to two *half-steps*. Together the whole-step and half-step intervals are the building blocks for most conventional scales (i.e. the major scale - see **Fig. 1.1.**). The whole-step is also equivalent to a *major 2nd.*

Whole-step-4th cluster — I have used this term in the *Pop Piano Book* to describe three-note voicing shapes with a whole-step interval between the bottom two notes, and a perfect fourth interval between the lowest and highest notes (see **Fig. 13.9.**).

Whole-step-&-5th structure — I have used this term in the *Pop Piano Book* to describe three-note voicing shapes with a whole-step interval between the bottom two notes, and a perfect fifth interval between the top two notes (see **Fig. 15.50.**).

Fingering guide for major and pentatonic scales

Here is a reference guide to the fingerings for the major and pentatonic scales, arguably the two most common scale sources used in mainstream contemporary styles. The convention here is to use the numbers **1**, **2**, **3**, **4** & **5** to denote the fingers to be used in each hand - **1** refers to the thumb and **5** refers to the 'pinky'. I believe it is helpful to think of scale fingering in terms of 'groups' i.e. blocks of notes on the keyboard, played by the right or left hand. Each scale will consist of two 'groups' and will be played by each hand as follows:-

When the **right hand** is playing an ascending scale, each fingering group (except the first) will begin immediately after a 'thumb turn' (i.e. passing the thumb under the other fingers to reach a higher note) and each fingering group will **begin** with the thumb. For example, a **C Major** scale ascending (see **Fig. 1.2.**) is typically fingered by the right hand as follows:-

Notes:-	*C*	*D*	*E*	*F*	*G*	*A*	*B*	*C*	*D*	*E*	etc.
R.H. Fingering:-	***(1***	***2***	***3)***	***(1***	***2***	***3***	***4)***	***(1***	***2***	***3)***	etc.

Note the parentheses around the fingering numbers - these indicate the fingering 'groups' mentioned above. The first group **(1 2 3)** begins with the thumb and ends with the 3rd (middle) finger. At this point the thumb is passed under the 3rd finger in order to reach the following note **F**, which then begins the next fingering group **(1 2 3 4)** and so on. If another octave of the scale is to be played, the thumb is passed under the 4th finger to play the next **C**, otherwise the pinky could play this note if the scale were to stop there or if we were to descend afterwards.

When the **left hand** is playing an ascending scale, each fingering group (except the first) will again begin immediately after a thumb turn (in this case passing other fingers over the thumb to reach a higher note) and each fingering group will **end** with the thumb. For example, the same **C Major** scale ascending is typically fingered by the left hand as follows:-

Notes:-	*C*	*D*	*E*	*F*	*G*	*A*	*B*	*C*	*D*	*E*	etc.
L.H. Fingering:-	***(5)***	***(4***	***3***	***2***	***1)***	***(3***	***2***	***1)***	***(4***	***3***	etc.

This is a situation where it is easier to use the pinky on the first note **C**, however when the note **C** is required in higher octaves, the thumb is used. After the first note **C**, the fingering group **(4 3 2 1)** begins with the 4th finger and ends with the thumb. At this point the 3rd finger is passed over the thumb to reach the following note **A** and begin the next group **(3 2 1).** Again if we are to continue into the next octave, the 4th finger would then be passed over the thumb to play the note **D** and begin the next **(4 3 2 1)** fingering group.

The beauty of the 'fingering group' approach is that it can be adapted to play a scale from any starting and/or stopping point (for example this approach can be used for modes, which can be viewed as displaced major scales) - regardless of where the scale starts and ends, the 'fingering groups' will be the same - although in practice the fingering may be amended as required at the very beginning and end of such a 'displaced' scale. The above guidelines on right and left hand 'fingering groups' will work exactly in reverse when each hand is playing a scale in a descending manner.

SCALE FINGERING GUIDE

Now we will list the scale fingerings and place parentheses around the 'groups', for all of the major scales in **Figs. 1.2. - 1.16.** Again don't forget that the numbers refer to the fingers (1 = thumb, 5 = pinky) required in each hand. Note that some scales start with a 'group' of three notes or less, which is actually the end part of a fingering group that repeats in its entirety later in the scale. Also in this situation the fingering at the very beginning of the scale may be varied to accommodate the 'short' fingering group used. The fingering number shown in bold type and underlined, is being used to play the tonic of the scale in question. Each major scale is shown in at least a 2-octave range, as follows:-

Major scales ascending - right hand fingerings and groups

Major scale	*Right hand fingerings and groups*
C, **D**, **E**, **G**, **A** and **B** (**Cb**)	*(**1** 2 3) (1 2 3 4) (**1** 2 3) (1 2 3 4) (**1** 2 etc.*
Db (**C#**)	*(**2** 3) (1 2 3 4) (1 **2** 3) (1 2 3 4) (1 **2** 3) (1 etc.*
Eb	*(**2**) (1 2 3 4) (1 2 **3**) (1 2 3 4) (1 2 **3**) (1 2 etc.*
F	*(**1** 2 3 4) (1 2 3) (**1** 2 3 4) (1 2 3) (**1** 2 3 etc.*
Gb (F#)	*(**2** 3 4) (1 2 3) (1 **2** 3 4) (1 2 3) (1 **2** 3 4) etc.*
Ab	*(**2** 3) (1 2 3) (1 2 **3** 4) (1 2 3) (1 2 **3** 4) (1 etc.*
Bb	*(**2**) (1 2 3) (1 2 3 **4**) (1 2 3) (1 2 3 **4**) (1 2 etc.*

Major scales ascending - left hand fingerings and groups

Major scale	*Left hand fingerings and groups*
C, **D**, **E**, **F**, **G** and **A**	*(**5**) (4 3 2 1) (3 2 **1**) (4 3 2 1) (3 2 **1**) (4 3 etc.*
Db, **Eb**, **Ab** and **Bb**	*(**3** 2 1) (4 3 2 1) (**3** 2 1) (4 3 2 1) (**3** 2 1) etc.*
Gb (F#)	*(**4** 3 2 1) (3 2 1) (**4** 3 2 1) (3 2 1) (**4** 3 2 etc.*
B (Cb)	*(**4** 3 2 1) (4 3 2 **1**) (3 2 1) (4 3 2 **1**) (3 2 etc.*

Now the same principles can be applied to the fingering of all the pentatonic scales (see **Figs. 1.52. - 1.66.**). However, due to the fewer notes and larger intervals present in the scale, these fingerings are most practical when restricted to the thumb and first two fingers (i.e. finger numbers **1**, **2** & **3**) of each hand. This allows the required 'thumb turns' to occur while accommodating the larger intervals needed. The fingering number conventions etc. shown below are the same as for the major scales:-

Pentatonic scales ascending - RIGHT hand fingerings and groups

Pentatonic scale	*Right hand fingerings and groups*
C, **D**, **E**, **F**, **Gb** (**F#**), **G**, **A**, and **B** (**Cb**)	*(**1** 2 3) (1 2) (**1** 2 3) (1 2) (**1** 2 3) etc.*
Db	*(**2** 3) (1 2 3) (**1** 3) (1 2 3) (**1** 3) (1 2 etc.*
Eb	*(**2**) (1 2 3) (1 **3**) (1 2 3) (1 **3**) (1 2 3) etc.*
Ab	*(**2** 3) (1 3) (1 **2** 3) (1 3) (1 **2** 3) (1 3) etc.*
Bb	*(**2**) (1 2) (1 2 **3**) (1 2) (1 2 **3**) (1 2) (1 etc.*

Pentatonic scales ascending - LEFT hand fingerings and groups

Pentatonic scale	*Left hand fingerings and groups*
C, **Db**, **Eb**, **F**, **Gb** (**F#**), **G**, **Ab** and **Bb**	*(**3** 2 1) (2 1) (**3** 2 1) (2 1) (**3** 2 1) (2 etc.*
D	*(**2** 1) (3 2 1) (**2** 1) (3 2 1) (**2** 1) (3 2 etc.*
E	*(**4**) (3 2 1) (2 **1**) (3 2 1) (2 **1**) (3 2 1) etc.*
A	*(**2** 1) (2 1) (3 **2** 1) (2 1) (3 **2** 1) (2 1) etc.*
B	*(**3**) (2 1) (3 2 **1**) (2 1) (3 2 **1**) (2 1) (3 etc.*

Note that some of these are at best compromise solutions and present technical challenges. For example, the fingerings for **Gb**, **Db** and **B** pentatonic involve 'thumb turns' from one black note to another. Have fun!

--- THE END ---

That's all folks!! I hope you enjoy and benefit from this book - if so, all the time and effort will have been worthwhile. The main thing that kept me going throughout the writing process was the firm belief that there was a need for this book! Since it was released, I have been lucky enough to receive numerous letters and calls from musicians around the world, who have felt they were empowered by this method (as well as some who have offered excellent constructive criticism)! Unfortunately it is not possible for me to meet all of the users of the Pop Piano Book - however I always like to hear how you are doing - please write to me at P.O. Box 56505, Sherman Oaks, CA 91413 when you have the chance.

I have a great many people to thank on both sides of the Atlantic who have helped me along my chosen path! My experience in the unique educational environment at the Grove School of Music shaped my commitment to helping people 'take control' of their music, and I would like to thank all the many friends and students here in Los Angeles for their assistance and encouragement. My move from London to California in 1987 was also made immeasurably easier by my family & friends back home, who have been consistently supportive of my music and education career here in the U.S.A. - I would like to thank them for making it all possible!

Remember - music is supposed to be FUN - but you'd better do it SERIOUSLY!

==== *Mark Harrison* ====

This book is dedicated to my parents, TOM and EILEEN HARRISON.